Advance Praise from the Chief Executive Officers of Fortune 500 Companies, Professionals, Business Owners, and Families

"Inspiring..."

"Finally, a financial management book worth the money. Insightful, inspirational, straightforward and thought provoking. A must for every family interested in its financial future. Brock is a financial planner's planner!"

—Robert M. McChesney
President, The University of Montevallo
Montevallo, Alabama

"I read with utmost interest. ... It doesn't matter what career path you choose or the degree of it ... if people would only perform their responsibilities to the best of their ability then that would be a first class achievement. ... I agree with Hank Brock that creating a win-win situation should be the ultimate goal in productivity. ... My best to Hank on his **Masterpiece!"**

—Allen Questrom
Chairman and CEO, Federated Department Stores, Inc.
New York, New York

"Extraordinary! *Money Happiness* shows great maturity and wisdom. Everyone, rich or poor, will find it worthwhile."

—John Schmidt
Pianist, Composer, Recording Artist
Salt Lake City, Utah

"The chapters of Brock's book bring the achievement of financial success and happiness within reach by teaching the proven principles of integrity, positive thinking, and hard work."

—Orrin G. Hatch
United States Senator
Washington, D.C.

"... Will hit home with every reader."

—Marty W. Smith
Chief Executive Officer, Thrifty Payless Holding
Wilsonville, Oregon

"Authoritative..."

"... **Extremely well done** with a new twist. ..."

—Allen Born
Chairman and CEO, Alumax Company
Norcross, Georgia

"Like Stephen Covey (author, *Seven Habits of Highly Effective People*), Hank applies the character ethic rather than the personality ethic as the key to lasting success. Hank then builds on that to add some profound insights about freedom's role in economic progress. While Covey applied correct principles to effectiveness in the realm of human relationships, Hank has applied them to effectiveness in the realm of money and happiness."

—Irv Hallman, CFP, CLU, ChFC
Certified Facilitator, Covey Leadership Center;
President, Hallman Financial Group
Honolulu, Hawaii

"From the looks of Henry Brock's information on tax planning, he doesn't need anybody telling him how to write his book."

—Robert C. Hardy
Author, "How to Get Rid of the Income Tax"
Oklahoma City, Oklahoma

"... **EXCELLENT!** I heartily agree that you must have a passion for your work to succeed at it."

—J. Willard (Bill) Marriott, Jr.
President and Chairman of the Board, Marriott International
Washington, D.C.

"Henry Brock is on the right track with *How to Enhance Your Career Opportunities and Rewards*. It's amazing the harder one works, the luckier one gets."

—Willard Holland
President and CEO, Ohio Edison
Akron, Ohio

"Invaluable..."

"*Money Happiness*, through seven basic principles, provides an invaluable road map to achieving the delicate balance of financial security and personal fulfillment. **I highly recommend it!**"

—Nolan D. Archibald
Chairman, President and CEO, The Black & Decker Corporation
Towson, Maryland

"**This is an incredibly helpful book** for the lay reader in money matters. Even the person who can't make change can feel adept at high finance, smiling all the way to the bank. Just reading the Table of Contents is worth the price of the book. The ABCD's of the Insight/Action sections are a practical approach to implementing the correct principles for money happiness. **What a mind jog!**"

—Elaine Cannon
Author, "Adversity"
Salt Lake City, Utah

"**Compelling, a gold mine of principles.** Hank Brock's philosophy for a good life is that 'Everyone must win!' His counsel has helped us succeed personally and in our business. Thank You!"

—Karen Altemeier Oliver and I. James Oliver
Altemeier Oliver & Company
Cincinnati, Ohio

"**Invaluable.** Hank clearly and simply explains how to build a solid financial foundation. We've watched Hank practice what he preaches over the years. He transcends the common thinking in his focus on freedom and happiness. The book's fast-reading, forthright style delivers a breath of fresh air."

—Jana Rees and William V. Rees, M.D., *Surgeon*
Salt Lake City, Utah

"In a downsized, risk-oriented, competitive global marketplace, accelerating in fast forward, where change is the rule, *Money Happiness* is **the steering wheel, seat belt and shoulder harness to guide us safely toward financial and personal security.**"

—Dr. Denis Waitley
Author, "Empires of the Mind" and "The Psychology of Winning"
Rancho Santa Fe, California

"Insightful..."

"**... Best work I've seen** to help young and old sort their feelings about money and achievement. ... Hank has been my trusted adviser for several years and I have relied heavily on his insights, which he has graciously shared in *Money Happiness*. ... **Marvelous indeed if read worldwide.**"

—Curtis L. Hoskins, CPA
President and COO, El Paso Electric Company
El Paso, Texas

"**Insightful.** I appreciate Mr. Brock's emphasis that character counts as an essential ingredient for lasting success. No one lasts long without it."

—Bill Boyan
President and COO, John Hancock Mutual Life Insurance Co.
Boston, Massachusetts

"Henry Brock's work is not a cookie-cutter formula or a get-rich-quick scheme. It is a journey into personal attitudes, goals, character and principles. This is what really counts when searching for money happiness!"

—Charles A. Coonradt
Author, "The Game of Work"
Park City, Utah

"... Helps people focus on things that really make a difference as opposed to the less significant conventional wisdom."

—Tom Scott
Vice President, VF Company
Wyomissing, Pennsylvania

"Hank's insights over the years have helped us through stormy seas to safe ground. We wish more could share this hope."
—Relda Thomas and Tony Thomas, D.D.S.
Templeton, California

"Easy-to-Read..."

"Portfolio risk is a subject that is often poorly understood, even by experienced investors. Hank's excellent coverage of this topic is presented in an easy-to-read style that is easily comprehended by the novice and advanced investor alike."
—Steve Shellans
Editor, MoniResearch Newsletter
Portland, Oregon

"Brock's investment information is **remarkably clearly written. I want to buy a copy!**"
—John M. Templeton
Founder, Templeton Funds
Lyford Key, Nassau Bahamas

"Relevant..."

"... Presents some very important advice and raises some very important questions. ... **I wouldn't change a word.**"
—M. Anthony Burns
Chairman, President, and CEO, Ryder System, Inc.
Miami, Florida

"Hank's incisive and trusted advice has worked for us for over fifteen years—it has given us peace of mind and security at a time when there is so much uncertainty. ... *Money Happiness* **is a deeply satisfying gift full of priceless guidance.**"
—Karla Ferguson and Greg B. Ferguson, M.D., *Anesthesiologist*
Kaysville, Utah

"I appreciate Mr. Brock's emphasis on honesty and results. **I want all six of my children to read this.** *How to Enhance Your Career Opportunities and Rewards* should be part of each high school senior's curriculum and new employee's orientation."
—Roger R. Hemminghaus
Chairman, President, and CEO, Diamond Shamrock
San Antonio, Texas

"I've learned over the years that the financial planning decisions leading up to choosing an adviser are just as important as which adviser is chosen. Hank Brock serves a crucial purpose by addressing these powerful prerequisites to financial success."

—Mark Hulbert
Editor, The Hulbert Financial Digest
Alexandria, Virginia

"The average person misses their ability as a competitive weapon. This book could open up their greatest resource, themselves."

—Ronald A. Rittenmeyer
Chief Operating Officer, Burlington Northern Railroad
Fort Worth, Texas

"Hank Brock makes some excellent points that relate to values, discipline, children and spouses. I could have benefited greatly in my life from some of his pointers."

—Loren Marc Schmerler
President and CEO, Bottom Line Management, Inc.
Atlanta, Georgia

"Sound Advice..."

"... Tells the truth about the characteristics of people who are successful and those who are not."

—Lynn Buchanan
Weyerhauser Company
Valley Forge, Pennsylvania

"**Good old-fashioned common sense.** A return to the financial management principles that are proven by the test of time."

—Jake Garn
Former U.S. Senator; First Senator in Space
Salt Lake City, Utah

"... An excellent birds-eye view of career planning. ... Brock's emphasis of being honest and candid are absolute keys."

—Alan Hoops
President and CEO, Pacificare Company
Cypress, California

"... **Excellent!** It provides a refreshing, realistic view of how to plan and succeed in business. It is 'basic training' in a world that has forgotten the value of honesty and commitment. It helped me re-evaluate my value as an employee. I plan to re-read and internalize its principles."
—Noel M. Howard
Executive Director, Merck and Company
Whitehouse Station, New Jersey

"Really sorts out what's important about life and money. Easy reading, and full of insights."
—William H. Child
Chief Executive Officer, R.C. Willey Home Furnishings
Salt Lake City, UT

"*Money Happiness* fills in the gaps for an average person like me to genuinely change my practices and approaches in my financial life. **It showed me how to achieve peace of mind when it comes to money.**"
—Ted L. Wilson
Former Salt Lake City Mayor
Salt Lake City, UT

Your COMPLETE GUIDE TO
Money
Happiness

by Henry S. Brock

Legacy
PUBLISHING COMPANY, INC.

Your Complete Guide to Money Happiness
How to Achieve Financial Success, Security, and Peace of Mind

By Henry S. Brock

Published by:
Legacy Publishing, Inc.
2533 N. Carson Street, Suite 2737
Carson City, NV 89706

This is a work of non-fiction.
All characters and events portrayed in this book are fictional, and any resemblance to real people or incidents is purely coincidental.

PRINTING HISTORY
First Printing 1997

Corporate Discounts Available Direct from the Publisher:

5-10 Copies	5%
11-30 Copies	10%
31-50 Copies	20%
51-100 Copies	30%
101-1,000 Copies	35%
Over 1,000 Copies	40%

Shipping extra. For ordering information, call 1-800-390-1647.

Publisher's Cataloging in Publication (*Prepared by Quality Books Inc.*)

Brock, Henry S.
    Your complete guide to money happiness : achieve financial success, security, and peace of mind / by Henry S. Brock.
    p. cm.
    Includes bibliographical references and index.
    Preassigned LCCN: 96-77754
    ISBN 0-9653886-9-7

    1. Finance, Personal--Planning. 2. Financial security--Planning. I. Title.

HG179.B75 1996   332.024   QBI96-40282

To Julie

"She sees a diamond."

Acknowledgments

First and foremost, I thank my wife and sweetheart, Julie, and our children, Danny, Andrea, Larry, Leslee, Carrie, Beth, and Thomas. I appreciate their sustaining support. I thank my father, Dan Brock, who, though he never had much of this world's wealth, was rich in wisdom, integrity, and courage. I thank my mother, Thella, who provided full-time love, and encouragement to venture.

I am indebted to those who have taught me so generously. I have learned most as clients have asked innumerable questions over the years. I have rejoiced with them in their progress and joys, and I have hurt with them in their pains. Intimate observation has taught much. Added to that is personal experience, often painful, which has taught more.

My thinking has been corralled by great leaders and successful businessmen, most notably Hugh W. Pinnock, CLU, retired financial adviser, who has shared countless hours of financial insights and counsel. As a trusted mentor and friend, he has generously and patiently taught me so many lessons on financial security and success over the decades that I am not sure where his thinking ends and mine begins. I attribute to him many of the pervasive lessons, for which I will be forever grateful.

My family and the firm have been an endless laboratory in real life. I express to them my deepest appreciation for their support along the extra miles.

I wish to acknowledge and express my gratitude to those who have contributed their enthusiasm and unique talents for this book. Melissa Thomas has been with me virtually every step of the way, researching, editing, and re-editing. She has provided cohesion and truly extra-mile service. Kathy Frandsen performed a monumental work editing the initial transcripts, Giles Florence provided critical insights and feedback in the final editing process, and Berneice Neeley transcribed thousands of pages. Missy Larsen and Angela Strong provided insight and much feedback as they coordinated the many critiques and suggestions for improvement, and Jeffrey Jones worked his magic on the illustrations. There are not enough words to adequately express my appreciation and gratitude to these individuals for their contributions, personal caring, invaluable assistance, and professional expertise. Without them, this project truly would not have been possible.

Making all their efforts possible was the support and follow-through of my staff and professional associates, who have maintained order in the firm during my absence while working on the book: Marcus Pinnock, Scott Hansen, Doug Jones, Eric Barlow, and Wendell Brock from our management team, and Susan Glad, Kathleen Johnson, Brenda Woods, Jeffrey Jones, Nicole Hunter, Erica Thorn, and Kathryn Briggs from our office staff. They have kept things running without a hitch. *I thank them.*

I also wish to acknowledge and express my gratitude to the following individuals who have read selected portions of the manuscript and have generously provided valuable critiques and suggestions in its preparation: Lee Anderson, MBA, CFP, ChFC; Paul Anderson, CPA; Robert C. Andringa, *President, Coalition of Christian Colleges & Universities*; Nolan D. Archibald, *Chairman, President and CEO, The Black & Decker Corporation*; Eric Barlow; Donald R. Beall, *CEO, Rockwell International*; Kristen M. Bihary, *Varity Corp.*; Allen Born, *Chairman and CEO, Alumax Company*; Matthew Bowman; Bill Boyan, *President and COO, John Hancock Mutual Life Insurance Co.*; J.G. Breen, *CEO, Sherwin Williams*; Andrea Brock; Wendell Brock, ChFC, CFP; Joe Brusatto, CLU, ChFC; Lynn Buchanan, *Weyerhauser Company*; M. Anthony Burns, *CEO, Ryder*; Elaine Cannon, *Author, "Adversity"*; Charles A. Coonradt, *Author, "The Game of Work"*; Jack B. Critchfield, *CEO, Florida Progress*; Earnest W. Deavenport, *CEO, Eastman Chemical*; Draza Esplin; Karla Ferguson and Greg B. Ferguson, M.D., *Anesthesiologist*; David P. Gardner, *former President, University of California System*; Jake Garn, *Former U.S. Senator; First Senator in Space*; Bob G. Gower, *Lyondell Petrochemical*; Irv Hallman, CFP, CLU, ChFC, *Certified Facilitator of Covey Leadership Center, President of Hallman Financial Group*; David Handy, JD, ChFC; Scott Hansen; Robert C. Hardy, *Author, "How to Get Rid of the Income Tax"*; Steven J. Harris, *Executive Director, Chrysler Corp.*; Orrin G. Hatch, *United*

States Senator; Roger R. Hemminghaus, *Chairman, President, and CEO, Diamond Shamrock*; Dennis Hendrix, *CEO, Panhandle Eastern*; Willard Holland, *President and CEO, Ohio Edison*; Alan Hoops, *President and CEO, Pacificare Company*; Curt Hoskins, *President, El Paso Electric*; Noel M. Howard, *Executive Director, Merck & Co.*; Mark Hulbert, *Editor, The Hulbert Financial Digest*; Nicole Hunter, ChFC, CMFS; Frank Johnson, JD; Norman S. Johnson, *Commissioner, United States Securities and Exchange Commission*; Doug Jones; Drew Lewis, *CEO, Union Pacific Corp.*; Mark Lucius, *Northwestern Mutual*; Bill Marriott, *CEO, Marriott International*; Robert M. McChesney, *President, The University of Montevallo*; Todd McChesney; John K. Mulholland, *Southern California Edison Co.*; Jack Murphy, *CEO, Dresser Industries*; Karen Altemeier Oliver and I. James Oliver, *Altemeier Oliver & Company*; Jon Pinnock, ChFC; Allen Questrom, *CEO, Federated Department Stores*; Jana Rees and William V. Rees, M.D., *Surgeon*; Ronald A. Rittenmeyer, *COO, Burlington Northern Railroad*; Steve Robinson, CFP, ChFC; Helen Sayles, *Liberty Mutual*; Dan Scarlet, ChFC; John M. Scheldrup, *Armstrong World Industries*; Loren Marc Schmerler, *President and CEO, Bottom Line Management, Inc.*; John Schmidt, *Pianist, Composer, Recording Artist*; Tom Scott, *Vice President, VF Company*; Steve Shellans, *Editor, MoniResearch Newsletter*; Sue Sherwood, *Niagara Mohawk Power*; Mike Sloan, ChFC, CLU; A.J.C. Smith, *CEO, Marsh & McLennan Companies*; Marty W. Smith, *CEO, Thrifty Payless Holding*; John M. Templeton, *Founder, Templeton Funds*; Relda Thomas and Tony Thomas, D.D.S.; David H. Thompson; Bryan Todd, JD; Jay M. Todd; Dr. Denis Waitley, Author, "Empires of the Mind" and "The Psychology of Winning"; Josh Weston, *CEO, Automatic Data Processing*; Ted L. Wilson, *Former Salt Lake City Mayor*. I sincerely hope they are pleased with the final product.

Also, thanks to Jennie Pinnock; Keira Dreher; Craig Nelson; and Craig Paulson. Debra Lund has been most helpful.

While I am indebted to the many persons above, I alone am responsible for the final content, advice, counsel, and philosophy herein. If there are any errors, they are mine.

Quick Reference Guide

Use this simple guide for easy access to major subjects.

Books Within a Book:

Read These Chapters:	Economics & Freedom	Cash Flow & Budgeting	Career Planning	Tax Planning	Risk & Insurance	Education Funding	Investments	Retirement Planning	Estate Planning
1. Complete Money Happiness Is Within Reach	X	X	X	X	X	X	X	X	X
2. Money Has a Character of Its Own	X	X	X	X	X	X	X	X	X
3. Can Money Buy Happiness?	X	X	X	X	X	X	X	X	X
4. Work with Your Money Personality	X	X					X		
5. Your Economic Engine	X	X		X		X		X	
6. The Freedom Budget		X				X		X	
7. The Weight of Taxes		X		X					
8. What Is the Mainspring of Human Progress?	X	X	X	X			X	X	X
9. Focus on Freedom	X	X						X	
10. Liberate Yourself From the Bondage of Debt		X							
11. Financial Causes and Effects	X			X					
12. The Basic Economic Unit of Society: Family	X		X						
13. Only Character Can Bring Money Happiness	X	X	X						
14. Enhance Your Career Opportunities and Rewards		X	X						
15. How to Be the Last Person Laid-Off Work		X							
16. How to Achieve Security	X	X	X	X	X	X		X	X
17. Most People's Major Investment: Real Estate							X		
18. Risk Management and Insurance					X				
19. Now, Cement Your Foundation					X				
20. Protect Your Assets					X		X		X
21. Enhance the Richest Part of Life: Retirement								X	
22. The Risks in Your Investment Portfolio					X		X		
23. An Introduction to Mutual Funds						X	X		
24. Do Your Estate Planning with Care									X
25. The Debt You Didn't Know You Have					X				X
26. How to Profit from Charitable Giving		X			X				X
27. How to Achieve Success	X	X	X	X			X	X	
28. The Economics of Higher Education			X				X		
29. Your Most Effective Tax Planning Strategies		X		X				X	
30. Mutual Funds, Variable Annuities, Variable Life				X	X	X	X	X	
31. Nine Keys to Successful Portfolio Management							X		
32. Your Success Level Reflects Your Thinking	X	X	X				X		
33. How Successful Investors Think							X		
34. How to Achieve Goals Habitually		X	X				X	X	X
35. How to Combine These Principles	X	X	X	X	X	X	X	X	X
36. Action Plan on the Seven Core Decisions	X	X	X	X	X	X	X	X	X
37. Action Plan on Governing Yourself	X	X	X	X	X	X	X	X	X

Table of Contents

Introduction: Where the Lessons Came From 1
The Three Keys to Get the Most From This Book • Lifetime Satisfaction Guarantee • Before You Read On

Decision One: Make Decisions by Happiness Criteria, Not Ego Criteria

1. Principles with a Promise:
Complete Money Happiness Is Within Reach 17
What Is Money? • A Bit of Happiness in Your Pocket • How Much Happiness Do You Want? • Can Money Buy Happiness? • Money Means Freedom • Violated Expectations about Money • Are You Money Anorexic? • Choose Your Own Level of Money Happiness

2. Money Has a Character of Its Own 27
The Law of Unequal Rewards • What Is True Financial Planning? • Ego Criteria • Happiness Criteria

3. Can Money Buy Happiness? 35
We May Love It or Hate It • For What Purpose Do You Pursue Money? • Opposition and Adversity Are Natural Laws • How Much You Have, or How Much You Appreciate? • Is Money Your Daily Bread, or Your Daily Dread? • Make Money Your Servant, Not Your Master • Can Your Money Success Allow Time for Happiness? • What You Want *Most*? Or What You Want *Now*? • Beware Get-Rich-Quick Schemes

4. Work with Your Money Personality 45
Why Do So Many People Fail Financially? • Procrastinate ... and Fail • Profile Yourself • The Excuse of the Ages

5. Your Economic Engine 53
What Type of Person Are You? • You Decide • The Surprising Advantage of Saving • Just Can't Save, No Matter What? • Your Financial Freedom Fund • The Amazing WYHTE Phenomenon • A Dollar Isn't a Dollar • To Do It or Hire It Done • 26-Point Checklist for Increasing Personal Cash Flow

6. The Freedom Budget 71

Set Correct Budgeting Priorities • The Paradox of Controls • Must-Haves and Name Brands • What Is a Bargain, Really? • A Budget Is a Plan • Essentials of Developing an Effective Budget • Know Your Spending Cycles • It's All a Game—a Real One • A Word about Credit Cards • The Emergency Fund • Immediate and Certain Security • Balancing Cash Reserves • Other Essential Reserves: Food, Clothing, Energy • Try a Separate Savings Account for Big-Ticket Items • Especially for Youth • Understand the Cost of Using Investment Income • The Bottom Line

7. The Weight of Taxes 85

The Way Our Tax System Works—Since 1913 • The Impact of Taxes on the Economy • How Much Goes to Taxes? • Understand Your Marginal Tax Rate

Decision Two: Focus on Freedom

8. What Is the Mainspring of Human Progress? 93

We Have Risen to Practical Self-Interest • The Fatalistic View • Can We Calculate the Value of Individual Initiative? • Does Equality for All Compromise Freedom for the One? • When Is the Use of Force Morally Right? • Can You Accept the Responsibility of Your Own Freedom? • No One Grants Us Freedom • The Responsibility of Freedom • We Must Own Our Choices • Hope of Reward Over Fear of Punishment • Our Words Must Be Precise and Clear • The Fruits That Flow from Freedom • Economic Progress Thrives on Incentive • Profit Is Not a Dirty Word • Governments Get Rights from Citizens • Freedom Cannot Exist without Property Rights

9. Focus on Freedom 113

Any Bondage Restrains Freedom • Understand Freedom: Correct Choices Abolish Boundaries • Don't Ignore the Bondage of Ignorance • Are You Stressed by the Bondage of Time? • Break the Chains of Bondage to Addiction • Will You Let Go of Your Bondage to "Things"? • Can You Afford Your Financial Bondage? • Quit Bondage to Bad Habits • Will You Avoid Bondage to Mistakes? • Deny Bondage to False Economic and Political Systems • We Often Vote Slavery Back In • Truest Compassion Is Not a Handout

10. Liberate Yourself from the Bondage of Debt 131

Borrower Is Slave—Debt Is Bondage • Use Family Councils to Explain Money Facts • Don't Ignore Debts • Debt Can Challenge Integrity • Easy Money Dulls the Work Ethic • Don't Consolidate Debts • Debt Is Inflationary • Slaves to Government • Debt Limits Our Ability to Serve Others • Debt Motivation: Impatience, Greed, Impulsiveness, Ego • The True Nature of Debt • How to Get Out of Debt with Minimal Pain • Chipping Away at Debt Methodically

11. A Brief Economics Lesson:
Financial Causes and Effects 149
An Economy Thrives on Free Specialization and Exchange • The Insidious Tax: Inflation • Who Benefits from the Minimum Wage? • Technology Replacing Labor: Job Evolution and Misplaced Panic • Who Can Veto the President or Congress? • A Game of Deception: Gambling and the Lottery • Some Unsurprising Results of Price Controls • Prepare for the Next Depression • Stewardship for the Environment • Closed Organizations Violate Innate Freedoms • Threats to Your Economic Future

12. The Basic Economic Unit of Society:
The Family 167
Avoid Financial Ruin • Teach Your Children • Two Kinds of Spouses • Children: An Asset, Not a Liability

Decision Three: Recognize that Character Counts

13. Why Only Character Can Bring Money Happiness 177
By the Bright Beacon of Principle • Greatness of Purpose Determines Character • Nine Attributes of True Character • Character Counts

14. How to Enhance Your Career Opportunities
and Rewards 195
The Number-One Success Force • What You're Really Worth • Should You Work Smart, or Hard, or Both? • Getting Results • The Taxation of Work and WYHTE • The Common Denominator of Success • How the Success Curve Really Works—Dispelling Another Myth • Fatal Flaws That Cause Executives to Derail • What about a Working Spouse? • What about Starting Your Own Business?

15. How to Be the Last Person Laid Off Work 209
Be Your Employer's Most Profitable Employee • Here's What Employers Look For • How to Evaluate Your True Net Worth

Decision Four: Build a Solid Foundation for Security

16. How to Achieve Security 223
Are You Adequately Prepared? • Demand Self-Reliance • Increase Job Security • Exercise Self-Control • Work Hard • Establish Reserves • Guard Against Ego • Consider Working for Yourself • Buy Insurance • Manage Risks • Avoid Debt • Develop a Self-Reliant Family • Tithing: The Ancient Law of Giving 10 Percent • A Calisthenic for Gratitude • Our Stewardship • The Formula for Financial Security

17. Homing in on Most People's Major Investment:
    Real Estate 237
    Why Own a Home • Buy a Neighborhood, Not Just a House • Character,
    Character, Character • How to Qualify to Buy a Home • The Most Efficient
    Way to Pay Off Your Home • Use Your Money Most Efficiently • Don't
    Mortgage Your Home

18. How to Solidify Your Foundation:
    Risk Management and Insurance 247
    What to Do about Risk • How Much Life Insurance Should You Have? Ana-
    lyze Your Needs • Why the "Theory of Decreasing Needs" Doesn't Hold Up
    • To Choose Term or Whole Life: An Analogy

19. Now, Cement Your Foundation 267
    Is Your Insurance Company Reputable? • How to Choose a Professional In-
    surance Adviser • Beware Replacement Schemes • Three Ways Insurance Self-
    Adjusts Under High Inflation • Compare Group with Personally Owned In-
    surance • Beware Low-Priced Term Insurance • So You've Been Rated?

20. Protect Your Assets 283
    The Frightening Prospects of Disability • Long-Term Care: Another Increas-
    ing Threat • Sound Strategies for the Most Secure Asset Protection

21. How to Enhance the Richest Part of Life: Retirement 295
    Three Sources of Retirement Dollars, Supposedly • Pertinent Facts about Re-
    tirement: Where Do You Fit in? • Is Retirement for You? • Abundant and
    Appealing Reasons Not to Retire • Your Retirement Deserves Careful Analy-
    sis • Inflation Will Rise, Fixed Incomes Do Not • Why Tax Rates Rise to 60
    Percent on Retirees • How to Maximize Retirement Benefits • How Chari-
    table Pursuits After Retirement Help Finances • A Creative Last Resort: The
    Reverse Mortgage • The Selective Incentive Plan • So, Are You Prepared?

22. What You Should Know about the Risks in
    Your Investment Portfolio 315
    Make Big Money with the Top-Performing Investment • Cash Is Opportunity
    • Know These Three Vital Investment Principles • How to Manage Away the
    Four Investment Risks • Balance—Because Nobody Knows Nuthin' • Calcu-
    late the Risks of Ideal Investments

23. An Introduction to Mutual Funds 331
    Choose the Right Mutual Fund for You • Fixed vs. Equity Investments • Mu-
    tual Funds: Load vs. No-Load Myths

24. Guard the Castle Gate:
    Do Your Estate Planning with Care 341
    Exactly What Does Your Estate Include? • What Are the Basic Elements of a
    Good Estate Plan?

25. The Debt You Didn't Know You Have 353
   Estate Taxes: One Problem Worth Having • Project Your Estate Taxes: Plan
   Your Strategy Ahead

26. How to Profit from Charitable Giving 369
   Develop a Desire to Give Back • Develop Your Strategies for Charitable Giving • All Strategy Aside

Decision Five: Climb the Right Ladder to Success

27. How to Achieve Success 383
   Do What You Love • Sink Roots Like the Bamboo Tree • Focus on End
   Results, Not Unpleasant Means • Simplify to Focus • Synergize Through In-
   terdependence • How to Attract Security and Financial Success

28. Do Your Homework Early on the Economics
   of Higher Education 395
   What Will a College Education Cost? • How to Pay for a College Education

29. How to Develop Your Most Effective Tax
   Planning Strategies 407
   Tax Principles: Tree vs. Fruit, Form vs. Substance, Recognition vs. Realization • 44 Strategies for Reducing Taxes • What Are Your Tax Risks? • Taxpayer Bill of Rights

30. Three Prudent Investment Tools:
   Mutual Funds, Variable Annuities, and Variable Life 425
   Similarities between Mutual Funds, Variable Annuities, and Variable Life •
   Differences between Mutual Funds, Variable Annuities, and Variable Life •
   How to Transfer Assets to a Tax-Advantaged Program • What about Munici-
   pal Bonds?

31. Nine Keys to Successful Portfolio Management 439
   Engage These Four Proven Portfolio Strategies • Put It All Together

Decision Six: Avoid Poor Thinking

32. Your Success Level Reflects How Well
   You Are Thinking 463
   Avoid Poor Thinking • Poor Thinkers Have a Victim Mentality • How Do
   We Learn Success Thinking? • Financial Success Is Not Achieved by Spending
   • Even Leaders Teach Poor Thinking • You Don't Strengthen the Weak by
   Weakening the Strong • Watch Success, Don't Listen to Failure • Poor Think-
   ing Surrounds Us • Throw out Imposters

33. How Successful Investors Think 473

How the Wealthy Invest Differently from the Average Investor • Watch Your Plan, Not the Markets • Why You Must Learn to Sell at a Loss • Why You Must Learn to Sell at a Profit • Greed and Speculation • Beware the Lien on Your Portfolio

Decision Seven: Make Your Dream Your Reality

34. How to Achieve Goals Habitually 483

Your Goals Must Ignite Something Deep Within • Develop Your Master Plan • Put a Cost on the Goal • Assess Your Willingness to Pay That Cost • Break Your Goal Down into Daily Steps • Establish Self-Enforcing Mechanisms • Measure Performance • Goals Must Be Aligned • Balance Your Pursuit of Excellence • Manage Systems • Systematize • Be Visionary

35. How to Combine These Principles for
Complete Money Happiness 491

Choose the Right Financial Planner • Constructing Your Financial Plan: Who Does What? • What Is the Financial Planning Process? • Measurable Benefits of Having a Financial Plan in Place

36. Action Plan on The Seven Core Decisions 507

37. Action Plan on Governing Yourself:
The 27 Foundation Strategies 509

Free Fax-on-Demand Documents from
The American Financial Resource Center, Inc. 513

Recommended Resources 515

Ready-Reference Index 525

Introduction

Where the Lessons Came From

This is a book about discovering those timeless correct principles that synthesize money and happiness, about finding lasting financial security, success, and peace of mind in a world of increasing uncertainty and commotion. Our hypothesis is that *there are* consistent and reliable natural laws which, if discovered and followed, will lead to *economic freedom* and away from various bondages that keep many people in chains of financial stresses, concerns and even slavery. No one who is in bondage is as happy as he or she could be. Microscopically few people would choose the stranglehold of economic mediocrity if they see a satisfactory and often exciting alternative. The foundation principles here offer many solutions.

I believe that, tragically, we, as individuals and as a nation, have allowed ourselves to become enslaved in many bondages. Many unwittingly engage in self-destructive thinking. Debt has become a way of life for all too many. Financially speaking, nothing could be more unhealthy and even terminal if not controlled. We need to discern sense from nonsense as we are constantly bombarded by financial fads, often perpetrated by individuals who do not have a clue about what leads to financial success.

The research in my financial laboratory only *started* with the struggles of my own financial life. It didn't stop there—not by any means. I have studied the stories of hundreds of people who attend our workshops each year, and have consulted with thousands of clients of more than 40 financial planning associates in our fee-based firm. From them, I hear accounts of wisdom and clear thinking as well as accounts of shortsightedness and fuzzy thinking. I have observed those who can't discern sense from nonsense. I watch as many succumb to the fads and fables of the financial planning industry, as well as much foolishness perpetrated by the media. And I see those who, in spite of great odds, seem to naturally find financial success at regular intervals.

Most influential, though, have been my own impressions and observations of our culture, which has lost its will to save, yet grows more and more acquisitive.

I grew up fourth in a family of seven children. My father, a photographer known for his competency and honesty throughout southern California, worked long hours in his own darkroom as well as doing commercial shoots for clients throughout the city. My father's studio was at the foot of our steep hill, and he returned every night to do his darkroom work after dinner. We often visited with him at those times, standing beside the print wash tank or big drum dryer, talking about life and getting his advice. Born in Los Angeles in 1908, he knew the city's history, the beginnings of Hollywood, the world wars, the Great Depression. He understood people, and he loved America.

Mother was a full-time homemaker who worked hard caring for home and children. The nine of us lived in a three-bedroom home with one bathroom, a small kitchen, and a "front room" that also served as the family room and dining room—typical of most homes in the Echo Park area of Los Angeles.

My parents encouraged me to learn a musical instrument in third grade, so I chose violin. Although I hated to practice, my parents refused to let me quit, wanting me to learn discipline. My mother often said, "Do something every day that you don't want to do, just because you don't want to do it." I didn't know that I was learning to stick with something, regardless of how unpleasant. I have since learned that enduring unpleasant tasks along the way is basic to achieving any significant goal.

My parents taught us to embrace adventure. We learned to work. My parents were always building and encouraging, always supportive. They attended our school orchestra concerts, parent-teacher nights, Cub Scout pack meetings, and worked with us on our studies, always encouraging us to venture out.

Learning to Work Hard

Shortly after I turned 11, I had my first actual job—selling subscriptions to *The Los Angeles Times*. Then in junior high school, I would get home from school about 3:30 p.m. and wait for Mr. Rees, who would pick up four or five of us kids in his old station wagon. He would drop us off in various neighborhoods in south-central Los Angeles and we would go around the block, knocking on doors and selling subscriptions to *The Times* for $3 per month.

It was the second worst form of sales imaginable, but we did it. (The worst form of sales is anything dishonest or unethical.) We would go to the door in an attempt to play on the people's pity and entice them to subscribe to *The Times* by telling them we might win a trip to Cape Canaveral to see a rocket blast off. I would say, "Ma'am, I've never been out of Los Angeles before. Would you like to help me out by buying a subscription to the *Los Angeles Times?*" Sometimes they'd take pity on us and subscribe, only to cancel at the end of the month.

This went on from four in the afternoon until 9:30 p.m. Monday through Friday. On Saturday we sold from 9 a.m. until about 2 p.m. I put in 25 to 30 hours a week—for about two years—earning about $1 an hour. It was good money in those days. I earned about $100 a month in 1964, which today would be equivalent to about $400 to $500 a month, a fair sum of money for an 11-year-old boy.

So, I got in the habit of working. I'd get up in the morning for school, and get home 14 hours later to go to bed, with hardly any time to do homework.

Discovering the Value of Things

One of the most frequent reasons people gave for not being able to subscribe to the newspaper was that they were on welfare. Yet standing there in their doorway, I looked in at their color television set. This was 1964-1965, and all our family had was an old used black-and-white TV that my father had found a few years before. I remember wondering why it was that these people who were on welfare could afford to have a color

TV while we who were not on welfare had only a black-and-white set. These were my earliest impressions of welfare. Why couldn't a father with children who were working have those nicer things?

I did not understand then, nor have I been able to determine since, how those people could afford color TVs and still be unemployed, spending hours each day and each night watching TV instead of working and earning an income. I was equally perplexed that they would not subscribe to a newspaper when the paper in our home was devoured daily.

My parents trusted us children to have employment, to be working, to be traveling many miles from home, mixing and mingling at those young ages.

At age 14 and as a sophomore in high school, I learned of a job opening about five miles away, at Kentucky Fried Chicken on Hollywood Boulevard. Though I was too young, the manager gave me the job because I was in high school.

After about a year's time I was reaching seniority at the store. One evening Mr. Ziskin asked me if I would be willing to close up the store. After this came the opportunity to become the night manager, complete with keys, and I enjoyed the increased level of responsibility and a 10 cent raise to $1.60 per hour.

It was there after school every day in the odor of hot grease, managing and scheduling kids older than myself, cleaning up after closing and not getting home until 10, that I began to recognize the commitment and sacrifice required for success. About that time, I attempted my own little business designing and constructing custom loudspeaker systems, but didn't get far.

A few years later, I was recruited to sell Amway, where I learned the difference an organized marketing plan can make. With Amway, I learned about communicating, selling, having a message, providing a valuable product, as well as how to approach people. Starting at age 17, I sold Amway products for two years, earning just enough to keep gasoline in the car, replace a few transmissions, purchase some clothes, and even have some date money. It was a tremendous learning experience: I had been very shy, and was becoming more comfortable being in front of people.

Confronting Self-defeating Behaviors

At age 16, I finally came to grips with my shyness. I did not relish most public settings and hated public speaking, yet even then I knew that communication skills were among the necessary elements of success. I built up my resolve, contacted the speech director in our small church and volunteered to speak on short notice if she ever had any cancellations. Because it was always a trial to find a youth willing to share a three- to five-minute thought at a church meeting, she welcomed my offer.

For the next few years I was called upon to speak many times in our church services, much to the dismay of the congregation. I was terrible! After one of my talks, my older sister Jill came up to me and said that in the five-minute period she had counted only 31 "uh's" and stutters. That was only six a minute, which she considered a tremendous improvement. Every Sunday I dreaded getting up—it was difficult, but it was something I felt I needed to do.

Today, I still prefer to be at the back of the room, and yet today much of my income is made from public speaking.

We all have fears to overcome. These were some of the difficult things that I had to overcome, shortcomings and weaknesses that would be self-defeating throughout my life if I did not work to overcome them.

Despite the long work hours, I did graduate from high school with an adequate GPA. After graduation on a Friday, I began college the following Monday at Cal State University at Los Angeles, majoring in business and immediately taking 300-level courses. But without the adequate prerequisites, I did not do well.

Two years later I served as a full-time missionary for my church, working with the inner-city Puerto Ricans and blacks of Philadelphia, Lancaster, and Pittsburgh, Pennsylvania. We learned and spoke Spanish constantly. The mission became the highlight of my life up to that point, with its 65-hour workweeks, plus 10 hours of weekly study.

Recognizing Real Motives

While in Pennsylvania I learned the value of losing oneself in one's work, dedication, devotion to a cause. I learned that people are willing to work harder for a purpose in life than they would ever work for money or recognition or any other superficial motives.

It was an amazing feeling to lose myself in the work so thoroughly that neither food nor sleep nor any cares of the world seemed of any consequence, day after day, month after month. The humble people with whom we worked epitomized fulfillment and happiness in spite of having so few earthly goods.

The people who are the most successful and the happiest are the people who are working in some endeavor for which they have developed a deep sense of purpose. They are accomplishing something that is bigger than themselves, something that will make a difference in the world in which they live. All of us, it seems, are willing to work harder and apply more dedication toward a purpose than we are for simple success as measured by the traditional definitions of the world.

As one who had come from an environment of little material substance, and who had made material success a goal in life, I have been reminded ever since that material success alone is not the pathway to happiness or fulfillment or peace. Nor is it a very lofty definition of success.

At age 21, I applied to study at Brigham Young University with only three months to earn money for tuition. That fall I arrived in town with enough in my wallet for my first semester tuition, a deposit on an apartment, and $20 leftover. By teaching Spanish at the Language Training Center, I earned money for rent, food, clothing, and books. There were never enough books. I must have bought a book a week about business. Gratitude for knowledge and for the privilege of learning charged my battery daily.

When I graduated I had a degree in accounting and a minor in business/economics with almost full minors in international relations, Spanish, English, and political science.

Giving in to Ego

With graduation came the usual recruiting scene. I was flattered when prospective employers flew me to various cities and took me to fancy dinners. So I committed the mistake most graduates make when they complete college. Impressed with the highest salaries, I took the most prestigious, ego-gratifying position offered. I had married Julie Herzog by then and ended up accepting a position with Exxon in Houston, Texas, as an internal auditor on their exploration and production audit staff. They treated me very well.

Exxon had put me on their fast track, and I made a number of audit finds which apparently surprised them and served to make my employment with them quite profitable.

But I had only been there a few weeks when I began climbing the walls from boredom. I quickly learned that the corporate world stifled me. It did not give me the opportunity to expand and grow the way I wanted to and needed to. While it's best for so many people, it wasn't right for me. Soon, I was on my way back to Provo to pursue a Master's degree in Business Administration.

One of the most valuable things I learned at Exxon came from my peers. While I had a bachelor's degree in accounting, two other individuals I worked with had their MBAs, one from the University of Chicago and one from Wharton. They were surprised that I was getting some of the more "plum" assignments. What this proved to me was that once you were hired, success in a career position was not going to be based on whether you had a bachelor's or master's degree or what school it came from, but simply on performance, whether you got the job done.

Willing to Go into Debt

Graduate school brought the usual struggles. We were broke and had a new baby. Julie was now a full-time mom. I was a full-time student. We borrowed money to make it because the graduate school would not allow me to work. I borrowed enough money so we could buy a house, which set off probably the first major disagreement Julie and I had after our marriage. She did not feel we should go into debt and borrow money, and I, being the "smart business school graduate" that I was, explained to her the principle of leverage. One of the ways to make money in this world was OPM, "other people's money." Thus began the process of engaging in some debt to get through graduate school, into a home, buying a car, and some of the things I thought were necessary to get going in a career.

Debt can be an insufferable taskmaster. At the time we had a U.S. president and a chairman of the Council of Economic Advisors who felt the economy should be growing faster than it was. I can remember them suggesting that they wanted *real* growth of 5 percent, which is certainly an unsustainable rate when you look at the rate of population growth and the rate of productivity increases (which are the two key measurements for determining the maximum rate by which sustainable economic growth can occur). The result was high inflation. The inflation rate hit double digits in 1979, continued in 1980, and on into 1981.

After graduating with my MBA, I started working on a commission basis, but my income didn't take off as fast as I expected. A couple of years later, I expressed to a trusted adviser my anguish over my situation. My income was consistently running about $1,100 a month. My fixed debt payments—mortgage, student loans, and car payments—came to about $2,900 per month. That didn't include food, utilities, clothing, gasoline, and other normal living expenses. I was carrying $61,000 in debt for a home mortgage and an additional $55,000 in unsecured debt. I had three children under the age of four. I was 28 years old and working 70 to 90 hours a week. I saw nothing but despair.

Some suggested I declare bankruptcy. They saw it as my only out. But my trusted adviser asked how I could ever advise others about money if I did such a thing. It would be like a marriage counselor who wanted a divorce. That did it. I resolved to somehow work my way out of the situation I was in.

I had one major problem: I hadn't yet learned how to operate a business profitably. I was still trying to make my millions by leveraging other people's money. I had read about it in all the best-sellers: William Nickerson's *How I Turned $1,000 into $3 Million in Real Estate in My Spare Time*, Robert Allen's *Nothing Down*, Mark Haroldson's *How to Wake Up the Financial Genius Inside You*. But as I watched the economic carnage of the early 1980s, I realized that those books urged people to borrow money in times of high inflation to purchase items with real dollars—and then pay for those items later with depreciated dollars.

What's wrong with that?

As inflation climbs, interest rates eventually do, too. And climbing interest rates ultimately cause an economic collapse—especially a real estate collapse. Then what happens? Inflation spirals downward. Assets that *had* value *lose* that value—but the debt still exists.

I found out, simply, that assets are soft and debt is hard.

Soft Assets and Hard Debt

Debt is "hard" in more ways than one. It took me two more years to get to the point where my monthly income was as great as my monthly outgo. All that time, I had to borrow to live. It was like trying to borrow my way out of debt, like trying to drink yourself sober. By the time I finally turned the corner, I still had a mortgage of $60,000—and my unsecured debt had risen to $110,000.

During this depth I turned to the faith I had been raised on as a child. It was the only place I had to turn. My parents hadn't let me quit the violin, because they thought quitting was habit-forming. So is persisting. And persisting is winning. As a child I had also learned to trust in God and the promise He made to all who will pay Him back a tenth of all their earnings: "*Prove me now* herewith, saith the Lord ... if I will not open the windows of heaven and pour you out a blessing that there shall not be room enough to receive it." (See Malachi 3:8-11.)

I knew I needed a blessing. And I knew I must pay my creditors if I was to expect that blessing, because He was their God too.

On more than one occasion I can remember in desperation feeling an impression that before I had a presentation to make to a potential client, I needed to go immediately and take what money I had right then and not wait until Sunday to pay my tithing. I would put it into an envelope, climb into my car at 10 p.m. and drive over to my minister's house just so I could get the tithing in his hands. Then I could go home and expect a blessing from God.

There was never any question as to who needed to be paid first to be able to expect a blessing. The debt to Him came before others—before food, before clothing. It is my conviction that without that help, I never would have made it. At the most improbable of times, on so many occasions, the means were provided for us to pay our bills and to survive yet another month.

On occasion, people tell me how they are struggling under the load of their debt. My heart goes out to them.

Finally, I had progressed to the point where I was paying my bills and not going further in debt. Within 12 months my newfound confidence and personal progress had the business profiting very well.

Still, I pledged to myself that I would never again borrow money. I committed to focus on my debt payments, which were now many thousands of dollars a month. I also committed to save an additional $3,000 a month. Impossible? No. By putting in 15- and 16-hour days, I did it.

As I began paying off my debt, I made three additional commitments: First, I would not borrow for home improvements, computers at the office, marketing programs. Everything would be paid for with cash. Second, I would not increase my family's living expenses as my income grew; we would continue to live modestly regardless of income level. Finally, as I paid off debt, the money I had been using to retire debt would be put into savings.

I have kept those three commitments.

It is exhilarating not to owe money to anyone. It is a refreshing feeling to have the monthly cash flow necessary to expand the business with cash instead of bank loans. The business may grow less rapidly, but its growth is sure. It's owned, not borrowed. It creates a different level of confidence.

And do you know what? I've discovered that I'm much tighter with my own dollars than I was when spending other people's money.

I learned some additional critical lessons during those years. I learned to avoid debt. I learned how to increase cash flow. In fact, late night creative ponderings helped me discover more than 150 ways to increase cash flow in a business or family setting. Truly, necessity is the mother of invention. When most business owners need cash, they immediately think they must run to the bank. Not so. That is the last place to turn.

I learned that the financial gurus who tell you to put other people's money to work for you are people who are usually selling books, seminars, and tapes. They appeal to greed and the desire to get rich quick. They tell you debt is the way to do it.

They are dead wrong.

Debt destroys, not builds. I have seen it destroy marriages. I have seen it destroy dreams. I have seen it destroy freedom. I have seen it destroy lives.

No one is smarter than debt. If something can go wrong, it will. Whenever you look at a business opportunity, regardless of your training, double your expenses and cut your income in half as you do a cash flow projection. (See Chapter 10.) Then cut your cash flow in half again. Then stretch it out six months further than you think necessary.

I learned that the hard way, too. I figured I knew my business pretty well. After all, I have a degree in accounting. I'm a CPA. I've got an MBA. I was good at my business—I knew marketing. I knew sales. I knew the tax laws. But a couple of unforeseen events could—and did— throw it out of gear.

I learned that today's financial pundits don't really know very much. I decided instead to listen to those who lived during the 1700s and 1800s— and through the Great Depression of the 1930s.

No one on Wall Street ever talks about the 1930s. Yet the Great Depression repeats itself every year in many people's lives. You never know when your personal depression is going to come along—and whether you survive it has a lot to do with whether you are in debt or *not*.

I had to learn from my own mistakes. There are always plenty of *good* reasons to do something stupid, especially in managing money. You can certainly make your own mistakes, too. But you don't need to. *Your Complete Guide to Money Happiness* contains collected insights and experiences of many people who now enjoy financial freedom and independence.

The Three Keys to Get the Most From This Book

First. Constantly ask yourself while you are reading: "How does this thought, this point, make me *feel?*" Be aware of your *feelings* as you read this book. The questions you must ask are: Does it seem right *to you?* Does it feel comfortable *to you?* Is it reasonable *to you?*

Don't ask whether the thought complies with all you have been taught, because very likely it won't. Don't ask, like the skeptic, whether the thought would find approval from the politicians, intellectuals, or societal norms of today, because it may not.

Simply, how does the thought make **you feel?** If it *feels* right and comfortable, then I believe your heart is telling you something. I believe the heart has within it a "director" that will lead us along the pathway to peace and happiness. And that is what this book is all about.

Second. Read with a pen in hand and make notes of thoughts and sudden strokes of inspiration that come to you as you read. Discuss them with *someone. Complete the exercise and questions at the end of each chapter.* As you do, you will be keeping a journal of the suggestions most relevant and pertinent to *your* circumstances and needs. Thus begins the process of translating the book's concepts and principles to the practical and the applied as they relate to *your* situation.

Third. Decide. Do. Take action. We all know a whole lot more than we ever do, especially in the financial realm. The key is to make decisions. Sooner or later, each of us must decide whether we will submit our lives to the timeless principles that guarantee ultimate financial success and security. I have identified seven core decisions which open the door to financial peace of mind. Only then do the strategies make sense. It has been said that knowledge is power. But in truth, knowledge without action is dead.

Order *TODAY* a copy of *Your Money Happiness Workbook.* Complete the worksheets and exercises. Study in more depth those topics that interest you by ordering the free *Instant Reports* available by Fax-on-Demand (see page 513). This book will teach correct principles, but then it is up to you to govern yourself. Stop procrastinating. Take action *now*. Plant the seed today and you will gain a bounteous harvest.

Lifetime Satisfaction Guarantee

Read the book. Mark it up. Order the Workbook. Use it. I hope you will treasure this book as an important addition to your library. But, if at any time in the future you feel this book has not been worth 100 times its purchase price—$2,495—to you in increased financial well-being, return it to me, the author, and I will send you your money back, no questions asked. You must register your purchase by calling 1-800-921-9284 or by ordering *Your Money Happiness Workbook*—see coupon at rear of book. (Sorry, not available to bookstores or discount/bulk purchasers.)

Ship to: Henry S. Brock
P.O. Box 171018
Holladay, UT 84117-1018

Before You Read On

Most of the ideas in this book are *not* mine. I did not pioneer the concepts. I am simply a focused student and devoted disciple. Upon observation, the correct principles you will read on these pages are self-evident. I have occasionally tried to disprove them in my own life, only to suffer the pain of defeat. I have watched countless others try to short-cut them; they, too, have failed.

The principles in this book are based on natural laws. Natural laws *always* supersede political laws and personal taste or style. They are timeless. They will work as well in 2026 as they did in 1996 and in 1886. Financial strategies and practices may change with time, ruled by the economy and tax code and interest rates—but the natural laws upon which they are based never change. They cannot. *If* you are firmly founded in these natural laws, you will succeed. If not, you cannot.

Why take my word for it? Read. Study. Ponder the principles I describe. Test them. Observe them in your own experiences and in the experiences of others. Use the worksheets to determine how the principles apply to your own circumstances. See if they don't "ring true."

This book discusses both principles and practices. Principles don't change. Practices do. All practices, strategies, tactics, and financial advisers should be evaluated on the basis of whether or not they comply with correct principles.

We can't separate our financial-selves from the whole person. Our money life does not stand alone, isolated in a "financial planning vacuum." To the financial statement must be added our thoughts, feelings, hopes, dreams. The dimensions of our lives that impact our finances include the psychological, emotional, and spiritual, in addition to the practical, logical, and intellectual. All aspects of managing one's life are integrated into one great whole.

Psychological and spiritual insights and feelings always impact our views on any significant subject—including the pursuit of money and happiness. For that reason, you will find some "religious" words scattered throughout my text—words like *humility, peace, joy, service, freedom, modesty,* and *happiness.*

I hope this book helps you beyond your most ambitious dreams. I sincerely hope you find something that will bring you increased fulfillment and security. It can become a very useful tool in your quest for financial success and peace of mind.

The length of the book demands that most subjects be treated only briefly. Throughout, you will be able to get more information on a variety of subjects free through our Fax-on-Demand service at my office (see page 513). I hope you'll take the opportunity to learn more about the subjects that interest you. You pay only for the phone call.

You will also find a list of Recommended Resources at the end of the book, as well as an exhaustive Ready-Reference Index. Finally, the Fax-on-Demand service also provides a free index listing longer special reports available for a nominal charge. Simply request the index if you are interested.

I have made every effort to present faithfully those correct principles that govern our financial lives, and to present accurately those strategies and tactics discussed herein. I alone am responsible for this work and assume full responsibility for any inaccuracies or weaknesses in the presentation of these concepts.

For ease and simplicity of expression, I have chosen to use the pronoun he or him, rather than he/she or him/her. Whether you assume traditional or non-traditional financial roles, apply the principles as they relate *to you.*

Turn the page and discover *money happiness.* Some have told me that is an oxymoron—a self-contradictory term. But I have learned that a financial, or temporal, plan suggests there must also be a psychological, emotional, spiritual plan of happiness. The two are inextricably related— compounded into one. It is the union of the two we must discover, because in that union lie the answers to peace and joy.

—Henry S. Brock
Salt Lake City, Utah
September 18, 1996

Decision One

Make Decisions by Happiness Criteria, Not Ego Criteria

In Chapters 1, 2 and 3 we will examine the relationship between money and happiness and consider how to establish a philosophy which integrates the two and abolishes self-defeating behaviors. In Chapters 4, 5 and 6 we will examine the practical application of those principles. Chapter 7 examines the problem of taxes in meeting financial goals.

Chapter 1

Principles with a Promise: Complete Money Happiness Is Within Reach

Happiness. Freedom. Security. Success. Money.

These are five of life's most sought after and highly treasured commodities. They motivate people. Desire for one or another of them has inspired mankind's loftiest and most noble art (poetry, painting, drama, music), its revolutions, and its progress, as well as its baser acts of war, deception, perversion, and crime.

The first and last of these, *happiness* and *money*, seem only rarely in balance with each other the world over. Some people, in fact, will insist that money and happiness are two words that can't be used together, that as a pair they are self-contradictory. Too little or too much money often means anything but happiness, not to mention its dominant role in divorce and other social ills.

My driving purpose in preparing, and my central thesis in writing, *Your Complete Guide to Money Happiness* has been to show the relationship between happiness, freedom, security, success, and money. Their relationship with each other is clearest when seen in the light of correct principles that integrate them. Though the principles are self-evident upon inspection, they seem to elude many. All thought and action bear fruit. The five fruits of *happiness, freedom, security, success,* and *money* are born of compliance with the specific laws and principles that govern those fruits. Like the fruit of good health, only certain paths will get us there.

Anyone, regardless of education level or economic status, who applies these simple and timeless principles, will eliminate misunderstanding and self-defeating money behavior. These principles, or *decisions,* are the road maps to happiness, security, success, and peace of mind.

1. *Make decisions by happiness criteria, not ego criteria.*

Most money unhappiness and financial problems in our society can be attributed to decisions motivated by ego, the need to impress, be in style, have the latest or largest or most elaborate, the need to feed our ego rather than engage in pursuits that genuinely make us happy.

2. *Focus on freedom.*

Happiness will elude anyone who chooses bondage over freedom. If we genuinely seek happiness, we will focus our attentions and actions on maintaining our own freedom and respecting and valuing the freedom of those around us. Freedom increases when we choose correctly and decreases when we choose incorrectly, for incorrect choices disempower us. We unwittingly succumb to bondages that enslave.

3. *Recognize that character counts.*

Character is the foundation for all money happiness. Such character is based on qualities of courage, honesty, gratitude, resilience, commitment, trust, effort, result orientation, and alignment of goals with correct principles. We will discuss each of these.

4. *Build a solid foundation for security.*

Anyone who would enjoy security, whether financial or any other kind, must be willing to be prepared. Prepared for what? We must be vigilant and ready for whatever life has to offer. Three qualities that most enable us to be prepared in this way are self-reliance, self-control, and service.

5. *Climb the right ladder to success.*

Though they seem mysterious to most, the four laws that govern success are fairly straightforward. First, do what you love; second, focus on end results that have meaning to you, not the unpleasant tasks that lead to those ends; third, simplify to focus; and fourth, synergize through interdependence.

6. *Avoid poor thinking.*

Success thinkers look for opportunities rather than excuses, accept responsibility, are positive despite the stress, seek mentors and role-models, and find reasons to be glad, grateful, and cheerful. Poor thinkers can't accept responsibility, but instead blame, feel victimized, seem bound by self-pity, let obstacles overwhelm them, and justify failure or poor performance.

7. *Make your dream your reality.*

Without a vision, we perish. Our purpose in living, our life's mission, must be made clear to us as we live each day. That is why we must have goals that direct our thoughts and actions toward our life's purpose. If our goals are not aligned with our purpose for living, we will not likely achieve it. To be successful in our pursuit, all success-actions must become habitual.

The way we choose to earn and manage money cannot be isolated from the rest of our life—our feelings, our thoughts, our hopes, and our purpose for living. Money must be integrated with the emotional, psychological, and spiritual aspects, rather than kept on a separate ledger. Practicing these principles of money happiness will influence other dimensions, yielding even greater happiness and further enriching your life.

What Is Money?

Before money was invented as *a medium of exchange*, people traded or bartered their goods. Rice or vegetables were exchanged for meat or milk or honey.

The initial forms of money were gold and silver; the value of coins increased with size and weight. The U.S. dollar was backed by gold until we eliminated the gold standard in 1964, and since then our dollar has been backed by the taxing authority and borrowing capacity of our government. Even so, the U.S. dollar is recognized throughout the world as the currency of stability and safety, which is one reason why so many people feel it is critical that our budget be balanced and that we have a strong and stable government.

To define money as a medium of exchange is handy for economists, but it primarily focuses on the fact that money is more convenient than bartering. I prefer defining money *as stored labor*—that way we recognize that we have traded our labor for money. The more money we have saved, the more labor we have stored. In other words, money is past savings accumulated for future consumption or production.

Why do I prefer this definition of money? Because it teaches respect for money. It recognizes that someone's labor was expended in order to acquire money. It equates more directly the efforts we spend for money with the value of that money. *Most people will spend money much more frivolously than labor*: They'll spend *three* hours working for enough money to buy dinner at a restaurant, but they'd never consider spending *one* hour washing dishes at the restaurant for that same dinner.

Try translating your purchases into the hours it will take to acquire them. If you believe you shouldn't spend your labor for things of little worth, you will start to better respect your money—and to use it more wisely. Seeing money this way helps us appreciate that our income requires either "man at work" or "money at work." In our younger years, for most of us, it is clearly "man at work" that generates our income. Ultimately, at retirement, it will be necessary for us to use "money at work" in order to live.

Regardless, we are all going to live either by "man at work" or "money at work." Decide in which combination you want to have it. If you believe money is for consumption, then you will spend your life living from "man at work." If, on the other hand, you have an appropriate balance between consumption and saving, then you may some day realize the benefits of living from your "money at work."

This becomes especially relevant at retirement. If you've stored enough labor in the form of money, then you'll have the resources you need. Your stored labor can be used to buy time when you can't work. You'll discover, as American statesman Benjamin Franklin said, there are "three faithful friends—an old wife, an old dog, and ready money."

A Bit of Happiness in Your Pocket

Money is *nice*. When it's in your pocket, it warms your heart; when it's not, everything seems colder. Money can do good for us and others, it can bring security, and it makes possible the conveniences and luxuries of life.

Money is also temporary; that is, it applies only to our temporal time on earth. We must be concerned with all temporal affairs—not just money, but security, safety, success, and self-reliance.

Does money bring happiness? Most of us have experienced happiness. Happiness is not fun, entertainment, or pleasure; these are fleeting. Even the latest model car gets old and wears out. Objects of fine art fall off the shelf and break. A ride at an amusement park may be thrilling, but it provides little lasting satisfaction. It is not something that is relived in the deep emotional experiences of the heart.

Happiness, on the other hand, relates to the joy we feel from experiences of such import or magnitude that they deserve to be remembered and relived in our minds. These meaningful experiences are usually tied to human relationships or service in great causes. Happiness of that kind is a life-long quest.

You can be sick and be happy. You can be unattractive, even ugly, and be happy. You can be poor and be happy. You can be disabled and be happy. You can be ignorant and be happy. You can be fat, skinny, tall or short and be happy. You can be unemployed, an orphan, married or single and be happy. You can be a minority, abused, or illiterate and still be happy. The one thing you can't do and still be happy is be out of alignment with correct principles.

I believe that the purpose of life is to find happiness. Surely all of us understand that the deeper our satisfactions and joys and happiness, the more fulfilling our life becomes.

What, then, is your "happiness quotient"? Is there a healthy balance between your search for true happiness and your quest for pleasures in life? The thrill and excitement of rides at an amusement park, like all pleasures, soon lose their appeal without family and friends along to add meaning to the occasion and create lasting memories. One must realize that fun is not happiness; fun is just fun. Joy is happiness.

How Much Happiness Do You Want?

Do you want happiness? Of course. How much do you want it?

If asked, virtually everyone will answer, "Very much." But that just can't be true. Let's quit kidding ourselves.

Some people want happiness more than others and work harder than others at achieving it. They get up early to help their children with homework. They plan a special family reunion. They make a greater effort to qualify for the inner contentment, serenity, and peace of mind that comes with happiness.

Achieving happiness, as in achieving anything, is founded upon our compliance with those principles and laws that lead toward it. Specific natural laws and principles in the universe lead toward the acquisition of any specific result. Those results, or "fruits" of our labor, can be picked and eaten only as we discover and then comply with the laws which lead to them.

The law of the harvest is immutable. If you desire the fruit of security, tranquility, and peace of mind, you must first plant the correct seeds and nurture them. If you desire success, you comply with success principles.

Can Money Buy Happiness?

Alexander Hamilton, one of our founding fathers and the first Secretary of the Treasury, penned in a December 1779 letter to John Laurens, "Money is an essential ingredient to happiness in this world."

Of course, money can't guarantee happiness, and may not even be necessary for obtaining it. In early 1995, my wife and I and a few of our children spent a week in the town of Encino outside of Irapuato, Mexico. The town had no electricity or plumbing. The homes were built of rock, with dirt or concrete slabs for floors. Every day the townspeople fetched their water in pails from a nearby reservoir they shared with their goats and other farm animals. At sundown the town was blackened. The town's children worked from sunup to sundown—and then some. It seemed a hard life of drudgery and meager existence. But, were they happy? Very.

Money doesn't necessarily buy happiness. Instead, happiness depends on our expectations—and on how high we set those expectations. Those who have high or violated expectations may be disappointed. Those with low expectations may not.

Happiness also depends on our attitude about our circumstances and surroundings. When I lived and worked in the ghettoes of Philadelphia, I entered many homes where there was despair, monotony, a lack of feeling, and general malaise. But in a home next door—a home that looked just the same from the outside—the people were happy, enthused, and full of life. The difference? It wasn't material possessions. It was attitude.

If happiness has more to do with attitude than with material possessions, how does money relate to happiness? Can it buy happiness? When we consider how much time we spend acquiring money, success, and security, it ought to have *something* to do with happiness.

Then what is the purpose of financial success? Of security? Of money?

Let's start with what the purpose is *not*. The purpose of success or security or money is not to have more than your neighbors. It's not to have a bigger home or car. It's not to have a fancier boat, or vacations to more exotic places. It's not to play golf twice a week or to have a box at the stadium or even to provide retirement. (Did God tell Adam and Eve, "Thou shalt work all the days of your life *until you retire*"?)

There is only one purpose for stored labor—and labor is worth storing only when we discover ways to achieve that purpose. What's the purpose? It's the same as the purpose for anything else: Joy. Happiness. The only justifiable purpose for money, then, is happiness.

My suggestion throughout this book is that money *can* and *should* buy happiness.

When we start to prioritize our use of money by this standard, our perspective changes. Our labors become consecrated to higher purposes. The goal of a new car or box seats or club dues becomes less important. Retirement is no longer the age of trivial pursuits, but life's greatest time of opportunity. We quit squandering money for things of little worth.

The whole exercise of financial planning takes on new meaning. We look at money in a new way. Can money buy happiness? Money buys college educations, experiences and opportunities for our children, security in a neighborhood that will afford our family greater opportunities. These are the fruits of money that contribute to happiness. They are worth working and saving for.

Money Means Freedom

Consider a simple example of the kinds of opportunities I'm talking about. Doug and Holly took their young daughter Alexis to the park to play on the jungle gym. Doug's money had bought a video camera. His stored labor had purchased a day off work. In other words, he exchanged his resources to buy an experience with his child. The video recording would provide years of joyful memories.

In *The Law of Financial Success,* Edward E. Beals wrote, "Money is the symbol of nearly everything necessary for man's well-being and happiness. Money means freedom, independence, liberty." If we choose to use the liberty purchased by money in order to do good, then our money may buy some measure of happiness. If we use money merely to buy *things*—if money results in acquiring things or pursuing purposes that worsen the lot of mankind—then our money will help us acquire disappointment, heartache, and misery.

We should seek financial success, then, with the intent to do good and to improve the common lot of man. That may start with your own small family, within the walls of your own home. It reaches out from there.

Violated Expectations about Money

We soon discover that if money buys happiness, that happiness is bought out of our *surplus, beyond* our basic needs of food, clothing, and shelter. Our surplus dollars are available for what we might consider the higher purposes in life. Defining our basic necessities reveals a great deal about us. Just how insatiable have our wants become? Too often, we allow our *wants* to become *needs*. (Have you ever considered whether you "need" a television to live?)

We set our own expectations, be they high or low. If we set high expectations, we may well end up disappointed, feeling poor. If our expectations are lower, we may well end up feeling grateful but complacent. How do you reconcile the two?

The danger of lowering your expectations and aspirations is that whenever you expect less from life, a little bit of you dies. You lose some of your vision—and it has been said that without vision, we perish.

This happens all the time in the ghettoes and the poorer nations of the world. But it also happens in middle- and upper-income households. When you lose the vision of what you or your family can become, you lose everything—including happiness.

What's the answer, then? Since happiness is bought with surplus, it's critical to properly define our needs so we'll know what's available for savings and surplus. In other words, we need to manage our expectations.

Are You Money Anorexic?

Some people have a "scarcity" mentality. They sabotage themselves. They believe there isn't enough for themselves, so they have little time or money to share with others. Other people feel unworthy of success, so they engage in all kinds of self-defeating behaviors. They are success-driven. They dress for success. They graduate from college. They work hard. But they consistently sabotage themselves to doubt and ultimate failure. Why? Their self-image is incongruent with the success they are striving for. As a result, they have a difficult time ever achieving success and happiness.

This distorted view is much like anorexia or bulimia: Victims of eating disorders sabotage themselves physically, while victims of money disorders sabotage themselves financially. They become so worried about survival—like the pig wallowing in the mud—that they can never allow their thoughts to soar like an eagle.

How do you blast yourself out of self-defeating thought patterns? How do you expand your perspectives, your vision, your horizon? How do you raise your expectations of life without setting yourself up for disappointment?

Have you lowered your expectations in order to avoid the potential defeat of being disappointed? Are you living the quasi-fulfilled life because of fear of disappointment and failure?

A person who has high expectations of a relationship that eventually fails often withdraws to avoid getting hurt again. Are you doing that in your financial life? In your overall pursuit of happiness? It doesn't need to be that way. If you discover the true principles and laws that lead to success, security, and money happiness, then you'll find success, security, and happiness.

Choose Your Own Level of Money Happiness

There's no quick fix. It simply doesn't exist. This book, then, does not offer a get-rich-quick program. It does not promise wealth without effort. (If that's what you are looking for, you have the wrong book. Go watch an infomercial on late night TV.)

Like the eagle, the greater your vision, the more your boundaries expand. I hope this book will increase your vision and extend your boundaries beyond what you now believe possible.

If you engage in poor thinking, you limit your options. You can't enjoy freedom. As you expand your vision, your boundaries disappear.

When I face a classroom full of new hires in my business, I point out to them that only six or seven of 10 will survive the first year in my business. Then I ask, "So, what are your odds of success?"

I usually get a room full of dumbfounded looks. They glance at each other and meekly suggest that their odds of success are 60 percent. These are bright, sharp, young college graduates—the cream of the crop. Yet that's what they consider to be their odds of success.

If that question were posed to me, my response would be, "Nonsense! My odds of success are 100 percent."

How do I know that?

You make your own odds of success. Statistics are irrelevant when it comes to you and what you are going to make of your life. You are in control. If you want something badly enough—whether it's success or money happiness or something else—you decide whether you will succeed.

That is why I don't believe that a person is merely the sum total of all his experiences. That definition suggests that "we are what we have been." If you are a growing person, then (by definition) the past is inferior behavior. No, a person is not the sum total of all his experiences; he is what he hopes to become. Hope is what determines our behavior.

If your mind is preoccupied by your inferior past, you may have little hope. But if your mind is preoccupied by your future, by your goals and aspirations, then your past is highly irrelevant and you have abundant hope. And your hope should be founded in the principles of happiness!

Your Insights, Feelings, and Action Items

A. As you read this chapter, what *insights* came that seem applicable to *you?*

    1._____

    2._____

    3._____

B. How did you *feel* as you pondered particular points of this chapter?

    1._____

    2._____

    3._____

C. What do you *feel* you should *do* as a result of this chapter?

    1._____

    2._____

    3._____

D. How might you solicit the aid of others in accomplishing "C" above?

_____

_____

_____

Chapter 2

Money Has a Character
of Its Own

Bill and Joli have three children. Bill was climbing the corporate ladder of success and was near the top of a major corporation, with increasing responsibility and increasing income. When he was first hired, he managed a department of eight people. Three years later, he managed a department of more than 120 people with an annual budget of $8 million.

Bill reported to work one Friday, just as he had done every other day. By mid-morning he had been laid off. What a shock! He returned home to a concerned wife. Deep depression and uncertainty set in. He felt suicidal. Thanks to an encouraging spouse, he began to count his blessings. It would mean more time with the children. Joli helped him realize that he always landed on his feet. He was able to see the big picture.

Within 24 hours, he felt better. Two days later when some former co-workers ran into him, he was happy as could be. He knew other opportunities would come along. A week later, those same co-workers were surprised to see him even happier than he had been a week earlier. That's resilience.

Money not only has a character and force of its own, it has its own behavior patterns. It's as though money is magnetized—it attracts itself in certain ways. It flows in certain directions.

Money begets itself. In *Letters to My Friend, A.B.*, Benjamin Franklin wrote, "Money is of a prolific, generating nature. Money can beget money and it can beget more."

If you want to make money, you *must* understand the principles that attract and repel money. You need to become a person who attracts money—not one who repels money.

Likes attract likes. You've seen it: People of a similar nature respond and congregate together. That's a natural law. Intellectuals get together for study groups. Athletes work out together and play games on Saturdays. Goal-striving people want to be with goal-striving people. Partiers want to party. Each is drawn to its own.

So, what kind of person do you need to be if you want to attract money?

Money flows in only two directions—toward *incentive* or toward *trust*. If you want money to flow toward you, you must provide one or the other. You will attract money only to the extent you are trusted—because that is how others will find in you their security. When you respect money, when you have earned money, when you view money as stored labor, when you see money as a stewardship, others will trust you.

You will also attract money to the extent you provide incentive—because that is where those who desire opportunity will send their money. Economic incentives or profits explain why capital in our economy changes hands at the rate of about 20 times a year—and why socialist and communist societies do not turn over capital anywhere near the same magnitude.

You will discover that, just as money has a character of its own, it wants to be taken care of. It nestles toward those who nurture it. Thus comes the discovery that your proper relationship with money is that of *stewardship*. You discover you really do not *own* anything. You are simply a caretaker of the material possessions under your control. You will not be taking anything with you.

The Law of Unequal Rewards

Have you ever heard of *the law of unequal rewards*? It goes something like this:

One man was given one talent by his master. Another was given two talents. A third was given five talents. The master went into a far country and later returned for an accounting of their stewardships. As each steward gave an accounting of his stewardship, listen to how each might sound like some of us:

The first said, "Master, I had just one talent, and I knew you profited where you did not sow." (What does this say about his attitude? The master was his employer, and was giving him a little responsibility. Perhaps that is *our* attitude about those who are succeeding in this world.) "So," the steward continued, "I took the talent you gave me and I buried it."

The master was angry at his servant. He would not invest in an employee who would not generate a return on that investment. The servant wasted his talent.

It was the second servant's turn. "You gave me two talents, and I multiplied them." The master smiled, "Good job. Here are two more. Here is some additional responsibility—more opportunities to grow and succeed and progress."

What happened to the steward with five talents? He had even greater responsibility. He reported to his master that he had grown and cultivated and magnified his talents. The master, seeing that he had a profitable servant, not only gave him five more, but took the talent from the one who had buried it and added it to the five—for a total of 11 talents.

At first blush, this law of unequal rewards may seem unfair. Some excuse it by saying, "The rich get richer and the poor get poorer." But when you understand stewardship, you discover why it is a necessary and natural law for financial success. Those who exercise proper stewardship over what is given them attract more—and it continues to compound.

This law of unequal rewards is the parable of talents as found in the New Testament and taught by Jesus. It suggests many things. It suggests that someone who works a 40-hour week is making an average effort and will receive his fair reward—but the one who comes in a little early and stays a little late, and who works a 50-hour week, will ultimately earn *twice* as much as the one who works a 40-hour week.

Why?

He'll be given additional responsibility. He exhibits drive and trustworthiness. He attracts rather than repels success.

We will likewise have to account for our stewardship. When we have earned our financial success through hard labor, we respect it more and appreciate the proper relationship of man to material wealth. As a result, we attract more.

Ralph is thankful to his wife, Roberta. He commented, "I've made the money, and she's saved it."

Roberta's philosophy? "I don't need a new car. It's eight years old. New tires are all I need. I'm not taking anything with me. I don't own anything. Nice little things fall off the shelf and break."

Roberta was comfortable with her philosophy of money. It was right for her. She wanted a home that was inviting to grandchildren and was "childproof."

Those who come by their money easily often engage in speculative ventures—a reflection of their lack of respect. As Cato the Elder wrote, "Make moderate use of gains: When all is cost, what took long time to get is quickly lost."

What Is True Financial Planning?

Financial planning doesn't consist only of cash flow management, budgeting, investments, retirement planning, tax planning, and estate planning. Financial planning is far more encompassing. It has to do with anything that relates to money or temporal welfare, something that is worth financial planning.

Just as with life planning, financial planning must be based on correct principles. There is little room for error. As the saying goes, *"However you build it, the ship must sail. You can't explain to the ocean."*

Natural laws dictate that eventually we will reap what we sow. That's the law of the harvest. The key is to discover those natural economic laws and to make them work for you.

So, what is true financial planning? What are you planning for? Are you planning for more money? More vacations? A fancier car? A bigger house? Think further.

Are you planning for security? For retirement? That's better.

Are you planning for happiness? That is what you should be planning for.

Financial planning is a journey. There are tunnels, potholes, detours onto dirt roads. Sometimes there's black ice. When you hit it, you spin out of control. You have to get through the hot and dusty desert of training, skill building, college, the early married years—sometimes there doesn't seem to be an end in sight. Like life, there's the occasional cool shade of a mountain forest or stream. But most of your financial life is hard work, with only occasional vistas from the mountaintop and the panoramic view of a beautiful sunset. If you think otherwise, you're setting yourself up for disappointment. But the journey is always worth it.

Ego Criteria

The number-one cause of financial problems in America is ego. That's why families get into debt. That's why spending is out of line. It is said that 75 percent of all divorces are the result of financial problems. Ego, selfishness, and self-centeredness cause problems deeper than any of the other things that cause us financial problems. *The key, then, is to make decisions according to happiness criteria, not ego criteria.*

Ego criteria focus on things, buying experiences that yield pleasure, fun, entertainment, and instant gratification.

A person driven by ego asks, "What will others think?" Such a person worries about the short-term. Puts others beneath himself. Feels competition and pride. Thinks "win-lose." Has a scarcity mentality.

A person driven by ego spends and consumes, no matter how much or how little he earns. Such a person is inward-centered. Self-absorbed. Ego-centric. He may be untrue to his greatest commitments.

Such a person lives in bondage, a slave to debt, television, and spending. Such a person strives for excessive achievement. More and more success. More and more things. To the ego-driven person, money is trivial—at least, it's treated that way ("easy come, easy go").

Happiness Criteria

Happiness criteria focus on relationships, on experiences that yield fulfillment, joy, peace, and happiness.

A person committed to happiness asks, "What can I do for others?" Such a person thinks long-term. Builds others. Helps others. Cooperates. Serves. Thinks win-win. Is centered on others. Has an abundance mentality.

A person committed to happiness balances spending with saving, no matter how much or how little he earns. Such a person enjoys freedom and is not addicted to spending and debt. That person spends time and money acquiring family memories, adequate success, and high balance. He is loyal to his greatest commitments.

A person committed to happiness sees money as stewardship. Since money is hard to come by, it should be let go with wisdom.

Financial Decision-Making Criteria

Happiness Criteria	Ego Criteria
Focus on relationships	Focus on things
Experiences that yield fulfillment	Experiences that yield pleasure
Joy	Fun
Peace	Entertainment
Happiness	Instant gratification
"What can I do for others?"	"What will others think?"
Thinks long-term	Worries about short-term
Builds others	Puts others down
Helps others and cooperates	Competition and pride
Serves	Egocentric
Abundance Mentality	Scarcity Mentality
Thinks "Win-win"	Thinks "Win-lose"
Centered on others	Inward-centered
Sacrifices something of the moment for what he wants permanently	Sacrifices what he wants most for what he wants at the moment
Balances spending with saving	Spends and consumes
Enjoys freedom	In bondage
Not addicted to spending and debt	Slave to debt
Sees money as stewardship	Money is trivial, "easy come, easy go"
Spends time and money on family memories, adequate success, and high balance	Strives for excessive achievement

We are all in complete alignment for the level of financial success we are achieving. We are also in perfect mental alignment for the level of happiness we are experiencing (barring chemically-induced depression). If those statements make you uncomfortable, perhaps it is because they place on *you* the responsibility for your own level of temporal success and happiness.

Accepting responsibility is an adult trait; the child in us prefers to blame others for our circumstances. No change can occur until you accept responsibility for your condition.

Some would teach that those in the ghetto are there because of the government, big business or the haves vs. the have-nots. That kind of thinking simply *keeps* people in the ghetto. Remember: Most of our forebears arrived on the shores of the ghetto—the Irish ghetto, the Italian ghetto, the Chinese ghetto. If you are there today, it is the quality of your thinking that will get you out—not a government program or some other handout. (You cannot accept a handout without becoming weaker. Avoid them at all costs and you will become strong.)

Remember, too, that as you climb the ladder of success, you won't be happy unless "the ladder is leaning against the right wall." You won't be happy unless you are making decisions according to happiness criteria.

Those who make decisions according to happiness criteria are cognizant of the great responsibilities and commitments they have made to others. They are commitment-conscious, not consumption-conscious. They are happiness-conscious, not fun-conscious.

Remember: Your awareness and focus is on your commitments—the important commitments you have made in your life. I challenge you to establish a sound philosophy about money and temporal welfare and to make decisions according to happiness criteria. If you do, I promise you will find money happiness.

Your Insights, Feelings, and Action Items

A. As you read this chapter, what *insights* came that seem applicable to *you?*
   1._____
   2._____
   3._____

B. How did you *feel* as you pondered particular points of this chapter?
   1._____
   2._____
   3._____

C. What do you *feel* you should *do* as a result of this chapter?
   1._____
   2._____
   3._____

D. How might you solicit the aid of others in accomplishing "C" above?

   _____
   _____
   _____

Chapter 3

Can Money Buy Happiness?

We May Love It or Hate It

Why do we pursue the acquisition of money?

As I have asked that question at seminars and focus groups and to clients over the years, the answers have been far-reaching. Among them: To make more money. To survive. To provide security. To provide for college and retirement. For accomplishment. To gain prestige. To buy things and experiences. To buy love. To keep up with the Joneses. To get ahead of the Joneses.

If you are preoccupied with money—if it is your sole ambition, the *end* of your pursuits—then you'll certainly be disappointed and will find little happiness. Only when you consider money a *means* to greater goods will your focus change to the good things money can be used for.

Some people consider money the root of all evil, taking as their source a misquote of the well-known biblical admonition that "the *love* of money is the root of all evil." If you consider money evil, you will fail in your efforts to plan your finances and to succeed in your work. You must realize that money is good—it is a means to worthwhile ends and purposes.

That doesn't mean you can rationalize your pursuit of money. If you tell yourself that you are pursuing money to relieve suffering in the world and to promote good, but you become prideful in that pursuit, you may discover the occasional emptiness that often accompanies any false endeavor. Your "success" may be hollow and empty.

Ask yourself what money means to you. (Since you spend one-third of your life pursuing money—working for a paycheck—that's no small question.) If you consider money to be evil, you will be bogged down. If you believe money can help buy happiness, it will be easier to save—and the strategies and tactics in this book will be more meaningful.

For What Purpose Do You Pursue Money?

What are *your* great purposes in life? What are your goals? Your aspirations? Your deepest motivations? One of the exercises in *Your Money Happiness Workbook* helps you identify why you are pursuing money and what your purposes in life are.

If money is your end purpose, happiness will elude you, because money can only be a means to an end. Until your purposes in life are aligned there can be no real meaning in even the most competent planning. And once they *are* aligned, an amazing power will unleash itself toward those purposes. People will expend far more effort in pursuit of a worthwhile cause in life than in the acquisition of the dollar.

What is important about money to you? What are the most vital things you can acquire? Are they temporal—having to do with worldly possessions? Or are they of a lasting nature? Whenever we ponder the importance of things or consider our purposes, we can benefit immensely from the great thinkers, philosophers, and prophets. From them we have learned the importance of asking life's greatest questions: Where does the greatest happiness and fulfillment come from? Is there meaning to life beyond what we can see? And in the context of these searching questions we might also ask: What lasting value have our possessions? Have I invested as much in my relationships? Gaining knowledge? Improving attitudes?

These questions naturally cause us to think about what occupies our time. Are we pursuing things that are temporary? Or things that are permanent and lasting? What in life is important to you? Does that change your relationships or knowledge or status or prestige? Are you spending time and *money* on the things that are really important to you?

In *The Seven Habits of Highly Effective People,* Stephen Covey introduces "the maturity continuum," a model that demonstrates how we progress from a state of dependence to independence to interdependence. Covey maintains that, contrary to popular thinking, the highest level of maturity is not found in independence, but in interdependence. When we discuss the maturity continuum as it relates to money, we discover that most of us have a lot of growing up to do. "He who dies with the most toys wins," teases the bumper sticker, but many of us live as though it's true. So when do we grow up?

We all grow up on our death bed. Career accolades have faded. Ego-stroking from others means nothing. That's when we realize that we won't be taking the gadgets and the toys with us. All we will be able to take is our knowledge, attitudes, thinking habits, and relationships.

Opposition and Adversity Are Natural Laws

Opposites are a part of life. You have to experience adversity in order to appreciate happiness. Can anyone really know happiness without experiencing adversity and misery? No. Happiness would not even exist—we would be in a state of static oblivion.

Natural, self-evident principles tell us that, in all aspects of life, we need to pass through the challenges and adversity to know the good. Our financial lives are no exception. We may bring adversities upon ourselves through foolishness, mistakes of judgment, and misguided attempts to find happiness in an incorrect manner. But even if we are doing all in our power to live according to correct principles and to avoid mistakes, life will still be fraught with adversity and trials.

Because all of life is full of opposites, one of our tests is how we respond to adversity. Anne Morrow Lindbergh wrote, "I do not believe that sheer suffering teaches. If suffering alone taught, all the world would be wise, since everyone suffers. To suffering must be added mourning, understanding, patience, love, openness, and the willingness to remain vulnerable."

People who handle adversity well see some positive result—and they aren't bitter after enduring adversity. Some who have had plenty of adversities have discovered they were blessings in disguise.

When my home burned in 1994, many people were incredulous that my family and I shrugged it off. There was nothing we could do about it. I was in Dallas at some meetings, and I received the telephone call after midnight telling me about the fire. I asked a few questions, then our conversation turned to other topics. My wife, Julie, explained that eight or 10 fire trucks had left. My daughter Andrea was on the nightly news. The neighbors had been over to help. Life would go on.

It took us 10 months to rebuild. During that time, we had to find another home to rent, but we resumed life as normal. I had worked for years to build our large, spacious, beautiful home, but it was not the central part of our lives. The children were safe. Relationships were intact. The things that mattered were in place. It was simply going to be a nuisance for a year.

When I was in college people told me they did not want to pursue financial success because they might go to hell. They rationalized their thinking with the biblical thought that it is more difficult for a rich man to get into heaven than it is for a camel to pass through the eye of a needle.

I've heard of people who don't want to get married because they are afraid they might get divorced. I've heard people say about having children, "I'm not having children because they're expensive, and besides, they might turn out like me!"

True to the law of opposites, children may be our greatest trials, but they also are usually our greatest joys. (Children certainly must be mentioned in any discussion about adversity and money!)

Don't let your fear of adversity diminish your spirit or cause you to withdraw from challenges and opportunities. If you do, you will die just a little. Understand that, as Anne Bradstreet wrote in *Meditations Divine and Moral*, "If we had no winter, the spring would not be so pleasant. If we did not sometimes taste of adversity, prosperity would not be so welcome."

Remember that personal character growth is always spelled c-h-a-l-l-e-n-g-e. Sometimes we say, "Who needs growth?" When life is most painful, we are usually growing the most. Like exercise, "no pain, no gain." Adversity may be easier to endure when we remember the purposes of it.

How Much You Have, or How Much You Appreciate?

Eventually, then, we discover that it isn't how much money we have that brings happiness. Our *attitude*—the attitude of gratitude, challenge, variety, and service—brings happiness.

"Happiness doesn't depend on what we have but how we feel toward what we have," wrote American publisher and agriculturalist William Dempster Howard. "We can be happy or miserable with much."

Coco Chanel, acclaimed fashion designer, maintains, "There are people who have money and people who are rich." And in the conclusion to *Walden*, Henry Thoreau wrote, "Love your life, poor as it is. You may perhaps have some pleasant, thrilling, glorious hours even in a poor house. The setting sun is reflected from the windows of the almshouse as brightly as from the rich man's abode."

President John F. Kennedy counseled, "Ask not what your country can do for you, but what you can do for your country." It was considered a great statement. An inspiring statement. Why? Perhaps we recognized in this call for *service* the root of what makes us feel good about ourselves.

I like the healthy attitude expressed by my client Roberta, who lived many years without much money and then retired with more than she knew what to do with. "It's all in your head," she said. "If you feel rich, you're rich. If you feel poor, you're poor. It's only money!"

Perhaps my sister Draza summed it up when she said, "That's the challenge in life—to live without money and be happy or to live with it and be happy."

Can people be happy if they are starving? Can people pursue the answers to life's greatest questions if they're hungry? People don't pursue happiness, spiritual fulfillment, or any other higher pursuit with an empty belly. Fill the belly first, and you can then listen to the preacher or pursue happiness, however you define it.

As Woodrow Wilson noted in 1912, "Business underlies everything in our national life, including our spiritual life. Witness the fact that in the Lord's prayer the petition is for daily bread. No one can worship God or love his neighbor on an empty stomach."

Is Money Your Daily Bread, or Your Daily Dread?

How can money be used? It can be hoarded selfishly out of a miserly greed, as with Dickens' Ebenezer Scrooge. It may also be hoarded innocently because of insecurity or distrust. Regardless, the result is the same. In a letter to J.P. Custis dated January 1780, President George Washington pointed out the folly in that when he wrote, "It is not a custom with me to keep money to look at."

Money may be consumed. Almost everybody's good at that. And one of the purposes of money is to consume it, since doing so provides the comforts of life.

Money may be squandered—which is what happens when we spend it on things that bring no lasting satisfaction. Sophisticated and designing men spend their waking hours inventing new ways to entice us and our children to squander our money. Modern advertising geniuses of Madison Avenue have caused us to redefine many of our *wants* as *needs*.

Money may be gambled away. Many pursue the dream of getting rich quick. The gambling industry has subtly renamed the term "gaming," which seems innocent enough until we look at its addictive nature. Some spend their labor to purchase lottery tickets—hardly the stuff prudent financial planning is made of.

Money may be invested. You can invest it in real estate—bricks and mortar. You can invest it in productive capacities—represented by stocks, bonds, or mutual funds. You can invest it in people or in education. All of these may have their place in a sound program.

Finally, money may be spread. English philosopher Francis Bacon quipped, "Money is like manure, of very little use except it be spread."

In Charles Dickens' classic tale *The Christmas Carol*, Scrooge discovers happiness only when he spreads his money and serves others. Most of us discover this pleasure poignantly during Christmas, Hanukkah, birthdays, and other occasions when we serve others. Unfortunately, we often forget it during the rest of the year.

Make Money Your Servant, Not Your Master

As we consider what flows from money, we discover, as Henry George Bohn wrote in the *Handbook of Proverbs*, that "money is a good servant but a bad master."

How is money a bad master?

Money is a bad master when we are preoccupied by acquiring it. It's a bad master when we forfeit our freedom to debt. And money is a bad master when we unconsciously find ourselves having to keep up with the Joneses.

Conversely, some of us think, as John D. Rockefeller stated in a 1905 interview, "God gave me my money. I believe the power to make money is a gift from God. I believe it is my duty to make money and still more money and to use it for the good of my fellow men according to the dictates of my conscience."

The question is not so much, "How can money be used?" but, "How will *you* use it? What are *your* purposes for it?"

It is essential that you understand your philosophy about money. Natural laws and principles dictate that the more healthy your philosophy about money, the more your use of money will be congruent with your pursuit of happiness. The poorer your philosophy about money, the more unhappy and miserable you'll be. As American clergyman Earl Riney said, "Dollars do better if they are accompanied by sense."

Can Your Money Success Allow Time for Happiness?

Success means something different to almost everybody. Society often defines success in terms of monetary wealth. While that's the definition we will use in this book as we discuss financial planning, it is important to note that success defined by material wealth probably has little or nothing to do with happiness.

Is it okay to pursue material success? If your intent is to do good, you need to keep in perspective the things that really matter. It has been said that "no other success in life can compensate for failure in the home." (David O. McKay, 1873-1970)

That warm and honest actor, Jimmy Stewart, said his favorite role was "devoted husband of Gloria," whom he married in 1949. What an example of *real* success.

American Express President Jeff Steifler was making $4 million a year and was at the pinnacle of his career in his 40s. He still had plenty of new mountains to climb, but he decided he was not going to remain at the top of American Express at the expense of his family.

Jeff Steifler changed his priorities. Perhaps his professional achievements hadn't been matched in his personal life. He wanted to spend more time with his 17-year-old son, an aspiring journalist. That required a less intense pace. His $4 million a year wasn't bringing him the happiness he craved, so he decided to get his life into alignment with his priorities. He retired.

Most of us can't retire in our 40s, because we don't have that kind of income. But we make the same mistake: We climb the ladder of success to the top, only to discover it was leaning against the wrong wall. We arrive, only to find we have missed out on life.

Stephen Covey suggests, "Rather than focusing on *things*, we should focus on preserving and enhancing relationships and on accomplishing results."

Yes, it's okay to pursue material success. In fact, that's what much of this book is about. But we also need to remember that "the greatest cause of failure and unhappiness in this life is trading what you want *most* for what you want at the *moment*."

What You Want *Most*? Or What You Want *Now*?

The fleeting pleasures of life may become so addicting and appealing that we trade our deepest commitments and priorities for something far less important that we want at the moment.

Success takes sacrifice. That applies to *any* kind of success—financial, career, family, or any other kind of success we pursue. And sacrifice means giving up something good for something better.

Sacrifice is not a decision between a good choice and a bad choice. It's a decision between two good choices. Those who succeed in any endeavor learn to go without what they want at the moment in order to achieve what they want permanently. This applies as much to financial success as it does to success in the family, in interpersonal relationships, among friends, in school, or in any other pursuit.

Is your ladder against the wrong wall? The pursuit of money and material things can destroy the best of marriages. Consumption beyond our means is unwise and only yields frustration. Advertisements make things so enticing that we often trade long-term success and security for what we want at the moment.

Sometimes the ego-stroking of climbing the ladder of success distracts us from those we love the most. The enticements of television, sports, Monday night football, and "happy hours" sap the energy that could have been devoted to success and happiness. There's nothing wrong with good entertainment. In excess, though, it makes us slaves to our inferior habits. These are the kinds of things that must be sacrificed if we want to achieve success in any realm.

Remember, too, that money must be earned *honorably*. It's often tempting to take shortcuts in the pursuit of financial success. These shortcuts are one of our nation's greatest ills. Easy money is never respected. In that case, in fact, money is not stored labor—it is stored manipulation and deceit. British author Ayn Rand wrote, "The man who damns money has obtained it dishonorably. The man who respects it has earned it."

Beware Get-Rich-Quick Schemes

Promises of shortcuts to money are all around us. They are promised on late-night television in 30-minute infomercials, in advertising for the lottery, in the publicity given the winners in "get-rich-quick" schemes, in magazines and books, and on audiotapes. Everyone wants to achieve success without putting out the effort.

Don't be deceived. American journalist and politician Horace Greeley remarked, "The darkest hour of any man's life is when he sits down to plan how to get money without earning it."

The extreme example of this type of thinking? Robbing banks or dealing drugs. But many of us use this kind of self-destructive thinking to a lesser degree. We think there's no harm in taking advantage of our neighbor because of his words, or in digging a pit for a colleague so we can rise above him. Fed by greed, we are unwise in our pursuits. Blinded by our own ambition, we succumb to the glib promises of easy wealth, and our money becomes theirs.

One of the executive lectures at a local college featured my friend William H. Child, chief executive officer of R.C. Willey Home Furnishings, one of the world's largest home furnishing chains. His topic: "Instant Success in 40 Years."

Bill knows what he's talking about. He recently sold R.C. Willey to the world's greatest investor, Warren Buffett of Berkshire Hathaway, Inc. Bill is a modest, self-effacing man who understands the principles of success. When I asked if his son Mike could join me and my children on a trip to the Winter Olympics in Lillehammer, Norway, Bill explained that his son would have to pay for the trip with his own money. Bill spent 40 years building his "instant success."

Contrary to what people think, those who have earned their money the hard way live modestly. Sam Walton, the founder of Wal-Mart Stores and a billionaire before his death, never grew beyond driving his pickup truck to and from work. Warren Buffett is known for stooping down to pick up a penny.

How modest are *you* with money? How much do *you* respect it? How hard have you worked to earn what *you* have?

"People of this country are not jealous of fortunes, however great, which have been built up by the honest development of great enterprises which have been actually earned by business energy and sagacity," said President Woodrow Wilson in an April 1908 address in New York City. "They are jealous only of speculative wealth, of the wealth that has been piled up by no effort at all; only by shrewd wits playing on the credulity of others. This is predatory wealth."

Any who will try to short-circuit the laws and principles of success will eventually but certainly fall prey to self-defeating behaviors that deny them the very success they seek.

Your Insights, Feelings, and Action Items

A. As you read this chapter, what *insights* came that seem applicable to *you?*
   1._____
   2._____
   3._____

B. How did you *feel* as you pondered particular points of this chapter?

1._____

2._____

3._____

C. What do you *feel* you should *do* as a result of this chapter?

1._____

2._____

3._____

D. How might you solicit the aid of others in accomplishing "C" above?

_____

_____

_____

Chapter 4

Work with Your Money Personality

Why Do So Many People Fail Financially?

Someone once wrote, "Don't wait for your ship to come in; swim out to it." Unfortunately, many of us seem to have missed the boat entirely—we sit back instead and tread water.

A glance at the statistics makes this painfully clear. Studies have indicated that out of every 100 people reaching age 65, only two are financially independent; 23 must continue to work; and 75 are dependent on friends, relatives, Social Security, or charity for support. This is across all economic bounds.

Other research shows that approximately one-third of all physicians reaching retirement age and wanting to retire, can't. They've failed to build up adequate reserves to maintain their lifestyle. They're locked into debt and a lifestyle they can't afford, so they must continue to work.

Still another study suggested that it is easier for the average 18-year-old to quickly put his hands on $100 cash than it is for the average 65-year-old who has worked for 40 years.

What an indictment these statistics make. Why, after all these years of work, do so many have so little to show for it? What is the number-one reason people fail financially?

I've posed that question to thousands of seminar participants over the years. The most frequent responses are failure to plan, too much debt, reckless or irresponsible spending. Sometimes they respond that people don't have goals or don't know what it takes to succeed. A few suggest that people fail financially because they don't understand the tax system.

What, then, is the *number-one* reason people fail financially? Procrastination.

Procrastinate ... and Fail

I'm going to discuss procrastination in detail through most of this chapter. But first, I want to discuss a little about your money personality in general.

Most books on financial planning discuss strategies, definitions, and products. But they ignore the *psychological* view of money—in other words, what motivates your individual money personality. Very little has actually been done to integrate the emotional self with the financial self. No wonder there's so much confusion, disagreement, dissonance and family conflict.

A financial planner or investment adviser who does not understand your financial psychology may put your money into investments that will leave you feeling anxious and unhappy.

In *Your Money Personality*, Financial Psychology Corporation President Kathleen Gurney, Ph.D., discusses 13 different financial traits that influence money behavior and investment decisions and identifies nine distinct money styles or personalities. A simple one-page questionnaire (included in *Your Money Happiness Workbook*) scores you on a number of financial traits, including:

- The level of involvement you want in your financial affairs
- How much pride you feel in how well you manage money
- How emotionally involved you get in financial decisions
- Your level of altruism
- How much anxiety you feel after making a financial decision
- Your need to use money to achieve power
- The level of importance you place on work ethic in achieving success
- How content you are with your finances
- Your propensity toward risk-taking
- Your level of self-determination toward your money
- How you feel about spending vs. saving your money

- How reflective or impulsive you are in making financial decisions
- Your level of trust in how other people handle your money

Your numeric scores tell a lot about your "money personality." If you score high in spending, for example, you enjoy spending your money; if you score low, you prefer saving it. If you score high in self-determination, you believe financial success comes primarily from personal effort; a low score means you attribute financial success primarily to luck.

Your Money Personality also identifies nine money styles: entrepreneurs, hunters, high rollers, safety players, achievers, perfectionists, money masters, producers, and optimists. Each is different, and each has its own character traits. Some money personalities blend well; others result in conflict.

The bottom line? Understanding your money personality helps you pursue financial goals and achieve financial success.

Your money personality reflects your self-esteem, your money management style, the type of financial statement you need, your ability to mix business and personal life. It impacts your level of contentment or frustration, how you deal with alien territory, your need for safety, your tolerance for risk, and your level of anxiety over financial decisions.

Profile Yourself

Dr. Gurney developed a "MoneyMax Profile" questionnaire that will rank you on the 13 financial traits and show how your score compares with national averages. It provides insight on how to deal with other money personalities. It makes recommendations as to the types of investments people in your money personality feel most comfortable with. It contains cautions about traps your money personality might fall prey to. It identifies your financial strengths.

Once you discover your money personality, you are far more aware of how you handle money. You are far more likely to understand how—and why—your spouse deals with money.

I recommend the "MoneyMax Profile" as a beginning point for any financial plan, because it gives you a level of psychological understanding you won't get any other way. For more information on the "MoneyMax Profile," call Fax-on-Demand at (801) 263-1676 and request free report #120, or see *Your Money Happiness Workbook*.

What happens once you've identified your financial personality?

Most adults have had enough experience with money to discern what is accurate if they will think about the correct principles. Truth stands up to reason. Try them.

It does not take a degree in finance to understand these correct principles. They are practical and actually quite simple. Read, understand, and then have the confidence to move forward.

Moving forward is the key—because moving forward defeats procrastination. And procrastination, as stated earlier, is the number-one reason people fail financially. It is the worst part of your money personality.

The Excuse of the Ages

How many of the following excuses have *you* used at these ages?

> We're 25. We can't accumulate money now. We're just getting started and we don't make a lot yet. We're entitled to a little fun while we're young. Besides, we've got plenty of time.
>
> We're 35. Our family is growing. Our mortgage payments are high. Once the children are older, it will cost less. Then we'll start to invest. We can't put aside a penny now.
>
> We're 45. Two children are in college, and it's all we can do to pay their expenses. This seems to be the most expensive time in our lives.
>
> We're 55. We know we should invest, but things aren't breaking like they used to. At our age it's tough to start new careers or get a better job. We'll have to sit tight right now and maybe something will break.
>
> We're 65. Who, us? Sure. Investing is a great idea, but Social Security doesn't go far. We should have started years ago. It's too late now. (Copyright, Successful Money Management Seminars, Inc., used with permission)

Sound familiar? I have heard them all. Bryan and Jana are a perfect example. They came into my office in June. We plunged into a marathon work session and finally agreed upon a sound and prudent savings program that would help them achieve their financial goals. Just as they were ready to get going on this wonderfully prudent savings program, Bryan reminded me, "Well, it's June, and we promised the kids we'd take them to Disneyland. Could we reschedule and get started on this when we return?"

So we rescheduled. We got back together in August. Guess what? It was time to pay for school clothes and tuition. So we rescheduled. We got back together in November. Uh-oh. Christmas was just around the corner. So we rescheduled. We got back together in January. Guess what? Christmas was a budget-buster. So we rescheduled. We got back together in March. Bad idea. Taxes were just around the corner. So we rescheduled and got back together in June!

Often procrastinators like to use the silly play on words: "Tomorrow never comes." But it *does* come for most of us. Will *you* be prepared?

Is there *ever* a good time to start a savings program? Is there ever a *good* time to implement a financial plan? No. There is *never* a good time. Only the *best* time. **Now.** Abraham Lincoln said it well: "You can't escape the responsibility of tomorrow by evading it today."

The following table shows the cost of procrastination. Notice what happens if you postpone saving from age 25 to age 35—that's only 10 years.

The Cost of Procrastination

$100,000 at Age 65
Assumes a 12 %
Compounded Rate of Return

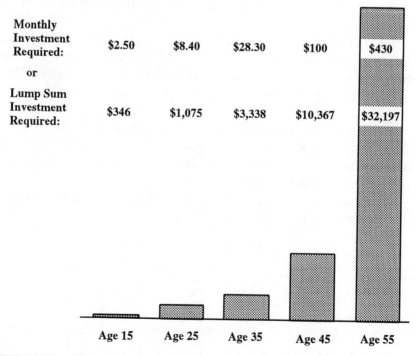

	Age 15	Age 25	Age 35	Age 45	Age 55
Monthly Investment Required:	$2.50	$8.40	$28.30	$100	$430
or Lump Sum Investment Required:	$346	$1,075	$3,338	$10,367	$32,197

Consider an example. At 25, Janelle only has to save $8.40 a month for every $100,000 she wants to have at retirement, assuming a 12 percent annual compounded return. Literally dozens of mutual funds have averaged 12, 15, 20 percent and more over the past couple of decades. Janelle assesses her financial situation and determines she can save 12 times that amount, or $100 a month. At that rate, she will have $1.2 million at retirement. And that assumes she *never* increases her monthly savings as her income rises.

Janelle could also make a single lump-sum deposit of just over $1,000. Assuming the same interest rate, it would grow to $100,000 by age 65. That's the magic of compound interest. (If your children start saving this much at age 15, imagine the impact!)

Now let's look at Dale, who postponed starting on his savings program until he was 35. Instead of saving in his 20s, he refurnished his home, took expensive vacations, and bought a new car. Now, at age 35, he has to save $28.30 a month for every $100,000 he wants at retirement. That's three and a half times the amount required at age 25.

What about Jack, who postponed saving until age 45? Instead of $28.30 a month, he needs to save $100 a month—again, more than three times as much. That amount jumps to $430 a month if he procrastinates until age 55.

How much of a leap does $8.40 to $430 a month represent? It means you need to save *50 times as much income per month* to achieve the same number of dollars at retirement. The point? As Victor Kiam put it, "Procrastination is opportunity's natural assassin." Do you have children who should be reading this message and understanding these principles?

And note that a late starter never catches up with an early starter. The table on page 51 shows two investors who are contributing to an IRA. Bill contributes from age 19 to age 26 and then quits. Bob doesn't start until age 27, and never catches up with Bill.

You have to decide *not* to procrastinate. You have to decide to start doing something about your program *now*.

The Late Starter May Never Catch Up

	Bill starts early			Bob starts late	
Age	IRA Contributions	Year-End Value	Age	IRA Contributions	Year-End Value
19	$2,000	$2,200	19	0	0
20	2,000	4,620	20	0	0
21	2,000	7,282	21	0	0
22	2,000	10,210	22	0	0
23	2,000	13,431	23	0	0
24	2,000	16,974	24	0	0
25	2,000	20,872	25	0	0
26	2,000	25,159	26	0	0
27	0	27,675	27	$2,000	$2,200
28	0	30,442	28	2,000	4,620
29	0	33,487	29	2,000	7,282
30	0	36,835	30	2,000	10,210
31	0	40,519	31	2,000	13,431
32	0	44,571	32	2,000	16,974
33	0	49,028	33	2,000	20,872
34	0	53,930	34	2,000	25,159
35	0	59,323	35	2,000	29,875
36	0	65,256	36	2,000	35,062
37	0	71,781	37	2,000	40,769
38	0	78,960	38	2,000	47,045
39	0	86,856	39	2,000	53,950
40	0	95,541	40	2,000	61,545
41	0	105,095	41	2,000	69,899
42	0	115,605	42	2,000	79,089
43	0	127,165	43	2,000	89,198
44	0	139,882	44	2,000	100,318
45	0	153,870	45	2,000	112,550
46	0	169,257	46	2,000	126,005
47	0	186,183	47	2,000	140,805
48	0	204,801	48	2,000	157,086
49	0	225,281	49	2,000	174,995
50	0	247,809	50	2,000	194,694
51	0	272,590	51	2,000	216,364
52	0	299,849	52	2,000	240,200
53	0	329,834	53	2,000	266,420
54	0	362,817	54	2,000	295,262
55	0	399,099	55	2,000	326,988
56	0	439,009	56	2,000	361,887
57	0	482,910	57	2,000	400,276
58	0	531,201	58	2,000	442,503
59	0	584,321	59	2,000	488,953
60	0	642,753	60	2,000	540,049
61	0	707,028	61	2,000	596,254
62	0	777,731	62	2,000	658,079
63	0	855,504	63	2,000	726,087
64	0	941,054	64	2,000	800,896
65	0	1,035,160	65	2,000	883,185
Less Total Invested		(16,000)			(78,000)
Net Earnings		$1,019,160			$805,185

ASSUMPTIONS:
1. $2,000 contribution made on January 2nd of each year.
2. Interest accrues at 10% compounded yearly.

Your Insights, Feelings, and Action Items

A. As you read this chapter, what *insights* came that seem applicable to you?

1._____

2._____

3._____

B. How did you *feel* as you pondered particular points of this chapter?

1._____

2._____

3._____

C. What do you *feel* you should *do* as a result of this chapter?

1._____

2._____

3._____

D. How might you solicit the aid of others in accomplishing "C" above?

_____

_____

_____

Chapter 5

Your Economic Engine

What Type of Person Are You?

"When the well's dry, we know the worth of water," Benjamin Franklin once wrote. Why do so many of us reach the bone-dry depths of our financial well before it occurs to us to save? The reason we fail isn't that we don't know what to do with our money. We just never get around to doing it!

Some people live completely for today: They live paycheck to paycheck; they never invest in advanced education or training; and they never seem able to sock away time, effort, or money for the future. At the other extreme are those who live completely for tomorrow, like the elderly lady who passed away while she had been living in poverty with $300,000 in saved cash under her mattress. Between these two extremes, we have to decide where we are going to fit.

There are basically two financial types of people in America, as represented by the two circles in the following table. One type will *spend first* and save what's left over, while the other type will *save first* and spend what's left over.

Two Types of People

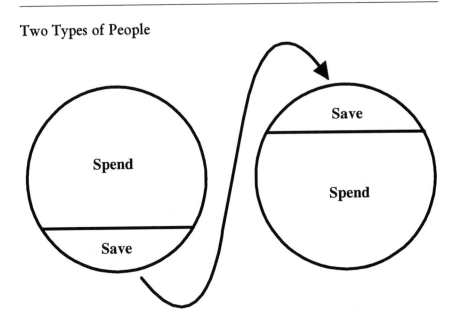

Observations:

1. Nineteen of 20 belong in the first circle; only one of 20 belongs in the second circle.

2. Those in the first circle always work for those in the second circle.

3. Those in the second circle share in the stocks and profits of America.

So, which type of person are you? Take a good look at your approach to budgeting.

I can always tell which type of person someone is when he explains how he prepares his budget. People in the first circle will do something very logical. They total up all the checks they wrote over the past few months and tell their financial adviser to the penny how much went for gasoline, food, clothing, shelter, utilities, entertainment, vacations, health care, insurance, contributions, etc. All of the dollar amounts which were spent are neatly categorized into these budgeted accounts. After they have totaled up all the money they need for their different categories, they then arrive at an amount left over for savings.

It *seems* perfectly sensible, doesn't it? Is that how *you* have developed *your* budget?

You Decide

In my experience, about 19 out of 20 families develop their budget with this "Circle-One Mindset." *Yet, all they have done is fix their past impulse buying and unwise spending habits into a rigid discipline.* They have merely institutionalized past spending habits. A budget developed in such a manner merely perpetuates past spending habits, whether those habits were good or bad in the first place. This is a dangerous course to take, for, in the words of Samuel Johnson, "The chains of habit are too small to be felt until they are too strong to be broken."

Developing a budget in such a manner *rarely* leaves many dollars for savings. If spending is a higher priority than saving, will there ever be dollars left to save? Or can you always spend what you earn? Are there always more wants to satisfy?

A few prudent families, those in the second circle, will arrive at a budget in an entirely different manner. They will usually come into our office and tell us they want to save 10, 15, or 20 percent of their income. After taking that percentage off the top, budgeting becomes a process of *reallocating* the remaining dollars according to spending *priorities* and goals.

Only about one family out of 20 falls in this second category. Interestingly, that ratio is similar to the number of people who are financially independent at retirement, about 5 percent of the population.

It is also important to note that the people in the first circle *always work for* the people in the second circle. That is, the people in the first circle are the employ*ees* of the world, while those in the second circle are the employ*ers* of the world. It's not that they all own businesses, but that they own the stocks and bonds, and are participating in the profits of America. They own corporate America. They have a different mindset.

When the *Exxon Valdez* ran aground in Alaska, the people in the first circle were merely concerned about the environment. The people in the second circle were not only concerned about the environment, but they were also concerned about what it did to the value of their Exxon stock— they realized that some Exxon stock was probably held in their mutual funds, retirement plan, or personal portfolio.

By now you may have realized what type of person you are. The question is, what type of person are you going *to be?* Before you will ever accumulate any wealth and have financial security, you must commit yourself to a *"Circle-Two* Mindset." Many people I know that are truly getting ahead are saving 15, 20, 25, or even 30 percent or more of their income. After all, in the words of John Boyle O'Reilly, "You're worth what you saved, not the million you made." *You decide* what type of person you will be.

The Surprising Advantage of Saving

Many years ago, I visited with a young couple, Greg and Karla, as they were about to finish college. Before they graduated, we determined that if they would maintain their college level standard of living for just five years and sock the dollars away rather than incurring debt to buy home furnishings and a new car, the interest working for them would put them forever ahead of all their peers.

Some years later, I was with them in their home when a neighbor came by. Upon introduction, she quipped, "Oh, you're the one who tells Greg and Karla when they can buy some furniture." I don't know what Greg and Karla had been saying about me to their neighbor, but I presumed she was referring to the fact that they had lived there for some years and did not have any furniture in their living room yet.

Finally, after a few years of patience and frugal living, Greg and Karla bought a nice ebony bench for the living room. With the bench came a beautiful grand piano.

What was most amazing about it was that Greg wrote out a check for the piano, and the next year he wrote out a check for a new car. A couple of years later, he wrote a check for a backyard swimming pool—all this within seven or eight years of graduating from college and without ever dipping into his retirement plan monies. He was determined he would forever have interest working for him rather than against him. You can too. I have seen this done many times, even with people earning modest incomes.

To start, save at least 10 percent of your income. Perhaps you think, "There's no way I can do that." In that case, I would pose this scenario to you: Suppose we are just coming out of a recession. What happens during recessions? People get laid off work and unemployment goes up. So, you go into the office and your boss says, "Joe, take your pick. You either have to take a 10 percent cut in pay, or we have to lay you off work."

Which would you choose? You would choose the 10 percent cut in pay, wouldn't you? And in so doing, would you go bankrupt? Lose your home? Default on all your payments? No. *Somehow you would make it.* Maybe you'd start taking a brown bag lunch to work, sewing a few clothes, and going to the one-dollar movie theaters, but somehow or other *you would make it*. Wouldn't you? So, living on 10 percent less is really a matter of *decision*, of *commitment*.

Of course, saving is easier to talk about than to do. Fortunately, several techniques can help. Remember that it is important to pay yourself first, so make it as easy as possible to direct money into your savings account.

How? Forced savings. The smart person will ask his employer to take money from his paycheck and put it into a 401k plan. Perhaps he will ask his bank to transfer money from his checking account into his savings account at a set amount each month. An even easier approach would be to authorize an automatic monthly deposit from a bank account into a mutual fund or cash-value insurance policy.

Just Can't Save, No Matter What?

Make it as difficult as you can to get at the money. If it is easy to withdraw money from the account, you probably will. Better to tie up the money in mutual funds, insurance policies, or a retirement plan.

Tell me, who will have the most money at retirement? John puts his money into an investment earning 10 percent interest. Bill puts his money into an average investment earning 5 percent interest. Gary, who isn't as bright as the other two, puts his money into a bottle, where he earns zero percent interest.

John and Bill can access their money easily. Gary, on the other hand, has made it hard to get to his money. As he puts his hand into the bottle to grab some cash, he can't pull his closed fist back out without releasing the money.

So, who will have the most money at retirement? The ones who are earning 10 and 5 percent but can access their money easily, or the one who is earning zero percent but can't get at it?

Interest can't make money for you without principal. You have to sock away the principal and put it in a place where it is difficult to access. Focus on the principal of the thing! *Only then* can compound interest do its job.

It all boils down to this: What are your priorities? What do you really want out of life? Whether you realize it or not, you have chosen which type of person you are going to be. Sit down with your spouse and have a thoughtful discussion to determine whether you are going to change for the better or stay as you are—the ball is in your court.

If you still insist your family does not have enough money each month to meet your "needs," please *do not expect the ultimate lifestyle or security of those who sacrifice now and save.* As we said earlier, sacrifice is not foregoing something bad for something good; it is foregoing something good for something better.

Saving, not spending (as some would have you think), *is the engine that drives all economic progress:* for the individual, for the family, for the community and for the nation. If you want to progress economically and are willing to commit to save first and then spend, you can reach your goals and achieve financial security.

Which type of person will you be?

Your Financial Freedom Fund

Fewer people today plan for a traditional retirement; rather, they are looking forward to the day when they achieve financial independence, when they are working because they want to, not because they have to. These people do not consider retirement as the purpose of their nest egg. They are looking for financial freedom.

I encourage people to think in terms of building their "Financial Freedom Fund." It directs their thinking toward their personal "Financial Freedom Day," which may be years before their actual retirement. The objective is *freedom*, not retirement. When you focus your thinking this way, your mind begins imagining all sorts of worthwhile and adventurous pursuits, only one being retirement.

Build your "Financial Freedom Fund," not your retirement account. The key is having a Circle-Two Mindset.

The Amazing WYHTE Phenomenon

"The real price of everything," writes Adam Smith in *Wealth of Nations,* "is the toil and trouble of acquiring it." This is precisely the reasoning behind the WYHTE phenomenon. W-Y-H-T-E stands for "What You Have To Earn."

I have never seen the WYHTE phenomenon discussed in any of my numerous college texts on finance. I have never seen it discussed in any magazine, newspaper or professional journal. And yet the WYHTE phenomenon impacts *every* one of us *every* day of our lives. If you learn to make it work for you, it can be worth many, many tens of thousands of dollars to you over your lifetime. If it works against you, it can make the difference between a nice standard of living and always living from paycheck to paycheck.

So, how does it work?

Assume you want to spend $1.00 and you are in a 25 percent tax bracket. What must you earn to spend that dollar? Most people, including business owners and even some accountants, would say $1.25. But the answer is $1.33. Why?

If you earn one dollar, and one-fourth goes to taxes, you only have 75 cents to spend. If you earn $1.25, and one-fourth goes to taxes, you only have 94 cents to spend. But one-fourth of $1.33 going to taxes would be $0.33, leaving you $1.00 to spend.

What if you are in a 40 percent tax bracket and you want to spend $1.00? You need to earn $1.67 before taxes in order to have $1.00 left over.

As your tax bracket increases, so does the amount you must earn in order to have $1.00 to spend. Those in a 50 percent tax bracket, for instance, must earn $2.00 in order to have $1.00 left after taxes.

WYHTE Phenomenon

WYHTE		$1.33		$1.67		$2.00
Less Taxes at:	25%	– .33	40%	– .67	50%	– 1.00
Spend		$1.00		$1.00		$1.00

Remember, the only relevant tax rate for financial decision-making is your *total marginal* tax rate, as we will discuss in greater detail in Chapter 7. Your total tax bracket includes both federal *and* state taxes *and* FICA taxes (plus county and city if they apply). Your first dollars are perhaps taxed at a lower tax rate of 15 percent, but those first dollars are being used for the basic necessities of life: food, clothing, and shelter. When you make financial decisions, you are using your last dollars. Whether that discretionary decision is to take the family out to dinner one night or to go on vacation, those last dollars are being taxed at your marginal tax rate, which might be 40 to 45 percent, or higher.

So, what does the WYHTE phenomenon mean to us? Let's look at an example:

My boy, Danny, comes to me one evening and says, "Dad, I need a new bicycle."

I respond to him, "Danny, how much is it?"

"Well, Dad, it's $100."

"Sorry, Danny. It's not worth it."

"Dad, it is too worth $100."

"I agree, Danny, it *is* worth $100."

"What do you mean, Dad? You just said it is worth $100, but you said it wasn't worth it."

"Danny, listen very carefully. The bicycle *is* worth $100, but it is not worth $200. *And I have to earn $200 to buy you a $100 bicycle.*"

What You Have to Earn to Spend $1.00

Your Marginal* Tax Bracket	WYHTE
25%	$1.33
30	1.43
35	1.54
40	1.67
45	1.82
50	2.00
55	2.22
60	2.50
65	2.86

* Add your Federal, State and Local Tax Rates (see Workbook), *plus* your FICA and Medicare Tax Rate, *plus* self-employment taxes (if applicable). If collecting Social Security, see pages 306-308.

A Dollar Isn't a Dollar

It is important to decide how the WYHTE phenomenon will fit in your life. You may choose to take advantage of it in some ways and ignore it and let it work against you in other ways. Realize, however, that opportunities to let it work for you are abundant. Consider the following, assuming you need to earn $2.00 for every discretionary dollar you want to spend:

Taking the family to dinner. You can pay $50 at restaurant A or $30 at restaurant B for a similar meal. So, you think that by going to restaurant B, you will save $20. But actually, you had to earn $100 to go to restaurant A, while you had to earn $60 to go to restaurant B. By going to restaurant B, you actually saved $40.

Planting a garden. Suppose you can buy all of your seed and water for $10, and your garden will yield $300 worth of fruits and vegetables at the end of the summer. You might think you are saving $290 on your summer grocery bill. But, in order to spend $10 on the garden, you had to earn $20, and in order to spend $300 on the grocery bill, you had to earn $600. So, you were actually able to have that standard of living while earning $580 less that year, not to mention you probably had better food while you were at it!

Shopping the sales. Maybe you don't believe it is worth your while to drive that extra few miles to buy a pair of shoes on sale. Suppose you buy a $100 pair of shoes for only $50. You assume you saved $50. But, you had to earn $200 to buy the shoes at the regular price, and $100 to buy them on sale, for a savings of $100. Are you beginning to see how these things can add up?

Going on a vacation. Regularly, you plan your vacation a month or six weeks in advance. You order the necessary tickets and discover the vacation will cost you $3,000. But, by planning even further in advance, doing a little extra telephoning and getting your tickets at a better discount, you are able to go on the same vacation for $2,000. To have gone on the vacation according to the original plan, you would have had to earn $6,000. By planning ahead, you only had to earn $4,000. So, once again, you were able to maintain that standard of living while earning $2,000 less that year.

Fees for services. This is where we see many mistakes made by physicians, attorneys, engineers, and other highly compensated professionals who bill their time out on an hourly basis. For instance, you might be able to build a deck onto your back porch for $500, as opposed to paying a contractor $2,000 to do the job. You had to earn $1,000 to do it yourself, while you'd have to earn $4,000 to pay the contractor. So, under the WYHTE phenomenon, you figure you saved yourself $3,000.

To Do It or Hire It Done

Here's the catch. Many professionals assume they could earn more in the amount of time they could have built the deck than it would cost to pay someone else to do it.

Phil, an attorney who charges $100 an hour for his services, made this classic blunder. Phil was eager to remodel his basement family room, a job which would take about 25 hours. Although he had the skills necessary to do the job himself, he figured he could earn $2,500 in those 25 hours, while he would only have to pay the contractor $2,000.

WYHTE Examples:

		Price	WYHTE
1. Bicycle		$100	$200
2. Restaurant	A	$50	$100
	B	30	60
	Savings	$20	$40
3. Garden	Store Bought	$300	$600
	Garden	10	20
	Savings	$290	$580
4. Shoes	Regular Price	$100	$200
	Sale Price	50	100
	Savings	$50	$100
5. Vacation	Regular	$3,000	$6,000
	Budget	2,000	4,000
	Savings	$1,000	$2,000
6. Fees for Services		$2,000	$4,000
	Do-it-Yourself	500	1,000
	Savings	$1,500	$3,000

7. Other applications:

Change your own oil	Buy quality so it lasts
Clip coupons	Don't pay interest
Buy in bulk or quantity	Plant a garden
Cook from scratch	Only one spouse working
Plan vacation early	Trade for services
Do your own yardwork	Bar-B-Que vs. restaurant

The problem, however, is that the $2,500 he could earn was a pre-tax amount, while the money owed to the contractor was figured in after-tax dollars. For those 25 hours, Phil's take-home pay was only $1,250, while he actually had to earn $4,000 to pay the contractor. Put another way, Phil's net earnings are $100 an hour—after taxes he only has $50 to spend.

This extends itself to the situation of a professional hiring a plumber or some other contractor to do work he could have done himself. Maybe he earns $70 an hour from his practice and the plumber costs $50 an hour, so the professional figures it is better to hire the plumber. But, in order to hire that plumber at $50 an hour, the professional has to earn $100 an hour, since half of that $100 will be lost to taxes.

Of course, this is all assuming the professional could do the job as expeditiously as someone he might hire to do it. Perhaps you may not have the skills to do these repairs on your own—then you may need to hire out the job. But, if you *can* do the job yourself, the savings will be worth it.

You can make the WYHTE phenomenon work for you in the little things you do every day. For instance, change your own oil. How many of us could do this in 10 minutes flat while in college, but quit after graduation?

Clip coupons. Purchase generic brands rather than labels. Buy in bulk or quantity. I know many fairly wealthy people who buy in bulk at the large warehouse grocery stores.

Shop the sales for 50 percent discounts on off-season items (skis, winter clothing, summer clothing, tools, yard care equipment, tires, lawnmowers, snowblowers, etc.). It is *equally accurate* to think of it as paying 100 percent more (or double the price) when you buy "in-season."

Buy quality so that it lasts. The objective of the WYHTE phenomenon is not to buy cheap, but to understand what something truly costs and make wise decisions accordingly. Better to buy quality used than cheap new.

Only have one spouse working. Whenever two spouses work, the second income is added onto the first income and *100 percent* is being taxed at the highest marginal tax bracket. If 40 percent of the second spouse's income is lost to taxes, and a good portion of the rest goes toward a wardrobe, child care, eating out more often, buying pre-prepared microwaveable dinners, and other work-related costs, someone earning $10 an hour may bring home only $1.

From a purely financial standpoint, it is important to understand the economic implications of having two spouses work. The family might have had more income and less stress if the first spouse merely worked two or three extra hours per week. I have observed this even when the second spouse is earning $20, $30 or $40 per hour. (The economics of the working spouse will be discussed in greater depth in Chapter 14.)

You can think of your own examples of making the WYHTE phenomenon work for you or against you, but remember that it impacts every candy bar or lunch that you buy. Decide in which ways you simply aren't going to worry about it. Maybe you won't clip coupons or change your own oil. Perhaps you could shop some sales or would enjoy planting a garden. The point is, if you don't figure out how it is going to work *for* you, it is going to work *against* you.

The WYHTE phenomenon explains why a farmer and a young district attorney can have a $40,000 difference in take-home income but the same outwardly observable standard of living. Living a mile away from town, the farmer grows his own garden, paints his own fence, makes his car last 15 years, etc. By doing so, he is able to have the same standard of living on $20,000 a year as the young attorney who makes $60,000 a year in the county seat.

Likewise, you might observe a young family with three, four, or even five children, where the father is a bus driver and somehow they make ends meet. Yet, another family with only one or two children and both spouses earning $80,000 a year is somehow just living paycheck to paycheck. The first family probably buys bulk and cooks from scratch, while the second family struggles.

What are we doing to our children when we teach them to buy based on labels? How much do we pay to have that little tag on the backside of our jeans, or that little symbol stitched on our golf shirts? What do we pay to drive that flashy car when we factor in the WYHTE phenomenon? These are the types of things that often make the difference between the lifestyle of one family and the lifestyle of another.

Some of my clients know that if they can get a well-known label to put on one of their manufactured products, they can sell it for 50 to 100 percent more. They laugh all the way to the bank as they take *our* money and deposit it in *their* bank accounts. Once again, instead of saving for ourselves, we are paying others first. They end up with the nice lifestyle, while we remain slaves to our ego and spending habits.

On occasion a client will tell me, "Well, I don't like the WYHTE phenomenon, so I don't want to do that," as though it is a recommendation within a financial plan. Whether we like it or not, the WYHTE phenomenon impacts every financial decision we make—*only* when we know the truth are we free to make correct decisions. The question is, *how will you apply it in your life?*

26-Point Checklist for Increasing Personal Cash Flow

Necessity truly can prompt our inventiveness. It certainly did in my case. After dealing with debt in my own life and finally breaking free, I have discovered a few ideas about how to increase cash flow.

Many of the cash flow strategies and approaches I now offer my clients are a direct result of my own late-night ponderings as I wondered how to operate a business profitably. Some of the toughest lessons I learned over the years were blessings in disguise. As I sit down with a client to discuss cash flow strategies, I can relate to what he's going through. *I have been there.*

Let's look at a few of these strategies.

Understand the WYHTE phenomenon. It can either work for you or against you. Make it work for you. Don't pay interest; plant a garden.

Examine your "keep up with the Joneses" attitude. One big reason families have cash flow problems is from "keeping up with the Joneses." What about you? Is ego causing your financial problems?

Teach your children work and self-reliance. Having your children do chores around the house brings multiple benefits. Because of the WYHTE phenomenon, you will receive large returns on your investment as your children's efforts essentially translate into tax-free income. But even more important, teaching your children to work makes them far more responsible and effective.

I remember well meeting with the senior vice-president of a major company who "loaned" money to his children for college. Because the children did not have to earn the money themselves, they never learned to appreciate the value of their father's loan, nor did they feel any pressing need to repay it. As a result, this high-ranking company executive was left with only scraps for his retirement fund.

Budget efficiently. One of the biggest drains on cash flow is buying on impulse and feeding our egos instead of our savings accounts. Put savings first. Determine what is really important to you, and be willing to budget accordingly.

Simplify lifestyle. How we spend money is not how we live, just as our lifestyle is not our life. Money doesn't buy some of the greatest things in life. Throw out, clean out, don't buy, simplify.

Save on major purchases. Lifestyle is often a reflection of how you spend money. Set a good example for your children by shopping around to save on major purchases. Be familiar with wholesale warehouses, which often offer good quality merchandise at a substantial discount. Always ask for a discount on whatever item you may be purchasing. You will often be surprised to find businesses very willing to satisfy your request. (As I write this ... last night at the home center I simply asked, "Since this is off-season for garden supplies, could you give me your best price possible?" The sales clerk asked the manager, who approved the sale price of the prior month. I got 50 percent off, saving me hundreds of dollars, just for asking.)

Examine debt consolidation. Consolidating debts runs contrary to the counsel I will give in Chapter 10, because it merely postpones your problem and lengthens your debt payoff schedule. But, it may be a means of improving your short-term cash flow, and may be appropriate in some situations.

Pay off debt. If you *really* want to increase your cash flow, pay off your debts. Debt payments devour 15 to 20 percent of the average family's household income. If you are willing to save up and wait for things you want, you will save paying interest. After paying cash for your car, immediately start to save for the next car. If you buy a car with monthly installments at interest, you are in bondage. You have no cushion. You can't respond to life's emergencies. All of your dollars are going to cover the debt. If you are free to pay in cash, you can generally negotiate a better deal.

Learn to wait. Learn to save for what you want. Put your dollars in a savings account instead of paying interest. Then you will have interest working for you.

Refinance your mortgage. This generally is prudent when the interest rate on your mortgage is 2 percent greater than the current market rate, and you intend to remain in your home for more than five years. If there is less than a 2 percent spread, you need to make a more careful analysis because of points, appraisal fees, etc. Realize that mortgage loan brokers are paid on commission as well—half a percent lower interest rate generally is not worth it.

Engage in an accelerated mortgage payoff plan. See Chapter 17.

Examine strategies to save taxes. Familiarize yourself with the tax breaks available to you. There are money-saving tax strategies associated with having children, getting married, making charitable contributions, and gifting to your children, just to name a few. (See Chapters 25 and 29.)

Make interest tax-deductible. Perhaps you might decide to take your consumer loans, auto loans, loans for travel or college or other purposes and make them tax-deductible by putting them under a home equity loan. This may be most unwise and needs to be done very carefully. (Refer to the counsel in Chapter 10.)

Utilize tax-deductible retirement plans. Longevity at your job can be especially important for vesting in employer-funded retirement plans, particularly if your employer will match your monthly deposits. Find a job you enjoy and stick with it.

B.J. has been in the work force for over 30 years, bouncing around from one job to the next. He never settled his roots or built up employer-provided benefits. Now, all he has for retirement is $4,000 in a couple of IRAs.

Use tax-sheltered savings programs. Savings accounts, CDs, money market funds, stocks, bonds, and mutual funds are all taxable. Consider putting those dollars into some kind of tax-sheltered or tax-advantaged accumulation program: an IRA, a variable annuity or cash-value life insurance.

Consider capital gains bypass strategies. With this option, individuals approaching retirement can avoid the capital gains tax on the sale of a highly appreciated stock, real estate, or business interest. Remember, saving 35 percent on your taxes is equivalent to a 50 percent increase in retirement income. (To understand why this works, review the section on the WYHTE phenomenon.)

Engage in tax-free exchanges. Exchange like-kinds of properties rather than selling properties. This spares you a hefty tax bite.

Maximize pension income. Two-thirds of all employees choose the wrong pension payout option. If they understood the concept of pension maximization, this would not be the case. Most retirees choose a pension plan with both a life and survivor benefit option. However, the benefit is 20 to 30 percent less than a life only option, and if your spouse dies first, your children are basically disinherited. You have no control over your survivor benefits.

With a life only option, however, you can put the additional 20 to 30 percent in retirement income into a life insurance policy on the retiree. This provides income for either spouse should the other die, and ensures control over your survivor benefits. (For a more thorough discussion, see Chapter 21 and *Your Money Happiness Workbook*).

Increase retirement income via charitable giving strategies. This is tied in with a capital gains bypass trust. By placing assets in a charitable remainder unitrust, you may be able to increase your retirement income level. (See Chapter 26.)

Consolidate insurance policies. Sometimes people have a collection of very old, very small insurance policies with a $10,000 to $30,000 face value. Each of these has an annual fee and administrative costs associated with it—consolidation may reduce these costs. Additionally, insurance policies of $100,000 or more typically have price break points or premium discounts. Sometimes consolidating policies makes sense. Engage in this only with competent professional advice, because replacing policies is usually not in your best interest. Do not let a policy lapse without the new policy being in force.

Save on insurance premiums. Periodically you can save money on your homeowners insurance and auto insurance premiums. It usually goes against your best interest to replace a whole life insurance policy.

Increase rates of return on investments. See Chapters 31 and 33.

Consider career planning strategies. If you feel you are undercompensated, ask yourself why. What can you do about it? I have found the two biggest killers for underemployed individuals are lack of knowledge and poor self-confidence. Often, with a little bit more of both, you can do a lot in the way of improving your income and financial quality of life.

Also, consider the risk you are willing to take in your career. With a low-risk career, your compensation may be lower, and vice-versa. What are you willing to put on the line? (For a more thorough discussion of career planning strategies, see Chapters 14 and 15.)

Measure your value to your employer. It is essential to know how your performance is being measured. To improve your value to your employer, develop a means to define your job description in quantitative terms. Ask your employer (and yourself), "What objectives do you want me to achieve, and when?" (See Chapters 14 and 15.)

Negotiate a raise or bonus. Never tell your employer *why* you need more money. A raise is based on your job performance, not the size of your car payments or your daughter's tuition bill. Show your employer that you were able to increase your productivity over the past year. If you deserve it, prove it, and you won't be turned down. (See Chapters 14 and 15.)

Change employment. Perhaps consider a new job, and always be prepared to change where you work, if necessary. Keep your education and job skills sharp. You are your greatest investment. Keep learning!

Start a business. In starting a business you are able to avail yourself of additional perks and benefits. In evaluating whether or not you are cut out to run a business, review the section on career planning. Do you have the personality? Training and education? Remember that 80 percent of all businesses fail within the first five years. That is not the way to increase cash flow.

Your Insights, Feelings, and Action Items

A. As you read this chapter, what *insights* came that seem applicable to *you?*

   1._____

   2._____

   3._____

B. How did you *feel* as you pondered particular points of this chapter?

   1._____

   2._____

   3._____

C. What do you *feel* you should *do* as a result of this chapter?

   1._____

   2._____

   3._____

D. How might you solicit the aid of others in accomplishing "C" above?

_____

_____

_____

Chapter 6

The Freedom Budget

Set Correct Budgeting Priorities

If you want security and peace of mind, it is critical that you set appropriate budgeting priorities. I have committed to the following priorities, as outlined by N. Eldon Tanner:

"Wise financial counselors teach that there are four different elements to any good budget. Provision should be made *first* for basic operating needs such as food, clothing, etc.; *second*, for home equity; *third*, for emergency needs such as savings, health insurance, and life insurance; and, *fourth*, for wise investment and a storage program for the future."

These priorities reflect real *needs*. Only after they are met does a sound budget address other *wants*.

The Paradox of Controls

As we recommend budgeting to clients, they will often recoil at the notion, and one spouse or the other will become frustrated and discouraged about the financial planning process. The common illusion about the budgeting process is that the budget will take away all flexibility and freedom.

In reality, the budgeting process actually *enables* freedom.

How?

The budget provides a plan, without which a family is not free to reach its objectives. One of the apparent contradictions in life, often difficult to understand, is that laws provide us freedom. Sometimes we think that laws constrict us and hold us back. This may be the case with over-regulation and over-micromanagement. But appropriate laws and rules tend to help us achieve our goals and objectives. When we know the truth we are free to reach our goals.

Take, for example, the simple exercise of traveling from one side of a major metropolitan city to the other. If there were no stoplights, would we be free to climb in our cars and go from one side of town to the other? No. Without stoplights, we would have nothing but traffic jams and auto accidents. The rules and laws of an ordered society give us the freedom to travel with a high level of confidence. A good budget will likewise free us to reach our financial goals.

Perhaps you have felt you couldn't get across town, financially speaking, and have ended up in budget traffic jams and snarls. I have seen many clients in the same situation. Mary, for example, was intent on accumulating enough capital to retire comfortably in just a few years. But she had procrastinated far too long. After a lifetime of poor spending habits, she was unwilling to submit herself to a budget. As a result, she would not know the freedom of a comfortable and secure retirement.

Paradoxically, only when we *submit ourselves* to greater laws do we actually become free. And by holding on to our supposed freedom to spend and impulse buy, we become slaves, addicted to habits that are difficult to break. (Remember, *good* laws increase freedom; *bad* laws decrease freedom.)

Some people just can't give up their addictions, no matter the pain. They don't learn their lessons. They can't see that a budget actually frees, rather than constricts. Tom, for instance, expressed these thoughts: "We had a brush with bankruptcy a few years ago and it was really hard on our marriage. Now that we have some money, we don't want to scrimp and save. We want to live without financial worries for a while. My wife doesn't want to be stressed out over money, and we need to enjoy life a little. We don't want to put *all* our money into savings and lose *control*."

This is another case where we do dumb things for good reasons. We always think we have a good reason to spend money. Many of our mistakes in budgeting are due to our immaturity and lack of experience.

Jason did not want to buy health insurance for Jenny, his new bride of just a few weeks. They were in their early 20s, deeply in love, and anxious to be enjoying life together. Jason was hesitant to buy health insurance for his wife because they were just making ends meet, yet they had adequate money for health insurance. Fortunately, a young financial adviser and good friend insisted that he acquire the insurance. Within months, Jenny was severely injured. Their health insurance took care of the claim, which otherwise would have destroyed them financially.

Must-Haves and Name Brands

What are some of the biggest challenges in effective budgeting? Ego. Having to "keep up with the Joneses." Impulse buying. Being unwise and immature. Feeding our desire to "have it now."

Successful people distinguish between needs and wants.

Dwight D. Eisenhower recognized these characteristics in so many of us when he quipped, "Some people wanted champagne and caviar when they should have had beer and hot dogs."

I remember when my oldest boy, Danny, came to me at age 11 and insisted he had to have British Knights, the "in" tennis shoes at the time. My wife and I felt a good pair of $40 Nikes was adequate, but because Danny was such a hard worker and always earning money on the side, we made a deal with him. We would pay $40 toward his tennis shoes, and he would have to pay the difference. By making Danny contribute his own money to the deal, we hoped he would learn the true cost of the item. He saved his income, bought the British Knights, and reported for school.

About a year or two later, after the conversation was long forgotten, the experience repeated itself. This time, Danny had to have the "right" pair of jeans—Girbauds. We went through the same conversation: Julie and I would pay for the Levi or Lee price of jeans. If Danny wanted the other brand, he would have to pay the difference. Fortunately, he had learned his lesson.

I can only imagine that when he showed up at school with his British Knights tennis shoes, his entire fifth-grade class formed a circle around him, pointed their fingers at his feet and exclaimed in unison, "Oh, Danny, we notice you're wearing British Knights!" Evidently, such was not the case.

In fact, apparently hardly anyone noticed, because when the opportunity arose to purchase Girbaud jeans, Danny decided he could do without them. What are we teaching our children?

Are we strict enough with ourselves? When we are going over the family budget, how ego-driven are our expenditures? "Perhaps parents should be more like the father of the college boy who wired home, 'No mon, no fun, your son.' His father wired back, 'How sad, too bad, your dad.'" (N. Eldon Tanner)

What Is a Bargain, Really?

As we develop our budget, are we engaging in the process of rationalization? *Most people buy on emotion and then justify their purchase with logic.*

How often do we impulse buy at the supermarket or stereo store, only to spend the drive home racking our brains for a way to explain the purchase to our spouse? As Franklin P. Jones once quipped, "A bargain is something you can't use at a price you can't resist."

Usually, it takes a mutually agreed upon budget for a married couple to preserve and enhance their relationship. In money matters, particularly in budgeting, it is critical that sound and open communication and mutual *respect* exist between husband and wife.

My wife, Julie, enjoys telling our friends how we sat together in the city park shortly after our engagement to review my balance sheet (with all the student loans, my net worth was a big negative). Few couples discuss family finances before marriage, yet such a discussion can help lay a solid foundation. Over 75 percent of divorces are caused by financial disagreements. Yet if the groundwork is laid before marriage, much of this can be avoided.

"Keep your eyes *open* before marriage—afterwards keep them half *shut*," advised Benjamin Franklin. Unfortunately, most of us only see what is right with our fiancee, and after marriage all we can see is what's wrong, when the opposite thinking should prevail.

Respectful communication. Sound and wise budgeting. Accepting responsibility for our actions. Avoiding impulse buying. Understanding that a budget will actually free rather than restrict. All are fundamentals to developing a financial plan and committing to live it.

A Budget Is a Plan

N. Eldon Tanner tells the story of the man who sent his daughter on an overseas study abroad program. When she kept writing home for more money, the father finally called her to ask for an explanation. After some discussion, she explained, "But, Dad, I can tell you where every penny has been spent."

Exasperated, he replied, "You don't seem to get the point. I'm interested in a budget—a *plan* for spending—not a diary of where the money has gone."

Many people today think they are budgeting when they are merely keeping a diary of their expenditures on the family computer.

Essentials of Developing an Effective Budget

We know that a good budget will free, not restrict, but for some reason the idea of developing a budget still makes some of us as uncomfortable as the thought of a tax audit or a root canal.

How do we develop an effective budget without feeling like we're pulling teeth?

There are five primary elements involved: First is goal-setting, for "where performance is measured, performance improves." Second is saving. Third is *healthy* spending based on priorities and goals. Fourth is accounting for what is spent. Fifth is constantly evaluating progress. You must continually analyze your budgeting situation, remain flexible, and readjust if necessary.

Even with all these elements, there is one essential key to any successful budget:

Commitment.

I once heard an author comment, "The difference between being involved and being committed is like ham and eggs: In contributing to the meal the chicken is involved; the pig is committed."

Be committed to your budget. This comes more easily as you see the progress toward your goals and feel the new-found mental freedom and peace of mind a budget affords.

Make the commitment. Take the first step.

Start by estimating your monthly income for the next 12 months. If you are on salary, this step will be easy, as it is your monthly net income. Commissioned employees will face a greater challenge. I suggest taking the average of your monthly income from the previous year and using it as your projected monthly income for the upcoming year.

Once you have determined that number, you know how much you have to save or spend each month.

Know Your Spending Cycles

After deciding how much you will save off the top, calculate your average monthly expenses, again using the previous year as a base. Divide your expenses into 12 to 25 categories. On a piece of grid paper, or other organized print, list your expense categories horizontally at the top of the page with the dollar amount allowed per month under each expense. Because you are now committed to a savings plan, your monthly expense total will probably exceed your average monthly net income. (Remember, your categories must cover all the money you receive each month). Give each spouse an allowance or miscellaneous account to build in flexibility, a cushion, and freedom money.

Now prioritize and adjust expenses according to your goals. Be creative on how to be more efficient. Reallocate your dollars according to what is really important to you. Take the broad perspective and ask yourself, "Did I really mean to spend so much in that category compared to this category? In light of the WYHTE phenomenon, are there some ways I can be more efficient or effective with my dollars?" The brainstorming process will yield surprises. The effort is worth it. Sleep on it a few days. Let the ideas germinate. Then revisit it.

If you are married, the next practical, but optional, part of preparing your budget is to identify which spouse will take responsibility for the monies in each expense category. For example, John might initial the "Home" column, while Linda might initial the "Entertainment" column. You may also split the money in a category and have *hers* and *his* portions.

Transfer the information you have collected to a manageable worksheet, either the one in *Your Money Happiness Workbook* or one of your own creation. List your total monthly income at the top of the page. Then list your savings and expense categories across the page, along with the dollar amount allocated for each category.

Every time you write out a check, in addition to recording it in your checkbook, flip out your budget worksheet and record the amount of the check under the proper expense category. For instance, if you write a check for $100 to pay your electric bill, record $100 under your expense category headed "Utilities." Deduct the $100 from the amount originally allotted for "Utilities" and record the new balance.

This budget gives you the flexibility of adjusting the amounts allocated to each expense category each month. If you find yourself spending less under the "Food" category but more in the "Entertainment" category, go ahead and readjust these figures the next month.

It's All a Game—a Real One

Julie and I try to teach our children there is a game stores and advertisers play, so we should too. *Their* goal is to see how much of *our* money they can get away from us in exchange for things *they* want us to buy. *Our* goal is to see how much of *our* money we can keep, or how little we can pay for what *they* want to sell.

There is a lot of strategy to the game. The rules are integrity, honesty, and fair value. Stores and advertisers can be very cunning in convincing us that our *wants* are really *needs*. We need to be smart and discerning. Sometimes we are foolish and buy on emotional impulse. Then the store passes "Go" and collects $200. Sometimes we are wise and we outsmart them. Then we buy Park Avenue.

We teach our children our American free-enterprise system is good, because it is founded on freedom and healthy competition, which gives us endless variety and drives prices down. But we must do our part and be smart consumers, budgeting according to our priorities, not our impulses.

A Word about Credit Cards

The minute you put something on your credit card, record it on your monthly budget worksheet under the correct expense category. If you charge $80 at Wal-Mart, record it in its category and deduct $80. That way you will never overextend your credit and will have the cash to pay off your card in full each month. Beware of credit cards. Use them as seldom as possible.

Finally, remember the bottom line of effective budgeting, illustrated by Charles Dickens in *David Copperfield*: "Annual income twenty pounds, annual expenditure nineteen ninety six, result happiness. Annual income twenty pounds, annual expenditure twenty pounds ought and six, result misery."

The Emergency Fund

It is essential for family financial security that cash reserves or emergency funds be maintained, but there is a great deal of misunderstanding on this subject. An emergency fund should only be dipped into for *true* emergencies: a disability, a major medical problem, unemployment, a death in the family, and other unanticipated expenditures. A new car, education, a new washing machine, Christmas, and school clothes are not emergencies and should fall within the normal monthly budget. They can be planned and saved for in advance.

Set aside cash reserves equivalent to six months of living expenses or three months of gross income as a safety net. Appropriate places for cash reserves would be a savings account, certificates of deposit, cash values of insurance policies, money market funds, etc. The most important criterion for a cash reserve is that it is easily accessible *at full value.*

It Is the Principal That Counts:

Even if your Emergency Fund earns less than the Inflation Rate, you become financially stronger. (Assume 6% inflation and 5% after-tax return.)

Year	Annual Income increasing @ 6% Inflation (beginning-of-year)	Savings Amount @ 10% of Income (beginning-of-year)	Balance of Savings Account earning 5% after-taxes (end-of-year)	Savings Account as a percent of Annual Income (end-of-year)
1	$50,000	$5,000	$5,250	9.9 %
2	53,000	5,300	11,078	19.7
3	56,180	5,618	17,530	29.4
4	59,551	5,955	24,660	39.4
5	63,124	6,312	32,520	48.6
6	66,911	6,691	41,172	58.0
7	70,926	7,093	50,678	67.4
8	75,181	7,518	61,106	81.3
9	79,692	7,969	72,528	91.0
10	84,473	8,447	85,024	100.7
.	.	.	.	.
.	.	.	.	.
.	.	.	.	.
15	113,044	11,304	166,752	147.5
.	.	.	.	.
.	.	.	.	.
.	.	.	.	.
20	151,278	15,128	320,190	211.7

Immediate and Certain Security

I am amazed and alarmed when I hear some people suggest their emergency fund is their credit cards, a home equity loan, stocks, bonds, or mutual funds.

What's so bad about that? Plenty.

What is the very time you might have a personal emergency, such as unemployment? When during the economic cycle might you be laid off work: when the economy is robust and growing, or when the economy is down and we are in a recession? Stocks and mutual funds might work as a cash reserve four years out of five, but there is too high a correlation between an economic downturn, a falling stock market, and unemployment. If an economic downturn thrusts you kicking and screaming into the ranks of the unemployed and you have nothing but devalued stocks to fall back on, your cushion may as well be made of concrete. You are free-falling without a safety net, and you will hit hard.

Likewise with credit cards and home equity loans, read the fine print. A banker may be able to pull your home equity loan at any time if he discovers you are unemployed or something has occurred in your financial situation that restricts your ability to repay that loan. Besides, who wants to be going into debt for a financial emergency?

Now, there is a price you pay for having cash reserves. This is called the "liquidity premium," or the price you pay for accessibility. The places you deposit your cash reserves—CDs, money market funds, and the like—are unlikely to provide any real long-term returns. In fact, after taxes and inflation, you will probably lose money.

For instance, assume you have $10,000 in your emergency fund earning 5 percent interest. At the end of the year, you have $10,500 in your account. But from that $500 it will be your privilege to pay $150 in income taxes, so now your $500 in interest earnings has been reduced to $350. How much do you need in your account to keep up with inflation, if it is at, say, 5 percent? $10,500. But you only have $10,350. You have lost $150 after taxes and inflation.

Balancing Cash Reserves

Nevertheless, having adequate cash reserves to fall back on in emergencies is critical. You simply need to pay the liquidity premium, just as you pay insurance premiums, in order to have the insurance and security of having readily available cash. And remember that cash reserves must be accumulated before *any* type of serious investment program can be embarked upon. Furthermore, just as you don't want to have too *little* in cash reserves, you don't want to store too *much* there either.

Having said that, I have found people who have a moderate risk-tolerance level, yet they have hundreds of thousands of dollars sitting in CDs simply because they do not know where else to put their money.

They are losing on those sleeping dollars, which ought to be working harder.

On other occasions, I will be teaching at a seminar and someone will raise his hand and say, "Yes, but my CDs are safe because they're FDIC insured." I like to refer to this as *going broke safely*!

With the potential shadow of increasing economic commotion looming on the horizon, we have all the more need for increased reserves, self-reliance, and independence. How is your safety net?

Net Interest Rates
After Tax and After Inflation

Year	Money Market Mutual Funds (Annual Yield)	*minus*	Taxes at 35%	*equals*	After-Tax Return	*minus*	Inflation Rate	*equals*	Net Return
1980	11.20%		3.92%		7.28%		12.5%		− 5.22%
1981	14.70		5.15		9.55		8.9		0.65
1982	10.50		3.68		6.82		3.8		3.02
1983	8.80		3.08		5.72		3.8		1.92
1984	9.99		3.50		6.49		3.9		2.59
1985	7.71		2.70		5.01		3.8		1.21
1986	6.26		2.19		4.07		1.1		2.97
1987	6.11		2.14		3.97		4.4		− 0.43
1988	7.08		2.48		4.60		4.4		0.20
1989	8.87		3.11		5.76		4.7		1.06
1990	7.82		2.74		5.08		6.1		− 1.02
1991	5.70		2.00		3.70		3.1		0.60
1992	3.40		1.19		2.21		2.9		− 0.69
1993	2.71		0.95		1.76		2.7		− 0.94
1994	3.74		1.31		2.43		2.7		− 0.27
1995	4.99		1.75		3.24		2.9		0.34
1996	5.30		1.85		3.45		3.1		0.35

Total 17 Year Net Return   6.21%
Average Annual Net Return   0.37%

Other Essential Reserves: Food, Clothing, Energy

I can't stress enough how important it is that a family have reserves of food, clothing, and energy. I am neither a doomsayer nor a survivalist, but there are sound economic reasons why a family should develop not only cash reserves but reserves of other types. I have seen families experience personal financial difficulties. Those reserves become valuable, and not just when a natural disaster or massive strike hits. These are not the types of disasters that most often require us to call upon our reserves.

Certainly, they are reasons to have reserves, but more often our reserves are needed due to unemployment, disability, health problems, or simply moving. Sometimes our reserves come in handy when a brother or sister has had setbacks and could use our help in his or her time of need.

Besides cash reserves, having a year's supply of food and clothing stored gives a family a sense of security. Food doesn't go stale when used and replaced regularly with fresher food.

As with any investment, your year's supply of food and clothing will grow in value at least with the inflation rate. This is not hoarding, but actually helps the economy: People tend to purchase these items in bulk when prices are down, thus helping to keep demand more stable while supply is high. Conversely, when supply is low and prices have risen on various goods, that is the time to draw upon your reserves.

When buying in bulk, it is common to get $1,400 worth of food for $1,000. That is like a 40 percent *instant, tax-free, risk-free* return.

We all need to prepare ourselves and our families for unavoidable emergencies. This means being wise, prudent, and frugal. It is not a doomsday matter nor a crisis mentality, but simply an orderly approach to self-reliance. We never know when an accident or illness, unemployment or commodity shortages may affect our family. Depressions, hurricanes, earthquakes, famines, wars, floods and such are all possibilities. It clearly makes sense to save in times of plenty for times of want.

Self-reliance in all of these things provides security for the individual and the family. It is an integral part of a total program including debt avoidance and a willingness to work.

Try a Separate Savings Account for Big-Ticket Items

An emergency fund of cash reserves needs to be set aside for true emergencies and is not appropriate for big-ticket items such as a new car, a new washing machine, college funding, etc. It is important that the family establish a separate fund for Christmas, cars, furniture, and the types of things which are shorter-term than retirement and not emergencies. Big-ticket items are *not* emergencies. They can be predicted in advance and should be saved for separately.

Especially for Youth

Start saving now! Remember, procrastination is the number-one reason people fail financially. Can you see how anyone can be wealthy if he simply makes it a habit to save even a small amount on a regular basis?

Develop this and other sound financial habits while you are young. Don't insist on learning everything the hard way through personal experience. The wise person learns from the experiences of others. He doesn't need to touch the hot stove and get burned!

Understand the Cost of Using Investment Income

An important aspect of cash flow planning is understanding the cost of using investment income to support your current lifestyle, rather than re-investing dividends for long-term growth. This is a case where perhaps some of us are sacrificing what we want most, long-term financial independence, for what we want at the moment. That is no way to plan your financial future.

Let's look at an example. John and Carol have a combined income of $40,000, while their expenses total $38,000. Naturally, John and Carol are very proud of their ability to save $2,000 a year.

There's just one problem.

While John and Carol believe they are saving $2,000 a year, they need to take a closer look at where their "savings" are coming from. Probing deeper into their financial situation, their financial planner soon discovers that $3,500, a good chunk of their income, is coming from investments, while the remaining $36,500 is earned wage income.

So what?

This is where the cost of using investment income comes into play.

John and Carol have a lifestyle expense of $38,000, yet their total earned income is only $36,500. They are actually working with a $1,500 deficit, or a negative net cash flow.

What does that mean?

It means they have to dip into their investment returns to help pay for their lifestyle expense, instead of reinvesting those dollars and allowing the buildup of compound interest to provide for their future needs. They are not saving any *new* money at all, but are merely spending $1,500 of their investment dollars on today's lifestyle.

A glance at the figures 20 years down the line illustrates how dramatically disadvantageous it is for John and Carol to be spending $1,500 of their investment income now. Saving $3,500 per year at a 10 percent interest rate for 30 years will accumulate to a total of $633,302, while $2,000 at a 10 percent rate for 30 years will only reach $361,887. Thus, John and Carol are not merely losing $1,500 of their annual investment income. They are throwing away $271,415 in future dollars.

Is dipping into investment income now worth the loss of accumulated interest later? What do you think?

The Bottom Line

You've read the strategies, learned some key budgeting principles, and hopefully picked up some valuable information on cash flow. Now comes the commitment. You must be committed to a disciplined savings program if you ever hope to get ahead financially. You can read about saving, talk about it, and think about it. But that's wasted energy if you don't *do something about it!*

Now is the time. Period. There are always reasons to put off saving. The excuses don't go away. But the longer you wait, the less likely you are to achieve true money happiness. Accept the challenge to start saving now—your dedication and firm commitment to a prudent savings program will put you forever ahead. What are you waiting for?

Your Insights, Feelings, and Action Items

A. As you read this chapter, what *insights* came that seem applicable to *you?*

1._____
2._____
3._____

B. How did you *feel* as you pondered particular points of this chapter?

1._____
2._____
3._____

C. What do you *feel* you should *do* as a result of this chapter?

1._____
2._____
3._____

D. How might you solicit the aid of others in accomplishing "C" above?

_____
_____
_____

Chapter 7

The Weight of Taxes

The Way Our Tax System Works—Since 1913

In 1913, the states ratified a new Constitutional amendment that would forever affect future generations of wage-earners.

That amendment gave the U.S. government the power to tax our income.

Chief Justice John Marshall of the U.S. Supreme Court had denounced such taxation almost a century earlier, claiming, "The power to tax involves the power to destroy." What did he mean? He meant we are in bondage to the extent that we are taxed. What many people often do not realize is that we don't work for ourselves. We have a lien on our income, and we don't work for ourselves until that lien is satisfied in full.

That lien, simply put, is money owed to the IRS in taxes.

People will come into my office and insist they are completely out of debt. To prove their point, they will show me a balance sheet with no liabilities. Yet, I'll observe they have a closely-held business interest in which their basis is almost nothing and has appreciated to $1 million or more. Or, they might have some highly appreciated stocks, bonds, mutual funds, real estate, investment portfolios, an IRA, a pension plan, or a 401k plan. And they either don't understand or they forget that there is a lien on all of those assets. They don't truly own those assets, nor can they do anything with those assets—consume them, spend them, or even pass them to their heirs—until that lien is met.

The Impact of Taxes on the Economy

Sometimes the media will attempt to console us by suggesting that we look at some of the countries with tax rates much higher than ours to justify raising our tax rates. Yet, if you go to Copenhagen, Denmark, as I did a few years ago, you will discover it is full of vacant, see-through buildings. I am not talking about a mere occupancy problem. I'm talking about *vacant*! Why?

The strength of an economy is based upon economic incentive. Unless there is economic incentive, economies do not grow. Lowering tax rates increases economic incentive to work, invest, and grow the economy. Ironically, this will actually raise government revenues, and is not a "risky tax scheme." It was President John F. Kennedy who said, "It is a paradoxical truth that tax rates are too high today and tax revenues are too low, and the soundest way to raise the revenues in the long run is to cut taxes now."

When people are taxed and stripped of the fruits of their labor, economic incentive is diminished—the economy freezes.

In 1986, for instance, I wanted to do a small remodeling job in my basement. But major tax reform had just been passed, increasing my tax bill beyond the amount I would have had available to spend. So much for home improvements.

When President Clinton proposed his national health care program and talked about businesses funding it, I remember asking my wife, "Julie, where are these dollars supposed to come from? Our existing health insurance plan costs so much less than the tax would be. Which employee am I going to have to lay off in order to pay the payroll tax to provide health insurance for the rest of my employees? If Congress is going to mandate that I provide insurance for my employees through this tax, I have to determine which of my employees is expendable because I have to support all these others." (Please don't take issue with the political merits of my example—I am simply observing the reality of natural economic laws at work.)

How have taxes become such a powerful influence over our business affairs and personal lives? It didn't start out that way. Our definition of government has changed since 1913. We have steadily moved away from a government close to the people to a centralized government. That is one of the reasons we have a massive federal tax system today. It's like the story of the Arab and the camel.

An Arab sat in his tent protecting himself from a sandstorm. His camel poked his nose inside the tent. When the Arab tried to shoo the camel out, the camel begged, "Just my nose." The master replied, "Ok, just your nose." A while later, the camel put his head inside the tent, and the master said, "Nothing more. Just your head." Soon after, the camel had his forelegs inside, and before long the whole camel was inside the tent.

We have the same problem with our tax system and our tax code. Congress passes a law, and the public lets them do it.

It all begins very innocently. Perhaps the government assures us a new tax is just temporary—they just want to pay for a new public works project. But, once the project is finished, does that tax get rescinded? No.

From this temporary tax, perhaps the government moves on to a permanent property tax increase or even a value-added tax (VAT), like those found in most European countries. A value-added tax is like a national sales tax which is levied upon each point in the distribution chain: The manufacturer adds a tax when he sells his product to the jobber; then there's an additional tax when the jobber sells it to the wholesaler, when the wholesaler sells it to the retailer, and again when the retailer sells it to the consumer.

The most insidious thing about such a tax (and a reason some politicians like it) is that it is hidden in the cost of goods—consumers don't see it being taken out of their pockets, yet it forces up prices and inflation. It diminishes our ability—our right—to enjoy the fruits of our labor.

So what happens? Eventually, we are letting the entire government camel inside our tent!

What are we supposed to do about all this? The good news is that there are steps we can take to reduce our individual tax burdens. As Judge Learned Hand of the New York State Supreme Court maintained, "No man owes a duty to pay more taxes than are required. ... There is nothing sinister in so arranging one's affairs as to keep taxes as low as possible."

How Much Goes to Taxes?

How large, really, is the tax bite? How much are we paying? Of course, we all pay differently, but add up some of the more common taxes, which include:

1. Federal Income Taxes: Ranging from 15 to 39.6 percent, depending on income.
2. State Income Taxes: Usually 6 to 8 percent of income.
3. FICA and Medicare Taxes—Employ*ee* Portion: 7.65 percent, up to about $65,000 income; 1.45 percent thereafter.
4. FICA and Medicare Taxes—Employ*er* Portion: Same as above. Did you realize 15.3 percent of your income is going for this tax alone? What could you do with that money if your employer could pay it to you?
5. Sales Taxes: 6 to 8 percent of purchases, though you spend money that has already been taxed once.
6. Gasoline Taxes: Average 34 cents *per* gallon.
7. Property Taxes: Usually 1 to 1.2 percent of assessed valuation of your home. Also levied on car, boats, etc.
8. Corporate Income Taxes: About 5 percent of every product or service you buy.
9. Inflation (Yes, it *is* a tax. More on this later.): 3 to 5 percent of income, *plus* 30 to 50 percent of any returns on investments.
10. Estate Taxes: A tax on passing property to your heirs at death. Starts at 37 percent on estates above $600,000 and goes to 55 percent. (That includes home value, life insurance proceeds, investments, all assets.) Another double tax because everything owned was purchased with after-tax dollars.
11. Special Use Taxes, Fees, "Sin" Taxes, etc.: Too many to detail.

Add them all up. No wonder it is determined that we work for the government until "Tax Freedom Day," which usually occurs around mid-May each year.

Understand Your Marginal Tax Rate

Before attempting tax reduction strategies, it's essential you understand that the only *relevant* tax bracket for financial decision making is your marginal tax rate, not your average tax rate.

So, what is your marginal tax rate?

We have a graduated income tax system. As our income increases, our tax rate increases. The first portion of our income might not have any taxes on it. Then taxes kick in at 15, 28, 31, 36 and 39.6 percent under the 1991 tax code. And on top of these federal rates, we must add our FICA, state, and local income tax rates to arrive at our *total* tax rate.

Simply stated, our marginal tax rate is the rate at which our very last dollar of income is taxed.

Now, let's say Bill and Joan come into my office and I ask what tax bracket they are in. Bill tells me he's making $100,000 a year. I conclude, "You're in a total tax bracket of approximately 35 percent." (That is 28 percent federal plus the state rate). Shocked, he says, "No, I'm not in the 35 percent tax bracket!" I reply, "Yes, you are."

He argues, "But, I didn't pay $35,000 last year in taxes. I only paid about $12,000 or $15,000. So I'm not in a 35 percent tax bracket." Then I try to explain to him that because of our marginal tax rate system, his first portion of income was taxed at zero; his next portion was taxed at 15 percent, up until about $40,000. Then he was taxed at 28 percent for the amount above $40,000 of taxable income.

What he is looking at is his *average* rate, not his *marginal* rate. And his average tax rate is completely irrelevant for financial decision making—when we make a decision we are *always* impacting the very last dollars, the dollars on the margin.

Your Marginal Tax Bracket

All of your financial decisions are made with marginal or incremental dollars. These "last dollars" are taxed at your marginal tax rate.

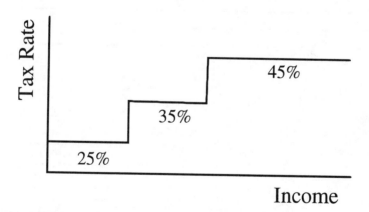

If we get a raise or our spouse goes to work, 100 percent of the dollars that come from that raise or second income are taxed at our *top* tax bracket. And that 35 or 43 percent rate doesn't include FICA or Social Security taxes. If for some reason we get other income, interest or dividend income, or we structure our investments so they are fully taxable, then that investment income is also fully taxable at our top or marginal tax bracket.

So, the only relevant tax rate for financial planning, investment planning, or tax planning is your *marginal* tax rate.

Your Insights, Feelings, and Action Items

A. As you read this chapter, what *insights* came that seem applicable to *you?*

  1._____

  2._____

  3._____

B. How did you *feel* as you pondered particular points of this chapter?

  1._____

  2._____

  3._____

C. What do you *feel* you should *do* as a result of this chapter?

  1._____

  2._____

  3._____

D. How might you solicit the aid of others in accomplishing "C" above?

_____

_____

_____

Decision Two

Focus on Freedom

In Chapter 8 we will examine freedom and its role in economic progress for the nation, community, family, and individual. In Chapter 9 we will discuss various bondages and self-defeating behaviors that keep people from achieving success and security. In Chapters 10, 11 and 12 we will apply the principle of freedom to understanding the bondage of debt and other economic lessons that impact us daily. You may wonder why a thorough discussion of freedom is included in a book about finance—because freedom is at the very foundation of success, progress, incentive, and human nature.

Chapter 8

What Is The Mainspring
of Human Progress?

The title of this chapter and much of the content is taken from Henry G. Weaver's The Mainspring of Human Progress, *published by the Foundation for Economic Education, Inc., Irvington-on-Hudson, New York, and is used by permission. Passages in quotation marks are taken directly from Mr. Weaver's work. In 1979, Arch L. Madsen, President of Bonneville International Corp., presented me with a small paperback copy of this book. I devoured the book within days. This brilliant treatise, first published in 1947, deserves wider contemplation; I commend it to you in its entirety.*

In this day of electronic gadgets and quartz watches, many don't understand what a mainspring is. The *mainspring* was the principal spring in a watch that drove the mechanism by uncoiling. The mainspring is what kept the watch going. When we talk about *the mainspring of human progress*, we are contemplating just what it is that keeps human progress and economic welfare going.

Why is it that throughout recorded history, for 6,000 years, there was little advancement in our economic condition—then, during the past

200 years, was unleashed the greatest economic force the world has ever known?

Decade after decade, century after century, millennia after millennia passed without any perceptible improvement in the lot of mankind. Mankind continued to be ravaged by disease. People spent virtually all their time trying to gather enough food to barely survive at a subsistence level. They continued to use rudimentary mechanical tools to eke out a daily existence. Various governmental systems were tried, but little changed. Civilizations and empires rose and fell with little improvement in the general lot of mankind.

History books are full of the facts of these civilizations—their wars, governments, leaders, arts, and cultures. But little comment is ever made about why the civilizations rose and fell and why they were never able to improve the lot of the common man.

We Have Risen to Practical Self-Interest

Millions of our forebears lived in squalid, disease-ridden hovels, fighting the ravages of the elements. Why did all that change so suddenly 200 years ago?

Today we have an intricate global network of human beings linked in a cooperative effort. Americans consume coffee from Brazil, gold and diamonds from South Africa, oil from the Middle East, electronics from Japan, silk from China, and chocolate from Switzerland. In turn, we ship those countries machinery and wheat.

"This is the kind of world in which men and women naturally want to live, and it is the kind of world they begin to create when they are free to use their individual energies and are free to cooperate among themselves voluntarily. ... We are bound together in the imperative desire to survive. 'Do unto others as you would have them do unto you' is not only a sound moral precept, it is also hard-headed advice of practical self-interest. Whoever injures another injures himself because he decreases the opportunities for gain that come through cooperation and exchange.

"But how can we reconcile the principle of cooperation with the conflicts of competition? ... There is nothing inconsistent between the two. Competition is the practical manifestation of human beings in free control of their individual affairs arriving at a balance in their relationships with one another. Free competition is within itself a cooperative process."

The Fatalistic View

The old world view was that man derived his rights from the government, and that the king received his rights either from the divine or from the strength of his military might. Man believed that the gods, based on their disposition at the time, bestowed a good crop or health or love. That perception—a *fatalistic* approach that the needs of the individual are *subservient* to the common good of society—endured for 6,000 years. In fact, it is still found today.

"The new approach to the bee-swarm is found in socialism or communism ... both refer to collectivism. The only difference is the variation in viewpoint as to what procedures should be used to bring it about. ...

"In the middle of the 19th century, Karl Heinrich Marx with the support of the wealthy Frederick Engels presented the ancient will of the swarm superstition, then put it in modern dress embellished with pseudo-scientific theories. His voluminous writings include *The Communist Manifesto* (1848) and *Das Kapital* (1867). ...

"The so-called Industrial Revolution was just beginning to make headway in lifting the burden of heavy labor off the back of mankind. But Marx misinterpreted the trend. He mistook the new tools of freedom as being tools of further oppression. He contended that capitalism under the machine age would devour and increase the share of the wealthy and that the working man would be reduced to a pitiable destitution unless all the peoples of the world organized on a uniform socialistic basis."

In the early 1840s, French economist Frederic Bastiat reached the opposite conclusion. He said, "In proportion as capital is accumulated, the absolute share of the total production going to the capitalist increases, and the proportional share going to the capitalist decreases. Both the absolute and proportional share of the total production going to the laborer increases. The reverse of this happens when capital is decreased."

Can We Calculate the Value of Individual Initiative?

In other words, under capitalism, the *dollar amount* going to the owner increases, but the *portion of the total dollars* going to the owner decreases. But *both* the dollar amount *and* the portion of total dollars going to employees increases—something that cannot happen if we assume a static-sized pie, as presumed under socialism or communism. But this phenomenon *can* happen when there is a dynamic, increasing-sized pie, as presumed by a win-win relationship.

Here are some hypothetical figures to illustrate Bastiat's theory. The figures are used merely to indicate the direction of a relationship that occurs when capital accumulation increases:

National Product	Units to Owners	Units to Employees
50 units	10	40
75 units	12	63
100 units	14	86

"The trend Bastiat predicted in the division of the national product is just what happened" under capitalism. But under communism, "the ruthless tactics of the dictatorship necessary to get it started become increasingly ruthless in its efforts to conceal the errors and defects of a scheme that can't be made to work."

The inevitable result? Human energy and individual initiative are put in a straitjacket; poverty and distress lead to war. "It may be internal rebellion or it may be war of aggression against other people. Those in power naturally prefer the latter course. It provides the opportunity to draw attention away from failures at home with the alluring possibility of taking wealth from others and getting away with it. ...

"In establishing a communistic state, it is possible to take advantage of everything that has gone before and to borrow techniques and ideas from other countries. It is also possible to set up and maintain bureaus of scientists and research workers under the control of the state, but even under such a policy, a communistic state will lag behind those countries in which the opportunity for free initiative extends to the entire population instead of to the chosen few. ... "

Does Equality for All Compromise Freedom for the One?

"In all fairness, it must be said that communism recognizes human equality and the brotherhood of man, in theory at least. But it fails to recognize the real nature of man."

To the communist, "individuals are merely cells of a larger organism, the tribe, the people, the mass. ... As the human will and freedom is quashed, the socialist becomes the 'humanitarian with the guillotine.' ... But the misguided benevolence of complete social and economic power leads to ruthless suppression of religious freedom, personal freedom, freedom of expression, and even freedom of thought."

These cause-and-effect relationships are critical to an understanding of the mainspring of economic progress—for the nation, the family, and the individual. History shows us "a succession of convulsive efforts and collapses as if a living thing were roped down and struggling," because that's precisely what was happening. Human energy couldn't get to work at producing and distributing the necessities of human life.

Why?

Because "whenever men started to develop farming and crafts and trade, government stopped them." It wasn't intentional; its honest aim was to help. But the effect was the opposite—"efforts to help were based on a false notion that human energy and individual initiative can be directed and controlled by an overriding authority using the brute force of military and police power. ..."

"Force and fear have their uses ... but they are ineffective in stimulating ambition, creative effort, and perseverance.

"Human energy cannot operate effectively except when men are free to act and to be responsible for their actions. But liberty does not mean license, for no one has the right to infringe on the rights of others. Certain restraints are necessary."

What are those restraints? According to Weaver, there are two—*legal*, in which laws are passed and enforced, and *moral*, in which individual discipline and reasoning demonstrate consideration for the rights of others.

When Is the Use of Force Morally Right?

"Legal restraints ... are useful in curbing activities which are clearly injurious and which are generally recognized as being opposed by all decent people. [But] legal restraints are inadequate when we get over into the area of questionable practices which cannot be sharply defined, which cannot be easily detected, and generally disapproved. ... Laws on the statute books can never be an adequate substitute for moral restraint based on enlightened self-interest which means a recognition of one's duties as well as one's rights."

No, simply making more laws isn't the answer—especially in areas that *should* be governed by morality. Why? It not only increases bureaucratic red tape without accomplishing the intended result, but it weakens respect for the truly necessary laws. That's not all—it de-emphasizes personal responsibility. It says that legalized force is a substitute for "self-control and individual morality." That goes *against* personal freedom—

and retards economic productivity. It's the basis of socialism, communism, and fascism.

"Call it anything you please but it is still a pagan concept based on a misunderstanding of human energy. It is an attempt to make a static world in a dynamic and changing universe. It is an attempt to make the gasoline engine run on steam or the steam engine run on gasoline. In brief, it is an attempt to do the impossible.

"It is difficult for us Americans to understand the stagnating effects of regimentation and how it leads to greater and greater oppression. It is generally outside the range of our experience because we have lived in a new kind of world where human energy and initiative have usually worked under the natural control of the individual, which is the only way it can ever work."

For more than 200 years, "during the greatest demonstration of progress the world has ever known, each American has been mostly free to decide for himself how to earn money and whether to save or spend it, whether go to school or go to work, whether to stick to his job or leave it and get another or go into business on his own, whether to plant cotton or corn, whether to rent or buy or build a house, how much he would or would not pay for a shirt or a car, and what he would take for the jersey calf or the old jalopy."

As such, Americans have lost a deeper understanding of our true heritage of freedom as the mainspring of our own economic progress.

Can You Accept the Responsibility of Your Own Freedom?

The only real revolution was the one "against pagan fatalism, the revolution for human freedom."

A vivid example is the children of Israel, who "turned against Moses, blaming him for all their troubles. When food was scarce, they howled that he was starving them. When he didn't bring them water, he was killing them with thirst. One wonders how Moses stuck it out."

For 40 years, Moses kept telling the people they were responsible for themselves. But, as Weaver writes, "Slaves are passive. They submit. They obey. They expect to be fed. They wanted Moses to be their king so they could hold him responsible and blame him for everything."

Isn't that like some of us today in our attitude toward our government? Toward our employer?

Moses kept insisting they were free, responsible for themselves, that no man could rule another. But the children of Israel kept on murmuring, drifting back into idolatry. "Finally, as a last resort, Moses reduced the teachings of Abraham to a written code of moral law. Known as the Ten Commandments, it stands today as the first and greatest document of individual freedom in the recorded history of man." Why? Because each of the Ten Commandments is "addressed to the individual as a self-controlling person responsible for his own thoughts, words, and acts." Each recognizes freedom as "inherent in the nature of man."

What Moses wrote was "too revolutionary to find acceptance in the pagan world of his time. The ancient Israelites wanted a king rather than a code of personal conduct."

Unfortunately, many of us today behave like the children of Israel in the days of Moses. Like them, we want to be taken care of instead of taking responsibility for our own freedom. Can *you* accept the responsibility of *your* freedom?

Subsequent civilizations behaved much the same way. But finally we come to the Magna Charta: In 1215 at Runnymede, the British armed forces so frightened King John that he signed an agreement to respect feudal customs.

No One Grants Us Freedom

"The Magna Charta was an admission from the king that his power was not unlimited. In the statement of British liberties, it has preserved the best values of the feudal system and has served as the foundation for building the British empire. ...

"But a grant of freedom is a denial of the fact that the individual is naturally free. A thing that can be given to one person can also be taken away. The point is that freedom exists in nature. It is the individual person's inherent, inalienable self-control, a natural function of the human being, the same as life itself. Man is endowed with liberty by the Creator just as he is endowed with life and the power of reason.

"To speak of liberty as a grant of permission by one person to another person or by a so-called government to its so-called subjects is within itself a denial of the principle of individual freedom. Such a denial is based on the assumption that human beings are incapable of taking care of themselves, that they must be held subservient to an authority which controls their actions and is responsible for their welfare."

In the years that followed, the Dark Ages continued. The New World was explored by Columbus, Magellan, Ponce de Leon, Cortez, and others. The North American continent was colonized, and British kings staked their claims. For 200 years the kings of England were *negligent* in governing the American colonies; *without* their attention, the colonies grew and prospered.

But then along came the benevolent and caring King George. He was a humanitarian, very interested in the welfare of his American subjects. He began interjecting himself into the planned economy of the Americas. At one point he was concerned about the price and distribution of tea.

"He had the tea shipped to the American colonies at a controlled price, a little less than they had been paying, a little more than a free market would have supported.

"Did the colonists applaud this wise measure for the good of all? They did not. They raided the ship and threw the tea into Boston harbor. This act of violence and willful destruction of property was immediately condemned by leading patriots, including Benjamin Franklin and John Adams. The incident would have been smoothed over except that King George and his bureaucrats unwittingly came to the aid of the rioters. The port of Boston was ordered closed to all outside commerce. The Massachusetts charter was revoked and other consequences were invoked upon the colonists.

"But when the king's troops were moved into Boston to take things over, the Americans did not consent. They stood their ground and fought the British regulars. The great fact in history is this: The American Revolution had no leader. This fact is the hope of the world because human freedom is a personal matter. Only the individual can protect human rights in the infinite complexity of man's relationships with each other. Nothing on earth is more valuable than the person who knows that all men are free and who accepts the responsibility of freedom."

The Responsibility of Freedom

America's godfather was a man by the name of Thomas Paine. With his own money he printed a pamphlet, *Common Sense*, giving his views on freedom. It wasn't copyrighted; the first edition didn't even bear his name. He didn't want profit. It was widely reprinted; in a nation of 3 million people, an estimated 300,000 bought copies. Translated into present-day terms, that would correspond to a sale of 30 million copies in the United States.

In it he told the colonists:

> We have it in our power to begin the world over again. A situation similar to the present has not happened from Noah until now. ...

These are the times that try men's souls. The summer soldier and the sunshine patriot will in this crisis shrink from the service of their country. ... Tyranny, like hell, is not easily conquered. ... What we obtain too cheap we esteem too lightly. ... It would be strange indeed if so celestial an article as freedom should not be highly rated.

Weaver writes that Paine's "ringing words cut through the gloom of defeat. In every colony courage rose to meet the challenge and George Washington declared that Thomas Paine was worth more than an entire army. This plainspoken man was the leader and the spirit of the new revolution. In America, England, and France, he was the greatest political influence of his century.

"Soon thereafter came the Continental Congress and the Declaration of Independence. ... Some 13 years later we ended up with the Constitution, ... providing for the first time in history the appropriate checks and balances to yield government of and by the people."

But still the colonists were suspicious of any government. In effect, our forebears said to the revolutionary leaders, "We don't mind joining a voluntary federation with a limited organization to look after overall problems, but we are not as much interested in the good things you could do as we are in the bad things you or your successors might do if there were too much centralized power.

"We don't want to drift back to the same sort of situation that brought on the war. The whole idea is to protect the freedom of the individual citizen—not only from outsiders, but from insiders, and especially from people in public office. It's got to be government by law, not government by violence. The government must be run according to law, not the whims and fancies of those in office."

Weaver continues: "The colonists were not naive. They understood what could happen with the subtle encroachment of government into personal freedoms. They also contended for the first time in human history that government received its powers and rights to govern from the consent of the governed. For the first time ever, all authority was vested in the people, and our Constitution so states that the rights of the government are only those which are specifically enumerated to it by that Constitution. All other rights are reserved to the states or to the citizens." The government is the servant, not the master.

The colonists determined that "amendments were the price of ratification." They guaranteed freedom of speech, freedom of the press, religious freedom, and the right of trial by jury. In addition, public officials were forbidden to seize or to search a person or his property or private papers except under certain definite circumstances prescribed by written law.

"For the first time in history, property was to be given full legal recognition and was to be extended to the humblest citizen without reference to class distinction, social position, or status of birth. Private property could not be taken for public use without just compensation to its owner.

"Cruelty was outlawed once and for all. Any accused person was to be considered innocent until his guilt proven. The individual's life, liberty, and property rights would be held secure against unjust acts—not only by other individuals, but by government itself.

"These early amendments are known collectively as the Bill of Rights, but the name is misleading and tends to confuse a careless mind. ... Our so-called Bill of Rights is really a statement of prohibitions against the government, and it defines the uses of force that will or will not be granted to public officials. It is based on the principle that human rights are born in every human being along with his life and are inseparable from life itself. People cannot be given that which already belongs to them and only to them."

We Must Own Our Choices

"Here in America men in public office were to be the recipients, not the donors, of permission; servants, not the masters."

That is why such progress has occurred during the past 200 years. "If our progress is to continue," writes Weaver, "it is important that we do not forget the things which have brought us thus far. Economists and statisticians take the end of the Civil War as the milepost marking the beginning of America's first great era of accelerated progress. In terms of the increased output and higher standard of living, that is true. But the seeds of that progress had been sown by the preceding generations."

In the progress of a nation, just as in its decline, there is always a lag between cause and effect. The histories of Greece, Rome, and Spain show it clearly: Progress or decline at any given time depends on what was happening in the minds of men and women earlier. Failure to recognize this extremely important point seems to account for most of the mistakes and misery of mankind through the ages.

America's progress in the years ahead depends on America's thinking today. Her long-range prospects depend not on the older generations, but on the thinking of the younger ones who will be leading this country 20, 30—even 50—years from now.

"As individuals, what is their outlook on life? Are they fatalistic, or self-reliant? What is the influence of the home—and how does it compare with that of 50 and 100 years ago? What's going on in the schoolroom? What is the philosophy of our educators and of people in public office?"

Hope of Reward Over Fear of Punishment

"No one nation or race has a monopoly on creative and inventive talent. But new ideas, like natural resources, don't amount to much unless something is done about them.

"Much of what we have today has old-world origins. America's first century of industrial progress was largely a matter of getting something done with ideas that had been collecting dust for centuries. When creative workers find themselves entangled in artificial restrictions and bureaucratic red tape—added to the natural, unavoidable difficulties surrounding their work—much of America's potential talent will die on the vine.

"Even the irrepressible genius can accomplish very little without the help of others. To extend the benefits of a new invention or discovery requires complex networks of supporting talents, skills, and physical facilities." Progress, then, depends on maintaining conditions that provide widening opportunities and incentives to use and exchange.

In America, those opportunities and incentives have been more far-reaching than anywhere else in the world. Why? We've been free to invent, free to try out new ideas and new methods, free to back up the other fellow's business, free to go into business on our own, free to take a chance of making a profit or going broke.

"The only sound program for free competitive enterprise, the only program that has a chance to succeed, is one which concerns itself first, last, and always with maintaining freedom for the individual citizen, let the chips fall where they may," writes Weaver.

"It's a matter of keeping the way open so that any business or trade group, large or small, may be continually challenged, kept on its toes, even put out of business by any runner-up who can demonstrate an ability to serve the customer better. It may be argued, and frequently is, that free competition is a cruel process. But it's not nearly so ruthless and cruel as the opposite philosophy—a philosophy that through the ages kept the majority of people ill-housed, ill-clothed, and dying of famine and pestilence."

It's a fact: Human effort is motivated by hope of reward on the one hand and by fear of punishment on the other. The ideal combination? Rewards that are great and reasonably attainable, punishments that are not too severe. In America, our potential rewards seem limitless; our penalties are limited to personal insecurity and business bankruptcy. "At the other extreme is the totalitarian state, which promises security at the expense of freedom and which attempts to encourage initiative by the threat of the concentration camp and firing squad. ...

"Not having to worry about being robbed of his life or his property, the American has been free to concentrate his energies on the production of useful goods and services.

"Although we have just barely reached the threshold, we've gone far enough to disprove the age-old superstition that for one person to make a profit, the other must suffer a loss. Under the American formula, the soundness of the golden rule becomes increasingly apparent, and, for the first time in history, the paradox of higher wages, lower prices, more things for more people, and we're only just getting started."

Obviously, we're far from perfect. As we plan to overcome our faults, Weaver suggests that we ask ourselves three questions:

How much are our shortcomings due to the political structure under which our nation was founded?

How much are they due to the distance we've strayed from that political structure?

And, finally, how does our record compare to that of countries that have tried the opposite approach?

"In drawing the comparisons," Weaver notes, "it's important to bear in mind that we've been at it just over 200 years as against thousands of years of experience of various forms of regimentation.

"Today we hear a lot of talk to the effect that our original form of government has been outmoded ... and that we are now in the midst of a new world revolution. ... [In truth], the American Revolution for human freedom is the only thing that's really new, and it did not end with the surrender of Cornwallis or the signing of the Constitution. It's still going on, and the counter-revolutionists, the enemies of freedom, are on the march. Their major attack is not the open battlefield. It is in the fifth-column technique of skillfully boring from within, a program of infiltration and attrition.

"The principal secret weapon is traceable to Lenin, who allegedly instructed his followers to first confuse the vocabulary. Lenin was smart.

He knew that ... thinking requires words of precise meaning. Confuse the vocabulary, and the unsuspecting majority is at a disadvantage. ...

"Lenin was an able strategist, and his instructions have borne fruit. There is evidence on every side. The result is that the communication of logical thought has become increasingly difficult. We are living in a world of sugarcoated fallacies, cliches, false meanings, and double-talk.

Our Words Must Be Precise and Clear

"We in America are up against the problem of protecting ourselves against the ju-jitsu tactics of those who would have us commit suicide by using our own strength to destroy the very thing responsible for that strength. Without regard for moral principles of decency and fair play, their techniques are skillfully designed to take advantage of our virtues and to turn them into weaknesses. Our habit of self-criticism, which is so largely responsible for our progress, makes us particularly vulnerable to distorted propaganda. ...

"The fact that we are a progressive and open-minded people always on the alert for new ideas makes us susceptible to old ideas when they are attractively camouflaged as something new. Being a hospitable, tolerant, and fair-minded people, we are inclined to consider both sides of every question. ... But when it comes to the eternal verities of moral truth, there are no two sides to the question. Right is right and wrong is wrong. And any concession to the pagan viewpoint, either in the name of expediency or open-mindedness, paves the way for the destruction of all moral values."

With fewer than 6 percent of the world's population, we in America have developed more new wealth than all the other billions of people in the world combined. The benefits of this great wealth have been more widely distributed here than in any other country at any time.

The Fruits That Flow from Freedom

"In addition to, or rather as a result of, such accomplishments, we have more schools, more libraries, more recreational facilities, more hospitals. Americans have gone further than any other people in the elimination of abusive child labor practices, the reduction of backbreaking drudgery, enlightenment, health, longevity, well-being, and good will toward others. Ours is the only continent on which there has never been a general famine. Even in the depths of our worst depression, Americans who were on relief were living better than the fully employed in other countries. There was more laughter and more song in the United States than anywhere else on earth. In shops, streets, factories, elevators, on highways and on farms everywhere, Americans are friendly and kindly people, responsive to every rumor of distress. Someone in America will always buy food and share his gasoline or his tire tool with a person in need. It would seem that insecurity, the price of freedom, has bred a degree of human sympathy that is without parallel in the history of mankind. It is only in America that rank-and-file citizens over and over again have made millions of small sacrifices in order to pour wealth over the rest of the world in such far-away places as Armenia and Japan.

"With the shortest working hours on earth, we have greater *opportunities* for self-improvement and personal advancement. ... Taking advantage of opportunities is up to the individual. It can't be any other way. There are no substitutes for faith, self-development, individual effort, responsibility.

"Life is no bed of roses. The end of man is not self-indulgence, but achievement. There are no shortcuts, no substitutes for work. Human life came into being and aspires to advance in the face of conflict, struggle, pain, and death.

"In the last analysis, no person's security can exceed his own self-reliance. When anyone denies this self-evident truth, the chances are he has for too long depended on someone to do his fighting for him."

Economic Progress Thrives on Incentive

We discovered that the mainspring of human progress is freedom, economic opportunity, and incentive. Though free enterprise isn't the ideal economic system, it currently is the best system that exists on earth. We can operate under it as a practical reality. It is based on freedom, not force. It is based on economic incentive and a growing pie, not on a static size pie.

On a flight in 1987 from Hartford, Connecticut, to Salt Lake City, Utah, I visited with a contractor who did small home remodeling jobs. As he expressed his work ethic and commitment to quality service, I thought of the small remodeling job I wanted at home. Then it occurred to me that my wife and I had calculated that we couldn't do it because of the increase in taxes I'd be paying that year as a result of the recent change in the tax law.

Which provides more incentive to work hard—to remodel my home, or to pay taxes? We were excited about home remodeling, but paying taxes didn't provide the incentive. Which is more economically efficient—

for me to hire a worker, or to run my money through the government overhead and then have the government disburse it to him on welfare?

Many have poked fun at President Ronald Reagan's economics, suggesting that the well-off simply hoarded increased earnings and there was no "trickle-down" to the general economy. But in this case, the contractor was going to go without a job because we would have to pay increased taxes instead.

In 1962 President John F. Kennedy discovered that when he lowered the tax rate on society, tax revenues actually went *up* because of the increase in economic production. The same was discovered when President Reagan lowered tax rates in 1981 and ushered in the expansion of the 1980s.

Economic incentive is fundamental to all economic progress. To understand this, however, it is important that the average American develop an increased understanding of the purpose of profit. In a communist or socialist system, recognition is given solely to the component of production called labor. In a capitalist society, three components of production are recognized—labor, natural resources, and capital.

In order for individuals to save money to provide the capital for new business start-ups, business growth, and expansion, it is necessary for them to have economic incentives. It is necessary that there be a return on their investment. This is called profit.

Profit Is Not a Dirty Word

Unfortunately, many of us are not well-versed in the purpose or necessity of profits. We think profits are those dollars left over at the end of the year, that after a company such as General Motors takes in all of its revenues from the sales of automobiles, and then pays out all of its expenses, profit is what is left over. It is as if those dollars have no use or purpose and therefore the game is for labor to try to get as much of those profits as possible in the way of wage rate increases.

This is all fine and good in a competitive market economy, but the danger is that in the pursuit of the golden egg, they kill the golden goose. If those putting up capital for the business cannot get a return on their investment, they will withdraw their capital and the business will die. In this sense it is important for us to understand that profit is not the unused monies that are left over, but literally an *expense*.

Profit is an expense just as much as any other business expense, and if that expense is not met, the owners of the business will withdraw their capital and go elsewhere.

In a capitalistic society, capital comes from two sources: debt and ownership. Debt is represented by the bonds or money loaned to a business enterprise. Everyone understands that interest on borrowings is a business expense that must be met—that money must be repaid. However, those who own the business only get what's left over. Without the economic incentive of profits, that business will close.

As Charles F. Abbott once said, "Business without profit is not business any more than a pickle is a candy." When you read of General Motors' or Exxon's profits of billions of dollars each year, do not be misled. Recognize that those billions of dollars of profit reflect tens of billions of dollars invested by millions of shareholders. Those profits merely represent the 8 to 15 percent rate of return in the stock market today.

Recognize also that in America, most of us are capitalists who own the businesses reporting those profits. Before you object to that statement, think about it. You most likely own shares of stock in General Motors, Ford, Exxon, IBM, or other major corporations in America in your IRA, your mutual fund, your retirement plan, your pension plan, etc.

Governments Get Rights from Citizens

In this chapter I think we've developed a perspective on the role of government in a growing economy. Rather than debate the proper role of government in society, I will simply observe that the economy that grows the most will be in the nation which provides its citizens the greatest level of freedom and economic incentive.

Note also that the government gets its rights from the citizens. We do not get our rights from the government. We have merely stated prohibitions on the government as to what its rights include. Simply understanding and appreciating this fact gives us a whole new vista or perspective on our independence and freedom, yet this is twisted and warped in our society.

For example, take the First Amendment to the Constitution: "Congress shall make no law respecting an establishment of religion, or prohibiting the free exercise thereof; or abridging the freedom of speech, or of the press; or the right of the people peaceably to assemble, and to petition the Government for a redress of grievances."

Note that this amendment is one-directional. It *prohibits* government from getting into *our* freedoms. It does not prohibit religion from getting into government. No one of us or any segment of us is to be prohibited from making our opinions felt either in the halls of Congress or in the voting booth, in spite of what some self-anointed interpreters of the Constitution may say. *We are free* men and women!

Freedom Cannot Exist without Property Rights

Socialism and communism are essentially the same. They both have the same ends: the redistribution of wealth. They both have a government-planned economy. Everyone is employed by the government.

The terms *socialism* and *communism* were used interchangeably until about 1912, when Lenin suggested to the Third International Convention that redistribution of wealth could be achieved through a revolutionary, rather than an evolutionary, process. That is when communism took on a distinction: It took a different means to the end. But that's the only difference. The purpose, the end result, the philosophies are the same.

Both advance the fatalistic notion that the governed receive their rights from government—that the government bestows all rights and owns and maintains all property. Remember: A free enterprise economy or market economy only operates as long as rights are vested in the people and the government maintains only those rights delegated to it by the people.

Here is an important distinction: The people can only delegate to the government those rights they themselves possess in the first place. The creation cannot exceed the creator. What does this mean? Should our government have the right to confiscate private property from one class of people and give it to another? Do I have the right to enter your home, take your television, and give it to Joe because he "needs" it? No, no matter how generous I want to be with your money.

Property rights may be taken in various ways—by taxing authority, confiscation for the presumed greater good, legislation, or, as in a socialist state, by simply denying that the property rights exist at all.

When the Declaration of Independence was written, it originally stated that our inalienable (God-given) rights include "life, liberty and property." Within the 13 colonies at the time, the right to property was such a given assumption that Thomas Jefferson was persuaded to change the words to "life, liberty, and the pursuit of happiness." Nevertheless, before the states would ratify the Constitution, the people forbade government to encroach on their rights to property in the Bill of Rights. The motto on their revolutionary flag said it all: "Don't tread on me."

The right of property has not, will not, and cannot exist in a communist state. It is curtailed and minimized in a socialist state. Whenever the right to private property is curtailed, freedom ceases to exist.

What is property? *Property* has the same definition as money: It is stored labor. If you do not have stored labor, and you do not have private property, you cannot enjoy the economic fruits of your labor, your freedom.

Why is private property so important? It is not just important, it is necessary to a free society, to a republic, to a democracy, to any type of freedom. Why? When you do not have the right to private property, you are disenfranchised from the system. Even if you have the right to vote, you lack political power unless you have the right to private property. No political freedom can truly exist without property rights.

Private property rights are sacred. Note this quote of Justice George A. Sutherland of the U.S. Supreme Court: "Property, per say, has no rights; but the individual—the man—has three great rights, equally sacred from arbitrary interference: the right to his life, the right to his liberty, the right to his property. ... To give a man his life but deny him his liberty, is to take from him all that makes his life worth living. To give him his liberty but take from him the property which is the fruit and badge of his liberty, is to still leave him a slave."

In fact, property rights, economic freedom, and political freedom are so inextricably interlinked, that astute observers knew that once eastern Europe embarked on a road granting economic freedoms, political freedoms would follow.

Astute observers also realize that to the extent that communist China, Russia, or any socialist or communist state allows any level of free enterprise or the right to private property, to that extent political freedom exists and greater political freedom will follow.

To the extent that economic freedom is allowed, freedom exists. To the extent that economic freedom and economic incentive are curtailed, political freedom is relinquished.

Let's never forget the price our forebears paid for the only true revolution that has occurred in the history of mankind—the American revolution of freedom, which is still going on today in the countries of the world. Truly freedom is the mainspring of human progress, and economic incentive is the mainspring of economic growth, whether for the nation, the community, or the individual.

Your Insights, Feelings, and Action Items

A. As you read this chapter, what *insights* came that seem applicable to *you?*
   1._____
   2._____
   3._____

B. How did you *feel* as you pondered particular points of this chapter?
   1._____
   2._____
   3._____

C. What do you *feel* you should *do* as a result of this chapter?
   1._____
   2._____
   3._____

D. How might you solicit the aid of others in accomplishing "C" above?

   _____

   _____

   _____

Chapter 9

Focus on Freedom

Any Bondage Restrains Freedom

No one can achieve happiness—including money happiness—if he is in any kind of bondage. Bondage is the great enemy. It is at the root of all failure. Freedom is necessary if man is to achieve success expressed by worthwhile goals and aspirations.

Freedom from bondage is the eternal struggle. Our struggle is not to achieve "peace." Peace is easily obtained. Look at the People's Republic of China: Almost a third of the world's population lives there in peace. By setting up peace as the supreme virtue, those who would dominate us—who would take care of us—diminish our focus on freedom. They would have peace at all costs.

When we take our eye off of freedom, our love for it diminishes. Our capacity to appreciate it is lost. Americans have lived with so much freedom that many are becoming complacent, lazy, eager for the government to take care of them.

"We have heard much of the phrase *peace and friendship,*" explained President Dwight D. Eisenhower, Supreme Commander of the Allied Forces in Europe during the Second World War. "This phrase in expressing the aspirations of America is not complete. We should add *peace and friendship in freedom*. This I think is America's real message to the rest of the world."

Too often we mistakenly think of freedom only in its political sense. While this book is about economic freedom, we soon understand that all freedom is so interrelated that political freedom cannot occur without economic freedom. And economic freedom cannot occur without a citizenry that understands the foundations of *all* freedom.

As we lose that understanding, we become slaves. We find ourselves in bondage. We rationalize our bondage because we enjoy our lazy habits and appetites.

When pushed from *without*, the patriotic American has always awakened to his sense of freedom. In 1775, Patrick Henry of the Virginia House of Burgesses passionately proclaimed, "Is life so dear, or peace so sweet, as to be purchased at the price of chains and slavery? Forbid it, Almighty God! I know not what course others may take, but as for me, give me liberty, or give me death!" President Franklin D. Roosevelt maintained that Americans "and all others who believe in freedom as deeply as we do, would rather die on our feet than live on our knees."

But is the greatest threat to freedom from *without* our country's borders?

I don't think so. The greatest threat to individual freedom may come from within, threatening our pursuit of happiness—for no happiness may be had without freedom. The deeper the personal freedom, the deeper the personal happiness.

Understand Freedom: Correct Choices Abolish Boundaries

There is no such thing as "*free* choice," for all choice has a cost or consequence. We may have freedom of choice, but no one has freedom from consequences. Every act has a consequence: When we choose the act, we choose the consequence. When we make wrong choices, we lose our freedom—for the consequences disempower us. That applies regardless of how we lose our freedom—whether it's to addiction, the breaking of political laws, or the breaking of natural laws. We lose our freedom, and we are in bondage.

If we lose our freedom when we make incorrect choices, then we are actually free *only* to make correct choices. As we persist in making correct choices, aligning ourselves with natural law and correct principles, our freedom actually increases. The horizon of possibilities expands.

Boundaries are abolished. (For example, in the scientific realm we understand that all progress is dependent on compliance with the natural laws of physics, chemistry, etc.)

When we understand this, we understand that compliance with natural laws and principles frees us; it doesn't constrict us.

It is an incredible irony: As we "give up" freedom and willingly submit to correct principles, our actual freedom increases. As we hoard our freedom, we lose it.

The key to happiness, then, is to align your life with correct principles. The principles that lead to happiness are natural laws that do not change with societal customs, public opinion polls, or Supreme Court decisions. In that sense we can't break the law; we only break ourselves against the law.

They are old laws, not because they are tradition, but because they are proven. Some who do not understand this have attempted to foist upon us the concept that "anything goes." Freedom has come to be a justification for anarchy.

The deeper the personal freedom, the deeper the personal happiness.

Let's consider freedom from the perspective of some of the great bondages that may enslave us.

Don't Ignore the Bondage of Ignorance

One of the first great bondages is ignorance. It is up to us to get all possible training, knowledge, and learning. There are three levels of knowledge.

Levels of Knowledge

The lowest level of knowledge is provided in our great universities. It is received from professors and teachers, through books, through theories, and in laboratories that *mimic* real life.

Often the wisdom of the intellectuals is respected above all else. Academia or science can announce a new finding, and it can destroy something accepted as common knowledge just a few years earlier. We see it often with new diets and new medical procedures; economic theories are no different.

Intellectuals often deride common sense because it cannot be proven. They maintain that a mere correlation does not mean cause-and-effect. That may be true, but to deny common sense is not exactly the sign of an intelligent argument, either.

Want a wonderful example? A widely respected federal judge, considered one of the great intellectuals on the bench, recently said that we should legalize marijuana in order to lower the crime rate. Most people laughed. The press, however, reported it as a profound argument—a new development to be seriously considered. (Of course, we can lower the crime rate by legalizing all sorts of things—drug use, robbery, embezzlement, murder. Soon, we would have no crime at all!)

His statement was a classic. Clearly, if he had been thinking, he wouldn't have thought that!

How then do we avoid fuzzy thinking? How do we discern sense from nonsense?

The second level of knowledge is real-world experience. Depending on the intensity, depth, and breadth of experience, it takes at least five years out of college to get your feet wet—and 10 to 20 years to be an expert on anything. Real-world experience adds wisdom and perspective to what we learn in college. It is the wisdom of the world.

Actually, if you are wise, you often *unlearn* much of what you were taught in college. At that point, knowledge becomes your own, no longer your professor's. You learn to be cautious and not believe everything you read or hear. (As you will learn later in this book, for example, follow the financial press, and you are almost sure to be misled. Journalists are journalists because they know how to write a story, not how to make money.)

The third and highest level of knowledge is divine truth—absolute and correct principles, or divine wisdom. It is the wisdom of God. It is knowledge and understanding beyond our experiences, outside ourselves. It comes as inspiration is coupled with the two previous levels of knowledge. It is the least sought after realm of knowledge. Many people never get it.

Because it doesn't come through the scientific method, skeptics—and even some intellectuals—scoff at it. But this wisdom is self-evident. Timeless. It consists of natural laws and correct principles at work. The cause-and-effect relationship is sure.

Accept Responsibility for Your Growth

A financial adviser can help you get ahead in life, succeed to a higher level, and reach your goals *only* when you are willing to accept the responsibility of your decisions.

A person who wants freedom makes himself aware of his *blind spots*—self-defeating behaviors that are holding him back. We all have them.

The person who wants freedom is not only willing to expose his self-defeating behaviors, but invites correction. He knows that is the only way to grow—and to free himself from the behaviors that keep him in bondage.

I grew up in this bondage, not knowing what it took to succeed financially—and had many self-defeating behaviors. So I regularly sought out a trusted mentor who could help me learn the difficult lessons I needed.

Does it hurt to be corrected? You bet. Is it bruising to the ego? Of course. Sessions with my mentor were often brutal. In fact, for several years we visited almost monthly; then, I didn't go back for five or six months. When he asked why, I had to confess that it had taken me that long to recover from our previous visit!

Successful people everywhere are those who want to grow and develop. Sadly, few people are willing to submit themselves to the honesty of brutal self-appraisal. To be free, *you have to have an accurate self-image.*

Ironically, the most successful people, those who achieve the most, are humble and down-to-earth. They are the ones who are always learning and growing. They are the ones who are pleasant to be around. They are less likely to be sabotaged in their career path.

To be free, one must have a correct view of himself, circumstances, environment, opportunities, natural laws, and correct principles.

Only Positive People Have Freedom

It is essential that we begin with a correct view of ourselves. A negative or cynical person does not have freedom. A negative person cannot practice agency or exercise choices. A negative person lacks options. He closes doors on himself because he cannot "see" the choices available to him. He fatalistically accepts himself as a product of his circumstances. He is reactive, and acted-upon.

Only positive people have choices, flexibility, options. Their horizons expand. *They determine not to be a product of their circumstances, but a product of their decisions.* Positive people accept responsibility. They are proactive, not reactive. They don't get trapped in poor thinking.

Who Are We?

Who, then, are we? In his bestselling book, *The Road Less Traveled*, M. Scott Peck gave a scary thought:

We are going to find that the simple notion of a loving God does not make for an easy philosophy. If we postulate that our capacity to love, this urge to grow and evolve, is somehow breathed into us, then we must ask to what end and what is to grow? What are we growing toward? What is the end point? What is it that God wants of us? ... All of us who postulate a loving God and really think about it eventually come to a single terrifying idea: God wants us to become himself or herself or itself. We are growing toward godhood. God is the goal of evolution. It is God who is the source of the evolutionary force and God who is the destination. That is what we mean when we say that he is the Alpha and the Omega, the beginning and the end. When I said that this is a terrifying idea, I was speaking mildly. It is a very old idea but by the millions we run away from it in sheer panic, for no idea ever came to the mind of man which places upon us such a burden. It is the single most demanding idea in the history of mankind, not because it is difficult to conceive; to the contrary, it is the essence of simplicity. But because if we believe it, it then demands of us all that we can possibly give, all that we have.

I believe there is within each of us the divine. To the extent that people accept Charles Darwin's *theory* of evolution, society will accept and excuse animal behavior, for that becomes the end of life. Likewise, to the extent that people accept a divine parentage and M. Scott Peck's statement that we are "growing toward godhood," then people will see purpose in life. It is indeed a scary thought, but the only one that truly uplifts and ennobles. In the end, we all must decide for ourselves who we believe we are.

Ultimately, we can discern the incorrect belief because it will lead toward the thoughts and behaviors of bondage and slavery. The correct belief will lead toward freedom and empowerment. (All truth leads to empowerment and freedom—*true* knowledge *is* power. Just as all ignorance leads to bondage and slavery.) Have you decided who you are?

Other Ignorances

You must avoid ignorance about yourself—but you must also avoid ignorance about your circumstances and environment. If all a young girl of the ghetto "sees" is despair and misery, she will remain in the ghetto. But that is not her true environment: Within blocks of her home is the library, the newspaper, and opportunity. It is ignorance of her true environment—the freedom in America—that keeps her in the ghetto. It is hope and vision that sets her free.

We all face the challenge of misinformation that leads to ignorance. I am troubled by a press that is more concerned with *creating* news than reporting it. I remember arguing with syndicated columnist Jack Anderson one Sunday afternoon in May 1976. I had been living in Washington and observing the open meetings of the Democratic Party national platform committee, but when I picked up the newspaper the next morning, I hardly recognized the event I had seen myself. I felt the press sometimes went too far. Jack Anderson argued that the press is the watchdog of the government, and therefore should be free to disclose almost any information it could obtain.

"Then who watches the watchdog?" I argued. He never gave a satisfactory answer.

For almost 200 years the press held itself to the supreme standard of *objectivity* in reporting. In recent years, the press has admittedly changed the standard from objectivity to subtle *advocacy*, using the sophisticated argument that it "takes courage to change the world." They have never publicized this new emphasis. Insightful readers detect the slant. The press's credibility is lowered.

The world is full of "cunningly devised fables." Do we follow them? How do we discern them?

Regarding ignorance bondage, Jesus said, "Know the truth, and the truth shall make you free."

Are You Stressed by the Bondage of Time?

Time bondage occurs as we overcommit ourselves, when we don't have the ability to say "no," when we allow others to force their priorities on us. What is most important to us becomes subservient to what is most urgent to another.

The fruit of time bondage is stress and inadequate balance in our lives. How can we have peace and progress toward our goals when under so much stress? How can we have a happy home—and quality relationships with spouse and children—while under stress?

We are constantly taking care of the urgent rather than the important—putting out fires instead of planning so we avoid the fires in the first place.

Unfortunately, relieving stress usually requires a short-term *increase* in stress. Whenever someone wants to lower stress, here's what happens:

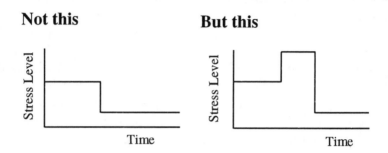

Have the courage to address whatever is adding stress to your life. How? Start with these three simple ideas:

1. *Simplify.* Learn to say "no." Cut out the nonessentials. Go ahead— identify your nonessentials. Then get rid of them. It is easier to simplify than to delegate.

2. *Delegate.* This takes time, because you have to train those to whom you are delegating. Only delegate the *essentials*. Don't delegate the nonessentials. Dismiss them. And remember: Delegation without accountability is abdication.

3. *Systematize.* Only when you get a system for the routine aspects of life can you create the time for the truly important things. Free time is more important than you think. For example, increased productivity toward attaining any goal—financial or otherwise—happens only when you have first *created* free time.

At one point my business wasn't growing like I wanted it to. I was always running a thousand miles an hour. Associates filled my calendar with appointments addressing *their* priorities. Progress was slow. I spent all my time putting out fires. Many important things were not getting done. Only when I mandated a four-day workweek in the office—and spent one day a week at home—did I start to address some of the truly important matters.

I think of my physician client, Tony, moving to a smaller home. The complexity of his large home simply didn't allow him to pursue the things that would make him most happy. So he determined to simplify life.

As the stress of time bondage increases, financial success and security diminish. Why? You don't have the emotional energy or resources to achieve financial success.

Break the Chains of Bondage to Addiction

Addiction—to anything—derails the best-laid plans for financial success. It might be an addiction to alcohol, tobacco, drugs, pornography, excessive television, spending, or food. Addictions are self-destructive. They dull the work ethic and diminish our sensitivity. They wreak havoc upon our goal-striving mechanism.

Unfortunately, one of the characteristics of addiction is that the addict believes he can stop the behavior at any time. Too often, the addict fails to recognize there is even a problem or can't see the detrimental effects, which is a self-destructive behavior that prevents achieving happiness or temporal security.

The 12-step program of Alcoholics Anonymous has been adapted to other programs to address many addictions. It is a proven program with amazing results for those who devote themselves to it.

Will You Let Go of Your Bondage to "Things"?

The "things" I am referring to here are material possessions we purchase to provide satisfaction and luxury. Satisfaction and luxury in themselves are not bad. But excessive ownership of things, or dwelling on them, creates bondage.

When Karl and Sue reached retirement, they sold their business for a substantial profit and built a beautiful home on the hill. They furnished it lavishly with money they had never before had. What's wrong with that? Now they want to travel and experience the world. They can't. They want to serve others in foreign lands. They can't. They have to stay home and guard their things. They are afraid to leave their possessions. Karl and Sue are in bondage.

"Things" must be maintained and insured. We worry about them. They get scratched, dented, and must be repaired.

Things form their own kind of bondage. They become master, and we become slave. When you keep your life simple and avoid overabundance, you are free—free to travel, free to experience life, free to serve others, free to achieve.

Can You Afford Your Financial Bondage?

It is impossible to understand financial freedom without discussing debt. You will find an in-depth discussion of debt in Chapter 10.

For now, understand one principle: Bondage precludes happiness. To the extent that you allow yourself to slip into the chains of debt or any other bondage you will forfeit your temporal security, success, and freedom.

It is easy to think that people do stupid things for stupid reasons. They don't. People do stupid things for good reasons. Otherwise, they wouldn't do stupid things. Remember, there is always a *good* reason to do something stupid. Like get into debt. And become a slave to financial bondage.

Quit Bondage to Bad Habits

The bondage of bad habits is one of our most insidious captors. Our lifestyle becomes a prison. Consider your health, eating, fitness, spending, and travel habits—are they positive? The trash we put out in barrels on the street each week to be hauled away is as unique to us as our fingerprints.

Look at your own lifestyle habits. Are they habits of freedom, or bondage? How can you tell the difference? Bad habits take away freedom. Good habits increase freedom. (*That* is the definition of "good" or "bad" I will use throughout this book.)

Will You Avoid Bondage to Mistakes?

What about mistakes? There are innocent mistakes of judgment, and there are conscious mistakes in which we pit our will against unchanging principles. Either way, we suffer the consequences of our mistakes. And the way to free ourselves from mistakes is to change.

As bondage to our mistakes increases, the ability to achieve financial success decreases. Why? For one thing, it takes an enormous amount of time and emotional energy to repair and recover from mistakes—whether they were purposeful or innocent. Those who achieve the greatest success consistently try to keep their entire life in alignment with correct principles. I have never seen anyone achieve money happiness whose life is strewn with the wreckage of repeated mistakes and other abandoned principles. The laws are universal. Even the multi-millionaires fall when they make mistakes. Their debris is all over the tabloid pages.

Deny Bondage to False Economic and Political Systems

Despite all the intellectuals, political pundits, and theorists, the masses understand which system is best. Former U.S. Secretary of Education William Bennett gave a great test for discerning a good governmental system. He calls it "the fence test." Here's how it works: Put a fence around a country and look to see whether people are trying to get in or trying to get out. There is a fence around most all countries, including the United States, those of eastern Europe and communist China. Where do the people want to go? This is such a simple observation that schoolchildren understand it—but many adults don't.

I believe that times are rapidly changing; it is critical that we all earnestly avoid bondage to political systems. To keep yourself free from bondage, learn to recognize those economic and political systems that threaten freedom. There are keys to recognition, as I learned in my youth.

Using their divergent backgrounds, my parents' talk salted the plainest evening meal into a feast of ideas. Our family could gather around a can of ice cold pork and beans and resolve problems with Hollywood, the Watts riots, peace marches, campus takeovers, protest demonstrations and pending political appointments, with clear distinctions between right and wrong stated plainly enough that we children could understand. We listened, we absorbed, and we participated.

There are many "isms": communism, socialism, fascism, neo-Nazism, and others. The threat is that *any* extremist group, including organized crime and gangs, by virtue of their passion, will take cunning and secretive steps to promote their ideology. Though I am not intimately acquainted with socialism, fascism, and neo-Nazism, their tactics are probably similar to those who espouse communism, though not nearly so experienced, refined, and financed.

Communists and fatalists are *still* at work, behind the scenes, in closed organizations throughout this country.[1] There, they share a common thread: They foment dissent and division. It started with the labor strikes of the 1930s, and continued at a fever pitch through the 1960s with demonstrations, riots, marches, protests, and rallies.

When television brings you the image of 10,000 people demonstrating in a public square, ask tough questions. Who organized the protest? What is their goal? What is the *real* issue—the hidden agenda? Scrutinize news coverage of the event: Is it unbiased, or is it sympathetic to the "cause"?

---

[1] Information about the CPUSA agenda and their continuing activity in America is available from the library at the Hungarian Center in Los Angeles and from the Progressive Bookstore near 7th and Alvarado Streets in Los Angeles. Suggested reading: *The Secret World of American Communism*, by Harvey Klehr, John Earl Haynes, and Fridrikh Igorevich Firsov, published by Yale University Press; *Stalin's Letters to Molotov*, a collection of his personal writings, edited by Lars T. Lih, Oleg V. Naumov, and Oleg V. Khlevniuk, published by Yale University Press.

A key tactic of the Communist Party of the United States (CPUSA) is to use the constitutional guarantee of freedom of assembly to protest. The CPUSA and its "clubs" have an amazing ability to amass a crowd almost instantaneously to stage public demonstrations. At one time, they controlled almost 30 "front" organizations in Los Angeles. Behind the scenes, it is known to foster an undercurrent of dissension, muddy the waters of civic tranquility, create extra expense and legal problems, and stall public progress.

Always eager to infiltrate labor unions, the CPUSA targeted teachers unions as *the* prize avenue for influencing future generations. In the early 1960s, they began making such progress in these unions that today many teachers and parents are bewildered at the new history and civics lessons their children are taught.

They have never deviated from their favorite tactic used since the McCarthy era of the early 1950s: Use humor and ridicule to undermine the opposition. Intimidate any clear thinking citizens by sarcasm, twisting half-quotes out of context, making jokes. And of course, silence those knowledgeable by calling them "conspiracy-thinkers."

Lenin told his followers to confuse the vocabulary. Their buzz-words are terms we, as Americans, would *think* lead to freedom. Though they are all words we recognize, the meanings have been perverted to meet their tailored agendas: *peace, discrimination, tolerance, diversity, freedom, free speech, liberation, choice, academic freedom, victimless crimes and lifestyles,* and many others. What do all these words mean today?

The fatalist agenda still consists of, but is certainly not limited to: revisionist history, new agendas for our schools, lowered patriotism, ridding public places of any reference to God and religion, pitting women against men (and vice-versa) and race against race, and encouraging class warfare. There are particular circumstances when the leadership of groups that fight to rid America of the right to bear arms, battle for *extreme* environmentalism, push humanism, existentialism, evolution, sexual rights, and many other causes in the name of "freedom" have been unknowingly inundated with the full agenda given to them by members of closed organizations. When you see protests on TV, ask yourself how all these people are instantaneously organized to protest on the issue of the day.

Who finances the CPUSA? There have been two primary sources: Moscow, and wealthy Americans. Among them are writers, professors, intellectuals, businessmen, and Hollywood actors and producers.

"'The millionaires in all countries,' wrote Lenin, 'are behaving on an international scale in a way that deserves our heartiest thanks.' No one should be surprised that the Communists continue to get their most effective cooperation from the frightened, ignorant and despairing rich, driven by dark impulses beyond their own control to conspire in their own destruction." (Arthur M. Schlesinger, Jr., 1917-)

Beware All Ideologies That Threaten Freedom

Discerning the tactics or the agenda of closed organizations is not a matter of being conservative or liberal, but a matter of loyalty toward our country, America, and its way of freedom.

Do we see closed organizations at work when a student demands the "right" to ban a religious song from the high school graduation ceremony? Do we see them at work when a citizen, surrounded by publicity, demands his "right" to forbid a nativity display in town? Are these individuals consciously participating in the communist agenda? Probably not. Do they realize that the fatalists even infiltrate the groups to which they, themselves, claim allegiance? Almost certainly not. But still they participate in advancing that agenda.

The most committed individual leaders would soon wither *without an organized group behind them*. Who is that organized group? The closed organization? That organized group easily and enthusiastically keeps the issue alive, contributes money to cover court costs, and brings up new or related issues that impede speedy and fair resolution. They are not interested in peace or the public good; their goal is to stir contention.

Their pattern of protest was designed to create schisms in America that were unknown before the 1960s. For the first time in its history, America has within it "haters." It seems that today there is always one group or another, twisting legitimate public concerns to serve their private long-term agendas.

An important way to discern truth from error is to recognize some techniques of disinformation.

One tactic is to grossly exaggerate the number of participants in publicity about public protests, often three to 10 times the actual number. They will slant the wording of their public opinion polls to yield results. They have deceptive social scientists to announce new "findings."

A more important tactic is that planned demonstrations are backed by planned press techniques. The sponsors' reporter will have their story written, slanted, and copied *before* the event even happens—and then will work with his organization to make the occasion newsworthy by encouraging unruliness or defiance of police. As reporters arrive on the scene, they are handed a printed copy. The result of this "calculated courtesy"? The Associated Press, United Press International, and other news services have sometimes (unwittingly) endorsed the activities of small groups above the public interest, (hopefully) unaware that they were printing intentionally slanted reports.

Our protection against *any* misinformation? Adopt a healthy sense of skepticism toward what we see in the press. Do what we can to see the events as they actually happen—congressional sessions are carried live on television—and decide for ourselves on the right and wrong of issues debated in public. Be careful of those who would interpret the day's events for us in their "news, analysis, and commentary." (During the Vietnam War and protest years of the '60s, it was enlightening to watch Walter Cronkite at 6:00 p.m., and then get the story straight at 6:30.)

Recognize when people apply dual meanings to words like *tolerance* and *discrimination*. Have the courage of our own convictions. Focus our personal values to make sure that what we internalize is accurate. Teach our children responsible independence. More important than any ideology, support those for public office and judgeships who are good, honest, and wise. (Those three traits are more needed today as the criteria for public officeholders than any ideological issue.)

Author Michael Novak wrote, "For all its deficiencies, capitalism is better than socialism for the poor, more likely to raise them out of poverty, liberate them from disease, and allow them to exercise their own initiative and talents. For the past 150 years intellectuals have written hundreds of books trying to deny this lesson, but the poor know better. Just watch in which direction they invariably migrate. They seek opportunity and liberty. They seek systems that allow them to be creative as God made them to be."

We Often Vote Slavery Back In

Sometimes we vote ourselves into bondage. We want entitlements. We forget that "a government that is big enough to give you all you want is big enough to take it all away." (Barry Goldwater, former U.S. Senator)

And we want regulations for the *other* guy. We should understand that, as former U.S. President Gerald Ford reminded us, "A necessary condition to a healthy economy is freedom from the petty tyranny of massive government regulation." The purpose of government is not to put us into bondage, but rather to protect our liberties. Yet we unwittingly allow it to do just that—put us into bondage—whenever we ask the government to take care of us. To the extent that we vote ourselves a largesse from the government trough, we place ourselves into bondage.

All those living in a welfare state are always slaves to the extent that income is shifted from one person to another.

All those who are not eating at the trough of the government but are being taxed to support the system have *involuntarily* given up freedom. In a quasi-welfare state, we are taxed heavily. To the extent we are taxed we have given up our freedom, the fruits of our labor. Thirty to 50 percent of the fruits of our labor is going to support the government middle man and bureaucracy and our taskmasters, the nonworking. The slave involuntarily gives up the fruits of his labor to his taskmaster.

The nonworking, all those who are beneficiaries of the government's largesse and entitlement programs, have *voluntarily* given up their freedom—and that dependency drains their strength. Just as one who doesn't exercise his muscles becomes flabby and weak, so does the person who allows himself to wallow in dependency.

Truest Compassion Is Not a Handout

This understanding is not meant to be merciless or judgmental; it is simply how economic incentive works. We do not help people when we rob them of the dignity and self-respect that comes from work. We do not help our brothers and sisters when we establish a system which tempts them not to work but to live off the dole, becoming soft and dependent.

In his first inaugural address on March 4, 1801, President Thomas Jefferson gave a definition of good government that still applies: "a wise and *frugal* government which shall restrain men from injuring one another, which *shall leave them otherwise free to regulate their own pursuits of industry* and improvement, and *shall not take from the mouth of labor the bread it has earned.* This is the sum of good government, to close the circle of our felicities." (Italics added.)

To achieve temporal security and financial success, we must maintain free enterprise. Francis J. Dunleavy of IT&T said it this way:

> Like so many in American life, businessmen have made their share of mistakes, and often the decisions they made were not popular with those who feared change, but ... it is worth remembering that 200 years ago the American Revolution started as a businessmen's revolution. That is, after all, what the Boston Tea Party protests were all about. It

is also worth remembering that 100 years ago it was the businessman who began translating the "heroic age of invention" into a better life for Americans and the world. In our own day it has been the businessman with his practical development of medical technology, the computer, the jet, the Xerox machine, the new sources of energy, antipollution devices, and much else who has continued to enhance the quality of life, not only for the select and the wealthy, but for all of us. This is what the American revolution with its dedication to free enterprise promised. And it would be tragic if America were to allow progress to be blunted.

The poorest people in America's ghettoes have more opportunity to succeed than do three-quarters of the world's population. Our capitalist system has yielded greater literacy, cleaner water, more freedom from disease, better health care, more education, and a brighter future than any nation in the world.

British Prime Minister Winston Churchill wrote, "The inherent vice of capitalism is the unequal sharing of blessings. The inherent virtue of socialism is the equal sharing of miseries." And capitalism provides a more equal sharing of opportunity than any other system the world has ever known.

You can achieve temporal security, financial security, and money happiness for yourself and your children only if you and enough other Americans stay vigilant in protecting our freedoms. And you can achieve temporal security, financial security, and money happiness only when you align yourself with *all* the principles of freedom, not those of bondage.

Your Insights, Feelings, and Action Items

A. As you read this chapter, what *insights* came that seem applicable to *you?*

   1._____

   2._____

   3._____

B. How did you *feel* as you pondered particular points of this chapter?

   1._____

   2._____

   3._____

C. What do you *feel* you should *do* as a result of this chapter?
 1._____
 2._____
 3._____

D. How might you solicit the aid of others in accomplishing "C" above?

_____

_____

_____

Chapter 10

Liberate Yourself from the Bondage of Debt

If you stopped to think about what things really cost you when you purchase them with credit, you would choose *today* to liberate yourself from the bondage of debt.

Borrower Is Slave—Debt Is Bondage

Interest never sleeps nor sickens nor dies; it never goes to the hospital; it works on Sundays and holidays; it never takes a vacation; it never visits nor travels; it takes no pleasure; it is never laid off work nor discharged from employment; it never works on reduced hours; it never has short crops nor droughts; it never pays taxes; it buys no food; it wears no clothes; it is unhoused and without home and so has no repairs, no replacements, no shingling, plumbing, painting or whitewashing; it has neither wife, children, father, mother, nor kinfolk to watch over and care for; it has no expense of living; it has neither weddings nor births nor deaths; it has no love, no sympathy; it is as hard and soulless as a granite cliff. Once in debt, interest is your companion every minute of the day and night; you cannot shun it or slip away from it; you cannot dismiss it. It yields neither to entreaties, demands, or orders; and when you get in its way or cross its course or fail to meet its demands, it crushes you.

J. Reuben Clark, Jr.
Ambassador to Mexico during the Great Depression

From ancient times to modern day, countless leaders have counseled against the plague of indebtedness and the shackles it places on our ability to progress. "Think what you do when you run in debt. You give to another power over your liberty," remarked Benjamin Franklin.

Unsuspecting or irresponsible borrowers may find themselves ensnared by this financial captivity, struggling futilely to escape its clutches. Unnecessary interest payments will stalk frivolous borrowers relentlessly, inhibiting communication within a family, disheartening its members, and draining emotion which could have been used for success and progress. It saps the energy of the soul.

Use Family Councils to Explain Money Facts

Parents and children should hold a "Family Council" to discuss family financial matters. It is important for family members to work together on financial issues.

I recall a father who brought in his family of nine children, some of them married, to discuss the financial facts of life. As they all sat around the conference room table, we discussed how the younger children wouldn't have the funds to go to college if the older children didn't pay off their student loans to father. We discussed the importance of exercising prudence and exhibiting patience by waiting for those things that they wanted. All came away much wiser, and a true spirit of family cooperation and unity prevailed.

Contrast this with another situation. Another of my clients, also a father, brought his wife and two children into such a council. They were drowning in debt, yet the wife adamantly refused to cut back on her lifestyle. She was intent on keeping up with neighbors, though her husband's salary could not support it. He worked two extra jobs and had little time to spend with the family—it was all he could do to keep his nose above water. He also purchased things on credit unwisely, causing further heartache and anxiety. It was most unfortunate that one spouse would not support positive change in the family.

Our failure to obey the Tenth Commandment—"Thou shalt not covet"—is a primary cause of family debt. How often do we hear our children beg and plead for the expensive toys their friends have? How many times do we watch with envy as a neighbor pulls up in a new car or takes an exotic vacation? Wanting what others have seems to be an inherent part of human nature—the grass is always greener on the other side of the fence. So, we go into debt for things that don't make us happy.

Don't Ignore Debts

Clearly, when you are in debt, you become a slave. You are in bondage. "If there is any one thing that will bring peace and contentment into the human heart and into the family, it is to live within our means," insurance executive Heber J. Grant once expressed. "And if there is any one thing that is grinding and discouraging and disheartening, it is to have debts and obligations that one cannot meet."

As grinding and discouraging and disheartening as debt may be, it is still dishonorable to ignore our debts. There are those who will borrow money with no intention of paying it back. Perhaps in later stages they realize they are in such a hole they have lost hope of getting out. So, they declare bankruptcy without giving a second thought to their creditors. One need only put oneself in the position of the creditor to know how dishonorable such a solution is.

Equally wrong is the tendency of some to lash out at banks when the crushing experience of unwise debt accumulation causes bankruptcy. Bankruptcies aren't caused by banks any more than murders are caused by guns. The problem isn't with credit. Rather, who is holding the credit? In whose hands does the credit reside? Is he or she responsible with its use? Do we close down all the banks because some have been unwise?

Debt Can Challenge Integrity

People who are deeply in debt may have their integrity challenged. They may begin to cut corners in the way they manage their finances or career. Maybe they are tempted to embezzle from their employer, or begin to question their value system in some other way. A sage said, "But he that hasteth to get rich shall not be innocent."

In spite of repeated warnings, I still observe people who continue to "borrow from Peter to pay Paul." Many come dangerously close to losing their homes or businesses and spend much of their time running around to simply manage their debt. They have not learned their lesson and will someday pay the consequences.

Easy Money Dulls the Work Ethic

When people receive money they have not earned by the sweat of their own brow, they do not work as hard.

Who will work harder: the salesman who is paid a living allowance to get started, or the one who is on commission only? While there are notable exceptions, the salesman with a guaranteed wage is generally more likely to coast and be less diligent in his efforts.

I have also seen this in start-up companies. When those starting up the company receive investment capital from others, they often do not work as hard in making the company profitable and are not as tight with their budget as when they use their own money to finance the venture.

The same is true of borrowed capital. Those who repeatedly borrow money, whether for student loans or for consumer goods, are often not those with the greatest work ethic, when they should be working harder than their counterparts to get themselves out of debt.

Anyone who receives something for nothing, when he or she hasn't expended the appropriate effort to receive it, is hurt spiritually and morally. This might be what Shakespeare was referring to in *Hamlet*: "Neither a borrower nor a lender be, for loan oft loses both itself and friend, and *borrowing dulls the edge of husbandry.*"

Don't Consolidate Debts

Once again, this is an area where decisions by the numbers often yield the wrong result. People frequently suggest to me that by consolidating their loans, they can lower their monthly payments and lighten their debt burden.

More often than not, I observe that all debt consolidation frees up is one's borrowing capacity. The individual then continues with his compulsive buying and his addiction to purchasing items on credit. Within six months or a year, he is in an even worse fix than he was before. All he has done is increase his interest rates and extend his bondage. As has been said, "It is impossible for anyone to borrow himself out of debt."

Debt Is Inflationary

Those people marketing consumer products and services understand that if they can get you to buy on credit, they can sell for a much higher price. This has much to do with the rising inflation rate in the economy overall. But it has even more to do with our personal inflation rate—the escalating cost of living for our own families.

The automobile industry has developed still another approach to enable them to raise the prices of their cars, by encouraging people to lease rather than to buy. This is a most expensive and unwise practice.

When we purchase things for cash, we put a brake on our spending. When we purchase things on credit, not only do we pay interest, but we end up purchasing an item far greater than we can afford in the first place. Over time, this contributes to the inflation rates for our individual families.

As John H. Vandenberg observed: "People seldom see how much an item costs anymore. It's how much a week. When people have trouble meeting their credit installments, they begin traveling from loan company to loan company. That's like trying to drink yourself sober."

A colleague of mine told of advising Alan, a client who wanted to buy an expensive imported car. He had committed him to buying a car for cash, rather than credit. After some time, Alan had finally saved enough money for the purchase. He called his financial adviser and announced that he was now going to make his purchase.

But the consultant had one last request.

He asked Alan to go to his bank, withdraw the money in cash, and then go to the auto dealer to make the purchase. When Alan got to the dealership and looked at the car, and then looked at the substantial cash in his hand, he decided the car wasn't worth what he had to pay for it.

I have observed similar experiences over the years. People who have the cash or can write a check for the purchase of an item usually end up making much more modest purchases than those who buy on installment credit. Perhaps you have seen the bumper sticker, "Don't laugh. It's paid for." There is much truth in that statement.

Slaves to Government

The mass of the people in America today have voted themselves into slavery. They have tolerated our leaders putting us into bondage to national debt and taxes. The responsibilities of government have so enlarged over the past 80 years since the federal income tax was passed as to multiply our tax burden many fold since that time.

What is the cause of this? One of our wise founding fathers, Thomas Jefferson, made this comment about independence: "I place economy among the first and most important virtues and public debt as the greatest of dangers to be feared. ... To preserve our independence, we must not let our rulers load us with perpetual debt—we must make our choice between economy and liberty, or profusion and servitude. If we can prevent the government from wasting the labors of the people under the pretense of caring for them, they will be happy."

How accurately he described our day, almost 200 years ago!

Abraham Lincoln added this thought: "As an individual who undertakes to live by borrowing soon finds his original means devoured by interest and next to no one left to borrow from—so it must be with a government."

Debt Limits Our Ability to Serve Others

Avoiding debt bondage is a "happiness" law. When we undertake debt, we diminish our capacity for "happiness" experiences. One such experience we may be deprived of is the opportunity to serve our fellowmen who are struggling in difficult foreign countries as well as right here in America.

Have we forgotten the great sacrifices many of our parents made to provide us opportunities? Do we feel so entitled to the blessings bestowed upon us that we cannot in gratitude reach out and extend those blessings to others? How is it possible for us to reach out to them if we are struggling under bondage ourselves?

Are we too caught up in our day-to-day worlds? Are we so detached from the history of our forebears and the struggles they had in taming the American wilderness that we forget the obligations we owe to yet other generations now seeking a better life?

Surely debt is one of the great reasons we are not able to avail ourselves of the blessings which come to those who are in a position to help.

Debt Motivation: Impatience, Greed, Impulsiveness, Ego

What is the number-one cause of money problems in the American family today? Spending more than we make? Being in too much debt? Yes. But what is even more fundamental than those? *Ego.* This is why the WYHTE phenomenon is working against us. We have to have it now: things with little labels on them, impressive cars we can't afford. We are not teaching our children to wait and save for things because we can't even wait for them ourselves.

I remember a college professor many years ago who observed that he could generally tell the odds of a new business's success based on how nice the furnishings were in the reception area. The businesses that spent money on appearance and image before they could afford it were those businesses doomed to failure.

Isn't it ego that causes so many financial problems in our families? And what is another word for ego? Pride.

What are we teaching our children? They come to us and they want to have something right now: They ask for a loan or an advance on their weekly allowance. If we give in, are we teaching them to wait? No. We are teaching them to go into debt. What kind of financial bondage do you think we have raised our children to be in by the time they are 25 or 30?

I remember when my son Danny, at age 14, wanted to buy a stereo. He *had* to have it. He confronted me about advancing him the money for it. I knew that Danny was a hard worker and a saver who always had money in his pocket from mowing lawns and doing odd jobs. There was no question that I would get the payment back from him in a very timely manner.

He explained to me that he needed to buy the stereo right away because the model he wanted was on sale at about 40 percent off. (Remember cash equals opportunities?) He had saved up about $175, but that was only half of what he needed. I explained to him that I would not lend him the money—he needed to save up for it.

When he insisted the stereo sale would be gone and there wouldn't be any left, I reminded him other sales would come. Dollars would be available later to buy another stereo on sale. He needed to learn to save and wait to buy his stereo—impulse buying would not work.

Seeing the disappointment on his face, I suggested that maybe he could "lay it away." He didn't understand that term so I explained it to him. We went to the stereo store and asked them if we could lock in the sale price with a "layaway." They didn't understand what a "layaway" was either! So we had to explain it to them. They wrote up his ticket, took the stereo he wanted and put it on a back shelf. Every couple of weeks, he deposited his earnings toward the purchase of his stereo. Six or eight weeks later, he proudly brought the stereo home, having earned it on his own.

The question is, what are we teaching our children about impulse buying when we even give them an advance on their allowance or their earnings? What are we teaching them about living for ego?

Once again, coveting, that least talked about of the Ten Commandments, becomes a noose around our necks. Uncontrolled wants are insatiable. If you allow your wants to preoccupy your mind, you will never be satisfied. You will never find peace of mind, security, or happiness, only bondage and misery.

The True Nature of Debt

We have examined some philosophical reasons to stay out of financial bondage. Now, let's get down to the hard facts and talk about some correct principles of debt:

Assets are soft and debt is hard. Let's look at two balance sheets—one belonging to John and one to Bill. John has assets of $1,000,000 and Bill has assets of $500,000. John has a debt of $500,000 and Bill has zero debt. Therefore, John and Bill each have a net worth of $500,000.

Now here's the question—which one has the *better* net worth?

Assume the interest on John's debt is zero or that even if John does have some interest to pay on his debt that his increased assets generate enough income to pay that interest. Who has the better net worth?

If you're thinking like a banker or accountant (I can say this because I am one), you might conclude that they both have identical net worth, or perhaps you'll conclude that John has the better net worth.

But what if the value of their assets were to drop by one half? Then what would their net worth be? John's net worth would be zero and Bill's net worth would be $250,000.

So, the first lesson that we learn about debt is that *assets are soft and debt is hard.*

Unfortunately, too many people must learn this lesson the hard way. They learn it when they have leveraged themselves to the hilt in real estate, the economy turns south and they lose their shirts. Perhaps they learn it after they've bought a new car, and then they must turn around and sell it some months later, only to discover they can't sell it for as much as they owe on it. These are *very* painful lessons to learn in real life. Yes, assets are soft and debt is hard. Sometimes very hard.

Bankruptcy is not a function of net worth; it is a function of cash. Let's assume now that John has assets of $900,000, cash of $100,000, debt of $500,000 and a net worth of $500,000. Now let's assume that Bill has assets of $1,000,000, cash of zero, debt of $300,000 and a net worth of $700,000.

Which one has the stronger balance sheet? Which one has the better net worth?

We are tempted to say that Bill has a better net worth, and there are many who would agree. Yet in this situation, John is in a better position because Bill is going to visit his attorney tomorrow morning to declare bankruptcy. Bill simply cannot make his payments. John has enough cash to make his payments for many, many months into the future. He is working on saving enough money to make payment number 26 into the future, while Bill can't make his mortgage payment tomorrow morning and is therefore going into a state of foreclosure.

So, the second lesson that we learn is that *"bankruptcy is not a function of net worth; it is a function of cash."*

Very often we talk with people who wonder how millionaires can go bankrupt. That is because bankruptcy is not determined by one's net worth. It is determined by how much cash one has. You only pay bills in America with cash.

Financial integrity is spelled C-A-S-H. Do you have a "financial integrity rating?" Yes. It's called your credit rating. And that credit rating is spelled C-A-S-H. Having a cash fund, an emergency fund, cannot be stressed enough. Cash is the flip side of debt.

Big money comes from financial opportunities, not compound interest. How is big money made in the business world? One of the hardest things to teach at financial planning workshops is that big money doesn't come from earning compound interest—an interesting observation, considering that my whole career is spent discussing with people the virtues of compound interest. Compound interest is what I sell. That is what I encourage people to invest in—in mutual funds and stocks and bonds and savings accounts—and yet big money is not made from compound interest. Big money is made from financial *opportunities*, like being able to take advantage of a certain real estate deal or an estate sale where you know there is potential for a substantial profit.

What other opportunities might readily available cash provide? Consider the following scenario:

You're going to buy a car and the salesman asks how you intend to pay for it. Looking a bit puzzled, you say, "What do you mean how am I going to pay for this?" He responds, matter-of-factly, "Are you going to finance this through the dealership or at your bank or credit union?" "Well I just thought I'd write you a check," you reply. "You do take cash, don't you?"

And how does the salesman react to this? Do you think that you've got his attention for the rest of the day? Do you think you might have a little bit easier negotiation on the price? Cash determines whether or not we are able to take advantage of the opportunities of the day.

The WYHTE phenomenon is equivalent to a surcharge on all your purchases. What is the impact of the WYHTE phenomenon on debt? We discovered as we discussed the WYHTE phenomenon that we have to earn $2.00 in order to pay $1.00.

Correct Principles of Debt

			John	Bill
1.	Assets are Soft	Assets	$1,000,000	$ 500,000
	Debt is Hard	– Debts	500,000	0
		Net Worth	$ 500,000	$ 500,000

			John	Bill
2.	Bankruptcy is	Assets	$ 900,000	$ 1,000,000
	not a function	Cash	100,000	0
	of Net Worth	– Debts	500,000	300,000
		Net worth	$ 500,000	$ 700,000

3.   Financial Integrity is spelled C-A-S-H

4.   How BIG money is made:

Opportunities
Opportunity is spelled C-A-S-H

5.   WYHTE impact on Debt:

Equivalent to a
16% - 24% - 36% Surcharge on Purchases

6.   10% - 20% Risk Free return?
(Actually, 20% - 40% when you consider WYHTE.)

Guaranteed!
Pay off Debt.

7.   Home Equity Loans:

Sleeping in Your Car.

8.   What is the #1 cause
of money problems
in America?
1. _____*EGO*_____
2. _____
3. _____
4. _____

Suppose we go into a stereo store, and we look at the shelves full of receivers, tape decks, tuners, and amplifiers. Next to them, what kind of little sign do we see? One that says "Mastercard" or "Visa"—they will gladly take a credit card.

Well, let's assume that you buy something with that credit card and you finance $1,000. If $1,000 is your average outstanding balance, how much do you have to pay in interest on that average outstanding balance over a year's time? $180? What did you have to earn to pay that $180 in interest? $360.

Now tell me, do stores put that little Mastercard sign there because they expect to sell more stereos or fewer stereos? Many more. And yet we've just discovered that on a $1,000 average balance we have to earn $360 in order to pay the $180 in interest. How many people read that sign as saying, "*Special Today, 36% Surcharge*"? Would you be buying more or fewer stereos if you saw it that way?

The WYHTE phenomenon's impact on debt is equivalent to having a 24 to 40 percent *surcharge* on all your purchases. Can anyone who has interest working against him rather than for him ever hope to keep up? Is he ever going to get ahead financially? How can that person ever expect to have the same lifestyle as someone who is not paying interest?

Paying off debt is like getting a 10%, 20%, 40% risk-free, guaranteed return. In our brochures advertising a financial workshop, we will often point out that people will learn at the seminar how to make a 10 to 20 percent risk-free, guaranteed return. Have you ever wondered how to make a 10 to 20 percent rate of return *guaranteed, risk-free*?

People come into our office all the time with $10,000 they want to invest, yet they have $5,000 or $10,000 or $20,000 sitting out there in auto loans and credit card debt. Well, we think we are pretty good at helping people manage their money, but I'll tell you that I cannot make 15 to 20 percent guaranteed, risk-free. CDs are at about 5 to 6 percent at this writing. And while you can make some healthier returns in mutual funds and in some other places, I certainly can't deliver for my clients 15 to 20 percent risk-free.

So how do you get that kind of return? Well, of course, you pay off your debt. Paying off your debt has the precise, to the penny, impact on your net worth as *earning* that same amount of interest. Why invest in a 5 percent certificate of deposit when you have a 10 or 15 percent note on the car? It doesn't make sense! (Because of the WYHTE phenomenon, someone would have to earn 20 to 40 percent in a taxable investment, risk-free, guaranteed, in order to equal the return by simply paying off his consumer debt.)

Now, on the one hand I am talking to you about getting out of debt, and on the other hand, I am stressing that you have enough cash. These are flip sides of the same coin. First get a three- to six-month reserve of cash, and then begin paying off your debt with major extra installments. You don't do it all at once. You have to have cash in case you have an emergency. So you take a balanced approach at building cash reserves and paying off your debt.

Equivalent Guaranteed Return by Paying Off Consumer Debt:

Your Marginal Tax Bracket*	Interest Rate on Debt						
	6 %	8 %	10 %	12 %	14 %	16 %	18 %
15%	7.1%	9.4%	11.8%	14.1%	16.5%	18.8%	21.1%
20	7.5	10.0	12.5	15.0	17.5	20.0	22.5
25	8.0	10.7	13.3	16.0	18.7	21.3	24.0
30	8.6	11.4	14.3	17.1	20.0	22.9	25.7
35	9.2	12.3	15.4	18.5	21.5	24.6	27.7
40	10.0	13.3	16.7	20.0	23.3	26.7	30.0
45	10.9	14.6	18.2	21.8	25.5	29.1	32.7
50	12.0	16.0	20.0	24.0	28.0	32.0	36.0
55	13.3	17.8	22.2	26.7	31.1	35.6	40.0
60	15.0	20.0	25.0	30.0	35.0	40.0	45.0
65	17.1	22.9	28.6	34.3	40.0	45.7	51.4

* Add Federal, State, Local Income Tax Rates

Incurring debt during inflationary periods is unwise. One of the old adages is that you buy on credit during times of inflation and you do not save cash because it is better to spend money than to keep depreciated dollars. You'll hear it is better to buy things before prices rise. This is false, and paves the road to sure destruction. Yet, I hear this all the time from many financial advisers.

In reality, someone gets in debt just as inflation rises and, with a very short time lag, interest rates also rise. The economy takes a dive. Some people are laid off work, and they don't have any cash reserves. All they have is debt. Others get stuck with higher interest payments and can't survive. So, the rising interest rates which surely come along with rising inflation always cause an economic downturn in that scenario. And that downturn becomes a catastrophe for the families it hits.

Don't believe the so-called insights of some people who believe debt is the way to go during times of high inflation. We observed this scenario in the late '70s and early '80s and we will observe it again in future years because most people have no sense of history, and are therefore doomed to repeat it.

It is enough to be concerned about the economic difficulties ahead for our nation, but it is even more important to be concerned about the difficulties that may affect our families when we are unwise.

Home equity loans are *not* the answer. What is the hottest product in the banking industry today? Home equity loans.

Why?

Bankers like them because they have very low loan-loss ratios—it's good, profitable business. We have accountants recommending them. Why? Because they are looking at the tax implications, and interest on home equity loans is tax-deductible. And we have financial planners from my own industry recommending them. Why? Because some planners want to pull money out of your home and put it into some investment they are selling, under the guise of making your dollars work harder for you. It is a most unfortunate recommendation.

What is a home equity loan actually worth? Suppose you take a $10,000 home equity loan. On that loan you pay 10 percent interest, or $1,000. Over a year's time, you have a $200 to $400 tax savings because of that interest.

What are we doing when we mortgage the roof over our children's heads for a lousy $200 to $400 in tax savings? We are mortgaging our home! I hear advertisements all the time from banks and credit unions offering home equity loans as the means to purchase cars, clothes, and vacations—people are treating their home equity like a credit card!

Nowadays you go into an auto dealership and they ask you how much equity you have in your home, as they are wondering how they can finance your car for you. So what's happening? It used to be that when you bought a car and couldn't make payments on your car loan, you lost your car. These days if you can't make payments on your car loan, what do you lose? Your house. And so where do you sleep? That's right—in the car.

I hope that we are using some level of common sense when we think about home equity loans. Many institutions should be embarrassed for how they are marketing these loans.

There appear to be no critics of home equity loans. Financial planners, accountants, and bankers all seem uniform in their praise. Unfortunately, even husbands and wives do not think clearly on this issue. As Charles B. Neal, Jr., has observed:

> A young couple entered into married life with the best of intentions. As all good consumers do, they bought heavily on the installment plan and did not save a nickel to ward off emergencies or predictable major expenditures. When payments became burdensome, they consolidated into bigger loans. Then collection procedures brought on family fights. They separated and blamed each other. ... Never has a major threat to family life appeared on the social horizon with less critics than has the installment buying, borrowing, spending, and debt.

It has been estimated that 75 percent of all divorces result from clashes over finances. If debt and financial problems are such a threat to the most critical of all institutions, the family, where are the critics who are bringing a level of sanity to this discussion? Where is the sense from the nonsense?

It used to be that we were told over and over again to get our homes paid for, free and clear, and not to mortgage them. A second mortgage used to mean that a family was in financial straits. Now it has been renamed and repackaged as something enticing. But the day may come when the misery will be the same.

What's the difference between a second mortgage and a home equity loan? The second mortgage is for those already in financial straits; the home equity loan is for those who will be.

How to Get Out of Debt with Minimal Pain

Now that we have developed a better understanding about some of the difficult lessons of debt, how do we get out of debt most painlessly? The most simple process I've ever learned is basically a two-step process:

Step number one: You have to exercise some discipline and stop borrowing! You have to *want* to get out of debt. Stop increasing your debt burden. Stop using the credit card. If you don't exercise step number one, forget about step number two.

One or more of the following strategies may help. You may wish to enlist the aid of your financial adviser or spouse in implementing these tactics.

- **Cut up all credit cards but one.** Keep the least expensive credit card but try not to use it unless you can't pay with cash or a check.

Determine that whenever you do use it, you have enough in the bank to cover the charge.

- **Think long and hard before applying for a home equity loan.** If you have one, get it paid off. If getting a home equity loan means the difference between whether or not my daughter goes to college, I would do it.

- **Eliminate buying major items on credit by creating a category in your budget for such things.** An automobile or durables like refrigerators should be paid for with cash. Consider the WYHTE phenomenon—a car purchased on credit will cost 40 to 80 percent more when you add up all the interest payments. Do you ever get ahead that way?

- **Make a plan for all the things your family wants to buy and rank them by priority.** Use a different account to purchase the various items on the list. Priorities on the list will change, but the underlying principle remains the same. Save for the highest priority on your list. Once you get that, begin to save for the next item.

- **Cancel your overdraft protection for your checking account.** It is too easy to write checks for more money than you have. For most people, this convenience seldom outweighs its consequences.

- **Hold a family council and discuss the debt problem with members of the family.** Ask them to sustain you in your commitment to resolve your debts.

Step number two: Please look at the debt elimination calendar in *Your Money Happiness Workbook*. Begin by listing all your monthly payments and ranking them by dollar amount from the largest payment down to the smallest. Maybe your largest payment is a mortgage. Then you might list car payments, student loans, and some credit cards. Finally, you get to your smallest payment, perhaps just a little $17 monthly payment to Sears.

Double your payment on that $17 a month. Now you're making payments of $34 a month. Remember that the first $17 covers all of the interest due on that debt, plus a little bit of principal, right? So the next $17 that you've added to it goes completely toward principal. The debt will be paid off within 20 to 24 months, and all you did was simply increase your total current monthly payments by $17. Of course, all these months you are continuing to make payments on all your other debts as well.

With that debt paid off, take that $34 and add it to payments on the next debt. The next debt will be paid off within 10 to 15 months. Once that debt is paid off, take the original $34, plus the amount of that next debt, and apply all of that toward the next smallest debt.

In the interim, you may have paid off one or two of your other debts. Perhaps not. It doesn't matter, because if you follow this method, you will have all your debts paid off within five years no matter how much debt you now have. I have seen people in the absolute worst financial situation who have been out of debt within five years by following this plan.

How to Get Out of Debt:

1.   Stop Borrowing

2.   Rank Debts According to Payment Size, and Double the Smallest Payment.

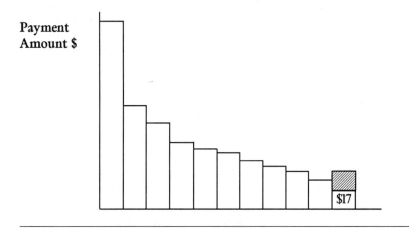

Payment Amount $

$17

Chipping Away at Debt Methodically

If you take all those payments that are going toward all those debts and begin applying them to your home mortgage, you can typically have your home mortgage paid off within another two to five years after that. This works because of the way compound interest works. And yet, all you did was simply increase your total monthly debt service by the amount of that smallest debt, that $17. What makes it appealing is that 100 percent of that extra payment is going toward principal.

This debt payoff methodology is based upon the size of your monthly payment. Others may argue that you should pay off the debt with the highest interest rate first. If you would rather do it that way, fine. Ranking them according to the payment method I have outlined simply seems to be easier for many people, though a combination of the two approaches also makes sense. This is the simplest, most painless, and most effective methodology I know of for a family struggling under the burden of debt to get out from under that load.

Since getting *into* debt was an emotional and not a logical process, involving some deep-rooted habits, digging your way out takes significant determination. Many financial advisers have counseled those about to be ruined by financial bondage: Control is lost. Spouses leave, taking children with them. Careers are threatened. Suicide is considered or attempted. Creditors are undaunted and merciless.

Those willing to seek help and exercise diligence and humility (no ego) may become free again. As they progress, they become empowered. Their minds become clearer. Enthusiasm returns.

If you are in debt and require help, seek people out who will provide it for you—a family member, a trusted counselor, or another adviser. Invite them to get tough with you. Creditors will even help if you are *immediately* open and honest, and they see your genuine effort. Here, the ancient counsel to "agree with thine adversary quickly, lest he cast thee into the dungeon" may be particularly appropriate, as a "soft answer turneth away wrath." Do not let creditors languish in uncertainty, as this will only compound the problem. Freely submit yourself, cooperate, and pay the price—the rewards will be forever worth it.

Above all, understand that freedom, peace, and contentment come into our hearts when we live within our means. Peace, prosperity, and success come to those who have interest working for them rather than against them, since "interest never sleeps." Heed the inspired counsel of countless sages past and not the enticing advertisements of those who would enslave us. Get out of debt, live within your means, and pay as you go. "Pay your debt and *live*."

Your Insights, Feelings, and Action Items

A. As you read this chapter, what *insights* came that seem applicable to *you?*

1._____

2._____

3._____

B. How did you *feel* as you pondered particular points of this chapter?
   1._____
   2._____
   3._____
C. What do you *feel* you should *do* as a result of this chapter?
   1._____
   2._____
   3._____
D. How might you solicit the aid of others in accomplishing "C" above?

   _____

   _____

   _____

Chapter 11

A Brief Economics Lesson: Financial Causes and Effects

In a sea of economic commotion and uncertainty, is there any way to find a safe harbor where the water is calm and shipwrecks are few? Yes. Increase your understanding of these principles, so you can face the future with confidence. Then you can avoid the threats to your financial security.

Natural economic laws are understood as we examine the minimum wage law, price controls, free specialization and exchange, technology replacing workers, gambling and the lottery, inflation, depression, recession, socialism and communism, and government control of the economy. These all affect our ability to succeed financially, individually and as a nation. The workings of these economic laws are sure—it does little good to debate them. As you understand the economic laws affecting these issues, you learn to live above many of the threats to your financial future.

An Economy Thrives on Free Specialization and Exchange

In order to live, you need wheat and milk. Let's look at what happens in a basic farming community between Farmer John and Farmer

Joe. Farmer John is able to produce 100 bushels of wheat and 40 gallons of milk based on his acreage, the quality of his soil, his equipment, and the climate. Farmer Joe is able to produce only 60 bushels of wheat but 110 gallons of milk with his resources.

Each farmer spends exactly half of his effort on producing wheat and half on producing milk. Given the figures above, if Farmer John sacrificed his milk production and devoted all his effort to wheat, he would be able to produce 200 bushels. If Farmer Joe devoted all his efforts to wheat, he'd produce only 120 bushels of wheat. But if he spent all his efforts on milk, he'd produce 220 gallons.

If Farmer John spent all his effort on wheat and Joe spent all his effort on milk, and they traded, what could happen?

Let's say John put all his effort into wheat, but he needed some milk. Joe put all his effort into milk, but he needed wheat. If John traded half of his wheat—100 bushels—how much milk would he get? He'd get 110 gallons of milk. He'd still have 100 bushels of wheat, which is what he had originally—but he'd now have *almost three times as much milk* as he had before.

What about Joe? If he traded half his milk to John, he'd still have 110 gallons of milk—as much as he had originally. But he'd have almost *twice as much wheat* as he had before.

What has happened? Both John and Joe are better off than before. What does this teach about specialization and exchange? Specialization and exchange—or synergy, or interdependence, or a win-win relationship—is the *foundation* of an increase in wealth.

The principle of specialization and exchange is a key reason why the American economy has grown during the last 200 years while the European economy has not grown nearly as much. The European economy had imposed artificial tariffs and boundaries between countries, affecting its ability to specialize and exchange. In contrast, our wise founding fathers made the U.S. Constitution forbid tariffs within interstate commerce. The standard of living increases in direct proportion to free trade (specialization and exchange).

As long as certain people, certain economies, and certain companies have competitive advantages, the principle of specialization and exchange will be a natural economic law. As long as Argentina grows cattle, Brazil grows coffee, South Africa produces diamonds and gold, and the U.S. grows wheat, for example, the principle of specialization and exchange will improve the general welfare of all mankind.

It explains why allowing immigration into the U.S. has always improved the standard of living for all. It explains why a planned economy will never result in an improved living standard. It reflects the adage that 50 percent of something is better than 100 percent of nothing. Specialization and exchange flourishes under abundance thinking and shrivels under scarcity thinking.

It will be the number one reason for the rise in the standard of living into the 21st century, if the world operates on a level of free trade. To the extent that the world will *not* tolerate free trade, improvements in standard of living will be limited in all areas of the globe, including the U.S.

Even *within* a company or a family, specialization of tasks and mutual interdependence will result in improved security, success, and well-being for all.

To the extent that we in America allow our unskilled, low-income jobs to go to China and Taiwan, we will *improve* our overall standard of living, *even* for our unskilled. Why? Because we will provide China with what we produce most efficiently—and we will acquire from China the things it produces most efficiently.

The more workers there are, the more the production; the more the production, the more the economy grows, and coupled with the principle of specialization, the more we have an improved standard of living for all.

It is important to understand that sustainable real economic growth is approximately equal to the population growth rate plus the growth rate in productivity. Historically the population growth rate has been between 1.5 and 2 percent per year, and the productivity growth rate has been between 0.5 and 1 percent per year. That would suggest that sustainable real growth in the United States is around 2 to 3 percent per year.

I remember the late 1970s when we had a chairman of the Council of Economic Advisers announce he wanted real growth in the economy at 5 percent. He dramatically increased the money supply. Insightful observers immediately began to suspect inflation, and that was, indeed, the result.

Sustainable real growth is a measurement for an improvement in standard of living. The growth rate of productivity is equal to labor working more effectively or technological improvements and automation. While the productivity growth rate in the United States averages between 0.5 and 1 percent per year, in China in recent years it has averaged 20 percent per year due to the unleashing of free enterprise.

Perhaps it is easier to understand this principle if we consider productivity on a farm. In yesteryear, a large family meant an increased standard of living for the household. The same holds true in a town of 100 versus a town of 500. It holds true in a nation or a world where there is free trade. This is not debatable. Those who would debate it would deny the proof of history. They would let their fear and anxiety say, as they always say, "But today is different," and they offer the rationalization which fits their scarcity view of the world.

This is an emotional view of the world. The only accurate and logical view of the world is the proven view of the law of abundance.

Specialization and Exchange

	1/2 Effort toward each	All Effort toward Wheat	All Effort toward Milk	Specialization & Exchange
Farmer John	100 Bushels	200 Bushels	0 Bushels	200 Bushels
	40 Gallons	0 Gallons	80 Gallons	0 Gallons
Farmer Joe	60 Bushels	120 Bushels	0 Bushels	0 Bushels
	110 Gallons	0 Gallons	220 Gallons	220 Gallons
Combined Standard of Living in the John-Joe Economy	160 Bushels 150 Gallons	320 Bushels 0 Gallons	0 Bushels 300 Gallons	200 Bushels 220 Gallons
Total Units	310 Units	320 Units	300 Units	420 Units

The Insidious Tax: Inflation

Someone has said, "Inflation means that your money won't buy as much today as it did when you didn't have any."

We smile, but inflation is no laughing matter. Some people even think that a small amount of inflation is good. They think it demonstrates that demand is slightly higher than supply—or that the economy is growing.

Inflation is an increase in the price of a good or service without any corresponding increase in the quality of the good or service. In other words, you pay more money for the same exact item.

When you consider that definition, it's sometimes difficult to accurately measure inflation. Why? The government tries to establish the inflation rate using a static basket of goods that it measures each month. What is wrong with that? The basket of goods *does* change. Take automobiles, for example. The price increases—but you may also get "extras" like power steering, automatic transmission, and anti-lock brakes. Additionally, as certain prices increase, the consumer changes the mix of the goods he is buying: If the price of potatoes goes up, people switch to rice.

So let's look at inflation. First, inflation is a tax. American economist Milton Friedman called inflation "the one form of taxation that can be imposed without legislation." If we have 5 percent inflation, we have 5 percent tax. In fact, when we calculate the after-tax, after-inflation rate of return, the "tax" of inflation is even higher.

Want an example? Let's say your rate of return on an investment is 10 percent, and let's say you are in a 40 percent tax bracket—how much of your 10 percent return vaporizes into taxes? Forty percent of it. That leaves you with a 6 percent return.

Now let's say we have a 4 percent inflation rate. Your 6 percent return now becomes a *2 percent return*—4 percent of it vaporizes into inflation. Do you see what just happened? You lost 80 percent of your anticipated return to taxes and inflation. In other words, if you are in a 40 percent tax bracket and inflation is at 4 percent, *you are in an 80 percent tax bracket*. Your real return—after taxes, after inflation—is 80 percent less. Four percent inflation destroyed as much of your return as a 40 percent tax rate.

Inflation is a highly regressive tax, impacting lower-income and high-consuming people the most.

Inflation is caused by a number of factors. A key factor is that the government wants it to be that way.

Think about it: Who is the greatest beneficiary of inflation? The government. Why? The government borrows. The government is the largest debtor. If inflation is high enough, they can repay their debt at pennies on the dollar. That means they can also increase the money supply and float debt to keep the government operating. Sir Fredrick Leath-Ross, English economist and financier, said, "Inflation is like sin. Every government denounces it, and every government practices it."

There is another reason why the government benefits from inflation. The government is financed in two ways: directly by income taxes, and indirectly by debt and inflation. As long as we tolerate the government running deficits and financing their expenditures through borrowing, we are going to maintain the tax of inflation.

Deficit spending can work in the short term. Why? It is an artificial stimulus to the economy—it produces a "high" that we get addicted to. It is the same thing as deficit spending within a family. They buy things, see a welcome improvement in their standard of living, and are then driven to buy even more on credit. It causes an artificial *short-term* improvement in their outward standard of living. But the day of reckoning comes.

When we play accounting games like the government does and we do not show that debt on our balance sheet, we are fooling ourselves. We do not understand that in the long term, we either get our spending under control or the deficit gets too far out of hand. If that happens, we have either fiat money and spiraling inflation or dramatically increasing taxes. That all falls upon the backs of future generations, namely our children.

John Maynard Keynes, the economist of Great Britain, wrote in his *Essay in Persuasion*, "Lenin is said to have declared that the best way to destroy the capitalist system was to debauch the currency. By a continuing process of inflation, governments can confiscate, secretly and unobserved, an important part of the wealth of their citizens. ... Lenin was certainly right."

There are two different kinds of inflation: *cost-push inflation* and *demand-pull inflation*. In cost-push inflation, there is a shortage of supply, so costs increase. Want an example of cost-push? A drought in the Midwest causes a shortage of food, so farmers must charge more for the food they *are* able to produce in order to cover their costs. The increase in price is passed along to everyone along the manufacturing and distribution chain, until you pay more at the supermarket. Or, the cost of labor increases.

In demand-pull inflation, demand is so great that people will pay more for the same product. In the national economy as a whole, the cause of demand-pull inflation is best illustrated by the government increasing the money supply, resulting in too many dollars chasing too few goods.

How can you predict inflation?

Three basic resources go into any product in a capitalist economy: raw materials, labor, and capital. Approximately 89 percent of the cost of any good or service is labor. Capital and raw materials make up the other 11 percent. That applies to everything in the economy—all the way from harvesting the raw material in the mine or forest to manufacturing, transportation, wholesaler, and retailer.

If 89 percent of the cost of any good or service is labor, and you want to predict inflation, what should you look at? Labor rates. The cost of labor is reported monthly on the front page of the *Wall Street Journal* in a graph entitled "Hourly Earnings." Watching labor rates helps predict cost-push inflation.

Which indicators help predict demand-pull inflation? The supply of money, which is reflected in the price of money. What's the price of money? Interest rates.

If you are interested in predicting inflation over the next six months to two years, look at short-term interest rates—the prime interest rate, and the rate on Treasury bills. If you are interested in predicting inflation over the next five to 10 years, look at long-term interest rates—those on Treasury bonds and home mortgages.

Regardless, remember that the price of money (interest rates) is always going to be determined by people wanting to lend out their money and have that money paid back to them, adjusted for inflation, plus one or two percentage points based on the risk premium. The premium is going to be lower with government T-bonds; it is going to be a little higher with mortgages.

Is that going to give us a better answer on the prognosis of inflation than you can get from any economist in the country? Yes. Why? What determines the price of money? Massive supply and demand forces in the economy. So, we are dealing with an equilibrium point to get those prices.

Who Benefits from the Minimum Wage?

At first glance, minimum wage seems like a good law. But let's take a closer look. Who is a minimum wage designed for? The skilled or unskilled laborer? Unskilled. So we are looking at the unskilled laborer vs. the skilled laborer vs. technology or automation.

Are labor unions in favor of or against minimum wage? They are in favor of minimum wage. Why? Is it because unions view themselves as protectors of the downtrodden? Who makes up unions? Skilled or unskilled workers? Unions are made up of *skilled* workers. Do not assume that unions, full of skilled workers, have organized themselves on behalf of unskilled workers.

Now let's look at our options. Assume that an unskilled worker can assemble two widgets per hour, a skilled laborer can produce five of the same widgets in an hour, and automation can produce 10 of the same widgets in an hour.

Let's say that, based on supply and demand, the market will tolerate a price of $2 per widget. Who determines market price? Is it the manufacturer? Wholesaler? Retailer? Absolutely not. It is the consumer, and the consumer determines price by his demand for widgets. The competition is *not only* widgets made by other manufacturers, but *whatever else* the consumer can buy with that $2.

So, supply and demand determine the price of that unit. And prices determine how we will allocate scarce resources—like timber, minerals, and iron ore, for example. Is labor a scarce resource? Is there a limited supply of labor? Yes. There is also a limited supply of different qualities of labor. Prices, then, determine how labor is allocated.

Labor and the Costs of Production

The scarcer the resource, the higher the price of that resource. If you want to have a higher price paid for *your* labor, then, you need to provide a scarce resource or talent. Eighteenth-century economist Adam Smith called the free-market system the "invisible hand"—an invisible hand operating in a free economy that provided the most efficient allocation of scarce resources. And, he maintained, the invisible hand operated best without any governmental intrusion, artificial coercion, or economic restraints. In other words, the invisible hand of supply and demand—the price system—gives the most efficient allocation of these scarce resources.

Supply and demand determines the price of the widget, which we have said is $2. Let's assume the unskilled laborer is earning $1 an hour. The skilled laborer, who is represented by a union, is earning $2 an hour. And the automated plant costs the equivalent of $3 an hour.

Based on those figures, what does it cost to produce each $2 widget?

	Unskilled $1.00/hr.	Skilled $2.00/hr.	Automation $3.00/hr.
Output per hour	2 widgets/hr.	5 widgets/hr.	10 widgets/hr.
Cost per widget	50 cents	40 cents	30 cents

It costs the manufacturer 50 cents a widget to use unskilled labor. It costs 10 cents less to use skilled labor and 20 cents less for automation.

Remember, the price of this widget is $2. What is the implication? They'll make the most money if they are automated. So the company will automate.

Now let's assume that, as a result of labor negotiations, the skilled person now charges $3 an hour. And, for our example, we will assume the cost of automation is now $6 an hour.

How much does it cost to produce each widget now? It still costs 50 cents for the unskilled laborer to produce the widget. But it costs 10 cents *more* for skilled labor or automation:

	Unskilled $1.00/hr.	Skilled $3.00/hr.	Automation $6.00/hr.
Output per hour	2 widgets/hr.	5 widgets/hr.	10 widgets/hr.
Cost per widget	50 cents	60 cents	60 cents

What has happened? The union, which negotiated wages up to $3 per hour for skilled workers, just negotiated their workers out of a job. Did the employees vote for that union package? Yes, they wanted the raise. Are they happy now? No. They get laid off. Who gets the work? The unskilled.

Let's assume now that this is not a union shop; it is a service company (like McDonald's) that is not represented by a union. Who is going to have the job here? The skilled or the unskilled? No question. The unskilled worker will be employed.

All of a sudden, union people are losing their jobs. What do the unions do in response? Lower the wage? Never! They do not want their skilled workers being paid a lower wage. Instead, they petition Congress and the president, and say that, in the interest of fairness to society, it is not right that the downtrodden—the unskilled workers—earn only $1 an hour. No, say the unions—they should be given a minimum wage, and that minimum wage should be raised to $2 an hour.

Okay. Now unskilled workers are earning $2 an hour. What is the cost to manufacture each widget *now*? It's *twice* as much as it was before—$1 per widget. What happens to the unskilled? They lose their jobs. Perhaps the skilled workers get hired back.

What happens? When the minimum wage is increased, employers have to either raise the price of goods, automate, or shift to more skilled labor. Either way, the unskilled become unemployed.

Whenever the minimum wage goes up, unemployment increases. In the 1970s, the minimum wage rate was raised quite high relative to the limits of supply and demand. Unemployment of the unskilled skyrocketed.

Technology Replacing Labor:
Job Evolution and Misplaced Panic

During the past 200 years, millions of manual workers have been replaced by machines. During this same period, the number of jobs has steadily grown, as has the real income of most people in the industrialized world.

Let's be clear: Economic growth and financial enrichment have occurred *because of* technological change, not in spite of it.

When the sewing machine was invented, everyone feared that tailors would be put out of business. When the computer was invented, everyone feared that typewriter manufacturers would be put out of business. When the cotton gin was invented, everyone feared that cotton pickers would be put out of business. When the electric light was invented, everyone feared that candlemakers would be put out of business. When the automobile was invented, everyone feared carriage manufacturers would be put out of business.

Those were misplaced fears. The economy thrived and new jobs were created—many times the jobs.

It is the same today. The speed of technological advancement has caused some to fear that people will be put out of jobs. In reality, technological change *improves* employment.

In George Eliot's *Middlemarch*, discussed in *The Economist*:

> Victorians thought that the railway would change their lives, and they were right. But they were wrong in thinking it would deprive all of them of their livelihoods. For every stagecoach driver the train put out of work, it created many other jobs—not only on the railway itself but in businesses and shops that were now connected to the outside world. The town's improved productivity would deliver growth—and eventually jobs. Even if some of these changes proved painful, in the longer run jobs were safer in a town such as Middlemarch that was connected to the railway than in towns that were not.
>
> "Misplaced Panics," *The Economist*
> February 11, 1995, p. 13

Today, as in Victorian times, embracing technology means "connecting with the larger world and the enriching, job-creating opportunities that the free movement of people and goods can offer." (Eliot)

Who Can Veto the President or Congress?

While the American public *thinks* economic policies are determined by the President, Congress, or the Federal Reserve Board, there is a select body of voters that maintains virtually instantaneous veto power. They aren't elected, and many are citizens of other nations.

They are those people who finance the U.S. deficit by buying government bonds. They come from all around the world; many are Japanese and middle-easterners. Because of them, we are able to live in our excesses without re-igniting inflation. (Foreign buyers of government bonds are the major reason we haven't had our day of reckoning with our massive deficit.)

But if our government proposes unwise policies that will drive up inflation, chances are world bondholders would swiftly begin selling their bonds, driving bond prices down and interest rates up, perhaps even plunging the country into recession. They can be tough disciplinarians.

In the early 1990s Sweden saw how swiftly this could occur. After a particularly unwise bill was signed into law, their bond market rapidly drove interest rates up to almost 200 percent on government bonds, forcing the government to reverse itself.

The U.S. bond market is *four times* the size of the stock market, with trillions of dollars of government debt. With our enormous deficit, bondholders are rightfully concerned about inflationary spending policies.

Currently, interest on the national debt is about one-fourth of the federal budget. What would happen if interest rates doubled within just a couple of years, as they did 1979-1981? Our economy is more highly leveraged today than it was then. The U.S. government has engaged in short-term borrowing (Treasury bills) to finance long-term projects. This mismatch means rising interest rates are felt more quickly as it rolls over its debt.

Corporations and people understand that you don't borrow short-term to invest long-term. That is like buying a home with a one-year mortgage. So what happens? If government spending exceeds the government's ability to tax or borrow, all it can do is turn on the printing press and inflation skyrockets.

A Game of Deception: Gambling and the Lottery

We have all seen the sensational news reports about people who've struck it rich after buying a lottery ticket. What could be so wrong with them?

The lottery works on the principle of *something for nothing*. It is poor social, tax, economic, and political policy.

You may hear the argument that the lottery is an effective way to raise capital for various government expenses—even expenses as worthy as education. But as a government revenue-raising mechanism, it is clearly regressive. Want proof? Low-income people are the ones who buy most of the lottery tickets. Higher-income people buy fewer tickets. (This is a government-sponsored predator program against those who engage in the poor thinking described in Chapter 32.)

The lottery is also an extremely expensive way of raising money. Why? The traditional process of collecting taxes costs about 2 cents for every dollar that is raised. The lottery? It costs about *70 cents* for every dollar raised. A lot of that expense goes into advertising and promoting the lottery.

The lottery only contributes about 2 percent of the budget for those states that have legalized the lottery. The same could have been accomplished by increasing the sales tax by 0.5 percent. And statisticians contend you are *seven times* more likely to be struck by lightning than to win the lottery.

And that's not all: The lottery is a precursor to gambling. The state that advertises and promotes the lottery is promoting gambling. Supporting the addiction and slavery that goes along with gambling. Promoting the ruse of something for nothing. (Of course, the gambling industry has been one of the staunchest supporters and benefactors of the lottery; they have artfully renamed gambling "gaming.")

As the late Thomas E. Dewey said, "The entire history of legalized gambling in this country and abroad shows that it has brought nothing but poverty, crime, and corruption, demoralization of moral and ethical standards, and ultimately lower living standards and misery for all the people." Witness the flight of businesses, a middle-class, and economic growth in Atlantic City, New Jersey, since it legalized gambling in the late 1970s, and witness the influx of robbery, assault, prostitution, and organized crime.

The lottery is inefficient, regressive, and enslaving. It is dumb policy. Period.

Some Unsurprising Results of Price Controls

In 1973, President Richard Nixon fixed wages and prices. All the aisles of the nation's supermarkets bore red-lettered signs stating that prices had been fixed by emergency declaration and could not change.

Nixon did it because inflation—which had reached 6 percent—was ravaging the economy.

Two things happened. When price fixing was being considered, some companies dramatically raised their prices in anticipation. When prices were fixed, then, they were fixed at an artificially high level. So the black market started selling products at a lower price on the side.

Second, shortages occurred. Why? As the costs to manufacture grew, other companies refused to provide product at the fixed price. We started seeing empty shelves in the stores. The only way people could get merchandise was, again, through the black market.

Price and wage fixing are always clamored for whenever inflation raises its ugly head. The economy takes on the appearance of a socialist state. Whenever wages and prices are fixed in the economy, shortages occur, dislocations occur, and economic incentive is curtailed. Such controls are *always* scrapped eventually. That scenario only persisted a few months. What stopped it? Price controls were rescinded. Wage and price controls simply will not work. Period.

Prepare for the Next Depression

Just as businesses, real estate, stocks, bonds, and other assets lose value in a recession or depression, so does your greatest asset—your income.

Allen Booth lost his job during the Depression because another man offered to do the same job for less money. Could that happen again? Of course. Would a business owner be justified in hiring another employee for less money? Of course—he may need to do it to compete, or to survive.

Let's take it a step further. Do most employees resist downward adjustments in wages? Of course! So what happens? When business values, income, or sales go down but wages stay the same, what happens? Layoffs. Would you rather be laid off, or take a downward wage adjustment? *Always* be prepared for one or the other.

Will we go through another recession or depression? Yes. Remember, though, in order to affect you, a recession or depression doesn't need to be economy-wide. It may occur only in your industry. Or only in your company. If it happens, and you become unemployed, are you prepared? It has been said that "when the other guy loses his job it's a recession; when you lose yours, it's a depression."

Is it difficult to predict a recession or depression with much accuracy? Ask 10 economists, and you will get 20 opinions. It is said that economists have predicted 17 of the last three recessions!

Stewardship for the Environment

Economics is the study of scarce resources, but those resources are scarce only because we currently have insufficient labor and a standard of living too low to capitalize on the resources available to be mined, grown, harvested, discovered, recycled, etc.

As long as free enterprise is left unfettered to do its job, we will have scientists and engineers and businessmen who will be discovering how to harvest oil deeper, use solar energy more efficiently, harvest the ocean, and explore the universe. The only way the earth will not do its job to support us is if we return to the fatalistic notion of political and economic government paternity, and sabotage ourselves through self-destructive thinking.

If we return to slavery, either to government or other forms of bondage, our lives will be reduced to the squalor of our ancestors. Has this happened before? Yes. Great civilizations of the ancient world demonstrated understanding of astronomy, legal systems, surgery, extensive canals and water systems, and other complexities. The Greeks, Romans and Incas built extensive highways stretching thousands of miles and facilitating far-reaching free trade. Yet these advanced civilizations succumbed to various bondages and ultimately failed.

Man's appropriate relation to the earth is that of stewardship, not worship. We are to care for it as it cares for us. But some worship the earth like the pagans and put it above the people for whom it was created. We must remember not to misplace our adoration. I, for one, already have a mother.

Closed Organizations Violate Innate Freedoms

In Chapter 9, we talked about false economic and political systems that subvert our freedom and place us in bondage. Based on incorrect principles, they will eventually self-destruct. In the meantime, these closed organizations continue to have profound impact on our economic, political and social environment.

Their destructive forces can be discerned promoting anarchy in the name of freedom (rights without responsibilities). They promote destructive bondage and slavery in the name of free speech, tolerance, diversity, gaming, alternative lifestyles and liberation. They deem as "oppressors" law-abiding citizens who would suggest *responsibility* for actions or enforce *consequences* for laws. They would make us slaves to ignorance through revisionist history and so-called "academic freedom." Their "cunningly-devised fables" are clothed with an aura of intellectualism.

They are supremely competent in their capabilities. As the "humanitarian with the guillotine," they believe their ends justify their means. Yet when you meet them, they are big-hearted and sincere.

Threats to Your Economic Future

The coming years will bring increasing commotion. If you are unprepared, economic and financial volatility will make your problems worse. If you are prepared, informed, and have built your financial program on rock, you have no reason to fear what is ahead.

What *is* ahead? Let's take a look:

Increased psycho-media risks. Select industries may be sacrificed in order to sell newspapers and magazines. If your industry or company gets in the cross-hairs, you are dead (see page 270).

Class warfare. We have an increasing risk of a wealth tax, increased income taxes on the most productive in society, and riots and strikes incited for political gain by closed organizations. Those who went to college—who got training and education, took risks, worked hard, saved their money—may be targeted by those who did not.

Increasing natural disasters. Drought, hurricanes, earthquakes, and blizzards may cause company and geographic shutdowns, resulting in increasing volatility in investment markets as well as shortages of food and the supply of raw materials.

Spiraling budget deficit. Spiraling inflation and volatility in the financial markets may cause capital to dry up as investors are unwilling to finance the budget except at super-high interest rates.

Diminished financial incentive. Inflation, a confiscatory tax structure, and instability may result in diminished financial incentives to grow a business, hire employees, and take risks.

Curtailment of freedom and economic incentive. Stifling government regulations, red tape, and involvement in a myriad of complex laws will cause those who would invest in a company to look elsewhere.

Tort risks. The average American *already* pays more than $1,000 per year in the increased cost of goods and services to pay the unnecessary costs of frivolous and exorbitant lawsuits, claims, class-action suits, and damages. Everyone is at risk, and everyone pays for it.

Sin taxes. Taxes will be increased to cover the increasing costs of social programs gone awry and the natural consequences of lifestyle: We will be financing increased numbers of latchkey children, teenage mothers, prisons, AIDS carriers, and substance abusers. While most people despise drug dealers, the entertainment industry (rock bands, Hollywood sitcoms, etc.) are usually subtle, but occasionally overt in their role as *the new drug pushers* to children. The additional taxes paid by those involved in the societal shifts cannot begin to pay for the increased governmental programs or costs to society.

Diminished productivity. An increasing number of people simply do not know how to work. And people who do not know how to work are vulnerable in a layoff.

Debt. Those in debt will be especially vulnerable to economic volatility, unemployment, or loss of their homes. What do we do as individuals if our highly leveraged economy hits a flash point and begins a domino collapse? What might cause such a flash point? Perhaps another president who re-ignites inflation, causing investors to begin selling their government bonds. Do you recall when the Mexican peso collapsed in late 1994 and the United States stepped in with $20 billion to support their economy? Unlike Mexico, there is no economy in the world large enough to save us.

A society without laws. At this writing, a new threat called "jury nullification" is gaining ground. The press is presenting it as though it has broad support. It says that jurors should vote however they want in determining guilt, regardless of whether facts prove a law has been broken. (Proponents call this "vote your conscience.")

An article in the *Yale Law Review* argues it is the "moral responsibility of black jurors to emancipate some guilty black outlaws," and that the slum drug dealer or thief who robs a wealthy white family should be acquitted. Their argument is that these criminals are actually *victims* of unfair laws. Sophisticated lawyers know how to stack a jury. The rule of law is lost. Where there is no consequence, there is no law. Anarchy reigns. No one is safe. The laws of our elected representatives are rendered impotent.

Isolationism. Without free trade, our standard of living is suppressed. That is not all: Isolationists are more prone to war. History shows those countries with a closed society are more apt to be the aggressors in pursuing the wealth of their neighbors.

Closed organizations. These secret societies have learned to manipulate a sympathetic press and society with their agenda. Without discernment, their rumors, "facts," *sophisticated* arguments, "rights," and "calculated courtesies" become social norms and are foisted upon the unorganized majority. They distort, disrupt, deceive.

They talk about the rights of owls, children, and anything else that cannot accept responsibility. The result? Diminished rights for everyone. By detaching rights from responsibility, they rob freedom from those who are responsible citizens. Rights can only belong to those who can be responsible, because without one you cannot truly have the other. (The correct relationship of responsible citizens toward those who cannot accept responsibility is that of sacred stewardship.)

Closed organizations are subtly promoting most of these threats to our future.

Covetousness of the idle. People who will not work—but who want the same things as those who will—will lead to increased crime, threats, robbery, rioting, and class warfare.

Usurping power from the governed. Increasingly, the governed are being led to believe that they get their rights from the government. The opposite is true: The government gets its privileges from the consent of the governed. Regulators write regulations with the force of law (legislative function), execute their enforcement (executive function), and adjudicate resolutions (judicial function) without any checks and balances. They have become all-powerful dictators over their serfdom.

Insidious taxes. Tax on wealth lays a heavier burden on the backs of the productive while the unproductive reap the benefits. Natural economic laws dictate that this system proliferates the poor. You simply can't give people incentives not to work, then expect them to work. By the same token, you can't punish the workers and expect increased productivity and an improved standard of living for all.

Divorce. If you want to kill your financial program, security, and growth, get divorced. The traditional family will always be the most efficiently designed and supreme economic unit, unequalled in its power to yield a superior standard of living.

Speculation. A something-for-nothing attitude causes increased volatility in the financial markets. This get-rich-quick mentality is promoted in the financial press, magazines, on late-night television, and elsewhere because it sells magazines and appeals to the greed motive.

Ignorance. As our schools have issued revisionist history books, they teach politically correct attitudes about society, yet leave untaught the founding principles upon which our nation was established. Our children are left ignorant of their heritage of freedom. They don't understand true economic and political principles about our inalienable rights and responsibilities as citizens. As a result, they will be left unprepared to counter the onslaught of *sophisticated* arguments.

How can you be prepared for the future?

Simple: Put your own house in order. You may not be able to influence political, social, or economic trends, but you can comply with the suggestions in this book for building your own financial security. When *you* are prepared, *you* will not fear.

Those intent on self-destructive lifestyles always destroy themselves. That's the natural result of breaking oneself against correct principles.

But if you make correct principles work for you, you will survive. Those correct principles include freedom, prudence, balance, conservatism, savings, self-reliance, work, and all other laws that naturally yield money happiness, security, success, and peace of mind.

The economic principles discussed in this chapter are natural economic laws. They occur just as surely as the sun rises in the morning. In their pursuit of power and gain, closed organizations will use whatever means necessary to achieve their ends, which includes usurping the rights of free people. The economy will never grow in the absence of free specialization and exchange. Wealth cannot survive without economic incentive and freedom. And no individual can be completely secure without adherence to correct principles.

Your Insights, Feelings, and Action Items

A. As you read this chapter, what *insights* came that seem applicable to *you?*

1._____
2._____
3._____

B. How did you *feel* as you pondered particular points of this chapter?

1._____
2._____
3._____

C. What do you *feel* you should *do* as a result of this chapter?

1._____
2._____
3._____

D. How might you solicit the aid of others in accomplishing "C" above?

_____
_____
_____

Chapter 12

The Basic Economic Unit of Society: The Family

The traditional family is the most efficient economic unit in society. Most people don't realize this. Despite the corporate models of excellence, no organization has ever improved on the family for its economic efficiency. The best explanation for this may lie in the family's innate self-reliance. Some might refer to the division of labor. Others mention the emotional support and synergy. Perhaps it's because of the family as an emotional refuge and morale builder.

What makes the family so economically efficient is the way it functions naturally. Within the family unit, we can observe the economic principle of *specialization* and *exchange*. Members of a family contribute economically to the unit in both ways. Each member *specializes* in a role, or several, and each *exchanges* or shares labor (service) according to his role.

Specialization in families is largely a matter of capability. Exchange results from members interacting as a community. Family members of different ages and genders are each suited for making their own contributions to the welfare of the whole. Each parent complements the other's labor and service, just as each child does, depending on age and other characteristics. With large families, the quantity of exchange and the range of specialization are both enhanced. In the agricultural economy, larger families meant potentially greater wealth, as all shared the labor.

The economic value of the family extends far beyond the family circle—it benefits the whole society. For example, the birth of children strengthens the Social Security system and affects the production and consumption of goods. In the family unit, the economic efficiencies are also clear.

A child who does chores contributes time and saves his parent from either doing the labor himself or having to pay to have it done. We don't often calculate the economic value of having children. They are usually considered liabilities rather than assets, since they don't "earn" a living.

It may seem mercenary to consider children in this light, yet no one chooses to have children just so they can do chores. We have children do chores because it prepares them to be contributing members of society. That's an additional economic benefit. The two benefits synergize to make a whole that becomes greater than the sum of either part.

The economics of having children do chores for an allowance is one of the family's great efficiencies. In families, the wage that is paid for labor need not go through the tax siphon. You will recall how the tax siphon creates the WYHTE phenomenon. To illustrate, say your son mows your lawn in an hour and earns $4. He saves you the hour, and your time is worth $50 an hour. Though he is only being paid $4 an hour, *how much was his time actually worth?* His actual contribution was many times what he was paid.

In order to have economic health reach its optimum, both self-reliance and the WYHTE phenomenon dictate that the economic unit which has significant non-cash income will rise to a higher level than those that don't. The reason for this is that whenever labor is translated *directly* into assets or standard of living, the transfer is the most efficient possible. Typically, by contrast, labor is *first* translated into cash, which must go through the tax siphon, reducing the value of the labor by as little as 30 percent or as much as 50 percent.

Divorce is devastating, because, among other things, it disrupts this efficiency between family members, removing one of the major means of both specialization and exchange. One of the truly significant downfalls to any financial plan occurs with divorce.

Avoid Financial Ruin

If you want to avoid major financial setbacks, possibly ruin, avoid divorce. First, communicate openly and regularly on money matters with your spouse. I recommend a formal, weekly "Family Council" to discuss finances, schedules, special needs of children, vacations, family rules, household needs, goals, etc. Second, develop an understanding of each other's money personality. An excellent means to achieving this is by completing the MoneyMax Profiler. Third, don't go into debt. Fourth, don't covet. Control your ego, for it is usually the *ego* which causes financial problems, selfishness, and debt. Distinguish between *needs* and *wants*. Fifth, develop a family budget which both spouses agree upon. Sixth, consider whether a second working spouse in the home is actually adding anything to the family budget, especially if there are children in the home (see page 203).

If within *your* marriage you conclude that mother should be a full-time homemaker, support and encourage her. It can be a challenge with the competing voices of society today, yet, as has been said, "Motherhood is near to divinity. It is the highest, holiest service to be assumed by mankind."

Just a note for husbands about wives regarding money happiness: Financial happiness can only come when, instead of trying to make her better, you try to make her happy. Accept your spouse's own program for growth. When you focus on making her happy, rather than better, financial happiness will increase in the home.

Ideally, discuss money *before* you get married. Before two people marry, they should understand *exactly* how each feels about budgeting, debt, spending, and saving and should establish sound and prudent financial philosophies.

Teach Your Children

Raise secure and financially stable children. For one thing, teach them to stay out of debt, by refusing to loan or advance them money on their allowance. When you advance them money, what are you teaching? You are teaching them instant gratification, you are teaching them to go into debt. They may be only eight or nine years old, but they are learning the lesson. At age 25 or 30, where will they be? In debt. Teach them patience, and that they don't deserve immediately the lifestyle and possessions of their parents.

When we deal in financial matters or loans within the family, my counsel is that you either be dealing with family members on a strictly professional basis or simply make the money involved a gift. Some people just refuse to mix money and blood, because they realize that *whenever* you attach strings to anyone else, *those strings become chains on you.* Think twice before doing it.

Do not let your children quit, because they will become quitters. What happens later? They will quit college. They will quit high-opportunity careers. They might even quit a marriage. There are all kinds of negative consequences—not just economic ones—for people who have not learned to overcome and persevere.

The only people I know on the earth who are independently wealthy are children. It must be nice. One of my clients, Dr. Adair, referred to the baby his wife was expecting. He said, "I want twins, Mimi and Gimi, because 'Me Me' and 'Gimme' are all I ever hear from my children."

As the basic economic unit of society, the traditional family has a variety of forces threatening it. As the most efficient economic organization, the family that will summon the resources and exercise self-reliance will succeed.

Two Kinds of Spouses

Married couples express empathy in two common ways. One way strengthens and supports the spouse, and the other weakens and undermines. The first is true empathy, and the second is unconscious collusion, leading to mediocrity.

Collusion starts out looking like empathy when one spouse expresses discouragement or frustration about, say, his job and the people there. His spouse may sympathize tenderly, but at some invisible point her support or loyalty for him turns into resentment, criticism, or negativity toward those who frustrated him. (This phenomenon can apply to either him *or* her.) This begins an unconscious, destructive downward spiral of poor thinking that they jointly nurture over days, weeks, and months. She thinks she's being supportive, but the truth is, they are weakening each other. This spouse is *reactive*, and accepts "martyr" talk.

The wise spouse expresses empathy, remains supportive, shows sympathy, gives comfort, on a level in proportion with the spouse's concern. But before it continues too long, this wife would help her husband do a reality check, reminding him of his goals in spite of the incident or problem. She encourages and inspires, without pandering to him or contributing any kind of self-pity. At some point she'll even tell him to quit feeling sorry for himself and to get back to work. This spouse discerns the self-defeating negativity and *proactively* wants "champion" talk.

The most wonderful kind of synergy can exist in marriage. But the problem is that for many couples it isn't there. Couples can help each other by reminding one another that greatness in one spouse reflects, even declares, itself in the other. At times all that's needed is a moment or two of reflective listening. But there are times when long patient hours of genuine support will be required. Putting aside blame and accusation usually will enable such empathy to remain real, rather than becoming unconscious collusion in negativity.

Children: An Asset, Not a Liability

One of the biggest threats to our current standard of living is our falling population growth rate. People, including children, are an asset, not a liability. While the extreme environmentalists and the Vatican duke it out over population control,

> The real issue is the assumption that curbing population growth is critical for economic development. That premise is preposterous. A growing population is not a drag on economic development. When combined with freedom, it is a stimulant. (Malcolm S. Forbes, Jr., editor-in-chief, *Forbes* magazine, September 12, 1994)

The fatalists are at it again. The brilliant Forbes continues with this insight:

> Behind all the talk of the need to "stabilize" the number of people on this earth is the not-so-hidden agenda of expanding the power of the state. Now that socialism is discredited, statists are looking for excuses to justify and to expand the scope of intrusive government.

Forbes understands the principle of specialization and exchange. He continues:

> A growing population helps *improve* the quality of life by enabling people to devote their talents to tasks for which they are best suited rather than to eking out subsistence livings. In a free society people are an asset, not a liability. Poverty and malnutrition persist only in those areas where governments dominate and suffocate economic activity.

The facts just don't register with the doomsayers.

> The real threat is not that the Earth will run out of land, topsoil, or water, but that nations will fail to pursue the economic trade and research policies that *can* increase the production of food, limit environmental damage, and ensure that resources reach the people that need them. Indeed, embracing the myth of environmental scarcity could ironically prompt the United States and other countries to adopt policies that virtually guarantee that the apocalyptic future that environmentalists foretell really does come true. (Stephen Budiansky, *U.S. News and World Report*, September 12, 1994)

During the 1980s, the rate of world food output grew *three times faster* than the population growth. Food is becoming more plentiful throughout the world, as evidenced by the fact that the world price of food has dropped by more than one-half in real terms since 1970. The United States and Europe have deliberately idled over 57 million acres of productive farm land under government programs in order to increase the income of farmers. Almost 200 million acres of grasslands in South America could be brought into production if free trade were allowed.

Budiansky continues:

> A recent study by Paul Waggoner of the Connecticut Agricultural Experiment Station in New Haven backs up the claim that food production is for the foreseeable future limited only by human ingenuity, not natural resources. The gross productive potential of the Earth—set by available land, climate, and sunlight for photosynthesis—is sufficient to produce food for a staggering 1,000 billion people. Even without irrigation, available water is sufficient to grow food for 400 billion, and a conservative estimate of sustainable fertilizer production implies ample supplies to produce food for 80 billion.

The 1997 estimate of world population is at about 5.7 billion people. It is estimated that by the year 2050, there may be as many as 10 billion people on Planet Earth. The solution lies with facts and freedom, not fables and fear. *Fatalism is the enemy.* (For more information on this, call Fax-on-Demand at (801) 263-1676 and request free report #280, "Children are Assets, not Liabilities.")

Your Insights, Feelings, and Action Items

A. As you read this chapter, what *insights* came that seem applicable to
   you?
   1._____
   2._____
   3._____

B. How did you *feel* as you pondered particular points of this chapter?
   1._____
   2._____
   3._____

C. What do you *feel* you should *do* as a result of this chapter?
   1._____
   2._____
   3._____

D. How might you solicit the aid of others in accomplishing "C" above?

   _____

   _____

   _____

Decision Three

Recognize that Character Counts

In Chapter 13 we will examine why natural and sure laws dictate that character is not merely important, but essential for lasting success. We will apply that lesson in Chapters 14 and 15 as we observe how to improve career opportunities.

Chapter 13

Why Only Character Can Bring Money Happiness

By the Bright Beacon of Principle

Countless enterprises will bring money. Some will even bring great wealth. But money happiness can come only from having character. The bottom line to successful, happy living will always be character.

The words of UCLA basketball coach John Wooden ring true: "Be more concerned with your character than with your reputation. Your character is what you really are; your reputation is merely what others think you are."

Character is built only by adherence to correct principles.

What are *principles?* They are natural laws. They are like a beacon on a hill. They are timeless—not because they are merely old or traditional, but because they are proven. Anyone who tries to test them will find out how certain they are. Principles are self-evident.

Cecil B. DeMille, speaking of the principles outlined in "The Ten Commandments," said, "It is impossible for us to break the law; we can only break ourselves against the law."

In his last public address before his assassination, Abraham Lincoln observed, "Important principles may and must be inflexible."

If you want to achieve primary greatness—that is, from the inside out—correct principles are the only true recipe. They are the only sure path to growth. Those who, as DeMille said, seem intent on breaking themselves against natural law and correct principles by engaging in self-destructive behaviors, eventually come face-to-face with the truth.

As you surrender yourself to a great purpose, you become great in its accomplishment. That is what determines character—and the future. Is it easy? Of course not. *It is a forever quest.*

Greatness of Purpose Determines Character

It also requires a change of perspective for some. People who want to achieve money happiness must focus on *being* rather than *seeming*. To do it, you have to begin with your heart and your mind instead of your clothes and your car. As Stephen Covey has observed:

> The inside-out approach says if you want to have a happy marriage, be the kind of person who generates positive energy and sidesteps negative energy rather than empowering it. If you want to have a more pleasant, cooperative teenager, be a more understanding, empathic, consistent, loving parent. If you want to have more freedom, more latitude in your job, be a more responsible, a more helpful, a more contributing employee. If you want the secondary greatness of recognized talent, focus first on the primary greatness of character.

Money alone can't yield happiness—but money plus character may. The deeper the character, the deeper the happiness. Conversely, anything minus character will equal suffering, just as anyone who lacks character will yield suffering for himself and all those around him.

Politicians lacking character will equal suffering of the electorate, just as business owners, ministers, teachers, lawyers, doctors, news media, or spouses lacking character will equal suffering throughout their spheres of influence. In politics, for example, an element of the media would like to foist on the rest of us the notion that character doesn't matter in public life. The question is simply whether or not the politician can do the job. Any electorate that believes that will get the same results as the person who would marry another without character. The person who does not understand character, integrity, loyalty, or fidelity in the marriage relationship cannot be expected to understand it as a civil servant.

What will the consequences be for America if society repudiates character and goodness at the ballot box?

Character is not merely important; it is essential. Some would have us believe otherwise, but as someone once said, "You can't do wrong and feel right; if you're doing right, nothing can ever go permanently wrong."

If you haven't defined the principles that guide your life, *now is the time to do it*. Your reputation precedes you at every turn—so decide *early* what reputation you want to have. Get clear about your values. Know which wall you are going to lean your ladder against. As Tom Scott, vice president of the VF Company, observed, "Once you start going down one path, it's hard to get on another."

Decide not only how much success you want, but how you want to achieve that success. Once you do, it will be much easier to achieve your life's objectives. You won't drain your emotional energy fretting over decisions that conflict with your values. Instead, your integrity will be intact and your career will naturally progress.

As much as we might not like to admit it, there *are* absolutes. There are natural laws. There are commitments we need to make. As football coach Grantland Rice told his players, "When the one great scorer comes to write against your name, he marks not that you won or lost, but how you played the game."

As we apply these principles and see them affect our lives, we become more self-aware, more awake to our own possibilities. From earliest times, thoughtful people have searched for their own identity. In 600 B.C., Siddhartha Gautama was led by a greatness of purpose. He sought enlightenment, deeper understanding. He objected to the Brahmin prejudice that hereditary bloodlines should determine social position. Once Siddhartha became enlightened he was called Buddha, "the Awakened One." He told his followers, "I am neither a god, an angel, nor a saint. I am awake." We must become awake also, to those powerful and enlightening principles that help us to choose a greatness of purpose, to actually *be* rather than *seem*.

Character is developed *consciously*. The path is simple:

Sow a thought and you reap an act.
Sow an act and you reap a habit.
Sow a habit and you reap a character.
Sow a character and you reap a destiny.

Anonymous (quoted by Samuel Smiles,
1812-1904, in *Life and Labor*)

Nine Attributes of True Character

Courage

Courage is not the absence of fear. Courage is the *conquest* of fear, according to Mark Twain. A courageous act may be frightening—but the courageous person has the resolve to overcome fear. The more you act with courage, the easier it becomes. And it's never too late to develop courage.

There are those in history who have made their indelible mark on succeeding generations through their acts of courage. Courage breeds amazing power. Ten men will wither at the sight of one who speaks up with courage.

Andrew Jackson wrote, "One man with courage makes a majority." And Winston Churchill, who led Great Britain through World War II, observed, "Some men change their party for the sake of their principles; others their principles for the sake of their party."

Is courage *always* manifest by standing up and speaking for what's right, or by performing some heroic deed? No! In fact, that's seldom the case. Courage is far more often manifest in quiet daily acts of resolve through personal habits. In a sense, courage precedes the eight other attributes of character.

Courage brings with it the willingness to take risks in order to make things happen. It takes great courage to risk failure—and then to try again. Remember: Your altitude in life will not be based on how many times you fail, how many mistakes you make, or how often you fall down. It will depend on how many times you get back up. As long as you get up one more time than you fall, you have succeeded.

It takes courage to "just say no."

Don't give up when you fall. Don't stay on the ground. Have the courage to take risks, even if it occasionally means failure. The great inventor Thomas Edison pointed out, "People are not remembered by how few times they fail, but how often they succeed. Every wrong step is another step forward."

In my early years in business, I was certain no one had ever failed more often than I. Try as I might, I couldn't get it right. If every mistake cost me $1,000, I had made hundreds of them. But every mistake, although painful, taught me one more thing that wouldn't work as I endeavored to build my practice.

How can you develop courage? Read about it. Study it. Ponder it. Then start by taking small, courageous steps in your personal affairs. Gradually courage will start to work within you.

Honesty

It doesn't take long to discover that honesty will propel you to success in spite of yourself. You may lack many of the other things people consider necessary for success—such as great intelligence or creativity—but if you can be trusted, you will succeed.

Honesty goes beyond being ethical and fair. It's not merely an accounting to someone else—it's an accounting to yourself.

Natural economic law dictates that businessmen must be honest. Why? Because in no other career is a person held to such an immediate standard of honesty. In the marketplace of consumers, people vote with their wallet every day. That vote determines which businesses they will patronize and which they will avoid. No one is held to such an immediate and exactingly high standard—not politicians, professionals, teachers, the news media, or even the clergy.

When dollars are exchanged for products or services, the consumer expects and requires that honest value be given. Anything less is unacceptable. Those who offer less are quickly found out and avoided.

Former Secretary of the Treasury William E. Simon observed, "The whole point of free enterprise, of capitalism, is vigorous, honest competition. Every corner cut, every bribe placed, every little cheating move by a businessman in pursuit of quick plunder instead of honest profit, is an outright attack on the real free enterprise system."

Whether you are a businessman or an employee wanting to climb the ladder of success, honesty is not simply important. It is essential.

But no matter how hard some people try, they just can't seem to develop the habit of honesty. They are perpetual liars and rationalizers. Some are forced into honesty by the discipline of the marketplace or by regulatory agencies—but those who are always looking for the opportunity to be dishonest will fail. Ultimately, you must make the *internal* commitment to honesty because you value honesty.

An important element of honesty is **congruence** or wholeness, born of loyalty to the complete person. Are you more concerned with your outward appearances or with your reality—your character? The answer you give is a measure of your **integrity**—your congruence.

Those who are congruent are trusted. Those who focus on image are eventually discerned for what they are—phony. I'm reminded of Alex, a

28-year-old yuppie, with his leather driving gloves, Cross pens, wool overcoat, and BMW-535. Only three years out of college, his incongruence made anyone of substance suspicious of doing business with him. He would have been better off to focus on his strengths: He was hardworking, bright, and optimistic.

Don't try to take a shortcut to success by placing image above substance, seeming above being.

Attitude

Attitude refers not only to having a positive attitude, but a *host of other mature attitudes* that create mental health.

While I was growing up, there was a little piece of white paper tacked to the wall above the only telephone in our home. On it, my mother had written in pencil, **"Altitude is due more to attitude than intellect."** I must have read that thousands of times during my adolescence. It became one of the subconscious lessons taught in that home.

Intellect is nothing if you can't control your attitude.

Today, I still find myself asking, "What's my attitude? How hard am I working? Am I positive? Loyal?" In our financial planning firm, we hire on *aptitude*. But six months later, we discern success by *attitude*.

Want a checklist for your attitude barometer? Ask yourself these questions:

- Am I working harder than I ever have? (That's the most observable indicator.)
- Am I enthusiastic, positive, excited, looking forward to each day?
- Am I focusing on things I can control? Or am I draining energy on things I can't?
- Do I think my "intellect" has let me figure things out better than those above me? Or am I willing to listen to those with equal intellect, but more experience in the school of hard knocks and success?
- Do I covet others' success without wanting to pay the same price they did? (Coveting is the sign of a lazy mind.)
- Am I resting on my laurels? Discovering my blind spots? Improving on my weaknesses?
- Do I think life's fair? (Life is unfair at times to *all* of us, but that is exactly why life is fair. So, the question to ask is, do I cry over my misfortune? Or do I charge through it and pay the price?)
- Do I spend even one minute listening to others with poor attitudes? How much of this do I tolerate?

- Do I have an inflated opinion of people with average or mediocre success?

And, finally, here's the *ultimate* question to ask yourself if you're interested in removing the roadblocks to your progress: In what other ways to I dam myself by my inadequate thought processes?

You may think you have a good attitude, but you may be unaware of self-defeating comments you make that betray less-than-complete thinking. Occasionally, have the courage to request a reality-check from a trusted, successful friend or adviser.

Here are some things to look for:

Are you **positive**, uplifting, and building of others, yourself, and your company? Or are you negative and complaining? Are you cheerful and pleasant to be around? Cooperative?

How about your competency? How much are you improving your job skills? Are you constantly branching out, developing, expanding skills, and taking on additional responsibility? Do you take pride in always doing your very best? Do you study on your own hours to become better at your career?

Do you take **initiative**? Must you be asked to do every little thing, or do you seek out more work to do? Do you require constant oversight, or can you be trusted to work hard while alone? Do you show initiative by creatively finding new and better ways to do the job? Are you focused on *solutions*, or problems? Stephen Covey pointed out, "The way we see the problem *is* the problem. It becomes obvious that if we want to make relatively minor changes in our lives we can perhaps appropriately focus on our attitudes and behaviors. But if we want to make significant quantum change, we need to work on ... the way we see the world."

Are you **enthusiastic**? Not much is achieved without enthusiasm. For success, knowledge is important; enthusiasm is imperative.

Are you negative? Negative people are naturally logical, analytical, critical and *justifiably* see why things can't work—and thus begins a downward spiral that feeds on itself. The positive see why things *can* work—and an equally justifiable upward spiral begins that also feeds on itself. Achievers flee cynicism because it holds down their belief system. They quickly become weary of cynics and pseudo-intellectuals.

Are you a **team player** or a prima donna? Successful people are involved in company and family activities and recognize the importance of relationships. Prima donnas are driven by pride and competitiveness, not achievement.

Gratitude is perhaps the rarest attitude of all. Do you take things for granted? Do you wind down and get sloppy in your work habits? Do you express a careless attitude in work and action? Or do you appreciate your co-workers, your associates, your company, and your opportunities to learn and grow? None of us is a robot. We are all human beings.

Some are always looking for greener pastures. But the people who maintain a mature and vivid sense of gratitude for what they already have live life with greater contentment and the ability to improve right where they are.

Grateful employees are pleasant to be around. Everyone likes working with appreciative co-workers. Why? The grateful person seeks growth and improvement; he'd rather submit his ego to the pain of correction than forgo the learning. You will improve the most when you not only tolerate, *but seek*, painful correction.

I have seen people with great blessings lose this sense of gratitude and become expectant. When people expect blessings and opportunities, a sense of entitlement replaces the grateful life. Regardless of the quantity of material possessions, the happy, full life—the life in which "one's cup runneth over"—is a life of gratitude. I've seen people in apparent poverty, bursting with joy and gratitude. I was reared in such a home.

Examples of lost gratitude are all around us. Greg, for instance, showed great promise during his first three years with a publishing company. He was rapidly promoted to positions of responsibility. He was eager, efficient, organized, loyal, anxious to please, learning, growing, humble, and grateful. Gradually, he became expectant—he felt entitled to success. He lost his eagerness, his reliability slipped, and he became important in his own eyes. Assignments began slipping through the cracks, undone. His usefulness to the company dwindled, and he was told so. Fortunately, he was able to regain his original attitude.

How is your attitude? Are you positive, learning, growing, dynamic? Do you believe in yourself and your ability to accomplish a given task? Your level of success will be in proportion to how well you think. How well you think is due more to your attitude than your aptitude—talent is virtually irrelevant to success when compared to the magnitude of your attitude.

Quit resting on your talent laurels. Instead, demonstrate a positive attitude in your thoughts, work habits, focus, and refusal to accept or make excuses for average performance. "Altitude is due more to attitude than intellect"—worthy of an inscription on our foreheads.

Resilience

The resilient person overcomes. The resilient person is persistent, patient, and permanent. He can't quit, no matter how tough things get.

Unfortunately, quitting becomes a habit. Children learn to quit when they are young. When they're on a Little League soccer team and they don't get asked to play as much as the other children, we let them quit. When they don't like their orchestra teacher, we let them quit violin lessons. When they dislike an elective class, we let them drop it. If we allow our children to quit, we are teaching them to quit—and later, when they get in a difficult career situation or a difficult marriage, they quit again.

Some years ago my son Larry was on a trip with the Boy Scouts to the National Jamboree. He called from a pay phone in New York City asking me to please get him a flight home. He couldn't stand the Scoutmaster. I wasn't about to let him come home for the simple reason that he wanted to.

Perhaps you've had children who wanted to quit high school, or just drop out of a class. Their rationalization: "It's only an elective." Sometimes people need to do things just because they said they would do them, no matter how unpleasant the task. Being an **overcomer** isn't a sometimes thing. As Green Bay Packers coach Vince Lombardi said, "Winning is a habit; unfortunately, so is losing."

In his 1941 address at Harrow School, Winston Churchill said, "Never give in. Never give in. Never, never, never, never. In nothing, great or small, large or petty, never give in except to convictions of honor and good sense."

Some people are just determined to overcome. They are the ones who succeed. President Calvin Coolidge once said, "Nothing in the world can take the place of persistence. Talent will not. Nothing is more common than unsuccessful men with great talent. Genius will not. Unrewarded genius is almost a proverb. Education will not. The world is full of educated derelicts. Persistence and determination alone are omnipotent."

I think of an associate who came to me deeply discouraged and wanting to quit. I responded, "Scott, *you couldn't quit if you tried*. It's not in your character. You know you're doing the right thing, and no matter how hard it is, you won't quit."

His response? "You know, Hank, I think you're right, but I just needed to hear it."

Along with persistence comes **patience**. The person intent on getting rich quick discovers his path is strewn with thorns, needles, detours, failures, and losses. Patience is one of the supreme virtues for those who want to build wealth. Real success does not come overnight. It occurs by doing a job well day in, day out.

Success, like trees, takes time. Softwood trees may grow three to six feet per year; they're popular with many homeowners because they shoot up rapidly. But they don't last. They're brittle. They break, get diseased, and die. Hardwood trees, on the other hand, grow much more slowly, but are resilient to disease and drought. Their roots sink deep. Once mature, they may provide shade for a century or more.

Are you a softwood or a hardwood? Will you break at a small breeze or gust of wind? Or can you withstand a hurricane? All of us will have hurricanes in our lives. The question is, can you ride out the storm?

Much resilience comes of the little understood and seldom discussed virtue of **permanence**. Permanence becomes an anchor, a bulwark against storms. Smart people seek something to hold on to—not because they are weak, but because they understand strength. Great strength comes from sinking in roots, settling down, planting trees and gardens, owning a home, developing family traditions, discovering the family tree, holding family reunions, and maintaining deep friendships from the "old neighborhood."

Smart families who understand sources of strength still seek elements of permanence. So it is with acquiring and maintaining solid, long-term elements of a sound financial program: A rock-solid foundation is built one brick at a time.

Can you imagine lasting peace of mind and security in a temporary home, a temporary insurance policy, and a temporary job? If you want to achieve success, think permanently. Then slowly, with patience and determination, pay off your home mortgage, establish a permanent insurance program, put away adequate reserves, and acquire broad career training. These form the bedrock upon which you may anchor other financial instruments.

Alignment

Alignment is a necessary characteristic of success—and you can look at it from two perspectives.

First, **principles and goals must be in alignment.** Are your goals in alignment with correct principles and natural laws? If they are not, beware. The principles won't fail; you will.

For example, are you in alignment with your family? The family is the most important and basic unit of society. You can't be in alignment with the rest of your life yet out of alignment with your family and expect lasting success.

The second aspect of alignment is **focus.** That is, are your thoughts, actions, and efforts in alignment with your goals? Automatic Data Processing CEO Josh Weston shared with me his "shorter hand" for success: "Focus, persistence, and hustle." Are you focused on your principles and goals? Are you on-task? Or on-tangent?

It is easy to lose focus. It is easy to get sidetracked. But, remember: Tangents consume both time and emotional energy. Tangential time and energy are forever lost. Not to mention the massive amounts of both time and energy to get back on track.

Have you ever focused the sun's rays through a magnifying glass onto a leaf or a sheet of paper? What's required to start a fire? Stillness, concentration, focus. Contrast that intensity with the efforts of a person running to and fro with every new tangent that presents itself. That person is never in one place long enough to kindle a flame.

Focus is one of the characteristics that separates significant success from average success. It is the harnessing and marshaling of all one's resources—brains and brawn, creativity and brainstorming, decisiveness and action.

Evaluate your acts during the day and with each activity ask yourself: Is this the highest priority activity that will lead to my goal?

Too often we are working on something urgent rather than important. We are allowing others to dictate where we are focusing our time. How can anyone achieve excellence if in each aspect of his life he has not identified what he should be focusing upon and then working toward that end?

From the lowest apprentice in a small family company to the top board rooms of the largest Fortune 500 companies, *focus* is one of the key attributes of character and success. Work to improve your weaknesses, but focus on your strengths. Realize that a miraculous power is unleashed in your life when you truly commit yourself and focus on end results.

Commitment

The committed person is **loyal.** He focuses on commitments he has made. He never goes halfway. He is capable of making and abiding by long-term commitments. Get out of his way, because he is moving forward.

Few things carry more weight with me than knowing I have a loyal associate or employee. If I owned a manufacturing company, my major investment would be in plants and machinery—but in a service company such as mine, my greatest assets, my associates, walk out the door at the end of every working day.

I can own plants and machinery, but I can't own associates, so this naturally presents a dilemma. How do I choose the person I am going to invest in? I make a significant capital expenditure each year in recruiting and development. I send associates to dozens of training conferences around the country. How do I decide who I am going to invest in? Loyalty.

Let the people around you know where you stand. Communicate your loyalty to them in word and action. Be careful about those to whom you commit your loyalty—but once you do, be loyal.

Once someone has served you well, stay with him. If you are ever wondering precisely to whom you should be loyal in the workplace, look at who signs your paycheck. If you can't be loyal to your employer, in both speech and action, *get out!* Otherwise, don't expect job security or a reputation of integrity.

Exhibit loyalty, and loyalty will come back to you. It is one of the most reciprocating of all character attributes. Jesus taught this principle when he observed the difference between a shepherd, and a hireling who flees when he sees the wolf coming, leaving the sheep to be scattered. Don't be like the hireling. (See John 10:12-13.)

Decide early in your career not to be a half-wayer, but rather to be a person of **commitment** and will. Be the person who gets the job done. During World War II, it is reported that General William ("Bull") Halsey needed a message delivered to some troops who were trapped across enemy lines. He asked his lieutenant to bring him someone who would go through enemy lines to deliver the message. When a young soldier was brought to him, Halsey asked if he would deliver the message. The soldier responded, "I'll try, sir."

Halsey said, "I don't want you to try. I want you to deliver the message."

The soldier repeated, "I'll do my best, sir."

The general began to get upset. He said, "I don't want you to do your best; I want you to deliver the message."

The soldier was now getting the point; he courageously retorted, "I'll do it or die, sir!"

At that, the general became angry and shouted, "I don't want you to die! I want you to deliver the message!"

Do we have that same kind of commitment in our personal lives? Do we live with that commitment to our spouses, our children, our friends, our employer, our ideals, our professed value system, our goals?

Don't go halfway. Like the sign in the window of the cabinetry shop— "Finishers Wanted"—finishers are still wanted throughout society. You have to finish high school. You have to finish college. You have to finish the project you start. You have to be committed.

The excellent person is a person of commitment.

Trustworthiness

Those who are trustworthy attract money; those who aren't repel it. Be congruent. Demonstrate integrity. Make promises, then keep them. Learn to say no to those promises you can't keep. Confidently announce when you have been unable to complete an assigned task. Be clearly responsive to others who count on you by reporting frequently the status of any outstanding assignments. Don't allow assignments given you to drop into a black hole.

Demonstrate loyalty to those who aren't present—your spouse, coworkers, friends. Never expect to be trusted in your business affairs if your colleagues see that you can't be trusted in your marital, social, or private affairs.

Never betray a confidence. There *are* things you take to the grave. (This was cited as one of the top reasons executives derail on the way to the executive suite. See page 202.)

Do you make mistakes? Of course. We all do. The question is, do you own up to them? Confess and move forward, repairing as best as possible the harm done.

Effort

Work. Drive. Go the extra mile. Make the effort.

There is no escaping honest-to-goodness **hard work**. It is a necessary element to money happiness, and it hasn't changed throughout the centuries. In his famous letter to Major Ramsay, Abraham Lincoln wrote of a woman whose two sons wanted to work. "Set them at it if possible," Lincoln urged. "Wanting to work is so rare a merit that it should be encouraged."

There is no substitute for hard work. Children can't appreciate what their parents give them until they become adults—and have to work for what they get.

All possessions are valued only to the extent that we worked for them—for, as American Revolutionary Thomas Paine wrote, "What we obtain too cheaply, we esteem too lightly."

Growth, both personal and professional, comes only of **challenge** and struggle—effort that puts us out of our comfort zone. Ninety-five percent of the population have probably seen their best days by the time they are 30 years old.

Think about it: During their 20s, people are struggling their way through college, trying to get on their feet financially, adjusting to a new career, marriage and perhaps small children.

Challenge translates into growth.

But by the time people are 30, they settle into a career. They have quit growing and taking on new challenges that would cause continued struggle. They become couch potatoes in their comfort zone.

"The reason a lot of people don't recognize opportunity," Thomas Edison wrote, "is because it usually goes around wearing overalls looking like hard work."

There is nothing sacred about the 40-hour workweek. I've never personally seen anyone achieve much success in a 40-hour workweek. It just isn't done. It will always be the person who goes the extra mile—50 to 60 hours a week—who will achieve greater success.

Don't make the mistake of thinking that long hours automatically mean hard work. Once, while I was putting in grueling hours, a trusted counselor told me, " ... and you need to start working." As I left his office I indignantly thought, "How could he say such a thing? If he only knew ... !" But, he was reminding me that the highest definition of work was not measured by effort, but by results.

How is your effort? Do you stay focused on a task until it is done, or are you easily distracted? Do you prioritize your tasks daily? Are you a hard worker, a smart worker, or both? Do you understand your job description thoroughly and seek training as needed? There is no getting around it: It takes real effort to succeed.

There are no shortcuts to success. The law of the harvest is immutable. Ultimately we will always reap what we sow. And you can't speed up the harvest. You've got to plant in the spring of your life to harvest in the fall. You can't plant in August and expect a harvest in October.

You have to sow the seed into fertile ground, a believing mind, not on stony soil. Then you must cultivate it, fertilize it, water it, and nurture it with time and patience. Ultimately, you'll have a harvest.

If you sow corn, you won't harvest rice. If you sow barley, you won't harvest wheat. If you sow strife in the workplace, you won't harvest loyalty.

If you **go the second mile**—put in the effort—you will harvest a reward.

Ever wondered where the concept of the "second mile" came from? In the days of the Roman Empire, a Roman soldier could ask any subject of the empire to carry his luggage one mile, but no more. So Jews who carried the luggage the first mile were under conscription. It was slavery.

Then along came Jesus, who told them to carry the luggage an extra mile.

What happened?

Those who carried the luggage only the first mile demonstrated that they were slaves. But those who went the second mile demonstrated that they were free men. Their attitude transformed them from being a servant to being the master.

There is no reward in the first mile. There is no satisfaction. There is no progress up the corporate ladder. It is only when we go the extra mile that we demonstrate our freedom and our true attitudes.

Do you only do the bare minimum required? Or do you volunteer to do whatever it takes to get the job done? Are you satisfied with mere work effort or activity regardless of results achieved? Or, are you dissatisfied with anything less than the needed results?

Work clears the mind, soothes the soul, calms the spirit. There are lots of reasons you should work—and many of them have nothing to do with money. As John Rushkin said, "The best reward for a person's toil is not what they get for it, but what they become by it."

The children of this generation need to learn *how* to work as never before. Our firm interviews hundreds of job applicants each year, and the ability to work hard is a diminishing trait. Sometimes I wonder if it wouldn't be a blessing to have children without good looks or athletic ability—then they would have to get through life on what really counts.

Success demands high energy, supreme drive, effort, intensity, work.

Results

Early in my career, I remember some associates debating the question, "What should someone focus on—*results* or *activity*?" Some argued that we should focus on *activity*, and the *results* would come. Others suggested that if we focused on *results*, we would engage in the *activities* that led to those results.

The answer? *Always focus on results.*

Why? When you focus on activity, you start to believe that activity will yield the results. Eventually, you will wake up and find that you have little or no results to show for your work. You have been spinning your wheels.

Those who focus on results achieve the highest levels of success. The distinction is subtle, but it can make *all* the difference. When you focus on *results*—that is, your ultimate goal—your life becomes energized. You have motivation and drive. You will engage in the activity necessary to achieve that goal. **Focus on the end results, and the means will take care of themselves.**

The basketball player sets his eyes on the hoop; he does not focus on how he extends his arm muscles, lifts the ball over his head, and releases the ball from his fingers. Yes, there is technique—but that technique is learned as a result of focusing on the goal in mind.

People who accept the premise that they should be measured by their results are people who accept responsibility. They do not want to be paid for trying; they want to be paid for getting the job done. They do not mind being measured by their productivity. They do not rationalize or make excuses. They let the results speak for themselves.

Responsibility for results is a character trait that is most demanding. Some employees always report they are "doing it." Others report, "It's done."

Quit being a *doing* person. Become a *done* person.

Every job includes unpleasant tasks. Do you avoid them, or do you tackle them head-on? Do you accept responsibility for the job you were hired to do?

Some people put forth tremendous effort but spin their wheels. Productivity is key. How much work do you get done, and how long does it take? How well is your work done? How efficient an employee are you? What is your output per hour? Your employer wants results, not motion.

An old aphorism says, "However you build it, the ship must sail. You can't explain to the ocean." This applies whether you're building a company, or building children into responsible adults. It takes a lot of effort.

Some would rather intellectualize about success than achieve it. American educator Booker T. Washington said, "The world cares very little about what a man or woman knows; it's what the man or woman is able to do that counts."

You will achieve greatness only to the extent that you are willing to accept **responsibility** for your decisions, your efforts, your actions, your speech. Once you accept responsibility, you begin changing your circumstances. If you were born poor, the first step isn't getting out of the ghetto. It's not getting on welfare. It's not even opportunity. No. The first step to rising from the ghetto is accepting responsibility for your condition—then adding the vision, the belief, the faith that you *can* change your circumstances.

Stephen Covey says that you can "decide within yourself how circumstances will affect you. Between what happens to you, or the stimulus, and your response to it, is your freedom or power to choose that response." That is response-ability.

Rather than accepting responsibility, too many of us rationalize and make excuses. Some even have excuses for mediocre performance in all aspects of life—career, financial success, mental exertion, family success, physical fitness, even spiritual strength.

Are you focused on results? Can you accept responsibility for your thoughts, speech, and actions? None of us is perfect—but are you striving? Are you gaining ground? Are you getting better?

Character Counts

So there you have it, nine traits of character:

> Courage
> Honesty
> Attitude
> Resilience
> Alignment
> Commitment
> Trustworthiness
> Effort
> Results

Character counts. It counts in those who would achieve lasting success. It counts in those who would find peace in a troubled, commotion-filled world. It counts in those who would aspire to money happiness. It counts in those who would lead us in the political or economic realm. It counts in those who would teach our children in schools and in those media people who filter the news they report. It counts among sociologists, psychologists, university professors, business owners, clergy, police, etc. It counts in a marriage and among friends. In short, it counts everywhere.

And those who say it doesn't, who would say all that is necessary is whether the person can do the job, may be excusing their own lack of it. At least, they certainly don't understand why character counts. Be wary of those people.

These are the nine traits that lead to money happiness. Along the way, remember that it is possible to try *too* hard for success. It can lead to self-destructive shortcuts. Rather, become a person of value, and success will follow. To become a person of value, begin from the inside out. Become a person of character. Become a person not only of economic value, but of moral value. Others will notice and reward you with success.

Your Insights, Feelings, and Action Items

A. As you read this chapter, what *insights* came that seem applicable to *you?*

1._____

2._____

3._____

B. How did you *feel* as you pondered particular points of this chapter?

1._____

2._____

3._____

C. What do you *feel* you should *do* as a result of this chapter?

1._____

2._____

3._____

D. How might you solicit the aid of others in accomplishing "C" above?

_____

_____

_____

Chapter 14

How to Enhance Your Career Opportunities and Rewards

Too often traditional financial planning concentrates on things like insurance, taxes, budgeting, retirement planning, and estate planning. It skips the basics.

How?

Look at budgeting, for example. Budget discussions always focus on the bottom line—where the dollars are going. Budgeting most often deals with cutting expenses to improve net family profit and boost the rate of savings. Seldom do financial planners talk about increasing the *top* line— how to improve your income—which is where the largest dollars are actually available.

Your most valuable asset is your ability to earn money. Yet most Americans spend more time managing their investments, maintaining their home, and managing their business than they do managing their career. That's a dangerous pattern: Since your career determines how much money you earn, career planning is a critical part of successful financial planning.

The Number-One Success Force

To succeed in career planning, you need to understand the number-one *"Success Force"* (the attribute, according to Joseph Sugarman, that propels you to succeed in spite of yourself.) You've seen them: people who lack all obvious attributes of success—college education, raw talent, native intelligence, positive attitude, good self-image, belief in themselves—but who are *always* employed. They're the last ones laid off. They're successful by many definitions.

So what *do* they have? They have the number-one success force: honesty. As an example, look at Joseph Sugarman. Joseph Sugarman is not a household name, but he became wealthy. He was the founder of Joseph Sugarman and Associates, the first marketing company to run full-page ads in airline magazines in the 1970s. He's also the first person who accepted credit card transactions over the telephone, letting people order merchandise without a signature on file. Today, that's common practice.

Until then, Joseph Sugarman had a very interesting business career. He found out that if he didn't have things in writing, people stuck it to him. Even when he had it in writing, in fact, the dishonest found a loophole and stuck it to him anyway. (If you're doing business with a snake, having it in writing doesn't make much difference.)

He learned that going through life was a matter of discovering who the honest people were and doing business with them. As he did business with honest people, he learned he didn't have to have things in writing. He achieved significant success. (For insightful reading, get a copy of Sugarman's book *Success Forces.*)

What You're Really Worth

While on a vacation years ago, Sterling W. Sill and his family stopped at a service station. Bottled sodas were a dime—so he put his coins into the pop machine. The pop bottle rolled out of the machine, along with a dime too much change. His initial thought? "Great! I finally beat one of these machines! I deserve this dime."

What happened? As he started to walk away, a voice said to him, "So you will sell your integrity for a dime?" The mental struggle was over. He found the attendant, and returned the coin.

Weigh that story in light of what you read about in almost every newspaper in this country today. Look at the people who embezzle thousands of dollars from their employers, who rob convenience stores, who steal from their neighbors in ordinary break-ins—and more deceitfully, who steal time while on their employer's payroll, who "borrow" supplies from the office. Now ask yourself the question: What is your integrity worth? How much will you sell it for? Will a dime buy yours? Will a million dollars?

I remember when my son Danny rented a drum set from a local music store. The salesman induced Danny by saying that a certain percentage of his monthly rent would go into an account that he could use to purchase anything else at the music store. Eighteen months later, Danny eagerly went to the music store to see how much credit he had. The same salesman curtly informed him that all he qualified for was the drum set he had originally rented.

Danny had quizzed the salesman in great detail from the beginning to make sure he understood the arrangement. Was the salesman honest? No. What kind of reputation did the store have because of that salesman? Not a very good one.

Is that the kind of employee I want to hire? In my business, my associates manage other people's money. Do I want to hire someone who misrepresents me? Do I want to hire a wheeler-dealer? Do I want to hire someone who cuts corners? Absolutely not. By many, it's considered a virtue to be in the "fast lane." Be careful of them.

If one of my associates ever absconded with a client's money, the associate would be in jail. But it wouldn't stop there: Our firm's reputation would be destroyed. That's why I have to be very sensitive about the integrity and ethics of the people I work with. And by watching people, I know—just as any other employer learns—who will be honest and straight.

Should You Work Smart, or Hard, or Both?

It's easy to understand the highest definition of work when you understand the lowest definition of work. What's the lowest definition? "If I've punched in on the time clock, I am working." People who subscribe to the lowest definition assume that if they've punched in, they're earning their day's wages.

A slightly higher definition regards work as "activity." These employees are going through the motions on behalf of their employer. Mere movement, by itself, is just one step above the living dead.

What's next? An even higher definition of work says that work is effort—and a person who believes that makes a sincere effort to accomplish some task. He's dedicated. He may work up quite a sweat. He may even dedicate a great deal of mental and physical exertion for his employer. Generally, he will believe he has given his best—and that he deserves all the rewards of those who have given their best. He is certainly blameless. But that's not the highest definition of work.

What's the highest, then? The meanest, toughest, rudest, most exacting, most unforgiving definition of work—to which few are willing to submit—involves *results*. Simply stated, it's the achievement of predetermined results.

Twenty years ago in Philadelphia, a co-worker told me he had never worked so hard in his life. I remember thinking that we *were* working hard—but we were spinning our wheels. My co-worker was the hardest-working person in the organization—but was he accomplishing results?

Getting Results

It doesn't matter how many doors a professional salesperson knocks on—it's the actual sales that count. It doesn't matter how many hours a film editor spends in the cutting room—it's the box office receipts that count. It doesn't matter how many touchdown attempts are made or how many balls are lobbed at a basket—it's the final score that counts. Results are measured after every game. Who won? What was the player's shooting average? Batting average? Earned run average? The highest level of success comes only to those who are willing to display results for everyone to see.

Teachers may be paid less than other professionals because it's very difficult to measure the results of teaching. A private school instructor can assess a prospective student, then promise to raise the student's competency to a certain level. But the *result*, the actual increase in competency, may occur many years later. Contrast that with a surgeon who removes an infected appendix. The *results* are immediate—and obvious. And that may be why society is willing to pay a surgeon more than it is willing to pay a teacher.

One of the misconceptions about the nature of work is that we should work smart, not hard. That is one of the silliest statements I've ever heard. How can you expect to succeed to the level of someone else who is not only working smarter than you are, but is also working *harder* than you are? Are you a hard worker? Can you put in long and hard hours? Are you willing to be judged by your *results*? I don't know who suggested to our society that a workweek of 40 hours is something sacred, but whoever it was, he prescribed the path to career mediocrity.

Working hard is especially important if you are underemployed—not getting the kinds of opportunities or making the kind of money you want. Hard work—along with knowledge and self-confidence—will improve your situation. It might not happen with your current employer, but if it doesn't, it will happen when someone *else* sees the kind of employee you are. American television executive Grant Tinker said it well: "First we will be best, and then we will be first."

The Taxation of Work and WYHTE

One of the great misconceptions about careers and financial success is that success is measured in dollars. In the business world, the score is kept in dollars. But that's a tremendous mistake.

Why? When you equate everything to dollars, you look only at the size of your paycheck, when what you *should* be looking at is your standard of living and your ability to achieve your life's goals. When you keep score in dollars, your career measuring stick becomes how much money you are being paid instead of whether your career is helping you reach your life's goals.

That raises an interesting question: Is work taxable?

Remember, money is "stored labor." The more money you have, the more you have stored of your lifetime accumulation of labor. That's how most of us achieve our lifestyle: We first trade our labor for money, then trade our money for lifestyle. But whenever your work is traded for money, it must first be taxed. So every time you trade labor for money and then money for lifestyle, some is siphoned off into taxes.

Is there an option? Yes. It *is* possible to structure your career and family finances so that you're *not* trading your labor for money. How? The goal becomes to trade labor *directly* for lifestyle—without it first becoming money—and avoid the tax siphon. (Review the WYHTE Phenomenon, see page 58.)

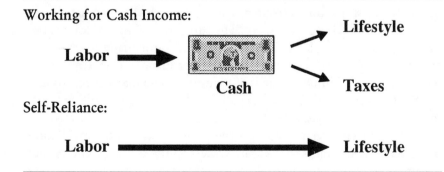

There are many ways to maximize the way you achieve lifestyle *other than* with a paycheck. Consider the economics of a nonworking spouse. Look at the economics of having children—and of having children do the family chores. Think about the principles of frugality, simplicity, nonconsumption, and trade. Do you see how you can maximize your lifestyle without trading labor for money?

Most college graduates allow their ego to define success by their starting salary. But an important part of career planning is figuring out what lifestyle you want—and how you'll achieve that lifestyle. If you define money as success, you'll get one type of result. If you define lifestyle, confidence, and security as success, you're likely to have an entirely different set of results.

The Common Denominator of Success

By definition, success comes to relatively few. If everyone was successful, there would be a new definition of success.

So what's the common characteristic of successful people? Is it intelligence? Education? No. "Nothing is more common than an educated derelict." What about effort? Can't be—we all know people who make a huge effort but spin their wheels all day long. Is it persistence?

The most profound writing on this subject is found in *The Common Denominator of Success*, a speech given in 1940 by Albert E.N. Gray. Gray observes that no matter the job description, everyone faces unpleasant tasks. And those same tasks tend to be unpleasant for most people. Simply stated, if you don't want to do them, and no one else wants to do them, they're not going to get done. But they *have* to get done.

Here's where economics steps in. The law of supply and demand dictates that the most unpleasant tasks are the most highly paid tasks. A business owner has the unpleasant task of figuring out how to borrow money and risk his home to finance a business. A salesman has the unpleasant task of calling a prospect. The surgeon had the unpleasant task of doing homework through many late nights—for many years—while friends were going to movies, living it up, or just plain relaxing. A garbage collector or plumber makes more money than many professionals.

So it's the needed but unpleasant tasks that people are willing to pay for, *not* the pleasant tasks. Never think that great monetary reward will ever come to you even if you do the pleasant tasks most excellently, because everyone wants to do that. Success comes to those who will do the unpleasant task. If you will do an unpleasant task even adequately, you will achieve greater monetary success than a person who does only the pleasant task most excellently.

So why are certain people *willing* to do unpleasant tasks, while others are *unwilling*? Because only a few people are motivated by pleasing *results*; most people are motivated by pleasant *methods*.

People who are motivated by the pleasure of *results* are willing to endure whatever hardship or unpleasant task is necessary in order to achieve the desired result. People who are motivated by pleasing *methods* are satisfied regardless of results, as long as those pleasant methods can be used.

People motivated by results seem to have a greater vision than those motivated by methods. Have they seen the bigger picture? Are they willing to sacrifice more?

Average people are motivated by pleasant tasks or methods. Only a few people are motivated by the pleasure of results and are willing to endure the hardships necessary to achieve them. This is the law of supply and demand in the career sense.

So, where do you stand? Can you tolerate the highest definition of work? In other words, are you driven by results rather than methods?

How the Success Curve Really Works— Dispelling Another Myth

Many people think the "success curve" is some type of compound interest curve. In other words, they think that if salary grows with inflation, they'll achieve an exponential curve of success. The rate of increase on the curve is the inflation rate—and that's all they'll ever achieve. They'll merely keep up with inflation.

That may be what the average worker's *income curve* looks like, but it's not what a *success curve* looks like.

A success-driven individual will sometimes earn less than the rate of inflation. His income may even fall as he is paying the price of success. But while his wage is falling, he is building a far greater type of income— something I call "professional equity."

Here's how it works: A person working for a salary or wage is renting out his time. When you rent out your time, what do you get? You get money. Once you are paid that month's wage, do you ever get paid for it again? No. You've rented out your time, and you've been paid the rent.

Now let's look at the person who is taking on the risk of building professional equity, or career ownership. During the first four to eight years of his career, he'll suffer unpleasant methods while he works on results—but all of a sudden, things will click, and professional equity takes over.

Does he rent out his time? No. He builds equity in his career through his professional knowledge, experience and insight. Once he learns it, he never forgets it. He knows how to do it again. It's interesting to watch people as they turn this corner in their career: Everything clicks, the lights go on, and they start to realize that there are few questions they can be asked that they haven't answered before. They "know it, and they know they know it."

When you discover that you've been asked every question, and that you know the answer, something happens to your self-confidence. Then you *own* your career.

The Success Curve

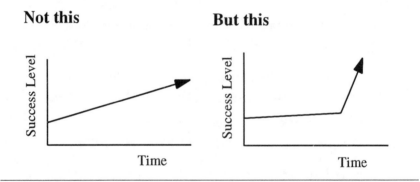

Not this

But this

Fatal Flaws That Cause Executives to Derail

Morgan McCall, Jr., and Michael Lombardo did a study at the Center for Creative Leadership on "derailed executives." They boiled 65 factors down to 10 categories or reasons for failure. The top three categories include: (1) insensitive to others—abrasive, intimidating, bullying style; (2) cold, aloof, arrogant; (3) a betrayal of trust.

It's interesting to note that not one of these has to do with specific performance problems. These are executives who were on the fast track to success. None of them had all the flaws listed in the study.

I've seen executives under stress who have become abrasive and intimidating. Whether in a large Fortune 500 company with 20,000 employees or a small financial planning firm, there is no place for insensitivity. Everyone deserves respect. Those of us who become so focused on a particular task or objective at hand must make a special effort to be sensitive to the needs of others.

An egotistical executive is on a sure path to failure when he thinks that because he is the boss, he doesn't need to treat other people with respect. Still other executives become arrogant, considering their strengths and brilliance as an excuse to intimidate others, or put others down. If you want to succeed, *be building.* If not, someone will always undermine you.

Finally, there is perhaps management's only unforgivable sin—betraying a trust. A trust may be betrayed by breaking a confidence, by not following through on promises made or actions to be taken, or by "one-upping" or undermining a colleague. Often a root cause of betrayal is lack of loyalty toward those to whom you should be committed. The study indicated that even big mistakes don't hurt executives who know how to handle adversity.

Of the 10 categories of fatal flaws, one dealt with the inability to manage interpersonal relationships. No matter how competent or brilliant one might be, interpersonal relationships will set the ceiling of one's ability to progress within an organization. Those people who are sensitive, caring, considerate, generous, loyal, team-building, positive, adaptable, trustworthy, and building of colleagues and subordinates will find their pathway easier.

What about a Working Spouse?

If you're not achieving the desired financial income in your career, how about encouraging your spouse to work?

Plenty of people in this country think that's an obvious solution. If you're one of them, think again. Personal reasons aside, let's focus on the *economics* of a two-income family. Only when we know the economic truth about our decisions are we free to make truly correct choices.

Take a realistic look at the impact of a second working spouse on a family's financial profile:

Increased taxes. *All* of the second working spouse's income is taxed at the top marginal tax bracket of the first working spouse. Here's what that means: Even if the first working spouse only pays 15 percent of income in taxes but is in a 28 percent marginal tax bracket, then *all* of the second spouse's income is being taxed at 28 percent *or above* (see Chapter 7). *Plus,* don't forget to add state income taxes.

Increased FICA and Medicare taxes. The first working spouse is most likely to exceed the Social Security limit of about $65,000. What does that mean? Simply, the 7.65 percent FICA and Medicare taxes are assessed *again* against the very first dollar a second working spouse makes.

The result? Even if a second working spouse earns a fairly minimal amount, 40 to 45 percent usually goes to federal, state, and Social Security taxes right off the top. Only 60 cents of every dollar can go toward living expenses.

Increased expenses. That 60 cents has a lot of work to do. Because a second working spouse usually means some hefty additional expenses: A second car. Increased auto insurance premiums for commuter rather than pleasure driving. Additional gasoline, parking fees, maintenance costs, repair bills, and tolls. A second career wardrobe. Bigger food bills (rather than cooking from scratch or buying in bulk, working parents who are too tired to fix dinner start relying on restaurants, frozen foods, or microwaveable meals, all at a price). And don't forget child care expenses— including camps and special programs during the summer, when many child-care providers take a break. A second working spouse who starts out with a wage of $15 an hour may end up contributing only $1 or $2 per hour to the family income by the time all expenses—including increased taxes—are deducted. Is it worth it?

Those are just some of the financial costs. Now let's consider the *other* costs. What happens when a parent isn't home when the children get home from school? Who helps with homework? Who provides discipline? Who ensures safety and security? What are they watching on television? Are they being exposed to violence? What happens to a worried parent's job performance?

Seriously consider these impacts on your family. Then what about the economy as a whole? Economists tell us that an increase in the number of two-income families has driven up consumer prices. That means we all pay more for houses, automobiles, and other goods and services. Rather than volunteers in the local schools, we now pay taxes to hire teacher's aides, etc.

If a second spouse is working for reasons other than to add to the family income, such as professional pursuits, then the discussion obviously goes beyond economics. I simply find that seldom does a second wage earner put a family ahead financially, *especially* if there are children home.

I recall a two-physician family, where each doctor earned well over $100,000 per year. After calculating all of the above, they figured that the second spouse was only adding about $12,000 per year to the family budget. They rightly wondered, "What's all this effort for?" Then they rightly concluded to have one spouse stay home with the children, and the other spouse was freed up to work about three extra hours per week, which made up for the lost income. This is the common result of a thorough analysis.

Admittedly, spouses work for more reasons than finances. If you are working for other reasons, such as variety, challenge, professional growth, etc., then weigh those reasons against the reasons not to work. But be certain that if you are working for economic reasons you do so with an accurate picture of the situation.

Once you know the truth you are free to make correct decisions. At such times, isolate the economic issues from the personal or professional issues so you can understand clearly the basis of your decisions.

Net Take-Home Pay of Second-Wage Earner, *Excluding* Additional Expenses (child care, clothing, etc.)

Marginal Tax Bracket*	\$10,000	\$20,000	Annual Income of Working Spouse \$30,000	\$40,000	\$50,000	\$60,000
25%	$7,500	$15,000	$22,500	$30,000	$37,500	$45,000
30	7,000	14,000	21,000	28,000	35,000	42,000
35	6,500	13,000	19,500	26,000	32,500	39,000
40	6,000	12,000	18,000	24,000	30,000	36,000
45	5,500	11,000	16,500	22,000	27,500	33,000
50	5,000	10,000	15,000	20,000	25,000	30,000

* Add Federal, State, Local Income Tax Rates (see Workbook), *plus* FICA & Medicare Rates, *plus* Self-Employment Tax Rate, if applicable.

What about Starting Your Own Business?

Another option you might have considered is starting your own business. Will it work? The answer depends on the business—and on you. Successful entrepreneurs have certain traits. Most of all, they're calculated risk-takers.

Can you accept risks? Your answers to a few simple questions will reveal a lot. Do you have trouble sleeping if you don't know where your mortgage payment is coming from next month? Do you feel unemployed if you don't receive a regular paycheck? If you answered yes to either question, starting a business may not be for you.

You also need to take a careful look at the business itself. Bruce Phillips studied business failure rates—and, based on the failure rate per 10,000 businesses, he came up with the five riskiest and the five safest.

The safest? In order, the least failures occurred in private education, health services, legal services, insurance (among both agents and brokers), and personal services.

The riskiest business is amusement and recreation services, including restaurants. In order, the top five are rounded out by oil and gas extraction, lumber and wood manufacturing, general building contractors, and home furnishings stores.

Part of your decision is intangible: What's your reason for wanting to start the business? Does that reason reflect your personal values? There are some tangibles, too, that should figure into your decision. Find out:

- How much will you need to get the business started?
- What is the break-even point for the business—both in terms of time and money?
- What are the monthly operating costs—including payroll, taxes, rent, and utilities?
- What legal requirements, such as licensing, apply?
- What resources do you have to support the business until it reaches the break-even point?
- What's the market potential?
- What's the competition?
- What will be your measure of business success?
- At what point will you determine it's time to get out of the business?
- What options are available if you want to get out? Can you liquidate? Transfer?

I've learned that the two key questions to ask yourself when considering such an investment of time and resources are: (1) What is the *worst* that could happen? and (2) Could I live with that? Be brutally realistic in your introspection.

Armed with the answers, only you can make the decision. Just make sure you go into it fully informed, with a solid plan and a secure safety net. For some Recommended Resources, see page 515. Then get expert counsel.

Career planning is full of opportunities. As I said earlier, your greatest asset is your ability to earn an income. Invest in yourself before your portfolio. Expand your definition of financial planning. Work on your top line, your gross income, as well as your bottom line.

While you are being brutally honest with yourself, you will discover that you have several self-defeating character attributes. So what. We all do. If you are like me, you probably acquired some from your upbringing and some from your own foolishness and stupidity. If needed, now is the time to *unlearn* much of what you've been taught. It's your life—be responsible for it. Begin with these simple insights and understandings. Ponder them and make them a part of your own thinking. Take ownership. As you do, you will feel an increased sense of control, security, and peace over your career.

Your Insights, Feelings, and Action Items

A. As you read this chapter, what *insights* came that seem applicable to *you?*

1._____
2._____
3._____

B. How did you *feel* as you pondered particular points of this chapter?

1._____
2._____
3._____

C. What do you *feel* you should *do* as a result of this chapter?

1._____
2._____
3._____

D. How might you solicit the aid of others in accomplishing "C" above?

_____
_____
_____

Chapter 15

How to Be the Last Person Laid Off Work

Be Your Employer's Most Profitable Employee

The average American worker thinks along these lines: "My union needs to negotiate for more money. I should be paid more. It really bugs me that the company is making so much off of me." This type of thinking is a problem because it pits you *against* your employer rather than *with* him or her.

This potentially divisive attitude says something to your employer: That you're not grateful for your job. That you're not a team player. That you have a zero-sum, scarcity mentality. That you won't be around very long. Knowing all this, how much is your employer willing to invest in you?

If you want to be the last person laid off in an economic downturn, you need to be your employer's most profitable employee. The company invests in the most profitable employees, sends them to special schools and workshops and conferences, and gives them plum assignments and opportunities to prove themselves. If you want job security and opportunities, you must *want* to be your employer's most profitable employee. You *want* your employer to make as much money "off you" as possible!

Once, while lecturing to a class at the business school of one of America's fine universities, I posed the question: "How many of you would like to be overpaid when you graduate?" I was surprised at how many raised their hands.

If you want job security, be sure you are underpaid.

Why? Your employer must make a profit on your services, or there is no reason for him to take the risk of being in business. The more underpaid you are, the more profitable you are—and the more secure your employment.

If you are paid just what you are worth, you will eventually be un-employed; no employer can tolerate a break-even situation.

Worst of all, don't be overpaid. If you are, you will be the first one laid off.

Measuring your value. One of the smartest things you can do is find out how your performance is being measured. Then you'll better understand your value to your employer.

Sit down with your employer—today, if you haven't already done so—and ask him to outline your job definition in quantitative terms. Find out *in detail* what objectives you should meet, and when. Then meet or exceed them by working hard. Results should be measurable. How does one know if he's achieved a goal, or a desired result, if it isn't measurable?

Ask how you will be evaluated. Get your employer to develop as specifically as possible how you will be evaluated and then periodically seek ways to improve. Then work on your productivity.

Might other employees balk at your efforts to rise? Of course, if they are satisfied with mediocrity. You will raise the standard for everyone, and who wants that? You decide. One is a sure path to mediocrity; the other is the only path to success.

Negotiating a raise. Once you meet the objectives, can you ask for a raise? Definitely! But if you *want* the raise, there's a specific way to ask for it.

Never explain why you need more money—your child is going to college, your spouse is quitting work, you just bought a house and must furnish it, all your credit cards are maxed out, you just bought a new four-wheeler. Think about it. Whose problems are those? They're your problems, not your employer's problems. It's not your boss's job to bail you out of your financial problems, or to support your new lifestyle.

Even more important, are those "reasons" related to your job? No.

Here's the key: If you want to get a raise, go to your employer with some objectively measurable, definable criteria that show you increased your productivity. In other words, talk *results*. When you can show that your productivity increased, that you are coming to the table with results, you're almost guaranteed the raise.

Use your talents. The rich get richer, and the poor get poorer. Remember the law of unequal rewards spelled out in the New Testament's parable of the talents?

As you recall, one man was given a talent. He buried it, and it was taken away from him. Another man was given two talents; he magnified them, and was given two more. A third person was given five talents. When he magnified them, he was given five more—*plus* the talent of the one who had lost his.

On the surface, the law of unequal rewards may seem unfair. But in a very real sense, it is extremely fair. Why? Because the master who dispensed the talents had a responsibility to see that they were given to people who were going to do something with those talents. The talents needed to be given to people who were going to recognize their stewardship to improve the common lot of society through those talents.

The same thing applies to a corporation, a business, an educational institution, or even a family. The opportunities and rewards come to those who are the most loyal, who are the most profitable, and who are willing to follow the highest definition of work.

Here's What Employers Look For

The *real* way to achieve success in your career is to become the most profitable, the most valued employee to your employer. Let's review those characteristics of career management which will help you succeed, because no matter your career path or your occupation we cannot adequately stress their importance. You need to be:

Honest. Remember the number-one success force? *Honesty is the first law of success.* Do you call in for extra sick days? Do you "borrow" supplies? How long are you gone for lunch? How do you use long-distance telephones? How trustworthy are you? What is your reputation?

Do you put in an honest day's work for the agreed-upon wage? Regardless of what the wage is? Remember—if you are receiving a paycheck, you agreed to that wage. If you feel you are underpaid, address that issue—but don't decide to short your employer on effort because you feel shorted on your wage. If you are underpaid and still go the extra mile, your wage will ultimately catch up with you—either with that employer, or through the good reputation that lands you a better job.

Hard-working. Are you lazy? A successful employee doesn't just look for the easy way to do things; he looks for the right way, the best way. Some people put out tons of effort and yet spin their wheels, while others get the job done. Look around. See who gets the job done. Then model those people.

Some people are always *doing* the job. Some have it *done*. When the boss asks about a task, don't be one who says, "I'm doing it." Be the one who says, "It's done."

A lot of people think they're working because they're at the office. They're not. They're the living dead.

Loyal. Who are you loyal to? That's who will be loyal to you. If you're confused, look at who signs your paycheck or pays the rent for the office in which you work. *That's* who you should be loyal to.

Never get into a case of mistaken loyalties toward co-workers. They may be great friends, but they don't issue the paycheck that makes your monthly mortgage payment. Don't misplace loyalties or confidences. As I've said, if you can't be loyal, get out. Employers invest only in loyal people; they merely endure the others until someone better comes along.

Some will tell you that it's smart to not let your employer know what you're thinking. To keep your employer guessing. To keep your options open. To keep your cards close to the vest. Perhaps this is why, with the younger generations, loyalty is one of the two rarest character attributes.

But contrary to popular wisdom, I am convinced that the very smartest employee is the one who is very open with his employer—who lets him know he's on the team, and that he's going to stay on the team, and exactly where he stands. What happens? Who does the employer invest in? Who is going to have paths open? Who is going to have opportunities sent his way? Who is going to be sent to advanced training and special workshops? The loyal people are the ones who get ahead.

This assumes, of course, that you work for someone you can be loyal to. Don't work for someone who asks you to compromise your ethics or integrity.

Productive. What is your output per hour? Are you overly analytical? Do you suffer from "analysis paralysis"? Are you over-socializing or fueling idle chitchat in the hallways?

The average worker becomes a master at expanding the work to fill the time allotted. The profitable employee gets it done, then looks for something new to do.

Stable. Employers want someone with low job turnover. Punctuality. Dependability. Do you have an emotional, family, financial, or health problem that drains your time? Does your employer ever pay you for getting nothing done?

Committed for the long term. Can your employer count on a long-term return for his investment in you? If your employer is not willing to invest in you, why not? Have you had too many jobs in your history? How's your attitude? Loyalty?

There are all kinds of unseen forces that immediately combine to come to the rescue and aid of a person who has commitment. Commitment is sensed immediately in a person of single-minded focus and purpose.

Goal-driven. A very successful businessman and mentor once confided to me that 95 percent of all young men he mentored stopped achieving by the age of 30. They had seen their best days.

Why?

Is it because they stopped growing? Your best work is done while you are growing—and growth happens only when you face challenges and struggles. No pain, no gain.

Is it because their growth occurred while they were young—struggling through college? Adjusting to marriage? Starting a new career?

At 30, most people have settled into an eight-to-five routine with two hours a day thrown in for a commute. Are you one of those? Or do you regularly self-evaluate? Keep striving? Are you as goal-driven as you were during your college or early career days? Or, are you settling for a lesser dream?

Responsible. Employers want people who accept responsibility. Are you reliable? Do you seek out responsibility, volunteering for assignments that could damage your chances if you fail—but could bring tremendous opportunity for success?

Your boss is swamped. Your boss *wants* to delegate. Are you the one your boss can count on? Take the load off others—both your boss and your co-workers. They'll notice.

Competent. Some people know, and know they know. They are both safe and useful. Other people know, but don't know they know. They are safe, but not very useful. Still others don't know, and know they don't know. They are safe, but not useful. Finally, some people don't know, but think they know. They are dangerous.

Where do you stand? Do you ask others to honestly tell you about your "blind spots"? Are you studying, growing?

Experienced. Do you have relevant experience in your chosen career or line of work? Sometimes the most valuable type of experience is the experience of overcoming. Think about obstacles you've conquered, times you didn't quit when everyone told you you should.

Any work experience is better than none. If you've had any employment—whether it's working the counter at a fast-food restaurant or digging ditches—you'll be looked on more favorably by a prospective employer than if you've been sitting around waiting for the phone to ring.

Educated. Highlight whatever education you've had—college, vocational school, technical school, or even self-study. Education and training are a great "laziness barometer." Why? Because it's so much easier to do *anything*—watch TV, play golf, etc.—rather than study.

Another important part of education is finishing. Be a finisher. Complete your formal education. A lot of people get right down to the wire but never quite graduate.

Even worse, many people graduate but think they're done learning. Read, read, read. Only 40 percent of all Americans have bought even one book in the past year—but only half an hour of daily study can make you a national expert in virtually any chosen field within five years. The person who *won't* read is just as illiterate and ignorant as the person who *can't* read.

Self-motivated. Are you reading? Are you sharpening your skills at home on your own time, or only on your boss's payroll? Do you have the initiative to accept responsibility for your career? Do you make it a point to learn new skills?

Basically, you either need to burn the midnight oil or be early to rise, just one of the unpleasant things others aren't willing to do. You have to become a self-motivated person. This does not mean being perpetually on an emotional high. Usually, motivation is self-generating, and grows gradually by taking small, incremental steps toward increasing discipline and accomplishing tasks and goals.

The motivated person is one who is experienced at achieving strenuous goals. Each time he does, he gets a new burst of energy and a "runner's high." His self-esteem is more durable.

Persistent. We learn to quit as children—when our parents let us quit Little League baseball because we weren't getting up to bat often enough. Let us quit soccer because we were the last one picked for the team. It's time to be responsible enough to overcome those habits.

Don't turn tail and run when things get tough. Just because you have a difficult colleague, a burdensome boss, a challenging marriage, or frightening financial woes, don't quit. And don't tell others about the myriad of struggles you've endured. Just keep it to yourself, and be the one who doesn't quit. Remember that persistence is omnipotent. You have to believe that sooner or later you reach the top, no matter how steep the mountain.

You need to wake up some morning and discover that you are not a quitter. Your winning attitude will then carry over into your marriage and all other aspects of your life.

And be sure you aren't teaching or allowing *your* children to become quitters. Sometimes they need to persist just to persist!

An extra-miler. Never stop at the minimum; do the maximum. Magnify your job description. Always ask, "Can I do more?"

Going the extra mile demonstrates freedom, because in the workplace, the first mile is conscription. That's what is required. When you go the *extra* mile, you show that you're free—free to perform at the higher standard of your own free will.

Being an extra-miler underscores a principle of career planning that few people understand: *The servant is always, always the master.* If you're merely coasting along, your employer is the servant—he's paying you more than you're worth. But when *you're* the servant—the one who goes the extra mile, the one your employer can't do without—then you're in charge. It's that simple. Go the extra mile and it will come back to you. If not, others will be bidding for your services. The servant always sets the terms. The master is always dependent on the servant, not the other way around.

Creative. Can you work beyond the stated parameters? Can you create opportunities for yourself and others in the company? Can you find ways to win? When you run up against a brick wall, do you go over, around, or through? Or do you throw up your hands in exasperation?

At the first sign of a problem, do you cry, "It can't be done"? Think how that sounds to your employer, 20 years older, who built his business on the philosophy that, "If it's impossible, it might take a little longer." Never, never tell your boss that something can't be done. If he is someone who has worked his way up from nothing, knows the business from the inside out and has personally done every task that gets done, he's not going to like to be told that something is impossible. He's more likely to ask you to get out of the way so someone else can do it.

Take your employer creative solutions and options—not problems. *Never* go to your employer with a problem until you have exhausted all your own creative possibilities and examined all potential solutions.

Teachable. A teachable person expands his competence because he is willing to learn. An unteachable person has topped off his level of competence because he thinks he knows it all. Stop mouthing off like you know it all.

Let others *under*estimate rather than *over*estimate you. Keep a low profile. Be humble and modest in your style. Remember: "The nail that sticks up gets hit."

Positive. Do you have a positive attitude and create a positive work environment? Or are you a complainer, even under the false—and silly—guise of "constructive criticism"?

Don't be negative, and don't associate with negative people. Don't tolerate them, go to lunch with them, or let their garbage thinking even enter your mind. If you do, your mind will become like the vacant lot, a collection of other people's trash.

A good rule of thumb? Never, ever listen to a person who hasn't succeeded. Don't measure colleagues by the logic of their constructive criticism or their analysis of the situation at work. Instead, evaluate them on the basis of their own success. I would rather follow the illogic of a success than the logic of a failure any day.

Discover that negative people *cannot* exercise their free will. They don't have freedom of choice. Why? Because they can't even *see* the options! That's why people of *vision* lead organizations—they can see the options, the choices, the opportunities. Their horizon is beyond ours.

Profitable. Do you really want to be your employer's most profitable employee—the last person to be laid off? Then develop a reputation of being the most profitable employee.

What happens then? Others will be bidding for your services. And as they bid for your services, they will bid up your wages.

If your employer loses on you, he'll remember. I know a person who went from employer to employer, always with the attitude, "My employer makes so much money off me." But after four or five employers, no one had ever made a dime of profit off this employee. And that's not all: Since he was preceded by his reputation, soon no one would hire him.

Not too rough. Learn to accept criticism. Become more interested in personal growth than you are in protecting your own ego. Seek to have your rough edges knocked off. When you want improvement more than you want to protect your fragile ego, you won't be afraid of the pain of challenges.

Not too smooth. On the other hand, don't be too polished or smooth; you'll lose credibility. If you want to be trusted, be down to earth.

It is often better to have the image of a hard-working, sleeves-rolled-up hustler, than that of an established, "I've arrived" type of person. Trust is born of congruence, another form of integrity.

Conservative. Are your dress, language, grammar, and grooming conservative? Have you matured to that level? Or are you still dressing like the kids did in college? If you're in the business world, get rid of your layered haircut and argyle socks. Meet or exceed the standards of *your* occupation. Above all, be clean and well-groomed.

Balanced. Does your life reflect integrity through your wholeness? Employers want a balance among an employee's work, family, social, physical, and spiritual lives. Don't discuss your religious, social, physical, or academic pursuits *until after* you have established a close and solid relationship with your boss or colleagues. These should never be part of a job interview. Exhibit that you are a whole, well-rounded, balanced person.

Mature. Voice your opinions and feelings with understanding, not aggression. Learn to disagree without being disagreeable. And remember: There are always two sides to every issue. Never be insistent about something that's really just an opinion.

Thinking. Your success will be determined more by how well you think than by any other factor. Think the way an employ*er* would think—not the way an employ*ee* would think—and you will discover a secret to rising within any organization. Think the way happy people think. Read the thoughts of great thinkers—then ponder them until they become your own. Think with a journal; a magical thing happens when a thought is written down. Meditate. Ponder. Read inspirational books.

Appreciative. Gratitude is the rarest of all character attributes. Someone gave you a job, an opportunity, when he could have chosen someone else. (Still could!)

It's amazing what a simple thank-you can do. An associate's employees in Ohio once gave him a list of things they wanted. On their "wish list" was installation of a water fountain on the far side of the factory.

That was easy. It was installed within a few days. You know, he got more thank-yous for that very simple, inexpensive water fountain! What happened to him as a result? He listened. He learned to do the little things, and to do them as quickly as possible. Why? Because those things were appreciated. Express your appreciation often and with sincerity.

Your boss is human too. He sacrifices to give you an opportunity. Just like you, he's motivated by many things other than making money. Employers are motivated by the same things that motivate everyone else—and it's not just the bottom line. Obviously, they have to cover the bottom line if they want to stay in business. But once that happens, they are motivated by friendship, appreciation, gratitude, mentoring, coaching, and making a difference in someone's life. If you don't recognize that, you'll be defeated by your own cynical attitude.

Involved. Often it is an unwritten rule to attend office parties and gatherings. When an employer invests in an office party or gathering, be sensitive to the rule of the company. Although they may say "it's optional," companies like to see who the "players" are and how they mix with others in a social setting. They don't invest in gatherings for mere fun. There is usually a very serious business reason involved. If you don't show up, you may be saying, "Relationships don't count." If you aren't naturally outgoing, this may be a time to fake it—or work on changing.

How to Evaluate Your True Net Worth

Once you become the most valuable employee, an interesting thing happens to your net worth. And too few understand that principle. They don't account for their nonfinancial assets when they figure their net worth.

Soon after graduating from college in accounting, I expressed to a mentor frustration about my debt level and my ability to handle it. My mentor insisted, "You're not in debt." I sadly shook my head. "Yes, I am. I have liabilities that total far more than my assets. I have a negative net worth."

I was thinking like an accountant. Don't be thinking like an accountant or a banker if you really want to understand your true net worth.

My mentor was right, and I was wrong. I wasn't in debt. I had a positive net worth.

Why? Because net worth includes plenty of things that don't show up on your financial statement—such as your attitude, your education, your training, and your experience. They're the things that no one can take away from you. And they include your value to your employer. With those in your plus column, you're *way* ahead.

Your Insights, Feelings, and Action Items

A. As you read this chapter, what *insights* came that seem applicable to *you?*

1._____

2._____

3._____

B. How did you *feel* as you pondered particular points of this chapter?

1._____

2._____

3._____

C. What do you *feel* you should *do* as a result of this chapter?

1._____

2._____

3._____

D. How might you solicit the aid of others in accomplishing "C" above?

_____

_____

_____

Decision Four

Build a Solid Foundation for Security

Chapter 16 will discuss the principles upon which you may find lasting security, freedom from fear and anxiety, and peace of mind. In Chapters 17 through 26 we will apply those principles to build a financial foundation solid enough to hold significant success, or to weather any storm.

Chapter 16

How to Achieve Security

E veryone wants and needs to feel secure.

But what exactly *is* it that provides security? And how do you get it? Does it start with a huge bank balance? Maybe. But money in the bank is only a small part of security. As Henry Ford maintained, "If money is your hope for independence, you will never have it. The only real security a man can have in this world is a reserve of knowledge, experience, and ability." Security has much more to do with being *prepared* than with having a huge bank balance. Insecurity breeds fear, and *fear vanishes when you are prepared.*

Are You Adequately Prepared?

If you are prepared for the contingencies that may befall you or your family, you know you will have the emotional strength and temporal resources to face whatever happens.

Jesus tells the story of 10 virgins who were waiting for the marriage. When the bridegroom came to call the virgins into the wedding feast, the five wise virgins had oil in their lamps and were allowed to enter. They were prepared. The five foolish virgins, who were unprepared, did not have oil in their lamps. They didn't merely run out of oil. Instead, like many of us, they ran out of *time*. They were procrastinators.

The greatest enemy of preparation is procrastination. You probably *know* a lot more about how to manage your financial life than you actually *do*. The problem is not lack of knowledge; the problem is lack of *action*.

Do you feel an urgency, or do you slumber?

The five foolish virgins were not prepared when the moment of opportunity came. The door to the wedding feast was shut. That's how it is with preparation. You never know when opportunity will present itself—just as you never know when financial setbacks may occur. And when adversity hits, it often hits hard.

Demand Self-Reliance

Self-reliance is important at every level: as an individual, family, neighborhood, company, and community. There are many ways to achieve self-reliance; an extended family, for example, can inventory the skills of all family members, then trade services with each other.

The person who is self-reliant is proactive. He takes responsibility for his own condition and does not wait for circumstances or other people to provide him with security. He realizes that security will never be found in other people or through government programs.

The dependent person is passive and reactive. He is acted upon. A proactive person initiates action.

When you achieve a greater level of self-reliance, you and your family are not so dependent on the fortunes or misfortunes of your employer, your community, or even the national economy.

There is a story of dependency told where I live near the shores of the Great Salt Lake. Every day the brine shrimp factory processed its harvest and then discharged the shrimp waste. Soon the seagulls were crowded around the discharge area. Eventually, they got fat and lazy.

Years went by. The baby gulls, raised in fatness around the discharge area, didn't know how to hunt for food.

One day, the shrimp factory closed. Did the seagulls understand what happened? Did the baby gulls know why they were starving? No. But starve they did.

Are you becoming dependent on others? If so, what are you doing to yourself? To your children? Do you blame the "shrimp factory"—your employer, the government, or the economy—when the fatness gets turned off?

What Henry Ford said about business also applies to the individual: "Business is never so healthy as when, like a chicken, it must do a certain amount of scratching for what it gets."

What are you doing, then, to achieve self-reliance and independence? These are the bedrock principles of security.

Increase Job Security

What about security on the job? There are several different ways to increase job security. The first is *always* be underpaid. (See Chapter 15.)

Another key to job security is productivity. Be especially wary if you have been given a significant raise: Your employer is looking for heightened results. *Never* mistake a good employee review as an excuse to slack off.

Still another key is to be the servant. Why? *The servant is always the master.* In the example of the underpaid employee, who is the master? Is it the employer? No. It's the employee: The employer *needs* the employee to achieve profitability.

What about the overpaid employee? Who is the master? The employer: He is working and running a business to provide charity to the overpaid employee.

When you are truly the servant, you continue to climb the ladder of success. Ultimately, one of two things will happen: You will always be appreciated and financially rewarded, *or* you will build a reputation and be bid away by a competitor who will appreciate and reward you.

Service is one of the first laws of security. In fact, service *is* security. Just as the employee who is the most profitable has job security, the employee who is constantly going the extra mile has increased security. It has been said that if you want to like someone, serve him. It is hard to dislike someone you serve. This applies to family, office, and social relationships. Providing opportunities for your children to serve others probably teaches them more and makes them more economically valuable than providing them opportunities for education, cultural exchange, job experience, or travel.

Exercise Self-Control

Self-discipline, or self-control, seems to be the gatekeeper governing all the good or bad that passes into our lives. *All* the positive character traits, *all* the virtues, must pass through the single gate of self-discipline. None of the virtues can be yours without it. They can all be yours with it. What does that have to do with self-reliance and security? Your economic tree can't bear economic fruit if it doesn't have the deep roots of self-reliance and independence born of a proactive discipline and self-control.

Most people are only willing to change when the painful consequences of continuing on their current course, are perceived as greater than the pain of starting anew.

As Jeffrey Locker observed, "There are two pains in life: the pain of discipline and the pain of regret. Basically with every decision we make we must weigh the pain of discipline (what will it take to do what I'm attempting to do), versus the pain of regret (what are the painful consequences if I don't get myself to do the activity). Which pain do you think will usually be perceived to be the more painful? The pain of regret is also more painful, because it is final."

Focusing on these true principles and internalizing them brings about desired change. Among the Muslim students of Islam, there are the most devout, who are called *hafiz*. The *hafiz* study diligently to memorize the entire *Koran* so they can recite it correctly by heart! Motivated by their reverence for the sound of these holy words of Allah, these students model what is required if we would gain the necessary self-control and self-discipline to govern our lives.

If you are not proactive and in control of yourself, other people and circumstances will determine your economic life. *That* is insecurity.

Work Hard

Service—in other words, security—requires work. Like most children, I was required to do my daily chores. When I complained, my mother would insist, "Do something every day you don't want to do, just because you don't want to do it." I hated it. But I did it. Fifteen years later, while a university student, it paid off. I discovered I needed to do my homework rather than go out.

Develop a reputation as a hard worker:

> Every morning in Africa, a gazelle wakes up. It knows that it must run faster than the fastest lion or it will be killed. Every morning a lion wakes up. It knows that it must outrun the slowest gazelle or it will starve to death. It doesn't matter whether you are a lion or a gazelle: *When the sun comes up you had better be running.*

People need to work in order to have self-respect. Idleness breeds lazy actions, lazy thoughts, get-rich-quick schemes, and trouble with society.

When people need welfare assistance, its purpose should be to sustain *life*, not *lifestyle*. The aim of welfare should be to help people help themselves. As the ancient Chinese proverb says, "Give a man a fish, and you feed him for a day; teach a man to fish, and you feed him for a lifetime." People should expect to work for their assistance. Working for what they get blesses their own lives, blesses the lives of others (the beneficiaries of their work), and provides self-respect.

Is that harsh? No. Have I helped anyone when I make him dependent? No. I have merely made him a slave. Were the seagulls by the shrimp factory being truly helped? No.

Establish Reserves

A key to achieving self-reliance and security is to establish reserves in all areas of your life. Do it for yourself and for the members of your extended family. (Your extended family should be able to turn to you for help before they turn to the government or charity.)

Establish reserves of cash for "a rainy day." Get your home paid off. Build up emotional reserves so you have an emotional well to draw upon when all else is drying up.

Establish reserves of skills and abilities. Get the tools you need to manufacture, repair, and maintain the necessities of life.

Put away a year's supply of food, clothing, and energy. Sound impossible? Instead of storing enough food to maintain your usual eating habits, consider storing only what it would take to sustain life. Why? What about unemployment? Whenever there is a flood or earthquake or blizzard, the store shelves are immediately emptied. There are long lines. How long might a trucking strike last? What, then, are some of the necessities? Wheat. Sugar or honey. Dried beans. Rice. Salt. Dry milk. Remember: It's less expensive to buy in bulk and cook from scratch.

Be creative. Your pantry could be constructed so that canned goods are added from the rear and roll forward. That way, your food can be rotated. Many canned items have a shelf life of years, and with an appropriate rotation program, you may have a year's supply as soon as you buy it.

Consider a garden. Look at the space you have: Even a planter box in an apartment building can yield food.

Some consider having a year's supply "hoarding," but it actually helps the economy. How? It smooths the ebbs and flows of supply and demand. People tend to buy when prices are down, helping to support prices. Then they consume reserves when prices are up, controlling the rise of prices during periods of shortage. In this sense, buying food in bulk is just smart family economics.

The same holds true for a year's supply of clothing, energy, and other resources. It may be illegal to store a year's supply of gasoline on your premises, but you may be able to store enough coal or wood for a stove that could heat part of your home through an oil crisis.

Guard Against Ego

What does ego have to do with security? Plenty: *Ego causes high consumption, which demands high expenses.* You purchase name-brand items when a generic would do as well. You go into debt. You fail to put money into savings.

Instead of having a more modest home that you can pay off, you buy a bigger home than you truly need. Instead of driving an economical car, you sink far too much into something more flashy. The number-one cause of financial problems in America today is *ego*.

Consider Working for Yourself

Too many people think that working for a big company builds security, and that working for yourself yields insecurity. That's no longer always true.

Rapid economic changes mean there may not be as much security in large corporations as there once was. Working for yourself or working on commission can often give you the skills and attributes necessary for self-reliance.

It's not easy. Starting up a business may take months, or even years. It will be hard work. But it may ultimately give you a greater level of security and self-reliance.

Buy Insurance

Too many people have an *insecure* security program. Why? They rely on employer-provided benefits, such as health insurance, group term life insurance, and disability insurance.

As an employee, are you in control of those programs? Can they be changed or cancelled at any time? If something happens to your insurability, can you then get insurance on your own?

Whenever possible, own your insurance personally. The contract should be between you and the insurance company. Whenever possible, get permanent, noncancellable, guaranteed renewable insurance. Get a *reliable* program from reputable agents and companies that avoids cracks in your foundation. Get a *broad* program consisting of adequate health, life, property and casualty, disability, and general liability insurance. Consider dental and long-term care insurance. Get a *secure* security program.

Manage Risks

Manage your risks to balance conservatism and prudence. In your investment portfolio, avoid speculation. Shun greed. Avoid the something-for-nothing mentality. Forget about making the fast bucks (you'll only be susceptible to con artists).

If you want to achieve security, understand your risks. Then plan for those risks. Later in this book, the chapters on investment portfolio management, protecting your assets, and estate planning will help you do just that.

Avoid Debt

Any solid financial program that will permanently provide a real level of security must have a solid foundation. Whenever you take on debt, you develop cracks in your foundation. Debt makes you vulnerable. Debt can collapse everything you have worked to build.

Develop a Self-Reliant Family

The family is not only the fundamental social unit of society, but the fundamental economic unit as well. Ideally, the family should have a good mix of cash and non-cash income. The more self-reliant the family, the more non-cash income—and the greater the economic progress.

You need cash income to purchase the things your family can't produce for itself. But the more you use cash, the greater the tax siphon—in other words, the payback on your labor is diminished. The more your family can produce or manufacture its own items, the more moderate the tax drain. Your family can keep all the fruits of its labor, and economic progress is enhanced. The skills developed through self-reliant living also serve as a buffer during periods of unemployment, disability, or other setbacks.

Am I suggesting that everyone goes back to a farm or returns to the wilderness and lives off nature? No. I *am* suggesting that you convert as much of your labor as possible straight into goods, supplies, and skills. Whenever your labor is first converted into cash, the fruits of your labor are diminished by the 20 to 50 percent tax bite. I *am* suggesting that as an economic unit, family finances operate best when the division of labor recognizes the value of self-reliance.

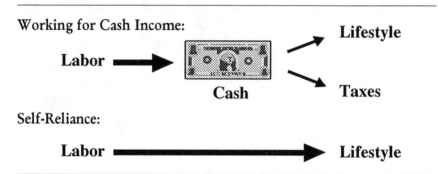

Working for Cash Income:

Labor ➡ Cash ➡ **Lifestyle**
                    ➡ **Taxes**

Self-Reliance:

Labor ➡ **Lifestyle**

Self-reliance is more than just skill development and the ability to provide for one's own. It is, in fact, the most sound financial strategy of all.

Remember, too: Self-reliance and self-responsibility need to be tempered by compassion. Provide compassion after you encourage someone to do everything he can with every means possible. And that balance needs to be achieved in an environment of freedom. Forced compassion is no compassion at all. A sense of gratitude and service are necessary—and are the basis of sharing, compassion, cooperation, synergy, and interdependence.

Tithing: The Ancient Law of Giving 10 Percent

Giving 10 percent of your income to your church or synagogue makes your security sure. How? There are really two ways of looking at it. Externally, you'll reap tremendous economic benefits. Internally, you'll be a happier, more significant person. Regardless of which point of view you take, giving to charity is a fundamental financial law of security and success.

Just for a minute, let's look at a principle that too few recognize: *Service to others is the first law of economic security.* For example, if you're in business, what causes your customers to keep coming back? It is service—the service they do *not* pay for, the extras they do *not* expect, the service that is *not* already calculated into the purchase price. If you only provide them the level of service which they figure they are paying for, what loyalty have you generated? It is only when you go the extra mile, when you provide that service which is beyond the purchase price, that loyalty is born. That is why service is the first law of security.

Consider another example. What happens if you are an employee, or a neighbor, who gives unexpected service to others? When economic stress hits, others will remember you. That is a principle that dates back thousands of years, but it is as true today as it was then. In spite of what you may read about our detached communities, an extra mile of service is almost always reciprocated many fold. Perhaps it is precisely because of our detached communities that such service is so noticed, appreciated, and reciprocated.

You have heard that 10 percent of your increase should be given away in pure service to others—something that applies to financial increase as well as gifts of time. An amazing mental transformation occurs when you observe this law. Here is what happens:

Some people have an attitude, or mentality, of scarcity. Faced with an economic proposition, they always ask, "What's in it for me?" That attitude crops up between competitors in almost all business ventures, and is seen amongst employees everywhere.

Others live with an attitude of abundance. They are the ones who develop win-win propositions, who ask, in a spirit of teamwork, "How can *we* pull this off? How can *we* make this work?"

A Calisthenic for Gratitude

When you give 10 percent of all you have to others, you reap all kinds of benefits. First, you live your own life with a higher level of integrity and honesty. That attracts economic success—others want to do business with you. Your employer wants to keep you on the payroll, your customers want to do business with you, your clients want to seek out your advice. You will be the last one laid off—and the first one rehired.

The law of giving away 10 percent is called *the law of tithing*. Those who obey it stay in touch with the world; they become, or remain, sensitive to the plight of others who are less fortunate. They live a life of increased peace. They maintain a sense of humility and modesty, and find favor with others. They value the ethic of hard work, and demonstrate it to those around them. They avoid gambling and other excesses. I have seen this phenomenon occur unconsciously in people. All these character traits unconsciously combine into natural economic laws that compound their blessings. Best of all, they pass this character on to their children.

When you give 10 percent of all your income to your church or synagogue, you develop an abiding sense of gratitude for the 90 percent you keep. Never mind whether it might be tax-deductible—the *real* benefit is a sense of gratitude, an abundant life, and a greater sense of joy.

Perhaps you believe this law is a spiritual one; it is. I have had clients who sometimes had to choose between paying a bill—maybe the mortgage—and paying tithing. They knew who to pay—then they could prayerfully turn their problems over to their God, and in confidence request the promised blessings and help.

Some believe that these promises are sure. They have no doubt that they will be blessed. They have no doubt in God's ability to keep His promises. The Old Testament portrays ancient Israel's law of tithing:

> Will a man rob God? Yet ye have robbed me. But ye say, Wherein have we robbed thee? In tithes and offerings.
>
> Ye are cursed with a curse: for ye have robbed me, even this whole nation.
>
> Bring ye all the tithes into the storehouse, that there may be meat in mine house, and *prove me now* herewith, saith the Lord of hosts, if I will not open you the windows of heaven, and pour you out a blessing that there shall not be room enough to receive it.
>
> And I will rebuke the devourer for your sakes, and he shall not destroy the fruits of your ground; neither shall your vine cast her fruit before the time in the field, saith the Lord of hosts. (Malachi 3:8-11.)

While this promise was given in an agrarian setting, might it refer to how we may be prospered and protected in our career? Yes, the law is spiritual. But the law of tithing is also an economic law. As a financial adviser, I have observed this law countless times, and I am convinced of its sureness. Nothing opens up windows of opportunity quite like this does. It seems to make up for our other failings and compensates for our economic weaknesses. The result? You do better than you otherwise would. The rate of return cannot be calculated.

That great Canadian industrialist N. Eldon Tanner said that tithing "is not a gift or a charitable contribution. It is a debt. No matter how the tax code calls it a contribution, it is not paid out of our generosity. It is paid out of our obligation. ... Our full and honest tithing is our signal to the Lord that we recognize that He is the true owner of all things on the face of the earth and the source of all that which he has entrusted to our temporary care."

I remember some years ago observing a very prosperous Catholic who gave 10 percent of his gross income to his local parish. When I asked him about it, he told me that he felt he would be blessed with the other 90 percent. He had never missed the 10 percent, he said; in fact, he felt he did better without it.

Our Stewardship

We have a stewardship, a responsibility, to provide not only for our own, but for the poor, the needy, and the distressed in all parts of the world. While many of us live comfortably in our excesses, we have brothers and sisters throughout the world who have not been so blessed. They will be with us always. What are we to do? We are to help them dig wells. We are to teach them principles of temporal security. We are to teach them health care. We are to teach them effective farming methods. We are to teach them how to provide for themselves. Most of all, we are to love them.

Maybe you think the task is too great—and you feel too insignificant to rise to the task. Remember the story of the mouse and the lion? The mouse pleaded with the lion not to eat him. In exchange, he promised to return the favor some day.

"What could you ever do for me?" roared the lion.

"I don't know," replied the mouse, "but something will come along."

Remember what happened? The lion got caught in a net and couldn't escape. Do you remember the key to his survival? The mouse came along and painstakingly chewed through the ropes of the net until the lion got loose.

Also, remember the Chinese proverb, "It is better to light one small candle than to sit and curse the darkness." What is the cost of our tithing or our charitable contributions? Might the cost to us be no more than the cost of seed compared to the cost of a harvest?

A great individual once said, "A person makes no greater sacrifice when he pays his tithing than the farmer does when he sows his seed in the ground. Both require faith, and both bring their reward."

Go ahead. Give 10 percent of all of your earnings to your church or synagogue—a cause worthy of your labor. Then forget about any kind of return.

It won't be easy; it requires sacrifice and commitment. But it always brings results. At first, those results may not be discernible, but if you stick with it, you'll notice a few things over time. First of all, you'll suddenly realize that you really don't miss the 10 percent. The 90 percent you keep will stretch—will make up for what you give away. But that's not all: Your economic world will take on a new perspective. You'll find more meaning and reward as you work for the bread you eat. Your life itself will take on greater significance.

Perhaps you are in shock as you read my recommendation that you give 10 percent of your income to your church or synagogue. If you don't think you can pay 10 percent, then pay 1 percent. And when you feel like you can pay 2 percent, then pay 2 percent. And then pay 5 percent when you think you can do that. Just test the law—prove it.

The Formula for Financial Security

The formula for financial security, then, is self-reliance and independence born of a proactive sense of self-responsibility, grounded in self-discipline and self-control. Its enemies are procrastination and ego. Its allies are advance preparation, reserves, and skill development. It won't be found merely in FDIC insurance or in how many dollars are in your savings account. It will be enhanced with provident living. It is made sure through service.

When you understand the sources of economic security, you will invest more in education and training, self-reliance, and preparation. As you do, you will sleep better—and you will live with less stress, fear, and uncertainty. Security and peace of mind will be yours.

The Security Continuum

Low   High

◄———————————————————●————————————————————►

High Bondage "Things"	Skills High Freedom
Bad Habits Complexity	Simplicity Cash Savings
High Wants/Needs	Low Wants/Needs
Dependence Debt	Self-Reliance Independence

Your Insights, Feelings, and Action Items

A. As you read this chapter, what *insights* came that seem applicable to
   you?
   1._____
   2._____
   3._____

B. How did you *feel* as you pondered particular points of this chapter?
   1._____
   2._____
   3._____

C. What do you *feel* you should *do* as a result of this chapter?
   1._____
   2._____
   3._____

D. How might you solicit the aid of others in accomplishing "C" above?

   _____
   _____
   _____

Chapter 17

Homing in on Most People's Major Investment: Real Estate

Why Own a Home

Why do you own your own home? It's the American thing to do. You can paint your walls if you want. You can build equity and get a tax deduction. Buying a home is a good investment, generally. In fact, it's the biggest investment most Americans will ever make.

These are all good reasons to buy a home. Most likely, though, you own a home because you just feel good about it. Even without tax advantages and appreciation, the real reasons to buy a home are the security and sense of permanence ownership brings.

When Herschel and Esther had to go from owning a home for 22 years to renting for five years, it tore them to pieces. They felt they were throwing money down the drain. When they bought a home again, the feeling of ownership was wonderful. Yet for some people, owning a home is a totally foreign concept. They can't even imagine it.

When I was in Philadelphia many years ago, you could buy a home there for $1,700. And that was a three or four bedroom, two bath, three level row house. Now if you wanted one with windows in it, you had to pull off the tin and the boards, but you could get one of those for $5,000.

And yet, in spite of that price, it was very difficult to get many of the people there to understand why they ought to own something.

Some people have a highly transitory sense of life. They live paycheck to paycheck, with no investment in the future, whatsoever. Their attitude is completely "live for today."

It's important to understand that there *is* a future. And the very type of person who believes there is a future to prepare for is the type who will buy a home and reap the benefits. That is the type of person who plants a tree. The transitory person will never plant a tree because he is not going to be around to enjoy the shade.

If you want to enjoy the shade, you've got to plant the tree.

Buy a Neighborhood, Not Just a House

Once you've decided home buying is right for you, it's time to search for your dream house, right? Maybe. But even more important than the house itself is the neighborhood you choose.

A wise man once told me, "Hank, in spite of all you do, in spite of all you think of your prowess as a parent or your influence on your children, one-half of all they become is due to the neighborhood you live in."

One of the biggest mistakes people make is to buy a house instead of a neighborhood. A home is a house *plus* a neighborhood. Your neighborhood is where your children will pick up attitudes and philosophies toward higher education, politics, business, debt, spending, saving, free enterprise, sports, finance ... anything and everything. In the words of Winston Churchill: "We shape our dwellings, and afterwards our dwellings shape us."

As you drive around any city in America, you will see that neighborhoods have personalities. When people come into my office, and I learn what neighborhood they're from, I know a lot about them. At least I have some ideas. I can usually guess pretty well something about them or about their neighbors.

The neighborhood I grew up in had a very distinct personality—one that unfortunately bred far more gang members than businessmen. I was raised with six brothers and sisters in a three-bedroom home in the Echo Park area of Los Angeles. We had one bathroom. The kitchen was tiny. The living room, dining room and family room were all combined in an area smaller than my conference room at the office. I lived there for over 20 years. My family lived there for over 30 years. Needless to say, it was *not* in a fancy area of Los Angeles.

I can remember my minister giving me a lecture once when I was about 13 years old because somebody told him that I kept a knife in my pantleg. That was because walking to the neighborhood grocery store about three blocks away after dark was something I liked to do—I didn't want to give up that freedom.

I rebelled a little bit, but I was one of the fortunate people who sought heroes and role models outside my immediate neighborhood. I don't know where all the friends I grew up with are today. I wish I knew. Few of those kids likely got out of there in very good shape.

There's no way to overemphasize how critical it is to determine *now* what environment you want for your family. Ask yourself: What neighborhood "personality" do I feel most comfortable with? What attitudes do I want my children to be exposed to on a daily basis?

It is your job to pick the neighborhood where you want to raise your children. What many people don't realize is that there are well neighborhoods and sick neighborhoods. What's the difference? There are "sick" neighborhoods where people live heavily in debt, covet the big house, live beyond their means, indulge in bickering between spouses, give their children too much and teach by their actions instant gratification, irresponsibility, and ego.

Then there are "well" neighborhoods where people live modestly relative to their means, have peace in their homes, insist that their children work for what they get, and try to teach savings, thrift, and patience.

So, you buy a neighborhood first—*then* buy a house. What do I mean by buying the neighborhood? Simple. You buy the land, the school, and the neighbors, not the house.

This means doing as much research on the neighborhood as you do on the house. When Julie and I were investigating the area where we now reside, we attended church there, we looked at the schools and what portion of kids were going to college, and we spent time getting acquainted with people in the neighborhood.

Ask yourself many questions: Will there be a personality "fit" with your neighbors? An occupational "fit"? A work-ethic "fit"? A political/philosophical "fit"? Is it a mature, stable neighborhood where people own their own homes and maintain their properties? Is it an area where your children can sink in their roots and establish long-term, stable relationships?

How important is higher education to you? In some neighborhoods, 80 percent of the high-school graduates go to college; in others, only 20 percent. If this is important to you, investigate. It will definitely cost more to live in a neighborhood where most of the kids go to college.

This is why, when buying a home, you may get much more square footage per dollar in some areas than others. But keep in mind that the square footage you gain might be offset by losses in other areas. Is it worth it?

I've given this advice to many a client, and some of them don't believe it, and don't follow it. Perhaps one spouse or the other doesn't understand the principle of buying a neighborhood first and instead falls in love with a house. So, the couple will drive into different neighborhoods checking out houses. In some established neighborhoods, they'll see that an old house on a little lot costs just as much as a larger house in a new neighborhood. For many, the temptation is to buy the larger house in the new area.

Character, Character, Character

This is where the problem of new neighborhoods versus old and established neighborhoods comes into play. *Any* new neighborhood lacks character. It may take 10 to 15 years for a neighborhood to develop any level of character. Why? Many of the people that move into that neighborhood are more transient, or are getting moved around by their employer.

Half of the people in that neighborhood may not be there five or eight years later. There may be considerable turnover. There are going to be some people who settle in and sink their roots, and others who are just passing through.

I learned this lesson the hard way many years ago. I decided I was going to get a lot of house for my dollar, so I bought a larger house in a new neighborhood. Over the following five years, our neighbors were constantly coming and going, moving in and out. When I moved in, I had no idea what personality the neighborhood would adopt—it was still in the early stages of growth. I sold my house five years after moving in—for only $1,000 more than I paid for it.

That brings up another important point about new and old neighborhoods. If you buy in a new neighborhood, chances are the value of that neighborhood will appreciate slowly for a number of years, until it has a character established. If that character established is undesirable, the area may appreciate more slowly, level off, or even depreciate in value. If that character is desirable, then after 15 years that neighborhood will begin to appreciate at a much faster rate than before.

But what if you buy into an established neighborhood that already has a desirable character? You are buying in at the higher appreciation rate from the very beginning. You don't have to wait 15 years for the developing character of the neighborhood to determine its market value.

So, where do you buy? You buy in an established neighborhood that already has some desirable characteristics, even if you can only get half the home for your money. Financially speaking, you'll generally be better off to look for an older, established neighborhood and buy a smaller home—then fix it up, expand it, remodel it, and make it into the home you want to have.

After all, you can modify a home. You can't modify a neighborhood.

Now, all of this is great generalization, of course. Will any neighborhood have completely one or another characteristic? Of course not. You wouldn't want it that way.

Your family will get to mix with many different types of personalities wherever you live, and your children will likely have the privilege of mixing with other children of varied backgrounds and cultures. Few people want sterile sameness.

All I am suggesting is that neighborhoods have a large impact on the value system of your family, not to mention the value of your home itself. So choose wisely, from a position of awareness.

How to Qualify to Buy a Home

So you're driving through neighborhoods you want to live in, and perhaps you've found a home you'd like to buy. But how do you convince lenders you are eligible for a mortgage, and how large a mortgage can you qualify for?

Lenders will consider a number of factors, including your annual gross income, your long-term debt, and the amount you have available for a down payment. They will also want a detailed account of your current assets and liabilities.

Let's begin with the down payment. The larger the down payment you can provide, the smaller the mortgage loan you will have to obtain (and the more likely you are to get that loan).

If at all possible, try to make a down payment of 20 percent of the total price of the house. Many first-time buyers may discover they do not have nearly enough available cash to meet this guideline. Fortunately, there are other options.

You might consider taking out an FHA loan, which requires a much lower down payment of 3 to 5 percent, or may not require a down payment at all. Other lenders might also cater to first-time homebuyers by accepting low down payments. But keep in mind that the smaller the down payment, the higher other costs will be.

Another option would be to ask for help from family members. If you do, it is far better for them to give you the money rather than loaning it to you. Why? Because lenders will take into consideration your long-term debt when determining whether or not you qualify for a mortgage. If a family member loans you the money, it is automatically tacked onto your long-term debt total, reducing your chances of being approved.

In general, lenders will allow a household to devote up to 28 percent of its gross monthly income to cover housing costs, including the mortgage payment, property taxes and insurance. Debt payments, including housing costs and long-term debt, usually may not exceed 33 to 38 percent of your gross monthly income.

How expensive a home can you buy? The rule of thumb is that you can acquire a mortgage up to 2 1/2 times your annual gross income (the amount you make before taxes). So, if your combined household income is $50,000 before taxes, a prudent mortgage would be $125,000 or less.

It never hurts to prequalify yourself before you find the home you wish to buy. You can do this by running the numbers past a lending institution to see how much they will consider loaning you for a home mortgage. See if the numbers add up.

If you find you won't be able to qualify when you *do* decide to apply, consider taking one of the following steps to improve your status in the lender's eyes.

- Pay off your existing debts with the highest "payment-to-principal" ratio so you will be in a more favorable position.
- Wait until your income increases.
- Save up for a larger down payment so you will not need to borrow as much money for your mortgage.
- Work to provide some "sweat equity" to lower your down payment.

See the worksheet in *Your Money Happiness Workbook* to determine how much home you may qualify for.

The Most Efficient Way to Pay Off Your Home

Why do we spend time discussing how to qualify for a mortgage when Chapter 10 counseled against going into debt? Because for most of us it is probably appropriate—even necessary—to go into debt for a home. Owning a home is a way of life; it's not a luxury, but a necessity. In spite of this, not all families take the important steps to protect their mortgage, and most families do not make the most of their mortgage payments.

During the term of a typical 30-year mortgage, the chance of a 35-year-old homeowner's death is one in four. Many of those families would have to sell their homes if the breadwinner died.

If you or your spouse died prematurely, would your family have the financial resources to live where they choose? Would they want to remain in their home? Move to a smaller home? Rent an apartment? Families who have lost a loved one are already making painful emotional adjustments. The last thing they need is financial difficulties *and* the social/emotional adjustments of moving to a new neighborhood.

So, it is important to provide a way to cover mortgage costs in the event of the breadwinner's death. But, because most homeowners will live to pay off their mortgage, it is important to plan for that as well. You can kill two birds with one stone here. The mortgage acceleration plan can help you accomplish multiple objectives with the same dollar.

There are a number of bases to cover with your home mortgage. First, you should enter into a life insurance policy to provide a mortgage payoff and fund the family's living arrangements in the event of premature death. In addition, you could avoid substantial interest expense by putting additional dollars toward the early payoff of your mortgage.

Take the case of Scott and Sue. Scott and Sue had a home mortgage of $100,000 at 9 percent interest, with a monthly payment of $804. This was a conventional fixed-rate loan over 30 years. With interest added in, the payments on a typical mortgage will total almost three times the amount borrowed. If Scott and Sue paid their mortgage off over 30 years, they would end up paying over $289,000. So, they considered refinancing their loan in order to have it paid off in a 15-year period. That would have increased their monthly payment to $1,013, or $209 per month more.

Should they go with the 15-year mortgage or stay with the 30-year mortgage? One might suggest the more conservative approach would be to pay off the mortgage in 15 years, but that is not the way a creditor looks at it. In fact, whether the mortgage is paid off in 15 or 30 years really is irrelevant—either way, it looks so far into the future that you can't anticipate setbacks or progress that can occur in the intervening years.

Of far more concern to a banker is your monthly cash flow. In this case, the 30-year mortgage with an $804 monthly payment is actually considered a more conservative or lower-risk approach than the 15-year mortgage.

If both mortgages are at the same 9 percent interest, where does that extra $209 go? It goes 100 percent toward principal. But does somebody still need some life insurance in order to pay off the $100,000 mortgage upon the premature death of the breadwinner? Of course. Let's say a $100,000 term life insurance policy is going to cost around $20 a month.

Use Your Money Most Efficiently

Consider Scott and Sue's wisest alternatives for meeting their mortgage obligation. Assume that the $229 ($209 difference between the 15- and 30-year mortgage payments plus the $20 policy premium) was instead put into a permanent life insurance policy. Scott and Sue visited with their financial adviser, who explained to them that the $229 would purchase a $100,000 permanent policy that would pay off the mortgage in the event of the breadwinner's death. In addition, it would accumulate cash values on a tax-sheltered basis. Due to this accumulation, the total cash values inside the policy would roughly equal the remaining principal balance still owing on the home at about year 15 to 17.

What did Scott and Sue accomplish?

They were ahead in a number of ways:

- They provided for the mortgage to be paid off in the event of the breadwinner's death.
- They saved money by accumulating the approximate equivalent of the mortgage payoff amount in the same number of years as if they had a 15-year mortgage.
- They retained the increased interest deduction on their mortgage loan, providing a *further* tax/cash flow advantage.
- Because their cash is still accessible within the insurance policy, and not locked into the bricks and mortar of their home, it may also meet the objectives of an emergency fund, a college savings fund, or some other purpose.
- The cash values inside the policy grow on a tax-sheltered basis.

- The plan provides a convenient forced savings program.
- They retain the primary tax advantages associated with owner-ship of the home.
- The surviving spouse has the flexibility to decide whether or not to pay off the mortgage in the case of death.
- They will have additional cash available at retirement.

So, Scott and Sue not only achieved the same objectives as if they had a 15-year mortgage or made one extra mortgage payment per year, but they also benefited in other ways. They made the most efficient use of their money, and so can you.

Don't Mortgage Your Home

Many bankers, accountants, and financial planners are recommending home equity loans, the old "second mortgage." Don't succumb to their persuasive arguments—much wisdom is omitted. In my opinion, this is one of the questions to ask to discern whether or not a financial adviser complies with correct principles. Trust your *feelings* on this decision. (For a thorough discussion on this, review Chapter 10.)

Your Insights, Feelings, and Action Items

A. As you read this chapter, what *insights* came that seem applicable to *you?*
  1._____
  2._____
  3._____

B. How did you *feel* as you pondered particular points of this chapter?
  1._____
  2._____
  3._____

C. What do you *feel* you should *do* as a result of this chapter?
  1._____
  2._____
  3._____

D. How might you solicit the aid of others in accomplishing "C" above?
  _____
  _____
  _____

Chapter 18

How to Solidify Your Foundation: Risk Management and Insurance

Establishing security begins by building your financial plan on a solid foundation. Life, property, liability, health, and disability insurance are all part of that foundation. As you add the other elements of your financial program, you can't afford to have cracks in your foundation.

So, how do you build the kind of foundation that is solid enough to support a tremendous financial plan?

First, you need to learn more about risk. Risk can be part of investments in the upper part of your financial success pyramid. But risk should never be part of your foundation.

What to Do about Risk

The purpose of insurance is to minimize risk. Risk minimization is vital in providing for the security and safety of those you love.

There are three things you can do with risk: You can avoid it, absorb it, or transfer it.

First, do everything you can to avoid risk by using trusts and family limited partnerships. By minimizing risks in your lifestyle. By being competent. By being attentive. There are specific things you can do to avoid risk—they're discussed later.

If there are risks you can't avoid, see if you can absorb them. Increase the deductibles on your car insurance, homeowners insurance, or health insurance, for example. (In essence, you're insuring yourself for the amount of that deductible.)

If there are risks you can't avoid or absorb, transfer them through some kind of insurance. You'll learn how in this chapter.

How Much Life Insurance Should You Have? Analyze Your Needs

People of character purchase adequate life insurance to protect those they love.

I don't know your specific situation—but you may be able to analyze your own needs by looking at a typical situation. The average breadwinner needs a death benefit of $400,000 to $600,000.

Sounds like a lot, doesn't it?

Perhaps. Let's see what you'll need to cover with that money. As you look at what you'll need, *don't base your projection on your current lifestyle*. Look ahead—at least three to five years—to the job you want to have, the number of children you want to have, the home you hope to live in, the neighborhood you want to settle in. *That's* what you'll want to protect.

Funds Required at Your Death

Let's work through an analysis of your needs. Make notes of the amount that seems right for you. Then repeat the exercise for your spouse.

Immediate expense fund. You'll need some immediate cash to pay the bills presented after your death. That could include medical and hospital expenses, burial expenses, attorneys or executor fees, federal and state taxes, estate taxes, and probate court costs.

The typical funeral costs between $5,000 and $7,000, including burial expenses. Since most people die as a result of an accident or illness, there are also medical bills. Medical insurance usually doesn't cover 100 percent of those expenses. *Assuming* you have adequate health insurance, the medical expenses not covered by insurance will probably range between $1,000 and $5,000.

The total? Figuring $7,000 for the funeral and burial, and $3,000 for additional medical expenses, the total is $10,000.

Debt liquidation. You also need to plan for paying off installment credit, unpaid notes, school and auto loans, outstanding bills, credit cards, and other debts. As an average, those bills total $15,000 per working adult. Total your debt.

Emergency fund. You'll need an emergency fund to pay unexpected bills that you can't easily pay with your regular income—things like replacing the roof on your house, rebuilding the engine of your automobile, or paying for a medical emergency.

Let's look a little more closely at this emergency fund. It assumes you have a sound and prudent insurance program—because it's a separate stash of money that you don't use *except in an emergency.* You use it when you *have* to pay for something, and you have no other way to cover the expense.

Want an example? Your child is hospitalized after a bicycling accident, and you face a large deductible to the surgeon, anesthesiologist, hospital, and physical therapist. You need to fly to Virginia to attend your father's funeral. A creek running past your backyard floods your basement, causing $20,000 in damage—and your homeowner's insurance doesn't cover "ground water." You forgot to pay your auto insurance, your brakes locked up, and you ran into a luxury car. Your company cuts back, you are laid off, and you need the money to cover basic expenses.

How much money would you want available in case of those kinds of emergencies? Between $20,000 and $40,000 would be a minimum. You may need more, depending on the number of children you have, the size of home you live in, and your lifestyle. I recommend three months gross income or six months living expenses.

Mortgage/rent payment fund. How much would you need to pay off your mortgage? If you're renting, how much would you need to pay your rent for 10 years? (Before you answer, remember that rent increases with inflation; you need to build in an amount that yields *at least* the inflation rate after taxes.)

There's something else you need to consider: Do you want to stay in the home you currently own? Or would you like your surviving spouse and children to move to a more stable, secure neighborhood?

For example, let's say you're a new college graduate living in an apartment or a small starter home. Perhaps you and your spouse have dreamed of a nicer home or neighborhood and better opportunities for your children. Well, just because you happen to step in front of a truck, does that mean that your spouse's and children's dreams disappear? Of course not. So, you may want to allow a higher mortgage payment amount.

For now, assume you'll need $130,000 to $180,000.

Is this a lot of money? No. Will it buy a luxury home in a fancy neighborhood? Certainly not. But it will provide a modest home in a stable middle-income neighborhood. Settle on the amount you'll need for your locale.

Child care/home care fund. When your spouse dies, you will automatically have some additional expenses.

Like what?

When one spouse dies, the surviving spouse has to pay for chores and odd jobs the deceased spouse always did around the house—changing the oil in the car, preparing meals, making electrical repairs, doing minor remodeling, maintaining the house, mowing the lawn, changing the washers on the faucets, unplugging the drains, washing clothes, doing heavy landscaping and yard work, and so on. How much will the surviving spouse need? An average is about $2,000 a year for 10 years, or $20,000.

What if there are preschool children who need to be cared for? The surviving spouse can't simply quit work and stay home—then no one would cover the expenses. Instead, he or she will have to pay child care expenses until the children are old enough to take care of themselves.

Here's something else to think about: Often when a parent dies, children do not merely live in a one-parent family. Instead, they become virtual *orphans*. This is especially relevant when both parents work outside the home. Why? Because the surviving spouse has to spend that much additional time covering for the spouse who dies. If the surviving spouse wasn't working, he or she must now get a job. When the surviving spouse comes home from work, he or she has to maintain the household—do the shopping, cook meals, clean the house, do laundry, run the errands, and take care of home maintenance. There's not much time left for the children. What about hiring a nanny to take care of some of those tasks? How much would that cost?

Additionally, even if you're the sole breadwinner, you may want to replace *your own* earning power in case of the death of your nonworking spouse.

To see what I mean, let's use me as an example. I work 60 hours a week. Right now, I make it to most of my children's Little League games and most of their school programs; in fact, I'm there more often than most of the other fathers. When I get home at night, I visit with our older children while my wife Julie is tucking our small children into bed and reading them a story.

If Julie died, would I want to continue working 60 hours a week? Absolutely not! I would want to have the financial resources so I could cut back to 30 hours a week. I would want to be home when my young children come through the door from elementary school. I would want to hire someone else to do the maintenance around the house so I could tuck my children in and read them stories. Simply, I would want to be able to fill in for Julie. I do not want my children to be emotional orphans.

What does that mean? If I cut back from 60 hours a week to 30 hours a week, what's going to happen to my income? It will be cut in half. (This is an especially critical calculation if both spouses are working.)

What do I need to do to prepare for that possibility? I need to put enough insurance on my wife Julie to replace her earning capacity and reflect her economic value—and to replace my earning capacity and reflect *my* economic value as well.

Think about that. If you lose your spouse, perhaps you'll want to be able to take off a week for summer camp, take off on Fridays for Scout camps, be at Little League games and piano recitals, and be at the Christmas program.

Okay. Think about cutting your income by $10,000 to $40,000 a year. Multiply that by 10 years. Looking at it this way, you can see why $120,000 to $400,000 in insurance may be appropriate on a nonworking spouse just to cover child care, home care, and the lost earnings of the breadwinner so the children don't become emotional orphans.

Educational/vocational fund. The cost of a four-year undergraduate education or comparable vocational training will vary by state and type of school. You should plan on about $40,000 per child, or $10,000 per year. You'll need to plan on more if your child will be living away from home or attending a private college.

You may have a different arrangement with your children—you may offer to pay for 50 percent of their education, for example, or for tuition and books only. Your children may be responsible for their own housing, transportation, food, and clothing. Whatever your decision, make sure you plan for enough to provide the opportunity you had intended.

College-age children often have other expenses as well, and you need to plan for those. Perhaps you would like to provide your child the opportunity to enroll in a study abroad program in Europe or Asia. Or, do you want to consider the cost of graduate school, an internship or fellowship which might open doors of opportunity?

You may also want to plan for the expenses of your child's wedding; you should plan for $5,000 to $10,000, depending on what you want to cover. Some weddings run $30,000 and more. You decide.

Finally, estate taxes. What about federal and state estate taxes? If your estate is substantial, you should also consider the amount you'll need to cover estate taxes. Estate taxes generally kick in if you have an estate of $600,000 per person, or $1.2 million for a married couple. The minimum tax rate is 38 percent of the amount over $600,000, and it grows to 55 percent at $3 million. An estate of $700,000, then, would owe estate taxes of $38,000.

What's included in an "estate"? Generally, it includes the value of your home, death benefits on insurance policies you own, investment portfolios, retirement plans, cars, and all other personal property. When all that is figured, many people exceed the limit—and owe estate taxes. And insurance is the least expensive way to pay estate taxes. (For more on this, see Chapter 25.)

The envelope, please. Now you have some idea of the lump-sum expenses you'll have presented to you at the death of a spouse. You'll be handed a check from the life insurance company—and you're assuming that, after taxes, your money is going to keep up with inflation.

If inflation is 5 percent, and you're in a 40 percent tax bracket, you need to earn *at least* 8 to 9 percent on your money just to keep up with inflation—just so your money will still pay for the emergency funds, debt liquidation, mortgage, and college educations.

These lump-sum expenses total $285,000 to $360,000. Those are absolute minimums.

That's the lump sum your heirs need to be presented with if you die. But note *that sum doesn't include your usual living expenses*—the money you need from one month to the next, from one year to the next, just to pay the light bill, buy groceries, and otherwise maintain your lifestyle.

Funding cash flow needs. How much will it cost for you or your heirs to live from month to month? That depends on your lifestyle—but according to a U.S. Bureau of Labor Statistics study, it takes 60 to 70 percent of the breadwinner's income in order for heirs to remain in their own world. And this assumes educational expenses are provided for separately and the mortgage on the residence is paid. Since two-income families outspend their one-income counterparts, they should assume they'll need 70 percent of the family's income upon the passing of either spouse.

So, let's assume your annual income is $50,000. You multiply it by, say, 70 percent, giving a need of $35,000. Assuming you have two children under age 18, you subtract an additional $9,600 for Social Security income. (Assume Social Security will pay about $400 per month per child under age 18.) This leaves a need of $25,400. Next, look at the following chart to see how much capital you will need.

Amount of Capital Required to Meet Annual Income Needs

Annual Income Needed for Survivors	Expected Investment Returns			
	Conservative ◄————————————————►			Optimistic
	4%	6%	8%	10%
$15,000	$375,000	$250,000	$188,000	$150,000
20,000	500,000	333,000	250,000	200,000
25,000	625,000	417,000	313,000	250,000
30,000	750,000	500,000	375,000	300,000
35,000	875,000	583,000	437,000	350,000
40,000	1,000,000	667,000	500,000	400,000
45,000	1,125,000	750,000	563,000	450,000
50,000	1,250,000	833,000	625,000	500,000

Notes:
1. Do you want to be optimistic or conservative when providing a security program for loved ones?
2. If you want an inflation-adjusted income, first determine what you believe is a realistic return. Then subtract your inflation expectation to arrive at an after-inflation expectation of investment returns.
3. If your income need is greater than $50,000, simply add the numbers together. For example, if your need is $80,000 and you are assuming 6 percent, you will need $1,333,000 ($500,000 + $833,000).

Now, let's assume you pay off the immediate bills, and invest $250,000 at 10 percent. That would generate $25,000 in interest a year indefinitely, right? That's interest only. Are you ever going to dip into the principal? No.

Here's where a fallacy creeps in. You have assumed the interest will last forever—that you will never dip into the principal. Now let's look at reality. During the first year, let's say you'll need $25,000 to meet expenses. With inflation, you'll need $26,000 the second year. The third year, you'll need $27,000. The amount starts compounding. The next year, it's $28,500. Then $30,000. That's reality: Because of inflation, you'll need increasingly more every year.

What happens, then? You start dipping into principal. It's just a tiny dip—maybe $1,000. Then what happens? The principal that's left generates less interest. The next year, you have to dip in a little more—and what's left generates even less interest. The whole process snowballs until your money is gone—and it only takes about 11 or 12 years to disappear. So, even under these assumptions, your insurance proceeds will be gone and your surviving spouse would have to return to work.

When you are figuring out how much insurance you need, calculate your annual expenses. If you want an inflation-adjusted income, subtract your assumed inflation rate from your expected rate of return.

To complete a thorough analysis of your needs, see *Your Money Happiness Workbook* and visit with a qualified financial adviser.

Why the "Theory of Decreasing Needs" Doesn't Hold Up

You've probably heard that people need less insurance as they get older. After all, their children have left home. Their mortgage is paid. Survivors simply don't need as much. This is called *the theory of decreasing needs*. It simply doesn't work.

You might have an insurance salesperson recommend a decreasing term policy (one in which the death benefit declines over the years) or a level term policy (one in which the death benefit remains level). You might have a salesperson suggest that you simply cancel your policy as the term premiums get too expensive. You might even be told to cash your policy in at age 55.

All of those recommendations seem to make sense. Unfortunately, they don't hold in the real world.

Here's why:

Let's assume you have a level term insurance policy for $100,000. If inflation is 5 percent, your death benefit will have decreased to the purchasing power of about $21,000 between the time you buy it at age 25 and the time you are 55. By the time you're 65, your policy will have a value of less than $13,000. In other words, even *if* you need less money as you get older, you need to hold on to that full death benefit just to have a *little* coverage by the time you're 65.

Second, let's say you die when you're 60. What's your spouse's life expectancy? In the United States today, your spouse could very easily live an additional 20 to 30 years. Obviously, you'll need investments that are working for you—and plenty of death benefit from your life insurance.

Does Self-Insurance Work?

What about the argument that you'll ultimately become self-insured as your investments grow and accumulate? Your investments might not grow, and you might not build an estate. Your surviving spouse will still need insurance. On the other hand, your investments might grow, and you might build a significant estate. At the exact rate you build an estate and become self-insuring, your insurance need for *protection* purposes may decline, but your need to pay *estate taxes* is increasing. In that case, your surviving spouse will still need insurance to pay those estate taxes.

A great industrialist in my neighborhood discovered he had cancer as he was applying for a $50 million whole life policy. A $50 million whole life policy on a 55-year-old man has an annual premium of hundreds of thousands of dollars. Why would he want to pay those kinds of premiums? Because the best financial, tax, legal, and estate planning advice his money could buy suggested the lowest-cost way to fund his estate taxes was through the purchase of a life insurance policy.

Forbes magazine publisher Malcolm Forbes purchased all the life insurance he could until he was in his late 70s. Why? For estate taxes.

As mentioned, your heirs will have to pay estate taxes if your estate exceeds $600,000. That sounds like a lot, but it's not: At 8 percent interest, $600,000 would provide a $30,000 annual after-tax retirement income. That's not much to build a retirement plan on.

There are plenty of problems with the theory of decreasing needs. I've observed one of the biggest problems firsthand. I've seen many successful people who purchased insurance programs for their families when they were 25. By the time they were 40 or 45, they let their policies lapse. Then, at age 55 or 60, they suddenly realize they're going to have an estate tax problem. So they rush to buy million-dollar insurance policies. What happens? The premiums are horribly expensive for people that age. They kick themselves for letting that original policy—with plenty of coverage—lapse.

To Choose Term or Whole Life: An Analogy

Don and Kathy faced a dilemma. They knew they were long overdue for purchasing life insurance, but they couldn't decide whether to buy term or whole life insurance. Unsure about the distinctions between the two, they went to their financial adviser, David, for clarification. "Don, Kathy, the simplest way to understand term and whole life insurance is to use a little analogy," he explained. "Term and whole life can be compared to renting vs. buying a home." Don's wrinkled brow and Kathy's puzzled look told David he had his work cut out for him.

"When you rent a house, your rental payments start out low," David began. "But, thanks to inflation, those payments climb over time. The same thing happens when you buy term insurance. Your premiums start out low, but, because of your increased chance of dying with age, those premiums climb over time."

Make Fixed Payments

"Payments aren't the only comparison between term life and renting," the adviser continued. "Once you pay your rent, then live out the month in the house, your rental money's gone. Once you pay your term insurance premium, then live out the month, your premium money's gone."

"Yeah, but aren't whole life premium payments higher than term?" Don asked.

"Yes, at first," David said. "But look at it this way. If you buy a home with a conventional 30-year fixed-rate mortgage, your payments at first will be quite a bit higher than if you were renting. But once you qualify for that home and start making payments, those payments stay the same for the next 30 years. And as your income goes up, those payments get easier to make."

Kathy jumped in, "So you're saying once you've purchased a permanent policy, just like buying a house, the premium payments stay the same for the rest of our lives. And as our income goes up, those payments get easier to make."

Build Up Equity

"Exactly," David replied. "And that's not the only comparison between permanent insurance and buying a home. Once you make a rent payment, it's gone. But when you make a mortgage payment, you make an investment. You're building equity. It's only a small amount at first—but it grows with time. It compounds. There are two reasons why this happens: First, you pay down the amount you owe on your mortgage; second, the house appreciates in value."

David told them that, at some point, buying becomes less expensive than renting. The crossover happens when the net cost of renting is more than the net cost of buying a home (your mortgage payment minus tax savings minus the increase in equity. In other words, in time the increase in equity due to appreciation means you have no cost at all, but rather a *gain* on your purchase).

"The same thing happens with permanent insurance," he explained.

"How?" Kathy asked.

As the conversation continued, Don and Kathy found they could relate to the analogy. They discovered that, like home ownership, permanent insurance builds equity. And that equity is invested at a good, tax-sheltered interest rate. After seven or eight years of building equity (cash values), their net cost for permanent insurance would be less than for term life, *even* assuming they were investing the difference.

"What does that tell you?" David asked. "If you expect to live fewer than eight years, buy term insurance. Or if you're using the insurance to cover a temporary need—such as covering a short-term bank loan—then buy term. But regardless of your age when you buy the policy, if you're planning on living eight years or more, you'll have a lower long-term net cost by buying permanent insurance. By the way, Don and Kathy, you should buy life insurance as soon as you can. The younger you are when you buy your policy, the greater your eventual equity. For every $100,000 of death benefit, every year you wait to buy costs you about $5,000 (increased premiums plus loss in cash values over time)."

Getting Out Your Equity

He took the analogy one step further. "Don, if you want to get out the equity you've built in your home, what can you do?"

"You can borrow against your equity, or you can sell your home," Don replied.

"Right. You have exactly the same options with cash value insurance," David said. "If you want to get out the equity you've built in your insurance policy, you can either borrow against your policy, or you can sell it—surrender it to the company, which will pay you your equity.

"Here's where the analogy breaks down: If you want to borrow against the equity in your home, do you have to qualify for the loan? Yes. Do you have to have a job? Yes. Do you have to prove income? Yes. Do you have to have a solid credit rating? Yes. Does the bank establish a fixed monthly repayment schedule? Most of the time, yes. If you miss any of those fixed monthly payments, does the bank report you to the credit bureau? Yes.

"When you borrow against the equity in your insurance policy, on the other hand, you write down your policy number, sign your name, and indicate where you want the check sent. Seven to 10 days later, you get your check. There's no loan application. It's private. It's not disclosed—to credit reporting agencies, to courts, to anybody. You repay it if, when, and in the amounts you want."

That was enough for Don and Kathy. They were convinced they would live far longer than eight years. And they liked having the option to borrow against the equity in their policies. Whole life was the best vehicle for their insurance needs.

Amortizing Administrative Costs

There's another reason why term ends up being more expensive than whole life in the long run. There are certain costs incurred when a policy of any kind is put on the books. Those costs include the agent's commission, the medical underwriting, the marketing, and the advertising. They also include staffing, administrative expenses, and overhead. Those costs generally total more than the first year's premiums. And they have to be amortized over the life of the policy.

How much does that add to the cost of the policy? The average term policy stays on the books for four years. The average whole life policy stays on the books for 16 years. That's a 4-to-1 ratio.

The result? Those acquisition costs will be amortized over 16 years for a whole life policy. They'll be amortized over four years for a term policy. Which is higher? The answer is obvious. The typical buyer of term policies will buy four policies in the length of time a consumer pursuing a whole life strategy will have bought one. And whether he did or didn't, he has purchased a policy that is priced as though he had.

Insuring Your Insurance

What happens if, somewhere along the line, you can't make your premium payments? You become disabled. A recession comes along. There are layoffs at work. You have some financial setbacks. Somebody in the family needs help.

What happens then?

It depends. If you have term insurance and can't make your payments, you lose your policy. Your family's security program is gone. And if something has happened to your insurability, that security may be gone forever. Term insurance is an *insecure security* program.

If you have permanent insurance and you have paid the premiums for a couple of years, you may cut your premiums by having them paid from cash values. This pays your premiums for you and keeps your policy in force—perhaps for years, if you need it to. It makes your security program secure—regardless of setbacks you may have. I like *secure security* programs. No cracks in the foundation.

You may actually vanish the premium on many whole life policies within seven to nine years (and as early as five or six years with some high-cash policies). You *probably* won't have to make payments on it again—but the cash value will continue to build.

Protect Your Policy

In case of bankruptcy or creditor claims, cash value in a life insurance policy is traditionally considered protected property. (Cash values in annuities, your primary residence, and qualified retirement plans like IRAs, Keoghs, and corporate pension and profit-sharing plans are also traditionally protected.)

That's not the case with cash in banks, CDs, money market funds, stocks, bonds, mutual funds, real estate, or other similar investments. That cash is up for grabs in a bankruptcy. Consider that when you are considering buying term and investing the difference.

Benefit from "Forced" Savings

Simply stated, whole life forces you to save money.

One of my first clients earned his MBA at the same time I did. At that time, he was struggling like most graduates. He had four children, was just finishing his degree, and was going to work for American Express. He made $28,000 a year in 1979, and he budgeted $300 a month for life insurance. That was a lot of his income.

He took out a policy on himself, a small policy on his wife, and policies on each of his children. His goal was to start accumulating cash.

That went on for eight years. By then, he was earning $36,000 a year. He took a look at his insurance premiums. They were 10 percent of his annual income.

I recently went to visit him. Now he has six children. He has moved into an upgraded, but still fairly modest, home. The home cost him $80,000 some years ago, and he has $20,000 equity in it. He lives in a fairly modest neighborhood. He owes a little money on his car. He's trying to figure out how to put his six children through college.

He was considering buying some term insurance. So I opened up his current policy, and we took a look. We discovered that it was as if 100 percent of every premium payment he had made all those years had gone straight into cash value.

His whole life policy represented $35,000 in cash value. He only had $20,000 equity in his home. In other words, the most significant asset he has is the $35,000 cash value in his whole life policies. Yes—it was tough for him to keep paying that $300 a month. But when he saw what he had built, he decided to keep doing it.

In five years, that equity will more than double to about $70,000. Fifteen years from now, he'll have $150,000 in cash from those policies.

None of his neighbors will have that kind of cash. Why will he have it? He got started while he was young. He made a commitment. He stuck to it. He socked those dollars away. He and his wife forgot about it. They worked it into their budget. Over the years they had some financial struggles, and his wife went to work off and on, but they kept putting the dollars away. And now they are home free.

Let's Analyze the Numbers

So far we have been discussing term vs. permanent insurance from a subjective, nonquantitative viewpoint. But let's look at the numbers. On the following pages we have compared a permanent policy vs. a term policy and a side-fund invested into mutual funds. Note that the cash value of the permanent policy typically bypasses the investment side-fund in years seven through 10. And notice the difference at retirement.

Beware the Ultimate Rip-off

What's the ultimate rip-off?

Simply, the ultimate rip-off is someone who tries to convince you that any single kind of *insurance* is a rip-off.

Lots of insurance companies work hard to convince consumers to buy term and invest the difference. These companies insist that whole life is a rip-off.

Then there are whole-life agents who insist that term insurance is a rip-off.

The truth? There are advantages to both. Both have their place. What you buy should be dictated by your individual situation, not by an aggressive salesperson. *Anyone* who suggests an extreme position is either attempting to defy the fact that we have a competitive marketplace, or just does not understand insurance. (There is perhaps more financial pornography written on this subject than any other.)

Age: 35 **Male**   Annual Planned Premium $3,000.00

Initial Guaranteed Death Benefit of $250,000
Variable Life vs. Term Plus Side Fund
Assuming Current Rates and a Gross Rate of 12% (Net Rate 10.71%)
Portfolio Management Fee of 1.29% and a Marginal Tax Rate of 35%

Bill   Bob

					After-Tax		Combined
		Total			Side Fund	Term	Beg of Yr
		Account	Death	Term	Amount	Value at	Death	Death
Year	Outlay	Value	Benefit	Cost	Invested	12.00%	Benefit	Benefit
1	3,000	2,343	250,000	302	2,698	2,886	247,302	250,000
2	3,000	5,174	250,000	302	2,698	5,972	244,416	250,000
3	3,000	8,288	250,000	303	2,697	9,272	241,331	250,000
4	3,000	11,715	250,000	314	2,686	12,790	238,042	250,000
5	3,000	15,483	250,000	324	2,676	16,542	234,534	250,000
	15,000				13,454			
6	3,000	19,627	250,000	338	2,662	20,541	230,796	250,000
7	3,000	24,186	250,000	356	2,644	24,798	226,816	250,000
8	3,000	29,204	250,000	375	2,625	29,332	222,577	250,000
9	3,000	34,731	250,000	395	2,605	34,160	218,063	250,000
10	3,000	40,905	250,000	421	2,579	39,296	213,261	250,000
	30,000				26,569			
11	3,000	47,840	250,000	452	2,548	44,757	208,156	250,000
12	3,000	55,527	250,000	468	2,532	50,580	202,711	250,000
13	3,000	64,057	250,000	483	2,517	56,793	196,903	250,000
14	3,000	73,526	250,000	502	2,498	63,417	190,709	250,000
15	3,000	84,045	250,000	521	2,479	70,482	184,104	250,000
	45,000				39,143			
16	3,000	95,799	250,000	542	2,458	78,017	177,060	250,000
17	3,000	108,792	267,616	617	2,383	85,995	187,217	267,616
18	3,000	123,108	293,626	730	2,270	94,409	205,360	293,626
19	3,000	138,879	321,283	873	2,127	103,255	224,747	312,283
20	3,000	156,245	350,739	1,042	1,958	112,536	245,526	350,739
	60,000				50,339			
25	3,000	273,034	530,532	2,690	310	164,615	376,630	530,532
	75,000				55,854			
30	3,000	461,110	784,810	7,462	– 4,462	218,093	580,909	784,810
	90,000				45,107			
35	3,000	759,537	1,149,635	22,593	– 19,593	234,125	930,745	1,149,635
	105,000				– 15,027			

Compare

Age: **45 Male**   Annual Planned Premium **$4,000.00**

Initial Guaranteed Death Benefit of **$250,000**
Variable Life vs. Term Plus Side Fund
Assuming Current Rates and a Gross Rate of 12% (Net Rate 10.71%)
Portfolio Management Fee of 1.29% and a Marginal Tax Rate of 35%

John   **Jim**

| | | | | | | After-Tax Side Fund Value at | Term Death | Combined Beg of Yr Death |
| | | Total Account | Death | Term | Amount | | | |
Year	Outlay	Value	Benefit	Cost	Invested	12.00%	Benefit	Benefit
1	4,000	2,989	250,000	526	3,474	3,716	246,526	250,000
2	4,000	6,500	250,000	550	3,450	7,665	242,834	250,000
3	4,000	10,336	250,000	576	3,424	11,861	238,911	250,000
4	4,000	14,526	250,000	606	3,394	16,316	234,746	250,000
5	4,000	19,106	250,000	640	3,360	21,046	230,324	250,000
	20,000				17,102			
6	4,000	24,137	250,000	677	3,323	26,065	225,631	250,000
7	4,000	29,664	250,000	719	3,281	31,389	220,654	250,000
8	4,000	35,737	250,000	763	3,237	37,036	215,374	250,000
9	4,000	42,412	250,000	818	3,182	43,017	209,782	250,000
10	4,000	49,855	250,000	874	3,126	49,355	203,857	250,000
	40,000				33,252			
11	4,000	58,215	250,000	939	3,061	56,064	197,584	250,000
12	4,000	67,459	250,000	1,003	2,997	63,172	190,939	250,000
13	4,000	77,701	250,000	1,076	2,924	70,696	183,904	250,000
14	4,000	89,069	250,000	1,151	2,849	78,664	176,455	250,000
15	4,000	101,699	250,000	1,232	2,768	87,100	168,568	250,000
	60,000				47,861			
16	4,000	115,757	250,000	1,314	2,686	96,035	160,214	250,000
17	4,000	131,386	250,000	1,394	2,606	105,506	151,359	250,000
18	4,000	148,681	266,376	1,637	2,363	115,377	158,507	266,376
19	4,000	167,665	292,692	2,030	1,970	125,515	175,345	292,692
20	4,000	188,495	320,818	2,523	1,477	135,830	193,827	320,818
	80,000				58,954			
21	4,000	211,344	350,937	3,139	861	146,204	214,247	350,937
22	4,000	236,400	383,228	3,888	112	156,500	236,911	383,228
23	4,000	263,863	417,827	4,880	– 880	166,451	262,207	417,827
24	4,000	293,954	454,952	6,186	– 2,186	175,698	290,687	454,952
25	4,000	326,910	494,810	7,873	– 3,873	183,784	322,985	494,810
	100,000				52,987			
30	4,000	543,709	744,229	25,795	– 21,795	180,668	575,317	744,229

Compare

Age: 55 Male   Annual Planned Premium $7,000.00

Initial Guaranteed Death Benefit of $250,000
Variable Life vs. Term Plus Side Fund
Assuming Current Rates and a Gross Rate of 12% (Net Rate 10.71%)
Portfolio Management Fee of 1.29% and a Marginal Tax Rate of 35%

Ted   Fred

					After-Tax		Combined
	Total				Side Fund	Term	Beg of Yr
	Account	Death	Term	Amount	Value at	Death	Death
Year	Outlay	Value	Benefit	Cost	Invested	12.00%	Benefit	Benefit
1	7,000	5,364	250,000	1,149	5,851	6,259	244,149	250,000
2	7,000	11,439	250,000	1,238	5,762	12,858	237,979	250,000
3	7,000	18,048	250,000	1,342	5,658	19,805	231,484	250,000
4	7,000	25,249	250,000	1,452	5,548	27,118	224,647	250,000
5	7,000	33,102	250,000	1,574	5,426	34,808	217,457	250,000
	35,000				28,246			
6	7,000	41,696	250,000	1,706	5,294	42,893	209,898	250,000
7	7,000	51,114	250,000	1,843	5,157	51,394	201,950	250,000
8	7,000	61,450	250,000	1,988	5,012	60,332	193,594	250,000
9	7,000	72,810	250,000	2,136	4,864	69,733	184,804	250,000
10	7,000	85,492	250,000	2,290	4,710	79,624	175,557	250,000
	70,000				53,282			
11	7,000	99,777	250,000	2,441	4,559	90,043	165,817	250,000
12	7,000	115,661	250,000	2,570	4,430	101,048	155,527	250,000
13	7,000	133,387	250,000	2,715	4,285	112,665	144,666	250,000
14	7,000	153,249	250,000	2,862	4,138	124,932	133,197	250,000
15	7,000	175,385	265,463	3,366	3,634	137,515	136,896	265,463
	105,000				74,329			
16	7,000	198,587	294,127	4,317	2,683	149,956	153,929	294,127
17	7,000	225,019	326,435	5,573	1,427	161,919	175,051	326,435
18	7,000	253,936	360,995	7,152	– 152	173,026	199,228	360,995
19	7,000	285,568	398,168	9,141	– 2,141	182,778	227,283	398,168
20	7,000	320,161	438,237	11,692	– 4,692	190,481	260,151	438,237
	140,000				71,454			
21	7,000	357,970	481,434	15,013	– 8,013	195,168	298,966	481,434
22	7,000	399,276	528,043	20,184	– 13,184	194,650	346,058	528,042
23	7,000	444,378	578,313	27,340	– 20,340	186,442	404,004	578,313
24	7,000	493,609	632,560	37,348	– 30,348	166,958	476,466	632,560
25	7,000	547,327	691,056	51,415	– 44,415	131,072	568,513	691,056
	17,500				– 44,846			

Compare

Think about it: This is America. We have a free-enterprise economy. And in a free-enterprise economy, there is no such thing as the ultimate rip-off that lasts very long. If there were, the public would discover it. So would Congress. So would all the lawyers and CPAs and MBAs in the country. And soon, it wouldn't exist anymore.

I do have one simple observation for the people who are so avidly against whole life. Most of the really big insurance policies—million-dollar policies—are sold to men over the age of 50. And they are whole life policies. The premiums are $10,000, a year; some are hundreds of thousands.

People who can afford a $50,000 annual insurance premium are probably people who know how to invest their money. They are probably smart businesspeople. They can probably afford to hire the best legal advice, tax advice, and financial advice. So, if whole life is so awful, do you think those kind of people would buy it? And the average guy on the street gets the same benefits as the big guy.

The bottom line is this: Buy what makes sense for you. If you need $300,000 in death benefits, but can only afford $50 a month in premium payments, maybe you should buy $30,000 in whole life and $270,000 in term, then gradually convert the term to whole life. Most people do not buy the first place they ever live. It's okay to rent for a while.

Comparisons of Insurance Types
The higher the point score, the better.

	Term Insurance	Whole Life	Universal Life	Variable Life	Variable Universal Life
Low Initial Cost	9	4	5	4	5
Permanent Protection	No	Yes	Yes	Yes	Yes
Guaranteed Premiums	No	Yes	No	Yes	No
Guaranteed Death Benefit	No	Yes	No	Yes	No
Premium Flexibility	0	6	7	6	7
Choice of Investments	0	1	1	8	8
Current Returns	No	Yes	Yes	Yes	Yes
Higher Returns	N/A	7	5	9	9
Lowest Expenses over 20 years	3	8	7	7	6

Your Insights, Feelings, and Action Items

A. As you read this chapter, what *insights* came that seem applicable to you?

1._____

2._____

3._____

B. How did you *feel* as you pondered particular points of this chapter?

1._____

2._____

3._____

C. What do you *feel* you should *do* as a result of this chapter?

1._____

2._____

3._____

D. How might you solicit the aid of others in accomplishing "C" above?

_____

_____

_____

Chapter 19

Now, Cement Your Foundation

Is Your Insurance Company Reputable?

How can you determine whether an insurance company is reputable? How reputable a company is depends on many factors and tells you much about how you are likely to be treated at claim time or when you need service.

A few tell-tale signs:

Look for a company that has a high portion of its field force pursuing the Chartered Life Underwriter (CLU) designation, the sign of professionalism in the insurance industry. At great expense, they are actively promoting long-term training, service, professionalism, and ethical behavior.

Look for a company that has the reputation of adding new policy enhancements retroactively to existing policyholders, usually without charge. They truly reflect the concept of mutuality.

Be suspicious of any company that trains its agents to sell policies by merely replacing the policies of other companies. They are sly in their sales presentation and are very careful to do it legally, but usually it reflects ethical poverty.

Look for a company that grows its field force from scratch, rather than merely hires experienced agents away from another company. It is a tremendous investment to grow a field force, just as it is to plant a shade tree and wait for it to mature. Such a company will not engage in the short-sighted financial fads because it has a reputation to protect. Other companies and agencies may want to harvest where they haven't sown. It is really a matter of character, and you do not want an unscrupulous company taking license with your money.

Only do business with the most reputable of companies. As you can see, reputation has to do with many things besides financial strength, something few consumer advocates understand. Reputation is highly subjective, so get an experienced, trusted insurance adviser with a long-term ethical perspective. I've included *my* rankings in *Your Money Happiness Workbook* and the list is also available by Fax-on-Demand. Just call (801) 263-1676 and request free report #130, "Reputation Rankings of Major Insurers."

Another way to determine a company's reputation is, of course, through the ratings of financial strength. But, even with ratings in hand, you need to exercise caution.

A.M. Best is the only rating agency that regularly rated the insurance industry before 1980. Standard and Poor's, Duff and Phelps, and Moody's began rating a handful of insurance companies in the early to mid-1980s. These are credible rating agencies.

Standard and Poor's was initially extremely impressed with the strength of the insurance industry; relative to other types of companies they rated, insurance companies consistently deserved a triple-A rating. Recently, though, insurance companies haven't been rated as well. Moody's, in particular, has lowered the ratings of insurance companies that hold a high portion of real estate mortgages or real estate holdings.

Joseph M. Belth, author of *Life Insurance: A Consumer's Handbook*, provides one of the most accurate and insightful commentaries on insurance companies and the industry, while AARP and AAII are notorious for their lack of understanding.

Why aren't ratings always the final word? Recently, the insurance rating division of Standard and Poor's received a management directive to lower its ratings on a number of insurance companies. In spite of record profits and improved financial strength, these insurance company ratings were lowered. In other words, ratings that fall may not necessarily reflect a problem in the insurance company. Instead, falling ratings may reflect a change in the standards or emphasis of the rating agency.

Be careful which rating company you use. Some rating companies do not have the background of the major, reputable rating companies. They do very little, if any, qualitative or subjective analysis of many factors that influence a company's financial strength—such as the company's management team, agent force, goodwill in the marketplace, customer service, and fairness in how it treats its policyholders.

How, then, do these rating agencies rate a company? Often, they merely input quantitative data from the company's financial reports, do some computer calculations, come out with a scale that weighs various attributes, and then assign a rating. Rating an insurance company like that is like rating an NBA basketball team by plugging into a computer the players' heights, weights, and shooting percentages. It ignores the team's heart, its coaching, its tactics, its strategy, or any of a number of other nonquantifiable ingredients.

One problem with rating organizations and agencies is that their rating may become a self-fulfilling prophecy—something that happened on May 17, 1991, when Standard and Poor's downgraded the nation's 13th largest mutual insurance company, Mutual Benefit. A young, inexperienced reporter who had little background in finance was allowed to publish a front-page article in the *Wall Street Journal* which contained several factual inaccuracies about Mutual Benefit. Even though the "facts" weren't true, the article precipitated a run on the company. Two months later, Mutual Benefit sought receivership under the auspices of the New Jersey Insurance Department.

While no policyholder of Mutual Benefit lost any money, either in death benefits or cash values, the major insurance companies—among them Prudential, Metropolitan, and New York Life—did an audit of Mutual Benefit's asset quality. They determined the asset quality was there, so the industry stepped forward, avoiding federal intrusion, and decided to back or guarantee all death benefits and all cash values of Mutual Benefit.

Ironically, that guarantee made policyholders of Mutual Benefit owners of the strongest policies in the industry. Instead of having a policy backed by a single company, their policies were backed by the combined strength of most of the major insurance companies.

The industry and state regulators showed they could take care of their own without federal intrusion, in spite of a sensational press that needs to sell magazines and the pygmy-thinking of many self-appointed consumer advocates.

Nevertheless, this phenomenon adds a new element of risk to the insurance industry—it's called the *psycho-media risk*. It's what happens when the media gets involved. Risk in the insurance industry used to reflect only the financial strength of the company and how well their assets and investments were matched to their risks and obligations. Today, even an outstanding company can be damaged by irresponsible yellow journalism.

Subsequent in-depth investigation showed that Mutual Benefit did not deserve the sensational treatment it received in the press. But by then, the damage had been done. In the end, sadly, the press always gets the last word.

(For the latest *Instant Report* on the financial strength ratings of the major insurance companies and for more information on how to choose an insurance company, call Fax-on-Demand at (801) 263-1676 and request free reports #135, "The Ratings of the Major Insurers," and #140, "How to Choose an Insurance Company.")

How to Choose a Professional Insurance Adviser

The easiest way to choose an insurance adviser? Visit. You can tell a lot about an adviser by the company he keeps. The same thing applies to an insurance company.

Just last year, I was contacted to meet with a couple in their late 70s. An insurance agent was advising them to replace a million-dollar policy they had purchased to cover estate taxes. I was shocked. The adviser was being clearly unethical—and I naturally assumed that the home office would be concerned with the gross way the adviser was taking advantage of the elderly couple.

I called the home office of the replacing company, and spoke to the president and chairman of the board. He shrugged it off and passed me on to the director of marketing. The director of marketing said, "We can't be concerned about the propriety or impropriety of every application that comes to us."

I explained that this wasn't just any application. I told him these people were in their 70s, the policy was substantial, and the premium was $40,000 a year. Yet he wasn't concerned. Fortunately, most companies are more concerned about their reputation. Only after the couple's children and the insurance regulators got involved did the couple realize how they were being taken advantage of.

Check on the adviser's designation. A designation tells you a lot about commitment to ethical standards and education—and about the exams the adviser had to pass. It says a lot about continuing education. Insurance strategies can be complex. Make sure your adviser is a Chartered Life Underwriter (CLU). Few Certified Financial Planners, CPAs, MBAs, and attorneys have the background to advise clients about even basic insurance matters.

The Importance of Trust and Loyalty

Find a good, trusted adviser. Then be loyal to him or her. All efficient relationships are based on mutual trust and loyalty. On occasion, I've observed someone willing to replace a policy because a brother-in-law, friend, or cousin entered the insurance business. The replacement would have caused a loss of thousands. The person would be better off to simply write his brother-in-law, friend, or neighbor a check for a couple thousand dollars.

Would you make that gift with your family assets? What would your spouse say? Usually when that is pointed out, the silly thinking stops. Be loyal to any trusted adviser. Nowhere is loyalty more important than with your insurance adviser. (Be sure to study Chapter 35.)

Insurance is not a commodity. A *commodity* is something which is differentiated only by price. For example, wheat, barley, soybeans, iron ore, crude oil, and orange juice are commodities. Once you have found a professional and trustworthy adviser, you don't go shop his premium. Insurance is not a price or a premium. It is a service. I have seen consumers spend hours examining a 5 percent differential in premium or *illustrated* (estimated) cash values, when selecting the right adviser would have been worth 20 times that amount in value-added service.

Don't Be Confused By "Values"

Some insurance agents play confusing games by illustrating "interest-sensitive whole life" or "universal" policies. These policies typically have two stated values. One is the account value. The other is the cash surrender value. The difference is the surrender charge.

All too often, the agent illustrates the account value under the guise that "this is the amount you have working for you," and that "since you don't intend to surrender your policy, this cash surrender column on the illustration is not relevant."

That's not true. Your only true equity in the policy is the cash surrender value. That's how much cash value you actually own—and that's how much you can borrow against when you need money.

What's the account value, then? It's the money that is actually earning interest. It's the money that's actually invested. But you don't own it. It has been advanced to you by the insurance company. You can't borrow against the account value.

And don't forget that illustrations are just that. Illustrations of how the policy *may* perform. Don't attach a level of accuracy or truth to something which isn't there.

Buying No-Load Insurance for a Fee

Can you cut your insurance costs by dealing with an insurance company that sells insurance direct to the public without an agent, or that sells insurance on a fee basis with an agent? Those are becoming increasingly common. But they're also riddled with problems.

First, none of the large, reputable, financially stable insurance companies use this kind of marketing. Some of the companies that do are younger than my teenage children. I would not trust my life's security program on a 30- to 50-year insurance contract to a company that lacks financial strength, size, stability, longevity, or experience in various economic environments.

Second, compare the numbers in these companies. You will find their premiums are no lower than what you can get from some of the major reputable companies. That's not all: Their cash value buildup is no greater in year five, year 10, year 20, or year 30 than cash value buildup available from most of the major national insurers.

Third, if the premium is no less or the long-term cash value is no greater, then do you want to be getting your service from a receptionist at a toll-free number? Or do you want the services of a professional insurance adviser?

Does that mean some of these policies aren't good buys? Absolutely not. It simply means you need to do your homework. You need to spend some extra time making sure you sign with a solid company and are buying the professional service you need.

Simply stated, watch out. Take your time. Explore carefully. If, after investigating, you are thinking about buying direct from one of these companies, call your state insurance department. Just because a company advertises on television or radio doesn't mean it is licensed in your state. (If you have never heard its name before, be especially careful.) Find out its grades from a rating bureau like A.M. Best, Standard and Poor's, or Moody's.

Remember: These companies may offer cut-rate policies. But you usually get what you pay for. And you do not want cracks in the foundation of your financial plan.

Beware Replacement Schemes

It is often in your best interest to replace an existing term policy with a permanent policy. That assumes you're insurable, you're honest on the application, and you don't intend to commit suicide within two years.

Permanent insurance is another matter. Seldom is it in your best interest to replace a whole life, universal life, or variable life policy that has been in force for more than a year. Are there exceptions? Of course. You may replace a policy that performs poorly, one that you legitimately can't afford, or one backed by a company with an extremely poor reputation.

But a policy that has been in force for a year is accumulating cash—and has a year's head start on a new policy. Except in the *rare* case of a *very* poorly performing policy, it's extremely difficult for the new policy to ever catch up.

Last year, a colleague, Jane, received an interesting letter from a CPA. The CPA wanted to let Jane know that he and an insurance agent were going to replace a policy that Jane had put in place for some clients of hers. In his letter, the CPA told Jane not to call her clients. How ridiculous. Jane was duty-bound to call her clients!

First, Jane responded to the CPA. She pointed out that the CPA was giving advice beyond the scope of his license—in essence, he was engaged in the unlicensed practice of insurance consulting. Jane also pointed out that he assumed some legal risks as a result. Finally, she explained that the CPA's advice was misdirected. The CPA wouldn't back down.

So Jane called her clients, Jim and Marilyn. They had relied heavily on the CPA for advice in the past, so it was tough to convince them that the CPA and the insurance agent were unethical. They didn't have the couple's best interests at heart—they just wanted a commission.

It was a virtual tug-of-war. Jane advised against replacing the policy; the CPA insisted that the policy be replaced. Finally, Jane was able to convince her clients that if they replaced the policy, they would lose tens of thousands of dollars.

What happened? Fortunately, Jim and Marilyn held on to their original policy. Not only did the insurance agent lose the case, but he came very close to having his insurance license revoked because of some misrepresentations he made on the clients' application for insurance. And the CPA? He lost something even more valuable—his clients' trust.

Should You Replace Your Policy?

Sometimes called "leveraging," *replacement* involves lapsing or surrendering an old policy and replacing it with a new one. It may involve stripping an old policy, wherein the old policy stays in place, but you take all the cash value out of it. You use the money to pay the premiums on a new policy. (Since there's an unpaid loan on the old policy, it eventually gets cancelled.)

So, what's so bad about replacement?

Take a look at the new policy. *If* you pass the medical examination, you'll have to pay the acquisition costs of the new policy. Then there's a period during which the new policy can be contested. What's happening to the agent all that time? The agent is happily collecting the first-year commission from the new policy.

But what if your needs change? Wouldn't a replacement be appropriate?

That depends. Sometimes the policy alone demands replacement. You should *always* weigh the pros and cons of replacing an old policy and make *certain* you'll benefit by making a change. Make sure the replacement is in your best interest—not just in the interest of the agent.

If your needs change, you might be better off to make changes to your existing insurance portfolio with the in-force company. The cash value of the in-force policy will be considered old money, and there will be little or no new administration or commission charges.

Whenever it comes to replacing an existing policy, think twice. *Always* involve your existing agent. Understand that with a new policy, you'll start over with a new two-year clause for misrepresentations on the application and a new two-year suicide clause. And though *you* wouldn't make misrepresentations on the application, the kind of greedy agent that regularly replaces policies just might make one over your signature.

Finally, there's the bottom line: the value of your policy. It is *very* unlikely that a new policy can catch up with an existing policy, except in rare circumstances. Before you make a move, check out your existing policy carefully. You'll almost always find a number of modified payment provisions—if the policy is two or three years old and you're suffering a financial setback, you can probably decrease your premium payments for a while.

Three Ways Insurance Self-Adjusts Under High Inflation

College texts and the popular financial press would have you believe the value of a whole life insurance policy plummets under high inflation. In fact, you just saw how the value of a death benefit of $100,000 drops over a 30-year period because of inflation. But an insurance program may actually self-adjust under inflation. How? It happens in three ways.

First, assume you purchase a $100,000 whole life or universal life policy. The financial press often equates that to a fixed-income investment, such as a bond. But look at the facts. If you buy a $1,000 bond, your principal is returned to you at the end of 20 years. You get a check for $1,000. But, what's worth $1,000 today is worth only $367 in real purchasing power by the time the bond matures. That's not all: When you buy a bond, you pay for the entire thing at once. You make a single, one-time, lump-sum payment of $1,000.

How does that compare with life insurance? You buy life insurance on the installment plan. As the death benefit decreases in real value, so do the premiums. In other words, the premium you're paying for the death benefit is decreasing in real value over the years at the same rate that the death benefit is decreasing in value.

Now for the *second* way insurance self-adjusts: A life insurance policy usually has a guaranteed interest rate on the cash value buildup. The interest rate is guaranteed, whether it's a traditional whole life policy issued from a mutual company that participates in dividends, or a universal life policy issued from a stock company that may credit you with excess interest.

The result? During periods of inflation, interest rates follow inflation. Remember the late years of the Carter administration (1979 through 1981)? Inflation skyrocketed. So did interest rates. Mortgage rates hit 16 percent. Money market funds hit 18 percent. Prime rate hit 21 percent. In that environment, dividends and excess interest on whole life policies helped the cash value earnings adjust for high inflation. And as cash values adjust upward, the death benefit also grows.

Under a traditional policy issued by a mutual company, those cash values may purchase paid-up additions—free of any mortality cost, commissions, or any other fees or expenses. It's very common for a $100,000 policy issued at age 25 to grow to $400,000 by age 65. A similar thing may happen with a universal life policy.

What about the *third* way insurance self-adjusts? When you buy life insurance, don't look at it in terms of actual dollars. Instead, look at it as a percentage of your monthly or annual income. If you do, your death benefit will grow, because you'll be allocating more dollars to insurance over the years. You'll do the same thing with your insurance program that you'll do with your food, automobile, and utility budgets. Isn't it unrealistic to expect your utility budget to stay at 5 percent of your income, and your insurance premium to be fixed forever?

People who think insurance performs poorly under inflation don't consider the real world we live in. Let's look at a real-world example:

Zach buys a $250,000 policy at age 25. It costs him $200 a month, or about 5 percent of his monthly income. First of all, should that $250,000 death benefit last him throughout life? Absolutely not.

As Zach's premiums are decreasing in real dollars because of inflation, his income is keeping up with inflation. If he makes $30,000 a year at age 25 and his income grows at 5 percent inflation, he will be earning just over $62,000 at age 40. His $250,000 insurance policy should have been updated by then, because he'll probably need closer to $550,000.

Between the ages of 25 and 40, his insurance premium remains constant at $200 a month. What about his other expenses? What about utilities? If he was spending 5 percent of his family budget on utilities each month, is he still spending 5 percent of his family budget on utilities? Yes. But is it still the same dollar amount? No.

If Zach was spending 10 percent of his monthly budget on transportation, is he still spending 10 percent of his monthly budget on transportation? Yes. If he was spending 20 percent of his family budget on housing costs, is he still spending 20 percent of his family budget on housing costs? Perhaps. But here's the key: His family budget has increased. So, since his insurance premium is a set amount, it goes from 5 percent of his monthly budget to 2 percent of his monthly budget. That doesn't make sense.

If you want to keep your insurance program up with inflation, look at it as you do every other budget expense. Periodically review your program and update your insurance so you're paying 5 percent of your income in premiums. That's okay.

Compare Group with Personally Owned Insurance

It's a common question: Should you buy all the term life insurance you can through your employer-provided group plan by purchasing supplemental insurance? Or should you buy an individual term life policy?

That depends. Where can you get the coverage for the lowest cost? And, second, what non-cost factors should you consider?

If you can pass the physical exam for a life policy, you're in for a surprise: An individual term policy might have lower premiums than the term insurance policy you can get through your employer-provided group plan. Doesn't an employer-provided group plan benefit from group purchasing power—have some kind of quantity discount? Sometimes. But any group discount is usually overcompensated for: The insurance company must charge more for a group plan because it is issued without regards to insurability. In other words, people who sign up for all the group insurance they can get might not be able to get insurance on their own. This is called "adverse selection," and refers to the fact that a group policy contains a population that has inferior mortality expectations. So, naturally the rates are higher.

Age might also factor in—especially if the group plan has a set age or a fixed premium for a five- or 10-year period. If the group premium stays level for five or 10 years, and you're older, you might be able to buy a group policy for less than a personal policy. But as soon as you pass that age breakpoint, your group premium will jump—to about what you would pay for a personal policy.

Since you can often buy a personal policy for less than a group policy, it might be worthwhile to check out your insurability. But that's not all: There are a number of other factors you might want to consider. They're listed in the chart on the following page.

What do most of these factors boil down to? Who controls or owns the contract. It's important to understand that a group policy is not between the insured and the insurance company. The contract holder is actually the employer—the group that offers the insurance to group members. What are the ramifications? The employer can change the terms of the contract—just as the insurance company can. All you get is a certificate of coverage.

On the other hand, if you buy a personal policy, especially a permanent policy or at least a term policy that's annually renewable through age 100, you enjoy the privilege of a noncancellable contract. The insurance company can't modify it, regardless of changes in health, income, employment, or disability. You have all the control.

Even if you conclude that buying personal term insurance is better than purchasing that same coverage through your employer, you confront another question. Should you buy term insurance or whole life insurance? You might hear about a third option—re-entry term.

Comparing Group vs. Personally Owned Insurance

	Group	Personal
Unlimited amount of insurance	No	Yes
Proceeds excludable from your estate at death	No	Yes
Company guarantees level coverage	No	Yes
Employer (association) guarantees maintenance of coverage	No	Yes
Company guarantees premium rates	No	Yes
Insurance protection past age 70 or past retirement	No	Yes
If you're disabled, company pays your premiums, giving you increased insurance protection and increased cash values to meet needed expenses	No	Yes
Home Office supports an expert Legal Department that does estate planning daily	No	Yes
The insurance contract is transferable	No	Perhaps
Participation in company profits (dividends)	No	Perhaps
Professional agents provide services including updated information on changes in insurance laws	No	Yes
Conversion to a low-cost back-up policy in case of uninsurability and/or employment change	No	Yes
High limits on options to increase coverage in case of uninsurability	No	Yes
Conversion possible in case of disability	No	Yes
The odds of dying after retirement	2 to 1	
Life expectancy	Age 78	
Policy discontinued	Age 70	Death
Can the cost go up?	Yes	No

Beware Low-Priced Term Insurance

Re-entry term first came on the scene in the mid-1980s—perhaps you've heard it advertised on the radio. Since then, there have been a lot of re-entry term policies sold. Many annual renewable term policies (and even whole life policies) have been replaced with re-entry term.

What is it? Instead of having its premiums set at those of a competitive policy, re-entry term has initial premiums that are typically half of traditional premiums. It is very inexpensive. People buy it because they think they are going to save some money.

Well, so far, so good.

Not quite. With re-entry term, you keep the extremely low premiums as long as you'll have regular medical exams. Problems usually start about five years into the policy. If you forget to get your physical, your premiums are automatically bumped up—usually two or three times what you were originally paying. At that point, the re-entry premiums are 50 to 100 percent more than what traditional term premiums would have been. You seldom even get a note from the insurance company reminding you to get an exam. Your premiums simply go up.

When premiums increase, what does the typical policyholder do? He immediately runs out and tries to get another low-cost term policy. But, wait—if something has happened to his insurability and he has a hard time qualifying for re-entry, isn't he going to have a hard time qualifying for regular term or whole life? Yes. So, what happens? One of two things:

One, if he's still healthy, he lapses the policy. He immediately buys another term policy—and he can do that, because he's insurable. What about the insurance company? They couldn't be happier. That policyholder paid on a policy for five years, then lapsed it. The insurance company made money.

What if the policyholder isn't healthy and he can't pass a medical exam? He can't qualify for another policy. So, even though the premiums have skyrocketed, he hangs on to the policy. What about the insurance company? Right away, they know that the policyholder must be sick. Otherwise, he would have lapsed the policy when his premiums tripled. Now they know they have a sick population. So what happens the next year? They increase the premiums even more, to cover their risk.

So, what happens to the company? If the policyholder is sick, the insurance company has him paying through the nose for his coverage. If the policyholder is healthy and lapses his coverage, the insurance company makes a tidy profit. Or, if the policyholder just keeps re-entering year after year, the insurance company relaxes—they know they have a healthy risk pool.

Obviously, the insurance company comes out ahead in all three situations. But what about the policyholder? If he's healthy, he usually gets tired of re-qualifying every year. If he's sick, he's stuck for the rest of his life with a policy that is prohibitively expensive.

Is that the kind of predicament you want?

Now let's look at what you actually *buy* with re-entry term insurance. When the policy is never more than five years beyond the point when someone has qualified through a medical exam, how many of the death claims on that policy come from illness as opposed to accidents? Very few. Basically, what you have purchased is a very expensive accidental death benefit policy.

So, what percentage of deaths occur because of accidents? About one out of 12. What does that tell you? Even if you are paying half of a regular term life premium, you're paying six times what you should for an accidental death benefit policy. (It's not literally an accidental death policy, but it might as well be one. That's how it behaves.)

So You've Been Rated?

Okay. You have been determined to be a less than ideal risk. Maybe you have high blood pressure, diabetes, or a cancer history.

Your only option is an insurance policy that has been "rated." Should you buy it?

This is kind of a good news/bad news situation. The bad news? You'll pay a much higher premium. The good news? You have an insurance policy—and the insurance company believes you won't have to pay for as long as they had originally thought. (Why? Because they think you'll die sooner than others.)

The answer is yes. If you can, absolutely take the rated policy.

Imagine that you are considering buying a homeowners policy. You and your agent walk outside your house and cross the street. When you turn around to face your house, you see smoke coming out of your roof.

Would you buy the homeowners policy?

Absolutely—if the agent would sell it to you.

Well, you are just like that house. You have smoke coming out of your roof.

If you're rated, try to buy a cash-value type insurance policy. Guaranteed, locked in, the cash value may help self-support the policy and take care of it if you ever have a setback.

* * *

Several of the creative uses of permanent life insurance are suggested throughout this book. I make no apology. The most astute insurance consumers are the wealthy who recognize cash value insurance as one of the most versatile financial instruments available. It is one of the financial instruments which the wealthy use that is available to the average consumer.

Your Insights, Feelings, and Action Items

A. As you read this chapter, what *insights* came that seem applicable to you?

1._____

2._____

3._____

B. How did you *feel* as you pondered particular points of this chapter?

1._____

2._____

3._____

C. What do you *feel* you should *do* as a result of this chapter?

1._____

2._____

3._____

D. How might you solicit the aid of others in accomplishing "C" above?

_____

_____

_____

Chapter 20

Protect Your Assets

What is your biggest asset? Your ability to earn an income. What is your biggest risk? The loss of your income. *Sixteen times* as many mortgages are foreclosed on because of disability as they are because of death.

What does that tell you? Are you misinsuring?

Disability income planning is one of the major gaps for many people. The chart on the following page shows your potential earnings to age 65 without any adjustment for inflation. Note your age, then your family's monthly income. Follow the chart to see how much you'll earn by age 65. You'll see that your earning power is a significant asset—and one you'll certainly need to protect if you become disabled.

The Frightening Prospects of Disability

Each year, the odds of your becoming disabled before you retire are significantly greater than your chances of dying or losing your home to a fire. Each year, one in 105 people will die. One in 88 homes will catch fire. One in 70 cars will be involved in a serious auto accident. *But one in eight people will suffer a serious disability.* If you are between the ages of 35 and 65, the risk of your being disabled is twice your chance of dying prematurely. By the age of 42, your odds of being disabled are still four times your odds of dying prematurely. Yet while disability is the highest risk of all, only one-fourth of all Americans have individual disability income insurance.

Lifetime Earnings to Age 65, Without Inflation

Starting Age	Monthly Salary					
	$2,000	$3,000	$4,000	$6,000	$8,000	$10,000
25	960,000	1,440,000	1,920,000	2,880,000	3,840,000	4,800,000
26	936,000	1,404,000	1,872,000	2,808,000	3,744,000	4,680,000
27	912,000	1,368,000	1,824,000	2,736,000	3,648,000	4,560,000
28	888,000	1,332,000	1,776,000	2,664,000	3,552,000	4,440,000
29	864,000	1,296,000	1,728,000	2,592,000	3,456,000	4,320,000
30	840,000	1,260,000	1,680,000	2,520,000	3,360,000	4,200,000
31	816,000	1,224,000	1,632,000	2,448,000	3,264,000	4,080,000
32	792,000	1,188,000	1,584,000	2,376,000	3,168,000	3,960,000
33	768,000	1,152,000	1,536,000	2,304,000	3,072,000	3,840,000
34	744,000	1,116,000	1,488,000	2,232,000	2,976,000	3,720,000
35	720,000	1,080,000	1,440,000	2,160,000	2,880,000	3,600,000
36	696,000	1,044,000	1,392,000	2,088,000	2,784,000	3,480,000
37	972,000	1,008,000	1,344,000	2,016,000	2,688,000	3,360,000
38	648,000	972,000	1,296,000	1,944,000	2,592,000	3,240,000
39	624,000	936,000	1,248,000	1,872,000	2,496,000	3,120,000
40	600,000	900,000	1,200,000	1,800,000	2,400,000	3,000,000
41	576,000	864,000	1,152,000	1,728,000	2,304,000	2,880,000
42	552,000	828,000	1,104,000	1,656,000	2,208,000	2,760,000
43	528,000	792,000	1,056,000	1,584,000	2,112,000	2,640,000
44	504,000	756,000	1,008,000	1,512,000	2,016,000	2,520,000
45	480,000	720,000	960,000	1,440,000	1,920,000	2,400,000
46	456,000	684,000	912,000	1,368,000	1,824,000	2,280,000
47	432,000	648,000	864,000	1,296,000	1,728,000	2,160,000
48	406,000	612,000	816,000	1,224,000	1,632,000	2,040,000
49	384,000	576,000	768,000	1,152,000	1,536,000	1,920,000
50	360,000	540,000	720,000	1,080,000	1,440,000	1,800,000
51	336,000	504,000	672,000	1,008,000	1,334,000	1,680,000
52	312,000	468,000	624,000	936,000	1,248,000	1,560,000
53	288,000	432,000	576,000	864,000	1,152,000	1,440,000
54	264,000	396,000	528,000	792,000	1,056,000	1,320,000
55	240,000	360,000	480,000	720,000	960,000	1,200,000

Take a look at your chances of being disabled before the age of 65:

Odds of Disability Before Age 65

Age	For 3 Months	For 6 Months	For 1 Year	For 2 Years	For 5 Years
25	54%	34%	27%	22%	15%
30	52	33	26	22	15
35	50	33	26	21	15
40	48	32	25	21	15
45	44	30	24	20	14
50	39	28	23	19	14

How long will that disability last? If your disability is severe enough to last more than 90 days, chances are it will stay with you for several years, based on the age at which you become disabled:

Average Duration of Disability That Lasts 90 Days or Longer

Age	Duration (in years)
25	4.3
30	4.7
35	5.1
40	5.5
45	5.8
50	6.2
55	6.6

And here's another fact: Disability isn't always the result of an accident. Among people 40 years old, two-thirds of all disabilities are caused by illness. Only one-third are caused by injury. Among 60-year-olds, the percentages are even higher—84 percent of all disabilities are caused by illness.

Take a look at your own odds:

Disability by Illness vs. Injury

Age	Disabled by Illness	Disabled by Injury
40	67.0%	33.0%
45	71.3	28.7
50	75.7	24.7
55	80.3	19.7
60	83.7	16.3
65	85.7	14.3

Sources of Disability Income

If you become disabled, what are your alternatives? You could withdraw your savings. Think about that—how long would it take to deplete your savings if you weren't bringing home a paycheck?

Another option is to sell your assets. Would you want to sell your home and liquidate your investments if you were disabled? Sell your business?

What about Social Security? First of all, you have to be disabled for six months before you can apply. Then, to collect any disability income from Social Security, you'll have to meet three criteria. You must be *totally* disabled, *permanently* disabled, and unable to engage in *any* gainful occupation. (If you can push a broom in the city park, are you disabled?)

What about borrowing money? Who will loan it to you once they discover your income has stopped? And do you want to borrow without income? How long would the borrowed money last?

The best alternative is disability insurance.

How Much Is Enough?

How much disability insurance do you need? Use the disability needs analysis worksheet in *Your Money Happiness Workbook* to help figure it out. First of all, figure out how much money you would need if you were unable to earn a living. Include basic living expenses: mortgage or rent, food, utilities, transportation, etc. Then add in what you'll need to save for your own future, to educate your children, and to prepare for other emergencies; include cash reserves, college funds, your retirement plan, and retirement for your spouse, since disability benefits usually end at age 65.

When you purchase disability insurance, you'll need to determine an appropriate waiting period, based on your cash reserves. Do you have enough cash reserves for a 90-day waiting period? Or will you need a 60- or 30-day waiting period?

How long will you need the benefits to last? They should last for at least five years. The premiums are based in part on how long the benefit period is. If you can afford it, buy a policy with benefits that last to age 65 or your lifetime.

Your occupation partly determines both your premium level and your length of coverage. If you have a lower-risk occupation, you'll have lower premiums, and you can usually get benefits to the age of 65. If you're in a skilled trade, on the other hand, your benefits might be limited to five years.

How much will your benefits be? Typically, the monthly benefit can be as much as 60 percent of your present income. Why not more? If it were more, insurance companies would run the risk of people insuring themselves, then later putting in a false claim.

Finally, your age at the time you buy the insurance also determines your premium.

Here's the good news: Once you establish a disability policy, the premium usually stays level throughout your lifetime.

The Gray Contract: A Checklist for Analyzing Contract Provisions

Unlike life insurance, disability insurance is a "gray" contract. Collecting on a life insurance claim is fairly straightforward: If the insured is cold, you collect. Disability insurance is a little different. You'll have to answer all kinds of questions: Is the person totally disabled or partially disabled? How long has the person been disabled?

Because of that, you need to use a professional insurance adviser if you're buying disability insurance. The contract provisions are essential—and you need the benefit of a professional's training.

When you meet with a professional, here are some questions you should ask:

- How do they calculate pre-disability income to determine your loss?
- Do they adjust pre-disability income for inflation?
- Is the contract guaranteed not to be cancelled?
- Is the contract guaranteed to be renewed?
- How does the policy define disability?
- Does it include partial disability?
- Does it insure *your* occupation? Or, if you can merely do any work, will your claim be denied?
- What does the policy require to prove a disability claim? Will they accept your doctor's statement, or must you be tested by their physician?

What about workers compensation? If your employer offers it, do you still need disability insurance? Definitely. Disabilities may be caused by accidents or illness. Disabilities may occur on or off the job. Workers compensation only covers disabilities due to accidents that occur on the job. Far more disabilities occur due to illness or accidents that occur off the job, so never base your family's security program on workers compensation. Besides, it only pays a maximum of about $450 per week.

Workers Compensation Covers:

	Disabilities Due to Illness	Disabilities Due to Accident
Off the Job	No	No
On the Job	No*	Yes

* Some rare exceptions

What about health insurance—doesn't it cover disabilities? To a point, yes. But health insurance only covers hospitalization, physician fees, and the treatment of illnesses or injuries. It does *not* provide a monthly income so you can make your mortgage payment.

For a more detailed discussion about disability insurance and a list of the leading disability insurance providers, call Fax-on-Demand at (801) 263-1676 and request free report #145.

Long-Term Care: Another Increasing Threat

Long-term care insurance covers situations like home health care, care in an assisted living facility, adult day care, and nursing home care. It covers the risk that you will become mentally or physically disabled or incapacitated and will require skilled care at some point in your life. The expenses covered by long-term care insurance are not covered by health insurance or disability income insurance. And they can wipe out your entire life savings.

Unfortunately, few people plan for long-term care—yet 43 percent of all people age 65 or older will spend some time in a nursing home. Seven of every 10 couples age 65 or older have at least one spouse enter a nursing home.

In 1990, the average nursing home cost $36,000 a year. By the year 2000, it could well average $80,000 a year.

If it happened to you, how would you pay for long-term care? Private or company health insurance covers acute care only. What about Medicare? Medicare covers skilled care or skilled nursing facility—but only if the patient was in the hospital for three days first, and entered the facility within 30 days. Even then, full costs are covered for only 20 days. After that, it pays minimal costs for only 80 days. After 100 days, there's no coverage at all.

What about Medicaid? You have to spend down all your assets to poverty level before you qualify for Medicaid.

Speaking of assets, could you use them? Sure. But a single long-term illness could wipe out all your retirement savings—and more.

Generally, who pays the long-term care bill? Private insurance generally pays only 1.5 percent of all long-term care expenses. Medicare pays 1.6 percent. Other sources pay for 4.5 percent. Medicaid pays for 41.4 percent. Just over half—51 percent—of all long-term care expenses are paid by the patient.

Private long-term care insurance has become an increasingly critical element of a sound financial plan. It can provide continued financial independence, protection of assets, and peace of mind. It lets *you* maintain control over your life.

Think about it: Is there any risk you haven't already insured that could take away everything you already own? Have you insured your home? Your car? Do you have health insurance? Life insurance? Do you have disability income insurance? Then shouldn't you have a plan to pay long-term care expenses?

In evaluating a good long-term care insurance program, discuss the following with a professional agent:

- Are benefits flexible?
- Do you have a choice in different coverage options?
- Will the coverage provide home health benefits, allowing you to have skilled nursing care in your own home?
- Will the coverage include inflation protection as long-term care expenses increase?
- Does the policy cover Alzheimer's disease? (Many policies don't.)
- Is the policy guaranteed renewable?
- Does the policy allow for a time-out from paying premiums during any period when benefits are required?
- Will the policy provide you with upgrade privileges as new enhancements and policy descriptions become available?
- Does the company have a solid and liberal claims paying record?

Sound Strategies for the Most Secure Asset Protection

The risk of creditors gaining access to your personal assets increases as the size of your assets increases, as the size of your personal debt increases and as the risks of your lifestyle or occupation increase. With some careful planning, you can protect both personal and business assets.

Risk assets are assets that create risk and potential liability. For example, two common assets might be a mutual fund and a car. A mutual fund isn't a very risky asset—it has little opportunity to do damage. A car, on the other hand, *is* a risky asset—it has a greater opportunity to damage or harm. The more risk assets you own, the more important it is for you to protect all your assets against the potential liability of your risky assets.

For example, let's assume you're a plumber. While your employee is driving your company van and supplies to a job, he hits a little boy. The little boy dies. Because you personally owned the van and the supplies in the van, you may be held responsible for the death of this little boy.

The boy's parents sue you for $2 million because your employee ran a stop sign. You lose your business, your home, your savings, your cars, and your mountain cabin as you settle the $2 million lawsuit.

How could you have better protected your assets?

Consider Incorporating

One way is to incorporate. If you structure your plumbing business so it's a corporation, your personal car and home will be protected if you injure someone with your plumbing van. Retitle your van and insure it in the name of the corporation. Now the *corporation* is responsible for settling the lawsuit, because you were employed by the corporation at the time of the accident and the van was registered in the name of the corporation. Your personal assets are more insulated.

To protect your assets even further, you could create a family limited partnership. This is a limited partnership in which all the partners are family members. The family limited partnership owns the truck and the equipment, then leases it to the corporation. Now, when the corporation gets sued, the only thing it has is receivables. Not only are your assets no longer exposed, but the corporation's assets are no longer exposed, either.

And, of course, you could get insurance. Adequate property and casualty insurance are both asset protection strategies in and of themselves.

Asset protection strategies deal with how to protect your assets from frivolous claims. Basically, they include the following strategies:

- Limiting liability through incorporation of your business. Remember that there are strict operating guidelines which must be followed.

- Avoiding high-risk assets that may cause additional liability (high-risk automobiles, swimming pools, trampolines, a sidewalk that gathers ice in the wintertime, or high-risk businesses or occupations, for example)
- Retitling assets (transferring ownership of safe assets to a spouse or children who engage in a lower-risk lifestyle)
- Using family trusts, insurance, and liability insurance to their fullest extent
- Using family limited partnerships, business trusts, an irrevocable insurance trust, children's trusts, and other kinds of trusts
- Compartmentalizing—having each high-risk asset owned by a separate legal entity

Asset protection really requires the advice of a skilled attorney; a Chartered Property and Casualty Underwriter (CPCU) may also be of help. Some of the tactics listed above are beyond the scope of this book. I would like to discuss a few of the more relevant strategies.

Family Limited Partnerships: A Protective Shell

A family limited partnership is the "grand-daddy" of asset protection strategies.

When an individual transfers assets to a limited partnership, he forgoes his ongoing ownership of those assets, except indirectly through what ownership interest he might have in the partnership. But, as a general partner, he continues to control the asset, since only the general partners can control partnership decisions.

As an example, a man might transfer ownership of an asset to a partnership in which his children own most of the partnership interests. While the children then own the majority interest in the asset thereafter, the general partners continue to exercise complete control over it. Many people put their investments, homes, family cabins, insurance policies, and other low-risk investments into a family limited partnership.

Usually a separate family limited partnership is also established for the high-risk assets owned, sometimes for *each* high-risk asset owned—for instance, each apartment complex owned by a landlord.

A limited partnership provides several valuable benefits. Number one, as a general rule, limited partnerships provide excellent lawsuit protection. A family limited partnership may not be broken up or dissolved if one of the limited partners is sued. That's not all: Under most state laws, a distinct provision protects assets of the partnership from the individual creditors of a limited partner. Creditors only attach the limited partners' distributions, if and when paid. A properly drafted limited partnership will allow the general partner to retain all earnings for future business purposes, in effect giving the general partner the ability to leave creditors waiting forever.

Number two, a family limited partnership protects the estate. By transferring ownership of assets in limited partnerships, you can save millions of dollars in estate and inheritance taxes. While the general partner controls the partnership regardless of what percentage he owns, estate and inheritance taxes are levied only on the ownership percentage. Let's assume the parents own 2 percent of a limited partnership, and that the limited partnership owns their home, their investment portfolio, and their life insurance policies. Only 2 percent of all those assets can be included for estate tax purposes. (For more information, see Chapter 25.)

Evaluating Your Need for Property and Casualty Insurance

How much property insurance should you have? Most states require you to have *at least* $300,000 liability coverage on your auto insurance; current legal trends, however, indicate this is much too low. You should also have an equal limit in uninsured and underinsured liability.

If you have a lien on the car, the lender will require you to have comprehensive and collision insurance. If you have to make a choice between a low deductible and a low benefit, or a high deductible and a high benefit, choose the high deductible and the high benefit. That way, you self-insure for the amount of the deductible. It may cause a financial inconvenience or nuisance, but you won't risk financial ruin.

On a home, be sure your homeowners insurance includes replacement cost coverage. In other words, the policy will pay the cost of rebuilding the home—not its current depreciated value or the original purchase price of the home.

Over and above automobile, fire, and homeowners insurance, I recommend a general liability policy. This umbrella policy insures against the potentially greater risk of a loss of other assets—such as your investment portfolio or your earnings. It also will cover any liability limitations on your auto or homeowners policy. You can usually get a $1 million umbrella policy for about $140 per year. Wealthier individuals and professionals ought to have a $2 million to $5 million limit.

On both your automobile and homeowners insurance policies, it is important to differentiate between the *property* insurance and *liability* insurance portions. Property insurance, of course, covers your actual property. Liability insurance protects you against the consequences of your actions. For example, if somebody makes a claim against you for $2 million and your auto insurance is only $300,000, then they will come after you personally for any other assets you own—including your investments or your earning capacity. (In some states, they may actually be able to have your wages garnished for 10 years to satisfy a court settlement.) You need both property and liability insurance—but liability insurance should be covered first.

Remember: Asset protection strategies are used to protect your assets from frivolous lawsuits, malpractice claims, undeserving creditors, and the like. And because most states have "fraudulent conveyance" acts which invalidate transfers made in the face of actual liability, such strategies must be undertaken well in advance of need.

Asset protection strategies are for those situations when, due to unforeseen circumstances beyond your control, all you have built up over a lifetime may be wiped out because of an extreme judgment in a lawsuit, unwise legislation, unforeseen risks in an otherwise prudent business venture, and so on.

A small service station owner may be wiped out today for environmental concerns he wasn't aware of 40 years ago when the station was built. A sophisticated attorney may persuade a jury that even a highly competent and ethical physician should be held accountable for an unavoidable medical problem. An employer may be held liable for an employee's error, even though he did all in his power to establish systems and safeguards. You will be held liable when a neighbor's child jumps off your roof onto your trampoline and gets injured. *Those* are the situations for which you engage in asset protection strategies.

Your Insights, Feelings, and Action Items

A. As you read this chapter, what *insights* came that seem applicable to *you?*
   1._____
   2._____
   3._____

B. How did you *feel* as you pondered particular points of this chapter?
   1._____
   2._____
   3._____

C. What do you *feel* you should *do* as a result of this chapter?
   1._____
   2._____
   3._____
D. How might you solicit the aid of others in accomplishing "C" above?
_____
_____
_____

Chapter 21

How to Enhance the Richest Part of Life: Retirement

Dr. Jones was approaching retirement age, nervous about his preparation, or lack of it. After some unwise investments and tax shelters, he was concerned because he had lost a significant portion of his retirement dollars. Now within five years of retirement, he discovered that he would not be able to continue to support his current lifestyle. Locked inside this "lifestyle prison" of his own making, Dr. Jones had sufficient savings for only three years of retirement. He had hoped to offer charitable medical service in foreign lands. Yet he found himself incarcerated in a retirement of bondage.

A little prudent retirement planning could have gone a long way.

Three Sources of Retirement Dollars, Supposedly

Most of us count on retiring at or before age 65, right? You've thought about it. Maybe even made plans about how you're going to spend your free time. And you probably assume you'll be living off your retirement income.

But where are those dollars supposed to come from?

There are three sources of retirement dollars: personal dollars, employer-provided dollars, and government or social dollars.

But the harsh reality is this: The only dollars you will *really* be able to count on are those you come up with on your own.

What about government dollars? Won't they be there when you retire? Don't bank on it. With the burgeoning budget deficit, insecurity with Social Security is increasing all the time. It is likely that there will be cutbacks. These are not the dollars to be relying upon.

Likewise with employer-provided dollars. Certainly, I encourage you to take advantage of employer-sponsored retirement plans—corporate pension or profit-sharing plans, 401k plans, etc. These plans may help supplement your retirement income. But once again, studies indicate that these plans should not be relied upon as the primary source of retirement dollars.

So what *can* you rely upon? Yourself. If you want to have a full and secure retirement, get your home completely paid off prior to retirement, and develop a nest egg large enough to comfortably provide for your needs.

Think that's an unrealistic recommendation?

Consider this: Assuming we lived in a world without inflation, a 45-year-old with $50,000 a year of family income will need $725,000 in financial assets in order to retire at age 65 without a reduction in his standard of living. If inflation is at 4.5 percent, then he needs to have saved $1.7 million.

So, what are the *real* sources of retirement dollars? *Man* at work, or *money* at work. To the extent that you have money at work, you don't need to have man at work. If you don't have adequate money at work, then, yes, you will have to have man at work.

Pertinent Facts about Retirement: Where Do You Fit in?

It seems most retirees haven't set up a solid program of "money at work." The facts speak for themselves:

According to the Social Security Administration, at age 65, 45 percent of the population are dependent upon relatives; 30 percent are dependent upon Social Security or charity; 23 percent are still working; and *only 2 percent are self-sustaining*. (Self-sustaining defined as $35,000 a year of investment income).

In 1993, about 3.8 million elderly persons were below the poverty level. The poverty rate for persons over age 65 was 12.2 percent. An additional 2.3 million, or 8 percent of the elderly, were classified as near poor (income between the poverty level and 125 percent of that level). Thus, *one-fifth* of the older population was poor or near poor in 1993.

Here's part of the problem:

One out of every eight Americans, or 12 percent of the population, is age 65 or older. By the year 2010, 25 percent of the U.S. population—75,000,000 people—will be at least 55 years of age.

And the Social Security system just can't handle them all.

In 1945, the Social Security system was supported by 42 workers for every retiree. Due to the decreasing numbers of children that people are having, there were only 3.3 workers supporting each retiree on the system in 1984. By the year 2020, that number is expected to drop to 2.4 workers per retiree.

To compound the problem, people are living longer and retiring younger—at an average age of 61 instead of 65.

Serious misconceptions about retirement funding also pose a challenge.

In Merrill Lynch's fourth annual retirement survey, Americans between the ages of 45 and 64 were asked where they believed their retirement income would come from. Of those surveyed, 43 percent expected most of their income to come from their employer-provided pension plan, and 25 percent expected their largest source of income to come from Social Security. In other words, more than two-thirds of those surveyed believed their largest source of retirement income would be provided for them.

Only 18 percent thought most of their retirement income would come from savings, while 10 percent felt it would come from other sources. Only 4 percent anticipated their retirement income would come from earned income.

In reality, however, those with heads of households over 65 and $20,000 of income indicate that 32 percent of their income comes from savings, 24 percent from earnings, only 23 percent from Social Security, and 20 percent from a pension or retirement plan. Other sources account for 1 percent.

What do some of these facts tell us?

Simply stated, there is a lot of poor retirement planning going on. And that planning is based on some pretty unrealistic expectations about where retirement income will come from.

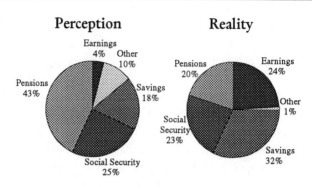

Perception

Earnings 4% Other 10%
Pensions 43%
Savings 18%
Social Security 25%

Reality

Pensions 20% Earnings 24%
Other 1%
Social Security 23%
Savings 32%

Source: Merrill Lynch 4th Annual Retirement Survey   Source: U.S. Department of Health and Human Services

Is Retirement for You?

We've seen how few people have adequate "money at work." Perhaps you might be happier having "man at work." Many people want to plan for a comfortable retirement, including travel and a fun lifestyle, and they want to retire younger so they can enjoy their retirement while healthy.

But others wonder, "Why retire?"

Do you have to retire at age 65? Was it written in a stone tablet some place that the end of life is to play golf, cheer for our favorite basketball team, or drive an RV across the country? These things are nice, but many retirees tell me that they get old quickly. Are they really what life is all about? Some people look forward to retirement, not as the age of trivial pursuits, but as the opportunity time of their life.

Steven Lecock, the Canadian economist and humorist, observed, "Let me give a word of advice to you young fellows who have been looking forward to retirement: Have nothing to do with it. Listen, it's like this: Have you ever been out for a late autumn walk in the closing part of the afternoon, and suddenly looked up to realize that the leaves have practically all gone, and the sun is set, and the day gone before you knew it, and with that a cold wind blows across the landscape? That's retirement."

Ernest Hemingway thought retirement the ugliest word in the human language. And Margaret Mead, the American anthropologist, maintained, "Sooner or later, I'm going to die, but I'm not going to retire."

Fewer and fewer people are retiring. While many of us might like to quit working altogether, some people must continue working at least part time to make ends meet. Others may continue to work for reasons of personal satisfaction.

Abundant and Appealing Reasons Not to Retire

Working beyond retirement age might appeal to you for a number of reasons. You will have ongoing socialization, an opportunity to keep mentally and physically active, and hopefully an escape from boredom. It may give you a reason to get up in the morning. It exposes you to a mixed age group. And, of course, it can help supplement other income sources. Plus, it may help you feel like you are contributing to society in a meaningful way.

The down side, of course, is that you will probably have less time for leisure activities, a possible reduction in Social Security benefits, and the inability to plan vacations, travel, and family time at your convenience.

Weigh the advantages and disadvantages, then ask yourself the following questions:

Are you ready to retire? Have you prepared financially? Not only do you have enough dollars set aside, but are those dollars invested in a portfolio that will provide an inflation hedge as well as downside risk protection? Do you have an estate plan? Have you raised your children to be financially independent? Or, are they still coming home to siphon from mom and dad?

Are you emotionally ready? According to Dr. Thomas H. Holmes, retirement can be a major source of stress for many people. The chart on the following page reflects the stress value of various life events. Those with asterisks are items which often accompany retirement. Have you prepared yourself mentally and emotionally to cope with these potential stressors? Has your spouse likewise prepared for the mental or emotional adjustment?

I remember well a CPA client whose wife was an author. She needed quiet time at home during the day in order to write. When he retired, his constant presence drove her nuts! Have you and your spouse talked things over, and made provision for the amount of time together and the amount of time away from each other? It is important to work out a schedule that meets both of your needs.

Are your hobbies, interests, or part time job engaging enough that you feel you have purpose? Don't expect to live a life of boredom, monotony, and lack of purpose, and then suddenly develop a purpose upon retirement. If you are a couch potato before retirement, you are not going to develop interests overnight.

Money Can Prevent Illness

Dr. Thomas H. Holmes, at the University of Washington School of Medicine, has developed a scale to measure the psychological stress that may be caused by various changes in life circumstances. **Dr. Holmes indicates an accumulation of 200 or more "life-change units" in a single year may be more disruptive than individuals can withstand, and make them susceptible to depression and other illnesses.**

Event

* **Death of Spouse**	**100**
Divorce	73
Marital separation	65
Death of close family member	63
Personal injury or illness	53
* **Retirement**	**45**
Change in health of family member	44
Sex difficulties	39
* **Business readjustment**	**39**
* **Change in financial state**	**38**
Death of close friend	37
* **Change to different line of work**	**36**
Mortgage over $10,000	31
Foreclosure of mortgage or loan	30
Son or daughter leaving home	29
Trouble with in-laws	29
* **Spouse begins or stops work**	**26**
* **Change in living conditions**	**25**
* **Revision of personal habits**	**24**
* **Change in work hours or conditions**	**20**
* **Change in residence**	**20**
* **Change in recreation**	**19**
Change in church activities	19
* **Change in sleeping habits**	**16**
* **Change in number of family get-togethers**	**15**
Change in eating habits	15

* These often accompany retirement and thus the values should be added together. They total 423, well over the 200 tolerance level. Adequate life insurance could reduce the "life-change units" to 198.

How is your health? Everyone has heard stories about workaholics who would take little relaxation, and then die when they had nothing to do. That is not uncommon, because of the stress factors and the lifestyle adjustment.

Finally, try practicing retirement with your spouse. Develop a weekly schedule, and try living it. Imagine what you would be doing day in and day out. Try living on the amount of income that you would have at retirement. Evaluate your physical activities and your diet. Get involved in those activities which you might be pursuing after retirement. Start looking for a new residence, if you plan to move when you retire. Work on developing social contacts outside your office environment.

Then, make the retirement decision that will work best for you.

Your Retirement Deserves Careful Analysis

Whether or not working past retirement age is on your agenda, adequate financial preparation for your retirement should be at the top of your list.

How much money will you need? People often tell me they expect to be able to live on 60 to 70 percent of their income after retirement. Is that a realistic assumption? Maybe not. For instance, many people assume that because the kids are grown and gone, their expenses will go down. Yet in reality, I often observe that such is not the case.

As grandchildren come, grandma wants to be sure she has the financial means to pamper them. Maybe she wants to take plane trips to visit her children and grandchildren a few times a year. Or, if they live in the same locale, she wants to feel free to take her daughter to lunch. And on the way to pick her up, she wants to be able to drop by the store and pick up a few goodies for the grandchildren.

It's very common to see grandma spending an additional $5,000, $10,000 or $15,000 per year on grandchildren, Christmas, birthdays, and other family get-togethers. And what about grandpa? Grandpa wants to buy season tickets to the local sporting events so he can spend time with his son or grandson. Then there are country club memberships. Golf dues. Vacations. All of these things can add up.

Plus, many expenses don't change upon retirement. For instance, your utility bills for your home won't change. They might even go up because you'll warm your home more.

There are a number of critical questions which require more analysis than a simple rule of thumb or guesstimate.

Questions to Ponder as You Consider Retirement

- Will your house be paid off? If not, how much will you owe on your monthly mortgage, taxes, and insurance?
- Will you have other debt for automobiles, etc.?
- Will you have dependents still living at home or at college?
- Will you have additional insurances to cover the loss of employer-provided benefits, such as health insurance, Medicare supplement insurance, long-term health care insurance, etc.?
- Will you even be able to get individual health insurance between the age that you retire and when Medicare becomes available at age 65? Will you be able to prove evidence of insurability?

Those are just the basics to consider when estimating your retirement needs. But what about expanding your options?

Adventures Worth Retiring to

For instance, perhaps you'd rather sell your home and move to a smaller residence or condo. If you do, there is a one-time, lump-sum income tax exclusion on the sale of your primary residence for $125,000 of gain. That $125,000 may be used to supplement your retirement portfolio.

Or, maybe you'd like to travel. In this case, you need to plan for travel expenses—airfare, hotels, or possibly a motorhome.

Might you want to engage in some charitable pursuits? Maybe you'll consider the adventure of providing service for the less fortunate in other lands. Some of the most rewarding retirement adventures I've heard of involve individuals who have helped dig a well in Africa, provide dental services in the Philippines, build a cistern for a village in Mexico, or teach basic health care concepts to Indians high in the Andes Mountains. Usually, these expeditions do not require unique skills or competencies.

As Americans, we take for granted much of what we have grown up with. The Peace Corps, your church, and a whole host of other charitable organizations have work you can do. Teaching others how to improve their lives can be a great adventure. You can go serve for four or six months and be home in time for fall football. Some retirees I know have done this repeatedly over many years. And they seem to be among the happiest.

A Whole New Life: The Second Career

Others find that retirement is a great time to begin a second career. They have developed broad expertise and knowledge over their lifetime, and they find new and improved positions the next time around. They are at or near the top of their profession, and they continue to develop new skills as they take on new challenges.

The specific plans you have for your retirement will help you determine how much you need to save, so don't be misled by oft-quoted rules of thumb. Consider whether or not you'd like to make a change. Be proactive, and be ready with a contingency plan in case your employer makes your decision for you. The more money you have in hand, the more flexibility you will have.

Start Saving for Retirement Now

Many people keep putting off the planning process, waiting until age 45 or so to start saving for retirement. Yet, one of the smartest retirement planning decisions you can make is to start saving early.

The table below shows how much you would have at age 65 if you started saving a set monthly amount at ages 20, 30, 40, 50, and 60. The table assumes a 10 percent pre-tax rate of return, a 28 percent tax paid on earnings every year, and an inflation rate of 3 percent.

Someone who starts saving $300 per month at age 20 will have a nest egg of $479,791 by age 65, in *real* terms. In order to save that amount by age 65, a 30-year-old needs to save $503 per month; a 40-year-old, $907; a 50-year-old, $1,918; and a 60-year-old, $7,200.

The lesson is simple—start saving now. While you're at it, drill this concept into your children. If you can convince them to start saving early, it will make a huge difference for their retirement. (Source: Integrated Concepts Group, Inc.)

Monthly Investment	Age you start investing:				
	60	50	40	30	20
$100	$ 6,664	$ 25,016	$ 52,926	$ 95,374	$ 159,930
200	13,327	50,031	105,852	190,748	319,861
300	19,991	75,047	158,779	286,122	479,791
400	26,654	100,062	211,705	381,496	639,721
500	33,318	125,078	264,631	476,870	799,652
600	39,982	150,094	317,557	572,244	959,582
700	46,645	175,109	370,483	667,617	1,119,512
800	53,309	200,125	423,410	762,991	1,279,443
900	59,972	225,141	476,336	858,365	1,439,373
1,000	66,636	250,157	529,262	953,739	1,599,303

Focus on the future, not the past. A positive attitude and optimism will invade your life when you contemplate what you could be doing in the years ahead. These are empowering thoughts. Take a pad of paper and begin writing ideas now. Let those idea-seeds germinate until they blossom into a full blown plan of action.

If the purpose of money is happiness, plan for your retirement accordingly. Twenty-five years is a long time, long enough for a whole other career or avocation. Make it full.

Inflation Will Rise, Fixed Incomes Do Not

Few people understand inflation well because each year their income rises in order to keep up with it. And as prices go up in the supermarket, people tend to be able to adjust accordingly.

But inflation becomes quite a slap in the face after retirement for those on a fixed income. Inflation can work for you, if you understand it. But it will work against you if you don't. Assuming 5 percent inflation, an individual retiring on $1,000 a month at age 60 will only have $290 per month of purchasing power 20 years later.

By then, that individual will require a monthly income of over $3,200 just to have the same $1,000 a month standard of living. So, his investment portfolio had better be invested into assets that provide an inflation hedge.

There are other ways to combat inflation as well.

For instance, what about real estate? If someone buys an apartment complex by the age of 35 or 40, and then works to have the mortgages paid off on that building by age 65, that apartment complex may provide an excellent inflation-adjusted retirement income. The problem is that the retiree must be healthy enough (looking forward 20 years) to provide the maintenance and upkeep on the rental properties during retirement.

If you can qualify to purchase an apartment or some real properties by age 35 or 40, you should have their mortgages paid off in time for retirement. And those mortgage payments would have been largely paid by those renting the property over the years. Additionally, because the mortgage payment is fixed, as rental rates increase with inflation, you may have an increasing positive cash flow on the rental property.

The Big Impact of Inflation on Retirement Planning

If you are *not* yet retired, how many years until you do?
If you *are* retired, how many more years should you plan for?

Monthly Income Needed to Produce Equivalent of $1,000 in Today's Dollars

Inflation Rate	Today	5 Years	10 Years	20 Years	30 Years	40 Years
3%	$1,000	$1,162	$1,349	$1,821	$2,457	$3,315
5%	1,000	1,283	1,647	2,712	4,468	7,358
7%	1,000	1,418	2,010	4,039	8,116	16,311

For example: If you think inflation will average 5 percent and you want to retire in 20 years on $3,000 per month in today's dollars, then you will need to develop a portfolio that will generate $8,136 income *per month* ($2,712 x 3 = $8,136). Alternatively, if you are retiring now and you think you may live another 20 years, then your portfolio which is generating $3,000 per month *today* will need to also grow so that it will generate $8,136 income per month in 20 years, just to keep your standard of living constant. This requires "inflation hedges," or equity investments.

Future Purchasing Power of $1,000 in Today's Dollars

Inflation Rate	Today	5 Years	10 Years	20 Years	30 Years	40 Years
3%	$1,000	$861	$741	$548	$406	$301
5%	1,000	778	606	367	222	134
7%	1,000	704	495	246	122	60

If your portfolio is not properly designed with appropriate "inflation hedges" but consists primarily of "fixed-income" investments such as CDs and bonds, then your purchasing power will diminish. Twenty years from now, your portfolio may still be sending you a monthly check for $1,000, but at 5 percent inflation, it will only purchase $367 worth of goods and services.

What else can you do to deal with inflation?

Inflation is a phenomenon that impacts a money society. In Chapter 5 we discussed how the tax siphon only occurs when we transfer our labor into money before translating the money into lifestyle. To the extent that we can transfer our labor directly into our lifestyle without it first becoming money, we not only avoid income taxes, we avoid the inflation tax. There is no inflation for those who live in a cash-free environment.

While this is most unrealistic for the major part of our living expenses, to the extent that you can develop self-reliance and skills, you will avoid the impact of inflation. This occurs because of your ability to grow a garden, use tools, own real estate and other tangible assets which hold their value in inflation. The key is *ownership, not loanership*. When you loan your money out to banks in the form of savings accounts, or to corporations and the government in the form of bonds, you will be repaid with greatly depreciated dollars.

You simply need to be aware of the drastic impact inflation can have on your finances during your retirement years—and plan accordingly.

History of Inflation Since 1970

Year	Inflation Rate	Declining Value of $1.00	Dollars Needed to Stay Even
1970	5.5%	$94.8	$1.06
1971	3.4	91.7	1.09
1972	3.4	88.7	1.13
1973	8.8	81.5	1.23
1974	12.3	72.6	1.38
1975	6.9	67.9	1.47
1976	4.9	64.7	1.55
1977	6.7	60.7	1.65
1978	9.0	55.7	1.80
1979	13.3	49.1	2.04
1980	12.5	43.7	2.29
1981	8.9	40.1	2.49
1982	3.8	38.6	2.59
1983	3.8	37.2	2.69
1984	3.9	35.8	2.79
1985	3.8	34.5	2.90
1986	1.1	34.1	2.93
1987	4.4	32.7	3.06
1988	4.4	31.3	3.20
1989	4.7	29.9	3.34
1990	6.1	28.2	3.55
1991	3.1	27.3	3.66
1992	2.9	26.3	3.80
1993	2.7	25.9	3.86
1994	2.7	25.2	3.97
1995	2.9	24.5	4.08
1996	3.1	23.8	4.21

Why Tax Rates Rise to 60 Percent on Retirees

Not only are people often unprepared for the impact of inflation at retirement, but there is also a common misconception that they will be in a lower tax bracket when they retire.

In fact, just the opposite may be true.

Your marginal tax rate at retirement may jump to 50 or 60 percent or more, as it does for about 30 percent of the retired population in America. Many elderly retirees are actually worse off because they put their savings in IRAs and employer-provided retirement plans, and many younger people will be better off if they avoid IRAs.

Why?

The premise behind IRAs and qualified plans is that you will be in a lower tax bracket after you retire. That premise has become a cruel hoax for many elderly retirees who face higher tax rates now than when they were young.

With IRAs and other retirement plans, taxes on savings are postponed until retirement when people traditionally have been in the lower tax bracket. Yet, according to some simple calculations, middle-income elderly retirees face *higher* marginal tax rates on income from savings than *any* other group. Elderly retirees with only $40,000 of income from savings currently are taxed at the rate of about 65 percent.

Want an example?

Assuming $40,000 per year retirement income:

If your income increases by $1.00 (to $40,001), out of that one dollar of extra income, you will pay an additional:

> 28.0 cents federal income tax
> _7.2_ cents state income tax (average)
> 35.2 cents total

PLUS, under current law, that $1.00 of income will cause an additional 85 cents of Social Security income to be taxed, or an additional:

> 23.8 cents federal income tax
> _6.0_ cents state income tax (average)
> 29.8 cents

For a total additional tax bite of almost 65 cents just for earning one more dollar!

That's your marginal bracket! This tax rate stays in effect until all Social Security income is used up, or at about $60,000 of taxable income.

Many workers today are avoiding a 15 percent income tax rate when they put money into IRAs and other retirement plans. Yet when they withdraw their funds during retirement, they may be taxed at a rate that is two to four times higher!

In other words, these people are postponing the payment of taxes until the time when they are in the *very highest tax bracket.*

The primary reason people save is to have income during retirement. Yet, the special tax rates on the elderly mean that if you do save, more than half of your extra retirement income may go to the government.

Does that mean you should stop saving? No, of course not. Just be aware of the potential future tax bite when planning for your retirement. Be selective, and explore your options with this consideration in mind. It also means that perhaps you should reconsider the vehicles you are using to accumulate retirement monies. (See Chapter 30.)

The other cruel hoax about our Social Security tax system? As Social Security taxes (FICA and Medicare) are withheld from your paycheck, they are *not* tax-deductible—while contributions to IRAs and 401k plans *are* tax-deductible. Yet Social Security income *is* taxable for many retirees—like income drawn from IRAs, 401k plans, etc. So, unlike personal or employer-provided retirement plans, Social Security is contributed to with *already-taxed* dollars, and when the retirement benefit is received, those dollars are taxed *again.*

How to Maximize Retirement Benefits

Almost two-thirds of all retirees choose the wrong option when selecting their retirement benefit from their employer-provided pension plan.

Stan wanted to be sure income was provided for his wife, Iris, if he were to die prematurely. So, it seemed perfectly logical for him to choose a pension benefit that provided both a "life and a survivor" benefit option, even though when his retirement was actuarially calculated for both his life expectancy and Iris' life expectancy, the benefit would be 40 to 50 percent more for a "life only" option.

But what if Iris dies before Stan? When Stan dies, his children have essentially been disinherited. Why? There is nothing left over. Stan has no control over his survivor benefits.

Stan's co-worker, Victor, decided to choose a "life only" option instead. His retirement plan would provide benefits for him during his lifetime only. It would *not* provide any benefits for his surviving spouse, Laura, if Victor died first.

So, why did he choose this option? There are a number of reasons.

He can take the additional 50 percent in retirement income and use it to purchase a life insurance policy to insure his life. He did some investigating and discovered he could pay the premium and still have more retirement income left over than he would otherwise have had. Plus, if Victor dies first, the life insurance provides the lifetime benefit for Laura. If Laura dies first, there is still an insurance benefit for their heirs—their children weren't disinherited as they would have been under the other option.

If Victor had chosen the life and survivor option, it would have provided him a monthly income for both his life and Laura's life for $1,200 a month. Alternatively, the life only option provided a monthly income of $1,800 for Victor's lifetime only. Upon his death, it would terminate.

So, Victor simply took $400 of the $600 difference in monthly income and purchased a life insurance policy adequate to provide Laura comparable benefits during her remaining lifetime. And the remaining $200 a month would provide an increased retirement income.

Further Benefits of Life Only

What about other benefits of this strategy?

- Victor may purchase a policy whose premiums may vanish in eight to 12 years, resulting in a paid-up policy; then he would have the full $600 for additional retirement income.
- He has control over survivor benefits.
- He can change the beneficiary and provide for contingent beneficiaries.
- If Laura dies first, he can cash in the equity in his policy and *also* continue receiving maximum pension benefits. The cash values of the policy may supplement his retirement in later years. Under the life and survivor option Stan chose, if Iris died first, Stan would be stuck with lower benefits throughout his lifetime.

Note: It is essential that you have a life insurance policy issued on your life *before* you select the life only option. Unfortunately, that means this strategy is only available if you are in good health and can qualify for a policy.

Also, consider inflation adjustments to your company's plan, and factor that into your insurance calculation. And consider whether or not your spouse will be able to continue to participate in company-sponsored health insurance after your death.

This is a strategy which may allow you have the best of both worlds—a larger retirement income, while still providing for your spouse.

How Charitable Pursuits After Retirement Help Finances

Why do people engage in charitable pursuits? They want to make a difference in people's lives. They want to make a contribution to our society, or to the world. And they want to help those in less fortunate circumstances than their own. In my experience, people who are engaged in charitable pursuits after retirement live a much fuller, richer, happier life—they awaken each morning with a sense of purpose.

That might seem obvious to you. But did you know that these rewarding pursuits can also have a significant positive impact on your finances? For one thing, if you are offering extended assistance abroad, your expenses will go down for the period of time you are away from home. At the same time, your investment portfolio has the opportunity to season and grow for that additional year or more without being drawn upon. One year to 18 months of additional growth in a portfolio may mean as much as 8 to 16 percent higher retirement income upon returning home.

Why is there such a dramatic impact? Not only is the investment portfolio growing untouched, but there is one less year or so in which it must fund a retirement. It normally must fund the retirement for 20 years. One less year that it must fund means an automatic 5 percent increase. Plus, if the portfolio has earned 10 percent on your money, you may have a total impact of 15 percent greater retirement income.

The travel and living expenses you incur on such a charitable adventure are usually tax-deductible. So, it is worthwhile to at least consider taking advantage of opportunities to provide service during your retirement.

Perhaps you have a favorite charity. Perhaps you are interested in offering assistance in a country less fortunate than our own. Look into charitable organizations, a number of which organize aid expeditions to struggling countries. Enterprise Mentors, for instance, gives you the opportunity to help people in underdeveloped countries start a business.[1] Or, you might consider groups like the Center for Humanitarian Outreach and Intercultural Exchange (CHOICE) who help those in foreign nations become more self-reliant.[2]

You can also contact your church or local university for ideas. Look for a program that doesn't merely provide a bonanza to the recipients,

---

[1] Enterprise Mentors may be reached at (314) 453-0006; 510 Maryville College Dr., Suite 210, St. Louis, Missouri 63141.

[2] CHOICE may be reached at (801) 363-7970; 643 E. 400 S., Salt Lake City, Utah 84102.

but instead teaches them how to provide for themselves. As the old Chinese proverb goes, "Feed a man a fish, and you feed him for a day. Teach a man to fish, and you feed him for a lifetime."

Remember, idealism is not only for teenagers. You *can* make a difference. If you have lost some of your idealism, reignite it—your torch might light another. The options and opportunities are endless.

A Creative Last Resort: The Reverse Mortgage

One idea increasing in popularity these days is the reverse mortgage. A reverse mortgage is a financial instrument wherein you receive a monthly income for a number of years from the equity in your home. The loan is repaid when the borrower dies or sells the home.

The reverse mortgage may free up a large part of the equity in your home to retire on, and you don't have leave your good friends and neighbors and sell down to another neighborhood. You may remain in your home throughout your lifetime. It may allow you to keep a level of independence, and you don't have to pay back the loan until your death, or the sale of your residence.

How long can you get that equity income? Typically, you can receive the income for life. The amount of the payment to you is based on the equity in your home and your life expectancy. You do not have to apply it to all of the equity in your home—you may decide only to use a small portion of that equity.

While there are many advantages to a reverse mortgage, I normally recommend that these be used only as a last resort.

Basically, you're borrowing money from the bank, and you are going to owe that money back to the bank when you die, or when the home is sold. You owe the bank not only principal, but also the interest which has been compounding.

Placing that kind of debt against the home you have worked your entire lifetime to pay off can be traumatic. Plus, the reverse mortgage doesn't allow you to take advantage of the $125,000 income tax exclusion, and it may not free up as much money as selling the home would. Also, if you had to move from your home into a retirement home or a nursing home, it could force the sale of your home in order to pay off the mortgage.

So, when *would* I recommend a reverse mortgage?

Only if parents enter into it with their own children instead of with a financial institution. In this case, their children are simply purchasing the home, which they would have been inheriting. They are essentially providing their parents a monthly income except that by purchasing the home, the mortgage interest the children are paying may be tax-deductible to them in their higher tax bracket.

In this sense, the children are able to contribute to their parents' retirement while taking a tax deduction for the mortgage interest they are paying. Of course, the parents must declare the mortgage interest as income, but *if* they are in a significantly lower tax bracket than their children, it may still be a profitable exchange.

In this case, the parents have also been able to get the home out of their taxable estate, and any further appreciation is accruing to the children. The agreement includes the right of the parents to live in the home for as long as they choose.

The parents may pay a small amount in rent back to the children for the right of living in the home, which may also entitle the children to take a tax deduction for depreciation as they would on any rental property. So, the children may get tax savings from both the mortgage interest paid and the depreciation expense.

If the reverse mortgage works in your family's situation, it may be worth exploring. But, remember that the psychological peace of mind of the parents is an essential factor that cannot be discounted when analyzing the financial implications of this strategy.

(Because there are some technical caveats, it is critical that the strategies discussed herein are pursued only with professional assistance.)

The Selective Incentive Plan

You are probably familiar with qualified retirement plans—IRAs, corporation pension and profit-sharing plans, 401k plans, defined benefit plans and others. But did you know you have other options? One of them, the Selective Incentive Plan (SIP), offers some tempting benefits for both employees and business owners.

With the SIP there are no contribution limits or administrative costs, and the dollars invested compound income tax free. Your money can be accessed tax-free as well. Plus, the plan may yield a greater retirement income than qualified plans or personal investing. The dollars are also accessible prior to retirement and there is a death benefit included. It does not cause your Social Security income to become taxable, thereby avoiding the 60 percent tax rate at retirement. The plan offers many other benefits as well.

The Selective Incentive Plan coordinates retirement planning and wealth accumulation along with risk management, estate planning, and tax advantages. It is an important option to examine for anyone considering contributions into a 401k plan, IRA, other retirement plans, or investing personally. (If you are interested in learning more about the benefits of the Selective Incentive Plan, please call Fax-on-Demand at (801) 263-1676 and request free report #150.)

So, Are You Prepared?

Obviously, retirement planning involves a lot more than mere reliance on Social Security, a 401k, or an IRA. The one thing you can rely on is yourself. You are the architect of your own future. Think about what your retirement goals are and how you intend to spend your time. Keep in mind the effects of rising inflation and the potential 60 percent tax bite for retirees. Then plan for your future needs, realizing that you may need more at retirement than you perhaps anticipated.

Remember the real sources of retirement dollars: man at work or money at work. Put your money to work for you now and you'll retire with more than just a healthy income. You'll have freedom, security, and peace of mind.

Your Insights, Feelings, and Action Items

A. As you read this chapter, what *insights* came that seem applicable to *you?*
   1._____
   2._____
   3._____

B. How did you *feel* as you pondered particular points of this chapter?
   1._____
   2._____
   3._____

C. What do you *feel* you should *do* as a result of this chapter?
   1._____
   2._____
   3._____

D. How might you solicit the aid of others in accomplishing "C" above?
   _____
   _____
   _____

Chapter 22

What You Should Know about the Risks in Your Investment Portfolio

As we discuss various investments, always remember: The best investments you will ever make are in yourself, and tools. Here's why: A college graduate will, on average, earn about 75 percent more than a high school graduate. That disparity is projected to steadily increase, resulting in an ever-widening spread between high school graduates and college graduates.

But it doesn't end at graduation: One of our greatest handicaps is to stop learning. Why? Education quickly becomes outdated. A $20 investment in a book that you read and apply is more likely to generate greater dividends than any thousand-dollar investment in a mutual fund, stock, or bond.

Second, what about tools? The saws, pliers, hammers, wrenches, computers, rakes, lawn mowers, sewing machines, bread makers, and auto repair tools you own—the tools with which you can build a backyard deck, grow a garden, or repair your home—will always generate a higher rate of return than typical investments. Why? Because of the WYHTE phenomenon.

Even in good times, tools generate a 300 to 1,000 percent return on their investment. If you take care of them, they may last for many years. Regardless of the value of your time, your ability to manufacture or repair lets you skip the whole distribution chain: markup, distribution costs, and taxes.

Let's take, for example, the hamburger you buy in a fast-food restaurant. If the restaurant is profitable, only 16 to 18 percent of the cost of that hamburger actually went into the purchase of the food.

What does that mean to you? You get your paycheck, then surrender a 40 percent bite to taxes. Then you pay $2 for the hamburger—something you could have made at home for 40 cents. The $1.50 drink you buy cost the restaurant 7 cents.

Many go through life with the silly economic assumption that they can make millions in the investment market—while they fritter away their income because they don't use education, tools, and self-reliance. The important thing isn't your rate of return—it's how much you save in the first place. *It is the principal that counts.*

Make Big Money with the Top-Performing Investment

People often ask me what, besides you, is the top-performing asset? Is it real estate? Stocks? Bonds? International investments? Precious metals? Collectibles? Leveraged real estate? It's none of those.

Make no mistake. The best asset is, and always will be, *cash*. When held by someone who understands it, cash always outperforms any other asset.

You might argue that during the past two decades, stocks have performed at an average compounded annual rate of 13.4 percent, bonds at 8.2 percent, and money market funds—or cash—at only 3.8 percent. So why is cash the top-performing asset? Simple.

Cash Is Opportunity

When you have cash, you can take advantage of special opportunities that come along—opportunities that might yield 50 percent, 100 percent, 200 percent, or even more.

What kinds of opportunities can you take advantage of with cash? Word gets out when people have cash. People with cash are the ones who get the telephone calls from someone who says, "If you can come up with $100,000 within 48 hours, I know of a hundred acres on the outskirts of Las Vegas in the direction of growth which you can have in a foreclosure." If you have the cash, you get the piece of land.

Cash lets you negotiate when you buy a car. It lets you negotiate when you buy real estate. (A seller who knows you have cash and can close quickly will often discount the price significantly.) Cash lets you buy business materials and supplies at a significant discount. Cash lets you take advantage of sales and store liquidations as they come along. Cash lets you buy low when everyone else is selling.

When you have cash, you usually deal in a fairly risk-free environment. Prices are reduced because someone gets into trouble—with debt, with the Internal Revenue Service, with a business failure—and you are able to solve their problem. Does that mean you're taking advantage of another *person*? Not at all. You should always be fair. But cash lets you take advantage of *opportunities*.

Really big money is made from opportunities—and *opportunity* is spelled C-A-S-H. Cash is *power*.

Now, I happen to think my associates and I are pretty good at what we do—advising people on money matters. And, what do we all sell all day long? The miracle of compound interest, investments. But however good we are, we can't generate the 50 to 100 percent return which ready cash may enable in the hands of the astute. (The trick is to discern the difference between real opportunity and a financial fad, or worse yet, fraud.)

Know These Three Vital Investment Principles

Now that you understand the importance of cash, we can look at several principles that govern traditional investments: diversification, liquidity, and compound interest.

Diversification

Diversification refers to holding many different stocks, bonds, or properties. It's the most secure way to reduce investment risk. That's not as easy as it sounds: You need *at least* 17 different assets in your portfolio to adequately reduce your risk.

Effect of Diversification on Risk

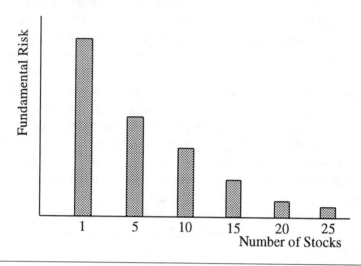

Liquidity

Liquidity refers to how easily you can convert your investments to cash. It goes beyond simply selling your assets—it refers to how quickly you can sell your assets and convert them to cash *at full value.*

Liquid assets, then, include savings accounts, certificates of deposit, money market funds, treasury bills, and the cash value of traditional life insurance. They're the assets you should keep in an emergency fund for cash reserves, as we suggested in Chapter 6.

Technically speaking, within the investment markets, stocks, bonds, U.S. government bonds, and corporate bonds are *not* considered liquid investments. Why? You never know whether you'll be able to get full value when you need to convert them to cash. That's the critical distinction.

What rate of return should you expect from liquid investments? Remember that the only relevant rate of return calculation is one that factors in the income tax implications. An investment portfolio manager won't manage your portfolio in terms of income tax implications, and that's okay. As an individual investor, though, if you want to compare apples to apples, you must always compare investments on an after-tax basis.

Let's assume a certificate of deposit is earning 5 percent. You invest $10,000. At the end of the year, how much money will you have? $10,500.

What happens to that $500 in interest? The bank sends you a 1099 form listing your interest. They also send a copy to the IRS. Then it is your privilege to pay about $150 to Uncle Sam. Your net interest is $350. Now how much is in your bank account? $10,350.

If it stopped there, it wouldn't be so bad. But, hold on. Inflation has averaged about 6 percent during the past 15 years. Now, how much do you need in your account just to stay even with inflation? $10,600. You only have $10,350. In other words, you lost $250 after taxes and after inflation.

This loss is called the **liquidity premium**—it's kind of like an insurance premium. You pay it so you can have a viable emergency fund. But it also explains why you shouldn't put *too* much in liquid investments—you'd be paying an unnecessary premium.

You should always figure in taxes, but you should always figure in inflation, too. If the inflation rate is 5 to 6 percent, you have to earn 9 to 10 percent on your money just to break even after taxes and inflation. This is called the **hurdle rate.**

The hurdle rate is an important concept in investing. It tells you that if you earn 9 to 10 percent on your money, and then subtract your total combined federal and state taxes of 30 to 40 percent, you net about 5 or 6 percent. If you then subtract inflation, you are just breaking even on an after-tax, after-inflation basis. You have a zero *real* return.

What does this tell you? If you want a real return, you need to beat the 9 to 10 percent hurdle rate.

Your "Hurdle Rate"
What you must earn just to break even after taxes
and after inflation (a net 0% return).

Your Marginal Tax Bracket*	The Inflation Rate							
	2 %	3 %	4 %	5 %	6 %	7 %	8 %	9 %
25%	2.7%	4.0%	5.3%	6.7%	8.0%	9.3%	10.7%	12.0%
30	2.9	4.3	5.7	7.1	8.6	10.0	11.4	12.9
35	3.1	4.6	6.2	7.7	9.2	10.8	12.3	13.8
40	3.3	5.0	6.7	8.3	10.0	11.7	13.3	15.0
45	3.6	5.5	7.3	9.1	10.9	12.7	14.5	16.4
50	4.0	6.0	8.0	10.0	12.0	14.0	16.0	18.0

* Add Federal, State, and Local Income Tax Rates.

What about federal bonds? Treasury bills are accepted as the definition of safety throughout the world. Why? Because they're issued by the U.S. government, and they mature in three months to a year. That's not really too risky—the U.S. government is not likely to fail within the next year.

On the other hand, lower grade corporate bonds, which mature in five to 30 years and are sometimes called "junk bonds," have a higher rate of return—partly because there is a risk of default. In other words, it is much more *possible* that the corporation could fail, so the risk premium is increased.

Let's look at the rate of return on a long-term U.S. government bond, considering both taxes and inflation (the hurdle rate). Let's assume you have a $1,000 bond that matures in 20 years. Let's assume inflation is 5 percent, that you're in a 30 percent total tax bracket, and that the bond is paying 8 percent.

How much interest will be generated each year? $80. You'll pay $24 in taxes each year on that $80, netting $56 after taxes. At the end of that first year, that $56 will buy $53.20 worth of goods and services because of inflation. In the second year, it will buy $50.54 worth of goods and services. In the third year, $48.01. And so on. At the end of 20 years, that $56 will purchase $20.08 worth of goods and services. So much for the interest.

At the end of 20 years, you get back the principal, and you receive a check from the U.S. government for $1,000. But because of inflation, that $1,000 will only purchase $358 worth of goods and services.

Okay—what's your total return? Over the years, you've received a total of $579 in inflation-adjusted dollars, paid to you in interest. But you've lost $642 in purchasing power from your original $1,000, for a net loss of $63. Your after-tax, after-inflation "return" is actually a loss.

The government, on the other hand, received taxes from you during those 20 years. That's not all: The government was also able to spend your $1,000—and give you back only $358. Why? Inflation.

Some have proposed that a little inflation is a good thing. Baloney. If a little is good, then more must be better. Nonsense. Just ask anyone who has lived under hyper-inflation. People forget that *any* inflation is nothing more or less than devaluing the dollar, making our currency and coinage more and more worthless. We notice it when it is rapid and painful. The government now manages it so it is slow and insidious. But the eventual destination is the same: a devalued currency. A portfolio must consider the effects of taxes and inflation.

Compound Interest

Why is compound interest so important?

Because with the power of compound interest, *anyone* can be a millionaire.

Here's how: Let's assume your average income is $25,000 a year. You commit to saving 10 percent of your income, or $208.33 a month. Starting when you are 25, you invest that $208.33 a month into a mutual fund that averages 12 percent a year. By the time you are 65, your fund would grow to $2,594,112 without taxes. (You can avoid the tax bite if you invest the money in an IRA, a corporate pension or profit-sharing plan, an annuity, or a variable life insurance policy.)

What about inflation? Inflation certainly diminishes the end value, but it also diminishes the value of what you're putting in. In other words, the $208 you put in each month steadily depreciates, too—until the final month's $208 would equal about $12.54 in today's dollars.

That's why you should invest 10 percent of your income every year—not a set amount based on your income when you start saving. If you invest 10 percent of your income every year, you'll automatically be saving an increasing amount as inflation goes up—and your multi-million dollar net worth will be in true inflation-adjusted dollars.

Anyone, *anyone* in America, can be a millionaire.

$10,000 Lump Sum Investment Will Grow to:

Rate	5 Years	10 Years	15 Years	20 Years	25 Years	30 Years
3%	$11,593	$13,439	$15,580	$18,061	$20,937	$24,272
4	12,167	14,802	18,009	21,911	26,658	32,433
5	12,763	16,289	20,789	26,533	33,863	43,219
6	13,382	17,908	23,966	32,071	42,918	57,434
7	14,026	19,672	27,590	38,697	54,272	76,122
8	14,693	21,589	31,722	46,610	68,484	100,626
9	15,386	23,674	36,425	56,044	86,230	132,676
10	16,105	25,937	41,772	67,275	108,347	174,494
11	16,851	28,394	47,846	80,623	135,854	228,922
12	17,623	31,058	54,736	96,463	170,000	299,599
13	18,424	33,946	62,543	115,231	212,305	391,159
14	19,254	37,072	71,379	137,435	264,619	509,501
15	20,114	40,456	81,371	163,665	329,189	662,117

Lump Sum Investment Needed to Accumulate $100,000

Rate	5 Years	10 Years	15 Years	20 Years	30 Years	40 Years
3%	$86,266	$74,409	$64,186	$55,368	$41,219	$30,656
4	82,197	67,556	55,526	45,639	30,850	20,829
5	78,357	61,391	48,102	37,689	23,154	14,205
6	74,730	55,839	41,727	31,180	17,426	9,722
7	71,303	50,835	36,245	25,842	13,150	6,678
8	68,053	46,319	31,524	21,455	9,950	4,603
9	64,998	42,241	27,454	17,843	7,548	3,184
10	62,096	38,554	23,939	14,864	5,741	2,209
11	59,349	35,218	20,900	12,403	4,378	1,538
12	56,746	32,197	18,270	10,367	3,347	1,075
13	54,280	29,459	15,989	8,678	2,565	753
14	51,941	26,974	14,010	7,276	1,971	529
15	49,722	24,724	12,289	6,110	1,518	373

Annual Sum Investment Needed to Accumulate $100,000

Rate	5 Years	10 Years	15 Years	20 Years	30 Years	40 Years
3%	$18,287	$8,469	$5,220	$3,613	$2,040	$1,288
4	17,753	8,009	4,802	3,229	1,714	1,012
5	17,236	7,572	4,414	2,880	1,433	788
6	16,736	7,157	4,053	2,565	1,193	610
7	16,251	6,764	3,719	2,280	989	468
8	15,783	6,392	3,410	2,023	817	357
9	15,330	6,039	3,125	1,793	673	272
10	14,891	5,704	2,861	1,587	553	205
11	14,466	5,388	2,618	1,403	453	155
12	14,054	5,088	2,395	1,239	369	116
13	13,656	4,804	2,190	1,093	302	87
14	13,270	4,536	2,001	964	246	65
15	12,897	4,283	1,828	849	200	49

How to Manage Away the Four Investment Risks

You must understand risk. Once you understand risk, you can grasp the most effective portfolio design. Unfortunately, most portfolio managers and financial planners concentrate on returns without understanding risk.

There are four basic kinds of risk: fundamental risk, technical risk, interest-rate risk, and purchasing-power risk. (A fifth risk, tax risk, is beyond the scope of this discussion.) Once you understand them, and understand how to manage them away, you'll have the basics of portfolio design.

(By the way, there's a risk tolerance worksheet in *Your Money Happiness Workbook*—answer the questions honestly, and it will help you understand how much risk you can tolerate.)

Acknowledge Fundamental Risk

You might have heard other terms to describe fundamental risk—terms like *micro-risk, business risk,* or *default risk.*

Fundamental risk is the risk that is inherent within a particular business enterprise, such as IBM, Apple Computers, General Motors, Exxon Oil Company, Bank of America, or Citicorp. It relates to a company's financial strength, position in the marketplace, and competitive strength, reputation, and good will. It is affected by how well managed the company is. It is determined in part by the economic, competitive, regulatory, and legal environment in which it operates. All these factors impact the fundamental risk of a particular investment. And this fundamental risk applies to stocks, bonds, CDs, money market funds, and all other kinds of investments.

Take CDs, for example. Fundamental risk applied to CDs would determine the risk that the company (the bank) will default on the CD. That was a much greater risk before the Depression, but since then we have had FDIC insurance.

What about a bond? The fundamental risk there is the corporation's possible inability to meet payments on the bond. What about stocks? There's a fundamental risk that the company may not be able to stay in business, grow, make a profit, and pay dividends.

How can you manage fundamental risk? An obvious way is to make sure you're investing in a solid business to begin with. This is called fundamental analysis. A not-so-obvious way is through diversification. To adequately diversify away fundamental risk, you need to invest in at least 17 to 20 different stocks or bonds in 17 to 20 different industries. You also need to invest in larger order sizes in order to achieve any kind of economies of scale in your transaction costs.

Mutual funds are a great way to manage fundamental risk. A mutual fund automatically provides professional management and diversification and manages away most of the fundamental risk in a portfolio.

Acquaint Yourself with Technical Risk

Technical risk is also called *macro-risk* or *market risk*—they are the risks that exist in the economy or market as a whole. Technical risk relates to how the stock market or bond market as a whole may be doing and how they respond to various economic factors. Determining technical risk involves measuring things like general unemployment, interest rates and their direction, the budget deficit, and other economic indicators.

How can you manage away technical risk? One of the surest ways is with asset allocation—also called *balance*. Balance isn't the same thing as diversification. Diversification means you own many different stocks or bonds; balance (or asset allocation) means you carefully determine which investment markets or asset classes you should invest into right now.

Asset allocation or balance requires that you ask, "How much should I invest in the stock market vs. the bond market, international markets, real estate, CDs, money markets, or precious metals?" As you allocate your assets among various kinds of investments, you achieve a greater level of balance—and you're able to manage away much technical risk. (More on this critical skill in Chapter 31.)

Pay Attention to Interest Rate Risk

Interest rate risk relates to where interest rates are headed—and how fast they're moving. The risk applies to both short-term interest rates (such as prime) and long-term interest rates (such as interest rates on mortgages or 30-year corporate bonds).

Whether interest rates are headed up or down, the change in interest rates causes significant fluctuations in financial markets. Interest rate risk causes a sure correlation with bonds and a strong correlation with the stock market. (That is because a number of other factors also determine how the stock market behaves, and may override the interest rate risk.)

When interest rates climb, the value of bonds falls (usually with the stock market). When interest rates fall, the value of bonds rises (with the stock market).

How can you manage interest rate risk? Simple—go for short-term holdings of fixed-income securities. In other words, instead of owning 30-year mortgages or 30-year corporate bonds, go to one- or three- or five-year bonds. Choose bonds or notes with a shorter maturity. The longer it takes a note to mature, the more volatile it is—and the greater the interest rate risk.

The other way to manage away interest rate risk is to go with fixed-income investments that don't have fluctuating principal, where your original investment doesn't decline in value. Bonds have fluctuating principal; CDs and money market funds do not.

Project Purchasing Power Risk

Purchasing power risk, sometimes called *inflation risk*, is the risk that your dollars today will be worth less in the future. To manage purchasing power risk, you need to find a way to hedge inflation.

Exactly how can you manage away purchasing power risk? Look for equity in a real or tangible investment—such as real estate, common stocks, precious metals, collectibles, and other equity investments. The most volatile of these are precious metals; the most illiquid are real estate and collectibles.

Here's something to remember: Real estate and common stocks are good inflation hedges during periods of moderate inflation. But during periods of sudden or high inflation, interest rates will rise so rapidly that common stocks and real estate will actually decline in value. Simply put, don't use common stocks or real estate as an inflation hedge when the inflation rate is high.

The problem with risk is that when someone asks if an investment is risky, he or she is usually referring to fundamental risk: "Will I get my money back? Is the business going to default? Am I going to lose my money?" If you are designing a portfolio and want to know whether a particular investment is risky, you need to determine which kind of risk you are concerned about—and which kind you want to manage.

The type of risk you want to manage will dictate which risk management approach you use. For example, a CD fully insured by the federal government has very low fundamental risk, but a very high purchasing power risk. Why? A CD is not likely to keep up with inflation and taxes. On a real after-tax, after-inflation basis, you'll lose money on a CD. You may recall, I referred earlier to "going broke safely."

On the other hand, precious metals have very high market risk, but low inflation risk.

Constructing a portfolio from this perspective allows someone to identify and focus on managing risks.

Four Types of Risk

	Risk Name	How to Manage It Away
1.	Fundamental Risk a.k.a. Micro Risk Business Risk Default Risk	Diversification
2.	Technical Risk a.k.a. Macro Risk Market Risk	Asset Allocation or Balance
3.	Interest-Rate Risk	Short-Term Investments Fixed-Principal Investments
4.	Purchasing Power Risk a.k.a. Inflation Risk	Equity, Tangible, or Real Investments

---

Balance—Because Nobody Knows Nuthin'

From what you've just read, it's natural to *assume* that information is the most valuable commodity you can have when managing your investments. That's why mutual funds make sense to most people: Mutual funds are managed by professionals. When you buy individual stocks and bonds, you can't possibly compete with investment analysts who are sitting on Wall Street and getting minute-by-minute investment information. (You'd do just as well throwing darts at a dart board as you would selecting stocks as an average investor on the street.) So, unless you are a stock-picker like Warren Buffett, it probably makes sense to consider mutual funds.

But information can also be its own worst enemy. That's why the principle of balance is so essential. How can an investment adviser in Cortez, Colorado, do just as well as the pros on Wall Street? Because the pros on Wall Street, despite all their information, don't know which direction the market is going. They see stocks, but not bonds. They don't see international markets, or precious metals, or real estate, or CDs.

That is why you need to balance your portfolio as scientifically as possible across several different asset classes. That is why balance is still one of the bottom-line principles for a successful portfolio. No one has a crystal ball. Never treat information as the supreme virtue. For all the information, knowledge, insights, and "truths" that exist, there is always a whole lot more that we don't know. Some things are simply beyond our finite minds, systems, and information-gathering capabilities.

Sometimes portfolio managers (like all of us) become so impressed with what they know, that they lose a healthy respect for what they do not know. In the short term, the market is run by emotion. Even professional investors on Wall Street make investment decisions based on emotion, then justify the purchase with logic. The profound Joseph Oppenheimer observed, "The stock market has a history of moving through irrational extremes because, on a short-term basis, stock prices are often more a reflection of fear, greed, or other psychological factors than of business and monetary fundamentals." William LeFevre, vice-president of Granger and Company, added, "There are only two emotions on Wall Street—fear and greed." Neither results in disciplined decision-making.

Calculate the Risks of Ideal Investments

So, when you consider all the risk, what are the ideal investments? Wouldn't the ideal investments have maximum growth, maximum tax advantages, maximum cash flow, maximum safety, highest rate of return, lowest risk, complete liquidity, and total shelter from taxes?

Consider this: How do you get more juice from an orange—by cutting it in half, or cutting it in quarters? There's only so much juice, regardless of how you slice the orange. It's the same with investments: Market factors, such as supply and demand, force an equilibrium point across all investments.

Investment Attributes

Which yields more juice? If you slice the orange in halves or quarters? No matter how you slice it, there is only so much juice. You decide how you want to fill the glass.

Certificates of Deposit:

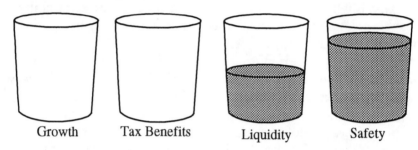

Growth   Tax Benefits   Liquidity   Safety

Growth Stock Mutual Funds:

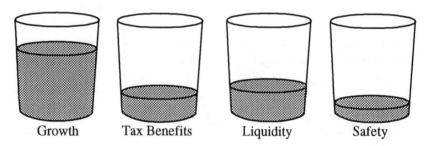

Growth   Tax Benefits   Liquidity   Safety

Directly Owned Real Estate:

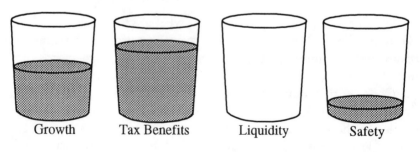

Growth   Tax Benefits   Liquidity   Safety

Let's look at it another way. You have four glasses to fill with orange juice, and there's only so much juice to go around. So you need to decide which glasses you want to fill. Do you want to fill the safety glass? The liquidity glass? The growth glass? Or the tax benefits glass?

If you want lots of safety, you will use all your juice filling the safety glass. You might have a little bit of juice left over to pour into the liquidity glass, but you won't have any juice to pour into the growth glass or the tax benefits glass. What "juice" (investment) would that describe? Savings accounts, CDs, and money market funds.

What if you are willing to tolerate less safety, and current income is not important to you? Then you might fill your growth glass, and pour whatever juice is left into your tax benefits glass. What would that describe? Growth stocks or real estate.

What if you split the juice evenly between the growth glass and the tax benefits glass? You'd have tax-sheltered limited partnerships, investments in oil or gas, or leveraged real estate. But no matter how you slice it, there is only so much juice.

Back to the original question: Is there a *best* investment—one that has a tremendous rate of return, is completely safe, and has all necessary tax advantages? No. There's only so much juice in the economy. The way an investment is structured or packaged determines how the orange is being sliced or which glasses are being filled. It doesn't produce any more juice.

Your Insights, Feelings, and Action Items

A. As you read this chapter, what *insights* came that seem applicable to *you?*

1._____
2._____
3._____

B. How did you *feel* as you pondered particular points of this chapter?

1._____
2._____
3._____

C. What do you *feel* you should *do* as a result of this chapter?

1._____
2._____
3._____

D. How might you solicit the aid of others in accomplishing "C" above?

_____

_____

_____

Chapter 23

An Introduction to Mutual Funds

Choose the Right Mutual Fund for You

A *mutual fund* is a selection of stocks or bonds, either U.S. or foreign, that are combined in a diversified, professionally managed portfolio sponsored by a mutual fund company and sold to the general public. It usually has complete pass-through of all dividends, interest, or capital gains. How can you select an appropriate mutual fund?

First, consider the range of mutual fund types. Mutual funds fall into many different *asset classes*. They may include T-bills; short-term bonds; long-term corporate, government or municipal bonds; blue-chip stocks; growth and income stocks; aggressive growth stocks; small-cap stocks; foreign stocks and bonds; or specialty funds (funds from select industries such as gold mining, automobiles, aviation, chemical, utilities, retailing, manufacturing, technology, banking, and insurance).

Your job is to determine which fund is right for you considering the phase of the current economic cycle; each fund behaves differently in each phase of the economic cycle. Each brings with it certain risks.

There are a number of different factors you should consider when choosing a mutual fund. Remember: An $18,000-a-year telephone "receptionist" answering an 800-line at the headquarters of a no-load fund company will not be able—or allowed—to answer many of these questions. That means you need to do your homework—talk to people who *are* able to give you the information you need. Then take the answers you get, and weigh them against your own goals and objectives as you study the prospectus and make your own investment decisions.

Learn to Assess the Risks

Because there are so many no-load mutual funds available, increasingly more people are investing with less professional advice. By law, mutual funds may report *only* their rates of return—**not** the risk associated with that rate of return.

What's the problem with that? Nine out of 10 people know how to measure rates of return. They were taught how to calculate percentages in third grade. But fewer than one in a hundred know how to calculate risk—even though risk is just as quantifiable. Calculating risk requires knowing how to calculate variance, standard deviation, beta, alpha, and so on.

Let's talk about a few of these risk measurements—*because discussing return without discussing risk is meaningless.*

Beta. *Beta* refers to how volatile a fund is relative to a market index. For example, Standard and Poor's 500 stock market index is assigned a beta of 1.0. A fund with a beta of 1.2 should rise 1.2 times as much as the market as a whole when the market is rising. When the market is falling, a fund with a beta of 1.2 should decline in value 1.2 times as much as the market as a whole. A lower-risk fund with a beta of 0.7 will rise only seven-tenths as much as the market will rise—but will fall only seven-tenths as much as the market falls.

Is that a useful, relevant measure? Absolutely! If you are quite confident that the market is climbing, you might want to choose a high-beta fund. If, on the other hand, the market is at or reaching an all-time high, you might want to choose a low-beta fund—because the market will eventually start to fall. (However, the amateur investor may have difficulty judging the current market status.)

Alpha. Another measurement is alpha. *Alpha* refers to the performance improvement the portfolio manager adds to a mutual fund. Alpha is calculated by taking the fund's actual performance, then subtracting the fund's expected performance (which is calculated by multiplying the mutual fund's beta by the excess index return for that fund's asset class. For more information, call Fax-on-Demand at (801) 263-1676 and request free report #181, "More about Portfolio Risk Measurements.")

It's not as complicated as it seems. Let's assume that the risk-free rate of return is 7 percent. The beta suggests that the expected rate of return for the fund should be 13 percent. But the actual return is 15 percent. That fund then has a positive alpha of 2 percent. Why? Because the professional portfolio manager has added value to the fund.

What if the expected rate of return is 13 percent and the actual performance is 11 percent? Then the fund has a negative alpha of 2 percent. In other words, the portfolio manager has subtracted 2 percent from the value of the fund.

Standard deviation. The most widely-used measure of risk is the standard deviation. The *standard deviation* specifies that about two-thirds of all expected performance periods will fall within the expected or average return plus or minus the stated standard deviation.

To translate: If the fund's average performance is 12 percent and its standard deviation is 11 percent (expressed simply as **11**), you can expect that approximately two-thirds of the time, the fund's performance will range somewhere between 1 percent (12 minus 11) and 23 percent (12 plus 11).

Two standard deviations equate to about a 95 percent probability. That means that 95 percent of the time, that fund's performance will range between –10 percent (12 minus 22) and +34 percent (12 plus 22). Can you begin to see how risk is statistically measurable?

Correlation coefficient. A fourth useful measurement of risk is the *correlation coefficient.* The correlation coefficient is a measurement from –1 to +1, representing the strength of the relationship between two variables, or asset classes. If the correlation coefficient is 1, there is a perfect linear relationship between the two asset classes—they are moving in the same direction at the same time. Conversely, if the correlation coefficient is –1, there is an inverse relationship between the two asset classes— they are moving in the opposite direction at the same time.

Correlations are used in Modern Portfolio Theory as a way of decreasing risk. By matching asset classes with inverse cross-correlations, the volatility of the portfolio as a whole can be decreased. When the correlation between two assets is highly positive, there is little reduction of risk by adding the new asset. However, when the cross correlations are inverse, the volatility of the overall portfolio can be decreased by adding the new asset.

Take Stock of Turnover

Another consideration when choosing a mutual fund is turnover. *Turnover* refers to how much of the portfolio is bought and sold each year.

Why is turnover so important? A portfolio with a turnover rate of 100 to 200 percent per year delivers a *lot* of taxable income every year. On the other hand, if a portfolio invests in growth stocks and has a turnover rate of 20 percent—meaning that one-fifth of it is bought and sold each year—then the portfolio has an average holding period of five years for its stocks and bonds. That means it behaves almost like an annuity—in which case the taxable income from the mutual fund might be very slight.

An excellent example of a fund with low turnover is the Lord Abbett Value Appreciation Fund. Managing turnover can have a very significant impact on a portfolio's after-tax performance.

Management vs. Track Record

It's important to consider what kind of management structure the fund has. Both individual and committee management structures have advantages and disadvantages. Generally, committee management results in better continuity—something that is especially in your favor if there is a solid team with an appropriate philosophy.

If you're selecting a fund based on long-term performance, make sure the manager who built the fund performance is still there. One of the biggest mistakes people make when investing in a mutual fund's track record is failing to find out whether the original manager is still there.

A perfect example happened in the mid-1980s with the American Capital Pace Fund. The Pace Fund's superior record during the '70s and early '80s disappeared when the original manager left. The result? A whole bunch of sorely disappointed investors who made their investment decisions based only on the fund's track record.

If you have to choose between a *fund* with a good track record and a *manager* with a good track record, choose the manager. It's okay to invest in a new fund that has no track record at all *if* the fund's manager has a long and solid track record.

A naive or inexperienced investor immediately asks, "How has the mutual fund performed?" That sounds like such a logical and intelligent question. People who want "the best investment" display a level of confidence in the track record, and assume that history predicts the future. It doesn't. With investments, as with most of financial planning, we're not dealing in the realm of truth, accuracy, the "best," or even with black and white. Instead, we're dealing in the realm of correct principles—we are looking for what is sound, prudent, conservative, diversified, and balanced. We're looking at ways to soundly measure and manage risk.

Even financial planners sometimes judge by a track record—mistakenly thinking that past performance is what's important. They develop unrealistic expectations—then pass those on to their investors.

Track records of the immediate past *may* be highly irrelevant, since investing does *not* rely on trends. They presume that a climbing market will continue climbing next year—regardless of the fact that the more it climbs, the greater the odds that next year it will fall. They presume that an industry sector that has declined over the last year or two will continue declining—even though the more it declines, the greater the chances are it will start climbing again next year. Picking a mutual fund that has performed well over the past year or several may mean that you are simply buying in at the top. In fact, a *Journal of Finance* study suggests that a fund that finishes the preceding five-year period in the bottom 60 percent of its peer group has a *greater* chance of being a top-half performer the next five years than a fund that had been in the top 40 percent.

Find the Optimal Size

When the fund is large, it's very difficult for the portfolio managers to do much more than replicate the market. It's very difficult for a multi-billion dollar mutual fund to purchase the shares of a small growth-stock company—then have that small growth stock impact the overall performance of the fund very much. And because a very large fund may take on the characteristics of the market as a whole, it loses much of its flexibility.

If the fund is too small, on the other hand, expenses may eat up too much of the portfolio return—something that can happen with funds as small as $10 million to $50 million. As a result, you won't achieve what you'd hope with a mutual fund. Small funds are more flexible and more appropriate if you're looking for a small-cap or aggressive growth stock fund. The problem is, of course, that once the small-cap or aggressive growth stock fund achieves superior performance and that performance is publicized, it becomes a large fund.

Flexibility

Flexibility is a significant issue, because you need to know what kind of investment options the fund may engage in. Will the fund purchase derivatives or options, engage in margin trading, futures, or short selling? Some of these strategies may make the fund riskier and more volatile.

Fixed vs. Equity Investments

Ted and Fred each had $100,000 to invest for retirement 25 years hence.

Careful Ted put his money into a super CD guaranteed to pay 6 percent interest for 25 years.

Aggressive Fred felt equity investments would provide an inflation hedge and better returns. Recognizing the risk involved, he diversified by putting $20,000 into each of five different investments. But he had trouble. One investment became worthless, and another never gained a cent over 25 years. The third returned only 5 percent. Fortunately, the fourth investment did a fair 10 percent return, and the fifth performed admirably at 12 percent.

Who did better, Ted or Fred?

Ted's $100,000 grew to a respectable $429,187.

And these were Fred's results:

$ 20,000	became worthless	$ 0
20,000	never grew	20,000
20,000	earned 5 percent	67,727
20,000	earned 10 percent	216,694
20,000	earned 12 percent	340,001
	Fred's total portfolio	$644,422

Fred gets a 50 percent higher standard of living for retirement by using equity investments. He was careful to diversify his holdings.

Mutual Funds: Load vs. No-Load Myths

How should you evaluate load funds compared to no-load funds? Sometimes it's not that easy to tell the difference. Recently, some full-load fund groups have reduced their front-end charges, while some formerly no-load fund groups have attached front-end loads to some of their funds. That's not all: The immense popularity of deferred sales charges and 12b-1 fees has further clouded the distinction between load and no-load funds. (12b-1 fees are increased expenses to pay those servicing the account.)

Despite the difficulties of defining load and no-load funds, a number of so-called industry "experts" still say that investors should only buy no-load funds. No-load funds may be better options for some investors, but not for everyone.

For one thing, that would eliminate some superior portfolio managers. To begin a mutual fund search by excluding some top managers hardly makes sense. It's probably smarter to try to separate good performing funds from bad ones, regardless of the load. After all, isn't everyone better off over time in a good performing load fund than in a bad performing no-load fund?

You should also consider service. Will you be dealing with an 800-number service representative who recently graduated from college and went through a "quickie" training course, or a trusted and experienced professional? Just how much can they pay those telephone reps, anyway? Why do they call them "load" or "no-load" funds? Why don't they call them "advice" or "no-advice" funds?

All funds have marketing expenses. A front-end load fund pays part of the load to the broker or financial planner. The no-load fund pays for national newspaper, magazine, radio, and television advertising. It's very expensive to run daily ads in the *Wall Street Journal* or in *Money* magazine. No-load funds also have to maintain an extensive 800-number service center. In actuality no-load really means no front-end load. Yearly management fees, which all funds charge, are sometimes higher in no-load than load funds.

The sales charge is just one of many factors you should consider when you are appraising a fund. Do not place too great a weight on it— or any other single variable. Why? You might fail to consider more important factors, such as risk levels, managerial ability, portfolio strategy, and service.

You should put the fund's sales charge in proper perspective. If your investment time horizon is relatively short, say two or three years, then you should more seriously consider a no-load fund than if you are expecting a five- to 10-year holding period.

Even more important than considering the relative cost of a sales charge is to consider the relative gain you can receive from paying such charges. A load represents payment for the services of the salesperson who sells the fund. If you get good advice, the fees can be a tremendous bargain. The danger, of course, is that you can pay the same charge to an uninformed salesperson as you'd pay to a dedicated and savvy financial professional.

That's not all: Because brokers get no added fees for moving an investor within a fund family, they have less incentive to regularly trade a load-fund account. As a result, load funds typically experience longer average holding periods than no-load funds. Load funds, then, may actually contribute to long-term thinking, while no-load funds may create greater potential for short-term trading.

Quantitative Analysis of Investor Behavior, a report by the independent firm DALBAR Financial Services, examined the period from 1984 to 1988. It shows that investors in no-load, direct market mutual funds averaged a 19-month holding period. Investors in load funds averaged a holding period of 44 months.

The study of investors' decisions to buy and sell during this period is revealing. No-load fund investors had a pattern of buying high and selling low. There was significantly more buying into no-load funds when stock prices were high than when they were low. What does that tell us? If investors bought while prices were high, sold while prices were low, and held their investments for only 19 months, their real return was less than the market.

During the decade of the 1980s, the *Standard and Poor's 500* was up 293 percent, while investors into no-load equity funds averaged a gain of 70 percent (that's *investor* performance, not *investment* performance).

It's important to note that repeated studies show there's no difference between the investment performance on load mutual funds vs. no-load mutual funds. They have performed similarly.

While these studies are repeatedly cited by the proponents of no-load mutual funds, it's important to understand that *investment* performance is not the relevant factor. *Investor* performance is the relevant factor. Let's look at the figures again: While the *Standard and Poor's 500* investment returned 293 percent during the 1980s, the average investor in no-load mutual funds earned an average return of 70 percent. That compares with the performance of money market funds. In fact, U.S. Treasury bills had a total cumulative return of 84 percent during the same period.

For example, in October 1987 when the S&P 500 index fell 21.52 percent, redemptions of no-load funds amounted to 7.55 percent of total assets, while redemptions of load funds were only one-fourth as much, or 1.87 percent. Conversely, in January of 1987 when the market jumped 13.43 percent, purchases of no-load funds climbed 4.62 percent compared to only 2.66 percent for load funds.

In other words, *real people buy high and sell low.* Absent a disciplined and experienced adviser or rules, most investors are emotional sheep, following the crowd. And this appears most pronounced in investors in no-load funds.

Once again, it's not the performance of the *investment* (load and no-load funds have performed comparably), but the performance of the *investor* that counts. (For a more complete report and analysis of the DALBAR study, call Fax-on-Demand at (801) 263-1676 and request free report #155, "Real People Buy High, Sell Low.")

I've heard investment advisers recommend that you go to the library and study it out for yourself. This *might* make sense for 5 percent of the population, but more often than not, all it perpetuates is the type of poor thinking described in Chapter 32.

It is important to remember one thing: Load funds are generally worth the money if you are getting good service and advice. Because they have a sales rep, people who buy load funds tend to get talked through market downturns better than people in no-load funds. Even better, those who utilize a professional mutual fund management service which provides discipline may find the fee a tremendous bargain.

Why is that important? When the market is down, people want to sell. It's human nature. It's even better to buy and hold and forget about your investments than to be whipsawed by the emotions of the market. The most successful investors I see are those who put their money in the market according to a disciplined portfolio management methodology and then forget about it.

The load may be a real bargain if you are getting a professional service. Interestingly, you pay a "load" for service almost everywhere you turn:

- You pay a 6 percent "load" when you buy a home or real estate.
- You pay points for the service of originating a home mortgage.
- You pay a 15 percent "exit fee" for the service you get at a restaurant.
- You tip a taxi driver 15 percent above the cost of the fare.
- You pay a "load" when you get a haircut or visit the beautician.

- You pay a service fee when someone delivers you pizza or helps with your luggage at a hotel.
- You tip your babysitter or gardener when they provide good service.

When viewed in this light, you should realize that you pay for service *all the time*. Paying a load in exchange for help in selecting a good mutual fund—one that is right for your circumstances—can be a real bargain. Those who would minimize the importance of this service may not appreciate all that is involved.

Your Insights, Feelings, and Action Items

A. As you read this chapter, what *insights* came that seem applicable to *you?*

1._____
2._____
3._____

B. How did you *feel* as you pondered particular points of this chapter?

1._____
2._____
3._____

C. What do you *feel* you should *do* as a result of this chapter?

1._____
2._____
3._____

D. How might you solicit the aid of others in accomplishing "C" above?

_____
_____
_____

Chapter 24

Guard the Castle Gate: Do Your Estate Planning with Care

It took some coaching, but the elderly woman finally agreed. First, she planned her funeral. She thought of all the details—the kind of funeral she wanted. Which mortuary should handle the arrangements. What kind of casket she wanted to be buried in. She even figured out how much she wanted her funeral to cost—then she prepaid the bill. Sound macabre? There's more.

Next, she went through the house and videotaped everything she owned of any value. She said who she wanted to inherit each item. Some people thought it odd. But guess what happened? When she died, everything went smoothly. Her children knew exactly what kind of funeral she wanted. They derived great peace from that funeral, knowing it was exactly as she had planned.

They also knew who was to get each item. There were no arguments, no bitter feelings. No problems at all.

At about the same time, another elderly woman in the same neighborhood died. She had done no estate planning. Nothing was arranged for. Nothing had been discussed.

Guess what happened to her children? They started arguing over the funeral. No one could agree on any of the arrangements. It finally happened, but her children were filled with contention and anger instead of peace.

Then, the fights got louder and more bitter as her children tried to distribute their mother's assets. Several became enemies. The family was pulled apart at a time when it should have pulled together. The difference? Estate planning.

You'll work all your life to accumulate an estate. Do you want to cause fights? Be taken for taxes? No. You want to make the most of what you have. Sadly, the average person spends 85,000 hours accumulating an estate, but fewer than 10 hours planning how to preserve it.

Exactly What Does Your Estate Include?

First, let's define just what's included in an estate. Your *estate* includes all you real and personal property, whether tangible or intangible. It includes your home, other real estate, your vehicles, jewelry, precious metals, coins, art, china, tableware, clothing, bedding, furniture, equipment, and other personal possessions.

Your estate also includes other personal property, such as bank accounts, savings accounts, annuities, CDs, stocks, bonds, mutual funds, interests in limited partnerships, business interests, retirement plan proceeds, and death benefit proceeds from life insurance policies you own. All your assets are totaled and included when your estate taxes are calculated.

So, why is it necessary to plan your estate? There are several good reasons.

Control Your Assets, or Someone Else Will

First, and most important, planning is control. You want to determine who will get what, how they will get it, and when they will get it.

How are assets distributed? Let's look at an example. Robert, whose children were grown and gone, decided that the simplest thing he could do was leave 100 percent of his assets to his wife, Ann. He figured she'd take care of distributing things fairly among their children.

What happened? Robert died unexpectedly at the age of 58. Ann was only 53. She remarried, and took 100 percent of Robert's assets with her.

Eighteen years later Ann died, leaving all her assets to her second husband. Twelve years later he died, leaving all his assets—which now included Robert's original assets—to *his* children. Remember: These are people Robert never even knew existed.

What about Robert's children? In essence, they were disinherited. That's clearly *not* what Robert had intended, but the way he designated his assets be distributed, that's exactly what happened. Think that doesn't happen very often? Think again. It's actually quite common.

So, how are your assets distributed to your intended heirs after you die? Your assets will probably go through probate, either by the operation of law or because their trust was not set up properly. Many people think that just because they've prepared a will, their assets won't go through the expense and delay of probate. Nothing could be further from the truth.

All wills must be presented to the probate court. The court determines whether the will is valid. The court, considering what is written in the will, then makes the final determination as to how assets (and minor children) are to be distributed to heirs (or guardians).

Your will may not necessarily have the final say. The probate judge does.

In certain cases, your assets will be distributed by "operation of law." That could happen, for example, if property was held by you and your spouse in joint tenancy with rights of survivorship. It could also happen if you've named a specific beneficiary—through a life insurance policy, retirement plan, tax-sheltered annuity, pension, or profit-sharing plan. In those cases, your assets pass directly to the beneficiary you designated.

Your assets may also be distributed by operation of law if you die without a will. In that situation, you're considered to have died "intestate." In essence, the state in which you live writes your "will" for you. Often, your state's "will" can be quite onerous. Consider the following "will" which contains some typical provisions, and which may be applicable to *you*.

My Last Will and Testament Drawn by Many-States, U.S.A.

Being of sound mind and memory, I declare this to be my last Will.

First: I give to my children the first $50,000 of any property I own, plus two-thirds of the remainder of my property, and to my spouse, what is left. It is my spouse's duty to support my children out of his or her share and render an accounting of how my children's share is managed. Furthermore, even if my children are grown and gone, the above allocations shall apply.

Second: I appoint my spouse as guardian of my children. But as a safeguard, my spouse shall report to the Probate Court each year and give an accounting of how, why, and where my children's money was spent. As a further safeguard, my spouse may be required to purchase a Performance Bond to guarantee that proper judgment is used in handling, investing, and spending my children's money.

Third: If my spouse dies before me, and any of my children are minors, I do not wish to name a guardian to care for my minor children; rather, I hope my relatives and friends will get together and select that guardian by mutual agreement. If they do not agree on a guardian, I direct the Probate Court to make the choice. If the Court wishes, it may appoint a stranger.

Fourth: Under existing tax laws, there are certain legal ways to lower death taxes. Since I prefer to have my money used for governmental purposes rather than for the benefit of my spouse and children, I direct that no effort be made to lower taxes.

IN WITNESS WHEREOF, I have set my hand to this, my Last Will, this date now uncertain.

_____

TESTATOR

On the surface, this may make sense. But examining further, does it really? For example, your children are either older or younger. If they're grown and gone, do you want two-thirds of your assets going to them rather than your spouse? If they're young children at home, do you want your spouse having to account to them for what he or she is doing with *their* money? The questions go on ...

You should also be aware that mutual funds, CDs, real estate, checking accounts, savings accounts, vehicles, stocks, bonds, many other assets normally do not pass according to the operation of law but will go through the probate process.

The message here is clear: Do something about your estate plan.

Don't let money stop you. A reputable attorney will usually prepare a simple will for $125 to $200. Don't rely on the will and trust "kits" offered for $10 on late-night television and in magazines. The court may consider them valid, but you will have forfeited the professional counsel you deserve.

Why is professional counsel so important? Assume that you go to the library and read an article on tonsillectomy. From that article, you figure out how to perform a tonsillectomy. Then you decide that you can do it easily and for much less money than a surgeon charges for the procedure. So you go to the bathroom mirror, open wide, and go to work.

Are you properly trained? Hardly. Can you perform a proper tonsillectomy? No way. So what makes you think you can properly interpret all the complicated estate laws from a $10 do-it-yourself kit?

Even if you're a surgeon who is completely trained in performing tonsillectomies, you're not going to do one on yourself. You'll hire another surgeon to do it for you.

Eliminate Expenses

Good estate planning can greatly minimize and often eliminate certain expenses after you die. One of those is estate taxes; you want to minimize them as much as possible. Another is probate costs.

Remember, though: As much as you want to eliminate expenses, that's still less important than how you distribute your estate.

Avoid Publicity

Still another reason for estate planning is to avoid publicity. When an estate goes to probate, all probated assets go through the courts and become a matter of public record, regardless of the size of your estate. Anyone can easily see what your spouse and children received from your estate. In some areas, those records are even published in local newspapers. That may leave your family at the mercy of unscrupulous individuals who may prey on them. By establishing a living trust, you avoid exposure to public records.

Protect Your Assets

Your assets need to be protected, both before and after you die. A good estate plan will contain instructions for what you want done during your lifetime in case you become disabled or incapacitated due to illness or injury. As people are living longer, more and more are spending time in rest homes with Alzheimer's and other degenerative conditions.

A good estate plan will also protect your assets from frivolous lawsuits, malpractice claims, and creditors, both before and after your death. The result is peace of mind—you'll know your affairs are in order and will be transferred as you want.

A good estate plan also protects your most important assets—your children. Your estate plan not only determines who will inherit your property, but determines who will "inherit" your children. By determining the guardian of any minor children you might leave, an estate plan does something for your children that they can't do for themselves. No one else can do it on your behalf, either. You may think you have a strong, stable family, and that one of your family members would rear your children if you die. Are you sure?

You might be surprised. If you haven't legally designated that, it's out of your hands. You're considered to be "intestate." The state in which you live decides what happens to your children.

Avoid Family Contention

An estate plan may help avoid family fights and disagreements after you are gone. I have watched the best-mannered, closest families argue over property and assets.

One of the most valuable things a family can do is sit down together and discuss exactly how the estate is structured. Children should know about a parent's will and trusts. Children should know who the executors are. They should know who the trustees are. They should know how things are going to be handled. That applies even if your children are grown and gone—and even if your only assets are your children.

What Are the Basic Elements of a Good Estate Plan?

An effective estate plan may include living wills, simple wills, pour-over wills, a living trust, or durable powers of attorney, among other things. It's important to understand the uses of each and to discuss with a competent estate attorney how each might apply to you.

Establish a Will

As discussed, a will usually determines who gets your tangible and intangible assets. It determines who will be appointed guardian of your minor children, and who will be your executor. The court process of distributing your property according to the terms of your will is referred to as *probate*.

If you don't have a will, the court will decide how to distribute those assets subject to probate. Usually, the court either tries to figure out what you would have wanted or simply distributes your assets according to state law. If you do have a will, the probate court will be more likely to execute the instructions in your will.

You've probably heard a lot about avoiding probate. But probate serves some very useful purposes:

- Probate provides for the distribution of your assets as you want, assuming you have a valid will.
- The probate court will limit the amount of time during which someone may challenge your will.
- The probate court will limit the amount of time in which creditors can make claims against your assets, letting your heirs know there are no further claims that may be filed against your estate.
- The probate court supervises the executors' activities.

Of course, probate has some disadvantages, too:

- Survivors may have limited access to their property or assets during the probate period; depending on the complexity of the estate, the probate period may last for years.
- There are costs associated with probate—court costs, attorney fees, executor fees, accounting fees, and appraisals—that average from 3 to 7 percent of the estate's value.
- In most states, probate files are open to the public.

A *pour-over will* works in conjunction with a living trust and distributes all your assets directly to your heirs according to the itemization specified in your will. All assets that are not designated for a specific heir pour over into your living trust. In other words, the heir is the trust, and assets are distributed under the terms of the trust.

As mentioned earlier, when your assets are held in joint tenancy, they will be distributed according to law without probate. In *joint tenancy*, each spouse owns 100 percent of the property. When one dies, the surviving spouse automatically takes over as sole owner. It's an undivided interest. In *tenancy in common*, however, each spouse owns 50 percent, and the 50 percent owned by each can be severed. That is, the husband or wife could sell his or her half of the property. It's a divided interest.

Even though joint tenancy is most common, it causes significant problems. If you want to establish a separate estate in the name of your spouse, the assets need to appreciate and grow in value separately throughout your spouse's life. If you try to transfer your assets within a few years of your death, things often don't go as you'd like.

Tenancy in common, however, lets one spouse sell his or her half of the property without the approval of the other spouse. All appreciation for that half accrues to the individual spouse—even through subsequent homes and other properties as they are purchased. That simplifies the estate planning process if one of the two intends to accumulate a sizable estate.

Because each spouse only owns half of the property, tenancy in common may also be helpful as an asset protection strategy. If either spouse gets sued, it is tougher to make a claim on half a home.

In reality, joint tenancy can be a nightmare. I recently had a case in a small, rural town. The father had placed all of his assets—including his checking accounts, savings accounts, and home—in joint tenancy with his daughter, who lived nearby. Another daughter, who lived in a distant metropolitan area, wondered what the implications were.

Her father explained that having his assets held in joint tenancy would bypass the time, expense, and delay of probate. That was true. But what else was true? When her father died, all his assets would become the sole property of the daughter who was named in joint tenancy.

What if the daughter named in joint tenancy then distributed the assets to the other children in the family? Wouldn't that be okay?

First of all, she's under no legal obligation. She might decide not to. But that's not all—she might not be able to do it without significant adverse consequences. Why? For one thing, that daughter can pass no more than $10,000 a year to her brothers and sisters without paying gift taxes. What a nightmare—one child being required to pay gift taxes just so she could share her father's assets with his other children!

Gift taxes start at 18 percent and go as high as 55 percent. You can exercise a one-time exclusion—but if you use it to pass assets to your brothers and sisters, you lose it for your spouse and your own children.

Remember: A will is just the beginning. It won't solve all your problems. It doesn't avoid probate, for example. It won't manage your assets after you die. A will simply designates who your heirs are—and, as soon as you die, it transfers your assets to your heirs. They have immediate and complete reign over those assets, after the probate process.

Establish a Trust

A *trust* is a relationship established when one party (a trustor) transfers property to a second party (the trustee) to be held and managed solely for the benefit of a third party, the beneficiary.

In almost all states, the law allows the same person to be the trustor, trustee, and beneficiary of a trust. For example, you might establish a trust, transfer your own property into the trust, manage your assets as trustee, and be the beneficiary of the trust during your lifetime. In that case, you'll designate a contingent trustee who will manage your assets according to your wishes when you die or if you become incapacitated. You'll also appoint a contingent beneficiary—usually your spouse, your children, or a charitable organization.

Trusts are often established to distribute assets after death. But they can also be set up for the management of assets while you're still alive. For example, you might set up a trust that will manage your assets if you are ever declared incompetent because of illness, Alzheimer's disease, or some other problem.

Unlike a simple will or the operation of law, a trust may reduce an estate tax liability if one exists. There are several types of trusts. In estate planning, the two most common types are living trusts and testamentary trusts.

Testamentary trusts. A testamentary trust is created under a will and has assets deposited into it upon death. It's most commonly used to provide for dependent children. It lets you designate who will manage your assets, for what purposes the funds may be used, and when your assets may be paid out to your heirs.

A testamentary trust allows you to manage your assets from the grave, but it only manages assets that are placed into it *after* the probate process or after operation by law. All assets still go through the expense and delay of probate.

Living trusts. The most common kind of living trust, the revocable trust, lets you transfer property outside a will. A revocable trust has both advantages and disadvantages. On the plus side:

- A revocable trust may allow your heirs to avoid the costs, time, expense, and delays of probate.
- A revocable trust lets your assets be passed privately—without the publicity associated with probate.
- You may change it or terminate your revocable trust as you desire.
- A revocable trust provides for distribution of your assets exactly as you wish. They may be given to your survivors immediately upon your death, or they may be distributed over a period of years.
- A revocable trust can provide for the management of your estate while you're living if you can no longer take care of it yourself.
- A revocable trust is the only way you can manage *all* your assets from the grave; assets don't depend on probate or operation of law.

What about the disadvantages of a living trust?

- A living trust may be expensive and take a few hours to set up. Fees range from $700 to $2,500; if your estate is simple, your cost will fall at the low end of the range.
- A living trust requires that you give up personal ownership of your own assets unless you name yourself and/or your spouse as the trustee.

Remember: *Your assets must be transferred into your living trust before you die.* If they are not transferred until after you die, your trust functions like a testamentary trust and you will not avoid probate.

Check with your estate attorney. You may think your estate plan is complete because you have a revocable living trust, but if it isn't funded, it's nothing more or less than a testamentary trust. Your attorney may not have transferred your assets into your living trust. It happens. For example, an attorney may not consider the time and expense of transferring assets when he or she quotes a fee for the trust. Then, the transfer simply doesn't get done. Sadly, some attorneys name themselves the executor—and they intend on making a living by managing the probate of assets after their clients die. (If an attorney does 500 inexpensive estate plans each year during the first five years of his career, he'll have a handsome income for years to come as he settles estates through the probate courts.)

Choosing Guardians, Trustees, and Personal Representatives

Guardians, trustees, and personal representatives are the three important people in any estate plan.

Choosing a guardian. A *guardian* is the person who inherits your children. The first step, of course, is to look at the person's individual character and situation in life. What is his home and family life like? Are his attitudes and philosophies similar to yours? What are his attitudes about higher education, religion, hard work, self-reliance, thrift, industry, discipline, and politics? How does he discipline his own children? Will he provide a home atmosphere that builds encouragement and self-esteem, or is he negative and critical? Will your children be treated as equals or as second-class citizens?

The second step is to remember the guardian financially as you plan your estate. Are you making adequate provision through insurance or other means so that the guardian can afford to take your children into his home? If not, your children may end up being passed from home to home, family to family, relative to relative, without any sense of stability or permanence. Your children may even be split up between several homes or relatives.

Remember—you'll need to cover more than just food and clothing. Your children take up space. The guardian may need to enlarge his family home, expand the dining room, add on two bedrooms, or finish off another bathroom. If you've got a large family, the guardian may need to buy a bigger home. Those are perfectly appropriate expenses that a guardian should be entitled to incur from your estate or the proceeds of your insurance policy.

Most important, you're looking for someone who will provide your children love, comfort, security, and a solid and strong self-esteem.

Choosing a trustee. *Trust* is the key part of the word—you must implicitly trust your trustee.

There are some basic questions you'll need answered, too. Does he have experience managing money—hopefully, more than just a little bit of money? Will he be able to handle the large sums of money likely to be generated from your insurance or estate?

Is he conservative? Is he prudent? Has he lived his own life within a budget? Will he seek expert advice when he needs it—such as in interpreting a complex trust document? Most important, can you trust him to look after your children's interests?

The guardian and trustee may be the same person, or they may be two different people. You might decide, for example, that your children would be best off in the home of your brother and sister-in-law, people who provide a loving, stable, disciplined family atmosphere. But they may not have experience in managing money, especially large sums. You'd choose them as guardians. As trustee, you'd choose your wife's brother—a bachelor in his late 40s who loves your children and has considerable experience in managing assets. If you do choose a separate guardian and trustee, make sure they are people who can work well together while still providing a respectful check and balance.

Choosing a personal representative. Being a guardian is a long-term commitment. So is being a trustee. A *personal representative*, on the other hand, is the person who executes the terms of your will. Generally, that takes six months to a year—then his obligations are over.

Obviously, you'll want someone who is trustworthy, conservative, and experienced in handling assets. Most important, your personal representative should be familiar with your will, familiar with your wishes, and committed to following your instructions. This may be the same person as your trustee.

Your Insights, Feelings, and Action Items

A. As you read this chapter, what *insights* came that seem applicable to *you?*

   1._____

   2._____

   3._____

B. How did you *feel* as you pondered particular points of this chapter?

   1._____

   2._____

   3._____

C. What do you *feel* you should *do* as a result of this chapter?

   1._____

   2._____

   3._____

D. How might you solicit the aid of others in accomplishing "C" above?

_____

_____

_____

Chapter 25

The Debt You Didn't Know
You Have

Estate Taxes: One Problem Worth Having

How does the estate tax system work? The estate tax—levied through the unified gift and estate tax system—is levied on a person who dies. It taxes his right to pass his property to his heirs.

Under the estate tax laws, each individual receives a $192,800 tax credit; a married couple gets a total of $385,600. What does that translate to? An individual can pass $600,000 to his heirs before they have to pay estate taxes. A married couple can pass $1.2 million without being taxed.

That might seem like a large estate. It was a decade or two ago. But today, a $600,000 estate is considered very modest.

An estate includes the value of your home, the death benefit on all insurance policies you own, the value in your retirement plan, and any other stocks, bonds, and assets you own. It's easy to exceed $600,000. Even if you don't exceed it today, you will in five or 10 years, thanks to inflation. Many married couples have more than $1.2 million in an estate when they retire—and they live 20 more years, during which time the estate continues to grow.

When estate taxes finally kick in, what is the minimum estate tax bracket? At $600,000, your estate tax bracket is 38 percent. At $1.2 million, it is 43 percent. It graduates from there; anything over $3 million is subject to a 55 percent tax.

The "706 Mortgage"

Within nine months of your death, your heirs must file IRS Form 706—the estate tax return—with the IRS. I call it the "706 mortgage." You will never complete this form for yourself. Someone else will, and it will be signed by your executor on your behalf. Let's look at some of the ways it compares to a conventional mortgage.

Due date. You know in advance when a conventional mortgage is due. Not so with a 706 mortgage, because you don't know when you and your spouse are going to die. That's not all: You don't know whether you'll die in an up-market or a down-market! In other words, you don't know whether you'll be selling your assets high or low. Because whenever it is, it's a forced liquidation. What price will you get for your assets as soon as everyone knows it's an estate sale?

Collateral. With a conventional mortgage, the mortgaged asset is predetermined, specific, and identifiable. As a result, you can plan for it. If you have any financial problems, you know that asset is escrowed or warranted. In other words, you have a choice.

A 706 mortgage, on the other hand, is a mortgage on all your assets. Everything you own is liened. The IRS gets to choose which assets it wants. (The IRS decides which assets to foreclose on, then bills your heirs for the rest.) You have no choice. And it can leave your heirs in a real dilemma. Let's look at some actual examples.

In June 1993, the Miami Dolphins got new owners. Why? So the children of their previous owner, Joe Robbie, could pay nearly $50 million in estate taxes. That's right: Joe Robbie's children sold the Miami Dolphins *and* their half of Joe Robbie Stadium to two Palm Beach investors. They did it so they could pay the enormous estate taxes on their inheritance.

In another example, 79-year-old Cliff Hansen sold his ranch—one of the last working ranches in scenic Jackson Hole, Wyoming—to developers. Did he want condominiums and hotels to replace his cottonwoods and cattle? No. As a matter of fact, he wanted a cattle operation to stay in the scenic open space. Did he need the money? No. Then why did he sell? So his children wouldn't have to pay the exorbitant estate taxes that would be imposed on his scenic meadow valley nestled at the foot of the majestic Tetons. (If the ranch was valued at $10 million, the children would have to cough up about $5 million in federal estate taxes. They'd have a real problem.)

Terms. On a conventional mortgage, you know the terms as soon as you sign the dotted line. You may pay off that mortgage with cash—or you may trade assets to pay it off. Then, too, you may refinance a conventional mortgage.

Finally, a conventional mortgage is being amortized—you're paying it off either monthly, quarterly, semi-annually, or annually over a certain number of years.

What about the 706 mortgage? Your heirs pay it in a lump-sum, single payment that's due *nine months* from the date of your death. It's all due at once; it's not amortizable. And the IRS only takes cash. There are no other terms. (In a small minority of cases, the IRS allows the amount to be paid over a period of 10 years, with interest, if certain conditions apply.)

Amount. The amount due on a conventional mortgage is predetermined by how much you finance. You know how much that mortgage is going to be, because you know how much you borrowed. Do you know the amount of the 706 mortgage? No. It will range anywhere from 38 to 55 percent of the fair market value of all your assets at death. That's pretty simple—you don't know when you're going to die, so how can you calculate fair market value at the time of your death?

Security. What do you get? With most conventional mortgages, you receive either cash or property—the property the loan was secured against—when the mortgage is paid. You borrow money, and you end up with cash or property in exchange for the mortgage. When you have finished paying the 706 mortgage, you get nothing. Those are the differences between a typical mortgage and the 706 mortgage.

Imagine that you decide to take on this kind of a mortgage. Your business is worth $5 million, and you decide to borrow 50 percent of the $5 million. That means you put a $2.5 million liability on your balance sheet, and you put $2.5 million cash on your balance sheet—right? Not if you have a 706 mortgage. With a 706 mortgage, you have $2.5 million in liability on your balance sheet, but no cash. None. Did you get anything for it? No.

Even if you *did* get something for your 706 mortgage, can you imagine borrowing 50 percent of your company's value with no terms? No due date? What if that $2.5 million was all callable at any time at the bank's discretion? And when the bank calls the loan due, it's due in a lump sum. Can you imagine doing that to your business? Of course not.

But that's what we're talking about. The IRS has a callable mortgage. Whenever you die that mortgage is callable, in a lump sum, without any advance notice. What kind of strings does that put on your business, your practice, your children, your heirs, your estate? It's a catastrophe—a nightmare.

Unfortunately, it's a nightmare borne by your heirs—and discovered only after you're gone. More commonly, it's a nightmare known as an estate tax problem. You can leave your heirs a nightmare or a legacy. It's up to you.

But basically the IRS says you can change your 706 mortgage—the choice is yours while you are alive. There are several options, including the option to pay no estate taxes. But the day you die, all options are cancelled. Your family is locked into whatever you have done, *or failed to do*. (For a summary of the 706 mortgage, see page 367.)

Your Options for Paying a 706 Mortgage

If you're stuck with a 706 mortgage, there are four possible ways to pay:

Cash—the 100% method. The first way is to pay 100 percent with cash. That not only depletes your assets by at least 50 percent, but when half of your estate dissipates at death, you're yoking your heirs with a problem.

First, as mentioned, the 706 mortgage is paid with after-tax dollars. So in order to pay $1 million in estate taxes on a $2 million estate, you have to earn $4 million before income taxes just so you'll have $1 million left over. It's an inevitable catastrophe.

An estate includes differently valued assets. Imagine the estate as a circle. At the perimeter of the estate are *illiquid assets*, such as a business or real estate—those that don't generate quick income. Closer to the center are assets that generate income more readily, such as highly marketable securities. In the very center of the estate is cash.

A lot of people think that you draw a line straight through the circle, then pay half of all the assets of the circle in estate taxes. But that's not the way estate taxes are paid. Here's what really happens: The IRS drills a hole right into the center of your estate. They take the center—the cash—first. If there's not enough cash, they take the most marketable securities next. Your family or heirs are left with the least marketable assets—usually interest in a business.

Now consider: What happens to that business interest when operating capital is gone? Cash is gone? Marketable securities are gone? What happens to a line of credit at the bank when the balance sheet has been stripped of cash? Does the bank like to lend money, using only illiquid assets as collateral? No. They want to know that there is cash.

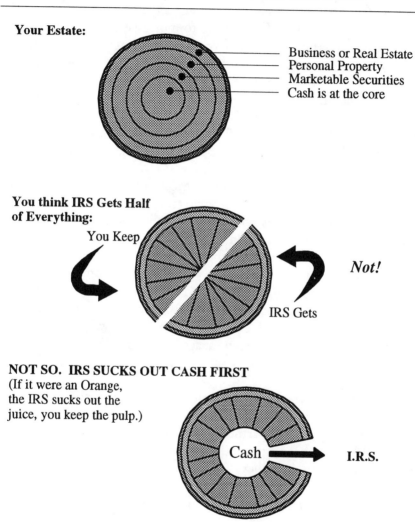

Your Estate:

Business or Real Estate
Personal Property
Marketable Securities
Cash is at the core

You think IRS Gets Half of Everything:

You Keep

Not!

IRS Gets

NOT SO. IRS SUCKS OUT CASH FIRST
(If it were an Orange,
the IRS sucks out the
juice, you keep the pulp.)

Cash → I.R.S.

Forced Liquidation. With forced liquidation, your heirs have to sell the business, stock, or real estate *immediately*. It may be an inappropriate time, and they may receive substantially less than if they were able to dictate the time and circumstances of the sale.

But they *don't* have time on their side—because they have to pay estate taxes. This is what happened to the Robbie family.

Loan—the 120% method. The third approach is the "120 percent method"—you get a loan from the government or from your bank.

There are very strict requirements for financing estate taxes from the government,[1] so that doesn't happen very often. What about taking out a loan from your bank? If you were to mortgage your business, your home, and everything else, then pay off the mortgage over a 15-year period, you would pay twice the amount of the tax because of interest. In effect, you'd eliminate all the assets it took a lifetime to build.

That's not all: How is the estate going to generate the cash flow to service that loan? If you borrow $1 million, you'll have to pay back $2 million over a 15-year period—all with after-tax dollars. The interest isn't tax-deductible. How will the estate generate enough capital to pay that back?

Life insurance—the 3% method. Most knowledgeable estate planning attorneys, CPAs and other advisers agree the fourth—and best—way to pay those taxes is with an irrevocable life insurance trust (or family limited partnership) and a life insurance policy. In essence, you get a 90 percent discount. Here's how it works:

Assume that at age 50 you have a one-time premium of $1 million. That $1 million would pay the tax on $17 million—or, in other words, it would cover 17 times its face amount. Put another way, you would need $17 million to equal the value of a $1 million single-pay insurance policy. At age 60 the return is 10-to-1, and at age 70, 5.5-to-1. (Even with a 5.5-to-1 return at the age of 70, you've achieved a one-time 80 percent discount on your tax bill.)

Alternatively, you may fund your policy on the installment plan, by paying annual premiums. This is known as the 3 percent method. And if you use a family limited partnership to own the insurance in lieu of an irrevocable insurance trust, you may have access to the cash values you are depositing into the policy.

Project Your Estate Taxes: Plan Your Strategy Ahead

With a little planning, there are several different ways you can insulate your heirs against estate taxes. Your heirs won't pay estate taxes on the current size of your estate. Instead, they'll pay estate taxes on the size of your estate after you and your spouse both die. How much will that be?

It's possible to come fairly close with estimates. The table on page 359 can help you figure out the size of your estate five, 10, or 20 years from now, assuming your estate is growing at 7 percent. It also assumes that you are not adding to your estate with ongoing savings. If you are 40 or 50 and will work another 10 to 20 years, you need to add the amount of your annual savings.

Dimitri's current estate is $500,000, which is a fairly modest estate. Because it's modest, he assumed he wouldn't have any estate tax problems. Then his adviser gave him a wake-up call: Within five years, that $500,000 estate will grow to more than $700,000. In 10 years, it will be almost $1 million. In 20 years, it will be a $2 million estate. *And that's if Dimitri doesn't add anything to it—just 7 percent annual growth.*

It's possible to estimate your estate taxes right now. It's also highly irrelevant. Why? Because odds are, you're not going to die today, tomorrow, this year, or even next year. Odds are, you may not die for five, 10, 20, or 30 years—or even longer. Average life expectancy is close to 80; many people reach 90 or 95. To get a relevant figure, then, you need to calculate your estate taxes based on the projected size of your future estate. And that may be a most relevant exercise.

Remember: Your heirs don't get any of your assets until the taxes have been paid. Even without additional savings, look at how an estate can grow:

Projected Estate Size
After-Tax Growth Rate. Ignores additional savings.

	Current Size				
	$500,000	**$1,000,000**	**$2,000,000**	**$5,000,000**	**$10,000,000**
At 5% Growth					
5 Years	$642,000	$1,283,000	$2,567,000	$6,417,000	$12,834,000
10 Years	824,000	1,647,000	3,294,000	8,235,000	16,470,000
20 Years	1,356,000	2,713,000	5,425,000	13,563,000	27,126,000
30 Years	2,234,000	4,468,000	8,935,000	22,339,000	44,677,000
40 Years	3,679,000	7,358,000	14,171,000	36,792,000	73,584,000
At 7% Growth					
5 Years	$709,000	$1,418,000	$2,835,000	$7,088,000	$14,176,000
10 Years	1,005,000	2,010,000	4,019,000	10,048,000	20,097,000
20 Years	2,019,000	4,039,000	8,077,000	20,194,000	40,387,000
30 Years	4,058,000	8,116,000	16,233,000	40,582,000	81,165,000
40 Years	8,156,000	16,311,000	32,623,000	81,557,000	163,114,000
At 10% Growth					
5 Years	$823,000	$1,645,000	$3,291,000	$8,227,000	$16,453,000
10 Years	1,354,000	2,707,000	5,414,000	13,535,000	27,070,000
20 Years	3,664,000	7,328,000	14,656,000	36,640,000	73,281,000
30 Years	9,919,000	19,837,000	39,675,000	99,187,000	198,374,000
40 Years	26,850,000	53,701,000	107,401,000	268,503,000	537,007,000

Your Heirs Can Use Insurance to Pay Estate Taxes: The Irrevocable Insurance Trust and the Family Limited Partnership

Any life insurance death benefit proceeds you own are included in your estate. If you own a $1 million insurance policy, it's very likely that half of that will go to estate taxes. If you're buying life insurance to pay taxes on a $3 million estate, then, you must buy twice as much insurance as you need for your current tax bill—because the insurance benefit itself will drive up your tax bill. But you *can* avoid an increased tax bill by *not* owning your life insurance.

Set up an irrevocable life insurance trust. One traditional way of "not owning" your life insurance is to have your insurance owned by an irrevocable life insurance trust. For instance, Klaus and Sonia set up an irrevocable trust that was owned by a separate trustee. After the trust was established, they transferred money into the trust irrevocably—that is, without the option or ability to ever withdraw that money again. The trust then applied for a life insurance policy on their lives, and the trust was named as the beneficiary of the life insurance policy. Klaus and Sonia may not access any of the cash values of the policy within the trust. But, they were able to cut their tax bill.

Establish a family limited partnership. Another approach to covering the cost of estate taxes is through the family limited partnership. This is the option Rachel and Jay chose. They formed a partnership in which they were the general partners (as the trustees of their living trust), owning 2 percent of the assets, and owning the other 98 percent as limited partners. They transferred money into the family limited partnership, which then applied for and became owner of an insurance policy on their lives. The family limited partnership was also named the beneficiary of the life insurance policy. Rachel and Jay then transferred their limited partnership interests to their children using annual gift exclusions.

Because Rachel and Jay are also the trustees of their living trust during their lifetimes, and because they are the general partners, they can control all assets of the family limited partnership (limited partners have no control over the assets). They can borrow from the family limited partnership, including borrowing the cash value of the insurance policy. They can also pay themselves a salary for managing the partnership.

When they die, their heirs (limited partners) get 98 percent of the proceeds of the life insurance policy tax-free, because the heirs owned it to begin with. The other 2 percent of the death proceeds go into Rachel and Jay's trust, so those proceeds may or may not be subject to estate taxes.

With both of these techniques, the life insurance is effectively owned by your children outside your estate, so it doesn't incur double taxation. But, with the family limited partnership, you have control of it during your lifetime. When you die, the assets in the family limited partnership are controlled according to the terms of your living trust by the successor-trustees of your living trust.

The family limited partnership is a very useful financial planning tool. In essence, there are three important purposes of a family limited partnership:

Income tax splitting. The family limited partnership is the most common way of shifting large amounts of income from parents (who pay high income taxes) to children (who pay little or no income taxes). Every partner in the family limited partnership owns a given percentage of the partnership and is taxed according to his or her percentage of ownership. If your children in the partnership own, say, 75 percent and are in the 15 percent tax bracket, you have successfully shifted the tax liability to those in a lower income tax bracket. Why? You're in a higher tax bracket—but you own only 25 percent of the assets in the family limited partnership.

Asset protection. Legally, the partners of the family limited partnership do not "own" the assets of the limited partnership. Instead, the assets are owned by the entity. Under the Uniform Limited Partnership Act, creditors of individual partners cannot dissolve the partnership nor attach its assets. Their sole remedy is a "charging order"—an attachment of the debtor distributions (if any) from the partnership. (Review Chapter 20.)

Estate minimization. The family limited partnership can also be used to remove future appreciation from your estate and to reduce the size of your estate. To remove future appreciation, transfer assets that will appreciate in value to a limited partnership, or accumulate all future assets in the limited partnership instead of personally. As a result, the size of your estate is minimized—and will be subject to fewer taxes.

Also, the family limited partnership is an excellent receptacle for any gifting program to your heirs. You've gifted away assets, but continue to control them, since only general partners have the right to manage the limited partnership. A family limited partnership is usually established as part of a comprehensive estate plan, and usually costs from $700 to $2,500 to initiate.

Unified Estate and Gift Tax Rates

If the amount with respect to which the tentative tax to be computed is:	The tentative tax is:
Not over $10,000	18% of that amount
Over $10,000 but not over $20,000	$1,800 plus 20% of the excess over $10,000
Over $20,000 but not over $40,000	$3,800 plus 22% of the excess over $20,000
Over $40,000 but not over $60,000	$8,200 plus 24% of the excess over $40,000
Over $60,000 but not over $80,000	$13,000 plus 26% of the excess over $60,000
Over $80,000 but not over $100,000	$18,200 plus 28% of the excess over $80,000
Over $100,000 but not over $150,000	$23,800 plus 30% of the excess over $100,000
Over $150,000 but not over $250,000	$38,800 plus 32% of the excess over $150,000
Over $250,000 but not over $500,000	$70,800 plus 34% of the excess over $250,000
Over $500,000 but not over $750,000	$155,800 plus 37% of the excess over $500,000
Over $750,000 but not over $1,000,000	$248,300 plus 39% of the excess over $750,000
Over $1,000,000 but not over $1,250,000	$345,800 plus 41% of the excess over $1,000,000
Over $1,250,000 but not over $1,500,000	$448,300 plus 43% of the excess over $1,250,000
Over $1,500,000 but not over $2,000,000	$555,800 plus 45% of the excess over $1,500,000
Over $2,000,000 but not over $2,500,000	$780,800 plus 49% of the excess over $2,000,000
Over $2,500,000 but not over $3,000,000	$1,025,000 plus 53% of the excess over $2,500,000
Over $3,000,000	$1,290,800 plus 55% of the excess over $3,000,000

Subtracted from this is the Unified Gift and Estate Tax Credit of $192,800, which is equivalent to a $600,000 exclusion.

Last-to-Die Insurance

Return per $1 Million Deposit (In Millions),
Based on Current Assumptions

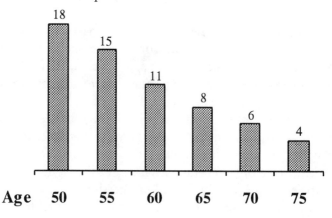

Age	50	55	60	65	70	75
	18	15	11	8	6	4

Understand the Value of "Gifting"

You and your spouse each may gift $10,000 a year to anyone you please. For example, if you have four children, you can gift a total of $40,000 a year. If you have five grandchildren, you can gift an additional total of $50,000 a year. If your spouse is alive, you can double that amount.[2]

That reduces the size of your estate—but it may not be the best strategy. Here's why: You could use the amount you are gifting to pay a premium on insurance policies within a family limited partnership. That gets your insurance out of your estate so it doesn't have to be taxed twice, multiplies the size of the gift, leaves you in control, and maintains available cash values.

On the other hand, it's almost impossible to gift fast enough. Clarence and Emma have a $5 million estate that's earning 10 percent a year. They have 10 children and grandchildren, so they gift $200,000 a year. But their estate is still growing at a rate of $300,000 a year. They aren't even gifting any of their principal. Their estate is growing from $5 million to $5.3 million and continues to compound. Simply stated, it's difficult to give away that much.

Someone with an estate of $1 million to $2 million could theoretically engage in a gifting program and largely diminish the size of his estate, but I've never seen anyone do it prudently.

Here's the reason. Let's assume your estate is $2 million. Is that really very much money to retire on for 30 years? No. And if you're 60, what are the odds of you or your spouse living another 20 or 30 years? Pretty good. And if you're going to live another 20 or 30 years, you'll live through four or five more inflationary/recessionary cycles. All kinds of things can happen to the economy. With so much uncertainty, it's not too smart to part with your retirement security blanket.

But what if you use a gifting approach to pay for an insurance policy? That *is* a smart strategy. Why? You're leveraging your gift 50-to-1—and taking care of the estate tax problem. Why does it work? Because you give the money away. You give the money to an irrevocable insurance trust, a family limited partnership, or your children. They apply for the policy. They own the money, and they own the policy. As discussed above, it's no longer subject to estate taxes.

Ways to multiply your gifts. Let's look at another approach. Howard and Elise, both in their mid-50s, were gifting $10,000 to each of their children and grandchildren every year. Their adviser, Floyd, convinced them they could multiply that gift. With that gift of $10,000 a year, they could purchase a second-to-die policy of approximately $600,000 per child. "My wife and I started doing this for our kids when we were 40," Floyd explained. "Because we started so early, we were able to use our $10,000 gifts to purchase a $3 million policy for each child. Within seven to nine years, those policies can be 'paid up.'"

What happened? Floyd multiplied a $10,000 gift to $3 million. *That's* some significant gifting. His children owned the policies. The cash values of the policies could be used to pay tuition, a down payment on a home, or anything else Floyd's children or grandchildren needed. So the cash was still there. He wasn't giving up the cash. In fact, the cash was growing at a very competitive tax-sheltered rate of return—and Floyd was giving a far larger gift!

Give Your Estate Away Twice

How would you like to give your estate away twice—*and have the IRS pay for it?* You can do it through a mechanism called a charitable remainder unitrust (CRUT) or a charitable remainder annuity trust (CRAT). Here's what happens: You set up a trust designating the entire amount of your estate for charity, which results in immediate tax savings for you. With the taxes you save, you then buy estate replacement insurance that replaces the entire estate for your heirs.

You can transfer virtually any type of asset into a CRUT. Within strict guidelines, the donor or the grantor of the trust (the person who establishes it) may continue to serve as trustee, but he owes a fiduciary duty to the charitable institution to manage the money well. The trust is required to pay out a minimum of 5 percent a year to the donor of the trust, so it generates retirement income for your life and for the life of your surviving spouse.

The CRUT is one of the most profound and creative estate planning strategies. It can completely absolve you of estate taxes due, while still allowing your children to receive your entire estate. (For more details on how to use this extremely effective estate planning tool, see Chapter 26.)

Multiply Your Exemption

Fred *waits* until he dies to allow Janice, his surviving spouse, to take advantage of the $600,000 exemption to generate retirement income for her. When Fred dies, his $600,000 goes to Janice, and she earns 10 percent on that money. In other words, Janice will have a $60,000 annual income for the rest of her life without dipping into the principal.

That's the typical use of the standard exemption—the *exemption equivalent*. But it may not be the best use.

Gary uses the same $600,000 exemption *now* to purchase a $4 million insurance policy with a single one-time premium. When he dies, his wife, Sarah, receives $4 million. She'll earn 10 percent on that money. In other words, Sarah will have a $400,000 annual income for the rest of her life without dipping into the principal.

What a difference! Fred and Gary had the same risk structure, same investments, same situation. The only difference is that Fred waited until death to utilize his $600,000 exemption. Gary leveraged his $600,000 *before* his death—and his wife now has seven times the annual income for the rest of her life!

Multiply Your IRAs

Jack had a pension plan of $1 million. When he retired, he rolled the money into an IRA and closed his pension plan. He had income from other assets, so he didn't really need to start using his IRA income by the age of 70 1/2, when he would be required by law to start using it.

Jack drew the money out over time. He paid a total of $350,000 in income taxes, leaving $650,000 when he died. Of that, $325,000 went to the IRS for estate taxes, and $325,000 went to his heirs. That's a very typical scenario.

Edward, on the other hand, decided to get smart. He surrendered his $1 million IRA in a lump sum, all at once. He paid $350,000 in income taxes, all at once. He then owned $650,000 tax-free. He put that $650,000 into an irrevocable trust and bought a single-premium life insurance policy for $6.5 million. Because the money was in an irrevocable trust, it was out of his estate. That means he didn't pay estate taxes on it—his heirs received the full $6.5 million when he died. That was *20 times* as much as Jack's heirs received—and it didn't cost Edward a penny more.

Multiply Your Single-Premium Life Policy

A single-premium life policy requires that you pay a lump-sum amount into a policy, which then purchases a death benefit. The cash value then grows at a preset rate. That growth rate is generally the focus of single-premium policies. If you buy a $1 million single-life policy that grows at 8 percent, your death benefit could be $1.9 million after several years.

But with a different focus, you can multiply the returns. If you want to multiply your estate and generate the maximum amount for your heirs, you can use your single-premium policy in an IRC Section 1035 tax-free exchange (or use other dollars), then use that same amount to buy a policy that focuses on the death benefit. Instead of having a death benefit of $1.9 million, it could be as much as $17 million, depending on your age. The cash value will grow at only about 6 percent, so you're giving up a little cash value growth to gain a lot of death benefit.

Here's the bottom line: You're actually worth less than half what you think you're worth. That's 45 cents on the dollar. Why? Because a massive 706 mortgage hangs over your estate. That money isn't going to your children—it's going to the IRS.

If you want to change that picture, you'd better do some advance planning. The approaches discussed in this chapter show you how. Get a capable financial planner to help—and you'll end up passing your estate to your children, not to the government.

Your Insights, Feelings, and Action Items

A. As you read this chapter, what *insights* came that seem applicable to *you?*
  1._____
  2._____
  3._____

B. How did you *feel* as you pondered particular points of this chapter?
  1._____
  2._____
  3._____

C. What do you *feel* you should *do* as a result of this chapter?
  1._____
  2._____
  3._____

D. How might you solicit the aid of others in accomplishing "C" above?
  _____
  _____
  _____

[1] Section 6166a of the Internal Revenue Code says that if the decedent's interest in a closely held business is greater than 35 percent of the adjusted gross estate, the portion of the federal estate tax attributable to that interest may be paid in installments. All conditions must be met for an estate to qualify as a closely held business.

[2] The Gift Tax Exclusion states that an individual can "gift away" $10,000 per year per donee from his or her estate. For example, a grandfather can give $10,000 per year from his estate to each of his 23 grandchildren without those grandchildren being taxed on the $10,000. According to Uniform Credit, the first $600,000 of an individual's estate after death can be distributed tax-free to the beneficiaries. Money gifted away from the estate during the life of the estate holder does not deplete the Uniform Credit. If a man gifted away a total of $480,000 to his grandchildren during his lifetime, and at his death there was $590,000 left of his $1 million-dollar estate, the entire $590,000 would be distributed tax-free to his beneficiaries.

Summary of Your 706 Mortgage

	"The 706 Mortgage"	A Typical Mortgage
Collateral	The Mortgage is on: All your Assets. Everything is liened. The IRS gets to choose (cherry-pick) asset they want. You have no choice.	The Mortgaged Asset is: Predetermined. Specific. Identifiable. Planned for. You have a choice.
Due Date	Unknown. You may think you are totally out of debt one day, and the next day you owe millions. It is "callable" at any time.	You know in advance specific Due Dates.
Terms	CASH. Lump-sum, Single-Payment due nine months from date of death. It is all due at once. No other terms.	Cash, Securities, Trade Refinance.
Amount	From 37% to 55% of the Fair Market Value of All your Assets at Death.	Predetermined according to amount borrowed.
What you got?	Nothing more than anyone else.	Cash or other property— Whatever was financed.

Chapter 26

How to Profit from Charitable Giving

Develop a Desire to Give Back

Charitable giving has all kinds of benefits. Start with the obvious: It provides a tax deduction for the year in which you make the donation. But there are other financial benefits. It can let you convert a low-yield, appreciated property to a high-income producing investment—without capital gains taxes. Or it can provide a continuous income throughout your life—and your spouse's life, too, depending on how it's structured.

There's more. Charitable giving offers you the pleasure of donating to a worthwhile cause. And you can even structure your gift so the charity has access to it while you're still alive.

Discussions about charitable giving often focus on the tax or financial implications for the giver. We'll look at those financial implications in a minute—but first let's talk about the real motivation behind charitable giving.

Take a look at what Andrew Carnegie had to say. He observed: "Surplus wealth is a sacred trust which its possessor is bound to administer in his lifetime for the good of the community." The man who dies rich, he said, "dies disgraced."

Thomas Jefferson agreed. "I deem it the duty of every man to put a certain portion of his income to charitable purposes, and it is his further duty to see it so applied as to do the most good of which it is capable."

Stephen Covey observed, "Intrinsic security comes from service, from helping other people in a meaningful way. One important source is your work. When you see yourself in a contributive and creative mode, you are really making a difference. Another source is anonymous service. No one knows it and no one necessarily will. That's not the concern. The concern is blessing the lives of other people. Influence, not recognition, is the motive."

Too many dismiss charitable giving with the idea that it's only for the wealthy. That's simply not true. Charitable giving is for everybody.

Some charitable giving strategies *do* work better for people of substantial means. But many work just as well for people of modest means. In fact, those who use these strategies—regardless of income—enjoy certain advantages not otherwise available. Even if there were no tax advantages, there would still be a solid financial case for charitable giving.

Try an example from Hollywood. Look at Jimmy Stewart's character in *It's a Wonderful Life*. He operated the old Bailey Savings and Loan. He helped people buy homes. He helped his brother. His neighbors. He helped people through the Depression. And he did it selflessly. It was pretty widely known that he wasn't fully remunerated.

He had discovered early in life—without any overt pursuit of tax advantages—that the first law of financial security is service. Giving of self.

What happened when *he* got in trouble? Those years of service came flooding back a hundredfold. Cynics might tell you that life doesn't work that way—that if you're in trouble, no one will come rushing to your aid. That no one would come to your aid when you need help. Maybe. Maybe half—or three-fourths—of the people out there *won't* come to your aid. But maybe the rest will.

Another example? One of my friends who owned a trophy store in Los Angeles learned that a competitor had suffered a severe medical setback and would likely be out of business within the year. How did my friend react?

He might have aggressively gone after his competitor's customers.

Instead, he contacted his competitor. He offered to take care of the competitor's clients for a year—then return those clients to the competitor when he was able to resume business. That's exactly what he did.

What happened? My friend benefited financially during the eight or 10 months while he serviced his competitor's clients. Did it end there? Absolutely not! Word got out. The local newspaper found out what he was doing, and ran a story about his service. Potential clients read between the lines—learned what kind of man he was.

In the end, his competitor went back to work and was able to re-establish his business. And my friend's business exploded, with more business than he could handle because people *wanted* to do business with him. They knew they would get an honest deal.

When you cast your bread upon the waters, it comes back to you many times over. That holds true whether you're figuring up a tax deduction or calculating how much you give. In fact, I'm sure it holds true more fully when you're *not* calculating—when you forget about the immediate financial benefits of your giving.

Jesus shared the fundamental truth, "He that findeth his life shall lose it; and he that loseth his life for my sake shall find it." (Matthew 10:39)

Develop Your Strategies for Charitable Giving

Without forgetting the higher motivation for giving, let's discuss some charitable giving strategies from a financial and tax perspective. Remember: Charitable gifting strategies are highly technical and should be undertaken only with competent professional advice.

Tax Deductions

One strategy is to take an income tax deduction for gifts to some charitable institution—your church or synagogue, educational institution, hospital, Boy Scouts, Girl Scouts, American Red Cross, Cancer Society, or some other nonprofit organization. Under the Internal Revenue Code, these are referred to as 501(c)3 organizations. Why is it a good strategy?

Its benefits exceed the tax deduction. Here's why: I have observed countless people who make those contributions. From what I have seen, they are less prone to squander their income in frivolous ways. They become more self-reliant. They better utilize the WYHTE phenomenon. They express gratitude, are humble, feel in touch with the rest of humanity. The end result? They're more careful with their money. So their money stretches further. In many other ways, the money they gave away comes back—multiplied.

Charitable Bequests

Assets willed to a charity upon your death are charitable bequests. Your taxable estate is then reduced.

I'd like to look in detail at several kinds of charitable bequests.

Charitable remainder trust. In a charitable remainder trust, the property is placed into the charitable trust irrevocably. When the donor dies, the property passes to the charity. While he is alive, however, the donor receives an income—typically paid on a quarterly basis. That income is normally taxable income.

When the donor makes the contribution irrevocably to the trust, he receives an immediate income tax deduction based on actuarial tables and on how much income he receives. As we mentioned in Chapter 25, there are two types of charitable remainder trusts: a *unitrust* and an *annuity trust*. Here are the basic differences:

A unitrust can receive ongoing contributions. An annuity trust can receive only one contribution. An annuity trust pays a fixed dollar amount—an "annuity," not less than 5 percent of the original value of the trust—each year, regardless of what the trust earns. It's best for older individuals who want the security of a guaranteed payment without having to worry about investment performance in the trust.

A unitrust pays either a fixed percentage of the trust assets each year or the net income of the trust, whichever is less.

What are the benefits of a charitable remainder trust? There are several. First, you might receive a higher retirement income than if you simply retained the assets. (In this setting, the Charitable Remainder Trust is sometimes referred to as a "Capital Gains Bypass Trust.")

I'm reminded of Randy, a rough-and-tumble engineer who sauntered into my office one morning looking for a way to bypass the capital gains tax on some closely-held corporation stock. He bought it for $10 a share, and it rose to $350 a share. I suggested he contribute the stock to a CRUT, and the CRUT could then sell the stock. Randy's capital gain of $340 a share would then be inside a charitable trust, which is not required to pay taxes on the gain.

"You mean you want me to give the whole thing to charity?" was his immediate response. "Yes and no," I replied. "You do turn the stock over to the charitable trust, but you will receive a tax deduction for a portion of the fair market value of your gift on the day you donate it, and when you have your CRUT sell the stock you'll pay no capital gains taxes." The mention of a tax break caught his interest. I continued, "As the CRUT invests your gift, you get an income for the rest of your life that is 50 percent larger than it would have been because you didn't have to pay taxes. And this strategy works for any other highly appreciated asset you might have, including real estate." Randy was finally convinced, and we were able to save him a substantial amount of taxes while increasing his retirement income dramatically.

Not only is the CRUT valuable for bypassing capital gains taxes, but it can also help you substantially minimize estate taxes. When you die, everything in the trust goes to the charity. All of those assets are removed from your estate as soon as you make the irrevocable gift to the trust. In other words, they're removed from your taxable estate long before you die. What does that mean? You can reduce an estate of millions of dollars to however small you want to make it. Taken to an extreme, you can avoid estate taxes completely.

Too often this strategy is considered only by people who have a significant estate or who are anticipating an estate tax problem. But it can be equally appropriate for someone who has a fairly modest estate but wants to give something to charity when he dies. What, then, happens to your heirs? Is there any way of increasing what your heirs—your children—might receive?

Let's look at an example. Tony and Maria have an estate of $3 million, and everything over $1.2 million is subject to estate taxes. For a $3 million estate, the average estate tax is 50 percent. Tony and Maria were considering a gift of $1 million into a charitable remainder trust.

They knew that if they left the $1 million in their estate, their children would only get $500,000; the children would pay the other $500,000 in estate taxes.

On the other hand, if Tony and Maria put that $1 million in a charitable remainder trust, how much will the charity get upon their death? $1 million. How much will their children get? Zero. The last thing Tony and Maria wanted to do was disinherit their children.

But their children could get a full $1 million. How? Through a wealth replacement life insurance policy that is placed in a trust for the children. The million-dollar life insurance policy replaces the entire $1 million for their heirs.

Who purchases the wealth replacement life insurance policy? Tony and Maria do—with the immediate income tax savings they get when they donate money to the charitable remainder trust.

Look at what happens. When Tony and Maria contribute to the charitable remainder trust, they can take a tax deduction against any and all other income they have up to 30 percent of their adjusted gross income.

If the tax deduction is more than they can use in the year they make the contribution, they can carry it forward for as many as five additional years, for a total of six years. With their income tax savings each year, they purchase the insurance policy. (Nine times out of 10, the tax savings will be more than enough to purchase a life insurance policy that can be "paid-up" within six years.)

Tony and Maria's annual income is $80,000. So, they can claim a charitable deduction of $24,000 a year. That saves them about $10,000 in actual cash savings—the amount they put into a life insurance premium. Over six years, they save $60,000. With their money, Tony and Maria pay the premiums on a "second-to-die" insurance policy that pays the death benefit upon the second death—enough to replace the entire amount they contributed to the charitable trust.

What happens? They give their full $1 million away *twice*: once to the charity and once to their heirs. In fact, their heirs get *double* what they would have. And the IRS paid for it! (Remember? Tony and Maria paid the insurance premiums, but they did it with money the IRS *would* have received in taxes.)

In fact, often the IRS loses on three taxes: They lose the capital gains taxes when an appreciated asset is sold from within the CRUT. They lose the income taxes due to the charitable deduction. And they lose the estate taxes upon your death because your assets were given to charity.

I've heard people say, "I'd rather have the government get my money." If you think the government will be more efficient in accomplishing good with your money than a charity, that's great. I've also heard people say, "I don't want my children to get all this money." Then give all your money to a charity—or include a trust or some other vehicle that will manage the money so your children don't get it all in a lump sum.

If you want to exercise stewardship over your assets, as discussed in Chapter 2, you'll want your assets to accomplish as much good as possible. A charitable remainder trust coupled with a wealth replacement trust may accomplish your objectives.

A special note: While this discussion used the example of an estate large enough to incur estate taxes, do not make the mistake of thinking that this strategy is only for large estates. Those with very modest estates may successfully apply this strategy, increase their retirement income, increase tax deductions, and still give their *full* estates to both their heirs and a favorite charity, thereby accomplishing something meaningful. Get expert advice on how this strategy might work for you. A word of caution: If you want the wealth replaced for your heirs through an insur-

ance policy, be sure you qualify for the policy *before* you make the irrevocable gift.

Give Your Estate Away Twice
(and have the IRS pay for it)

	Without CRUT *or* Insurance	With Insurance Only	CRUT with Estate Replacement Insurance
1. Taxable Estate Size (after exclusions)	$3,000,000	$3,000,000	$3,000,000
2. Minus Estate Taxes	− 1,600,000	− 1,600,000	-0-
3. Minus Charity	-0-	-0-	− 3,000,000
4. Plus Insurance	-0-	+ 1,600,000	+ 3,000,000
5. Net to Heirs	$1,400,000	$3,000,000	$3,000,000
6. Pre-Death Income Tax Savings	-0-	-0-	50,000+ a year for 6 years
7. Insurance Premium	-0-	15,000 a year for 6 years	28,000 a year for 6 years
8. Net Cost	53% of estate	3% of estate	-0-
9. Who Pays?	YOU BIG	You Tiny	IRS

Give Your Estate Away Twice

CRUT – Charitable Remainder Unitrust
(also known as a Capital Gains Bypass Trust)

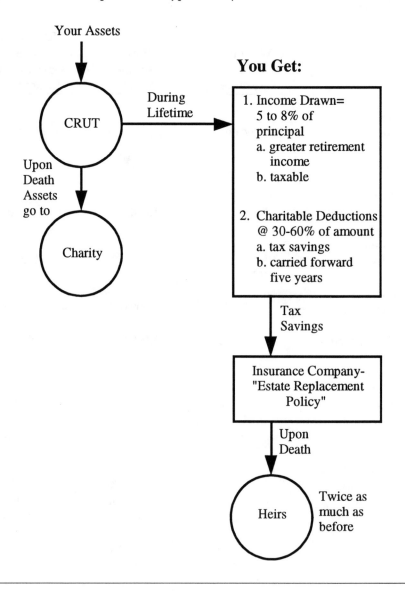

Your Assets

You Get:

CRUT

During Lifetime

1. Income Drawn=
   5 to 8% of
   principal
   a. greater retirement
      income
   b. taxable

2. Charitable Deductions
   @ 30-60% of amount
   a. tax savings
   b. carried forward
      five years

Upon Death Assets go to

Charity

Tax Savings

Insurance Company-
"Estate Replacement
Policy"

Upon Death

Heirs

Twice as much as before

Charitable lead trust. A charitable lead trust might be used when you have assets you want to leave to certain heirs, but you don't need current income. A charitable lead trust is the opposite of a charitable remainder trust. Here's what happens:

In a charitable remainder trust, the charity gets your assets when you die, and you get income or dividend income from the trust while living. In a charitable lead trust, the charity gets the income from the trust for a specified number of years (usually the remainder of your life), then the principal is returned to your heirs.

The charity does have another option: It can use part of the tax-free income from the trust to purchase a life insurance policy on you. When you die, the charity gets substantial proceeds from the life insurance policy. In other words, the charity gets a steady income stream while you're alive *as well as* a lump sum when you die. The charity might invest that lump sum, so it might continue to produce an income for the charity.

Life insurance trust. In a life insurance trust, one of two things happens: Either you give a charity an existing life insurance policy, or the charity buys a new life insurance policy on you. Either way, you're making a tax-deductible contribution to the charity in the amount of the premium. How does it work? The charity owns the policy irrevocably. When you die, then, the charity gets a significant donation—which may be a larger sum than you could have donated in cash.

In a variation on that, you might buy a single-premium whole life insurance policy through a charitable gifting program. Let's look at the benefits:

Oscar has $100,000 that he could put in a certificate of deposit at 6 percent. At the end of a year, he would have earned $6,000 in interest. Since he is in a 36 percent tax bracket, he would pay $2,200 in taxes, for a net gain of $3,800.

But Oscar discovered a better option. He instead put that $100,000 into a single-premium whole life insurance policy earning 7 percent in a charitable gifting program. At the end of a year, he earned $7,000 interest. But he didn't owe any taxes on it. He donated $3,200 to charity, and he kept the remaining $3,800. That's the same amount he would have netted from the certificate of deposit.

But wait—because Oscar gave $3,200 to charity, he also received a tax savings of about $1,500. Add that $1,500 in tax savings to his net of $3,800—for a total of $5,300.

The result? The charity received $3,200. Oscar netted $5,300—about 30 percent more than the after-tax earnings he would have received from the certificate of deposit.

Charitable foundations. A charitable foundation might be established by someone with significant financial resources. He then makes tax-deductible contributions to that foundation as long as the foundation is used for charitable purposes.

Gift of *appreciated* property. Another strategy is to make charitable contributions with appreciated property rather than with cash.

Here's how it works: After losing both parents to cancer, Gary donated to the American Cancer Society a marketable security consisting of appreciated stock. He originally bought the stock for $5,000, and now it's worth $10,000. If he wanted to sell the stock for its market value of $10,000 and give the proceeds to charity, he'd have to first pay taxes of $1,700, leaving only $8,300 to give to charity.

But by contributing the stock directly to the cancer society, Gary bypassed the taxable gain on the stock. The charity got the entire $10,000, Gary paid nothing in taxes, and he got a $10,000 charitable contribution deduction against his taxable income.

You can contribute almost any kind of appreciated property—real estate, art, jewelry, and so on. Make sure you get an independent third-party appraisal unless you have a readily marketable security. You then receive a tax deduction for the fair market value.

Gift of *depreciated* property. Remember to keep track of any contributions of gifts-in-kind that you make to the Salvation Army or any other charitable organization. List the items you donate—an old washer, dryer, refrigerator, used clothing, shoes, old games, and toys. You might need a third-party appraisal, but you can deduct the fair market value. (A fairly recent purchase in working order might have a fair market value of 30 percent of the retail price; older items and clothing usually have a value of only 10 to 15 percent of the new price.) The typical family discards hundreds, if not thousands, of dollars worth of items every year. Why not give them to an organization that can fix them up and use them? And for the 15 minutes it will take you to list your contributions and get a receipt, you might save $200 in taxes. That's a pretty good hourly wage.

If you own a business, remember you can donate your copier, telephone system, conference table, chairs, fax machine, computer, or other furniture and equipment. General office equipment can be used by virtually any charity—and the tax deduction you'll get might be easier than a yard sale or classified ad.

The bargain sale. You might also try a strategy called the "bargain sale"—you sell appreciated property to a charity at less than the fair market value. For example, you sell a $100,000 piece of real estate to a charity for $50,000. The charity realizes an automatic appreciation of $50,000. You get a tax deduction for $50,000—which will save you about $20,000 in taxes. And you've made a contribution at a level you can afford.

All Strategy Aside

It has been said it is more blessed to give than to receive. We have shown some of the ways that charitable giving has a financial planning perspective. I am not suggesting that is how to find happiness. The deepest happiness and joy comes only when we give without calculating what we will receive in return.

Perhaps you have felt your heart burn and tears come when you have sacrificed for a loved one, or helped a stranger along the way. That is the pathway to joy. It is strewn with opportunities to give of yourself freely, without anticipation of financial rewards. After all, no matter how much we think we accomplish, achieve, or earn ourselves, *we all reap where others have sown before us.*

This is a somewhat pedestrian chapter—it trivializes the special act of giving of oneself by focusing on tax strategies. Please don't confine yourself to the technical limitations of this chapter. While we can discuss giving from a tax and financial perspective, make no mistake about it. The more you can divorce yourself from the tax angle and the financial benefits of giving, the more you will *feel* the spirit of giving. That's when you will truly profit from the process.

Your Insights, Feelings, and Action Items

A. As you read this chapter, what *insights* came that seem applicable to you?
  1._____
  2._____
  3._____

B. How did you *feel* as you pondered particular points of this chapter?
  1._____
  2._____
  3._____

C. What do you *feel* you should *do* as a result of this chapter?

    1._____

    2._____

    3._____

D. How might you solicit the aid of others in accomplishing "C" above?

_____

_____

_____

Decision Five

Climb the Right Ladder to Success

While Chapter 27 discusses four key principles with which anyone may achieve great success, Chapters 28 through 31 elaborate on key strategies to achieve success in a financial plan.

Chapter 27

How to Achieve Success

B y definition, few people achieve success. Think about it: If everyone achieved success, the average would simply be raised.

In America today, we define *success* as rising above the norm in some way. While this book may be about economic success, it is important to remind ourselves that financial success achieved without the character traits that bring money happiness will only yield emptiness and loneliness.

There are four simple laws of success:

First, do what you love.

Second, focus on the end results that have meaning to you—not the unpleasant means by which you reach the end results.

Third, simplify to focus.

And, fourth, synergize through interdependence.

Let's look at each more closely.

Do What You Love

I met a young woman who had recently graduated from college in nursing. Nancy had spent some time as a nurse's aid in a local hospital, and her eyes absolutely lit up whenever she talked about her job. She loved nursing and found great meaning and purpose in her work.

Unfortunately, there were no nursing positions available in her area, so she got a securities license and decided on a career as a stockbroker. She had lined up a full-time position, complete with benefits, with a national brokerage house. Now she was asking me whether she should consider a part-time position at one of the local hospitals under less than ideal circumstances.

She was taken aback at my response: "You wouldn't be any good as a stockbroker, because you wouldn't devote the enthusiasm necessary to become expert. It would just become another tangent in your life."

I told Nancy to take the part-time position at the hospital. "You love what you do there," I reminded her. "They will see your devotion, and the next full-time position that becomes available will be yours. Besides, it will pay enough to make ends meet until the opening comes along, and you'll be happy."

Do something you love. *Only then* will you invest the time, energy, and enthusiasm to become very good—even expert.

Achieving success takes many hours, tremendous effort, and great enthusiasm. It can't happen for someone who considers his career a drudgery. If you work at a job you hate, you have placed money above happiness. It's that simple.

I often watch people start law school, only to discover after the first semester that lawyering won't be the fun career they saw on *Perry Mason* or *Matlock*. If they are brave, they get out and find something they love. If they are not, they stay—but they never achieve the success they hoped for. They make a decision based on ego criteria rather than happiness criteria. In law, as in anything else, you won't adequately compete if what you are doing does not completely motivate you, energize you, and enthuse you in the achieving of great goals.

The first rule of success is to find something you love so deeply that it virtually becomes a hobby. When you do, you will spend the time and effort necessary to truly become expert. And that happens only when you approach your work with deep compassion. It doesn't matter what it is, as long as you love it. American publisher B.C. Forbes observed, "There is more credit and satisfaction in being a first-rate truck driver than a tenth-rate executive."

Bill Marriott, CEO of Marriott International, shared with me his feeling that if you find something you love doing, the rest will take care of itself: "To be successful, you have to really love what you do." Put another way, those who directly pursue success may find it elusive. Those who pursue something they love will find success a natural byproduct.

If you have settled into a career rut, what will re-energize your life? Can you break the stifling habits? Can you blast out of your comfort zone? Are you doing what you love? What you would want to be doing? Or do you feel trapped by a paycheck?

By the way, don't get me wrong: Even when you are doing something you love, success requires great work and effort. Success doesn't come to a chosen few—rather, *very few choose success*, and the effort associated with it. Lasting success doesn't occur overnight. Growth comes slowly.

Sink Roots Like the Bamboo Tree

In China, there is a bamboo tree that seems to do nothing at all after its roots are planted under ground. Even when watered and fertilized with care, it shows no perceptible growth for five years. Sometime during the fifth year, a tiny sprout appears. *Then, within 60 days, the bamboo tree achieves a towering height of 90 feet.* Did the tree actually grow 90 feet in 60 days—or did it grow 90 feet in five years?

Preparation, testing, and nurturing takes patience and time. What we see as an outward show of true lasting success is the result of many years of cultivation in the personal private habits of the individual.

You've got to knock off a lot of rough edges. It takes nature millennia to grind stones smooth along a river's bottom. Those who polish gemstones know that a hard rock is placed in a tumbler and buffeted for weeks by coarse, medium, fine and ultimately a polishing grit before it becomes smooth and polished. Like grinding a stone, life is grinding. Adversity knocks off the rough edges—a little here and a little there. Only then is excellence achieved. That's why it is the private personal habits that count.

Even when you are doing something you love, you need to take time out to sharpen the saw. You can't spend all your time sawing. Spend some quiet moments of solitude to figure out what is truly important to you—then determine how you will achieve it, and go do it!

And even when you are doing something you love, you will make mistakes. That's okay. The first great freedom is the freedom to make mistakes. There are mistakes of judgment and mistakes of sin. Go see your clergy about mistakes of sin. What I am talking about here are the innocent mistakes of judgment, wisdom, insight, or experience.

In your pursuit of excellence, you have to be willing to venture out and take risks. Sometimes you will discover you did things right; usually you will discover you have done something wrong. Pain follows—but so does growth.

I know what I'm talking about here, because I have had plenty of experience with mistakes. As I started out in business, I was always trying to figure out how to do something better or more efficiently. After all, I knew how to do it. I had ideas. I was creative. I had worked continuously since the age of 11. I had started my first business at the age of 14. I had an MBA. I was a CPA. I had read a book a week for 12 years (at that time). Why shouldn't I know how to build a business?

Do you know what I learned? I learned that MBAs know nothing. I made mistake after mistake. I must have made hundreds of them—and, because I wasn't a quitter, I kept right on making them! Were they ever intentional? Of course not. Did I feel I had completely studied things out before I acted? Yes. Still I made mistakes.

You learn quickly from some mistakes; those are the mistakes you never repeat. Other lessons come more slowly. But if you are wise, you eventually learn. You read beyond worldly wisdom. You discern the flakes, the fly-by-nighters—and you stay away. Then you get blessed with wisdom, judgment, insight.

For many of us, our life is like the following autobiography. Read it aloud, slowly:

> Chapter 1. I walk down the street. There is a deep hole in the sidewalk. I fall in. I am helpless. It isn't my fault. It takes forever to find a way out.
>
> Chapter 2. I walk down the street. There is a deep hole in the sidewalk. I pretend I don't see it. I fall in again. I can't believe I am in the same place. But it isn't my fault. It still takes a long time to get out.
>
> Chapter 3. I walk down the same street. There is a deep hole in the sidewalk. I see it is there. I still fall in. It's a habit, but my eyes are open. I know where I am. It is my fault. I get out immediately.
>
> Chapter 4. I walk down the same street. There is a deep hole in the sidewalk. I walk around it.
>
> Chapter 5. I walk down another street. No holes.
>
> Author Unknown

Mistakes are like that. You have to pay the consequences. Don't be afraid to make mistakes, but don't keep making the same ones over again. The wise person will learn, too, from the mistakes of others; you don't have to learn everything for yourself.

Focus on End Results, Not Unpleasant Means

In his 1940 speech *The Common Denominator of Success*, Albert E.N. Gray said he realized the secret of success didn't lie in hard work alone. The secret of success, he said, is "the habit of doing things that failures don't like to do."

The difference between successful men and failures? Seldom understood, said Gray, is that "successful men are influenced by the desire for pleasing results. Failures are influenced by the desire for pleasing methods."

"The things that failures don't like to do are the very things that you and I (and other human beings, including successful men) naturally don't like to do," Gray explained. "In other words, we've got to realize right from the start that success is something that is achieved by the minority of men and is therefore unnatural and not to be achieved by following our natural likes and dislikes, nor by being guided by our natural preferences and prejudices."

Can you identify in your career what it is that people don't like to do? Right now, make a list of five things you and others like you don't like to do in *your* career.

Do you do them anyway?

If you want to be a success, you have to get into the habit of doing the things you don't want to do. Why? Because "it is easier to adjust to the hardships of a poor living than to the hardships of making a better one. If you doubt me, just think of all the things you are willing to go without to avoid doing the things you don't like to do."

Why does habit play such an important role in success? "Men are creatures of habit, just as machines are creatures of momentum. ... Habit is nothing more or less than momentum translated from the concrete into the abstract.

"What if there was no such thing as momentum? Speed would be impossible: The highest speed any vehicle could achieve would be the first speed at which it was broken away from a standstill. Elevators could not go up. Airplanes could not fly. The world of mechanics would find itself in a total state of helplessness.

"Then," asked Gray, "who are you and I to think that we can do with our own human nature what the finest engineers in the world cannot do with the finest machinery ever built?

"Every single qualification for success is acquired through habit. Men form habits and habits form futures. If you do not deliberately form good habits, then unconsciously you will form bad ones. You are the kind of man you are because you have formed the habit of that kind of man. The only way you can change is through habit."

Breaking any habit takes effort. So does establishing any habit. Why? Because all habits, whether good or bad, *feel natural*. It is disturbing and sometimes painful to leave that zone of familiarity. The same is true with success habits.

As uncomfortable as it may be, establishing good habits is crucial. Gray continued:

> Any resolution or decision you make is simply a promise to yourself which isn't worth a tinker's dam until you have formed the habit of making it and keeping it. And you won't form the habit of making it and keeping it unless right at the start you link it with a definite purpose that can be accomplished by keeping it. In other words, any resolution or decision you make today has to be made again tomorrow and the next day and the next and so on. And it not only has to be made each day but it has to be kept each day, for if you miss one day in the making or keeping of it, you've got to go back and begin all over again. But if you continue the process of making it each morning and keeping it each day, you will finally wake up one morning a different man in a different world. You'll wonder what happened to the world you used to live in.

Do you think the physician likes studying all night in college while his friends are relaxing? No. Does the business owner like mortgaging his home, laying awake nights wondering how he will meet payroll? No. Does the business owner like going without a paycheck? Absolutely not. Does the salesman like the rejection he must endure each day just to make a living? No.

But these people aren't motivated by pleasing methods. They're motivated by pleasing results—so they're willing to endure the unpleasant tasks. Focus on the essence, the end result.

Simplify to Focus

Charles Lindbergh was recognized for his courage as the first man to fly solo across the Atlantic. Within months before he did it, two others had tried but had disappeared at sea and were never heard of again. In just over 33 hours, Lindbergh landed at an airfield in Paris, France.

As he prepared to venture on that flight, he loaded his plane with so much extra fuel for the takeoff that people doubted he could get off the runway. The runway was lengthened. Then Lindbergh stripped his plane, *The Spirit of St. Louis*, to its bare essentials. He threw out the extra seat and everything else that could possibly be unbolted and removed.

If you want to achieve success, that is what you have to do. You have to cut through the nonsense and get rid of excess baggage—it dissipates the energy you need for success.

Get rid of emotional baggage. Forget real or imagined offenses. *You* are the one hurt by not forgiving others. *You* are the one that dissipates energy.

Successful people are forgiving people. They not only know how to readily forgive others, but they can also forgive themselves for mistakes they have made. The most successful people I know have developed the attitude of *forgiving in advance*. They have determined they will be "non-offendable." They refuse to waste their energy toward offenses they can't change. They realize they will be wronged, probably a great many times—but they realize, too, that *even remembering* the offense is like driving down the highway while looking in the rearview mirror. It simply isn't very efficient. It never gets you where you're going.

Get rid of physical baggage. If you want to be mentally alert and capable, you need to get in shape physically. Whether success is in career, business, or family, it requires the effort of a fit person. Get a tuneup. You can't achieve success running on five cylinders. You need all eight cylinders in a well-tuned vehicle.

Get rid of mental baggage. Just as you pursue a healthy body, get a healthy mind. Get rid of self-defeating thoughts. In today's health conscious society, most people wouldn't even *consider* eating garbage—but do you feed it to your mind? While the body has natural means to expel poisons, once poison is in the mind, it just sits there, waiting to be recalled. It's as dumb as lifting the hood of your car, removing the oil cap, and pouring sand into your crankcase.

Vacant minds become like vacant lots—filled with other people's petty garbage, litter, and debris. Successful people don't consume other people's cheap movies and gossip TV. The best thing to do is build something significant there and post a "No Trespassing" sign.

Get rid of stress. It is one of the great obstacles to winning. It dissipates the energy required. You've got to be able to do everything you can with everything you've got.

Get rid of the baggage of your weaknesses. If it's a personal or character weakness, overcome it. If it's a career or business weakness, delegate it.

Once you get rid of excess baggage, focus on your vision. Ask yourself, "What must I do over the next three years, professionally and personally, to be pleased with my growth?"

Pinpoint exactly what you want to achieve. Then make that *want* a *burning desire*.

Now simplify. Simplifying your life allows you to get rid of the nonessentials and focus on the results, just as Charles Lindbergh did.

Once you have simplified your life and thinking habits, you are better able to develop a detailed plan that contains just the essential elements. You can better use the resources available to you. When you have cut out all the nonessentials, you do not lose focus. You do not get off on tangents. You are able to stay with a task and follow through. You determine that *your* odds of success are one-to-one. What are *your* odds of success?

Cliff divers along the Pacific Coast near Acapulco, Mexico, have determined their odds of success. As the ocean climbs and recedes against the rocks, the divers actually dive when they see nothing but rocks beneath them. By the time they reach the bottom, the ocean has returned. It's as though their downward draft causes the water to appear! For this feat, they must have absolute confidence that their odds of success are one-to-one!

Synergize Through Interdependence

What is *synergy?* With synergy, 1 + 1 = 3. Synergy relies on the principle of specialization and exchange (see Chapter 11). It happens only in a state of abundance thinking and win-win relationships. It happens only through interdependence.

Alone, a person cannot be synergistic. Synergy requires teamwork, cooperation, humility. Interdependence and synergy require relationships, and relationships are based on *relying*. Therefore, synergy also requires trust and loyalty. Those are the traits that lead to interdependence and economic success.

Strength comes from interdependence. Alone we are as one—but the strength of many builds real success: Hold a twig in your hand; you can break it easily. Now hold a dozen twigs together, and see how hard they are to break.

Business schools teach competition. Competition fosters independence, not interdependence. It is the basis of pride and envy. Competition leads to win-lose relationships, pride, and inferior business relationships.

Interdependent relationships are based on trust. Contrary to popular thinking, trust is not something that is earned, but something that is *granted*. Just as beauty is in the eye of the beholder, trust is a gift the giver *bestows* upon the recipient. Yes, someone may violate your trust. But *you* determine whether you will ever trust that person again.

Long ago, I determined that it would be more efficient to consciously go through life trusting others. Though I get burned occasionally, it is still more cost effective than going through life with suspicion. I am not naive. I am simply being wise in choosing the company I keep—then I trust that company.

Relationships *do* count. Get involved. As you develop relationships, be a builder. If you want to be happy, go out of your way to find people you can lift. Be sensitive. Attract friends and loyalty. Be inclusive. Be a mentor. Broaden your circle of friends. Love people. Open your circle of friends to the newcomer. Get rid of your ego. Builders don't derail on their way to the executive suite because others sabotaged their progress. Egocentric, arrogant people get derailed.

You won't succeed by stepping on people, but by lifting people. That applies not only to your co-workers, but to your family, your community, the nation, and the world.

Realize that *secure people seek heroes*. Mature people seek role-models. This is a key ingredient of success. It is an efficient and effective means to growth.

The story is told of a man who got a flat tire in the middle of nowhere in a blinding snowstorm. He could faintly see the lights of a farmhouse in the distance. As he walked toward the farmhouse, he began to mutter to himself about how he would be waking the family from their sleep at 4 a.m. He imagined their anger at being disturbed.

The man finally reached the farmhouse and knocked on the door. The farmer peered out the window. But before the farmer could say anything, the man shouted, "I didn't want your darn jack anyway!"

Ultimately, *your success reflects how well you are thinking.* Don't think like the man in the snowstorm! Think according to the law of abundance, not the emotion of scarcity.

What's scarcity thinking? It sees a static-sized pie. It says that if you win, then I lose. It's the kind of thinking that destroys negotiations among employees, free trade, environmentalists, and advocates of population control. It's based on fear, and it sees the world as an intimidating place. It makes people get introspective, shrivel up, and die.

Scarcity thinking is illustrated by two small children arguing over who gets to play with a certain toy. You've seen it: They'll fight and kick and scream and tug at the toy. After a while, along comes a parent who says, "Let's go to the toy box and get a whole bunch of other toys."

The law of abundance is the opposite of the emotion of scarcity. It sees an expanding, dynamic-sized pie. It sees competition as a cooperative process of win-win relationships.

The law of abundance sees specialization and exchange among employees, between companies, within a society, and between countries, because it can see growth. Instead of drawing you inward, it lets you expand outward. It invites you to live the abundant life.

Instead of operating from a position of fear and feeling threatened when there's a new kid on the block, use abundance thinking. Approach others by saying, "Welcome. I've been waiting for you. I look forward to working together."

Scarcity vs. Abundance Thinking

The Scarcity Thinker focuses on the percent he is getting.
The Abundance Thinker focuses on the size of the pie.
Which would you rather have?

100%   50%

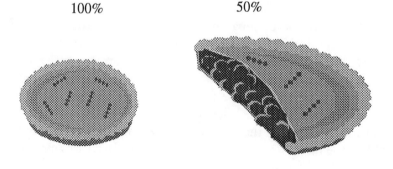

How to Attract Security and Financial Success

Money only flows in two directions. There are dollars looking for security, and dollars seeking success and achievement. Whether you are a worker in the career marketplace ("man at work") or an investor in the financial marketplace ("money at work"), dollars will seek you out and become yours only to the extent you meet *their* needs.

You will attract those dollars seeking security by providing *trust*. This explains why, in the career realm, the honest, loyal, and trustworthy person will succeed in spite of other apparent limitations. In the investment realm, these dollars search out trustworthy and reputable institutions.

You will attract those dollars seeking success or achievement by providing *incentive* and opportunity. The more profitable you are as an employee, the scarcer your unique competencies and talents, the more these dollars will find you. Increase your skills, develop a willingness to do the unpleasant but valued task, and others will place value on your services. The same holds in the investment realm.

You will repel dollars when you are dishonest, cynical, irresponsible, or developing traits opposite to any of those found in C-H-A-R-A-C-T-E-R.

* * *

The four laws of success are simple but essential: Do what you love. Focus on results, not means. Simplify. Synergize.

The Success Continuum

Failure

Success

Unskilled   Ignorance   Knowledge Skills Good Habits
Self-Destructive Behaviors   Attitude
Dishonesty   Focus   Honesty
Ego   Self-Gratification   Discipline   Patience
         Scarcity Mentality   Abundance Mentality
  Impulsive   Goal-Driven
Dependence   Independence   Interdependence

Your Insights, Feelings, and Action Items

A. As you read this chapter, what *insights* came that seem applicable to you?

1._____

2._____

3._____

B. How did you *feel* as you pondered particular points of this chapter?

1._____

2._____

3._____

C. What do you *feel* you should *do* as a result of this chapter?

1._____

2._____

3._____

D. How might you solicit the aid of others in accomplishing "C" above?

_____

_____

_____

Chapter 28

Do Your Homework Early on the Economics of Higher Education

According to a 1994 U.S. Census Bureau report, the average lifetime earnings for U.S. workers who did not graduate from high school is $609,000. That's only $15,225 a year.

You can do significantly better by graduating from high school. You'll average $20,500 a year, or 35 percent more. But look at what can happen if you graduate from college: People with a bachelor's degree earn an average of $35,500 a year—73 percent more than workers who graduate from high school and much more than double the earnings of high school dropouts.

Obviously, investing in your child's higher education yields a profitable return for your child, for you and for society.

Estimated Lifetime Earnings by Education Level for U.S. Workers

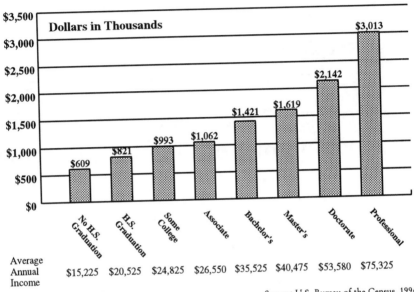

Dollars in Thousands

	No H.S. Graduation	H.S. Graduation	Some College	Associate	Bachelor's	Master's	Doctorate	Professional
Lifetime Earnings	$609	$821	$993	$1,062	$1,421	$1,619	$2,142	$3,013
Average Annual Income	$15,225	$20,525	$24,825	$26,550	$35,525	$40,475	$53,580	$75,325

Source: U.S. Bureau of the Census, 1994

What Will a College Education Cost?

That's not a simple question—especially if you're trying to predict costs 10 or 15 years from now. Why? Many factors can change—which involves a number of issues.

One issue to consider is taxes. Tax breaks for education may diminish as the budget deficit increases. And as the budget deficit increases, grant and financial aid programs from the government and student loan programs may decrease substantially.

Competition for scholarships may therefore get increasingly tougher. So will the competition for part-time student jobs. Some experts predict that competition will double. As competition for jobs increases, hourly wages will stay low—and the number of available jobs may drop. Finally, competition from international students will increase.

The result? Your child's college education will be more expensive than yours was. And it will be tougher for your child to finance that education.

How to Pay for a College Education

It may not be possible to accurately predict the cost of a future college education.

But one thing *is* possible to predict: Those who can best afford that education will be the ones who strategically plan ahead for it.

There are five basic sources of dollars for college funding:

- Scholarships and grants-in-aid
- Tax savings (which requires advance strategic planning)
- Compound interest dollars (also requires advance savings)
- Cash flow dollars (money you pay at the time of the education)
- Debt (money you pay back, plus interest)

Some of these sources—tax savings and compound interest—require time, patience, and advance planning. Others—cash flow dollars and debt—are very expensive.

The Naked Truth about Student Loans

Let's take a look at debt. It's last on the list for a reason: It should be your last resort. Why? Debt brings with it two significant expenses—interest, and lost career opportunities.

The first expense is interest. In fact, most think that the only cost associated with debt is the interest. Interest on educational loans is no longer tax-deductible, but because some guaranteed student loans are tax-deferred or have low interest rates, many people think it's wise to borrow their way through college. Some even think they can invest the student loan money elsewhere, then profit from the spread between what the investment earns and what they have to pay in income tax. This is not only inappropriate, because it's not the purpose of a college loan, but it also may be a fool's trap.

Borrowing to finance a college education also hampers career opportunities. How? The fixed costs of a high debt structure require a low-risk, secure career structure. What does that have to do with lost career opportunities?

People who make decisions by the numbers often end up with a career that looks like a paint-by-number kit. Careers have the same risk-reward relationship as investments. The lowest-risk careers, those that assure the most security, generally have the lowest financial opportunity or potential.

Stuart had the personality and aptitude to take on a career opportunity that required some effort and risk on his part. And given his aptitude, profile, and determination, he could have made a wonderful success at it. Within five years, Stuart could have been earning at least $50,000 a year; many in his profession earn more than $100,000 a year within five years of college.

But what happened? Stuart couldn't take the career opportunity because he was nervous—rightfully so—about repaying his college loans, starting within a few months after graduation. His student loans cost him his freedom to pursue opportunities.

It happens all the time: People can't take opportunities because they have fixed obligations that require a lower-risk financial structure. The ones who are not so encumbered are free to pursue their dreams and opportunities.

That's the cost of student loans that students don't understand. Often their parents don't understand it, either.

If you have to choose between borrowing and not going to college, *borrow*. It will be worth it. Then work very hard during the summer months and do everything you can to qualify for a very good part-time job so you can borrow as little as possible.

Applying for Grants-in-Aid and Student Loan Programs

You should apply for four different kinds of financial aid—federal, state, institutional, and private—even if you think you may not qualify. To apply for federal aid, use the Application for Federal Student Aid (AFSA); other types of aid generally require the Financial Aid Form (FAF) or the Family Financial Statement (FFS). Make sure you submit all completed forms by the required deadline. Remember that grants don't have to be repaid, while loans do. Also of significant note is that, with the looming budget deficit, it is anticipated that Congress will be shifting aid from grants to loans.

You may qualify for one of the following:

Pell Grant. Based solely on student need, the Pell is an annual grant ranging from $200 to $2,600. One in every five college freshmen today receives a Pell Grant. You must apply for a Pell Grant before applying for other kinds of financial aid.

Supplemental Educational Opportunity Grant. Based on need, the SEOG is granted by the college and depends on how much other financial aid the student receives. The grant is financed by federal funds that are distributed directly to individual colleges and may be at risk given the budget deficit.

The Stafford Loan. Guaranteed by the government against default and death, the Stafford Loan has two benefits. First, interest due on the loan is paid by the government while the student is in school. Second, the loan offers a six-month grace period before repayment begins.

The Perkins Loan. Administered by each participating college, the Perkins Loan offers a low interest rate to students based on financial need.

Parent Loans for Undergraduate Students (PLUS). Based on need, PLUS offers low-interest loans to parents of college-age students.

Scoping Out Scholarships

The best way to finance a college education, obviously, is with a scholarship. The most common, of course, is based on a student's academic achievement during his pre-college education. Some are available directly through local state boards of education or individual colleges and universities. Most private colleges today give their own institutional grants to most of their students, often based on merit as well as need.

Some of the best academic scholarships include:

National Merit Scholarships. Finalists from the Preliminary Scholastic Aptitude Test are awarded substantial monetary scholarships. While these are prestigious, they offer only a limited amount of money toward college expenses.

Presidential Scholars. Presidential Scholarships are awarded to students who score very high on the Scholastic Aptitude Test (SAT) and American College Test (ACT).

National Honor Society Scholarships. Each year, 250 scholarships of $1,000 are awarded to nominated members of the National Honor Society, a national high school organization based on academic achievement.

Harry S. Truman Scholarships. These are available to students already in college who have achieved a high level of academic performance in college.

What if your child isn't at the top of his class? That may not be a problem. Why? There are many kinds of scholarships that don't depend solely on academic performance. While your child will have to meet certain minimum grade-point standards, the following are available to those who may not qualify for academic scholarships:

Special-talent scholarships. These are awarded to students with exceptional talent or ability in a variety of fields, including art, photography, drama, leadership, science, and writing. High school counselors or college advisers can provide a detailed list of scholarships available.

Career interest scholarships. These are offered by colleges, associations, and corporations to students interested in pursuing specific fields of study.

For example, a number of government-sponsored scholarships are available to students pursuing a career in the health profession—as a physician, nurse, dentist, chiropractor, or veterinarian. For these, the government gives money to colleges and universities with strong pre-professional health departments, and the school grants the scholarship to the student.

Again, see your child's high school counselor or college adviser for details.

Athletic scholarships. Many colleges and universities seek outstanding athletes in major sports—and reward them with a variety of benefits, including free tuition, fees and lodging. Even athletes of average talent in minor sports can often land these scholarships. See your child's high school coach or guidance counselor for information.

Corporate-sponsored scholarships. A growing number of companies offer scholarships and other forms of financial aid to children of their employees as part of their benefits program. Check with your human resources office to see whether your company offers anything similar.

Student employment scholarships. Does your child have a part-time job? Check with his employer. Many businesses that hire college-age students, such as fast-food restaurants and golf courses, offer scholarships to their employees.

Membership scholarships. What trade groups, organizations, or associations do you *or* your child belong to? Many offer scholarships to their members.

The Boy Scouts, Future Homemakers of America, and 4-H Clubs all have scholarship programs for member students. So do a variety of trade groups, fraternal organizations, civic groups, and veterans' organizations—so check with any you belong to.

Do you belong to a union? Children of union members may be eligible for scholarships through the Teamsters, Letter Carriers, Postal Workers, Chemical Workers, Garment Workers, Seafarers, and Transport Workers unions.

Church-sponsored scholarships. Many churches—including the Catholic, Lutheran, United Presbyterian, Christian Scientist, and the Church of Jesus Christ of Latter-day Saints—offer a wide variety of scholarships and loans. Check with your clergy for details.

Minority or ethnic association scholarships. Various associations sponsor both college scholarships and student loan programs for the support of minority or ethnic students.

Military scholarships. The Army, Navy, and Air Force offer ROTC scholarships to hundreds of colleges every year, designated for students who will pledge some time to military service following graduation. Your child may also be interested in one of the five military service schools— West Point, Annapolis, the Air Force Academy, the Coast Guard Academy, or the Merchant Marine Academy.

For a complete analysis of literally thousands of scholarships, grants, and loan programs, both public and private, that might apply to your child's situation, call Fax-on-Demand at (801) 263-1676 and request free report #160, "The College Savings-Plus Information Kit."

Calculating College Costs

The projected total cost of a four-year education at a public college in 1997 is $46,400. That includes room, board, tuition, books, fees, and nominal living expenses. The average private college costs $96,900 for four years.

Nineteen years from now, the public education cost is expected to rise from $46,400 to $132,000; the private sector is expected to rise from $96,900 to more than $275,000. That assumes a 6 percent annual inflation rate—lower than what has actually occurred at the nation's colleges during the last few years.

Don't think you have to come up with all the savings. One of the wisest couples I know insist that their children contribute to their own education. As a result, their children are tighter with the dollars—whether they came from a certificate of deposit or a mutual fund or a life insurance policy. Those children know that whatever they use now won't be available later. Many of their friends who are financed wholly by their parents tend to be less careful. Their objective becomes, "How much money can I get out of mom and dad this semester so I can live in a great apartment and put gasoline in my car and go skiing on Saturdays and party while I'm in college?" Parents who hand responsibility to college-age children build responsibility in them.

To figure out how much your child's college costs will be, look at the college financial planner. First, calculate the number of years until your child enters college. Then look at how much one year of college will cost assuming 7 percent inflation. Multiply that figure by four.

The next three columns show what you need to save each year, assuming a 6, 8, or 10 percent rate of return *after taxes*. (If you're in a 30 percent tax bracket, you need to earn 9 percent in order to earn a 6 percent rate of return after taxes.)

College Financial Planner

Years Until Your Child Enters College	What College Will Cost Per Year @ 7% Inflation	Yearly Investment Required if 6% Return	Yearly Investment Required if 8% Return	Yearly Investment Required if 10% Return
1	$10,700	$10,094	$9,907	$9,727
2	11,449	5,558	5,504	5,452
3	12,250	3,848	3,773	3,701
4	13,108	2,996	2,909	2,824
5	14,026	2,488	2,391	2,297
6	15,007	2,151	2,046	1,945
7	16,058	1,913	1,800	1,693
8	17,182	1,736	1,615	1,502
9	18,385	1,599	1,472	1,354
10	19,672	1,492	1,358	1,234
11	21,049	1,406	1,265	1,136
12	22,522	1,335	1,187	1,053
13	24,098	1,276	1,121	983
14	25,785	1,227	1,065	922
15	27,590	1,185	1,016	868
16	29,522	1,150	974	821
17	31,588	1,120	936	779
18	33,799	1,094	903	741

NOTE: This table assumes that today's cost of one year in college is $10,000 for tuition, fees, room, and board, and that the inflation of college costs will be 7 percent. This table assumes after-tax returns. To calculate how much you will need, remember you will need only part of the cash when your child turns 18. You will need some each year throughout your child's education. So to determine how much you will need, look at the number of years until the midpoint of your child's college education.

Get an A+ for College Savings

Different types of savings accounts most often used for college funding include:

Certificates of deposit. CDs represent one of the most conservative and simple ways of saving money for college. The problem is that, after taxes and after inflation, there is usually little, if any, real return. Make sure you schedule the CD maturity date for a few weeks before your child's college tuition is due.

Series EE U.S. savings bonds. Interest on bonds bought in 1990 or later is tax-free for families with incomes below $60,000; you'll pay reduced taxes if your income is between $60,000 and $90,000. The minimum yield on bonds held for five years is 6 percent.

State savings plans. A number of states offer tax-free investment bond programs to help parents pay for college; few require that your child attend a state school. These bonds generally mature five to 20 years after purchase.

Zero coupon bonds. Zero coupon bonds don't pay semiannual interest. Instead, you buy the bond at a deep discount, then sell it for full face value at a later set date. For example, you may buy a $10,000 10-year zero coupon bond at 7.5 percent interest, and you'd pay only $4,852 for the bond. Ten years later, you would sell that bond for the full $10,000, profiting more than $5,000. The value of the bond may fluctuate widely in the interim, so be sure you won't need to liquidate.

Uniform Gift to Minors Act. You can fund a child's college education with an account called an UGMA account—an account made possible by the Uniform Gift to Minors Act. UGMA accounts are often established by banks or credit unions with mutual funds, savings accounts, and so on. Parents are limited to gifts of securities or cash. Annual unearned income of more than $1,000 in an UGMA is taxed at the parent's marginal rate until the child turns 14; after that, the income is taxed at the child's rate. The account can be an inexpensive way of shifting assets to a minor.

There is one disadvantage: When the child turns 18, all the money becomes his, and there is no way to stop it. He's free to spend the money on anything he wants. You as a parent have no guarantee that the money will be used in the way you intended—to finance your child's education. More than one parent has been dismayed when the child drives up in a fancy new sports car.

Life insurance. Why would you consider funding college with a life insurance policy? Why do people buy $500,000 policies on their children? Do they want to get rich if the unforeseen happens to their child? No, of course not.

Are they grossly overinsuring their child? Probably—unless they have a significant estate tax problem. Then why do they do it? To fund a college education.

You should use this strategy only if there's adequate life insurance on you as parents. When you calculate that "adequate" coverage, figure in the full cost of your child's college education. You might also want to use the cash value in your policy before you purchase a large policy for your children.

But there are reasons why it can be smart to purchase life insurance for your child. One is the unknown: Your child might become uninsurable at an early age. Two of my own nephews became uninsurable before the age of 12 because of diabetes and other medical problems. If you purchase the insurance early in the child's life, your child will always have that insurance.

A second reason to purchase life insurance on a child is that the premium is locked in forever at children's rates. If you buy a policy on a two-year-old, the premiums will always cost what they did when your child was two—even when your child is 50.

There's still another reason. If you buy early enough, the policy will be paid-up by the time your child enters college. Even if it's a whole life policy—with premiums due throughout the entirety of one's life—you may exercise a modified paid-up option and drop the premium payments to zero while your child is in college.

If you want to fund college with cash value insurance, you need to buy it at least seven years before you want to use it. In other words, it works best when purchased for children under the age of 12. If your child is older than 12 when you buy the insurance, you'll need to make excess deposits or excess premium payments straight into the cash value portion of the policy.

Cash value assets from life insurance policies grow tax-deferred, and you can borrow against the cash value, usually at a low interest rate. You can also surrender dividend additions to fund your child's education. Plus, you don't have to count the cash value policy among the assets you declare when applying for financial aid.

Several kinds of insurance policies can be used to finance college:

Variable life. Cash values will depend on the yield from investments in specifically selected funds, such as money market funds, stocks, and bonds. You may be guaranteed a minimum death benefit—usually the face amount at issue—but death benefits may increase if the chosen investments perform well.

Universal life. You can vary the amount of the premium you pay, as long as you meet the minimum payment. If you make excess deposits, you can build up the policy's cash value more quickly.

Single-premium life. If your child is enrolling in college soon, you can lower the amount of your assets with a single-premium life policy. (Policy cash values are not considered like other investments when applying for aid programs.) Surrender charges are high during the first few years, so you should plan to keep the policy for at least several years.

Why does insurance work to finance college? A typical insurance policy will earn 6 to 9 percent on its cash value growth. Because insurance earnings are tax-sheltered, you'd have to earn between 9 to 14 percent on your money to get the same return.

Some people use insurance for college expenses because of what it teaches their children. In my experience, those children whose education is financed from their parents' account seem to ask for all they can get. But those who finance their own college education are much more careful. That holds true when college is funded with an insurance policy: Most children will tap all other sources before using an insurance policy with their own name on it. They want those dollars to be available later for marriage, for a down payment on a home, for establishing a career, or for starting a new business. My youngest brother, for instance, bought his first insurance policy when he was 15. By the time he was in college, he looked for all other sources of income before tapping *his* "nest egg."

Whether you decide to use insurance, savings, scholarships or whatever source to fund your child's education, one thing is certain: You need to plan ahead. Don't wait until your children are nearing college age before deciding how you (or your children) will finance their education. Remember the words of Benjamin Franklin: "An investment in knowledge pays the best interest."

Your Insights, Feelings, and Action Items

A. As you read this chapter, what *insights* came that seem applicable to you?

1._____

2._____

3._____

B. How did you *feel* as you pondered particular points of this chapter?
  1._____
  2._____
  3._____

C. What do you *feel* you should *do* as a result of this chapter?
  1._____
  2._____
  3._____

D. How might you solicit the aid of others in accomplishing "C" above?

_____
_____
_____

Chapter 29

How to Develop Your Most
Effective Tax Planning Strategies

Tax Principles: Tree vs. Fruit, Form vs. Substance, Recognition vs. Realization

Before we examine some tax strategies, there are a few pervasive principles to consider. Understanding these areas of concern will help you determine which strategies are appropriate within the limits of the law.

Tree vs. fruit. Taxpayers may be taxed on income which they never received, but which was received by other persons and then given to them. The tree might be an investment portfolio or an income-producing business. The fruit is the income from the tree.

Using this analogy, if somebody receives any fruit of the tree, even if the tree is owned by someone else, that person enjoys some "ownership" in the tree as well. What does that mean to you? A lot, particularly in your estate planning. For example, some people think if they transfer municipal bonds to their child and have their child gift back to them the interest from those municipal bonds, they have those municipal bonds out of their estate. No such luck.

If you receive *any* of that interest income, even if it *is* owned by your children, the whole portfolio falls back into your estate—you are going to pay estate taxes on it. The only way to avoid payment of taxes on income produced by "the tree" is to completely transfer the property with no strings attached. The transferror must retain no control over either the property or the producers.

Some people try to claim, "I have no control over it. My child has no obligation to pay that to me." The tax courts have said that is inadequate. If they can even show by circumstantial evidence that you received money, it will get pulled back into your estate. (Believe me, it has all been thought of before.)

Form vs. substance. Another problem in income taxation is the principle of form vs. substance. People will often try to come up with tax loopholes and structure their affairs according to some fine print in the tax code. In doing so, they might develop a strategy which, by all form and procedures, seems like a means of getting away with tax avoidance. But, if the intent or *substance* of it is to avoid taxes in a way unintended by the law or which would be unfair to the rest of the populace, it just isn't going to hold up.

A few years ago, I came across an article titled "Common anti-tax arguments." In it were arguments protestors used to say they weren't really obligated to pay income taxes—all were based on form, not substance.

Common arguments of tax evaders include: "The 16th amendment, which grants Congress the power to levy taxes, was never ratified." "The IRS is actually a private corporation." "Paying income tax is voluntary." "A declaration of foreign citizenship or claiming to be a resident alien does away with any tax obligation."

Then there are those arguments that really stretch the limits: "The Fifth Amendment, proscribing self-incrimination, can be cited in not filing a tax return which might contain evidence of illegal conduct." "Income from cash or checks is not subject to tax because American currency became worthless after the U.S. did away with the gold and silver standards." "The 14th Amendment, which granted citizenship and due process to former slaves following the Civil War, can be interpreted to mean that only blacks must pay federal income tax." All, according to state and federal prosecutors, are false.

No matter what convoluted legal explanations you may hear, you should know that anybody who attempts to live by these arguments will end up in court or jail.

Realization vs. recognition. The cash-basis or "realization" method of accounting means that taxpayers report income and pay taxes on that income only if it is received during the taxable year.

One exception to this rule of tax payment is known as the doctrine of constructive receipt or "taxation upon recognition." Its purpose is to prevent taxpayers from determining the tax year when an item of income is received by them for federal income tax purposes. In other words, a cash-basis taxpayer is not free to arbitrarily select the year for which he will report income.

This doctrine states that income is reportable as soon as it is (1) credited to the taxpayer's account, (2) set apart for the taxpayer, or (3) otherwise made available to be drawn upon at any time by the taxpayer.

44 Strategies for Reducing Taxes

Now that you know what *not* to do, what *can* you do to save on your taxes? To reduce the "Success Penalty"?

For individuals:

Get married. Several years ago an associate and I drew up a financial plan on a wonderful, sweet couple who had been together six or seven years but hadn't married. We met with them to gather data in October, did the plan presentation in November, and suggested that if they got married before December 31, they could save significant tax dollars. We also recommended that they start having children. They chuckled and said, "Gosh, you guys are sure comprehensive!"

On December 30 they flew to Reno. We met again at the first of the year and they told us excitedly they had been married. About a year later they had a baby, and the father, who never considered himself a family man, can't come to the office without pulling out pictures of his children. Suffice it to say, that little recommendation was worth about $5,000.

Have children. Two hundred years ago when we had an agrarian society, people had large families—they needed the children to help work on the farm. And when the parents became too old to work, their children supported them. Do children still support their parents when they get older? Even in an urban society as we have today? Perhaps more than you realize.

Many more people are saving for retirement today than they were 200 years ago. Yet, how many will retire financially secure? Three to 5 percent. What are the others living on? Social Security. Does Social Security come out of thin air? No. Is it paid by the government? No. Who is it paid by? Your children. So children *still* support their parents!

Two hundred years ago we averaged four or five children per family. If we still had four children per family today, would the Social Security system be such a mess? Would parents still be able to retire and have their children support them?

The government never pays your Social Security check. Your children do.

Gifting money to your children. Gifting to your children does not save any income taxes by itself. When you give to a child, you do not receive a tax deduction. But, once your children have the assets, any earnings on those assets may be taxed differently based on your children's ages and their income.

Under current law, if interest, dividend earnings, or capital gains on investments owned by your child are less than $600, there's no tax on the earnings. If your child has between $600 and $1,200 of investment earnings, the income will be taxed at the child's rate. Anything over $1,200 is taxed at the parent's rate. If you are a business owner or self-employed, you can hire your children and pay them up to $3,800 income-tax free.

Transfer or gift appreciating assets to your children. If you are trying to lower your estate value for estate tax purposes, and lower your income for income tax purposes, you want to gift to your children your highly appreciating or fast-growing assets. These are assets generating a higher return—dividends, interest, or capital gains.

Mortgage interest. Currently, mortgage interest is fully deductible up to a maximum of a $1 million mortgage. Mortgage interest is tax-deductible on both your primary residence and a secondary residence. This is for debt used to purchase, construct, or substantially improve a residence.

Home equity loans or second mortgages. In most cases, these are fully deductible up to $100,000, whether or not they go toward home improvements.

Charitable contributions. If made in cash, charitable contributions are deductible up to 50 percent of your adjusted gross income in any given year. If charitable contributions are made "in-kind," they are deductible up to 30 percent of adjusted gross income.

Recently, my wife Julie loaded two pickup trucks full of items we no longer wanted and took them to a thrift store. Before doing so, Julie itemized everything—it totaled to a value of several thousand dollars. That amount is 100 percent deductible, up to 30 percent of my income.

So if I make $50,000 a year, 30 percent of my income is $15,000, and that's my maximum deduction.

What's another creative strategy on this? Let's say you're making a contribution of $1,000. Which is better, to pay it in cash or in appreciated stock? Appreciated stock. You make a contribution in kind by donating the appreciated stock. Just transfer title on the stock—don't sell the stock and then donate cash. (See page 378.)

IRAs. These are tax-deductible up to $2,000. If your spouse does not earn income, you can still deduct $2,000 for each of you. For it to be tax-deductible, what are the rules? There's an income test and an employer-provided pension test.

If either spouse has an employer-provided qualified retirement plan, including a corporate pension or profit-sharing plan or a 401k plan, then if you earn a certain amount of income, your tax deduction for your IRA is phased out. The phase out begins at $25,000 for a single person or $35,000 for a married couple filing jointly.

Annuities. Instead of putting money into a nondeductible IRA, you can put it into an annuity, where you won't have the $2,000 limit. Annuities grow tax-deferred, but are not tax-deductible. So, they are tax-advantaged during the accumulation years.

A common mistaken assumption that many people make is that IRAs or annuities are *merely* tax-deferred. In actuality, the dollars withdrawn at retirement are so much greater that many of the dollars are *tax-free*. (This assumes you remain in your existing tax bracket. However, look at what happens if your tax bracket jumps to 60 percent at retirement.)

Net Dollars After Taxes at 35%

Assumes: 10% return before taxes, 35% marginal tax bracket before and after retirement. Ignores possible 10% penalty for early withdrawal.

Number of Years until Withdrawal	Personally Investing $1,300 Annually	Nondeductible IRA or Annuity $1,300 Annually	Tax-deductible IRA, 401k, or Qualified Plan $2,000 Annually
5	$ 7,883	$ 7,950	$ 8,730
10	18,683	19,364	22,790
15	33,480	36,358	45,434
20	53,754	62,337	81,903
30	119,586	166,547	235,227
40	243,162	429,590	632,908

Net Dollars After Taxes at 60%

Assumes: 10% return before taxes, 35% marginal tax bracket before retirement, 60% after. Ignores possible 10% penalty for early withdrawal.

Number of Years until Withdrawal	Personally Investing $1,300 Annually	Nondeductible IRA or Annuity $1,300 Annually	Tax-deductible IRA, 401k, or Qualified Plan $2,000 Annually
5	$ 7,883	$ 7,392	$ 5,372
10	18,683	16,917	14,025
15	33,480	29,874	27,960
20	53,754	48,361	50,402
30	119,586	117,490	144,755
40	243,162	284,363	389,908

Cash value insurance. Using cash value insurance is a prudent way to accomplish several goals with a single vehicle. (See Chapter 18.)

Municipal bonds. These generate tax-free interest income. Before you place bonds in your portfolio, look at the yield between corporate or U.S. government bonds and municipal bonds in *Your Money Happiness Workbook*. Corporate and government bonds are fully taxable. Municipal bonds are income-tax free on a federal level and may also be tax-free on a state level. However, capital gains on a municipal bond are still taxable income. (See Chapter 30.)

Select investments that generate capital gains income over those that generate dividends and interest income. No matter what tax bracket you are in, you are better off going with capital gains. Usually the maximum tax rate on capital gains is equal to or lower than the tax on dividend or interest income. Currently, the maximum capital gains rate is 28 percent. What's the maximum tax rate on dividends and interest income? 39.6 percent. So from 28 percent and above you will pay more on dividends and interest income than you will on capital gains.

Invest in real estate. Real estate also grows tax-deferred. The two big tax deductions on real estate are mortgage interest and depreciation. Expenses each year for "all the ordinary and necessary expenses paid or incurred during the taxable year" are deductible—if property is held for the production of income (investment property). The property taxes paid on real estate investments are also deductible (subject to certain limitations). And with depreciation, you are able to claim a paper write-off or loss where there was no loss.

Can you take a tax deduction for real estate depreciation against your other earned income? It depends on how much you earn and whether you are a passive or active investor in the real estate. Daniel is a passive investor—he is not involved in the day-to-day management, operations, or maintenance of his real estate. So, he may take all his deductions up to the extent of his investment income. What does that mean? That means his rental income can essentially be tax-free to the extent that he has all these other deductions to offset it. If you are in a limited partnership, you are automatically a passive investor.

Marlene, on the other hand, is an active investor. She is involved in the day-to-day management, operations, and maintenance of the property. She can even pay someone else to do the day-to-day maintenance, but she is actively involved in purchase decisions, sales decisions, and strategic and operational policy decisions. She only meets with her partners once a quarter.

As an active investor, Marlene can take those deductions against her other investment income or against her other earned income. Since her W-2 or 1099 income is currently under $100,000, she can take up to $25,000 of deductions against earned income. As her income increases, that excess write off of $25,000 is offset at a rate of $2 for $1 between $100,000 and $150,000. If her income rises above $150,000, she cannot take it against her W-2 or 1099 income.

So, somebody who actively manages real estate and is earning between $100,000 to $150,000 a year will see his marginal tax rate jump from a federal bracket of 31 percent up to a tax bracket of about 47 percent.

Spread out real estate profits by making sales on the installment basis. If you are working on a cash basis, spread the income from the sale of real estate out over a period of time. You are taxed only on that portion you receive during the year. This can become a little complicated when taking into consideration the profits on the real estate, and the IRS has placed restrictions on installment sales.

Installment sales work only when a gain is realized on a property, but that gain from the installment sale is prorated and recognized over the years in which payments are received. The IRS provides the forms to assist you in determining how the gains are taken into account.

Please note that there are strict rules governing installment sales between "related" parties. Check with your tax expert on the restrictions regarding installment sales.

Schedule A deductions. Schedule A deductions include such things as medical expenses, property taxes, mortgage interest, charitable contributions, and miscellaneous deductions. They are often referred to as itemized deductions. These are sometimes calculated so they are deductible only if they exceed a threshold percentage of adjusted gross income (AGI). They come off your tax return after AGI and are not as valuable as before-AGI deductions. This is because deductions before AGI serve to lower your AGI, and therefore the threshold at which after AGI expenses are deductible.

Before-AGI deductions. The deductions that come off *after* AGI on Schedule A have to do with maintaining a household. Those that come off *before* AGI—investment expenses, business expenses, and so forth—have to do with generating income. Let's look at some before-AGI deductions:

Turning a hobby into a business. There are two IRS rules for turning a hobby into a business. One, you must show bona fide business intent to make a profit. Two, you must indeed actually show a profit three out of five years.

Several years ago, I was visiting with some neighbors, the Delaneys, in their home. They mentioned they had been contemplating a home business for some time and asked me for advice on what kind of business would be best for them. Glancing out their back window, I immediately had an answer. In a lot adjoining the house were five or six of the family's horses. Upon investigation, I discovered they had even more horses in a stable on the outskirts of town.

I suggested those horses could become tax-deductible by turning them into a business. The Delaneys could put them out to stud or put them out to foal; give horseback riding lessons to other children in the neighborhood; board other people's horses and write off much of their feed, barn, materials, and equipment; train horses; enter horse shows under the name of their business and sponsor certain classes in those shows, so their business becomes a marketing event; or join a horse association and market to those people. The Delaneys were enthusiastic about the idea and soon had a home business *and* a tax deduction.

Setting up a Keogh plan or pension or profit-sharing plan or contributing to a 401k plan. This strategy isn't just for business owners. In many cases, it is wise to contribute the maximum amount to a 401k plan at your work. (However, there are caveats—see Chapter 21.)

Offsetting capital gains with capital losses. Do some sorting of your capital gains vs. your capital losses. Long-term losses on assets held more than one year are only worth 50 cents on the dollar if they are being offset or subtracted against ordinary income. But when long-term losses are matched against short-term gains, they count dollar-for-dollar. So you have essentially doubled the value of any long-term losses if you are matching them against short-term gains.

Trade a raise for fringe benefits. If you take benefits instead of a raise, you don't have to report them as taxable income. Benefits you might consider include group health insurance, professional training and association dues, prepaid legal services, prepaid financial planning fees, group disability insurance, adoption benefits, group life insurance, etc.

Start a business. Write-offs or deductions on Schedule C from starting a business or from being a sole proprietorship or a partnership might include: travel expenses, advertising, marketing, gasoline, auto depreciation, auto insurance, auto repairs and maintenance, auto taxes, and business interest.

Business interest. If you are a businessperson, are self-employed, or have any 1099 income, where do you want all your interest expense to show up? On your Schedule C as a business expense.

Interest incurred from borrowing to further your business is fully deductible *before* AGI. If you had two loans—a $100,000 home mortgage and a $100,000 business debt—which would you want to pay off first? The home mortgage. Why? Because mortgage interest comes off after AGI on Schedule A.

Make the WYHTE phenomenon work for you. If you don't understand the impact of the WYHTE phenomenon, you are going to get hammered by taxes. The person who is a high consumer is impacted most dramatically by the WYHTE phenomenon and is also paying the most in sales taxes—a double whammy. People who live to consume will never be able to catch up with those who don't. So, one of the best tax strategies you can implement is to make the WYHTE phenomenon work for you. (See Chapter 5.)

Any time you perform labor on your own in a noncommercial enterprise, whether it is having a family vegetable garden or sewing clothes or building the deck yourself, you essentially have tax-free labor. As soon as you're laboring any place else, it's taxable. And that tax can be up to a 50 percent siphon.

This not only enters into the economics of the working spouse, but also the economics of having children. While we are putting out a lot of money to raise our children, we tend to view them as a liability because they aren't bringing in any cash income. In actuality, they *are* bringing in income if they're doing any type of chores or work around the house. And the kind of income they bring in is actually the best kind of income because it is tax-free. Raise them working, and they will be productive adults as well—contributors to, rather than a drain on, society.

Lease from a family limited partnership. When you receive earned income, you have to pay income taxes and FICA or Social Security taxes. Instead of drawing earned income, Terrence and Raina pay a portion of their income to a family limited partnership in the way of a lease payment for equipment leased to the business. That $1,000-a-month lease payment is going to their children and is taxed at their lower tax rate. Terrence and Raina also structured the family limited partnership so that it owns their business car, office furniture, equipment, and computer system—and they are also leasing those items from the partnership.

Even if the lease payment were not taxed at the children's rate but at Terrence and Raina's, they are avoiding FICA or Social Security taxes. Their FICA or Social Security tax would be 15.3 percent, since they are self-employed (receiving 1099 income). The same would be true if they were employees in a closely-held company. If they were not self-employed (receiving W-2 income), their FICA or Social Security taxes would be 7.65 percent. Terrence and Raina can take their 1099 income and either reinvest it into the business in some way or pay it on a lease payment.

Year-end strategic planning. There are two reasons why you might want to do end-of-year planning during December. One reason is to defer taxes one year, and the second reason is because your tax rate might change. Why might your tax rate change? Reasons internal to yourself: your anticipated income, your deductions, or the structure of your income may change. Reasons external to yourself: changes in the tax laws, etc.

Postpone income. You might postpone income, maybe interest income or revenues from your business. You might defer some income to next year by not sending out your December invoices until January 1.

Postponing income is like having an interest-free loan from the IRS for one year.

Take some expenses or losses early. If you have had a down year in the investment markets and you have some losses accruing in your investment portfolio, you might want to sell those off. You might also want to pay some expenses early. Pay all your bills in December: not only your December rent, but also your January rent; your property taxes or your mortgage interest; your charitable contributions for the next year. If you are setting up a billing system, the ideal is to have your income come in early enough in the year that you have plenty of time to spend it rather than invoicing people in November or December and having it all come in at the end of the year.

Shift professional income. Postpone it to the next year in the same manner in which you are managing your billings or payables.

Develop a charitable lead trust. A charitable lead trust would allow you to make charitable deductions today even though you aren't going to be making the contributions to the charity until five, 10, or 20 years from now.

Capital gains bypass trust. This is a good strategy for somebody who has highly appreciated property or assets—closely-held business interests, stocks, or real estate. Instead of selling these assets, paying taxes on them, and then investing the rest to generate a retirement income, contribute the property to a capital gains bypass trust, also known as a charitable remainder unitrust (CRUT). Sell the property after it has been put into the trust to avoid the capital gains taxes on it. That leaves you with approximately 50 percent more retirement income.

Want an example? Jerry has a $1,000 basis in a business he started 30 or 40 years ago. He built up the business and can now sell it for $1 million. The capital gains tax would be 28 percent, or $280,000, plus assumed state taxes of $70,000, for a $350,000 total tax bite. That 35 percent tax siphon would leave him $650,000 for retirement. Well, $650,000 at 10 percent interest will only generate $65,000 a year. But, if Jerry contributed the business to a CRUT and *then* sold the business, he would have $1 million invested at 10 percent interest, which would generate $100,000 a year, or 54 percent more. (See Chapter 26.)

Remember the WYHTE phenomenon—when you reduce income by 33 percent you have to earn 50 percent more on your money in order to generate equivalent income. So you have a 50 percent greater retirement by saving one-third on your taxes. Plus you get the charitable contribution deduction, and it's out of your estate.

You will have to consult with a professional to implement some of these more advanced strategies, but don't be intimidated. The results can be amazing.

Prepay state income taxes and property taxes in December. You can do this for one of two reasons: an interest free loan from the IRS for one year or because tax rates are going down next year. When don't you want to prepay expenses? When you see your tax rate going up, either because of tax laws or because your income is going up. Then you want to do exactly the opposite—accelerate income and postpone expenses.

Have a municipal, not traditional, money market fund. Rather than having a traditional money market fund, consider a municipal money market fund. Municipal funds earn less return but they are tax-free. Compare the interest rate difference to your tax rate.

Only have one spouse working. What taxes does a second wage-earner in a family have to pay? The *very first* dollar of the second earner's income is taxed at the *highest* marginal tax bracket of the first earner *plus* a minimum of 7.65 percent for Social Security. This means that a two-income family earning even $50,000 probably has the second income being taxed at 40 percent or more (federal and state income taxes *plus* FICA). If that second wage-earner is self-employed, the tax rate starts at the highest marginal rate of the first wage-earner *plus* 15.3 percent.

In terms of cash flow because of the WYHTE phenomenon, the second wage-earner would probably be better off to cook from scratch, buy in bulk, and allow the first wage-earner to work an extra one or two hours a day. That person can make more money by working one extra hour a day, five hours a week, than a second wage-earner can make by working full time when you factor in a second car, auto insurance at commuter rates rather than pleasure rates, gasoline, child care, wardrobe, dry cleaning, microwaveable foods vs. cooking from scratch, and more eating out for lunch and dinner. (See Chapter 14.)

For business owners:

Depreciate furniture, equipment, and buildings. Note that computer equipment becomes obsolete so fast that it is better to expense it rather than depreciate it.

One-time write-off of up to $17,500. A small business owner can purchase new equipment or furniture and trade depreciating the asset over time in exchange for writing off the asset all at once up to $17,500 per year. Somebody who has 1099 income might be advised to be purchasing up to $17,500 per year of equipment and writing it off lump sum, if that amount of equipment is necessary. It is wise to check with your accountant before implementing this strategy, as is it subject to certain limitations.

Defer collection of accounts receivable. Defer income.

Install a cafeteria plan or a section 125 plan. This plan allows employees to select various benefits which are tax-deductible to the employer but not reportable as income to the employee. This provides a win-win situation for the employer and employee.

Accelerate the payment of accounts payable. Accelerate the payment of expenses.

Consider high dividend domestic stocks. Rather than having cash balances sitting in a money market fund, a corporation might be better off to put some of those balances into low-risk, low-volatility, high-dividend paying domestic stocks. Why? Because 85 percent of the dividends on those high-dividend stocks are excluded from taxable income. This is only for regular "C" corporations on domestic stocks.

Accelerate your corporate growth rate. As you accelerate your corporate growth rate, you are incurring expenses in advance, sometimes many months in advance, of the receipt of that income. Unfortunately, you must have the cash flow to pursue this approach.

Install fringe benefit plans. These include group insurance, prepaid legal services, prepaid financial planning services, health insurance, disability insurance, life insurance, retirement plans, corporate pension or profit-sharing plans, Keogh plans for the self-employed, 401k plans, stock option plans, etc.

Write off travel expenses. For your car, you can either take mileage, or you can take actual expenses. Actual expenses include gasoline, repairs, maintenance, taxes, and depreciation. Whether you take actual expenses or mileage, you can only deduct expenses for the portion of the use incurred for business purposes—that does not include commuting to your primary place of employment. The rule for business expenses is that they must be reasonable, necessary, and customary.

Charitable contribution deductions. These may total up to 10 percent of profits for a corporation.

Use a medical reimbursement plan and/or a salary continuation plan. A medical reimbursement plan allows you to be reimbursed for all of your medical expenses, including insurance premiums and direct medical expenses, co-payments to the doctor and other medical expenses that you incur during the year. There are, however, restrictions—if you provide the plan for one employee, you must provide it for all employees.

Hire your children if they are of age. The rule is that they need to be paid market wages. You can't pay them abnormal market wages—that can backfire. I had some clients years ago who owned a large retail store chain. From the time their children were tiny, the parents were paying them $10,000 to $15,000 a year and taking these wages off on their taxes.

These children had well over $100,000 in each of their bank accounts by the time I met them.

This probably would have gone undetected by the IRS except that these children eventually became teenagers. One, in particular, got angry at her parents and made a little call to the IRS—it cost her parents a lot in back taxes, interest, and penalties. The nightmare those parents were trapped in was beyond anything they could ever imagine.

The problem was, the children hadn't earned the money and hadn't been given the money. They had not been paid a market wage for actual services. They were being "paid" a lot of money for nothing. The parents were just trying to siphon the money from their tax bracket to that of their children. It is hard for a 6-year-old to earn $15,000 a year in a retail store.

So, if you hire your children, you must pay them a market wage for actual services rendered. You can hire your children at any age. You don't have to wait until they are 14. They can be 10 years old and emptying trash cans, but they must be getting paid the actual market wage for actual services.

Step-up in basis, plus insurance. Under our current tax code, when you die, you get what is called a step-up in basis. Dora has a candy company in which her basis was $1,000, and she built that company to a value of $1 million. When she dies, her heirs get a step-up in basis from $1,000 to $1 million. That means if they sell the company for $1.1 million, their only capital gain is the $100,000 of growth between the $1 million when Dora died and the $1.1 million that they sold it for a year or so later. The same is true with third-generation inheritance. It goes on from heir to heir.

What's the catch? The only way to get the step-up in basis income-tax wise and to avoid tax on all that money is to include it in Dora's estate for estate tax purposes. So, with that $1 million, half will go off in estate taxes. How can she avoid that? Life insurance. When the estate tax bill comes due, the very event (death) that triggers the estate tax is the very event that triggers the solution to the estate tax (life insurance). In that case, Dora leaves the property in the estate if it is highly appreciated, rather than taking the charitable deduction route or gifting route. She avoids all the income tax on it, and she buys an insurance policy that essentially pays the estate taxes. In doing so, she escapes both the income tax and the estate tax.

Some of these tax strategies for business owners are exactly opposite of good cash flow strategies—unfortunately. Businesses which are cash-rich, or have the cash to be able to engage in these strategies, are in a better position to be tax-prudent.

For instance, it is tax-wise to defer the collection of accounts receivable, but you can't engage in that luxury if your cash flow dictates that you need to accelerate your collection of accounts receivable. Conversely, it is a tax strategy to accelerate the payment of expenses and payables, but you can't do that if you don't have the cash.

While cash flow might limit your ability to pursue some strategies, consider implementing some of the others mentioned. Many of the tactics can be utilized regardless of cash flow.

What Are Your Tax Risks?

A discussion of tax strategies would not be complete without considering tax risks. How aggressive are you with your taxes? Are you operating in a gray area of the law? Are you being very aggressive in your interpretation of the law?

Or, even if you are being conservative in your interpretation of the law, might the law change? Are you involving yourself in such a long-term strategy that over a five- or 10- or 20-year period the rules might change? You may end up regretting a particular strategy if the tax laws shift midstream. In that case, it behooves you to diversify yourself tax-wise as well.

What does that mean? Maybe it means you engage in a qualified pension or profit-sharing plan, which is fully deductible now but really gets hit with taxes upon retirement. Maybe it means you engage in an annuity or variable life insurance policy which is not tax-deductible now but can be pulled out tax-free later. Maybe it means you balance your tax strategies in other ways.

The ultimate tax strategy, of course, is self-reliance and making the WYHTE phenomenon work for you. Remember, because of sales taxes and the WYHTE phenomenon, consumption is one of the most heavily taxed enterprises in which you might engage.

When it comes to tax strategies, your best bet is to find a trusted adviser to help you make the most appropriate decisions for your individual situation. The strategies mentioned here are a good start. They will point out the possibilities available to you. A good adviser can also help you work through the highly technical aspects of some of these tactics. Explore your options. You *can* significantly reduce your tax bite ... and keep that government camel out of your tent!

Your Insights, Feelings, and Action Items

A. As you read this chapter, what *insights* came that seem applicable to you?

1._____

2._____

3._____

B. How did you *feel* as you pondered particular points of this chapter?

1._____

2._____

3._____

C. What do you *feel* you should *do* as a result of this chapter?

1._____

2._____

3._____

D. How might you solicit the aid of others in accomplishing "C" above?

_____

_____

_____

Taxpayer Bill of Rights

A synopsis of the most significant provisions in the Taxpayer Bill of Rights

1. *Disclosure of Taxpayer's Rights*—A document called "Publication 1: Your Rights as a Taxpayer" must be sent to all taxpayers contacted by the IRS with respect to taxes on a regular basis. This document must outline rights of taxpayers during an audit and procedures to follow during an audit or other acts by the IRS.
2. *Audit Interview Procedures*—A taxpayer has the right to record any interview by the IRS, has the right to an attorney or CPA present, and has a right to a full explanation of the audit process by the IRS representative.
3. *Reliance on Written Advice*—Any erroneous written advice to a taxpayer by the IRS is abatable.
4. *Taxpayer Assistance Orders*—These orders are issued by the Taxpayer Ombudsman on behalf of the taxpayer if the taxpayer is suffering a hardship due to the manner in which tax laws are administered.
5. *Basis for Evaluating IRS Employees*—IRS employees cannot be given production quotas or goals if they are involved directly in collection activities.
6. *Tax Due and Deficiency Notices*—A notice must be sent to taxpayers if they have any tax due.
7. *Installment Payment of Tax Liability*—The IRS can allow a taxpayer to satisfy tax liability in installments if the IRS decides it would facilitate collection.
8. *Levy and Distraint*—The IRS must wait thirty days after serving notice before it begins collecting taxes by levy.
9. *Administrative Appeal of Liens*—A taxpayer has the option to file a notice of a lien with the Treasury stating that the lien has been filed in error.
10. *Awarding Cost and Fees*—If a taxpayer wins a suit against the government in connection with any tax issue, he may be awarded administrative costs and litigation costs incurred in connection with the court proceeding.
11. *Civil Cause of Action for Failure to Release Lien*—If the government fails to release a lien, the taxpayer can bring a civil suit against the government.
12. *Improper Disclosure or Use of Tax Return Information by Tax Return Preparers*—Any tax preparer who uses confidential information from a tax return for any purpose other than to prepare the tax return is in violation of federal law and may be fined.

Chapter 30

Three Prudent Investment Tools: Mutual Funds, Variable Annuities, and Variable Life

Carolyn and Bill, both in their mid-30s, were eager to find an investment that would get their dollars working for them. Although the small hardware store they owned made a comfortable profit each year, they realized they weren't saving enough to build a solid foundation for their future. They wanted an investment that would preserve their capital and maximize their return, and they were not in a position to take on much risk. They also wanted good investment portfolio managers to oversee their investments. Carolyn and Bill wanted to choose the best investing structure for them—one that was the ideal vehicle for achieving their goals and objectives.

They met with their financial adviser, Andrea, who outlined three basic investment "vehicles"—mutual funds, variable annuities, and variable life. Mutual funds, variable annuities, and variable life insurance each have unique tax structures and other differentiating characteristics, she explained. Each has different tax implications, professional management, risk, flexibility, accessibility, fees, loads, charges, and expenses.

Similarities between Mutual Funds, Variable Annuities, and Variable Life

Portfolio Diversification

"One reason people invest in mutual funds is to diversify their portfolio," Andrea explained. Carolyn and Bill were amazed to learn that if they tried to construct their own portfolio of individual stocks and bonds efficiently, they would need to buy a round lot of 100 shares of between 17 and 20 different stocks or bonds in 20 different industries to adequately reduce their risk. That's not all: They would need to provide on-going surveillance, monitoring, and management—just like the professionals who have instant access to Wall Street information. Or, they could get the same effect by investing in mutual funds. Variable annuities and variable life also provide similar diversification.

Professional Management

Carolyn and Bill's management concerns were put to rest when they learned mutual funds, variable annuities, and variable life are all managed by professionals.

Risk

Carolyn was more interested in what kind of risk they could anticipate. "With mutual funds, the level of risk of each type of fund can range from extremely low to extremely high," Andrea stated. "Low-risk mutual funds include money market funds or short-term bond funds; higher-risk mutual funds include aggressive stock funds, international funds, and real estate investment trusts. The same kinds of risk profiles apply to the various accounts within variable annuities and variable life products."

Rate of Return

"What about rates of return?" Bill asked.

"Good question," Andrea responded. "Mutual funds, variable annuities, and variable life all have annual rates of return potentially ranging from a loss to a fairly significant gain, depending on the asset class, time of year, and phase of the economic cycle.

"In constructing a variable annuity or variable life contract, an insurance company often actually goes to a superior mutual fund company. The insurance company asks the mutual fund company to manage the accounts in that variable annuity or variable life contract. Those accounts, then, actually become a mutual fund. They are managed by a mutual fund manager and contain similar stocks and bonds."

"So what's the difference, then?" Carolyn inquired.

"Legally, a variable annuity and a variable life contract may be offered *only* by an insurance company. That's why there's a partnership between a life insurance company and a mutual fund company in managing a portfolio. It's a hybrid product."

"All three vehicles seem pretty similar in terms of the characteristics we've discussed so far," Bill noted. "Let's get down to the nuts and bolts. What makes one vehicle better for us than another?"

"Well, Bill, that leads us into the differences between these three accumulation vehicles," Andrea said.

Differences between Mutual Funds, Variable Annuities, and Variable Life

Number of Asset Classes

"With a family of mutual funds, you can typically choose between 20 and 30 different asset classes. They usually include the most popular asset classes, such as growth stocks, aggressive growth stocks, growth and income stocks, a balanced fund, a corporate bond fund, a municipal bond fund, a government bond fund, and a money market fund. They may also include some more obscure classes, such as a real estate investment trust, a small cap stock fund, or an international stock fund.

"Variable annuity and variable life usually provide only 10 to 20 different investment classes. They're usually the same as the most popular mutual fund classes, but there are fewer of them. Probably 95 percent of all mutual fund assets can be found in the 10 to 20 asset classes that are replicated in variable annuity and variable life policies.

"In your situation, 10 to 20 asset classes are probably enough," Andrea concluded. "Otherwise, you would need to choose a mutual fund."

Fixed Accounts

"Do the asset classes include a fixed account, Andrea?" Bill queried.

"Mutual funds don't," she responded. "Variable annuities and variable life do." She explained that a *fixed account* is a "guaranteed" account made available by the insurance company. Its dollars are usually locked up for a year, and it usually earns 2 to 4 percentage points more than a money market fund or CDs.

"Why is a fixed account important?" Carolyn asked.

"Because you may want it during the two to four years out of every 10 when you may want to be on defense," the adviser replied. "A mutual fund investor on the defense typically switches money into a money market fund—but, unfortunately, that money market fund may provide very low returns. Fixed accounts in a variable annuity or a variable life account usually achieve a much higher level of return during periods when you need to be on defense. This can be quite helpful."

Tax Issues

"You're probably wondering about taxes," Andrea presumed. Carolyn and Bill nodded. "Then let's work through the tax implications of each vehicle," she suggested.

Mutual funds. "Mutual funds are fully taxable. At the end of each year, you receive a 1099 detailing all dividends, interest, and capital gains you credited on the mutual fund.

"Transfers between mutual funds are also taxable, whether you're going from one family of funds to another, or keeping your funds within the same family. My brother had his money in the Putnam family of funds. He wanted to move money from one of their stock funds to one of their bond funds to their money market fund, but he was taxed with each transfer. This is where problems creep in: Your accountant starts dictating your investment program, because you are watching over your shoulder for the tax man."

Variable annuities. "Variable annuities provide tax-deferred growth," Andrea continued. "In other words, your money grows and compounds tax-deferred the entire time it's in the variable annuity account. When you start withdrawing money from the variable annuity, one of two things will happen:

- If you withdraw irregular amounts over a period of several years, the amount you withdraw is taxed as *last-in, first-out*, or LIFO. In other words, the first money you pull out of an annuity will be fully taxable at ordinary rates, until you've withdrawn enough interest income to return to your basis (the amount you originally invested). After that, you can withdraw money tax-free as a return of basis.
- If you *annuitize*, you calculate an exclusion ratio—which tells you how much of each annuity payment is income and how much is a

return of basis. (You can only annuitize if you have elected an annuity option, such as life only, life and survivor, or life and survivor with 10 years certain, etc.) You're taxed only on the interest portion of each payment.

"Any money you withdraw from a variable annuity before the age of 59 1/2 will have a 10 percent penalty assessed against any gain. Here's how it works: I had a client, Dan, who deposited $100,000 in a variable annuity, and it grew to $130,000. He withdrew $10,000. The entire $10,000 was considered interest income and was fully taxable. He also had to pay a 10 percent tax penalty on the $10,000—which makes a penalty of $1,000.

"Unlike a mutual fund, a variable annuity allows tax-free transfers among the accounts. That gives you the ability to move money back and forth between the stock account, the bond account, the real estate account, the money market account, and so on, without being taxed. This becomes a tremendous benefit as you are managing your portfolio."

"In summary, the variable annuity is like a tax-deferred mutual fund. If you won't need access to your money before you're 59 1/2, it may act just like a tax-deferred mutual fund—and when you withdraw it, you might discover that even though the dollars are taxed at retirement, the tax-free compounding nature of the variable annuity will give you a significantly greater retirement income than you would have had from similar mutual funds."

Variable life. "Like the variable annuity, the variable life policy offers tax-deferred growth. You are not taxed on the cash value buildup while it is accumulating. It grows and compounds tax-free," Andrea commented. She also told Carolyn and Bill they could access their money from a variable life policy without it being taxed. (In all cases, they *must* leave at least 10 percent or more of the policy's cash value in the policy to keep it in force until death; otherwise, the policy will lapse, and they may owe taxes.)

"The normal approach is to withdraw money from the policy until you reach basis," the adviser explained. Carolyn and Bill learned that unlike a variable annuity, money withdrawn from a life insurance policy is FIFO, or *first-in, first-out,* meaning the dollars withdrawn first are considered to be a return of basis. If they choose a variable life policy, Carolyn and Bill can withdraw basis tax-free. Once they have withdrawn their basis, they begin borrowing, and they are charged an interest rate on what they borrow. If Carolyn and Bill are charged 8 percent interest, the insurance company will credit their policy with, say, a 7 percent credit—giving them a net interest cost of 1 percent. They never need to repay the interest cost or the loan as long as adequate cash values remain in the policy to keep it in force. Instead, the loan and accumulated interest is repaid from their death proceeds. In this way, Carolyn and Bill can access their cash values tax-free for retirement or any other purpose.

Andrea also explained that they can transfer the money from one investment account to another without being taxed, giving them the freedom to manage their money without the annual tax siphon. They also have access to the cash value in their account at any age without penalty, even before age 59 1/2.

Additionally, while retirement income drawn from mutual funds and variable annuities causes Social Security income to be taxable (see pages 306-308), variable life does not.

The policy has several advantages: While Carolyn and Bill are meeting their death benefit needs, they are also accumulating cost-efficient dollars for retirement, they can use the money for an emergency fund, a college funding program, a mortgage payoff plan, and so on.

Once the dollars go in, the variable life policy allows tax-deferred growth and potentially tax-free withdrawal of money—an advantage regardless of which direction tax rates head over time.

Collateral Power

"We're considering buying a house," Carolyn said. "Can any of these investments be used as collateral for a loan?"

"Yes. Mutual funds can," Andrea replied. "Your banker will typically collateralize your mutual fund for 50 percent of its current market value.

"A variable life policy can also be presented as collateral—to the insurance company for as much as 90 percent of its cash value, or to a commercial lending institution (usually for a lower percentage of its value).

"A variable annuity, on the other hand, is not used as collateral. If it is, any money you borrow will be considered a withdrawal to be taxed at your normal rates, plus you'll pay a 10 percent penalty if you're under age 59 1/2."

Death Benefit

"What about a death benefit?" Bill asked.

"Mutual funds do not provide any death benefit; neither do variable annuities," the adviser explained. "Though if you die, a variable annuity will pay the greater of the fair market value of your account or what you have invested into the variable annuity. For example, suppose you had a friend, Glen, who invested $100,000 into a variable annuity on October 1, 1987, and then died on December 1, 1987. Even though the market crashed in October 1987 and the market value of Glen's account dropped to only about $70,000, his heirs would receive his full original investment—$100,000.

"On the other hand, variable life does provide a death benefit for the face amount of the life insurance policy. It can be used to provide protection for heirs, to pay estate taxes, or to fund a business owner's buy-sell agreement, among other things."

Fees, Loads, Charges, and Expenses

During the course of the discussion, Andrea also outlined fees and expenses for the three vehicles. Carolyn and Bill learned that mutual fund fees, loads, charges, and expenses average 1 to 2 percent a year, regardless of whether it's a load or a no-load fund, assuming the fund is held over, say, five years. "That is, while a load mutual fund pays a commission to the seller of the fund, no-load funds also have marketing expenses (for advertising in the *Wall Street Journal* or on radio, for example)," Andrea said.

She explained that variable annuity fees range from 2 to 2.5 percent per year; they reflect not only the portfolio management fees and marketing expenses, but an annuity charge levied by the insurance company.

In a properly structured variable life policy, fees may range from 3 to 7 percent a year, averaged over a 10-year period. These fees include all expenses: sales expenses and commissions, money management fees, administrative costs, and mortality charges. Because of the wide disparity in these fees, the purchaser should acquire the highest cash-value policy possible, which may require some shopping. "Though some policies might look good after 10 to 20 years, the acid-test is how much of your premium goes straight into cash value your *very first year*," Andrea noted. "For most policies, it is zero. For a few policies, it is 10 to 20 percent. And for one or two policies, it is as high as 60 to 70 percent." (For a free listing of how the various companies rank, call Fax-on-Demand at (801) 263-1676 and request free report #165, "Policies with High Year-One Cash Values.")

How the fees and expenses work. "The easiest way to understand this, Carolyn and Bill, is to look at three case studies," Andrea said. "Lori has a mutual fund, and her portfolio manager invests in a diversified portfolio of stocks that earn 13 percent during the year. Does Lori ever see that 13 percent? No. She wouldn't know she earned 13 percent unless she looked at the management fee in the prospectus. What Lori sees is about 12 percent—the net asset value (NAV). The change in net asset value is the percentage change reported by mutual fund rating organizations, surveys, newspapers, magazines, and so on. So a 13 percent gross rate of return minus 1 percent in management fees and expenses will result in a 12 percent increase in net asset value. After Lori subtracts approximately 40 percent for income taxes, she nets 7 percent. This 7 percent may be described as the compounding rate, or the rate at which her investments are growing until retirement.

"Now let's look at Richard, who has a variable annuity. With a 2 percent management fee and the same 13 percent gross rate of return, Richard will have an 11 percent change in his account value. Since it grows tax-deferred, he has a compounding rate of 11 percent. That's why people invest in variable annuities rather than mutual funds if they don't think they'll need the money for a while. An 11 percent compounding rate, even after retirement when taxes must be paid, still results in significantly greater dollars than the 7 percent compounding rate from Lori's identically performing mutual fund.

"What about Brent's variable life? His portfolio manager has the same 13 percent gross rate of return; Brent shopped around and found a policy with total fees and charges averaging 4 percent over 10 years. That resulted in a 9 percent change in the account value. Since there are no taxes, Brent's compounding rate is 9 percent.

"If we stopped here, Richard's variable annuity would come in first, with a compounding rate of 11 percent. But remember: When he retires, he'll be taxed on his variable annuity withdrawals. On the other hand, Brent can access his variable life policy money tax-free. Will taxes at retirement be greater than the difference between Richard's 11 percent and Brent's 9 percent? Probably. All it would require is for the retiree to be in an 18 percent combined tax bracket, federal and state. That makes Brent's variable life the winner.

"Now, Carolyn and Bill, this analysis has not considered the death benefit. If you need a life insurance policy to provide income for heirs, to pay estate taxes or for some other reason, you'll also have to subtract the annual cost of that insurance policy (or the pure term cost) from the variable annuity's 11 percent net return or from the mutual fund's 7 percent net return."

Andrea also explained that the fees, loads, charges, and expenses she cited included all applicable portfolio management fees, administrative costs, marketing expenses, and mortality costs averaged over 10 years. "It will usually take a variable life contract six or eight years to break even with the other choices, since those are the most expensive years of the contract," she noted. "That's when the contract is being set up, the death benefit is being funded, acquisition costs are being paid, and so on. If you think you'll live at least another six or eight years, then you'll probably be ahead with the variable life contract. If you don't think you'll live that long, then you probably won't qualify for the insurance policy anyway."

The bottom line? When you're analyzing which investment vehicle to use, choose the one with the smaller siphon. With traditional investments, gross returns go into the funnel; you keep what comes out the bottom. Unfortunately, there's a siphon on the side called *taxes* (combined state and federal), which may be 30 to 40 percent or more. If it's a cash value insurance contract, there are different siphons—mortality costs, marketing costs, and administrative costs. Which has the biggest siphon? That depends on your tax situation—and that's what you have to figure out.

Which Siphon Is Larger?

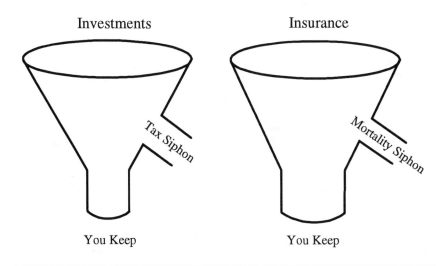

Mutual Funds vs. Variable Annuities vs. Variable Life

	Mutual Funds	Variable Annuity	Variable Life
1. Portfolio Diversification?	Yes	Yes	Yes
2. Professional Management	Yes	Yes	Yes
3. Risk	Lo – Hi	Lo – Hi	Lo – Hi
4. Returns	–10 to +40%	–10 to +40%	–10 to +40%
5. # of Asset Classes	20 – 30	15 – 20	15 – 20
6. Fixed Account?	No	Yes	Yes
7. Taxation:	a) Fully Taxable div., int., capital gains	a) Tax-deferred growth	a) Tax-deferred growth
	b) Fully Taxable transfers between funds	b) Upon withdrawal; LIFO, or, exclusion ratio	b) Tax-free withdrawal via –withdrawal to basis –borrow in excess of basis –loan repaid from death benefit
		c) 10% penalty if withdrawn before age 59 $^1/_2$	c) Fully accessible pre-age 59 $^1/_2$ w/o penalty
		d) Tax-free transfers	d) Tax-free transfers
8. Used for collateral?	Yes	No[1]	Yes
9. Death Benefit	No	No	Yes
10. Fees, loads, charges, expenses[2]	1 to 1 $^1/_2$%	2 to 2 $^1/_2$%	3 to 3 $^1/_2$%

Example:		Mutual Funds	Variable Annuity	Variable Life
	earns	12%	12%	12%
		– 1% fees	– 2% fees	– 3% fees
		11%	10%	9%
		– 4% taxes	– 0% taxes	– 0% taxes
	compounding rate	7%	10%[3]	9%[4]

Notes:

[1] Any borrowing with an annuity as collateral causes the borrowing to be taxable income, plus the 10% penalty.

[2] Includes all portfolio management fees, administrative costs, marketing expenses, mortality costs, etc. averaged over, say, 10 years.

[3] Annuity taxed upon withdrawal.

[4] Insurance may be drawn tax-free, also includes death benefit.

How to Transfer Assets to a Tax-Advantaged Program

All that considered, how could you transfer wealth from a taxable portfolio to a tax-advantaged portfolio?

During the mid-1980s, President Ronald Reagan's tax reform program largely eliminated tax shelters and significantly changed the tax code as we knew it. Its purpose was to simplify the tax code, establishing only two brackets instead of the 14 that existed. Brokerage houses and others responded to the loss of tax shelters by selling what was probably the hottest tax shelter at the time—single-premium life insurance policies. It let people deposit a lump sum—as much as $500,000 or more—into a single-premium life insurance policy. Their money could grow and compound tax-free, and they could access it—again, tax-free—by borrowing it from the insurance company.

In 1988, Congress decided that approach was oriented too specifically for upper-income people and abuse of the system. What happened? Congress said that if you invest in a single-premium life contract (what they called a *modified endowment contract*), you would be taxed as you would on an annuity. In order for an insurance policy *not* to be classified as a modified endowment contract (MEC), it had to comply with the following:

- For any given age, there was a maximum premium that could be deposited into a contract in any given year for a given death benefit. That prevented people from putting too much money into an insurance contract, thereby preventing them from having too large a tax shelter.
- Every year, the policy has to be checked to make sure that the premiums paid in do not exceed the MEC guidelines. A life insurance contract will fail the "seven pay test" if the accumulated amount paid under the contract *at any time* during the first seven contract years is more than the sum of the net level premiums that would have been paid if the contract provided for paid-up future benefits after the payment of the seven level annual payments.

Because of the modified endowment contract rules, you usually need to undertake a wealth transfer program over a period of at least five years. The modified endowment contract laws are detailed and can be confusing; ask a professional insurance adviser for an explanation if these laws apply to you. The fact that Congress passed a law on insurance indicates that there were some pretty good tax advantages associated with it. But

Congress *didn't* change the favorable tax status of insurance that has existed since the Depression—Congress simply tried to stop abuses by the wealthy. Congress presumed that the average American bought life insurance with an annual premium deposit, so that's what they want to happen. As long as you're making that annual premium deposit, you can get the full tax benefits of life insurance.

How do you use this strategy? First, get the most competitive variable life contract you can. For an updated list, call Fax-on-Demand at (801) 263-1676 and request free report #170, "Variable Life Competitive Rankings." Remember that the largest, most stable, most financially secure companies tend to be in the top rankings. Go with those.

Next, get the lowest death benefit possible for a given savings amount, then load the contract up with excess deposits up to double the base premium. In other words, the base premium—which buys the death benefit—will be only 50 to 70 percent of the total amount you are depositing each year into the contract. Virtually all of the excess deposits will go straight into the investment accounts.

One important caveat: While you're trying to get as low a death benefit as possible relative to the dollars you're putting in, don't drop the death benefit below what you need for your family's protection and for estate taxes.

Here's a modification on the strategy: If you have a variable life insurance policy that you bought primarily for the death benefit and not for the savings, and if you have extra dollars to save, deposit the excess into the life insurance contract rather than a mutual fund. Why? Because the portfolio management fee on the insurance contract is typically only 1 to 1.5 percent, which is about the same as you're going to incur with a mutual fund. But with a life insurance contract, it grows tax-sheltered and you can access your money without taxes. In other words, you can have the accessibility of mutual funds without the taxability of mutual funds.

Incidentally, I recommend that if you are purchasing over $500,000 of life insurance, it may be wise to split that amount equally between variable life and traditional life. Why? Though the variable life will offer greater long-term growth, the traditional policy will provide an anchor with its stable cash values, and will have lower expenses associated with it than a fixed account within a variable contract. Won't you get a lower return? Not necessarily. The traditional policy will allow you to be more aggressive in the variable policy.

What about Municipal Bonds?

I've purposely excluded municipal bonds from the discussion about taxation. While many people invest in municipal bonds because they generate tax-free income, it's important to understand the *cost* of that tax-free income.

Note the difference between the yield on a tax-free municipal bond and comparable-risk corporate bonds. The yield on the corporate bond will be higher than the yield on the municipal bond. How much higher? An amount equivalent to the average tax bracket of the investors in municipal bonds. In other words, the yield on the municipal bond will equal the corporate bond yield minus the average tax bracket of the investors in the marketplace.

Let's look at an example. If corporate bonds are yielding 8 percent and municipal bonds are yielding 5.2 percent, that suggests that 2.8 percent is being paid in taxes. The average investor, then, is in a 35 percent tax bracket (2.8 divided by 8 equals .35, or 35 percent). The so-called tax-free yield of a municipal bond isn't free at all.

So when should you buy a municipal bond? First, calculate where the average tax bracket is. If your marginal tax bracket is less than that, buy corporate bonds. If your tax bracket is equal, it doesn't matter. And if your tax bracket is higher than the differential, you should buy municipal bonds.

Tax-Free vs. Taxable Income

Your Marginal Tax Bracket	4 %	5 %	A Tax-Free Yield of 6 %	7 %	8 %	9 %
			Is Equivalent to a Taxable Yield of			
15%	4.7%	5.9%	7.1%	8.2%	9.4%	10.6%
20	5.0	6.3	7.5	8.8	10.0	11.3
25	5.3	6.7	8.0	9.3	10.7	12.0
30	5.7	7.1	8.6	10.0	11.4	12.9
35	6.2	7.7	9.2	10.8	12.3	13.9
40	6.7	8.3	10.0	11.7	13.3	15.0
45	7.3	9.1	10.9	12.7	14.6	16.4
50	8.0	10.0	12.0	14.0	16.0	18.0

Your Insights, Feelings, and Action Items

A. As you read this chapter, what *insights* came that seem applicable to *you?*

    1._____

    2._____

    3._____

B. How did you *feel* as you pondered particular points of this chapter?

    1._____

    2._____

    3._____

C. What do you *feel* you should *do* as a result of this chapter?

    1._____

    2._____

    3._____

D. How might you solicit the aid of others in accomplishing "C" above?

_____

_____

_____

Chapter 31

Nine Keys to Successful Portfolio Management

In an ideal portfolio, there are nine keys to performance. With them, you will be able to unlock the door to sound investment discernment.

1. *Asset allocation* uses Modern Portfolio Theory (MPT) to scientifically balance the portfolio—a proven way to increase returns and reduce risk.
2. *A contrarian approach* is used to determine when to increase or decrease holdings in a market class.
3. *Dollar cost averaging* (or its variation) is used to help you buy low and sell high.
4. *A modified market timing approach* is used to help you reduce risk.
5. *A disciplined and rigorous strategy* formulated on set rules is used to build the portfolio; emotional decisions are never used.
6. *Systematic monitoring and surveillance* keep track of the portfolio status and how the various investment strategies are interrelating.

7. *Certain trigger points* will automatically execute trades, making discipline easier.
8. *Regular reports* will measure the portfolio's success—measurement is integral in the portfolio's evaluation.
9. *Your individual objectives and personality* are reflected—including your risk tolerance levels, goals and objectives, cash flow requirements, desire for portfolio growth, and tax situation.

Read the list again. In reality, only the first four proven keys deal with actual portfolio management. The other five depend on disciplines and systems used to handle the personal aspect of the portfolio. They are what let you achieve your portfolio goals in the real world.

Engage These Four Proven Portfolio Strategies

In Chapter 22 we discussed portfolio risks. Understanding the risks enables you to move ahead with strategies that will make your portfolio perform the way you want it to.

The first four keys in the list above relate to portfolio design and strategy, which is where most strategic planners stop. The remaining principles bridge strategy with application, which is equally essential for success.

Asset Allocation

Asset allocation is the key to a successful portfolio. Why? According to the *Financial Analysts Journal*, almost all (93 percent) of successful investing depends on being able to select or weight how and when assets are spread among various investment markets. Very little (7 percent) of a portfolio's performance depends on the selection of individual stocks, bonds, or mutual funds.

A high-tech computerized model and data are necessary for scientific and successful asset allocation. One model is called *Modern Portfolio Theory (MPT)*; it was first observed by Harry Markowitz in the 1950s. A second model is the *Capital Asset Pricing Model (CAPM)*, established by William Sharpe of Stanford University. Together, these two models have been the foundation of portfolio design since the '60s. Based on their contribution, Markowitz and Sharpe received the 1990 Nobel Prize for economics.

Portfolio Success depends on

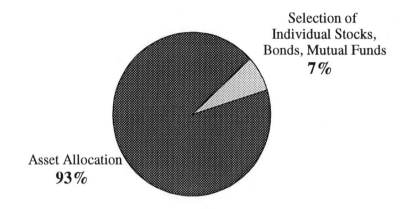

Selection of
Individual Stocks,
Bonds, Mutual Funds
7%

Asset Allocation
93%

To introduce modern portfolio theory and what it means, let's assume that Asset A, aggressive growth stocks, behaves as shown in the first illustration on page 442. It's volatile; it has its ups and downs over time. Now let's add Asset B, growth stocks; it has similar ups and downs over time. Together in a portfolio, these two assets produce returns illustrated by the dotted line. In other words, they are both volatile. Assets A and B, then, are *positively correlated*, or *directly correlated*.

Now let's introduce Asset C. In the same economic environment and the same time frame, Asset C behaves as shown in the second illustration on page 442. Combined in a portfolio, Assets A and C would produce returns that look like an average of the two assets. Over time, this portfolio is far less volatile. Assets A and C, then, are *negatively correlated*, or *inversely correlated*. In other words, they move in opposite directions in an identical economic environment.

How would this look in the real world? Let's assume you have two portfolios—Portfolio A and Portfolio B. You can choose between two investments: mid-maturity Treasury notes (a low-volatility, low-risk investment) and a real estate investment trust (a high-volatility, high-risk investment). During the past 10 years, the T-notes have had an average annual return of 7 percent with a standard deviation (a measurement of risk volatility) of 6. During the same 10 years, the real estate investment trust has had an average annual rate of return of 14 percent with a standard deviation of 15.

Cross-Correlation Is Positive

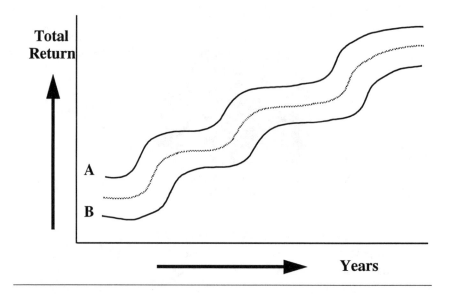

Cross-Correlation Is Negative

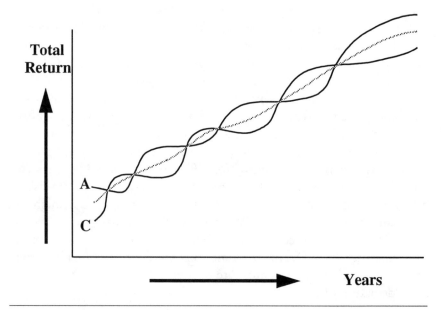

Let's assume that Portfolio A is 100 percent Treasury notes; it has no real estate investment trusts. Its average annual return, then, is 7 percent. Its standard deviation is 6 percent.

You know that a real estate investment trust is far more risky than T-notes, so in Portfolio B, 90 percent of the portfolio is invested in T-notes, and just 10 percent of the portfolio is invested in a real estate investment trust.

What's happened? You've added a highly volatile, highly risky investment to Portfolio B. So, will it have greater or lesser risk than Portfolio A? Do you think it has greater risk? Look closer. Portfolio B might have an average annual return of 9 percent instead of 7 percent—yet it might have a standard deviation of 5, as shown in the illustration below. In other words, you achieved a greater rate of return with less risk.

Maybe you thought that couldn't be done. Here's the key: In risk-return relationships, higher returns come with higher risks *only within the same asset class.* As soon as you introduce a different asset class, you must then consider the cross-correlation between the two asset classes.

Here's what you did, then. T-notes have a low level of volatility, and real estate investment trusts (REITs) are extremely volatile. But because they are inversely correlated and because REITs are so volatile, all it takes is 10 percent of a portfolio in a REIT to knock out much of the volatility in T-notes. You end up with a portfolio volatility level that is less than if you had invested solely in T-notes.

Increased Returns with Lower Risk

	Portfolio	
	A	**B**
Short-term Treasury Notes 7% 6 sd	100%	90%
Real Estate Investment Trust 14% 15 sd	0	10%
	7% 6 sd	9% 5 sd

Risk vs. Return vs. Cross-Correlations. Most people who design portfolios understand two things: *risk* and *return.* (Return is measured as a percentage, and risk is measured as a standard deviation.) But when you are talking about different asset classes, there is a third and probably equally important measurement: *cross-correlation.* Specifically, you need to consider the cross-correlation between different asset classes and whether the cross-correlation is positive or negative.

If the cross-correlation of two assets is positive, adding the additional asset class to the portfolio won't do much to lower the overall risk of the portfolio. But if you scientifically figure out which asset classes have a negative or inverse correlation, then you minimize the overall risk of the portfolio.

How? With modern portfolio theory (MPT) statistics. Though MPT was first observed by Harry Markowitz in the 1950s, it was difficult to implement on a practical level for over 30 years due to the extensive database and computing power required. Each asset class (stocks, bonds, real estate, CDs, precious metals, etc.) and mutual fund has its own MPT statistics, including how it cross-correlates with other asset classes. (See the table in *Your Money Happiness Workbook*.)

To have an analysis prepared on your portfolio is really quite simple: Check the list of Recommended Resources on page 515 for firms that will prepare such an analysis, see *Your Money Happiness Workbook*, or call Fax-on-Demand at (801) 263-1676 and request free report #175, "How to Get Your Portfolio Analyzed."

Assume your portfolio is at Point A on the scatter graph on page 445. Now assume that you let the computer come up with a number of other hypothetical portfolios. Each portfolio will have its own risk/ return characteristics, yielding a scatter graph, as shown. Once you have defined all of these portfolios, you can determine where you want to go with your portfolio. Any portfolio above the horizontal line that passes through your portfolio rate of return, and to the left of the vertical line that passes through your portfolio risk level, will have a higher rate of return and a lower level of risk. So you want to move to a portfolio in the upper-left quadrant from your current portfolio.

Now it's time to consider your risk tolerance. If your risk tolerance level is *much* lower than your current portfolio allows, then Portfolio B might be ideal for you. Or Portfolio C might be ideal. But there would be no sense in moving to Portfolio D. Why? It doesn't give enough increase in the rate of return when compared to the additional risk you would have to take.

That puts *balance* in a whole new light. "Balance" traditionally means you shouldn't put all your eggs in one basket. Traditionally, there's nothing scientific about it—you just put a few eggs into stocks, some into bonds, some into real estate, and some into CDs.

But that's not really "balance." Why? Because you don't know whether you're really lowering your risk. You might actually be making your portfolio *more* volatile. For example, I will often suggest that a client balance his portfolio across several mutual funds. He will respond that he has, only to name off five or six stock mutual funds with varying levels of aggressiveness, all of which are positively correlated. His market risk hasn't been addressed.

Applied MPT, on the other hand, lets you scientifically determine how to lower your risk and improve your risk-adjusted returns.

MPT requires significant number crunching that may use decades worth of historical data and perhaps a hundred classes of assets. Numerous measurements are taken. This type of advanced analysis used to be economically possible only for portfolios of more than $5 million—such as corporate trusts, pension trusts, and foundations. But, thanks to the personal computer, it can now be done on a portfolio as small as $50,000. (Because of the work still involved, it may not be cost-effective to run an MPT analysis on a portfolio smaller than $50,000.)

Moving from Current to Ideal Portfolio

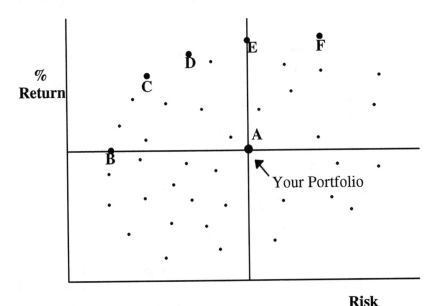

One important note: You don't get asset allocation within a single mutual fund. A mutual fund is required by its charter, its prospectus, and its stated investment objectives to stay within a certain asset class—such as aggressive growth stocks, equity income stocks, or corporate bonds.

The diversification within a mutual fund helps minimize the fundamental risk within a portfolio. Asset allocation does not even really address fundamental risk or diversifiable risks. Rather, asset allocation minimizes the market risk or the technical risk.

There *are* some asset allocation mutual funds available. Generally, however, they move strictly between stocks, bonds, and money market funds—they don't get into precious metals, international markets, real estate investment trusts, and other classes. And they are not personalized to *your* risk tolerance level, *your* investment objectives, *your* time constraints, *your* tax situation, or *your* cash flow requirements. They're simply a one-stop, one-size-fits-all approach, making them inferior investment vehicles.

At any rate, I have never seen asset allocation accomplished well within a so-called "asset allocation" fund, probably because asset allocation is a professional service that needs to be *client-specific* to be performed correctly.

Most asset allocation services available today also lack an understanding of the *art* of applied MPT. There are a number of problems:

- MPT does not account for current market extremes, including overbought or oversold conditions.
- As you consider the MPT optimization model, which economic "window" do you analyze? Most users simply look back 20 to 30 years, but should you be looking at a period of moderate growth, high inflation, recession, or what?
- Which asset classes do you use? What if you are limited to merely U.S. stocks, bonds, or money market funds?

Remember: Only about 7 percent of a portfolio's performance depends on the individual stocks, bonds, and mutual funds you select. That 7 percent effort addresses the fundamental risk. But 93 percent of successful portfolio performance depends on the timing, selection, and weighting of *asset categories*. Advanced asset allocation processes let you manage away much of the market or technical risk. How and when you allocate assets among classes is the key to successful performance!

A Contrarian Approach

A *contrarian investment strategy* means that you buy when others are selling, and you sell when others are buying. Basically, you figure out what everyone else is doing, then do the opposite. It takes real confidence to be a contrarian.

J.P. Morgan, the great American banker and financier, was once asked how he accumulated all his wealth. His response? "I buy my straw hats in the winter-time."

A contrarian approach is essential to managing money. It is necessary if you want to enhance profits during periods of low market risk (when the market is falling or bottoming out) or to lock in gains during periods of high market risk (when the market is climbing or reaching an all-time high).

Unfortunately, I have even seen this observation misstated in a publication of a national society of professional investment advisers. The general population thinks that the higher and the longer the market climbs, the better its "track record," the less risky it is. False. Yet that is when the small guy usually invests.

The higher the market is, the more risky it's becoming. The market is becoming less risky as it falls or is bottoming out, when everyone *thinks* it is heading lower. ("Everyone" is a relative term; we are looking at extreme ratios here.)

Being a contrarian is not merely a matter of psychology, as some think. There are mathematical relationships involved. If "everyone" thinks the market is headed higher, if all the bears have reluctantly given way and finally joined the ranks of the bulls, if debate has slowed and there is uniform agreement that we are in a raging bull market, then, is "everyone" invested? Yes. And if everyone is invested, can the market go any higher? Is there any more money on the sidelines to bid the market up further? No, and no. The market becomes overbought, and is ripe for a downward correction. The same holds for a bear market. When we reach an extreme ratio of "everyone" thinking the market is a bad place to invest, then is the time to buy.

Economic cycles are part of the cost of living in a free-enterprise economy. Regardless of how much one political party blames the other or big business, regardless of the rhetoric slung during a presidential campaign, economic cycles are generally not the fault of big business or the government. Economic cycles are a natural byproduct of a free-enterprise economy—an economy that naturally goes through periods of growth and expansion, contraction and recession. As the populace ages, as discoveries and technological advances are made, as people migrate, the economy naturally goes through dislocations and adjustments. So we have economic cycles. The question is, do you understand them and can you prepare for them or profit from them?

It is interesting that we understand the contrarian principle in other realms, but not in the investment realm. Some consumers understand it very well. They do all their Christmas shopping the week after Christmas. They buy snow-blowers in the spring and lawnmowers in the fall. Why? That's when the buys are best. It's the same for investments.

In *How to be Rich*, J. Paul Getty advised, "Buy when everyone else is selling and hold until everyone else is buying. This is more than just a catchy slogan; it is the very *essence* of successful investing."

Let's understand why contrarian investing is more than just a catchy slogan—and why there are fundamental mathematical, quantifiable reasons that it works.

There are a number of indices that let you determine investor sentiment—and figure out whether most investors are buying or selling. Those include market liquidity ratio, percent over moving averages, speculation intensity index, insider trading activity, the sentiment of various advisory services, the sentiment of institutional investors, market momentum, and the ratio of call-to-put options. Let's look at a few of these indices.

The market liquidity ratio. The market liquidity ratio tells you how many dollars are on the sidelines. Those are dollars that might be thrown into the market to bid prices up further. For example, if you see that the mutual fund industry is holding large cash balances, the public has large amounts sitting in CDs and money market funds, and institutional investors have large amounts of cash on the sidelines, that would indicate there is cash available to potentially bid the market up—because there are dollars available to bid prices up. If, on the other hand, cash reserves are at low levels, the market can't be bid up further and may have reached a peak.

Insider buys/sells. Corporate insiders must report any buys or sells of their corporate stock to the Securities and Exchange Commission. Historically, savvy corporate insiders tend to buy when their stocks are depressed and sell when their stocks are overpriced. Remember, though, it's all relative—you need to look at ratios. When the buy-to-sell ratio hits certain extremes, the market is probably in an overbought or oversold position.

Advisory service sentiment. How can you determine how advisory services feel? Read their newsletters. See the list of Recommended Resources on page 515 for some of the more popular newsletters available, including a newsletter that tracks newsletters. That may be helpful for an overall view of sentiment extremes, as well as how the various newsletters have performed.

Even with newsletters, if the herd is all going one direction, you probably want to do the opposite.

Institutional investors. Interestingly, the large institutional investors have been shown to be notoriously wrong in picking the direction of the market. If institutional investors believe the market is going higher, then, it might be a good time to sell. If they think the market is headed down, it's time to buy.

The popular press. This one might be the easiest of all. Just read *Time*, *Money* magazine, or anything else published by the popular press. They are notorious for popularizing a bull market for their readers *after* it has already had its run up, and for announcing the demise of the market when it has *already* hit bottom. Just do the opposite.

Depending on what these contrarian indicators are saying, you can increase or decrease your portfolio holdings to take advantage of market opportunities.

Let's look at the pie-chart portfolios on page 451. MPT analysis may draw on 30 years of data; each quarter, one new quarter's worth of data is added, and one quarter's worth of data drops off. Though MPT analysis is critical, it doesn't really tell you whether the market is currently overbought or oversold. Contrarian indicators do.

Let's assume you look at a number of contrarian indicators. If you see a strong signal for (against) a particular asset class, you might increase (decrease) your MPT weighting by 20 or 30 percent. If you see only a moderate signal, you might increase (decrease) your MPT weighting by only 10 to 15 percent.

The time to be contrarian is when the market reaches an *extreme* overbought or oversold position. Between those extremes, go with the market direction. That's a very important point: *Be contrarian at the extremes; go with the market in the interim.*

What's the biggest problem with being a contrarian? By human nature, we're all sheep. We like to follow the herd. We like to follow trends. You cannot do that when you are a contrarian. Look at what happens when there is a glut of single-family residences for sale in your county and massive vacancies in multi-family residential apartments. The herd mentality people—the sheep—are selling out. The insightful people—the contrarians—are buying properties for a song. To be a contrarian, you have to leave your fears behind and have the confidence to go against the pack.

Good Reasons for Stupid Decisions

Remember: There is *always* a good reason to do something stupid. If there weren't, no one would ever do anything stupid! Logic and analysis often override common sense and perspective. You might fall victim to the trap of believing that times have changed and the market can never crash again, because we have so many "safeguards." We have a global economy and a free trade agreement. And, because of all these things, you might think things are simply different. That's the kind of thinking that will set *you* up for a fall.

Look at the press. At best, the press mirrors the uninformed public. At worst, it seeks the sensational in order to sell newspapers or magazines. Want some examples?

- On January 8, 1973, the cover headline of *Time* boasted, "Gilt-Edged Year for the Stock Market." The high for the entire year occurred *three days* later—on January 11—at 1,051.7. From there, the market slid. By December 5, it was down to 788. It hit bottom a year later—December 6, 1974—at 577, a 45 percent loss.
- In September 1974, the cover of *Newsweek* called 1974 "The Big Bad Year." The market immediately began rebounding, and ended *up* a year later.
- The August 1979 cover of *Business Week* headlined with "The Death of Equities." Enough said.
- The September 26, 1988, cover of *Time* blasted, "Buy Stocks? No Way." A year later, the market was up more than 30 percent.

Get rid of emotion. Be contrarian. The laws of supply and demand tell us that when everybody wants something, it will eventually be priced beyond its intrinsic value. When everyone thinks the market is going up, it will soon be headed lower. When everyone believes that the market is not the place to be, now is the time to buy. They are such simple laws. Unfortunately, they are too easy to forget.

The Genius of Dollar Cost Averaging

Dollar cost averaging is an investing principle that is generally applied to a systematic savings plan.

In a portfolio, here's what happens: You invest a set dollar amount each month. Over time, you get a lower average cost per share. Why? Because when prices are high, the amount you invest buys fewer shares. When prices are low, it buys more shares. Over a full market cycle—from three to eight years—the average cost per share you buy is less than the average price that you can sell the shares at. It's a direct mathematical relationship.

For additional success, take the concept of dollar cost averaging one step further and apply it to an existing portfolio. Here's how: Regularly and consistently reallocate your portfolio to a pre-established mix among selected asset classes. That way, you'll be sure of buying low and selling high *over a full market cycle*. As a result, you will significantly enhance your portfolio's total return.

Suggested Asset Allocations

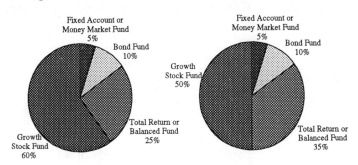

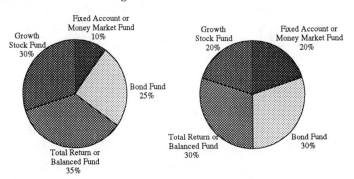

Dollar cost averaging is genius—but it can be a real no-brainer to pull off. For example, you can do something as simple as determine that a set portion of your portfolio will be in each of four asset classes, chosen from: stocks, bonds, money market funds, precious metals, real estate investment trusts, world bonds, or international stocks. Every three months you can re-balance so that a predetermined portion of your assets are in each of those asset classes: You sell off from those asset classes that have risen above the predetermined level of your portfolio, and move those dollars into the classes that have dropped below that predetermined level of your portfolio. What are you doing? You are being contrarian—selling off assets that are high, and buying assets that are low.

Though a personal adviser might adjust the suggested portfolio allocations for your particular circumstances and risk tolerance level, I suggest that the portfolio ratios on page 451 make sense for most people. These are long-term ratios that should continually be re-balanced to.

One word of caution here: Don't move a significant percentage of your money into CDs. Why? Over the long term, the market will significantly outperform CDs—you don't want to sell out of your best-performing assets and move the money into CDs, which are likely your worst-performing asset.

Apply Dollar Cost Averaging to a Savings Stream

Let's talk about applying dollar cost averaging to a savings stream. The following "Tale of Three Parents" is a tremendous example in point. (Source: John Hancock Distributors, Inc.)

"Bob, Bill, and Sue are three neighbors, each of whom has young children. All three parents wish to be able to provide a college education for their children, and realize that they must establish systematic plans that will help them to achieve their financial goals by the time the college years arrive. Each decides that with careful family budgeting, it would be possible to put aside $1,000 per month in a college funding program. They recognize that it may be extremely expensive to pay for four years at a top-notch private college by the time their children reach their late teenage years; so $1,000 per month may be needed to fully fund the plan over the next few years.

"All three know that over long periods of time the ownership of common stocks has proven to be an excellent way to provide for future needs. The last 10 years have been especially good years for stocks, and Bob, Bill, and Sue review this great decade in their decision making process.

The Dow Jones Industrial Average*
Performance demonstrated below represents past performance and may not be indicative of future results.

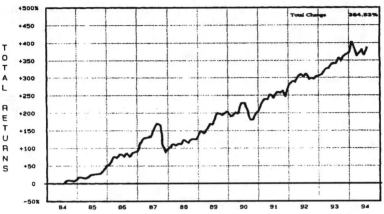

"But all three parents also know there are potential risks with owning stocks, especially if only a small number of stocks might be owned in a portfolio. Each parent goes through a series of 'what if' scenarios before determining how to start funding the college plan.

"Bob sees that an option would be to put the $1,000 per month into an FDIC insured bank account paying interest of 5 percent per year. The advantages of Bob's plan are that it is entirely predictable, and he can sleep at night knowing that his college fund is not subject to a loss. $1,000 per month placed into such an account would have a value of $12,330 at the end of the first year.

A Bank Account
Paying 5% Annually

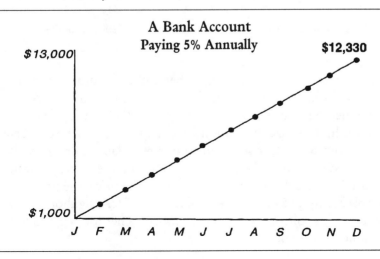

"Bill senses that stocks might provide greater returns over a period of time, and he is optimistic that he can select stocks that perform very well over time. He begins his plan by investing the first $1,000 in a stock that sells for $50. Each month he methodically buys $1,000 worth of the stock, and the stock moves up steadily, as he had anticipated. Of course, as the stock moves higher, Bill's $1,000 buys fewer shares per month than when it was $50 per share. During the first year, the stock proves to be exceptional; it rises to $70 by the end of the year ... obviously a great investment. At the end of the year Bob has accumulated 201 shares of the stock, and with the stock trading at $70 per share, his college fund now has a value of $14,070.

A Great Stock
$50 to $70

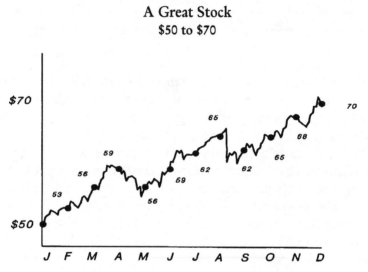

For illustrative purposes only and not representative of a particular investment.

"Sue agrees with Bill, and begins her college plan by investing the first $1,000 in her favorite stock, also a stock selling for $50. And like Bill, she methodically buys $1,000 worth of stock on the first day of every month, sticking conscientiously to her plan. But her experience is different from Bill's. Her stock does not rise, it falls ... dramatically. It goes down $5 per month for 5 straight months before it finally bottoms-out and rebounds. But it never gets back to the price Sue first paid. It climbs back only to $40 by the end of the year. Her neighbor Bob, who chose to put his college fund in the bank, scolds her for being so foolish with 'important money.'

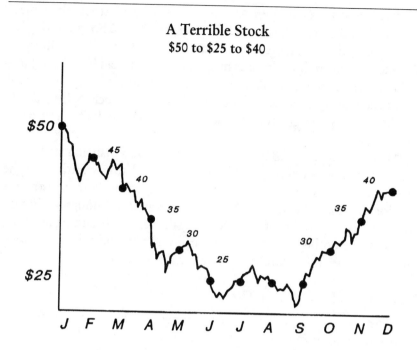

A Terrible Stock
$50 to $25 to $40

For illustrative purposes only and not representative of a particular investment.

"But, who is the foolish one of these three neighbors with similar goals? Was the 'obvious' winner the REAL winner? Perhaps not.

"Bob's account in the bank paid him 5 percent annually on the money in the account. Putting $1,000 per month into the account and collecting the interest resulted in the account having a value of $12,330 at the end of the year. **Bob: $12,330**

"Bill's account, having been invested in a rising stock, did better than Bob's account. In most months the $1,000 investment bought fewer and fewer shares, of course, because the price of the stock rose steadily, but the final result was an admirable one. Bill's selection of this great stock provided him with an account worth more than $14,000 at the end of the year. **Bill: $14,070**

"But what about poor Sue, whose stock began to fall immediately after she bought the first shares, and never recovered to its original price? Should Sue's young daughter be planning to work behind the counter of a fast-food restaurant while her friends are attending college in a few years? Perhaps not.

"Sue's first $1,000 bought 20 shares of her favorite stock, the same as Bill's $1,000. But as Sue's stock fell in price, her $1,000 bought more and more shares; in the middle of the year, when the stock was selling for $25, she was able to buy twice as many shares as she had bought in January! And when the stock finally began to climb, and reached $40 by the end of the year, Sue had accumulated 376 shares of stock. Selling at $40 per share, Sue's college account had grown to $15,040! **The Winner— Sue: $15,040**

"The key to planning for the future is to have a plan and stick to it. One of the most successful methods of accumulating wealth over the years has been systematic investing ... disciplined, regular investments over long periods of time ... *Dollar Cost Averaging*. Although no investment plan can assure a profit or protect against loss in declining markets, for parents who begin such a plan early enough, and who stick to it conscientiously, the future looks bright for their children."

Know the Role of Market Timing

Most people think the purpose of market timing is to increase a portfolio's rate of return. Not so. The purpose of market timing is to protect capital in declining markets so it is available for reinvestment in climbing markets. In other words, it manages your risk. Ideally, market timing gets you out of the market during declining periods, preserving your capital so you can use it when the market turns around and starts to climb again.

The market always goes through ups and downs, ultimately arriving at its five- or 10-year total return. The purpose of market timing is to let you know when the market is beginning to fall. Why? So you can sell out of the market and transfer that money into a money market fund, a defensive position. When the market turns around, you move the money back into the market—but this time from a higher beginning point, because your capital has been preserved for reinvestment.

Even though the *purpose* of market timing is not to increase your rate of return, that happens as an added benefit. Let's see why.

When the market is climbing, you're not receiving any greater returns than the market is as a whole. But there's a simple difference: When the market starts to fall, you go on the defensive until the market turns around. Then you buy back in. At the end of that five- or 10-year period, then, you have a higher total return than someone using a buy-and-hold approach.

Why does market timing make so much sense? If you can avoid down periods in the market, then return to the market for the strong periods, you'll have more dollars than if you buy and hold. That applies even if you're not in the market during its strongest periods—as long as you're also out of the market while it's underperforming.

A September 1991 *Forbes* article by Gary Schilling dramatically illustrated the importance of being out of the market. By avoiding the 50 worst months in the market, an investor went from an 11.4 percent return to an almost 20 percent return. The study also showed that most of the market's up movements were compressed into a very few and brief time periods. If an investor missed the 50 strongest months, his annual returns were reduced to just over 4 percent. But if he missed both the 50 strongest and the 50 weakest months, his rate of return would have increased to just over 12 percent. Avoiding the worst months was more important than participating in all of the strongest months.

The indicators most often used for market timing include interest rate swings and forecasts and selected moving averages. Usually market timing dictates that a portfolio is either 100 percent invested or 100 percent on the sidelines. Because this approach may result in whipsaws during periods of extreme volatility, a good portfolio adviser might use a three-tiered approach in connection with its contrarian indicators while staging advancements into and out of the market. (For a number of investment advisory firms that provide asset allocation and/or market timing services, see the list of Recommended Resources on page 515.)

Put It All Together

Now you know four key principles for achieving successful portfolio management. But at the beginning of this chapter, nine keys were listed. The first four dealt with proven portfolio management strategies. The next five show you how to make those strategies a reality in your portfolio.

This is where things usually break down. Plenty of people know the principles—but they don't know how to translate them into practical application. They don't know how to apply the principles to their own situation.

Be Disciplined

First, you have to use each of the four principles in a disciplined way—*without emotion*. The discipline with which you apply the investing rule is often more important than the rule itself. When your self-imposed rule tells you to do something, do it. It will *usually* tell you something that feels uncomfortable. But if it is statistically proven and historically sound and prudent, it will be right more often than your emotions.

Use Systematic Monitoring

Simply stated, you have to regularly monitor your investment strategies. Investing rules are interrelated—so a systematic monitoring has to happen on a regular basis. In fact, monitoring and surveillance need to be done every day if you want to protect your portfolio from any significant adverse economic developments.

While monitoring and surveillance need to be done every day, you probably need to reposition your portfolio only once a quarter. Why? A short-term perspective lets you get emotionally involved. The long-term, historical perspective lets you take greater advantage of larger movements, contrarian indicators, and the long-term strategies we have just discussed. If you can't or don't want to do the monitoring, utilize a professional to provide this service for you.

Get Automated

Discipline, monitoring, and surveillance must become automated. And automation usually requires that a computer system be involved to track trigger points, then effect simultaneous trades. If the process isn't automated, the success of the portfolio strategies will depend on emotion and on your own follow-through—and will be subject to greater human error.

Get Regular Reports

Your portfolio strategy should automatically generate regular reports to you—whether it's a pension plan, a personal portfolio, a corporate fund, or a foundation.

These regular reports let you measure the success of your strategy. How will you know if you're succeeding unless you have measurement information?

Just make sure you keep things in the proper perspective. Market timing, asset allocation principles, modern portfolio theory, and long-term gains require a three- to eight-year approach. You'll be sorely disappointed if you evaluate your portfolio on a quarterly—or even an annual—basis, because the market doesn't complete its cycles in that short a period.

Management reports must also be simple. They should generate consolidated quarterly reports that show the activity of all mutual funds on one simple statement. The statement should reflect all account activity, including balances among asset classes and within specific investments. Each quarter, you should have an investment inventory, asset distribution exhibits, and an analysis of your total portfolio.

Reflect Your Individual Objectives

All portfolio management is irrelevant if your portfolio doesn't meet your individual objectives and goals. Portfolio design should be custom-tailored—whether it's for a qualified retirement plan, corporate funds, a nonprofit organization, a trust account, or an individual account.

The successful portfolio should fit you like a surgeon's glove. It should reflect your personal goals and objectives; your personal risk tolerance levels; and your time horizon, whether it's one year or 20 years. It should reflect your cash flow needs—your need to draw an income from the portfolio. It should reflect the rate of return objectives necessary to achieve your "Financial Freedom Day" and other goals. It should reflect your goals regarding your phase of life, growth within the portfolio, and other resources you might have available to help achieve your goals. Such a design is available with reputable, experienced professional advisers.

Your Insights, Feelings, and Action Items

A. As you read this chapter, what *insights* came that seem applicable to *you?*
  1._____
  2._____
  3._____

B. How did you *feel* as you pondered particular points of this chapter?
  1._____
  2._____
  3._____

C. What do you *feel* you should *do* as a result of this chapter?
  1._____
  2._____
  3._____

D. How might you solicit the aid of others in accomplishing "C" above?

_____

_____

_____

Decision Six

Avoid Poor Thinking

Chapter 32 examines the relationship between your thoughts and your success level; this is exemplified in Chapter 33 by how you manage your investments.

Chapter 32

Your Success Level Reflects How Well You Are Thinking

Avoid Poor Thinking

All too often in life we come across people who are negative, closed-minded, who spend more than they earn and repeatedly fail to see the big picture. They perceive themselves as martyrs or victims of their circumstances, insist people are "out to get them," tend to feel violated for imagined injustices, and have a scarcity mentality that prohibits them from thinking win-win. These attitudes are found in all economic strata among people who clearly do not understand that our financial success depends upon how well we are thinking.

To achieve financial security and peace of mind, it is critical that we recognize the characteristics of poor thinking in ourselves and consciously make an effort to alter our perceptions. Poor thinkers see life as a zero-sum game in which the pie is a static size and there is only so much to go around. If life is a pie, poor thinkers always feel two or three blueberries short of their fair share. Remember feeling this way as a child?

Poor thinkers feel entitled to share in the success of others around them, believe they shouldn't have to repay money borrowed from more affluent family members, and have an expectant attitude without a willingness to pay the price. The glass is half empty, and everything wrong is someone else's fault. These characteristics seen in immature children are most distasteful in adults.

"The average man," A. A. Milne once noted, "is always waiting for something to happen to him instead of setting to work to make things happen. For one person who dreams of making fifty thousand pounds, a hundred people dream of being left fifty thousand pounds."

Poor Thinkers Have a Victim Mentality

Poor thinkers fancy "damages" for all kinds of imagined injustices simply because life is hard or unfair. But what's the real problem? They don't want to accept responsibility for their actions or thoughts. Instead, they wallow in self-pity because others aren't devoted to catering to their petty concerns.

Poor thinkers do not see the inconsistencies in their own thinking and therefore accuse others of twisting the truth. Because they do not see their incongruence, they can never rise above it. They do not have the options and choices that come with clear and positive thinking.

Poor thinkers frequently assign motives to others, not realizing that they have simply reflected their own motives.

People have to learn not to rail against their conditions, whether they are in a one-parent home, don't have food in their home, are unemployed, or have *any* other imagined *or* real injustices thrust upon them. Not railing against your condition is the first step toward losing your self-defeating behaviors and accepting responsibility for your growth. If you are going to feel self-pity or think that life is supposed to be fair, you will be cursed with a lifetime of feeling robbed. Your misery or malaise will only be exceeded by your inability to climb out of it. When people allow themselves to feel acted upon by their circumstances, they become slaves to their own reactive nature.

All of this is the result of the paradigm through which poor thinkers see life, the glasses they wear. When you engage in this kind of self-talk, it requires the most honest and brutal self-appraisal. There are many self-defeating habits or perspectives we might not even be aware we have. Anyone may be susceptible to poor thinking at any given time. The question is, do we recognize it?

One way to recognize poor thinking is to understand what makes successful thinkers different. The self-talk of a person who thinks successfully is, "I am responsible and proactive. I have the freedom to choose, regardless of the stimulus (whether it be a boss, a child, a law, the government, etc.)."

Therefore, the success thinker is independent. While the poor thinker considers himself a martyr, the success thinker is a champion—humble, grateful, and down-to-earth. He is positive and always seeks opportunities to contribute. No matter how much stress, pressure, or responsibility he may have, he lives life hopefully and optimistically. We have all seen the difference between martyrs who walk around with a downcast, hangdog look, and successful people who are cheerful and in control.

Poor thinking usually occurs when someone hasn't paid a dear price for what he or she has in life, or is overcompensated, or something comes too easily. On the other hand, you can see people with very little who have paid the dearest price and don't engage in poor thinking.

How Do We Learn Success Thinking?

Many middle-class Americans were lucky enough to have been raised in homes and neighborhoods where they observed, as small children, successful people succeeding. They had role model parents and neighbors. They had mentors who cared and opened doors. They were raised with high expectations regarding their own success, education, and opportunities.

Even if we were not raised in these circumstances, we can still overcome our situation. I know of two brothers raised in the same household who developed very different outlooks. One, a physician, earns more but spends less than his brother, a school teacher. The school teacher is constantly living on the edge of bankruptcy and feels he never has enough income, yet he is spending substantially more than the doctor with the bigger salary.

"People are always blaming their circumstances for what they are," George Bernard Shaw once asserted. "I don't believe in circumstances. The people who get on in this world are the people who get up and look for the circumstances they want, and, if they can't find them, make them."

Examine your upbringing, your culture. Is it one of savings, modesty, thrift, owning, self-reliance? Or, is it one of consumption, outward show, renting, poor thinking? We are responsible for ourselves and our descendants.

Financial Success Is Not Achieved by Spending

Do not ever engage in the mistaken notion that someone is financially successful because of his outward manifestations of spending. Financial success and security come from saving, not spending. This seems obvious, but we all erroneously assume others' outward standard of living reflects their success level.

As we discussed in Chapter 1, the purpose of success is not to have more than your neighbors. Remember, the purpose for money must be the same as *the purpose for anything in life*: to bring joy, happiness.

Shaw writes in *Man and Superman*, "This is the true joy in life, the being used for a purpose recognized by yourself as a mighty one; the being thoroughly worn out before you are thrown on the scrap heap; the being a force of nature instead of a feverish, selfish little clod of ailments and grievances complaining that the world will not devote itself to making you happy."

I know of a very successful individual with an annual income of multiple six figures who was so engaged in zero-sum thinking that he couldn't stand to see anyone else gain. A master of innuendos, he got his boss fired so he could take over his position. His desire to reap where he had not sown and harvest where he had not cultivated led his co-workers not to trust him. Those who really knew him knew he would some day self-destruct. This type of poor thinking is all over in our society. Do we discern it and avoid it? Or get caught up in it?

No one can or will discern what is going on in the world without a *clear* sense of right and wrong. Yet this is much of the problem because the notions of right and wrong have become so muddled, situational, and confused by double-tongued talk.

Even Leaders Teach Poor Thinking

I recently attended a speech by Mario Cuomo, former governor of New York, at the Regent Hotel in London in which he advised, "You can't do it anymore. You can't go to college and get married, and tell your wife to stay home and raise kids while you go to work, and buy a house. I'm not sure I could have made it with Matilda in this economy."

How defeatist! We used to have leaders who inspired us to arise out of the ghetto. Now, our leaders tell us we can't. No wonder people believe it. Why do they want to hold us down in dependency, which is slavery, rather than self-reliance, which is freedom?

A welfare state is slavery. One portion of the electorate is dependent on government programs. They have voluntarily given up their independence and freedom. The other portion of the electorate pays 40 percent of all the fruits of their labor, sweat, and tears to support their taskmaster: the dependent electorate and a government bureaucracy. They have involuntarily given up their independence and freedom. Either way, a welfare state makes slaves of all, as people live off the sweat of *someone else's* brow rather than their own.

In the same speech Cuomo continued, "Middle class people are mad. They say, 'I'm tired of paying for [all those social programs].' In the future, the middle third will combine with the bottom third and turn on the people in the top third. *It is inevitable!*"

As one who was born into the bottom third, lived the first 30 years of his life there, and finally rose to the top third, I resented Cuomo's misguided attitude. This type of failure-thinking perhaps is condoned when discussing the economy, but what if such thinking were applied to an individual career? Would any worker be around for long? Succeed to any level? If not, then how can such thinking be tolerated on a national level?

We credit Abraham Lincoln with the truth:

> You cannot bring about prosperity by discouraging thrift. You cannot strengthen the weak by weakening the strong. You cannot help the wage earner by pulling down the wage payer. You cannot further the brotherhood of man by encouraging class hatred. You cannot help the poor by destroying the rich. You cannot establish sound security on borrowed money. You cannot keep out of trouble by spending more than you earn. You cannot build character and courage by taking away initiative and independence. You cannot help men permanently by doing for them what they could do for themselves.

Now that was crystal clear thinking from long ago. And it is just as applicable today as it was then.

You Don't Strengthen the Weak by Weakening the Strong

I remember the popular book written years ago titled *Winning Through Intimidation*. Its whole point was that you should intimidate others for your own success based on how you dressed, the car you drove, and how you treated others. What an unfortunate attitude! Such actions can only reap short-term success at best.

Fortunately, another book, *Winning Through Integrity*, was written several years later. It did not, however, achieve the same bestseller status as its predecessor. What does that say about poor thinking in America, that we put intimidation above integrity?

The world is becoming increasingly "sophisticated." We see evidence of this trend in the advertising of Madison Avenue, among the intellectuals, and in the political and economic arena. Increasingly, people want to talk, dress, and act sophisticated. The unwary read newspapers and magazines which make sophisticated arguments for or against the issue of the day. Judges tolerate the sophistication of lawyers in *our* courtrooms.

Sometimes it might be well to remember that the root word of sophisticated is *sophistry*: "of or having to do with a plausible but deceptive, devious, or fallacious argument" (*American Heritage Dictionary*, 2nd College Edition). I wonder who would ever want to be known as such. Yet the sophisticated, proud of their title, announce themselves. The unwary fall prey.

It is important to check our own thinking, periodically. As I have often said, it is easy to think that people do stupid things for stupid reasons. They don't. People do stupid things for good reasons. We always have a good reason to do something stupid. Otherwise, we wouldn't do them in the first place.

Watch Success, Don't Listen to Failure

Never, never, never listen to someone who is not succeeding! A failure thinker will attempt to lead the way through his persuasive and logical arguments. His analysis of the situation or company environment will make complete sense. He will rely on an accepted and logical perspective. His strategy may even command the respect of others. But he will not succeed. This is not the path you want to follow. It will not lead you to success thinking and financial independence.

The one who is not succeeding thinks he can lead others to success by logic and reason. He thinks he's figured out the way. Don't listen to *anything* from that person. Better for him to keep quiet for five years and show the way by example. *Better for you to watch a success than to listen to a failure.*

In his book *Daily Reflections for Highly Effective People*, Covey notes, "If we want to change a situation, we first have to change ourselves. And to change ourselves effectively, we first have to change our perceptions. ... Change—real change—comes from the inside out. It doesn't come from hacking at the leaves of attitude and behavior with quick fix personality ethic techniques. It comes from striking at the root—the fabric of our thought, the fundamental, essential paradigms, which give definition to our character and create the lens through which we see the world."

He continues, "How much negative energy is typically expended when people try to solve problems or make decisions in an interdependent reality? How much time is spent in confessing other people's sins, politicking, rivalry, interpersonal conflict, protecting one's backside, masterminding, and second guessing? It's like trying to drive down the road with one foot on the gas and the other foot on the brake!"

I remember well a divorced contractor with three children coming into my office to discuss budgeting issues. He was terribly in debt and made it clear during the course of our conversation that he expected me to lend him some money, thereby placing himself in even greater debt. As it was, his relatives and others were already bailing him out of holes left and right.

I tried to explore other options with him, but it soon became clearly self-evident that he was wrapped up in a martyr complex, with his indignant sense of deprivation, injustice, and bitterness. He felt everyone had it out for him and was taking advantage of him. He did not exhibit any hope of digging his way out or any desire to change.

As we visited, I attempted to share with him some thoughts on the difference between successful and poor thinking, yet I still sensed he was going to spend many years struggling under the weight of never having a full and abundant life. All the strategies and tactics in the world won't help people if they can't learn to help themselves.

Poor Thinking Surrounds Us

Common sense is becoming less common. Poor thinking weaves its way into our daily thought processes. Much of our economic thinking is so destructive to the individual and to society that it might be considered "financial pornography." It's like the following poem:

> Vice is a monster of so frightful mien
> As to be hated needs but to be seen.
> Yet seen too oft, familiar with her face,
> We first endure, then pity, then embrace.

Alexander Pope
1688-1744, "Essay on Man"

We have done a lot of enduring and pitying since the 1960s, and some embracing, much of it destructive to self, family, and society. In the name of "tolerance" and "openmindedness" we have embraced a "politically correct" agenda which attempts to offend none for their differences and ends up introducing self-destructive thinking that denies any moral standards at all, legitimizing the illegitimate and amoral. Ironically, those of "tolerance" are most ready to label traditional values as "extremist." We are already seeing that the tremendous economic costs are only exceeded by the social costs. Our success level depends so heavily on our thoughts. Consider an example:

There were three applicants for the job to drive the stagecoach over treacherous terrain and down a narrow canyon pass. The first applicant was asked how close he could come to the cliff's edge without tumbling the stagecoach and its occupants down into the gorge below. He answered he could drive the stagecoach within three inches of the cliff and not go over.

A second applicant was summoned. When the same question was posed, the second applicant answered, "I could drive it so close that one of the rear wheels could be hanging over the cliff and yet I wouldn't fall over." The employer was impressed.

A third applicant was brought in and he responded, "I would stay as far away from the cliff as possible." Guess which one got the job?

Throw Out Imposters

Some of us do live our lives on the cliff's edge, always pushing the limits. We entertain destructive thoughts which eventually lead to acts. Those acts become habits. And those habits shape character. The most destructive thoughts are often the most enticing. In the economic realm they play on our greed, our emotions, and our desire to get something for nothing.

When a negative thought first knocks on the door of our mind, it is an imposter. Yet instead of banishing it immediately, we invite it in as though a treasured house guest and entertain it royally. Once we have entertained the imposter, it is much more difficult to ask it to leave. It is much easier *to avoid* the self-destructive, enticing thing when it first enters your mind as a thought, than *to resist* it when the thought has been entertained, contemplated, replayed, and acted upon. By then, it has become a habit, and is in the process of becoming part of your character.

Those who want to avoid the various bondages of addiction and mistakes know that they must stay as far away from the edge of the cliff as possible.

Conversely, if we fill our minds with the inspired thoughts of great men and women of centuries past, we will do well. If we fill our minds with the thoughts of those who have achieved notoriety in our own time, success is not so sure. Modern theories have yet to stand the test of time. And if they contradict the wisdom of the sages and prophets of the past, they are probably self-defeating delusions.

Look to those who built the most enduring monuments. Look to Abraham, Jesus, Mohammed, Buddha, and the founders of other great religions. Look to the Founding Fathers of the United States whose monument is a governmental system that has sparked the only truly great freedom the world has ever known.

In the world of art, we study the Michelangelos and the Da Vincis. In the world of inventions we study the Thomas Edisons and Alexander Graham Bells. In the world of political and economic freedom and social relationships, we study those who have built free civilizations—not those who are driving the world to hell with their foot on the accelerator.

Negative people do not have free agency or choices, simply because they can't "see" the choices. To the extent that people think negatively, their choices and freedom are curtailed. But those in the ghetto of poor thinking may get out if they are willing to submit their lives to hard work, integrity, belief, moral living, and *all* other correct principles. The horizon of our freedom expands the more we engage in choices which are congruent with timeless, correct principles. Your success level *reflects* how well you are thinking.

Your Insights, Feelings, and Action Items

A. As you read this chapter, what *insights* came that seem applicable to *you?*

  1._____
  2._____
  3._____

B. How did you *feel* as you pondered particular points of this chapter?

  1._____
  2._____
  3._____

C. What do you *feel* you should *do* as a result of this chapter?

  1._____
  2._____
  3._____

D. How might you solicit the aid of others in accomplishing "C" above?

_____
_____
_____

Chapter 33

How Successful Investors Think

How the Wealthy Invest Differently from the Average Investor

You already know that patience is one of the chief requirements for financial success. The impatient become greedy. The patient are those who understand that if you want to enjoy the shade, you have to plant the tree.

The average investor who does not have much money invests very differently from the wealthy. Why? The average investor feels a need to achieve a high rate of return, because he's been a consumer his entire life. Now he is 55, and he only has 10 years in which to fund his entire retirement. He's motivated by greed. He's impatient. And he wants to get rich quick. He's not focusing on his principal—he's focusing on his rate of return.

Now let's look at the wealthy investor. He has significant assets, so he feels no need to achieve a high rate of return. He can "afford" to be conservative. He focuses on his principal.

Let's look at an example. An average investor invests $1,000. Let's say he gets a 20 percent return every year. Even though that's a super percentage return, it is only $200 a year in interest, or $17 a month, or 45 cents a day, which feels like nothing. He wants a *50 percent* return on his money. *That* would feel significant!

Maybe you've said to yourself, "It's not worth the bother to invest at 5 percent over a year's time. It's just not worth the effort." That's the mentality of the small investor and children, the average investor, the investor who never accumulates anything.

Unfortunately, he attempts to force the investment. When the market is reaching an all-time high, he is saying to himself, "Oh, if I can just stay in the market a little bit longer, I can squeeze out a little bit more return." He tries to eke out that final 10 or 15 percent of the market. What happens? As he tries to "force the gain," he gets slaughtered. (It's been said that bulls can make money in the market, and bears can make money in the market, but the pigs get slaughtered.)

The wealthy investor, on the other hand, feels no need to take on the additional risk when the market is reaching an all-time high. He's not trying for spectacular returns. He's got a lot and doesn't want to lose it. He focuses on his principal. That is the number-one difference between how the wealthy invest and how the average invest. The wealthy have patience; the average tries to force the gain because of his own impatience and greed.

How can you break the cycle? Focus on your principal, on your savings rate, on how much are you accumulating. Let the return take care of itself. Focus on whether you are saving 10 or 20 or 25 percent of your income each year. Focus on how much you are socking away. Set that as your goal, commit to it, then forget about it—and just let your investments grow.

Watch Your Plan, Not the Markets

One of the silliest things I observe mutual fund investors do is look up their fund values in the daily newspaper. Why do they watch the market? Are they going to sell if the market is down? Does the fund's price movement matter *at all*? What difference does a daily change in value make? Perhaps it would make sense if they were stock traders, though terribly little. But mutual funds are *long-term* investments.

People shouldn't even invest in mutual funds if they aren't in for the long haul. Mutual funds are for reaching goals five to 20 years into the future, so what do daily (or even *annual*) fluctuations have to do with anything? *If* you believe the market will climb *over the years*, then you should invest, balance across several asset classes, and forget.

Pay attention to your financial plan and those things you *can* control. You *can't* control the market—and the more you look at it, the more you are likely to fret and make the dumb mistake of buying when the market is up and selling when it is down. Most susceptible to this poor thinking are *traders* of mutual funds: those who buy no-load funds high and sell low.

Avoid the meaningless price quotes: Even quarterly or annual statements are often only days away from a dramatically different story. Focus on your long-term prudent *plan, not* the markets.

Why You Must Learn to Sell at a Loss

Few people realize that paper losses are real losses. When my friend Lee's investment went down, his stockbroker tried to save face by telling Lee, "This isn't a real loss. This is just a paper loss. You haven't incurred a real loss until you've sold it." My response when Lee told me the story? "Baloney. When your asset has lost value, you have incurred a real loss. The new value shows up on your balance sheet, and whether or not you have recognized it for income tax purposes is irrelevant—you have lost. Your net worth has gone down."

But Lee insisted, "Yes, it's down, but I'm going to hold on to this stock until it goes back up." And what happened to his stock? It kept falling.

He just didn't understand that paper losses are real losses if the ship is sinking. This predicament requires a level of discipline and commitment to preset trigger points against which you will sell at a loss.

The question is not whether an investment has fallen. That is completely irrelevant. It has *nothing to do* with the decision you need to make. The relevant question is whether the investment is going to continue to fall, or whether it's going to start climbing. You must analyze where the investment is going in the future.

If it's going to keep falling, sell. Take your loss. If it's going to start climbing, hold on to it—*if* it's going to climb faster than your other investment alternatives. If not, sell it.

Why You Must Learn to Sell at a Profit

You must also learn to sell at a profit. Why? The same problem exists. Seth's investment was climbing. He invested $1,000, and his investment climbed to $2,000. His accountant said he couldn't afford to sell, because the tax bite would be too large. That's why accountants are accountants, and not portfolio managers.

Once again, the only relevant question is where the investment is headed. If it's going to fall, it's better to sell it and pay your taxes than to allow it to fall. On the other hand, if it's going to climb, you should hold on to it *if*:

- You don't have any better options. (If you do, you should probably sell this one and invest there.)
- Your portfolio is properly balanced. However, if too much of your portfolio performance is riding on the success of that single investment, then it may make sense to sell so you can improve your portfolio structure, minimize portfolio risk, and improve performance overall.

Greed and Speculation

Two emotions exist in the marketplace: fear and greed. Greed is impatient and short-sighted, and works against long-term success. When does greed most drive the market? When does greed most drive you? When the market's going up. We call this speculation.

What place does speculation have in a portfolio? The great Canadian industrialist N. Eldon Tanner advised, "Don't invest in speculative ventures. The spirit of speculation can become intoxicating. Many fortunes have been wiped out by the uncontrolled appetite to accumulate more and more. Let us learn from the sorrows of the past and avoid enslaving our time, energy, and general health to a gluttonous appetite to acquire increased material goods."

When you invest on speculation, you invest without fundamental value; you're completely dependent on the whims of the marketplace. What kinds of items have no fundamental value? Baseball cards. Art. Rare coins. Rare stamps. Race horses. The odds of items like this going up in value are based more on chance and investor psyche than on anything intrinsic in the investment itself.

There are only a handful of people who use the term "play the market":

- Stockbrokers and journalists who've never had any of their own money on the line, but who are giving advice to others. (That's right—they're literally "playing" with your money.)
- Speculators.

- The naive.
- Those who come by their money too easily.

Most of us have worked hard for what we have, which is why we shouldn't speculate.

What are the differences between speculation and investing? Speculation is focused on the short term; investing is focused on the long term. People who speculate are motivated by greed; people who invest are motivated by prudent accumulation. Speculation is emotional; investment is logical. Speculation is characterized by an insatiable appetite to get more, quickly; investment is characterized by patience. Speculation is intoxicating and addicting; investment is studied and reasoned. Speculation focuses on the rate of return; investment focuses on the principal. Finally, speculation doesn't understand risk; investment has calculated it.

When the speculative bubble bursts, it bursts big. Unfortunately, *those looking at the bubble from within, can't see it.* As the saying goes, "If you invest in fever, your profit is disease."

SPECULATION	INVESTING
short-term	long-term
greed motive	prudent, accumulation motive
emotional	logical
insatiable appetite	patience
intoxicating/addicting	could do without
focuses on rate of return	accumulating principal
doesn't understand risk	appreciation for risk

There are three basic priorities of investing: Number one is the **safety of principal.** Number two is **return**—either through income or growth. (Will Rogers quipped, "I am more interested in the return *of* my money than the return *on* my money.") And number three is **tax advantage.**

Many people foolishly focus on tax advantages above rate of return or safety of principal. A classic example are the investors who got burned in limited partnerships during the 1970s and 1980s. What happened? Everyone was focusing on the tax advantages of limited partnerships. They got shelter from tax, but lost their money.

I remember sitting down with Art Stowe in a data-gathering session in the mid-1980s—just as limited partnerships were heading for trouble.

As we looked over Art's limited partnership agreement, he asked me to evaluate it.

Here's what I found: Art made his original investment eight years earlier. And that was supposed to be the end of it. He shouldn't have had to invest any more in this real estate project. But every year he got a letter from the general partners demanding another $5,000 to $10,000; if he didn't pay, he would forfeit his interest in this tax shelter. Now he wondered whether he should keep paying.

I read over the partnership agreement. The partnership agreement specified that 100 percent of the expenses were to be attributed to the limited partners—but that the limited partners got only 50 percent of the income (gains). The other 50 percent of the income went to the general partners.

Where were the economic incentives for this program? Were the economic incentives of the general partners *in alignment* with Art's economic incentives? That's one of the criteria by which you need to evaluate any investment. Obviously, the general partners had no economic incentives to keep their expenses low. They weren't the ones paying the expenses. The partnership was structured from the beginning so that they could continue assessing the limited partners. There was simply no reason not to. When I pointed that out, Art responded, "Well, it needed to be structured that way, because we're the investors and we're the ones who need all the tax write-offs. The general partners don't need the tax write-offs." That, of course, was what the general partners had told him.

People invest that way all the time. A promoter or developer claims to not need the tax write-offs—but claims the investor does. So the investor takes all the tax advantages (losses), and the general partners or the promoters end up with most of the growth, income and real returns. Going back to the orange juice metaphor, the general partners get all the juice, and the limited partners end up with the pulp. That's not the way to accumulate money—you need to share the juice, not the pulp.

When are people most motivated by greed? When the stock market or the bond market or the real estate market starts climbing. When the press gets involved. When *Money* magazine and *Time* and your local newspaper start writing about a certain investment.

That's when the small guy gets into the market. He's motivated by greed and hopes to make a fast buck. But what happens? He simply bids up the prices during the last phase of a bull market. When the small guys start getting into the market, you know for sure that it is nearing a peak.

There is *no* place in a portfolio for speculation and its partner greed. A person who has worked hard accumulating his capital is generally smart enough so he *won't* risk it on speculation. The one who has a lot of capital *can't* risk it on speculation. And the one who doesn't have capital *shouldn't* risk it on speculation.

Simply put, no one should speculate. No one.

Beware the Lien on Your Portfolio

So, you think you're out of debt? Think again. People often come in and tell us that their balance sheet is completely debt-free—they don't owe a dime on their mortgage, cars, credit cards, or to anyone.

You need to understand that you have a lien on your portfolio, whether your portfolio is within a pension or a profit-sharing plan, an IRA, a variable annuity, or simply mutual funds. And that lien must be paid before you can own any of your money free and clear.

What is it? It is what you owe the IRS on your gains. You will never be able to do anything with "your" money until after the IRS has received their portion of "your" profits.

I encourage people to own their assets. It's often better to pay your taxes and own your property free and clear than it is to keep your money locked up forever, and never be able to do anything with it. In other words, sometimes it is better to go ahead and pay the tax man so that your money is available for better portfolio strategies, than it is to keep your money locked up in an inferior asset out of fear of having to pay taxes.

You and your professional financial adviser *do* need to understand the tax implications of any investment. All rates of return must be adjusted for their tax implications and should be compared using after-tax numbers. That is not the responsibility of your portfolio manager or investment adviser; it's your responsibility and your financial planner's.

Your Insights, Feelings, and Action Items

A. As you read this chapter, what *insights* came that seem applicable to *you?*

1._____

2._____

3._____

B. How did you *feel* as you pondered particular points of this chapter?

1._____

2._____

3._____

C. What do you *feel* you should *do* as a result of this chapter?

1._____

2._____

3._____

D. How might you solicit the aid of others in accomplishing "C" above?

_____

_____

_____

Decision Seven

Make Your Dream
Your Reality

Chapter 34 discusses why achieving goals habitually is essential for those who would find Money Happiness. Chapter 35 then discusses how to combine the principles and strategies in this book for success. Finally, an action plan is outlined for applying the key principles and strategies.

Chapter 34

How to Achieve Goals Habitually

Your Goals Must Ignite Something Deep Within

Why is it so important to become a goal-oriented person? Why is goal orientation one of The Seven Core Decisions? Because being goal-oriented is the process by which your abstract life mission and purpose is translated into a concrete reality. It is *how* we *become* our vision. Those who are not goal-oriented wander aimlessly—"If you don't know where you're going, any path will get you there."

So, goal achievement is the means for your vision to be translated into your reality. If you have had trouble living within a budget, getting out of debt, developing certain character traits, or following any of the other principles or strategies in this book, then becoming a goal-focused person is the *how* of success.

What distinguishes people who regularly achieve their goals from those who don't? People who are habitual goal achievers understand the goal-striving process and live a motivated life.

A goal has to have meaning. It must come from the heart. When you *need* to do something, it comes from your mind. But when you *want* to do something, it comes from your heart. You get emotionally involved.

Inspired. And only when a goal is deeply internalized emotionally—when you desperately *want* it—will you expend the tremendous energy required to achieve it.

In this sense, you can't *think* of a goal, you must *feel* a goal. There is no inspiration in logic.

How, then, can you become so motivated, so energized, so emotionally driven by your goals—your *wants*—that you're willing to pay the price to achieve them? That you are willing, as spelled out in earlier chapters, to break old habits, to blast out of your comfort zone, to endure unpleasant tasks along the way? How can you turn dreams into goals—and, eventually, into reality?

The Islamic religion has five pillars or practices that might serve to illustrate the importance of goals. One of the five pillars is the practice of praying toward Mecca, their holy city, five times every day. In these moments, the faithful turn their hearts and minds toward their God with full attention. Their devotion is exemplary. *Anyone*, whether religious or not, would gain tremendous strength and discipline by pausing a moment five times a day and focusing intently with both mind and heart on a single chosen purpose or goal.

Develop Your Master Plan

Take time to set a master plan. To start, ask yourself: Where do I want to be three years from now? Five years from now? What kind of person do I want to *be* (not *seem*) physically, mentally, socially, emotionally, spiritually, and financially? Create a vivid picture of yourself in these six different areas of your life. Determine whether you want to match that picture badly enough. It takes vision to see the future, vivid visualization to see yourself doing it, creative imagining, and emotional commitment.

Use that vivid mind-picture to develop a master plan. *Write it down—* "A goal not written is only a wish." Break your goal into yearly goals. Break your yearly goals into quarterly goals. From there, break your goals into monthly, weekly, and daily goals. Attach numbers. Make yourself accountable.

Put a Cost on the Goal

Have you ever really done that? You need to literally determine how much the goal will cost in terms of time, effort, and money. (Consider all three, because you'll have to spend all three.) Break your goal into daily steps. How much time, effort, and money will you need to spend each step of the way to achieve that goal?

Assess Your Willingness to Pay That Cost

You've attached a cost to your goal—are you willing to spend that much? If you want the goal, you have to pay the price, just as with anything else in life. What about burnout? Three factors help avoid burnout: focus, consistency, and intensity. *Your achievement will be dependent on the intensity and consistency of your focus on your goals.*

Break Your Goal Down into Daily Steps

Those are your Fixed Daily Activities (FDAs), your Key Result Areas (KRAs). Having daily goals creates a sense of urgency. A three-year, two-year, one-year, or even a quarterly or monthly goal does not exact nearly the accountability or demands.

Effective people plan their next day's activities the night before. They constantly prioritize their "to do" list, focusing on what is truly important, not merely urgent. They are careful not to put those things that matter most at the mercy of those that matter least. They are wise in not letting others' priorities usurp their own commitments. They are cautious before making commitments, but once having made commitments they do not let tangents distract them. They learn to say "no" to distractions.

Establish Self-Enforcing Mechanisms

Once you have attached a cost to your goal, determined that you are willing to pay the price, and broken the goal into increments, you need to establish some kind of self-enforcing mechanism. Why? When I have relied on myself alone to achieve my goals, I have fallen short. When I have established self-enforcing systems that made me account for my progress, I did better. Remember, though, you need to voluntarily submit yourself—in essence, give up your freedom to act in any other way than one that helps you meet your goal. You do this willingly when you deeply *want* your goal.

Want some examples of self-enforcing mechanisms? I have tried many. One of the most productive was posting my written goal on the wall of our bedroom where Julie could see it. I always share my goals with someone else, because that creates commitment. Publicize your goal. Let other people know about it. There's another reason why you should let people know about your goal: Significant goals require long hours, tremendous emotional effort, and occasional financial investment. Things will go much more smoothly if the important people in your life are on your team.

A goal is a *minimum*, not a maximum. It is something you are going to achieve, **no matter what**, unless you are dead or disabled. That is pretty intense. And if you're going to have that kind of intensity, the people around you need to be on your side. Your family, especially, needs to back you up. Ideally, they need to share your level of emotional commitment and drive. If the important people are not on your side, it will be much tougher to achieve your goal.

We have talked about Charles Lindbergh and how two pilots disappeared in the Atlantic not long before his attempt. An editor who read every newspaper clipping about Lindbergh's flight saw a cover story with the banner headline, "Lindbergh Flies the Atlantic Alone." In response, he wrote an editorial that began:

> Alone? Is he alone at whose right side rides courage? Who has skill sitting within the cockpit and faith upon his left hand? What is solitude to him who has self-reliance to show the way and ambition to read the dials? Does he lack for company for whom the air is cleft by daring, and darkness is made light by enterprise? True, the bodies of other men are absent from his crowded cabin. But as his aircraft keeps its course, he holds communion with those rarer spirits whose sustaining potency gives strength to his arm, resourcefulness to his mind, and contentment to his soul. Alone? *With what more inspiring companions could he fly?* (from *The Glory of the Sun*, by Sterling W. Sill, 1961)

When your spouse understands what is really required for you to achieve your goal, he or she will start helping you focus on what really counts.

Measure Performance

You have to keep score and be *accountable*. A goal must be measurable and quantifiable. If you can't measure it, you will never know when you have achieved it. So, you must work to make even subjective or qualitative goals measurable in some objectively determined way.

Remember: "When performance is measured, performance improves. When performance is measured *and* reported, performance improves most." This explains why even subjective goals need to become quantifiable in some way.

You must set a date, a deadline for achieving your goal. Without accountability and a deadline, you cannot know whether or not you have achieved the goal.

If you are keeping score on yourself, you may be tempted to cheat—just a bit. But what happens when you play these games with yourself? Isn't it a little like cheating at solitaire? When you set a goal, you need to be brutally honest with yourself and those around you as to whether you are reaching it.

Goals Must Be Aligned

If you want to achieve a goal, it must be *aligned* with your purposes in life, your deeply held beliefs. Let's imagine your goal is to become wealthy. If you consider money to be "filthy lucre," you are going to encounter some powerful, subconscious, self-defeating behaviors to keep you from reaching that goal. But if you consider money to be healthy and a tool for good, then you will probably achieve significant financial success.

Not only must your goals be aligned with your life's mission statement, but your *means*, how you accomplish the goal, must be aligned with your values. Your value system (honesty, integrity, etc.) sets the rules of "fair play" by which you will achieve your goals.

Balance Your Pursuit of Excellence

To be a success in reaching goals, you also need balance. This book talks a lot about financial or temporal goals. Your financial goals are only one aspect of the whole you. To be successful, you must be balanced. You need to pursue physical, mental, social, emotional, spiritual, *and* career or financial goals. When you are out of balance, you sell yourself short. Nothing works.

But is it even possible to pursue a high level of excellence in all aspects of your life so you are not out of balance? Yes. Is it tougher than working on an isolated aspect of your life? Without question. Does it take more time? Yes. Is it more emotionally demanding? Absolutely. Is it a challenge? Positively. But does it bring the ultimate sense of reward? Undeniably.

Manage Systems

People who achieve excellence in more than one area invariably follow a system. Simply, they reduce their goals to systems—then they develop systems in all areas of their lives. Certain hours are blocked out for certain things. Children, for example, know they will have their parents' undivided attention at certain times—and they can count on it. It's difficult getting the systems established at first, but it goes a long way toward guaranteeing success. *The successful person does not manage people—he manages systems so he can spend time with people.*

Goals: The Pursuit of Excellence
(Balance at a High Level)

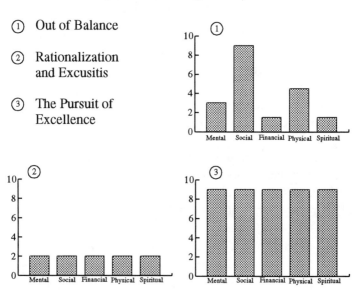

① Out of Balance

② Rationalization and Excusitis

③ The Pursuit of Excellence

Systematize

How serious are you about reaching your goals in life? If you are truly serious about your goals, you won't need to be taught the urgency of systematizing your operations. Constantly be thinking about how you can streamline your operations and all else that has to do with your success. *Success only becomes repetitive when it is systematized.*

To do this, you must not be an "unconscious competent" who is relying on luck for his success. I am especially concerned that work efforts must show your initiative and be systematized. As you develop systems for follow-up, you will achieve your goals.

For most people who don't report numbers on a regular basis toward achieving their goals, it takes a special kind of self-discipline to track your work hours, efforts, and results according to standards relevant for your career, eventually comparing those efforts to the standards you have personally established. Systems will help you do this. Systems can help you be more efficient and more effective with your time, thus increasing your earnings per hour. They provide a tracking vehicle, automate repetitive tasks, and provide quality control in your output. Only systems can provide the self-confidence and assurance that what you have accomplished in the past may be repeated.

Fine-tuning your systems assures you that your productivity can be increased from year to year. Early in my career I learned that I needed to find viable systems and then work those systems. The systems I chose were a significant part of my early success. I discovered that the systems worked, *but I didn't*. I didn't always work the system.

Later, one of the important realizations I came to was that I needed a system *that worked me*. So, I installed checks and balances with my wife, Julie, and I established other self-enforcing mechanisms and systems that would provide the constant flow of success I desired. By automating the processes, I was forced to work harder.

Systematize your practice, your career, your job position. Then work that system. If possible, establish systems that will work you. The person who will accept responsibility for his own success will systematize his life. People who have systematized their lives can spend more time with people.

Be Visionary

Perhaps you have heard the oft-repeated advice that a goal should be reasonable and attainable. That's true. But don't be held back by that advice. If you're too focused on making your goal reasonable, you may not reach high enough. Set a goal that requires you to really stretch. You may not dream enough. Robert Cavett said, "Any man who selects a goal in life which can be fully achieved has already defined his own limitations."

So you set a goal. You determine a price tag. You establish a target date. You double-check to make sure your goal is in alignment with your ultimate purposes in life, and that you are maintaining balance.

Achieving goals requires sequencing. If you want to get up at 6:00 every morning, you need to first master going to bed at 10:00. If you want to be honest with others, you must first develop the habit of becoming brutally honest with yourself.

It is time to take a critical look at your plan. Are your yearly goals congruent with your three-year master plan? Are you focused? Are your emotions involved? Have you internalized your commitment? Do your goals afford balance? Are they in harmony with your priorities?

There's a final question you need to ask about any goal. Is your goal significant? Motivating? Inspiring? Remember—a goal is not a "maintenance item." Buying a new car, for example, represents a maintenance item, not a goal. In other words, it is something you are naturally going to do as you are going through life. It is just like buying a new washing machine or buying a new living room set. You just do it.

A goal needs to recognize a real achievement. For most Americans beyond age 30, buying a car is not a major achievement in life. Is it really that inspiring? That significant? Is it something that causes you to leave a legacy?

If you want to achieve your goals in life, don't let anything stand in your way. Take responsibility for the hard work involved. Do not be distracted, but keep your eyes riveted on the goal. Achieving goals becomes a habit. *Not* achieving goals also becomes a habit. Make sure you establish the right one.

Your Insights, Feelings, and Action Items

A. As you read this chapter, what *insights* came that seem applicable to *you?*
   1._____
   2._____
   3._____

B. How did you *feel* as you pondered particular points of this chapter?
   1._____
   2._____
   3._____

C. What do you *feel* you should *do* as a result of this chapter?
   1._____
   2._____
   3._____

D. How might you solicit the aid of others in accomplishing "C" above?

   _____

   _____

   _____

Chapter 35

How to Combine These Principles for Complete Money Happiness

Of all the financial decisions you'll ever make, the most important might well be to put a financial professional on your side. Why? There are a number of convincing reasons.

A financial adviser will help you identify your goals and objectives, educate you about investments, insurance, estate planning, and taxes. A seasoned professional will help you improve your investment returns. A financial adviser can take care of the things you don't have time to take care of, help make your financial life simpler and more convenient.

So, what kind of adviser should you look for? Good question. There are all kinds. Some operate out of the trunk of their car. Some are part of a one- or two-man shop. Some belong to large firms that have access to specialists and resources—such as computer systems and data banks.

Financial advisers are no different from other professionals. Some are generalists, and some are specialists. Although the tag of *specialist* is no guarantee, it does suggest an additional level of advanced training, knowledge, or interest in a particular subject area.

There are specialists in estate planning, insurance, investments, retirement planning, employee benefit plans, business planning, and cash flow management, to name a few. Ideally, a financial planner should be well trained in at least one or more of these areas. But be careful: Some well-experienced generalists may know more than many self-anointed specialists.

A financial planner should specialize in a comprehensive financial planning methodology. Just as a CPA/auditor follows a specific method when auditing the books of a company, the financial planner should follow a specific methodology for gathering data, assessing and analyzing the data, preparing written recommendations, implementing those recommendations, and providing ongoing monitoring and follow-up. It is this specialty in a methodology that allows a comprehensive planner to quarterback an overall plan, and draw upon the resources of other specialists.

Choose the Right Financial Planner

What do you look for when choosing a financial planner? You need to find a financial planner with a rudder. A rudder?

A lot of financial planners consider it smart to travel on the "fast track." They've set their sails, and they're moving full speed ahead a hundred miles an hour with the wind in the sails. So, how do you find one with a rudder that can stay on course?

Unfortunately, many two- or three-man financial planning companies latch onto the latest fads. They're the ones sailing full speed ahead while large, national financial institutions seem to lack speed in comparison. They're old and stodgy. But what's really happening?

Conservative companies are steering with the rudder. They're conservative because they have a reputation to maintain. Because they don't want to get sued. Because they have the back-up—the legal and financial support staff—to provide the rudder for their financial advisers. They don't get tossed by the whims of financial fads.

Contrary to what the popular press may say, never assume that so-called objectivity and independence are the supreme virtues. Of far greater supremacy are conservatism, integrity, competency, trust. Of greatest importance is a rudder set to the timeless correct principles we have discussed. Find a planner with a rudder, one whose competence, integrity, outlook, and philosophies have been presented in this book. You will want one who has the character traits presented in Chapter 13, and who cherishes his individual freedom the way you do yours. A planner who isn't already on the road to security and success, can't lead you there. One who doesn't know how to set goals and achieve them himself will be ineffective in helping lead you toward yours.

A couple of tell-tale questions: (1) Does he think you should borrow out your home equity and invest it so it is "working harder"? If yes, stay away. (2) Does he believe you would be better off if you replaced your whole life policies, bought term insurance, and invested the difference? If yes, politely excuse yourself and leave. This book has taught you how to discern sense from nonsense.

Here are other questions you should ask:

How Much and What Kind of Service Do I Need?

Are you looking for comprehensive financial planning? Portfolio management? Estate planning? Insurance advice? Retirement planning? Asset protection strategies? Tax advice? Or something else? You need to find an adviser that specializes in the services you need—or that is part of a firm large enough to provide specialists for you. The vast majority—80 to 90 percent—of financial planners come from organizations of five or fewer. Many are not trained in areas other than life insurance sales or stock trading.

A financial planner may be able to provide you additional and broader services if he has a relationship with other financial planners within a large organization or a major financial institution. (For some, an affiliation with a major financial institution is looked upon as an evil conflict of interest. But, I often observe that such an affiliation provides an anchor and a rudder, which is preferable to having a loose gun on the deck of your financial ship.) Don't discount the value of these services.

Is the Adviser Properly Licensed?

To become a financial planner, certain state requirements must be met to show minimum knowledge of the industry. Financial planners give investment advice, and must therefore become registered as investment advisers. Financial planners often offer various insurance and securities products, so they must also pass the state insurance exam and several exams given by the National Association of Securities Dealers. Financial planners must also meet state and federal continuing education requirements for most designations and licenses.

What Is the Adviser's Designation?

The adviser's designation tells you about his educational background. Designations include Chartered Financial Consultant (ChFC), Certified Financial Planner (CFP), Certified Public Accountant (CPA), Chartered

Life Underwriter (CLU), or attorney (JD), among others. These signify backgrounds in finance, business, accounting, insurance, and law.

Remember, though, that background is only one aspect of a planner. For example, you might naturally assume that CPAs have greater background in income tax than other professionals. But that's primarily due to their experience, not their CPA designation. Did you know that the CLU exam has more questions about taxation than does the CPA exam? As another example, the ChFC exam is clearly a broader and more rigorous exam (and therefore accredited like other colleges and universities) than the CFP designation, though CFP is marketed better and is more popular.

Even areas of specialty don't mean everything. CPAs, for example, major in accounting. College accounting courses take a historical perspective. They look at recorded historical data—which the CPA then records, puts on a form, and prepares as a financial statement or a tax return. Every business owner should have a good CPA who can assist with financial statements and money management. But that's not the same as a financial planner. Even colleges recognize finance and accounting as different majors. Financial planning is applied economics. It takes a futuristic approach. It is analytical and has a long-term strategic perspective. It's proactive, not reactive.

The worst financial advice comes from journalists. They are notorious for describing an extreme market position, emphasizing the sensational in order to sell magazines. In my view, journalists are more concerned with making a story than reporting one. Seldom do I read the complete facts as given to the reporter, but rather a hazy half-truth intended to make a warped yet sensational point. Seldom do I find good judgment. Usually I find a pickle-sucker sitting on the fence pointing his finger of scorn at those in the arena who live with media judgments day to day. No wonder consumers feel like ping pong balls.

Planning your financial future by a magazine is like reading a medical dictionary and then performing surgery on yourself.

Is the Adviser Competent?

Ask how long the adviser has been in business—and the breadth and depth of his experience. An exam, degree, or designation will not make anyone an expert in financial planning. Even the designations listed above provide only a basic level of knowledge about financial planning. Expertise is seldom acquired under the tutelage of any professor, book, or designation. It comes only after long years of advanced studies combined with many years of intense application in the real world.

I regularly discover financial planners with years of experience and who have participated in extensive in-house training programs who have more prudent insights and judgment than others who simply hold the recognized designations. I'll take experience over designations anytime, though I would prefer a planner who had both.

But of more value than either designations *or* experience, is a rudder, an anchor, a philosophical commitment to timeless principles of wisdom, prudence, balance, and freedom.

Does the Adviser Have High Ethical Standards?

Look for membership in at least one industry organization that enforces a code of ethics. According to the Investment Advisers Act of 1940, a person in the business of giving investment advice must register as an investment adviser and must abide by established standards of ethical business conduct.

How do you deal with conflicts of interest, which exist with every professional, not just financial planners?

Everyone has biases, philosophies, professional opinions shaped by years of experience and exposure to ideas. For example, a physician may recommend medication instead of surgery if he owns the pharmacy attached to his clinic. Architects and contractors have conflicts of interest as they prescribe building approaches. CPAs and attorneys have conflicts of interest as they recommend services. Journalists would have us believe that they are the only ones *without* a conflict of interest (all they have to do is to sell newspapers and magazines). *But*, do *any* of the examples above indicate that the professional acted improperly? No.

So how do you deal with them? Ask. Have them disclosed to you. Request a comparison of various fees, loads, charges, and expenses that might be associated with each particular recommendation from your financial adviser. After understanding the impact of the up-front transaction costs of each alternative recommendation, you are in a better position to make a sound decision.

In my experience, contrary to what some would have us believe, the answer to this dilemma is not the legislating away of potential conflicts of interest, but reasonable disclosure. Attempting to legislate away potential conflicts of interest once again puts the government in the position of knowing what's best for the consumer. I believe that, with disclosure, the consumer is perfectly capable of choosing how to do business.

He realizes that he may be buying convenience, simplicity, service or a whole host of other things when he chooses to do business.

Is the Adviser Committed to Continuing Professional Education?

Laws governing finance and taxes are complex and constantly changing. Now add the fact that the economy fluctuates regularly. How many hours each year does the adviser spend staying on top of things? If he holds a professional designation or maintains membership in a professional association, he is probably required to complete a number of hours each year in formal continuing education.

Is There a Satisfied Client Base?

Ask if the adviser will give you client referrals. Want an easy way to find out if clients are satisfied? Find out how long the average client stays. Advisers may be hesitant to disclose the names of many clients for reasons of confidentiality or because they don't want them called all the time. In that case, perhaps some clients have allowed themselves to be quoted in a firm brochure. If you really need to talk to someone, go ahead and ask. The adviser should give you several names.

What Is the Average Client Like?

Assume you earn $50,000 a year. If the adviser primarily deals with people who earn $150,000 a year, will you get the attention you need? Does the adviser primarily work with professionals, business owners, middle-income clients, women? Do you fit the profile? Will the adviser meet your specific needs—or is he part of a firm that's large enough to handle all types of clients?

Is the Adviser a Full-time Professional?

Be wary of people who are part-time, lack membership in professional societies, ignore continuing professional education, and criticize others who do commit to high standards. There is a proliferation of those types—they are multiplying like rabbits.

Beware the friend who took a quickie course, got a quickie insurance license, and now wants to replace all your existing policies. You may be better off to write him a quickie check for a thousand bucks and send him on his way. It would be a lot cheaper.

How Is the Adviser Compensated?

Financial planners may receive fees, commissions, or both, in four possible ways. This distinction is important to you, because it may affect your cost and the service you receive.

"Fee-only" planners charge a fee for their services, but don't receive a commission when you purchase a product. The advantage is that you may get more objective advice. The disadvantage is that the planner may have little incentive to make sure you follow through by implementing the plan, and may lack the ability to coordinate all facets of its implementation. He may also be inexperienced when it comes to actually implementing the plan—dealing knowledgeably with insurance companies, stock brokerages, etc. And you will probably end up paying the product company an additional fee for implementation—after already paying the fee-only planner. In essence, you're paying twice for the same service.

"Fee-based" planners charge you a fee that's enough to fairly compensate for planning work, but they may also get a commission on any products you purchase. By law, their "engagement letter" must disclose conflicts of interest and all terms relating to the engagement, allowing you five business days for a full refund of any fees paid. The disadvantage here is that you will need to be sure you understand fees, loads, charges, and expenses of any recommendations offered. The advantages will probably include increased convenience, one-stop service, broader competencies, and increased influence when it comes to representing your needs with major financial institutions. And you'll probably not be paying double when it comes to implementing recommended product purchases: both a fee to the planner for oversight and a commission to the product salesperson.

"Fee-plus-commission" planners sometimes charge a fee, but most of their compensation comes from commissions. So, what's the difference between a "fee-based" planner and a "fee-plus-commission" planner? In my experience, the fee-based planner initiates *virtually every* engagement by charging a fee significant enough to provide a comprehensive financial plan. By contrast, the "fee-plus-commission" planner is set up to charge fees, but seldom does it unless you *insist* on paying him one—99 percent of the time he is commission only. As a result, although he will suggest a comprehensive engagement, he must be focused more on insurance and investment products.

"Commission-only" planners don't charge any fees; their only pay is commission from the products you purchase. (Remember, even most commission levels are government-regulated to balance consumer and industry interests.) Commission-only "planners" are seldom planners at all, but are focused solely on the products they sell. (Having said that, I have usually found very competent, thorough, and ethical CLUs, ChFCs and CFPs.)

Find a Planner Who Will Perform

What difference can the right planner make? Consider the following scenario: Chris was a CPA, had spent time with a "Big 6" accounting firm, and had risen during his 30-year career to become Chief Operating Officer of a company that employed many thousands. We visited, and I explained our services. We met in his home to gather some data, and as I was leaving he said, "Hank, by the way, here's a copy of a financial plan prepared by the accounting firm I was with years ago. We still use them for our corporate work. Maybe you'll find this plan helpful in your analysis."

I looked at the plan, which was less than six months old. I asked Chris, "Why don't you work with them? How much did you pay for this?" "Well, Hank, even though I paid $5,000 for this plan, it's just been gathering dust on my shelf. No follow-through. I'd rather start over with someone who'll get the job done."

True story, no kidding. He had the right CPA firm for the big corporate work, but they didn't get the personal job done. (Ironically, I had just finished an engagement with that Big 6 firm a year previous to teach them how to add a "Personal Financial Planning Division" to their practice.)

It's important that you understand the differences in compensation, but don't get hung-up on it. Keep it in perspective with the other eight criteria for selecting a planner. It's far more important to hire a planner who cares, who can be trusted, who is competent, who shares your philosophies, and who gets you ahead financially. This can't be stressed enough.

No one approach to planner compensation instantly converts anyone into a paragon of virtue, competency, and trustworthiness. Stay away from those self-righteous individuals who have the audacity to judge someone else's integrity by how he is compensated; they are usually projecting onto someone else their own cynical thinking and motives. A competent and trusted commission-only planner who gets you ahead is forever better than any fee-only planner who loses your money. Don't be self-defeating and small-thinking, like the person who focuses more on what the planner earns, than on what he's earning by following the planner's advice. A good planner will be worth every penny he earns. It's like the sign on the wall: "I have no argument with others who sell their services for less. They know what their services are worth."

The Key to Working Effectively with Your Planner

After you've chosen a financial planner, how can the two of you work effectively? The number-one element of an effective relationship is trust. If you can't trust a financial planner, don't work with him. So, let's talk about trust. I've found that some people go through life cynical, suspicious, unable to trust anyone, always trying to determine if others are worthy of their trust. But, contrary to popular wisdom, trust is not something that is earned. Instead, trust is something bestowed by the person granting it. No one will ever truly *earn* your trust. You decide of your own accord to trust others.

Trust is a gift. Like beauty, it is in the eyes of the beholder. When our trust is betrayed, it is up to us whether and when we will grant it again. Let's not fool ourselves. We don't bestow our trust when somebody has earned it, but when we simply decide to bestow it. Like forgiveness, it is a reconciliation that we arrive at within ourselves, not with another.

Am I suggesting that you work with anyone who comes along? That would be foolish. What I *am* saying is that once you have selected a financial adviser, the only way to have an *efficient* relationship is through trust. Yes—I might get burned sometimes because I trust people. But I determined long ago that the cost of possibly being burned occasionally is far less than the efficiency with which I can conduct business if I trust those with whom I work. Those who go through life always suspicious, cynical, and distrusting of others' motives usually lead a very inefficient, expensive, and often litigious life. And quality people won't do business with them because they've got more rewarding relationships to maintain.

What do you do if you feel your trust has been breached? After receiving his written financial plan, Jason Nakagama immediately began to "shop" the advice that had been given amongst several planners for "second opinions." Without any thorough data-gathering sessions or extensive discussions of issues involved, the newly consulted advisers were eager to take potshots at the written plan. After all, it was there for all to see, and if they could sufficiently plant any seeds of doubt, they might land themselves a client.

By the time Jason was through talking to all his "second-opinion-advisers," all that was left was to express his outrage at how "wronged" he had been by his initial adviser.

Never mind that those rendering opinions hadn't done thorough data-gathering, operated off insufficient assumptions, and weren't even licensed to render advice in those areas. The planner was left with no choice but to terminate the relationship, and Jason remained confused and paralyzed in his efforts to progress.

Craig and Regina had a similar experience when another planner tried to discredit a financial plan. But they called and communicated honestly and openly. They scheduled a meeting and listed seven concerns about what the other planner said was "bad advice." They provided their planner with the opportunity to explain in more detail why certain assumptions had been made in the plan.

As a result, they learned new facts about the tax code which the other planner hadn't explained. Understanding mathematics, they welcomed their planner's offer to work through the numbers with them in detail. They came away with an enhanced level of trust and appreciation for the adviser they had originally chosen, such is how mature and efficient relationships are maintained.

So do your homework *before* selecting your adviser, and then *let* him do his job, with your trust. No one is perfect. Everyone has faults for all to see. Avoid unrealistic expectations from your planner. Be mature and open in your communications. Take responsibility for your decisions. Realize that he is merely giving advice and recommendations and doesn't have a crystal ball of the future. Understand that it is not a risk-free world, and even the best-laid plans may go awry. Expect and understand what constitutes wise and prudent advice. Seek out experienced judgment and insight, rather than simply knowledge of facts and designations. Look for a personality "fit."

Constructing Your Financial Plan: Who Does What?

Once you choose a financial planner, what happens then? Financial planning addresses everything that has to do with money. With your adviser's help, you'll leave no financial stone unturned. Should you refinance your mortgage? Should you buy or lease a car? What should you do with the inheritance from your grandmother? How can you get more tax-sheltered dollars out of your professional corporation?

Where do the answers come from? They come from the "subsets" of financial planning—things like cash flow management and tax planning. Let's look at a few of the most common.

Investment portfolio management. Entire college courses are built around portfolio management. Simply stated, your planner makes sure your portfolio is "balanced." In other words, you need both long-term and short-term investments; liquid and illiquid investments; tax-advantaged and non-tax advantaged investments. You should have some fixed-income investments—such as bonds, certificates of deposit, and money market funds—and some equity investments—such as stocks, real estate, and other tangibles. This achieves the balance we've discussed. Since different kinds of investments behave differently during different phases of the economic cycle, current conditions will dictate how your assets are invested: Is the economy growing? Are we experiencing inflation? Recession?

As part of portfolio management, your planner will discuss the pros and cons of different kinds of investments—stocks, bonds, money market funds, annuities, mutual funds, real estate, tangibles, limited partnerships, and certificates of deposit, among others. You will look at the whole thing in light of how much risk you can tolerate.

Income tax planning. Tax planning actually spans all parts of your financial plan, such as investment strategies, retirement planning, and estate planning. Specifically, you need to make sure you're maximizing all available deductions, exemptions, and credits to minimize your tax bite.

Risk management and insurance. As you recall, there are three basic things you can do with risk: You can avoid it, absorb it, or transfer it.

First, find out what you can do to avoid risk. Your planner might advise using trusts, family partnerships, or family corporations. He should tell you how to protect your assets from frivolous malpractice claims, frivolous creditors, and similar problems.

You might be willing to absorb some of the risks you can't avoid. For example, you might increase the deductibles on your auto insurance, homeowners insurance, or health insurance. In essence you are self-insuring for the amount of that deductible.

Finally, if you can't avoid or absorb a risk, you should transfer it—usually through some means of insurance. Your planner should do a complete review and analysis of all insurance you own—life, auto, homeowner, health, dental, malpractice, disability, and so on.

Education funding. There are three basic sources of education funding: cash flow dollars, dollars from tax savings, and compound interest dollars. You won't want to use cash flow dollars. They're the most expensive. Income tax savings and compound interest dollars are far less expensive—but require advance strategic planning. That's what your planner is for.

Retirement planning. How much should you save for retirement? And how will you do it? Your planner will discuss tax-qualified retirement plans—including IRAs, Keoghs, 401k plans, 403b plans, corporate pension and profit-sharing plans. You'll also want to look at non-tax-qualified retirement plans, non-qualified deferred compensation plans, selective incentive plans, and tax shelters.

How do you know what's best for you? It's called "sensitivity analysis." It looks at your retirement goals. When you want to retire. Your income objectives. Inflation rates. Varying rates of return. The answers help determine how much you need to save—at what rate of return.

Estate planning. You'll start with wills. Trusts. Estate distribution issues. But that's not all. A good planner will help you construct a plan so you avoid estate taxes. Too few people worry about estate taxes. They're too far away. Too intangible. But the only way to avoid them is to strategically plan for them today.

What Is the Financial Planning Process?

Financial planning involves five basic steps: data gathering, plan preparation, plan presentation, plan implementation, and on-going monitoring.

Data gathering. Data gathering is a marathon. It usually takes place at your home. It may take two hours or all day. Your planner will need to examine all your documents: Tax returns. Balance sheets. Income statements. Employee benefit plan booklets. Retirement plan documents. Wills. Trusts. Insurance policies. Investment statements. Brokerage house statements. Bank statements. These are the tangible bits of information.

But there's also subjective information, such as: What are your lifestyle goals? How do you want to distribute your estate? At what age do you want to retire? How much income do you want during retirement?

Then there are the assumptions that need to be figured into the whole process. What's going to happen to interest rates? Where is the economy headed? How much inflation will occur? Your planner will want your feelings on these things to see if expectations are realistic.

Finally, your planner will consider your personal attitudes—toward risk tolerance, toward tax aggressiveness, toward simplicity in your financial affairs. By the time all the data is gathered, your planner has a very good idea of where you are now and where you want to be.

Plan preparation. Preparing your plan typically takes three to four weeks, as the planner does an analysis—the diagnostic work. The planner knows where you are, and where you want to be. Now he needs to figure out the most efficient way to get you there.

For example, maybe it's a family partnership. Or a family corporation. Or a family trust. He'll look at all the pros and cons—then prepare written recommendations. Some will be major strategic recommendations. Others will be minor tactical recommendations. They will all fit together.

Plan presentation. After all the recommendations are in writing, your planner will present them to you. During the first interview, he'll spread the plan out in front of you and skim over the major areas. Then you'll take the plan home. Read it. Study it. Go over it with your spouse. Jot down any questions you may have about it.

When you get back together with your planner, you'll go over the plan in detail. He'll answer your questions. Clarify details. As you agree on each recommendation, your planner will prioritize them into an "Implementation Check List." It's simply a "To Do" list for you and your planner.

Plan implementation. The first three steps move quite quickly. In fact, you will probably get through them in about a month.

Step four, implementing the plan, takes a lot longer—usually about five or six months. During that time, you'll meet with your planner to go over tax planning, retirement planning, estate planning, and insurance issues. Your planner may bring in other experts—such as attorneys—to help resolve certain issues.

In the end, your plan might have as many as 25 recommendations. A few recommendations will be major, broad, strategic recommendations, each worth thousands of dollars to you. The remainder will be fine-tuning recommendations—crossing the T's, dotting the I's, and making sure your financial affairs are really in order.

On-going monitoring and maintenance. Here the planner should be retained to provide periodic updates and on-going advice. Perhaps there are a couple of tax-planning sessions each year, portfolio reviews, insurance updates, etc. Perhaps you need some questions answered about whether you should refinance your mortgage, lease or buy a car, etc.

So, What's a Planner Going to Cost You?

Fees for financial planners and advisers may range anywhere from $500 to $20,000, depending on how complex your plan is—and, as a result, how much time it takes to prepare and implement. Most planners charge a fee between 1.2 and 1.5 percent of your annual income, plus travel expenses.

Normally, half of the fee is paid at the end of the initial data gathering interview. Most planners collect the other half of the fee three or four weeks later when the planner presents his written recommendations to you. The fee generally covers a six- to eight-month engagement, including implementation oversight. Your planner should give you a written "engagement letter" that explains the scope of the engagement.

Because your plan will contain tax advice, investment advice, and business management advice, you should run the fee through your business if you can. A part of the fee may be tax-deductible. That means you may get the equivalent of a 30 to 40 percent discount on the fee. If you don't own a business, part of the fee may be deductible as a miscellaneous deduction on Schedule A of your tax return.

Also, focus on what you are getting from your planner's recommendations, not on what he is getting in the way of commissions. Jack and Yolanda, for instance, became extremely upset over a 3 percent commission on an annuity. Yet, the most they could get on their bank CDs, where their money was currently deposited, was 5 percent taxable income, or only 3 percent after taxes. In the annuity, they were able to earn 7 percent *tax-deferred*. The planner's recommendation earned them *far* more than if they had kept their money in CDs. They benefited from the change and the planner did as well. It was a win-win situation. Their concerns were self-defeating.

Focus on what *you* are getting, not on what your planner is getting. If you are better off, great. It's okay if he is better off, also.

Measurable Benefits of Having a Financial Plan in Place

You hire a planner. You pay a fee. What do you get in return? You get two very different kinds of benefits. You get psychological benefits, and you get monetary benefits.

The psychological benefits are yours. You keep them. They include things like increased peace of mind, progress toward reaching your goals, without worry about unfinished business.

What about the monetary benefits? This is how most planners must justify their existence, their employment. For now, don't even consider the long-term strategic benefits of having a plan. For now, look at just the first couple of years. The *typical* client will usually see a cash-on-cash, measurable, identifiable return of anywhere from eight to 30 times the fee. In other words, if your fee is $1,000, you will see anywhere from $8,000 to $30,000 in identifiable returns within the first 24 months. What kinds of returns? Income tax savings. Improved returns on investments. Savings on legal fees. Savings on insurance premiums. Increased cash flow. Can your planner guarantee that return?

No, of course not! That would be most unprofessional. But a good planner *can* guarantee that, regardless of what you see during the first few years, you will absolutely benefit in the long term from a solid, well-thought-out financial plan designed by a professional planner.

And a good planner should be busy enough with an already active clientele that he will guarantee that, if at the conclusion of the exhaustive data-gathering interview, he doesn't feel he can accomplish something for you that will be *very* meaningful, then he will bow out of the engagement.

No planner worth his salt wants to do busy work. You don't want to hire him to do busy work, and he doesn't want to do it. He is in his career because he loves what he does. He knows that his clientele only grows when he has satisfied clients, and they refer him to their colleagues and neighbors. To do that, he's got to have meaningful long-term client relationships, where they get ahead financially.

Only then, do all prosper. Only then, does your planner stay employed by his employer: you. Only then, do you introduce him to neighbors and colleagues.

And that is as it should be, because like all laws governing money happiness, everyone benefits from complying.

Your Insights, Feelings, and Action Items

A. As you read this chapter, what *insights* came that seem applicable to you?

1._____

2._____

3._____

B. How did you *feel* as you pondered particular points of this chapter?

1._____

2._____

3._____

C. What do you *feel* you should *do* as a result of this chapter?

1._____

2._____

3._____

D. How might you solicit the aid of others in accomplishing "C" above?

_____

_____

_____

Chapter 36

Action Plan on
The Seven Core Decisions

Review The Seven Core Decisions for Money Happiness and then develop an action plan to make them effective in *your* life. Do this by summarizing *your* notes at the rear of each chapter indicated:

I. Make Decisions By Happiness Criteria, Not Ego Criteria (See Chapters 1, 2, 3)
   1._____
   2._____
   3._____

II. Focus on Freedom (See Chapters 8, 9)
   1._____
   2._____
   3._____

III. Recognize that Character Counts (See Chapter 13)
   1._____
   2._____
   3._____

IV. Build a Solid Foundation for Security (See Chapter 16)

1._____

2._____

3._____

V. Climb the Right Ladder to Success (See Chapter 27)

1._____

2._____

3._____

VI. Avoid Poor Thinking (See Chapter 32)

1._____

2._____

3._____

VII. Make Your Dream Your Reality (See Chapter 34)

1._____

2._____

3._____

Consider the insights which came to you as you read each chapter. Reflect on how you *felt* as you pondered the principles. Make a decision *now* to implement *your* action plan.

The collective thoughts within this book mean little if not put into effect in the manner most appropriate for *you*, and then, only to the extent and in the manner *you* deem appropriate. By now, *your* insights and feelings have dictated to you a personal and customized plan most appropriate for *you* to achieve money happiness. As your mind and heart have been dictating, I hope your hand has been writing a recorded history. When coupled with a sincere heart, this is how, I believe, personal inspiration is received. I believe it is beyond the wisdom of academia or the world, but perhaps a divine message for you.

Whatever it is, it came from within you and yet beyond you. I didn't put it there, but *your* insights and feelings did.

Now own it. Accept responsibility for it. Develop *your* action plan. This is the way, I believe, to money happiness, security, success, and peace of mind.

Chapter 37

Action Plan on Governing Yourself: The 27 Foundation Strategies

Now let's consider the key applications of the correct principles. These 27 Foundation Strategies will take the principles and apply them to building a sound financial program. After each strategy: (1) note *your* score on how well you are currently doing with that item (0-10, with 10 being Very Well), and (2) note *how* you will implement that strategy in *your* financial program. Consider whether you should focus your efforts onto those areas you score lowest, or those areas most important to you. Then, make your own "To Do" list by prioritizing the order in which you will address each item.

Implementation Checklist

Score	How?	Priority Order

1. Understand Your Money Personality (Chapter 4)

_____   _____   _____

2. Determine Which Type of Person You Are—Spender or Saver (Chapter 5)

_____   _____   _____

3. Determine How You Will Make the WYHTE Phenomenon Work for You (Chapter 5)

_____   _____   _____

4. Establish a Budget According to Your Priorities (Chapter 6)

_____   _____   _____

5. Enact Strategies to Increase Cash Flow (Chapter 5)

_____   _____   _____

6. Accumulate Cash and Other Reserves (Chapter 6)

_____   _____   _____

7. Use a Circle-Two Mindset to Build Your Financial Freedom Fund (Chapter 5)

_____   _____   _____

8. Understand Your Marginal Tax Rate (Chapter 7)

_____   _____   _____

9. Establish a Plan to Avoid Debt (Chapter 10)

_____   _____   _____

10. Evaluate the Threats to *Your* Economic Future (Chapter 11)

_____   _____   _____

11. Involve Your Family; Establish Regular Family Council Get-Togethers (Chapter 12)

_____   _____   _____

12. List Strategies to Improve Your Career Opportunities (Chapters 14, 15)

_____   _____   _____

13. Evaluate Financial and Non-Financial Issues Relative to a Working Spouse (Chapter 14)

_____   _____   _____

14. Establish Strategies to Achieve Self-Reliance (Chapter 16)

_____ _____ _____

15. Commit to Live the Law of Tithing (Chapter 16)

_____ _____ _____

16. Provide for Home Ownership (Chapter 17)

_____ _____ _____

17. Review and Update Your Life, Disability, Health, and Other Insurance Programs (Chapters 18, 19, 20)

_____ _____ _____

18. Establish Appropriate Asset Protection Strategies (Chapter 20)

_____ _____ _____

19. Match Your Financial Freedom Fund to Your Retirement Analysis (Chapter 21)

_____ _____ _____

20. Manage Away Portfolio Risks (Chapter 22)

_____ _____ _____

21. Complete Your Estate Plan (Chapter 24, 25)

_____ _____ _____

22. Pursue Charitable Giving Strategies (Chapter 26)

_____ _____ _____

23. Establish College Savings Funds (Chapter 28)

_____ _____ _____

24. Enact the Tax Strategies Right for You (Chapter 29)

_____ _____ _____

25. Examine Mutual Funds vs. Variable Annuities vs. Variable Life (Chapter 30)

_____ _____ _____

26. Put Proven Portfolio Strategies to Work for You (Chapter 31)

_____ _____ _____

27. Get Professional Help (Chapter 35)

_____ _____ _____

Prioritize the above items to develop *your* Implementation Checklist. Then start doing one at a time. Don't be overwhelmed—realize that some of the above items are as simple as making a decision or examining a strategy.

Use These Available Resources

1. Order *Your Money Happiness Workbook* if you haven't already done so. As you complete the worksheets you will want to examine various strategies and record your financial information for getting yourself organized.

2. Order the Fax-on-Demand Index of *free* "Instant Reports" by calling (801) 263-1676 and requesting document #101. Also request the *free* "Index of Special Reports." (The Special Reports are available for a nominal charge.)

3. Check out the list of Recommended Resources that follow, on page 515, for additional resources that might interest you.

4. If you ordered the *free* Catalogue of Services from The American Financial Resource Center, determine whether any of those resources might be helpful to you. If you didn't order it, call 1-800-594-8913 or write:

> The American Financial Resource Center, Inc.
> Free Catalogue
> P.O. Box 573655
> Salt Lake City, UT 84157-3655

Now, *do it*! I sincerely wish you and yours the very best as you pursue your personal quest for Money Happiness. If the messages within this book have made sense to you, then share it with others.

Free Fax-on-Demand Documents from The American Financial Resource Center, Inc.

The following reports are available to you instantly, 24 hours a day, seven days a week. Simply call (801) 263-1676 *from your fax machine* and request the report numbers you want. They will be faxed back to you instantly. Because the list is constantly being updated, be sure you order the free indexes (reports #101, 102, 105, and 106) to see what is currently available. Those in **boldface** are our most requested reports.

101: **Index of Instant Reports for Individuals**
102: Index of Special Reports for Individuals
105: Index of Instant Reports for Business Owners
106: Index of Special Reports for Business Owners
110: **The Personal Financial Check-Up**
120: **The MoneyMax Profile—Your Money Personality**
121: **A Cash Flow Checklist for Individuals and Families**
122: An Analysis of the Economics of Leasing vs. Buying
128: Understanding Financial Leverage
129: The Rule of 78s
130: My Reputation Rankings of the Major Insurers
131: The Problem with A.M. Best's Surrender Cost Rankings
135: The Financial Strength Ratings of the Major Insurers
140: How to Choose an Insurance Company
141: Stock vs. Mutual Insurance Companies
142: Whole Life vs. Universal Life: Issues to Consider
145: The Leading Disability Insurance Providers
150: **The Amazing Selective Incentive Plan—the Retirement Plan Everyone Should Consider**
155: Real People Buy High, Sell Low—A Study of Investor Behavior
160: **The College Savings-Plus Information Kit**
161: Locating the Right College *For You*
162: Locating the Right Scholarships and Grants *For You*
163: Locating the Right School Loans *For You*
165: Policies with High Year-One Cash Values
166: A Thorough Analysis of Mutual Funds vs. Variable Annuities vs. Variable Life
170: Variable Life Competitive Rankings
174: Questionnaire to Assess Your Risk Tolerance Level
175: **How to Get Your Portfolio Analyzed for Optimal Performance**
176: What Is Market Timing? And How Does It Work?

177: How to Optimize Your 401k Plan
178: How to Optimize Your 403b Plan
179: A Chart Comparing the Attributes of Various Investments
180: Table of Cross-Correlations of Asset Classes
181: More About Portfolio Risk Measurements
190: Imputed Interest on Intra-Family Loans
191: The 1031 Tax-Free Exchange on Like-Kind Properties
192: A Checklist of Creative Real Estate Financing Techniques
193: How to Own Real Estate
194: How the $10,000 Gift Tax Exclusion Works
195: Creative Estate Minimization with Private Annuities
196: Estate Freezes and Section 303 Stock Redemptions
197: Generation Skipping Trusts to Save Estate Taxes
198: You Can't Have Your Cake and Eat It Too—Section 2036c
199: Financing Estate Taxes with Section 6166a
210: The Business Owner's Financial Check-Up
221: A Cash Flow Checklist for Business Owners
225: How to Prepare a Business Plan
226: How to Get Capital to Start Your Business
227: Sources of Capital for Your Business
230: How to Start a Home-Based Business
240: Issues to Consider in a Buy-Sell Agreement
241: How to Value Your Company
242: Succession Planning for the Closely-Held Business Owner
280: Children are Assets, not Liabilities
281: The Government Fiasco in the Savings and Loan Bailout
282: How the National Education Association Agenda Affects Our Nation's Economic Future
310: Rules and Regulations Governing Financial Planners
315: What Do Financial Planning Designations Mean?
320: How to Get Ahead with the *Making Sense* Newsletter from the Center of Resources for Economic Education and Development (CREED)
325: Workshops for Executives or Professionals from the Center of Resources for Economic Education and Development (CREED)
330: Corporate and Association Seminars from the Center of Resources for Economic Education and Development (CREED)
331: Low Cost Pre-Paid Financial Planning as a Corporate Fringe Benefit
335: A Financial Planning Engagement with The American Financial Resource Center—Your Coach for Money Happiness
340: Other Services from The American Financial Resource Center

Recommended Resources

I cannot name all the excellent resources available that might relate to money happiness. The following includes a partial listing. Often the author has other good books available, though I've recommended what are, in my mind, the best.

Decide for yourself which of the following might be most useful to you, based on your individual situation. When you see an asterisk, it indicates those resources that are exceptionally valuable to those seeking permanent money happiness.

Decision One: Make Decisions by Happiness Criteria, Not Ego Criteria

* Christensen, James P. and Clint Combs with George D. Durrant. *Rich on Any Income*. Christensen and Combs, Incorporated, 4525 South 2300 East, Suite 202, Salt Lake City, Utah 84117. 1985. The best, simplest, and most practical system for budgeting I've found. I recommend it for all my clients. But consider its advice in light of Chapter 6.

* Clason, George S. *The Richest Man in Babylon*. Penguin Books USA Inc., 375 Hudson Street, New York, NY 10014. 1926. Another classic. Everyone should read why and how to start a savings program. Will motivate you to get started and get a *Circle-Two Mindset*.

Gurney, Kathleen, Ph.D. *Your Money Personality*. Doubleday, New York. 1988. Insights from her research into nine money personalities, what financial strategies work for you, and how to interact with other personalities.

Hartman, Taylor, Ph.D. *The Color Code: A New Way To See Yourself, Your Relationships And Life*. Color Code Unlimited, 2028 East 7000 South, Suite 203, Salt Lake City, Utah 84121. 1987. A simple, yet most insightful means to understand your personality and relationships.

* Maltz, Maxwell, M.D. *PsychoCybernetics*. Pocket Books, A Division of Simon & Schuster, 1230 Avenue of the Americas, New York, NY 10020. Probably the best book ever written on self-image psychology.

Peck, M. Scott, M.D. *The Road Less Traveled*. Simon & Schuster, Rockefeller Center, 1230 Avenue of the Americas, New York, NY 10020. 1978. An inspiring discussion of traditional values.

Pond, Jonathan D. *1001 Ways to Cut Your Expenses*. Doubleday Dell Publishing Group, Inc., 1540 Broadway, New York, N.Y. 10036. 1992. A checklist of how to save money on everyday items. How to apply the WYHTE phenomenon.

* Sheldon, Charles M. *In His Steps*. Zondervan Publishing House, Grand Rapids, Michigan. 1967. The largest bestseller of all time, with over 60 million copies sold. A life-changing story *completes* any financial plan as it causes the reader to examine the motives that drive his life.

Decision Two: Focus on Freedom

Friedman, Milton. *Capitalism and Freedom*. The University of Chicago Press, Chicago, Illinois 60637. 1962. An excellent treatise on the connection between various economic/political systems and freedom, success, and progress.

Hamilton, Alexander, James Madison and John Jay. *The Federalist Papers*. The New American Library, Inc., 1301 Avenue of the Americas, New York, NY 10019. 1961. The thinking *behind* our constitutional form of government, which too many of us take for granted. Helps us appreciate their profound thinking and discern nonsense today.

Hattemer, Barbara, and Robert Showers. *Don't Touch That Dial*. Huntington House Publishers, P.O. Box 53788, Lafayette, Louisiana 70505. 1993. How the media is used to purvey subtle messages of many self-defeating behaviors.

Hayek, Friedrich A. *The Constitution of Liberty*. The University of Chicago Press, Chicago. 1960. A profound discussion on our constitutional system.

Klehr, Harvey, John Earl Haynes and Fridrikh Igorevich Firsov. *The Secret World of American Communism*. Yale University Press, New Haven. 1995. Lots of documented material about the pervasiveness of their influence in America, unknown generally before the fall of the Soviet Union. Not a light read.

* Lewis, C.S. *The Screwtape Letters*. Macmillan Publishing Company, 100K Brown Street, Riverside, New Jersey 08370. 1961. A classic with insights on how to discern the subtle and hidden agendas of others.

Lih, Lars T., Oleg V. Naumov and Oleg V. Khlevniuk. *Stalin's Letters to Molotov*. Yale University Press, New Haven. 1995. A collection of Stalin's letters to his trusted comrade, only made available after the fall of the Soviet Union. Documents the thinking of a man who sent three times as many people to their death as Hitler.

Mundis, Jerrold. *How to Get Out of Debt, Stay Out of Debt & Live Prosperously*. Bantam Books, 1540 Broadway, New York, N.Y. 1988. An excellent treatise discussing not just the pitfalls of debt but practical and effective concepts.

Novak, Michael. *The Spirit of Democratic Capitalism*. Madison Books, 4720 Boston Way, Lanham, Maryland 20706. 1982. Thoughtful and insightful.

Rand, Ayn. *Atlas Shrugged*. Penguin Books USA Inc., 375 Hudson Street, New York, NY 10014. 1957. The bestseller that still deserves wider reading. An engaging read. Highly recommended.

* Skousen, W. Cleon. *The Making of America*. The National Center for Constitutional Studies, P.O. Box 37110, Washington, D.C. 20013; (202) 371-0008. 1985. An inspired work about our founding fathers and their monument: America. Should be read by every high school student (and up) who loves his country and wants to love it more.

* Weaver, Henry G. *The Mainspring of Human Progress*. The Foundation for Economic Education, Inc., Irvington-on-Hudson, New York. 1947. This classic looks at economic history and correlates how economic and political progress *only* occurs within the environment of freedom.

Decision Three: Recognize that Character Counts

* Carnegie, Dale. *How to Win Friends and Influence People*. Pocket Books, 1230 Avenue of the Americas, New York, NY 10020. 1936. The classic. A must-read for anyone who lives, works, or socializes with other people.

* Cline, Dr. Victor B. *How to Make Your Child a Winner*. Walker Publishing Company, Inc., New York. 1980. Most practical guide to translate financial responsibility (and *any* responsibility) to your children.

* Covey, Stephen R. *The 7 Habits of Highly Effective People*. Fireside, Simon & Schuster Building, Rockefeller Center, 1230 Avenue of the Americas, New York, NY 10020. 1989. A modern-day bestseller that may become a classic—tremendous insights into correct principles.

Covey, Stephen R. *Principle-Centered Leadership*. Fireside, Simon & Schuster Building, Rockefeller Center, 1230 Avenue of the Americas, New York, NY 10020. 1990. For those who would lead others according to timeless, correct principles.

Mandino, Og. *University of Success*. Bantam Books, Inc., 1540 Broadway, New York, NY 10036. 1982. Finally, a collection of his writings and books—full of timeless, correct principles on success.

Sugarman, Joseph. *Success Forces*. Contemporary Books, Inc., 180 North Michigan Avenue, Chicago, Illinois 60601. 1980. Discusses the key forces that propel one to success in spite of himself. Very engaging—you'll see yourself here.

Decision Four: Build a Solid Foundation for Security

Bolles, Richard N. *What Color Is Your Parachute?* Ten Speed Press, P.O. Box 7123, Berkeley, California 94707. 1970. New editions published annually. Read this while the economy is good to protect your career when the next recession hits.

Brimacombe, J. William. *Ready, Set, Retire!* Financial Freedom Press, P.O. Box 6285, Bend, Oregon 97708-6285. 1994. My favorite book devoted to retirement planning. Lots of sound advice.

* Brosterman, Robert. *The Complete Estate Planning Guide*. New American Library, 1633 Broadway, New York, NY 10019. 1964. This bestseller has been updated several times. Don't be misled by the title—it is really about comprehensive financial planning, with excellent chapters on investments, insurance, real estate, etc. One of my favorites.

Condon, Gerald M., Esq. and Jeffrey L., Esq. *Beyond the Grave: The Right Way and the Wrong Way of Leaving Money to Your Children (and Others.* HarperCollins Publishers, Inc., 10 East 53rd Street, New York, N.Y. 10022. 1995. Discusses the philosophies and practical issues of estate planning.

DeVos, Rich. *Compassionate Capitalism.* Penguin Books USA Inc., 375 Hudson Street, New York, NY 10014. 1993. Great insights about sharing and the purpose of success.

Eldred, Gary W., Ph.D. *The 106 Common Mistakes Homebuyers Make (and How to Avoid Them).* John Wiley & Sons, Inc., New York. 1994. Not just for first-time homebuyers—gives sound advice about the biggest financial decision you'll ever make.

Esperti, Robert A. and Renno L. Peterson. *The Loving Trust.* Viking Penguin, Inc., New York, NY 10010. Excellent treatment of the latest creative estate planning concepts.

Hallman, G. Victor and Jerry S. Rosenbloom. *Personal Financial Planning.* McGraw-Hill, Inc., New York. 1983. An excellent, broad-based, descriptive book into the uses and tactics of financial products and strategies. Unlike the authors of many bestselling financial planning books, the authors here know what they are talking about.

Kaye, Barry. *Save a Fortune on Your Estate Taxes*; also *Die Rich and Tax Free!* Forman Publishing, Inc., 2932 Wilshire Blvd., Suite 201, Santa Monica, California 90403. 1990. Makes seemingly-complex strategies simple for the layman.

Parrott, William W. and John L. *You Can Afford to Retire!* Simon & Schuster, New York. 1992. Another good book on retirement planning.

Whitney, Victor P. *Estate Planning in the 90's.* Fiduciary Publishers, 557 Greenway Drive, North Palm Beach, Florida 33408. 1989. A practical, reliable, and *short* book giving the essence of good planning.

Decision Five: Climb the Right Ladder for Success

Band, Richard E. *Contrary Investing for the '90s.* St. Martin's Press, 175 Fifth Avenue, New York, N.Y. 10010. 1989. The clearest book available on Contrarian Investing and why it works. Examines key indicators for several asset classes. Read this before you invest.

* Bettger, Frank. *How I Raised Myself from Failure to Success in Selling.* Fireside, Rockefeller Center, 1230 Avenue of the Americas, New York, N.Y. 10020. 1947. The classic on career development, whether or not you're in sales.

Brandt, Steven C. *Entrepreneuring: The Ten Commandments for Building a Growth Company.* The New American Library, Inc., 1633 Broadway, New York, NY 10019. 1992. The best little bible available for entrepreneurs. Excellent treatise on how to prepare a business plan.

Edwards, Paul and Sarah. *The Best Home Businesses for the 90s.* G.P. Putnam's Sons, 200 Madison Avenue, New York, NY 10016. 1995. A practical how-to book for those looking for freedom and income.

Graham, Benjamin. *The Intelligent Investor.* Harper & Row Publishers, Inc., 10 East 53rd Street, New York, N.Y. 10022. 1973. The classic from the school of fundamental investing.

Hagstrom, Robert G., Jr. *The Warren Buffett Way: Investment Strategies of the World's Greatest Investor.* John Wiley & Sons, Inc., New York. 1994. Not only investing insights, but commentary on a quality person.

Hulbert, Mark. The Hulbert Financial Digest Inc., 316 Commerce Street, Alexandria, VA 22314. The newsletter that monitors and evaluates other investment newsletters.

Kaplan, Martin, CPA, and Naomi Weiss. *What the IRS Doesn't Want You to Know: A CPA Reveals the Tricks of the Trade.* Villard Books, New York. 1994. Read this to understand your tax rights, risks, and pitfalls.

Price Waterhouse LLP. *The Price Waterhouse Personal Tax Adviser.* Irwin Professional Publishing, Chicago. 1995. Updated annually, gives quick answers to the most sought after tax questions.

Ries, Al and Jack Trout. *The 22 Immutable Laws of Marketing.* HarperCollins Publishers, Inc., 10 East 53rd Street, New York, NY 10022. 1993. The place to start marketing systems for the small business owner.

Shellans, Steve. *MoniResearch Newsletter.* P.O. Box 19146, Portland, OR 97280; (800) 615-6664. The newsletter that monitors and reports on mutual fund market timers and (increasingly) asset allocators.

Smith, Adam. *The Money Game*. Random House, Inc., New York. 1967. Recommended to understand the economy and successful investing. Read before you invest.

Decision Six: Avoid Poor Thinking

Brown, W. Steven. *13 Fatal Errors Managers Make and How You Can Avoid Them*. The Berkeley Publishing Group, 200 Madison Avenue, New York, NY 10016. 1985. So many executives derail because they just don't get it.

Carnegie, Dale. *How to Stop Worrying and Start Living*. Pocket Books, 1230 Avenue of the Americas, New York, N.Y. 10020. 1944. The classic to rid yourself of much psychological baggage.

Halloran, James W. *Avoid The 20 Fatal Pitfalls Of Running Your Business*. Liberty Hall Press, New York. 1991. For the entrepreneur or seasoned business owner, a checklist of traps.

Hill, Napoleon. *Think & Grow Rich*. Ballantine Books, New York. 1960. The classic on success-thinking.

Murphy, Dr. Joseph, D.R.S., Ph.D., D.D., LL.D. *The Power of Your Subconscious Mind*. Prentice-Hall, Inc., Englewood Cliffs, N.J. 1963.

Peale, Norman Vincent. *Positive Imaging: The Powerful Way to Change Your Life*. Ballantine Books, New York. 1982. This book, and another of his classics, *Creative Imagining*, will set anyone on the road to an increased vision and belief system.

* Peale, Norman Vincent. *The Power of Positive Thinking*. Ballantine Books, New York. 1952. He has a gift to inspire, lift, and help you see your real potential.

Schwartz, David J., Ph.D. *The Magic of Thinking Big*. Simon & Schuster, Inc., Rockefeller Center, 1230 Avenue of the Americas, New York, NY 10020. 1959. The classic on expanding your success thinking and avoiding those self-defeating thoughts that hold you down.

Stevens, Mark. *36 Small Business Mistakes—and How to Avoid Them*. Parker Publishing Company, West Nyack, New York. 1978. A practical checklist for the business owner.

Decision Seven: Make Your Dream Your Reality

* Franklin Institute. *Finding Your Values/Reaching Your Goals.* (Video). Franklin International Institute, Inc., 2200 West Parkway Blvd., Salt Lake City, Utah 84119; (800) 654-1776. 1990. Practical, useful explanation of the process. A great investment.

Lakein, Alan. *How to Get Control of Your Time and Your Life.* The New American Library, Inc., 1301 Avenue of the Americas, New York, NY 10019. 1973. The classic on time management, efficiency, and effectiveness.

* Smith, Hyrum W. *The 10 Natural Laws of Successful Time and Life Management.* Warner Books, Inc., 1271 Avenue of the Americas, New York, NY 10020. 1994. Really about how to live a value-directed life—perhaps the best ever written on time and life management.

Relevant Associations

American Bar Association (ABA), 740 15th Street, NW, Washington, D.C. 20061; (202) 662-1000.

American Institute of Certified Public Accountants (AICPA), 1211 Avenue of the Americas, New York, NY 10036-8775; (212) 596-6200.

American Society of Chartered Life Underwriters (CLU) and Chartered Financial Consultants (ChFC), 270 South Bryn Mawr Avenue, Bryn Mawr, PA 19010-2195; (610) 526-2500. Affiliated with the accredited American College at Bryn Mawr, PA.

Institute of Certified Financial Planners, 7600 E. Easternman, #301, Denver, CO 80231-4397; (303) 751-7600. Affiliated with the College for Financial Planning, Denver, CO.

International Association for Financial Planning (IAFP), Suite B 300, 5775 Glenridge Drive NE, Atlanta, Georgia 30328-5364; (404) 845-0011. Will give referrals of financial planners in your area. Check them out using criteria in Chapter 35.

Society of Asset Allocators and Fund Timers (SAAFTI), 7112 West Jefferson Street, Suite 300, Lakewood, CO 80235; (303) 989-5655. An association of professional portfolio managers.

Tactical Asset Allocators
(as of 6/30/95)

Flexible Plan Inv., Ltd. 3883 Telegraph Bloomfield Hills, MI 48302	Tammy Shap Jerry Wagner 810-642-6640	Min: $50,000 $10,000 for qual. plans	2.6% first $150,000. Subtract 0.1% for each $50,000 thereafter until reaching 0.9% @ $950,000
Five Star Management Co. P.O. Box 573646 Salt Lake City, UT 84157	Nicole Hunter Henry S. Brock 800-550-6323 801-263-0702	Min: $25,000 Assets: $30M	2.2% first $100,000 1.8% next $100,000 1.6% next $300,000 1.4% next $500,000 1.2% next $1,000,000 1.0% next $3,000,000 0.8% beyond $5,000,000
LBS Capital Management 311 Park Place Blvd., #330 Clearwater, FL 34619	Roy Stringfellow 813-726-5656 800-477-1296	Min: $25,000 Assets: $500M	2.0% first $500,000 1.5% next $500,000 1.0% next $1M
Monitrend Asset Mgt. Co. P.O. Box 020817 Staten Island, NY 10302	Lillian I. Asciutto 718-494-9072	Min: $50,000 Assets: $20M	2.0% first $500,000 1.5% next $500,000 1.0% thereafter
MRM Asset Allocation 901 Spoede Rd. St. Louis, MO 63146	800-233-1944 314-567-7734	Min: $50,000 Assets: $550M	2.0% to $5,000,000 negotiable thereafter
Potomac Fund Mgmt. 19522 Club House Rd. Gaithersburg, MD 20879	Rich Paul 800-346-5231 301-330-6000	Min Fee: $150 Assets: $125M	2.5% first $100,000 2.0% thereafter
RTE Asset Management Rightime Econometrics 1095 Rydal Rd. Rydal, PA 19046-1711	800-552-0551 215-572-7288	Min: $25,000 Assets: $1.2B	2.20% up to $100,000 2.00% next $400,000 1.75% next $500,000 1.50% next $1,000,000
Schield Management Co. Suite 410 390 Union Blvd. Denver, CO 80228	Corey Colehour 800-275-2382 303-985-9999	Min. fee: $200 Assets: $245M	One-time set-up charge: $75 2.0% up to $250,000 + $40 1.5% next $250,000 + $40 1.0% + $40 thereafter
Trendstat Capital Mgmt. 6991 E. Camelback, Suite D-210 Scottsdale, AZ 85251-2435	Tom Basso 602-970-3600	Min: $50,000 Assets: $52M	2.00% first $500,000 1.75% next $500,000 1.50% thereafter
Zweig/Avatar Cap. Mgmt. Div. of Avatar Assoc. 900 Third Ave. New York, NY 10022	Marietta Goldman Marty Zweig 800-447-9226 212-753-7710	Min: $150,000 Assets: $116M	2.50% up to $300,000 2.25% next $200,000 2.00% next $250,000 declining scale thereafter

Ready-Reference
Index

Symbols

401k plan, 308, 411, 412, 414, 419, 502
  don't rely on, 296, 313
  qualified plans vs. SIP, 312
403b plan, 502
706 mortgage, 354–358
  amount, 355
  collateral, 354–355
  due date, 354
  methods of payment, 356–358
    cash, 356–357
    forced liquidation, 357
    life insurance, 358
    loan, 358
  security, 355–356
  terms, 355

A

Abbott, Charles F., 108
Abundance, 231
  law of, 152
  and specialization and exchange, 151
Abundance mentality, 31, 32, 390, 392
Accelerated mortgage payoff plan, 66
Accounts payable, accelerating
  payment of, tax benefits of, 419
Accounts receivable, deferring collection of, tax benefits of, 418
Action plan:
  on governing yourself, 509–512
  on the seven core decisions, 507–508
Activity vs. results, 192
Addiction:
  and budgeting, 72
  to compulsive buying and debt, 134
  and deficit spending, 154
  and financial success, 121
  and gambling, 160
  and loss of freedom, 114
    breaking chains of bondage, 121

Addiction (Cont.):
  self-destructive, 121
Adversity:
  and opposition, as natural laws, 37–38
  and personal character growth, 38
  relationship to happiness, 37–38
After-tax returns:
  emergency funds, 78
  net interest rates, 80
Alignment, 186–187
  with correct principles:
    character and goals, 18
    relationship to happiness, 21
    relationship to success, 122
  and financial success, 32
  and focus, 187
  of goals, 487
  and happiness, level of, 32
  of life and priorities, 41
  of principles and goals, 187
Alpha, risk measurement, 332–333
Alpha and Omega, 118
America:
  Bill of Rights, 102
    and right of property, 109
  capitalist system in, 128
  colonies:
    and King George, 100
    negligent government in, 100
  Constitution:
    checks and balances, 101
    First Amendment to, 108
    freedom of assembly, 123
    and income tax, 85
    ratification of, 109
    rights of government, 101
  economic incentive in, 107
    purpose of profit, 107
  false economic and political systems in,
    122–126
    who finances, 124
  free enterprise system, 77, 103

America (*Cont.*):
  freedom in, 113
  government, responsibilities of, 135
  heritage of freedom, 98
  number-one cause of financial
    problems in, 31, 136, 228
  Revolution, 100
  businessmen's revolution, 127
  ongoing nature of, 104
  specialization and exchange in, 150
  two financial types of people in, 53
    save first, 53
    spend first, 53
Anarchy:
  and closed organizations, 162
  freedom as justification for, 115
  society without laws, 164
Anderson, Jack, 119
Annuities, 411
  charitable remainder annuity trust
    (CRAT), 364, 372
  fixed, 372
  tax-sheltered, 67
  variable, 425–438
    as a cash flow strategy, 67
Appreciation, real estate, 240
Appreciative, 217–218. (*See also*
    Gratitude)
  attitude brings happiness, 38–39
Aptitude vs. attitude, 182, 184
Asset classes, 427
Asset protection strategies, 283–
    294, 289–292, 345–346
  disability income insurance, 283–
    288
  family limited partnership, 291-292,
    360–361
  incorporation, 290–291
  long-term care insurance, 288–289
  property and casualty insurance,
    292–293
  trusts, 348–350
Assets:
  allocation of, 440–446, 451
  allocation, or balance, 324
  distribution of, upon death, 342–345
  gifting to children, 410
  lien on, 86

Assets (*Cont.*):
  and net worth, 138
  and bankruptcy, 138
  soft assets and hard debt, 138
  retitling, 291
  transferring to a tax-advantaged
    program, 435–436
Attitude, 182–185
  vs. aptitude, 182, 184
  checklist, 182
  effect of neighborhood on, 238
  happiness depends on, 22, 38
  vs. intellect, 182
  negative, 183
  positive, 183, 216
Attorney, 494 (*See also* Designations)
Attract money, 28–30, 189
  law of unequal rewards, 28–30
  money flows in two directions:
    toward incentive, 28
    toward trust, 28
Auto insurance, saving on premiums,
  68

B

Balance, 217, 444–445, 487
  or asset allocation, 324
  between consumption and saving, 20
  between happiness and pleasures, 21
  and happiness criteria, 31
  portfolio, 326
  and time bondage, 119
**Balance sheets, review with spouse
    before marriage,** 74
Balanced budget, U.S., why critical, 19
Bamboo tree, 385–387
Bank accounts, as forced savings, 57
Bankruptcy:
  and cash value life insurance, 259
  dishonorable to ignore debt, 133
  function of cash, not of net worth,
    138–139
  and responsible use of credit, 133
Bastiat, Frederic, 95
Beals, Edward E., 23
Before-AGI deductions, 414
Being vs. seeming, 178, 179, 182, 484
Belth, Joseph M., 268

Beneficiary, 348–349
Benefits:
  pension, life and survivor vs. life only, 67
  retirement, life and survivor vs. life only, 308–309
Beta, risk measurement, 332
Bill of Rights, 102
  and right of property, 109
Bohn, Henry George, 40
Bond market, 159
  and technical risk, 324
Bondage, 1–2
  of debt, 66, 131–148
  and ego, 31
  forms of:
    addiction, 121
    bad habits, 122
    false economic and political systems, 122–126
    financial, 121–122
    government, 126–128
    handouts, 127
    ignorance, 115–119
    mistakes, 122
    "things", 121
    time, 119–120
  restrains freedom, 113–114
  and taxes, lien on income, 85
Bonds:
  don't use for emergency fund, 78
  taxable, 67
Bradstreet, Anne, 38
Brine shrimp, 224
Buddha, 179
Budget, 71–83
  and avoiding financial ruin, 169
  bargains, 74
  and cash flow, 65
  communication between husband and wife, 74
  and credit cards, 77
  deficit, 396, 398
    and Social Security, 296
    threat to economic future, 163
  emergency fund:
    cash reserves, 77–80
    liquidity premium, 79

Budget (Cont.):
  five primary elements, 75
    accounting for what is spent, 75
    evaluating progress, 75
    goal-setting, 75
    healthy spending, 75
    saving, 75
  how to develop, 75–76
  key element, commitment, 75
  know your spending cycles, 76
  for life insurance, 259, 276
  must-haves, 73–74
  name brands, 73–74
  needs vs. wants, 73–74
  paradox of controls, budgeting process enables freedom, 71–73
  a plan, not a diary, 74–75
  priorities of, 71
  a real game, 77
  two financial types of people in America, 54–56
Budiansky, Stephen, 172
Builder, being a, 31, 32, 203, 391
Business interest, and taxes, 415
Business interests:
  avoiding capital gains tax on, 67
  closely-held, lien on, 85
Business, starting a, 69, 205–206
  and taxes, 415
Buy happiness, 22–25, 35–44

C

Cafeteria plan, tax benefits of, 418
Capital gains:
  bypass strategies, 67
  bypass trust, 68. [See also Charitable remainder unitrust (CRUT)]
  tax benefits of, 417
  offset with capital losses, 414
  pass-through of, and mutual funds, 331
  tax, 67, 372–373, 412, 417
Capital losses, 414
Capitalism, 95–96, 126, 128
  and Frederic Bastiat, 95
  Marxist view of, 95
  three components of production, 107

Capitalism (*Cont.*):
two sources of capital, 108
debt, 108
ownership, 108
win-win, 95
Career planning:
business, starting a, 205–206
common denominator of success,
200–201
employee, being most profitable, 209–
211
fatal flaws, 202–203
how to be last person laid off, 209–219
how to enhance opportunities and
rewards, 195–207
number-one success force, 196
personal net worth, evaluating, 218
results, importance of, 198–199
strategies, for increasing cash flow, 68
success curve, 201–202
what employers look for, 211–218
what you're really worth, 196–197
working smart vs. hard, 197–199
working spouse, 203–205
and WYHTE phenomenon, 199
Carnegie, Andrew, 369
Cash, 316–317
and bankruptcy, 138–139
and financial integrity rating, 139
and financial opportunities, 139
income, 168, 229–230, 415
income, from investments, cost of
using, 82
and inflation, 142–143
and opportunity, 316–317
paying 706 mortgage with, 356–357
purchasing items with, vs. credit,
135, 145
reserves, 77–80, 142
balancing, 79–80
liquidity premium, 79
save separately for big-ticket items,
81
Cash flow:
and home mortgage, 244
needs, funding with life insurance, 252
projections, and business opportunities, 10

Cash flow (*Cont.*):
strategies for increasing, 65–69
value to employer, measuring, 68
WYHTE phenomenon, 65
Cash value insurance, 255–264, 271–
272, 404, 405, 412, 429–431
funding education with, 403–405
Cavett, Robert, 489
Certificates of deposit, 403, 452
as cash reserves, 79
"fixed-income" investments, 305
and fundamental risk, 323
and interest rate risk, managing away,
325
and risk, managing, 326
risk tolerance level, going broke safely,
79–80
taxable, 67
Certified Financial Planner (CFP),
271, 493
Certified Public Accountant (CPA),
271, 493, 494
Chains of habit, 55, 122
and budgeting, 72
and impulse buying, 72
Challenge, and growth, 38, 190
Chanel, Coco, 38
Character, 18
and correct principles, 177
greatness of purpose determines, 178–
179
and habits, 470
of money, 27–33
and money happiness, 177–194
and money personality, 47
nine attributes of, 180–194
of old vs. new neighborhoods, 240
personal growth, 38
Character counts, 18, 193
Charitable contributions, 410–411
corporate deductions, tax benefits of,
419
Charitable giving, 40, 230, 369–380
appreciated property, 378
as a cash flow strategy, 68
bargain sale, 379
benefits of, 369–371
charitable foundations, 378

Charitable giving (*Cont.*):
depreciated property, 378-379
life insurance trust, 377-378
strategies for, 68, 371-379
charitable bequests, 372-379
tax deductions, 371
Charitable lead trust, 377
tax benefits of, 417
Charitable pursuits, after retirement,
302, 310-311
Charitable remainder annuity trust
(CRAT), 364, 372
Charitable remainder unitrust
(CRUT), 68, 364, 372-376, 417.
(*See also* Capital gains bypass trust)
Chartered Financial Consultant
(ChFC), 493
Chartered Life Underwriter (CLU),
267, 271, 493
Chartered Property and Casualty
Underwriter (CPCU), 291
Child care, life insurance provisions
for, 250
Children, 409
an asset, not a liability, 168, 171, 415
hiring, tax benefits of, 419-420
lessons for, 169
work and self-reliance, 65
Choice, freedom of, negative people
don't have, 216
Choice and consequence, 102, 114-115
free choice, not freedom from
consequences, 114-115
and freedom, 18
and sacrifice, 42
Churchill, Winston, 128, 180, 185,
238
Circle-one mindset, 55
Circle-two mindset, 55
Clark, J. Reuben, Jr., 132
Class warfare, 163, 467
and Communist agenda, 124
Closed organizations, 123, 162, 164-
165
tactics and agenda of, 125-126
College education, 395-406
cost of, 396, 401-402
earnings with, 395-396
first level of knowledge, 115-116

College education (*Cont.*):
funding approaches, 397, 502
grants-in-aid, 398-399
insurance, 403-405
savings, 403-405
scholarships, 399-401
student loans, 397-399
vs. high school, 315
vs. real-world experience, 116
Collusion, unconscious, 170
Commitment, 188-189
Commitment-conscious, vs. consumption-conscious, relationship to
happiness criteria, 33
Committed, 213
Commodity:
definition of, 271
insurance is not a, 271
Communism, 95-96, 109, 123-127,
149
Compassion, true, 230
not a handout, 127-128
Competency, 183
Competent, 213, 494-495
Competition, relationship to cooperation, 94
Compound interest, 321
anyone can be a millionaire, 321
cost of using investment income, 82
vs. financial opportunities, making big
money with, 139
focus on principal, 57
magic of, 50
and paying off debt, 146
Congruence, 181
between self-image and success, form
of integrity, 24
Consequence:
all choice has a cost, 114
and mistakes, bondage to, 122
Conservative, 217
Constitution, U.S.:
checks and balances, 101
First Amendment to, 108
freedom of assembly, and Communist
Party protest tactics, 124
and income tax, 85
ratification of, role of property rights
in, 109

Constitution, U.S. (*Cont.*):
  rights of government, 101
Consumer advocates, 268, 269
**Consumption-conscious vs. commit-
  ment-conscious, relationship to
  happiness**, 33
Contrarian investing, 447–450
  determining investor sentiment:
    advisory service sentiment, 449
    insider buys/sells, 448
    institutional investors, 449
    market liquidity ratio, 448
    popular press, 449
**Controls, paradox of, budget enables
  freedom**, 71–73
Coolidge, Calvin, 185
**Cooperation, relationship to competi-
  tion**, 94
Correlation coefficient, 333
Courage, 180
Coveting, 137, 182
  primary cause of family debt, 132
Covetousness, 165
  and avoiding financial ruin, 169
Covey, Stephen R., 36, 41, 178, 183,
  193, 370, 468
Creative, 215
Credit cards:
  and budgeting, 77
  don't use for emergency fund, 78
  stop using, first step to get out of debt,
  144
  and WYHTE phenomenon, impact on
  debt, 139–141
Cuomo, Mario, 466

D

Death taxes. (*See* Estate taxes)
Debt, 7–10, 131–148
  and avoiding financial ruin, 169
  causes slavery, 135–136
  challenges integrity, 133
  for college education, 397–398

  consolidation of, 66, 134
  consumer, paying off, risk-free
    guaranteed return, 141
  dishonorable to ignore, 133

Debt (*Cont.*):
  and financial security, 229
  government, 159
    and inflation, 153
  home mortgage, 243
  how to get out of, 144–147
    payoff methodology, 145–146
    stop borrowing, 144–145
  inflationary, 134–135
  is bondage, 131–132
  lien on income, 85
  limits ability to serve others, 136
  liquidation of, life insurance provisions
    for, 249
  motivation, 136–137
  paying off, 66
  and personal net worth, 218
  qualifying for home mortgage, 242
  reverse mortgage, 311
  threat to economic future, 164
  true nature of, 138–144
    assets are soft and debt is hard, 138
    bankruptcy is not a function of net
      worth, 138
    big money comes from financial
      opportunities, 139
    financial integrity is spelled
      C-A-S-H, 139
    home equity loans are not the
      answer, 143
    pay off debt for risk-free,
      guaranteed return, 141
    unwise to incur during inflation,
      142
    WYHTE phenomenon, a surcharge
      on purchases, 139
  and work ethic, 134
**Declaration of Independence, and
  property rights**, 109
Decreasing needs, theory of, 254–255
Deficit, U.S., who finances, 159
Delegate:
  people delegate rights to government,
  109

  to reduce stress, only the essentials,
  120
DeMille, Cecil B., 177

Depreciation of furniture, equipment,
& buildings; tax benefits of, 418
Depression, prepare for the next, 161
Depression, Great; repeats itself, 10
Derail, fatal flaws, 202-203
Designations, 270, 493-494
attorney (JD), 494
Certified Financial Planner (CFP),
271, 493-494
Certified Public Accountant (CPA),
271, 493-494
Chartered Financial Consultant
(ChFC), 493
Chartered Life Underwriter (CLU),
267, 271, 493-494
Chartered Property and Casualty
Underwriter (CPCU), 291
Master of Business Administration
(MBA), 271
Dewey, Thomas E., 160
Dickens, Charles, 40, 77
Disability income insurance, 283-284
Disinformation, techniques of, 125
Diversification, 317, 324
effect on risk, 318
and managing fundamental risk, 324
portfolio, 426
Dividends, cost of using income from,
82
re-investing for long-term growth, 82
taxation of, 89
Divine truth, third level of knowledge,
absolute and correct principles,
116
Divorce:
and financial problems:
discuss finances before marriage 74
ego 31
home equity loans 144
and financial ruin 168-169
threat to financial future 165
Dollar cost averaging, 450-456
applying to a savings stream 452
Dunleavy, Francis J., 127

E

Early retirement, 58

Earth:
productive capacity of, 172
stewardship for, 162
Easy money, 42
dulls the work ethic, 134
Economic cycles, 447
Economic engine, saving drives
economic progress, 53-69
Economic freedom, 110
Economic future, threats to, 163-166
Economic incentive, 110, 163
and attracting money, 28
fundamental to economic progress,
106, 107
and handouts, 127
and price and wage fixing, 161
profit, 107-108
strength of economy based upon, 86
wealth cannot survive without, 166
Economic progress, 106-107
Economic system, free enterprise, 106
Economics, 149-166
of a free economy, 93-111
of free trade, 149-152
of gaming/gambling, 159-160
of impact of taxes, 86-87
of inflation, 152-155
of minimum wage, 155-157
of population control, 172
of a regulated economy, 93-111
of specialization and exchange, 149-
152
of technology replacing labor, 158
of working spouse, 63-64, 203
Edison, Thomas, 180, 190
Educated, 214
Education. (See College education)
life insurance provisions for, 251
Education needs, capital accumulation
for. (See College education)
Effort, 189-191, 197
commission vs. wage, 134
hope of reward vs. fear of punishment,
104
parable of talents, 29
vs. results, 190, 192
something for nothing, 42, 134
Ego:
and avoiding financial ruin, 169

Ego (*Cont.*):
 and cash flow, 65
 criteria, 31, 32
 debt motivation, 136–137
 keeping up with the Joneses, 65
 needs vs. wants, 73
 number-one cause of money problems,
  136, 228
 and security, 228
Ego criteria, 18
Eisenhower, Dwight D., 113
Eliot, George, 158
Emergency fund, 77–78, 139
 bad vehicles for, 78–79
 capital accumulation for, 78
 cash reserves, sources of, 318
 life insurance provisions for, 249
 reasons for, 77
Employee, being most profitable, 209–
 211
Employment, changing, as a cash flow
 strategy, 69
Engels, Frederick, 95
Enthusiasm, 183
Entitlements, 126–128
Environment, stewardship for, 162,
 172
Equality, and freedom, 96–97
Equity:
 home equity, and budgeting, 71
 home equity loans, 67, 143–144, 145
 don't use for emergency fund,
  78, 79
 permanent vs. term insurance, 256–
 258
 professional, 201
Equity vs. fixed investments, 336, 501
Error vs. truth, techniques of
 disinformation, 125
Estate:
 give away twice, 364
 joint tenancy, 347–348
  problems with, 347–348
 operation of law, 343–344
 planning, 341–352
  avoid family contention, 346
  avoid publicity, 345
  basic elements, 346
  choosing a guardian, 350–351

Estate, planning (*Cont.*):
 choosing a personal representative,
  351–352
 choosing a trustee, 351
 control your assets, 342–345
 eliminate expenses, 345
 establish a trust, 348
 establish a will, 346–348
 professional counsel, importance of,
  344–345
 protect your assets, 345–346
 probate, 343, 346–347
 taxes, 88, 353–367, 358–362
  and theory of decreasing needs, 255
  life insurance provisions for, 252
  multiplying your exemption, 364–
  365
  multiplying your IRA, 365
  multiplying your single-premium
   life policy, 365–366
 tenancy in common, 347–348
  advantages of, 347–348
 what's included, 252, 342
  intangible assets, 342
  tangible assets, 342
Ethical standards, 495–496
 and professional designations, 270
Evolution, theory of, 118
Excellence, pursuit of, 487
Exchanges, tax-free, 67
Excuses:
 of the ages, 48
 vs. responsibility, 193
Executor, 346, 347, 350, 354
Expectations:
 danger of lowering, 24
 happiness depends on, 22
 managing, 24
 violated, about money, 24
Expenses, taking early, tax benefits of,
 416
Experience:
 vs. designations, 495
 real world, second level of knowledge,
  116
Experienced, 214
Extra mile, 190, 191, 211, 215, 225,
 231

F

Failure, financial, reasons for, 45–50
False economic and political systems,
　122–126
Family:
　alignment with, 187
　basic unit of society, 167–173
　conflict, and money personality, 46
　councils, 145, 169
　　to explain money facts, 132–133
　economic value of, 168
　finances, discuss before marriage, 74
　financial security, emergency funds,
　　77
　impact of debt on, 132, 144
　　coveting, 132
　lifestyle, and WYHTE phenomenon,
　　64
　number-one cause of money problems
　　in, 136
　reserves of food, clothing, energy, 80
　self-reliance, 229–230
　specialization and exchange, 167
　success, and sacrifice, 42
　two kinds of spouses, 170
Family limited partnership, 290, 360–
　361. (See also Limited partnership)
　asset protection, 291, 361
　estate minimization, 361
　income tax splitting, 361
　tax benefits of, 416
Fatal flaws, 202–203
Fatalism, 95, 171, 172
　and America's youth, 103
　government, rights of, 95, 109
　negative person lacks options, 117
　revolution against, 98
Federal income tax, 88, 204, 205, 319
　origin of, 85
　responsibilities of government, 135
　and retirement, 307
　and working spouse, 418
Federal intrusion, and insurance
　industry, 269
Federal Reserve Board, 159
Federal taxes, and marginal tax rate,
　60

Fence test, discerning good govern-
　ment, 122
FICA taxes, 205, 308
　employee portion, 88
　employer portion, 88
　and family limited partnership, 416
　and marginal tax rate, 59, 60, 88
　and working spouse, 204, 418
Financial adviser. (See also Financial
　planner)
　selection of, and correct principles,
　　12, 245
Financial aid. (See Grants-in-aid; Student
　loans)
Financial bondage, 1, 121–122
　and ego, 137
Financial causes and effects, 149–166
Financial failure, reasons for, 45–50
Financial Freedom Day, 58, 459
Financial Freedom Fund, 58
Financial incentive, 163
Financial integrity rating, credit
　rating, 139
Financial planner, 491–506. (See also
　Financial adviser)
　compensation, 497
　　commission-only, 497
　　fee-based, 497
　　fee-only, 497
　　fee-plus-commission, 497
　cost of hiring, 504
　designations, 270, 493–494
　keys to working with, 499–500
　reasons for working with, 491–492
　selection of, 492–499
　　client profiles, 496
　　compensation, 497–498
　　competence, 494–495
　　continuing education, 496
　　designation, 493–494
　　ethical standards, 495–496
　　full-time professional, 496
　　licenses, 493
　　performance, 498–499
　　questions to ask, 493–498
　　satisfied client base, 496
　　service, 493
　　and your money personality, 46

Financial planning:
  benefits of, 504–505
    monetary, 505
    psychological, 504
  building a solid foundation, 247
  process, 502–503
    data gathering, 502–503
    on-going monitoring and
      maintenance, 503
    plan implementation, 503
    plan preparation, 503
    plan presentation, 503
  subsets of, 501–502
    education funding, 502
    estate planning, 502
    income tax planning, 501
    investment portfolio management,
      501
    retirement planning, 502
    risk management and insurance,
      501
  tax rate relevant for, 89
  view of money, 23
  what is, 30–31
  who does what, 500–502
Financial security. (*See also* Security)
  family, 77
  first law of, 370
  formula for, 234
  personal, 55, 58
Financial success:
  how to attract, 393
  not achieved by spending, 465–466
First Amendment, to U.S. Constitu-
  tion, 108
Fixed annuities, 372
Fixed Daily Activities (FDAs), 485
Fixed vs. equity investments, 336, 501
Focus, 187, 389–390
Food production, 172
Forbes, B.C., 384
Forbes, Malcolm S., Jr., 171
Forced liquidation, paying 706
  mortgage with, 357
Forced savings, 57, 259–260
  mortgage acceleration plan, 245
Ford, Gerald, 126
Ford, Henry, 223, 225
Forgiveness, 389

Form vs. substance, tax principle of,
  408
Franklin, Benjamin, 20, 28, 53, 74,
  100, 132, 405
Free choice, 471
  but not freedom of consequences, 114-
    115
  negative people do not have, 216
Free enterprise, 103, 106, 109, 110
  and economic cycles, 447
  for security and success, 127
Free trade:
  and food production, 172
  and standard of living, 150, 151, 152,
    164
Freedom, 91, 113–129, 163
  and budgeting, 71–83
  closed organizations violate, 162
  economic, 1, 110
  extra mile demonstrates, 191, 215
  financial, 58
  vs. force, 97–98
  fruits of, 105
  and happiness, 18
  and money, 23
  necessary restraints, 97
  negative people don't have, 216, 471
  no one grants us, 99
  personal, 96–97
  and property rights, 109
  responsibility of, 98, 100
Friedman, Milton, 153
Fringe benefit plans, installing, tax
  benefits of, 419
Fringe benefits, tax benefits of, 415
Fundamental risk, 323

G

Gambling, 40, 159–160
Gaming, 40, 160, 162
Gangs, 123
Gautama, Siddhartha, 179
Get-rich-quick:
  and debt, 10
  schemes, 42–43
    idleness breeds, 227
  speculation, 165
Getty, J. Paul, 448

Ghetto, 32, 193, 466
  and environment, 118
Gifting, 363–364.
  to children, 410
  appreciating assets, 410
  and family limited partnership, 361
  gift tax exclusion, 367
  to minors, 403
  multiplying your gifts, 363–364
  taxes on, 348
Goal-driven, 213
Goals:
  alignment with correct principles, 187
  and budgeting, 55, 72
  how to achieve, 483–490
    align goals with your purposes in
      life, 487
    assess your willingness to pay the
      cost, 485
    balance your pursuit of excellence,
      487
    be visionary, 489–490
    break goal down into daily steps,
      485
    develop your master plan, 484
    establish self-enforcing mechanisms,
      485–486
    ignite something deep within, 483–
      484
    manage systems, 487–488
    measure performance, 486–487
    put a cost on the goal, 484–485
    systematize, 488–489
  and your money personality, 47
Goldwater, Barry, 126
Government:
  checks and balances, 101
  and debt, 135–136
  definition of, 86
  entitlements, 126, 127
  good government, definition of, 127
  and income tax, 85–88
  and inflation, 153–154
  regulation, 126
  rights of, 101, 108–110, 165
    and Bill of Rights, 102
  role of, 126
  servant, not master, 101

Government-planned economy,
  socialism and communism, 109
Grant, Heber J., 133
Grants-in-aid:
  Pell Grant, 398
  Supplemental Educational Opportu-
    nity Grant, 398
Gratitude, 184. (See also Appreciation)
  rarest character attribute, 217
  and tithing, 231–233
Gray, Albert E.N., 200, 387–388
Greatness of purpose, determines
  character, 178–179
Greed, 229, 476–477
  and debt, 10
  debt motivation, 136–137
  and speculation, 165
Greeley, Horace, 42
Growth, 190, 213
  accepting responsibility for, 116–117
  and challenge, 38
  corporate, 419
  economic, 151, 158
  and economic incentive, 110
  personal, 184
Growth rate, corporate, tax benefits of
  accelerating, 419
Guardian, choosing a, 350–351
Gurney, Kathleen, 46

                    H

Habit, chains of, 55
  and budgeting, 72
  and impulse buying, 72
Habits, 122, 470
  achieving goals, 19, 483–490
  bad, 122, 388
  and budgeting, 55
  and character, 179
  good, 122, 388
  inferior, and success, 42
  natural, 388
  persisting is habit-forming, 8
  quitting, 185
  quitting is habit-forming, 8
  and success, 387–388
Hamilton, Alexander, 22
Hand, Learned, 87

Happiness criteria, 18, 31–32
Happiness quotient, 21
Hard-working, 212
Harvest, law of the, 22, 30, 190
Health insurance, budgeting for,
    71, 73
Hemingway, Ernest, 298
Henry, Patrick, 114
Herd mentality, 449. (*See also* Sheep)
Hobby, turning into a business, tax
    benefits of, 414
Holmes, Dr. Thomas H., 299, 300
Home:
    buy a neighborhood, 238–240
    character, importance of, 240–241
    how to qualify to buy, 241–242
    mortgage, paying off debt 146
    most efficient way to pay off, 243–244
    second mortgage, pitfalls of, 245
    why own, 237–238
Home equity:
    and budgeting, 71
    and reverse mortgage, 311–312
Home equity loans, 67, 143–144, 145,
    245, 410
    don't use for emergency fund, 78, 79
Homeowners insurance, saving on
    premiums, 68
Honesty, 181, 211. (*See also* Integrity)
    with creditors, 147
    number-one success force, 196
Honor:
    and earning money, 42
    and ignoring debts, 133
Hope:
    determines behavior, 26
    of reward, vs. fear of punishment,
    103–105
House, buy a neighborhood, not just a
    house, 238–240
Howard, William Dempster, 38
Hurdle rate, 319, 320

I

Idleness, 165, 227
Ignorance, 165
    bondage of, 115–119
Impatience, debt motivation, 136–137

Impulsiveness, debt motivation, 136–
    137
Incentive, 393
    in America, 103
    economic, 86, 110, 127, 161, 163,
    166
    and attracting money, 28
    mainspring of economic growth,
    110
    economic progress thrives on, 106–
    107
    financial, 163
    money flows toward, 28
    and progress, 103
Income, postponing, tax benefits of,
    416
Incorporation, asset protection
    strategy, 290–291
Individual Retirement Account (IRA),
    259, 307, 308, 321, 411, 412
    don't rely on, 313
    illustration, 50
    multiplying, 365
    qualified plans vs. SIP, 312
    tax-sheltered, 67
Industry regulators, insurance, 26?
Inflation, 252, 254, 306, 319–320, 321
    borrowing during, 8
    causes of, 153
    cost-push, 154
    and debt, 134–135, 142–143
    definition of, 152
    demand-pull, 154
    government benefits from, 153
    hedge, 305, 325–326
    how to predict, 154–155
    impact of value-added tax on, 87
    impact on retirement, 296, 304
    insurance under, 254, 275–276
    and liquidity premium, 79
    rate of, 253
    tax of, 88, 152–155
Initiative, 183
    value of, 95–96
Insidious taxes, 165
    inflation, 152–155, 320
Insurance, 228, 247–265, 501
    cash value, 412
    and cash reserves, 78

Insurance, cash value (*Cont.*):
  as forced savings, 57
  funding education with, 403–405
  tax-sheltered, 67
casualty, 290, 292–293
companies, 267–270
consolidation of policies, 68
disability, 283–288
estate replacement, 364
funds required at your death, 248–254
  cash flow, 253–254
  child care/home care, 250–251
  debt liquidation, 249
  educational/vocational, 251–252
  emergency, 249
  estate taxes, 252
  immediate expenses, 248–249
  mortgage/rent payment, 249–250
group, 276–278
health, 288
  budgeting for, 71, 73
homeowners, 292
how much, 248–254
last-to-die, 362
liability, 292
life, 243, 248–264, 360–361
  budgeting for, 71
  and charitable remainder trust,
    373–374
  funding education with, 403–405
  how much, 248–254
  paying 706 mortgage with, 358
  and pension maximization, 67
  and retirement benefits, 308
  and step-up in basis, 420
long-term care, 288–289
no-load, 272
personal, 276–278
premiums, saving on, 68
property, 290, 292–293
purpose of, 247
rated, 280
replacement of, 270, 273–274
single-premium life, 365–366
  to finance college, 405
term life, 254
  decreasing, 254
  level, 254
  re-entry term, 278–280

Insurance (*Cont.*):
  term vs. permanent, 255–265
  under inflation, 275
  universal life, to finance college, 405
  uses of:
    706 mortgage, 358
    education funding, 403–405
    estate taxes, 255, 360–361
    protection needs, 255
  values, 271–272
  variable life, 425–438
    to finance college, 404
  whole life, 255–265
  whole life vs. term, 255–265
Insurance adviser, 268, 287
  how to choose, 270
Insurance policies, consolidation of, 68
Insurance premiums, saving on, 68
Integrity, 181, 196–197. (*See also*
    Honesty; Congruence)
  debt challenges, 133
  financial, 139
Interdependence, 37, 151, 390–392.
    (*See also* Specialization and ex-
    change)
  specialization and exchange, 150
  synergize through, 18
Interest rates, 159
  and debt consolidation, 134
  and inflation, 8, 142
  guaranteed, in life insurance policy,
    275
  on mortgage, 66
  net, 80
  and paying off debt, 147
  price of money, 155
  risk, 324–325
Interest, tax-deductible, as a cash flow
    strategy, 67
Investing:
  budgeting for, 71
  and cash reserves, 79
  cost of using income from, 82
  and debt, 141
  impact of estate taxes on, 88
  impact of inflation on, 88
  and marginal tax bracket, 89
  rates of return, increasing, 68
  in yourself, 69

Investing, priorities of, 477–479
Investment hurdle rate, 319, 320
Investment income, cost of using, 82
Investment principles, 317–321
Investment risks, 323–326, 327–329
  investment juice, 327–329, 478
Investment vs. investor performance,
  338–339
Investments, 412, 425–438
  annuities, 411
    variable, 425–438
  attributes of, 328
  equity, 501
  fixed, 501
  fixed vs. equity, 336
  income from, cost of using, 82
  limited partnerships, 360–361, 416,
    477–478
  mutual funds, 331, 425–438
  portfolio management, 501
    asset allocation, 440–446
    automation, 458
    contrarian approach, 447–450
    discipline, 457–458
    dollar cost averaging, 450–456
    individual objectives, 459
    market timing, 456–457
    nine keys, 439–460
    regular reports, 458–459
    systematic monitoring, 458
  rates of return, 68
  real estate, 412–413
  risks, 315–330
  strategies, 440–460
  top-performing asset, 316–317
  variable annuities, 425–438
  variable life, 425–438
Investor behavior, 338–339, 473–480
  greed, 476–479
  how successful investors think, 473–
    480
  lien on your portfolio, 479
  speculation, 476–479
  watch your plan, not the markets,
    474–475
  wealthy vs. average investors, 473–474
  why sell at a loss, 475
  why sell at a profit, 475–476
Involved, 183, 218

IRA, 50, 67, 259, 307, 308, 321, 411,
  412
  don't rely on, 313
  multiplying, 365
  qualified plans vs. SIP, 312
Isolationism, 164

J

Jackson, Andrew, 180
Jefferson, Thomas, 109, 127, 135, 370
Jesus, 29, 119, 371
Job evolution, 158
Job security, increasing, 225
Johnson, Samuel, 55
Joint tenancy, problems with, 347–348
Jones, Franklin P., 74
Joy, 21, 23, 31, 32, 379, 466
  and law of tithing, 232
Juice, investment, 327–328, 478

K

Keeping up with the Joneses, needs vs.
  wants, 73
Kennedy, John F., 39, 86, 107
Keogh plans, 414, 419, 502
Key Result Areas (KRAs), 485
Keynes, John Maynard, 154
Kiam, Victor, 50
Knowledge:
  knowledge is power, 11
  levels of, 115–116. (*See also* Levels of
    knowledge; Ignorance)

L

Labor, 156–157
  and technology, 158
Ladder of success, 33, 41, 42, 181, 225
Language, conservative, 217
Law of abundance, 152, 392
Law of the harvest, 22, 30, 190
Law of tithing, 230–233
Law of unequal rewards, 28–30, 211
Lawless society, 164
Laziness, 113, 227
  barometer for, 214
  and coveting, 182
  vs. hard-working, 212

Lease:
vs. buying, 135
within family limited partnership, 290, 416
Leath-Ross, Sir Fredrick, 153
Lecock, Steven, 298
LeFevre, William, 327
Lenin, Vladimir Ilyich, 104–105, 109, 124, 154
Levels of knowledge, 115–116
first level, college education, 115–116
second level, real-world experience, 116
third level, divine truth, 116
Leverage, 7
and U.S. economy, 159, 164
Life insurance. (See also Insurance, life)
budgeting for, 71
paying 706 mortgage with, 358
Lifestyle:
bondage of bad habits, 122
and career planning, 200
and debt, 45
and family councils, 132
vs. life, and welfare, 227
projecting insurance needs for, 248
self-destructive, 166
simplifying, as cash flow strategy, 65
and stored labor, 199
teaching children, 169
transferring labor into, 305
using investment income to support, 82
ways to maximize, 200
and WYHTE phenomenon, 64
Limited partnership, 290, 291, 360–361, 416, 477–478. (See also Family limited partnership)
benefits of, 291
general partner in, 291
and high-risk assets, 291
ownership of assets in, 291
Lincoln, Abraham, 49, 136, 177, 189, 467
Lindbergh, Anne Morrow, 37
Lindbergh, Charles, 389, 486
Lion and mouse, stewardship, 233
Liquidity, 318–319, 448
Liquidity premium, 79, 319

Load mutual funds, 431
vs. no-load, 336–340
Loan, paying 706 mortgage with, 358
Loans, student. (See Student loans)
Local income tax, 205, 319
and marginal tax rate, 88
Local taxes, and marginal tax rate, 60
Lombardi, Vince, 185
Long-term care insurance, 288–289
Losses, taking early, tax benefits of, 416
Lottery, 40, 159–160
success without effort, 42
Loyal, 188, 189, 212, 271
happiness criteria, 31

M

Mainspring of human progress, 93–111
Malachi, 8, 232
Man at work, 393
vs. money at work, 20
and retirement, 296, 313
Management vs. track record, of mutual funds, 334–335
Marginal tax rate, 59, 88–89, 319
at retirement, 307
and working spouse, 203, 205, 418
Market timing, 456–457
purpose of, 456
Markowitz, Harry, and modern portfolio theory (MPT), 440
Marriage: (See also Family)
discuss money before, 74
economic efficiency in, 141
economics of working spouse, 63–64, 203
family council, 132–133, 145, 169
respect, 74
tax benefits of, 409
two kinds of spouses, 141
Marriott, Bill, 384
Marshall, John, 85
Marx, Karl Heinrich, 95
Master:
government is servant, not master, 101, 102
money is servant, not master, 40

Master (*Cont.*):
  vs. servant, 191
  law of unequal rewards, 29–30
  servant is always master, 215, 225
Master of Business Administration
  (MBA), 271
Master plan, 484
Mature, 217
Maturity continuum, 36
McKay, David O., 41
Mead, Margaret, 298
Measuring value, 210
  to employer, 68
Media, 2. (*See also* Press)
Medical reimbursement plan, tax
  benefits of, 419
Medicare tax, 205, 308
  employee portion, 88
  employer portion, 88
  and marginal tax rate, 60
  and working spouse, 204
Milne, A.A., 464
Minimum wage, who benefits from,
  155–157
Misery, 40, 464
Misinformation, 119, 126
Mistakes, 180, 189, 203, 385–387
  bondage to, 122
Modern Portfolio Theory (MPT), 440–
  446
  and contrarian investing, 449
Modest, 43, 216
Modified endowment contract (MEC),
  435–436
Money:
  character of, 27–33
  definition of, 19–20
    medium of exchange, 19
    stored labor, 19
  purpose of, 22–23, 466
  servant, not master, 40
  uses for, 39–40
  why pursue, 35–37
Money at work, 393
  vs. man at work, 20
  and retirement, 296
Money happiness, 17–26
  choose your own level of, 25–26
  and success, 41–42

Money market, municipal vs. traditional funds, tax benefits of, 418
Money personality, 45–50, 169
MoneyMax Profile, 47–48, 169
Morgan, J.P., 447
Mortgage, 415
  706 vs. conventional, 354–356
  accelerated payoff plan, 66
  home equity loans, 143
  how to qualify, 241–242
  interest, 410
  life insurance provisions for, 249–250
  paying off debt, 146
  refinancing, 66
  reverse mortgage, 311–312
Mortgage acceleration plan, 243–244
Mouse and lion, stewardship, 233
Municipal bonds, 412, 437
Mutual Benefit Life Insurance Co.,
  269–270
Mutual funds, 331–340
  asset allocation with, 446
  asset classes, 427
  choosing, 331–336
  collateral power, 430
  death benefit, 430–431
  definition of, 331
  diversification, 426
  don't use for emergency fund, 78
  fees and expenses, 431–433
  fixed accounts, 427–428
  flexibility, 336
  load, 431
    vs. no-load, 336–339, 431
  management, 426
  no-load, 431
  rate of return, 426–427
  risk, 426
    measurements of, 332–333
  size, 335
  tax issues, 428
  vs. variable annuities vs. variable life,
    425–438
    differences, 427–433
    similarities, 426–427
  watch your plan, not the markets,
    474–475

N

Natural disasters, 163
and essential reserves, 80
Natural laws, 1, 12, 21, 40
choice and consequence, 114–115
law of the harvest, 30
law of unequal rewards, 29
likes attract likes, 28
opposition and adversity, 37–38
Neal, Charles B., Jr., 144
Needs vs. wants, 24, 39, 77, 169
and budgeting, 71
and success, 73
Negative, 183, 216, 471
cross-correlation, 442
person does not have freedom, 117
Neighborhood, 238–241
new vs. old, character of, 240–241
"sick" vs. "well", 239
Neo-Nazis, 125
Net worth:
and bankruptcy, 138, 140
and debt, 138, 140, 141
personal, evaluating, 218
Nixon, Richard, 160
No-load insurance, 272
No-load mutual funds, 332, 431
Novak, Michael, 126

O

Odds of success, 25–26, 390
Oppenheimer, Joseph, 327
Opportunity, 103, 106, 139
and borrowing to finance college, 397
business, cash flow projections for, 10
cash is, 316–317
Opposition, and adversity, as natural laws, 37–38
Orange juice, 327, 478
O'Reilly, John Boyle, 55
Organized crime, 123
Overcomer, 185

P

Paine, Thomas, 100, 190
Parable of the talents, 28–29, 211

Paradox of controls, budget enables freedom, 71–72
Patience, 169, 186, 473
Peace of mind, 18, 21–22, 207, 313, 345, 504, 508
and budgeting, 75
and correct principles, 166
and debt, 137, 147
Peace vs. freedom, 113–114
Peck, M. Scott, 117, 118
Pension maximization, 67
Permanence, 186
Persistent, 214
Persisting, habit-forming, 8
Personal representative, choosing a, 351–352
Play the market, 476–477
Poor, 165, 193
law of unequal rewards, 211
Poor thinking, 19, 25, 170, 463–471
don't strengthen the weak by weakening the strong, 467–468
financial success is not achieved by spending, 465–466
leaders teach, 466–467
surrounds us, 469–470
throw out imposters, 470
victim mentality, 464–465
vs. success thinking, 465
watch success, don't listen to failure, 468–469
Pope, Alexander, 469
Population, 151, 171
Portfolio management, 439–460, 501.
(See also Investments)
cross-correlations, 443–445
return, 443–445
risk, 443–445
strategies, 440–460
turnover, 334
Positive:
attitude, 183, 216
and freedom, 117
cross-correlation, 442
success thinking, 19
Prepared, 18, 223–224
for emergencies, 81
for the future, 166
for the next depression, 161

Prepared (*Cont.*):
vs. procrastination, 49
Press, 116, 125, 126, 449, 478. (*See also* Media)
advocacy vs. objectivity, 119
misleading, 116
sensational, 119, 269, 270, 450
Price controls, 160–161
Principal, 57, 78, 316
safety of, and investing priorities, 477
and wealthy vs. average investors, 473–474
Principles, 1, 12, 17–26, 37, 40, 48, 114, 115, 116, 122, 166, 177, 179, 187, 471, 491
Private property. (*See* Property rights)
Proactive, 117, 171, 224, 226, 234, 303, 464, 494
Probate, 343, 346–347
advantages, 347
disadvantages, 347
Procrastination, 234
and budgeting, 72
cost of, 49
enemy of preparation, 224
and financial failure, 46–50, 81
Production, costs of, 156–157
Productive, 212
Productivity:
diminished, 164
and negotiating a raise, 68
Professional equity, 201
Professional income, shifting, tax benefits of, 417
Profit:
and attracting money, 28
an expense, 107–108
from charitable giving, 369–380
purpose of, 107–108
why sell at a, 475–476
Profitable, 209–211, 216
servant, law of unequal rewards, 29
Progress, economic, 106
Property, definition of, 110
Property rights, 102, 109–110
Psycho-media risk, 163, 270
Psychological, 12, 13, 19
benefits of financial planning, 504
stress, 300

Psychological (*Cont.*):
view of money, 46–47
Punishment, 103–105
Purchasing power risk, 325–326
Purpose, greatness of, determines character, 178–179
Purpose of money, 22–23, 466

Q

Quitting, 2, 170, 214–215
habit-forming, 8, 185

R

Raise or bonus, negotiating, 68, 210–211
Raise vs. fringe benefits, tax considerations, 415
Rand, Ayn, 42
Rated insurance, 280
Rating agencies, 268–270
Rationalization, 36, 38, 114
and budgeting, 74
Reactive, 117, 170, 224, 464, 494
Real estate, 237–245, 412–413
avoiding capital-gains tax, 67
and inflation, 305
inflation hedge, during moderate inflation, 325
installment sales, 413
investment trust (REIT), 441–443
passive vs. active investing, 413
Real-world experience, second level of knowledge, 116
Realization vs. recognition, tax principle of, 408–409
Reap, 179, 190, 379. (*See also* Law of the harvest)
what you sow, law of the harvest, 30
Recession, 161
and emergency fund, 79
and saving, 56
and world bondholders, 159
Reputation, 177, 179
insurance companies, 267–270
Reserves, 77–81, 227
cash, 77–80
food, clothing, energy, 80–81

Resilience, 27, 185–186
Respect, 203
  and attracting money, 28, 30
  between husband and wife, 74
  for money, 20
  of self, 227
Responsibilities and rights, 98–102, 162, 165
Responsibility, 192, 193
Responsible, 165, 213, 464
Results, 192–193, 198–199
  vs. activity, 191, 192–193
  vs. effort, 190, 192
  highest definition of work, 198
  vs. means, 387–388
  measurable, 210, 211
  vs. methods, motivation, 201
Retirement, 295–313, 409
  adventures in, 302
  analysis, 301–302
  benefits:
    life and survivor vs. life only, 67
    maximizing, 308–309
  charitable pursuits, 310
  facts about, 296–297
  Financial Freedom Fund, 58
  inflation, impact of, 304
  money at work, 20
  planning for, 502
  plans, tax-deductible, 67
  questions to consider, 302
  reverse mortgage, 311
  second career, 303
  Selective Incentive Plan, 312
  sources of retirement dollars, 295–296
  tax rates, rising, 306–307
  time of opportunity, 23
  why retire, 298–300
Retitling assets, 291
Return, and investing priorities, 477
Reverse mortgage, 311–312
Reward, 103–105
Rice, Grantland, 179
Rights and responsibilities, 98, 162, 165
Riney, Earl, 40
Rip-off, 260–264
Risk:
  career, 68

Risk (*Cont.*):
  fundamental, 323, 446
  inflation, 325–326
  insurance, 247–265, 270, 501
  interest rate, 324–325
  investment, 323–326
  management, 247–265, 501
  and security, 229
  market, 445, 446, 447
  measurements, 332–333
  portfolio, 315–329
  psycho-media, 163, 270
  purchasing power, 325–326
  tax, 421
  technical, 324, 446
  tolerance, 444
Rockefeller, John D., 40
Rogers, Will, 477
Roosevelt, Franklin D., 114
Rough, 217
Rushkin, John, 191

S

Sacrifice, 58
  and success, 42
Safety net, 78, 79, 80
Safety of principal, and investing priorities, 477
Salary continuation plan, tax benefits of, 419
Save vs. spend, 53–56
  and financial success, 465
Saving, 48–50, 53–69, 83, 303
  advantage of, 56–57
  for big-ticket items, 81
  for college, 403–405
  on major purchases, as cash flow strategy, 66
  on taxes, 409–421
  programs for, tax-sheltered, 67
  and WYHTE phenomenon, 58–60
Scarcity, 151, 152, 172, 209, 231
Scarcity mentality, 24, 31, 32, 151, 152, 209, 231, 392, 463
Schedule A deductions, 414
Schlesinger, Arthur M., Jr., 125
Scholarships, 399–401
  athletic, 400

Scholarships (*Cont.*):
  career interest, 400
  church-sponsored, 401
  corporate-sponsored, 400
  Harry S. Truman, 399
  membership, 400
  military, 401
  minority or ethnic association, 401
  National Honor Society, 399
  National Merit, 399
  Presidential, 399
  special-talent, 400
  student employment, 400
Scott, Tom, 179
Seagulls, 224
Second mile, 191. (*See also* Extra mile)
Second mortgage, 245, 410
Section 125 plan, tax benefits of, 418
Security, 18, 221
  and 706 mortgage, 355
  financial, first law of, 370
  how to achieve, 223–235
  how to attract, 393
  job, 225
  and service, 225, 370
  and work, 226
Security continuum, 234
Seeming vs. being, 178, 179, 182, 484
Selective Incentive Plan, 312
Self:
  -control, 18, 97, 99, 225–226, 234
  -defeating behaviors, 4–5, 18, 24, 43,
    116, 117, 171, 183, 207, 464, 487
  -defeating thoughts, 389–390
  -discipline, 225, 234
    and systems, 488
  -employment taxes, 205
    and marginal tax rate, 60
  -enforcing mechanisms, 485–486
  -image, 24, 117
  -insurance, 255
  -motivated, 214
  -reliance, 18, 81, 106, 224–225
    family, 167, 168, 229–230
    and inflation, 306
    teach children, 65
  -respect, 127, 227
Series EE U.S. savings bonds, 403

Servant:
  government is servant, not master,
    101, 102
  and master, law of unequal rewards,
    29–30
  is always master, 215, 225
  vs. master, 191
  money is servant, not master, 40
Service, 18. (*See also* Charitable giving)
  debt limits ability to serve others, 136
  first law of financial security, 370
  from a financial planner, how much
    and what kind, 493
  and security, 225, 230, 370
  and work, 226
Shade, enjoy the, 186, 238, 268, 473
Shakespeare, William, 134
Sharpe, William, 440
Shaw, George Bernard, 465
Sheep, 339, 449. (*See also* Herd mental-
  ity)
Shortcuts, 12, 42, 106, 182, 190, 194
Sill, Sterling W., 196, 486
Simon, William E., 181
Simplify, 18, 120, 389–390
  lifestyle, 65
Sin taxes, 163
Single-premium whole life, 377–378
  to finance college, 405
Sink roots, 186, 239, 240, 385–387
Slavery, 1, 126–128, 162, 191
  borrower is slave, 131–132
  and debt, 135–136
  and gambling, 160
  and welfare state, 466
Smiles, Samuel, 179
Smith, Adam, 58, 156
Smooth, 217
Social Security, 168, 286, 296, 297,
  307, 409–410
  criteria for collecting disability income
    from, 286
  tax (FICA), 204, 205, 308
    employee portion, 88
    employer portion, 88
    and family limited partnership, 416
    and marginal tax rate, 59, 60, 88
    mutual funds, variable annuities,
      and variable life, 430

Social Security, tax (*Cont.*)
and working spouse, 418
Socialism, 95, 149
and communism, government bestows
rights, 109
and welfare state, 127
Society without laws, 164
Sophisticated, 39, 119, 164, 165, 467–
468
Sophistry, 468
Sow, 179, 190, 191, 233, 268, 379.
(*See also* Law of the harvest)
reap what you sow, law of the harvest,
30
Specialization and exchange, 152. (*See
also* Interdependence)
economy thrives on, 149–152
family, and divorce, 168
and law of abundance, 392
and population growth, 171
and synergy, 390
Speculation, 30, 165, 229, 476–479
vs. investing, 477
Spending, 53–56, 72, 76
financial success is not achieved by
spending, 465–466
Spouse, working, 63–64, 89, 203–
205, 418
economics of, 63–64, 203–205
unconscious collusion, 170
Spread money, 40. (*See also* Charitable
giving)
Squander, 23
money, 39
Stable, 213
Standard deviation, 333
State income tax, 88, 203, 204, 205,
319
prepaying in December, tax benefits
of, 417
and retirement, 307
and working spouse, 418
State regulators, 269
State savings plans, 403
State taxes, and marginal tax rate, 60
Steifler, Jeff, 41
Step-up in basis:
and insurance, 420
and taxes, 420

Stewardship, 233
for the environment, 162
and money, 28–29, 31, 32
parable of talents, 29–30
Stewart, Jimmy, 41, 370
Stocks:
don't use for emergency fund, 78
high dividend domestic, tax benefits
of, 419
taxable, 67
Stored labor, 199
money as, 28
definition of, 19
property as, 110
purpose for, 23
and retirement, 20
Stress, 390
and retirement, 299
life-change units, 300
and time bondage, 119–120
Stress chart, 300
Student loans:
Parent Loans for Undergraduate
Students (PLUS), 399
Perkins Loan, 399
Stafford Loan, 399
Success, 5, 18, 41–42, 179, 186
common denominator of, 200–
201, 387–388
financial:
how to attract, 393
not achieved by spending, 465–466
first law of, 211
four laws of, 383
do what you love, 383–385
focus on end results, not unpleasant
means, 387–388
simplify to focus, 389–390
synergize through interdependence,
390–392
and honesty, 181–182
how to achieve, 383–394
ladder of, 181, 225
number-one success force, 196
odds of, 25–26, 390
portfolio, 439–460
purpose of, 22–23, 466
reflects how well you are thinking,
463–471

Success (*Cont.*):
    and systems, 488
    watch success, don't listen to failure,
        468–469
Success continuum, 393
Success curve, 201–202
Success force, 196, 211
Success penalty, 409
Success thinking, 464–465
Suffering, 37
    and lack of character, 178
Sugarman, Joseph, 196
Surplus, happiness is bought with, 24
Sutherland, George A., 110
Synergy, 18, 150, 167, 171, 390–392
Systematize, 120, 488–489
Systems:
    managing, 487–488
    and success, 488

T

Talents, 211
    parable of, 29–30, 211
Tanner, N. Eldon, 71, 74, 232, 476
Tax system, U.S., 85
Taxes, 85–90, 428–430, 435–436, 437
    before-AGI deductions, 414
    capital gains, 67
    corporate, 88
    deductions for charitable giving, 371
    estate, 88, 353–367. (*See also* Estate
        taxes)
    federal, 59, 88
        and working spouse, 418
    FICA, 87, 88, 204
        and family limited partnership, 416
        and working spouse, 418
    gasoline, 88
    how much, 87–88
    impact on economy, 86–87
    income, 501
        and family limited partnership, 416
    insidious, 165
    and investing priorities, 477
    marginal rate, 59, 88–89
        and working spouse, 418
    Medicare, 87, 88, 204
    on mutual funds, 428

Taxes (*Cont.*):
    principles, 407–409
        form vs. substance, 408
        realization vs. recognition, 408–409
        tree vs. fruit, 407–408
    property, 88
        prepaying in December, 417
    risks, 421
    sales, 88
    schedule A deductions, 414
    sin, 163
    state, 59, 88
        prepay in December, 417
        and working spouse, 418
    strategies for reducing, 66, 67, 407–
        423, 409–421
        for business owners, 418–421
        for individuals, 409–418
        on variable annuities, 428–429
        on variable life, 429–430
Taxpayer Bill of Rights, 423
Teachable, 216
Team player, 183
Technical risk, 324
Technology replacing labor, 158
Tenancy in common, 347–348
    advantages of, 347–348
Term life insurance, 276
    re-entry term, 278–280
Term vs. permanent insurance, 255–
    265
    administrative costs, 258
    analyze the numbers, 260
    equity, 256–258
    forced savings, 259–260
    insuring your insurance, 258–259
    payments, 256
    policy protection, 259
Theory of decreasing needs, 254–255
Theory of evolution, 118
Theory of scarcity, 392
Thinking, 217
Thoreau, Henry, 38
Threats to economic future, 163–166
Throw out imposters, 470–471
Time bondage, 119–120
Tinker, Grant, 199
Tithing, 9, 230–233

Tort risks, 163
Track record, 447
  vs. management, of mutual funds,
    334–335
Travel expenses, writing off, tax
    benefits of, 419
Tree, 473
  bamboo, 385–387
  vs. fruit, tax principle of, 407–408
Trust, character trait, 28, 391, 393
  and choosing advisers, 271
  money flows toward, 28
  and selection of financial planner,
    key to working effectively, 499–500
Trust, legal document, 348–350
  capital gains bypass, 68, 417
  charitable, 364
  charitable lead, 377, 417
  charitable remainder, 372–376, 417
  irrevocable insurance, 358, 360
  life insurance, 377–378
  living, 347, 349–350
  real estate investment trust (REIT),
    441–443
  revocable, 349
  testamentary, 349
Trustee, 348–349
  choosing a, 351
Trustor, 348–349
Trustworthiness, 189
Truth, 65, 72, 105, 118, 119
  divine, 116
  vs. error, and techniques of
    disinformation, 125
Turnover, portfolio, 334
Twain, Mark, 180

U

Unconscious collusion, 170
Unequal rewards, law of, 28–30, 211
Uniform Gift to Minors Act (UGMA),
    403
Universal life, to finance college, 405
Usurping power, 165

V

Value, personal, measuring, 210

Vandenberg, John H., 135
Variable annuities, 425–438
  asset classes, 427
  collateral power, 430
  death benefit, 430–431
  diversification, 426
  fees and expenses, 431–433
  fixed accounts, 427–428
  management, 426
  vs. mutual funds vs. variable life, 425–
    438
  rate of return, 426–427
  risk, 426
  tax issues, 428–429
  tax-sheltered, 67
Variable life, 425–438
  asset classes, 427
  collateral power, 430
  death benefit, 430–431
  diversification, 426
  fees and expenses, 431–433
  to finance college, 404
  fixed accounts, 427–428
  management, 426
  vs. mutual funds vs. annuities, 425–438
  rate of return, 426–427
  risk, 426
  tax issues, 429–430
Victim mentality, 464–465
Vision, 19, 25, 216, 483, 484, 489–490
Visualization, 484

W

Wants vs. needs, 169
Washington, Booker T., 193
Washington, George, 39, 101
Wealthy:
  anyone can be, 81
  vs. average investors, 473–474
Weaver, Henry G., 93
Welfare, 3, 127, 227
Welfare state, 126–128, 466
Weston, Josh, 187
What you have to earn, 58
Who we are, 117–118
Whole life, 68
  and inflation, 275
  single-premium, 377–378

Whole life vs. term insurance, 255-265
administrative costs, 258
analyze the numbers, 260
equity, 256–258
forced savings, 259–260
insuring your insurance, 258–259
payments, 256
policy protection, 259
Wills:
establishing, 346–348
late-night television "kits", 344
living, 346
operation of law, 343–344
pour-over, 347
and probate, 343–345
simple, 344
Wilson, Woodrow, 39, 43
Win-win, 31, 32, 95, 150, 231, 390,
392, 419, 463, 504
Wisdom:
of academia, 115
of God, 116
of world, 116
Wooden, John, 177
Words/vocabulary, 104, 105, 124, 126
Work, 5–6, 189–191, 212, 226, 384–
385
smart vs. hard, 197–199
taxation of, and WYHTE phenomenon, 199
for yourself, 228
Work ethic, easy money dulls, 134
Workers compensation, 287, 288
Working spouse, 63–64, 89, 203–205
economics of, 63–64, 203–205
social costs of, 203–204
taxation of, 418
Write-off, business, tax benefits of, 418
WYHTE phenomenon, 58–60, 139–
141, 168, 316, 417, 421
and career planning, 199
examples, 60–64
and taxes, 415–416
and working spouse, 418

Yellow journalism, 270. (*See also* Press)
Youth, 81

Z

Zero coupon bonds, 403

Y

Year-end strategic planning, tax
benefits of, 416

About the Author:

Henry S. Brock heads one of America's largest fee-based financial consulting firms, The American Financial Resource Center, Inc., and Five Star Management Company, LLC. The firm provides financial advisory services, corporate and public financial workshops, and money management services nationwide for major corporations as well as thousands of midsize and small companies, professionals, and families. He also founded the non-profit Center of Resources for Economic Education and Development (CREED), whose programs and services assist people in the United States and abroad in gaining increased well-being. *Money* Magazine named Brock one of America's top financial planners, as selected by his peers. He is a Certified Public Accountant, Chartered Financial Consultant, Certified Financial Planner, Chartered Life Underwriter, MBA with an emphasis in investment analysis and taxation. Brock has taught thousands in his numerous seminars. He is married to Julie Herzog Brock, and they are the parents of seven children.

About the Center of Resources
for Economic Education and Development (CREED):

The Center of Resources for Economic Education and Development (CREED) is an independent non-profit 501(c)3 foundation. Its key purpose is to provide products, services and assistance to help families discover increased financial security and temporal well-being, both in the United States and abroad.

Its focus is to conduct workshops primarily in the United States and Eastern Europe, to help people better provide for themselves. It also publishes a periodic newsletter and special reports on timely and strategic economic, financial, and tax topics. Another key purpose is to help the small-business owner develop a stable and prosperous business, provide jobs for others, and grow without dependency.

The foundation provides opportunities for families and students to visit Eastern Europe and assist in teaching those peoples how to survive in a free-market economy. This inter-cultural exchange helps not only the recipients, but the givers, as all gain increased appreciation for each other. Members of CREED receive several membership privileges, including its newsletter and discounts on additional products and services.

Contributions are tax-deductible. For more information about CREED products and services, order the *free* CREED catalogue on the attached coupon, or call 1-800-635-2488 or visit our web-site at CREED.ORG.

About The American Financial Resource Center, Inc.:

The American Financial Resource Center, Inc., is one of America's largest fee-based financial consulting firms, headquartered in Salt Lake City, Utah. Since 1979, it has established an outstanding track record with clients across the nation, including successful business owners of public and private companies, professionals, families and retirees.

For the past decade it has also conducted well over 100 seminars and workshops annually for major corporations, professional practices, colleges and universities, churches, non-profit organizations and the general public.

The firm includes experienced attorneys, Certified Public Accountants, Chartered Financial Consultants, Certified Financial Planners, Chartered Life Underwriters, and investment advisers who believe in the firm's mission:

"Our mission is to provide superior and reliable financial consulting to our clients, as well as help in implementing that correct advice, in order to assist our clients in achieving their goals. All counsel will be honest, ethical, and even courageous when it is necessary to pursue an unpopular yet prudent path. We must be loyal to our clients, treating their personal affairs in utmost confidence. We will best meet these lofty objectives on behalf of our valued clients when we strive for excellence in all aspects of our personal as well as our professional lives. Then we may have great satisfaction as we view our clients gain increased security and financial well-being. We will serve best, as we care most."

For more information about The American Financial Resource Center, Inc., order its free catalogue of services by calling 1-800-594-8913 or visit its web-site at AFRC–INC.COM.

About Five Star Management$_{SM}$ Company:

Five Star Management$_{SM}$ Company provides portfolio management for the serious investor who wants to take advantage of the same sophisticated asset management research and technology developed for some of America's largest corporations, pensions, and trusts.

Five Star utilizes five key portfolio management principles, each proven statistically and by the test of time. These principles, when applied in a scientific and highly structured methodology, are proven to yield superior returns at a lower level of risk. Five Star integrates these proven principles into a disciplined portfolio program.

Five Star provides portfolio management services for Qualified Retirement Plans, Corporate Funds, Nonprofit Organizations, Trust Accounts, and Individual Accounts. Five Star customizes its service for your particular situation, considering your goals and objectives, risk tolerance level, investment time horizon, liquidity or cash flow needs, rate of return objectives, resources available, your phase in life, etc.

By enrolling in Five Star, you get the best of both worlds: proven investment principles and strategies within a disciplined portfolio management program, and the personal assistance of an established financial professional who is constantly available for consultation and reviewing periodic performance reports.

For the free report, "How to Achieve Successful Portfolio Performance" call Five Star at 1-800-550-6323 or visit its web-site at 5STAR-MANAGEMENT.COM.

$10.00 OFF COUPON

Your Money Happiness Workbook

Your Money Happiness Organizer

$10.00 OFF COUPON

☐ **Your Money Happiness Workbook**, for planning your future. Regularly $14.95, with purchase of *Your Complete Guide to Money Happiness*, **$10.00 off.** ... $ 4.95

☐ **Your Money Happiness Organizer**, for organizing your present. ... 14.95

Plus, I'd like the following FREE information:

☐ Catalogue of Services for the American Financial Resource Center, Inc. ... FREE

☐ How to Achieve Successful Portfolio Performance, Five Star Management Company ... FREE

☐ Catalogue of Products and Services, Center of Resources for Economic Education and Development (CREED) Please Check One (Confidential): ... FREE

  ☐Bronze Catalogue (Income below $75k or Assets below $300k)

  ☐Silver Catalogue (Income $75k to $150k or Assets $300k to $600k)

  ☐Gold Catalogue (Income $150k to $300k or Assets $600k to $1.2M)

  ☐Platinum Catalogue (Income above $300k or Assets above $1.2M)

☐ Information on CREED seminars in my area ... FREE

☐ Video Catalogue of CREED Products and Services ... FREE

Shipping . . . . $ 4.95

TOTAL _____

ORDER NOW! Your Workbook contains all the exercises, tables, and worksheets to use with your book. By phone, call **1 800 921-9284**. Please have credit card information ready.

Or, complete this coupon and mail to:

Legacy Publishing, Inc.
2533 N. Carson Street, Suite 2737
Carson City, NV 89706

Your Name_____

Address_____

City_____State_____Zip_____

Telephone (_____) _____

☐ Check enclosed

☐ Credit Card: ☐ M/C ☐ Visa ☐ Discover ☐AmEx

#_____ Exp. Date _____/_____

Signature

11 — 9/00